The Isle of Pines
and
Plato Redivivus

THE THOMAS HOLLIS LIBRARY

David Womersley, General Editor

The Isle of Pines
and
Plato Redivivus

Henry Neville

Edited and with an Introduction
by David Womersley

LIBERTY FUND

Printed in the United States of America

20 21 22 23 24   C   5   4   3   2   1
20 21 22 23 24   P   5   4   3   2   1

Library of Congress Cataloging-in-Publication Data

Names: Neville, Henry, 1620–1694, author. | Womersley, David, editor. | Neville, Henry, 1620–1694. Plato Redivivus.
Title: The Isle of Pines and Plato Redivivus / Henry Neville ; edited and with an Introduction by David Womersley
Other titles: Isle of Pines | Plato Redivivus
Description: Carmel, Indiana : Liberty Fund, [2020] | Series: The Thomas Hollis library | Includes bibliographical references and index. |
Summary: [See LC record]
Identifiers: LCCN 2020032902 (print) | LCCN 2020032903 (ebook) | ISBN 9780865979154 (hardback) | ISBN 9780865979161 (paperback) | ISBN 9781614872887 (epub) | ISBN 9781614876649 (kindle edition) | ISBN 9781614879343 (pdf)
Subjects: LCSH: Voyages, Imaginary—Early works to 1800. | Political science—Early works to 1800.
Classification: LCC G560 .N34 2020 (print) | LCC G560 (ebook) | DDC 335/.02—dc23
LC record available at https://lccn.loc.gov/2020032902
LC ebook record available at https://lccn.loc.gov/2020032903

LIBERTY FUND, INC.
11301 North Meridian Street
Carmel, Indiana 46032
libertyfund.org

CONTENTS

The Thomas Hollis Library   vii

Introduction   ix

Further Reading   xxxv

Note on the Texts   xxxix

Abbreviations   xli

Chronology of the Life of Henry Neville   li

Acknowledgments   lv

THE ISLE OF PINES   1

Two Letters Concerning the Island of Pines   3

The Isle of Pines, Discovered   5

Post-Script   37

PLATO REDIVIVUS   39

The Publisher to the Reader   41

Political Discourses and Histories Worth Reading   51

The Argument   55

The First Day   59

The Second Day   69

The Third Day   229

Appendixes

A: A Copy of a Letter from an Officer of the Army
   in Ireland (1656)   317

B: Neville's Major Speeches in Parliament (1659)   339

C: The Armies Dutie (1659)   351

D: The Humble Petition (1659)   375

E: Manuscripts Relating to Sir Henry Neville   383

F: John Somers, A Brief History of the Succession (1681) 395

G: Thomas Hollis's Life of Henry Neville   429

H: Corrections to Copy-Texts   433

 I: Textual Collation of the First and Second Editions
    of *Plato Redivivus*   439

Index   473

THE THOMAS HOLLIS LIBRARY

Thomas Hollis (1720–74) was an eighteenth-century Englishman who devoted his energies, his fortune, and his life to the cause of liberty. Hollis was trained for a business career, but a series of inheritances allowed him to pursue instead a career of public service. He believed that citizenship demanded activity and that it was incumbent on citizens to put themselves in a position, by reflection and reading, in which they could hold their governments to account. To that end, for many years Hollis distributed books that he believed explained the nature of liberty and revealed how liberty might best be defended and promoted.

A particular beneficiary of Hollis's generosity was Harvard College. In the years preceding the Declaration of Independence, Hollis was assiduous in sending to America boxes of books, many of which he had had specially printed and bound, to encourage the colonists in their struggle against Great Britain. At the same time, he took pains to explain the colonists' grievances and concerns to his fellow Englishmen.

The Thomas Hollis Library makes freshly available a selection of titles that, because of their intellectual power, or the influence they exerted on the public life of their own time, or the distinctiveness of their approach to the topic of liberty, comprise the cream of the books distributed by Hollis. Many of these works have been either out of print since the eighteenth century or available only in very expensive and scarce editions. The highest standards of scholarship and production ensure that these classic texts can be as salutary and influential today as they were two hundred and fifty years ago.

David Womersley

INTRODUCTION

Family Background and Early Life

Henry Neville was born in 1620 into a prominent Berkshire political family. His grandfather Sir Henry Neville (1561/62–1615) had been a leading politician during the reign of James I, had come close to being made secretary of state, and had served as ambassador to France. As we will see, the political career of Sir Henry Neville was significantly recalled by his grandson during the composition of *Plato Redivivus*.[1]

Neville was married young to a Berkshire heiress, Elizabeth Staverton. The marriage was cut short by her early death (a death which, so rumours suggested, ill treatment at the hands of her husband had hastened), and Neville acquired the bulk of the Staverton property. In 1636 he matriculated at Oxford, first as a member of Merton, then as a member of University College. As was normal in those days for gentlemen of birth and means, he went down without taking a degree.

The biographical sections of this introduction rely on the *ODNB* article on Neville by Nicholas von Maltzahn and the introduction to Caroline Robbins's edition of *Two English Republican Tracts* (Cambridge: Cambridge University Press, 1969), pp. 5–19.

1. See below, pp. 214–19. The measures and policies of Sir Henry Neville would also be quoted against Neville in Parliament in 1659; see Burton, *Diary*, vol. 4, pp. 346–47.

In the early 1640s Neville travelled in Italy for several years, living mainly in Florence and Rome (where he met Cardinal Bentivoglio); but he also visited Venice (a circumstance of importance given the use made of Venetian example in *Plato Redivivus*). For the commonwealth Whigs of the next century, this tour of Italy would hold great intellectual importance: they idealized it as a school of republican liberty. In Brand Hollis's copy of the 1698 edition of *Discourses Concerning Government* (as *Plato Redivivus* was then retitled) there is inscribed on the second front free endpaper:

> The following is a list tho' short & imperfect, of divers Englishmen, who were in Italy, together, or within a few years of each other, culling elegance & knowlege, & who after-wards espoused the Cause of Liberty and the Parliament and died or suffered for it.

The verso contains the following names, a veritable roll call of mid-seventeenth-century English republicanism:

John Hamden
Henry Marten
Thomas Chaloner
John Milton
James Harrington
Andrew Marvell
Algernon Sydney
Henry Neville.
Pym also had travells through Italy.[2]

Because of these Italian travels, Neville was absent during the early years of the Civil War, returning to England only in 1645.

The Civil War and Opposition to Cromwell

Neville's Civil War career is obscure until 1649, when he stood for election to Parliament. His political sympathies at this time can be gauged from the bawdy pamphlet he had published in 1647, *The Parliament of Ladies*. This squib pokes ribald fun at women prominent on the Par-

2. British Library 8025.f.62.

liamentarian side. Neville was no cavalier, but his youthful satire could never be entirely the servant of his political loyalties. In 1651 Neville was elected to the Council of State, and in April 1653 he was among those members of Parliament ejected by Cromwell—an episode he would recall with evident resentment in *Plato Redivivus*.[3]

Neville was profoundly disaffected from the Protectorate, and he expressed that disaffection in witty, inventive form in *Shuffling, Cutting, and Dealing in a Game of Pickquet* (1659). This pamphlet inaugurates a minor literary form, the political game of cards.[4] A few years earlier Neville may also have had a hand in the anti-Cromwellian *A Letter to His Highness from an Officer in Ireland* (1656). These years in the political wilderness also saw the growth of one of the two most important intellectual affinities of Neville's life, namely, that with the political theorist James Harrington. (The other affinity is with Machiavelli.) Harrington's *Oceana* had been published in 1656. Hobbes maintained that Neville had been in some respects a coauthor of that work.[5] Whatever the truth of that claim, it is certainly the case that the political works published under Harrington's name in the later 1650s, including but by no means confined to *Oceana*, left profound and multiple marks on *Plato Redivivus*, as the annotation in this edition bears witness.

Neville's disenchantment with the procedures of English politics, to which his enduring attachment to those Venetian institutions of the ballot and the rota attests, can only have been deepened by his experience of the election of 1656. Neville had stood as a candidate for Berkshire and was alleged to have polled sufficient votes to have won one of the seats, but the sheriff William Strode (who acted as the returning officer) declared,

---

3. See below, p. 282 and n. 567. On the significance of Neville's political career during the Interregnum in the formation of his political sensibility, see Skinner, *Liberty*, p. 16.

4. Although it was not so minor a form that it was unable to engage the interest of poets as important as Pope in *The Rape of the Lock* and Wordsworth in *The Prelude*. See Howard Erskine-Hill, "The Satirical Game at Cards in Pope and Wordsworth," in *English Satire and the Satiric Tradition*, ed. Claude Rawson (Oxford: Blackwell, 1984), pp. 183–95.

5. Aubrey, *Brief Lives*, pp. 318 and 322; Robbins, *Republican Tracts*, p. 7 and n. 4; Rahe, *Throne and Altar*, p. 322.

amid scenes of confusion and violence, that all the seats had been won by supporters of Lord Protector Cromwell. Neville took his case to law and had the best of the argument, but the lower courts were reluctant to pronounce on a matter that drew so near to the privileges of Parliament. The matter was eventually discussed by the Parliament of 1659–60, in which Neville sat as a member, but to no effect.[6]

Richard Cromwell's Parliament

Notwithstanding the disappointments of 1656, Neville was successful in the elections for the short-lived Parliament of 1659–60. There he formed part of a group of republican MPs who were disproportionately influential.[7] As well as Neville himself, the group included Sir Arthur Haselrig, Sir Henry Vane, Thomas Scot, John Weaver, and a "Captain Baynes." These men were articulate speakers blessed with well-stocked memories and clear principles, and they hunted as a pack. They also had a much stronger grasp of parliamentary procedure than was always the case with their fellow MPs. The number of occasions when Burton's *Diary* records with the phrase "*Altum silentium*" those moments when this Parliament lapsed into silence for want of a clear sense of what should happen next is very striking. Striking too is the number of occasions when, in short interjections, Neville tried to keep Parliamentary debates regular, focused, and on track.[8]

Expertise always attracts resentment, and Neville came under attack in this Parliament for alleged irreligion.[9] If proven, these allegations would have led to Neville's ejection. The matter was debated on 16 February 1659, but it led nowhere, as the diarist Thomas Burton recorded: "As to the charge against Mr. Neville, it fell asleep after five hours' debate, nobody knows how. Mr. Neville was present all the time."[10]

6. Burton, *Diary*, vol. 3, pp. 18–22, 51–53, 346, 498–500; vol. 4, p. 351.
7. Marvell, *Poems and Letters*, vol. 2, p. 294.
8. See, e.g., Burton, *Diary*, vol. 3, pp. 117, 476–77, 497, 546, 564; vol. 4, pp. 19, 150, 225, 231, 291.
9. Burton, *Diary*, vol. 3, pp. 296–305. The accuser was a Mr. Bulkeley.
10. Burton, *Diary*, vol. 3, p. 305.

The most substantial and important of Neville's speeches in this Parliament are reprinted in appendix B. Neville undoubtedly understood how great the political opportunity was (or seemed to be) in 1659, and his chief concern in these major speeches was to shape the constitutional settlement, discussion of which occupied most of Parliament's time. It is worth underlining, however, how hesitant and confused were the majority of MPs on this voyage into uncharted political water. On 14 February 1659 the Speaker had sighed, "We are indeed in a wood, a wilderness, a labyrinth."[11] It was a sentiment often echoed from the floor of the House:

> Till we go to the right constitution, we shall never know where we are. . . .
>
> I am afraid we are in a wood. No wonder the nation is puzzled, when the wisdom of the nation is puzzled in this place. Once out of the way, we see how hard it is to get in again. . . .
>
> I know not where we are.[12]

Where others were confused or despondent, Neville was clear and resolute. As he had said on 8 February 1659, "I am for a single person, a senate, and a popular assembly; but not in that juggling way. King, Lords, and Commons I cannot like."[13] Neville had no desire to revive the ancient constitution, which his Harringtonian principles revealed to him as hopelessly out of alignment with the underlying economic realities of England in the mid-seventeenth century. He tried repeatedly and patiently to educate his fellow MPs on this point, but never more explicitly and cogently than on 18 February 1659:

> We are upon alterations, and no thought now is to be taken of what was done by John of Gaunt, and such fellows. The Lords much outweighed before, and now the Commons and the people outweigh; and your King, not long since, before the Parliament, did oversway. So you build upon an ill foundation if you aim at the old way. You

11. Burton, *Diary*, vol. 3, p. 269.

12 Burton, *Diary*, vol. 3, p. 338 (Lenthall); ibid., p. 415 (Onslow); ibid., p. 564 (Knightley).

13. Burton, *Diary*, vol. 3, p. 132.

cannot build up that which God and nature have destroyed. We are upon an equal balance, which puts out Turkish government and peerage. Laws are made to preserve things that are, not things that are destroyed. You are invested with all legal power. If you will say, all power is in the sword, that is one thing; if in the people, that is another. But it is in the people, in you, in consent. You have laid a good foundation, a single person. It now concerns you to build upon that, and to bound him, that he may lay claim to no more power than now you give him. You are in a good way. Go on.[14]

But all this effort to imagine and construct a new constitution for England, with an appropriately constrained Richard Cromwell at its head as Protector, fell to the ground two months later. Cromwell was obliged by the army to dissolve Parliament, he himself was put under a form of mild house arrest, and on 14 May his lingering rule came to an abrupt end when the restored Rump Parliament destroyed his Protectoral seal.

Neville sat in the restored Rump Parliament for the five months of its existence, where he argued for the same constitutional form that he had advocated in the previous Parliament: a single magistrate (but not hereditary, not possessing a veto over legislation, and not in command of the militia); a second house (but not hereditary, and without any power to obstruct legislation passed by the lower house); and a popular assembly, where real power would reside. He was also once again a member of the Council of State. He may have had a hand in drafting *The Armie's Dutie* (1659), a pamphlet that was published on 2 May and signed with the six pairs of initials "H.M. H.N. I.L. I.W. I.I. S.M."—"H.N." could

---

14. Burton, *Diary*, vol. 3, p. 331. Compare the metaphorical expression of a desire for a comprehensive constitutional remodelling that Neville had placed in his own mouth in *Shufling, Cutting, and Dealing in a Game at Picquet* (1656): "I will not play for a farthing; besides that, I love not the Game, I am so dun'd with the Spleen, I should think on something else all the while I were a playing, and take in all the small Cards: for I am all day dreaming of another Game" (p. 5). But most MPs were not of Neville's mind concerning the irrelevance of John of Gaunt. It is striking how often the debates in the Convention Parliament of 1689 harked back to the Parliamentary history and language of the fourteenth and fifteenth centuries: see, e.g., Grey, *Debates*, vol. 9, pp. 47 and 85–86.

perhaps stand for Henry Neville.[15] On 6 July he presented *The Humble Petition*, which advocated a Harringtonian régime embodying principles of rotation and a careful separation of powers.[16] Like other such proposals, it did not progress, but the lack of practical outcome is the least important aspect of *The Humble Petition*. Along with Harrington's writings from *Oceana* onward until the Restoration and Neville's speeches in Parliament in 1659, it testifies to the intensity, the theoretical power, and the literary inventiveness which the republicans of the interregnum brought to their project of enforcing a break with the English political past—a project which at this time they also discussed at meetings of the Rota Club in Miles's coffee house, close by St. Stephen's chapel. These qualities of intensity, invention, and intellectual power would resurface strongly in Neville's writings of the 1660s and 1680s.

Restoration

In the early months of 1660 the momentum for the restoration of the house of Stuart became clear, and although Neville refused prematurely to throw in the towel (he introduced a late motion for the renunciation of Charles Stuart and defended his fellow republican Ludlow from suspension), when Monck's advance on London had made the Restoration inevitable Neville quietly withdrew, presumably to his Berkshire estates.

He appears not at first to have been molested by the new régime. His mail was opened, but (unlike his friend Harrington) he was not called in and examined until 1663, when he fell under suspicion of conspiracy and was imprisoned in the Tower along with Richard Salway and Colonel John Hutchinson (the husband of the writer and poet Lucy Hutchinson).

In May 1664 Neville was given permission to travel abroad, and he returned to Italy. What we know of his activities at this time is contained in letters he wrote to Bernard Gascoigne, the Florentine whom he had met during his first tour of Italy in the early 1640s and who had served in

---

15. See below, appendix C, pp. 351–74.
16. See below, appendix D, pp. 375–82.

the royalist regiment raised by Neville's brother Richard.[17] He spent time at the court of Ferdinand II of Tuscany where he befriended the heir to the duchy, the future Cosimo III.[18] He also travelled to Rome, where he had an affair of the heart. He was back in England by 18 November 1667, however, when Sir Winston Churchill (father of John Churchill, later Duke of Marlborough) deplored "seditious people whispering with many of the House, to give themselves reputation, and to the great scandal of our Members. *Meaning* Henry Nevile, *Major* Salloway, *and such.*"[19]

Return to England and Final Years

It must have been at this time, when he was newly returned from his travels in Italy, that Neville prepared for the press his first major publication, *The Isle of Pines*, which was published on 27 June 1668. The early publication history of this work is extremely complicated.[20] But whether this complication arose as a consequence of piracy or interference of some kind with the process of printing the work (as Harrington avers had been the case with *Oceana*),[21] or whether Neville himself was precociously aware of the potential for creative mischief afforded by the technologies of print culture, is unclear.

In 1669 Neville's Italian friend Cosimo de' Medici visited England, which provided an opportunity for their friendship to be extended and deepened.[22] The following year, on the death of his father Ferdinand II,

17. Crino, *Fatti e figure*, pp. 173–208. The archival research of Anna Maria Crino, too little known in the Anglophone scholarly world, has shed invaluable light on Neville's Italian experience and connections, as well as on the broader field of Anglo-Italian relations in the later seventeenth century more generally.

18. Cosimo III de' Medici (1642–1723), Grand Duke of Tuscany. Ferdinando II de' Medici (1610–70), Grand Duke of Tuscany.

19. Grey, *Debates*, vol. 1, p. 174. This comfortably predates Marvell's report on 25 November 1669 that Neville was "in town" (Marvell, *Poems and Letters*, vol. 2, p. 91).

20. For the very complicated publishing history of this text, see Gaby Mahlberg, "The Publishing History of *The Isle of Pines*," *Utopian Studies*, 17, no. 1 (2006), pp. 93–98.

21. Pocock, *Harrington*, pp. 7–10 and 156.

22. Lorenzo Magalotti, *Relazioni d'Inghilterra 1668 e 1688, edizione critica di editi e inediti*, a cura di Anna Maria Crino (Florence: Olschki, 1972); Lorenzo Magalotti,

Cosimo became grand duke, but this elevation did nothing to stem or reduce the flow of communication between the two men: gifts and letters passed between them freely. In 1675 Neville gave tangible proof of the depth and subtlety of his interest in Italian political culture when he seems to have taken a leading role in the publication by John Starkey of the first English translation of *The Works of Machiavelli*.[23] One element in this generous selection of Machiavelli's writings which was almost certainly Neville's handiwork was the spurious prefatory letter, "Nicholas Machiavel's Letter to Zanobius Buondelmontius in Vindication of himself and his Writings." This reads very much as, at one level, a playful practical joke. In what is perhaps a slightly heavy-handed clue as to its nature and purpose, the letter is dated 1 April 1537, ten years after Machiavelli had in fact died. But it would be a mistake therefore to dismiss the letter as nothing more than literary horseplay, even though that was to Neville's taste. For Neville used this spurious letter to fashion the image of a Machiavelli who was well-adapted to Neville's own inclinations and polemical purposes: a Machiavelli, that is, who was indignant at the various corruptions foisted on mankind by the Roman Catholic Church, who was staunchly republican in his politics, and who understood very clearly that government was a human contrivance that should be adjusted to serve the well-being and flourishing of ordinary men and women in this world, not the next.[24]

In August 1678, if the Earl of Danby's spies are to be believed, Neville was in France. He and John Wildman (1621–93), an old ally from the

---

Travels of Cosmo III, Grand Duke of Tuscany, through England in 1669 (1821); W. E. Knowles Middleton, *Lorenzo Magalotti at the Court of Charles II: His Relazione d'Inghilterra of 1668* (Waterloo, Ont.: Wilfrid Laurier University Press, 1980).

23. It was long believed that Neville was in fact the translator of the entirety of this book (see Hollis's clear statement to that effect in his brief life of Neville, below, p. 432). That now seems to have exaggerated the extent of his involvement (a more probable translator being John Bulteel), but the occasional vivacity of the language tempts one at some moments into seeing Neville's hand guiding the translation. See Raab, *English Face*, appendix B, pp. 267–72; Gaby Mahlberg, "Historical and Political Contexts of *The Isle of Pines*," *Utopian Studies*, 17, no. 1 (2006), p. 122; and Robbins, *Republican Tracts*, p. 15 and n. 1.

24. For a summary account of the interesting variants introduced into this text in the course of its successive reprintings in 1689, 1691, and in *The Harleian Miscellany* of 1744–46, vol. 1, pp. 55–66, see Robbins, *Republican Tracts*, p. 15 and n. 1.

opposition to the Protectorate, accompanied the Duke of Buckingham, George Villiers (1628–88), on what would prove to be an unsuccessful mission to try to persuade Louis XIV to fund their political activities (since his dismissal in 1674 Buckingham had become a disaffected critic of the Court). On his return to England, a confusion of identity with a Henry Neville of Holt, Leicestershire, nearly embroiled Neville in the Popish Plot.

Although Neville must have been a keen observer of that frantic and hysterical crisis, in those months he would have had little time for conspiracy, since he was busy writing his most important book, *Plato Redivivus*, published probably just after October 1680, although the title page bears the date 1681. According to Thomas Hollis, it was "very much bought up . . . and admired" by the current cohort of MPs.[25] In these three dialogues between an English gentleman (plainly a mask for Neville himself), a doctor (thought to represent the Restoration physician Richard Lower), and a noble Venetian (not conclusively identified, although allegedly based upon an actual person), Neville applied the Harringtonian principles he had imbibed in the late 1650s to this latest crisis in the English government. The book provoked an almost immediate response, and a second edition followed later in 1681, advertised as "with Additions." This second edition incorporated more overt anticlericalism, a fuller discussion of the demerits of any attempt to have the Duke of Monmouth recognized as heir to the throne, and most intriguingly of all, a fascinating paratext: the prefatory booklist of twelve "Political Discourses and Histories worth reading."[26]

The final years of Neville's life, until his death on 20 September 1694, were uneventful—or, at least, his activities left little or no trace on the public record. He lived quietly in London and avoided political entanglements, for instance, standing aloof from the Rye House Plot that would make Whig martyrs of William Russell and Algernon Sidney. His will,

25. See Hollis's life of Neville, below, p. 431. Close reading of Grey's *Debates* has failed to uncover any evidence that the language or arguments of *Plato Redivivus* were deployed in the House of Commons, but this of course does not rule out more subtle forms of influence.

26. For the variants between the first and second editions of *Plato Redivivus*, see below, "Textual Collation," pp. 439–70.

in its provision for gifts to friends and relations, and small legacies to the poor of Warfield and to servants, suggests a benevolent and charitable nature, although Neville was adamant that his burial should be free of "Jewish ceremonies."

Literary Life and Character: Neville's Writings during the Civil War and Interregnum

Neville's writings of the first phase of his literary career, from *The Parliament of Ladies* of 1647 to *The Armie's Dutie* of 1659—assuming for the moment that Neville did indeed have a hand in that work—show him exploring the expanded possibilities for literary production created by the Civil Wars, and also refining and stabilizing his political beliefs.[27]

The pamphlets with which Neville launched himself as a writer— *The Parliament of Ladies* (1647), *The Ladies, a Second Time, Assembled in Parliament* (1647), and *Newes from the New Exchange* (1650)—were, like all his works, published anonymously. They belong to a family of mid-seventeenth-century texts that, from a variety of political standpoints, reflected and commented on the disorders and inversions of the time by using that time-honored trope, found also in the literature of classical antiquity, of women usurping the place of authority naturally reserved for men.[28] It was just such a fragment of ancient literature, Aulus Gellius's relation of how Papirius Praetextatus acquired his name, that the earliest text in this group of pamphlets used as its point of departure.[29] *The*

---

27. For studies of the impact of the Civil Wars on the possibilities for and conditions of literary production, see, e.g., Margaret Anne Doody, *The Daring Muse: Augustan Poetry Reconsidered* (Cambridge: Cambridge University Press, 1985), especially pp. 30–56; Michael Wilding, *Dragons Teeth: Literature in the English Revolution* (Oxford: Clarendon Press, 1987); Thomas Corns, *Uncloistered Virtue: English Political Literature 1640–1660* (Oxford: Clarendon Press, 1992); Nigel Smith, *Literature and Revolution in England, 1640–1660* (New Haven, Conn.: Yale University Press, 1994); Joad Raymond, *The Invention of the Newspaper: English Newsbooks, 1641–1649* (Oxford: Clarendon Press, 1996).

28. These pamphlets as a group need (and would repay) bibliographical clarification and analysis. For the reasons for provisionally limiting Neville's authorship to the three titles specified above, see Mahlberg, pp. 94–95.

29. Aulus Gellius, *Noctes Atticae*, 1.23.

Parlament of VVomen (1640) is a Royalist text that mocks the incipient political disorders of the time through the image of a Parliament made up of a series of stock female characters: Mrs. Rattle, the tailor's wife; Franke Falldowne, the feltmaker's wife; Sisly, the saddler's wife; and so on.[30] The irrationality and sexual incontinence of these stereotypical figures is used to satirize the parallel enormity of the growing Parliamentary challenge to royal authority.

Neville therefore found this minor literary genre ready-made to his hand, but he took it in new directions. In the first place, he cut the initial reference to classical literature. Secondly, in the place of standard stereotypes he used the names of actual women associated with the Parliamentary cause. And finally, in the place of a general diatribe against the unnaturalness of inversion, Neville honed a more precise satire that took aim at two elements within the Parliamentary side: the Presbyterians and the House of Lords. The pamphlet as a whole was couched in a language of libertinism that invited, but did not insist on, translation into the realm of politics. The particular ground that Neville would occupy within the complicated space of Parliamentary resistance to Stuart kingship was foreshadowed in these slight but suggestive works. He would remain an adamant foe to the systematic hypocrisies of organized religion throughout his life. Moreover, although he was no friend to populism or levelling, neither was he a supporter of the hereditary privileges of the aristocracy. Neville's politics were aristocratic in a looser sense. As his speeches in Parliament in 1659 would show, he insisted on the need in a well-ordered constitution for an upper house, or senate, consisting of the better sort. But he saw no need for that upper house to be selected on hereditary grounds.

After the publication of *Newes from the New Exchange* in 1650, Neville published nothing that we know of until *Shufling, Cutting, and Dealing*

30. The pamphlet was reprinted in 1646, twice in 1647 (as *A Parliament of Ladies*), and in 1656. Other broadly contemporary instances of the trope of women in Parliament include *An Exact Diurnall of the Parliament of Ladyes* (1647), *Now or Never: or, A New Parliament of Women Assembled* (1656), *The Gossips Meeting* (1674), *A List of the Parliament of Women* (1679), *The Cuckholds Petition* (1684), and *The Parliament of Women* (1684).

in a Game of Pickquet (1656) and—although his partial authorship of this pamphlet is far from certain—*A Copy of a Letter from an Officer of the Army in Ireland, to His Highness the Lord Protector, Concerning His Changing of the Government* (1656).[31] The early 1650s had seen Neville taking an important role in public life as an MP and as a member of the Council of State. At the same time, his political ideas must have been deepened and enriched by his friendship with James Harrington, whose *Oceana* was also published in 1656, and in the composition of which Neville was thought by some to have assisted.

Neville was unable to reconcile himself to the Protectorate of Oliver Cromwell, and both the works he published in 1656 emerge from that position of disaffection and suspicion. Harringtonian politics also left their mark on the political vision of *A Copy of a Letter*, which deploys the key Harringtonian insight of the relation between the ownership of real property and the exercise of political power.[32] That new theoretical precision and penetration in questions of politics was accompanied by further literary refinement. *Shuffling, Cutting, and Dealing in a Game of Pickquet*, like *The Parliament of Ladies*, uses the names of real people (including Neville himself), but instead of taking a literary genre off the peg, Neville here seems to have created a new genre, that of the political game of cards. And *A Copy of a Letter* also shows Neville experimenting with literary possibilities that he had not previously attempted, such as forgery (the letter carries a feigned date) and the use of *personae*.

These were crucial years for Neville's political and literary development, years in which he broadened and refined his literary accomplishment while at the same time clarifying and stabilizing his understanding of politics in general, of English politics in particular, and most importantly of

31. One slight suggestion of common authorship, or at least of Neville's involvement in the composition of *A Copy of a Letter*, is the occurrence in that work of the language of cards applied to politics, which of course is the governing metaphor of *Shuffling, Cutting, and Dealing in a Game of Pickquet*; see *Copy of a Letter*, appendix A, p. 320, "turned up Trump." In *The Rehearsal Transpros'd; The Second Part* (1672) Marvell would also make satirical capital out of references to picquet (Marvell, *Prose Works*, vol. 1, p. 252; see also vol. 2, p. 305).

32. See, e.g., *Copy of a Letter*, appendix A, p. 326.

how the former might shape the latter. There is also a faint suggestion that Neville himself may have felt that, by 1659, his political principles had reached a point of stability. The epigraph to *Shuffling, Cutting, and Dealing in a Game of Pickquet* is an abbreviated version of the extremely common Latin tag *Tempora mutantur, nos et mutamur in illis*—"The times change, and we change with them."[33] But the epigraph given by Neville to his pamphlet reads simply: "*Tempora mutantur et nos*—." The dash can be read as a heavy hint that Neville, unlike Cromwell, would not under the pressure of circumstances change the republican political principles he had recently adopted on the basis of experience and study.[34]

The Isle of Pines (1668)

Perhaps during his period of travelling in Italy (1664–67), perhaps immediately after his return to England in November 1667, Neville composed, if not his most profound, then certainly his most widely read literary work.[35] *The Isle of Pines* relates the story of how George Pine and four

33. This is not in fact a quotation from classical Latin, although it bears some resemblance to lines of Ovid (e.g., *Metamorphoses* 15.165 and *Fasti* 6.771–72). It is first found in the early modern period in the *Postilla Deudsch* (Frankfurt an der Oder, 1554) of Caspar Huberinus, fol. 354; thereafter it is widespread. In an English context, see, e.g., Raphael Holinshed, *Chronicles* (1587), vol. 1, p. 179; May, *History*, tp; Albertus Warren, *A Just Vindication of the Armie* (1647), p. 13; Amon Wilbee, *Tertia Pars de Comparatis Comparandis* (1648), p. 20; Peter Heylyn, *Extraneus Vapulans* (1656), p. 311; Michael Hawke, *The Grounds of the Lawes of England* (1657), p. 105; Thomas Willis, *A Word in Season* (1659), tp; George Wither, *Furor Poeticus* (1660), tp.

34. The significant abbreviation caught the attention of at least one of Neville's antagonists: "Our Polititian must never sing *Tempora mutantur*, without a *Nos mutamur in illis*" (John Yalden, *Machiavil Redivivus* [1681], p. 45).

35. On republications and translations of this work, see Gaby Mahlberg, "The Publishing History of *The Isle of Pines*," *Utopian Studies*, 17, no. 1 (2006), pp. 93–98. Neville's work enjoyed a vogue across all of Europe, being translated into several languages. Daniel Carey's article "Henry Neville's *The Isle of Pines*: Travel, Forgery, and the Problem of Genre," *Angelaki*, 1 (1996), pp. 23–40, gives an excellent account of the significance of the variety of ways in which the text's translators wrestled with its complicated and contradictory generic markers.

women, shipwrecked on a large, deserted island in the Indian Ocean, over three generations furnish it with a population, and of how, nearly one hundred years later, the island and its population are rediscovered by Dutch merchants.

The text came to the public in a complicated way. Initially only the narrative of the original settler, George Pine, was published, on 27 June 1668, as *The Isle of Pines*. It was followed on 22 July by a larger text, *A New and Further Discovery of the Islle* [sic] *of Pines*, comprising the narrative of the subsequent rediscovery of the island and its inhabitants by Cornelius van Sloetten, a Dutch merchant, and the history of George Pine's descendant, William Pine. Finally, on 27 July, a conflated text was published as *The Isle of Pines*, in which George Pine's narrative was inserted at the appropriate point in William Pine's narrative of life on the island.

Why was this text published in such a piecemeal fashion? One possible explanation is that the first publication was pirated and that Neville then rushed to shore up his position by publishing the ancillary material as a separate book (i.e., *A New and Further Discovery*) before bringing out the third, complete and conflated version of the text. A second possibility, given the politically sensitive issues on which the text touches, is that these multiple texts were produced in an attempt to baffle or evade postpublication censorship. However, there is no direct evidence of either piracy or official interest in this text, which seems to have been licensed without difficulty. A third possibility therefore must be entertained, that Neville chose to bring *The Isle of Pines* to press in this complicated way as part of a ludic (but not therefore unserious) exploration of the rich possibilities of print publication that had opened up in the wake of the Civil Wars.[36]

A recurrent emphasis in the extensive secondary literature on *The Isle of Pines* is the difficulty of interpretation it presents to the modern reader.[37] As might have been expected, the resistant medium of this text has powerfully refracted the secondary literature. The spectrum of critical

36. See above, p. xix, n. 27, for a preliminary bibliography.
37. See, e.g., Amy Boesky, "Nation, Miscegenation: Membering Utopia in Henry Neville's *The Isle of Pines*," *Texas Studies in Literature and Language*, 37, no. 2 (1995), p. 180; Susan Bruce, *Three Early Modern Utopias: "Utopia," "New Atlantis," and "The Isle of Pines"* (Oxford: Oxford University Press, 1999), p. xxxvii; Peter Stillman,

opinion extends from those who, particularly struck by the playful *habitus* of the text, regard it as nothing more than a lighthearted and amusing *jeu d'esprit*,[38] to those who, more impressed by the depth and weightiness of the moral and political issues set in motion by the text than by its ludic manner, see in it a profound and satirical study of Restoration England.[39]

There can be no doubt that Neville's text addresses and mobilizes serious questions of patriarchalism, the hereditary principle, colonialism, race, sexual ethics and polygamy, libertinism, the dynamics of population growth, and the natural history of society. Equally it is undeniable that *The Isle of Pines* is a generically self-conscious and playful text, exploiting the emergent conventions of travel literature, the use of literary *personae*, mock geography, the mock-Biblical, and utopian and dystopian literary forms. The delicate critical questions that arise are of how to balance these two aspects of the book and of where to lay the interpretative emphasis.[40]

It is not immediately clear whether Neville's literary playfulness is calculated to encourage serious reflection on the important questions raised in *The Isle of Pines*, or whether—on the contrary—these important topics merely provide raw material on which he was able to exercise that taste for literary invention, mischief, libertinism, and fantasizing which we have already seen in his publications of the 1640s and 1650s. A clear satiric disposition and great literary high spirits are plainly at work in *The Isle of Pines*. But that does not, by itself, make the text a fully worked out and achieved satire. It is a work of genius, originality, and promise. But it is perhaps more a brilliant display of potential than the profound and finished masterpiece of sedition that some have discovered in it. George Pine's potency as a breeder of offspring taken with his incompetence as a

"Monarchy, Disorder, and Politics in *The Isle of Pines*," *Utopian Studies: Journal of the Society for Utopian Studies*, 17, no. 1 (2006), p. 152.

38. See, e.g., Hughes, pp. vii–xi; Robbins, *Republican Tracts*, p. 13.

39. See, most egregiously, Scheckter, passim.

40. Wiseman's view, that *The Isle of Pines* is "*both* a scurrilous narrative and political polemic," is accurate as far as it goes, but it stops short of addressing the critical issue (Susan Wiseman, "'Adam, the Father of All Flesh,' Porno-Political Rhetoric and Political Theory in and after the English Civil War," *Prose Studies*, 14, no. 3 (1991), p. 148).

statesman is sometimes said to constitute "a critique of England's current and future monarchs, of patriarchal rule, and of one dominant justifying argument for absolute monarchy."[41] Certainly it can be taken that way—but was it at the time? Did Charles II lose any sleep over *The Isle of Pines?* It is surely significant that, postpublication, no attempts were made that we know of either to arrest the printer or to bring charges of seditious libel. And if *The Isle of Pines* were really as implicitly seditious as some of its modern commentators have argued, would Neville—who had only just been permitted to return home from exile—have risked publishing it?

One detail of the text, elucidated in this edition for the first time, may supply a hint concerning Neville's attitude toward his own book. In the final part of Cornelius van Sloetten's narrative relating the events that occurred after he and his men had left the Isle of Pines, we are told of their visit to Calcutta and of the strange customs they discovered there:

> This *Calecute* is the chief Mart Town and Staple of all the *Indian* Traffique, it is very populous, and frequented by Merchants of all Nations. Here we unladed a great part of our Goods, and taking in others, which caused us to stay there a full Moneth, during which space, at leisure times I went abroad to take a survey of the City, which I found to be large and populous, lying for three miles together upon the Sea-shore. Here is a great many of those persons whom they call *Brachmans*, being their Priests or Teachers whom they much reverence. It is a custome here for the King to give to some of those *Brachmain*, the hanselling of his Nuptial Bed; for which cause, not the Kings, but the Kings sisters sons succeed in the Kingdom, as being more certainly known to be of the true Royal blood: And these sisters of his choose what Gentleman they please, on whom to bestow their Virginities; and if they prove not in a certain time to be with child, they betake themselves to these *Brachman Stalions*, who never fail of doing their work.[42]

This detail has caught the eye of commentators, who have seen in this description of the unconventional (to a European eye) sexual mores of

---

41. Peter Stillman, "Monarchy, Disorder, and Politics in the *Isle of Pines*," *Utopian Studies: Journal of the Society for Utopian Studies*, 17, no. 1 (2006), p. 158.
42. See below, p. 32.

the Indian princes a stroke in Neville's satire against Filmerian patriarchalism and the ideology of the hereditary principle. It surely is that. But
what has gone unnoticed is that Neville simply lifted the mildly indecent
second half of this passage verbatim from Peter Heylyn's *MIKPOKOΣMOΣ*,
"Augmented and Reuised" (1625), the second edition of the lectures on
historical geography that Heylyn had given at Oxford in the late 1610s.

This silent plagiarism concerning the sexual potency of the "Brachman stallions" is a detail that points us toward the true nature of Neville's
text. It is impudent, mischievous, astute, but winged for a short satiric
flight. Heylyn had a few years beforehand been the butt of Commonwealthman satire. In *The Rehearsal Transpros'd: The Second Part* (1672)
Marvell had traced Parker's blunder of saying that Geneva was on the
southern shore of Lac Leman back to Heylyn, "whose business it was by
his scandalous Histories to blacken the whole Reformation."[43] There is
huge cheek in Neville's act of textual theft, and also clever malice—how
the Laudian apologist and defender of absolutism Heylyn would have
hated finding his words in this indecent, slightly libertine book, had he
still been alive![44] But the presence of witty malice and literary adroitness
are not sufficient to make *The Isle of Pines* the kind of deep moral and political meditation that some have claimed it to be. Neville had assembled
some of the raw materials necessary for that profound book. But on the
showing of the family of texts published in 1668, he chose not to deliver
such a weighty work, preferring instead to write something short, irrev-
erent, fantastically complicated, and goading.

Plato Redivivus

If the brevity and bravura manner of *The Isle of Pines* makes it permis-
sible to be in two minds whether its technique was designed to support
its political and moral content, or whether that content was merely the

---

43. Marvell, *Prose Works*, vol. 1, p. 408; see p. 353 and n. 665 for the blunder over
the position of Geneva.

44. Heylyn died in 1662. For his political character, at least according to Algernon Sidney, see Scott, *Commonwealth Principles*, p. 125.

necessary scaffolding for a display of technique, the same cannot be said for *Plato Redivivus*, the suite of three political dialogues Neville published in 1680, at the height of the Exclusion Crisis and when the political nation was still in a state of shock after the Popish Plot. In this later work, literary sophistication and inventiveness were allied to a subtle and imaginative political vision and applied with impressive dexterity to the circumstances of a great crisis of state. *Plato Redivivus* is an expression of Neville's political intelligence at its most astute and innovative, and at the same time a demonstration of how dramatically his literary intelligence had developed since he had cut his authorial teeth on the witty but shallow lampoons he had published in the late 1640s.

The unsuccessful struggle by the House of Commons to pass a bill excluding from the succession the Roman Catholic heir presumptive to the throne, James, Duke of York, provoked a political earthquake. As is clear from the Parliamentary debates recorded by Anchitell Grey, MPs were shaken and alarmed to the point of paranoia by the scale of the mortal dangers that seemed to surround the nation in the final years of the 1670s.[45] At the same time, however, the magnitude of the crisis provoked a profound political debate concerning the ends of political systems in general, and the nature of the English constitution in particular. As Burnet would later recollect, looking back on that tempestuous period from the calmer waters of the next century, the arguments deployed by both sides had touched the deepest political questions:

> Those who argued for it [Exclusion] laid it down for a foundation, that every person, who had the whole right of any thing in him, had likewise the power of transferring it to whom he pleased. So the King and Parliament, being entirely possessed of the whole authority of the Nation, had a power to limit the succession, and every thing else relating to the Nation, as they pleased. And by consequence there was no such thing as a fundamental law, by which the power of Parliament was bound up: For no King and Parliament in any former

45. J. R. Jones, *The First Whigs: The Politics of the Exclusion Crisis 1678–1683* (London: Oxford University Press, 1961); J. P. Kenyon, *The Popish Plot* (London: Heinemann, 1972).

age had a power over the present King and Parliament; otherwise the Government was not entire, nor absolute. . . . Government was appointed for those that were to be governed, and not for the sake of the Governors themselves: Therefore all things relating to it were to be measured by the publick interest, and the safety of the people. . . . On the other hand, some argued against the Exclusion: That it was unlawful in it self, and against the unalterable law of succession; (which came to be the common phrase.) Monarchy was said to be by divine right: So the Law could not alter what God had settled. . . . Much weight was laid on the oath of allegiance, that tied us to the King's heirs: And whoso was the heir when any man took that oath, was still the heir to him. All lawyers had great regard to fundamental laws. And it was a maxim among our lawyers, that even an Act of Parliament against *Magna Charta* was null of it self.[46]

With men's minds thus perturbed, yet at the same time focused on fundamental political notions, Neville published *Plato Redivivus*: a book that, beneath its diplomatic, even courtly, surface, surreptitiously encouraged its readers toward radical political change.

The three speakers of these dialogues—an English gentleman, a doctor, and a Venetian nobleman—explore the problems of English politics during three days of discussions that range widely over Biblical, ancient, medieval, and modern history. Except for one short passage, in which the Doctor emerges as a passionate (although perhaps not deeply thoughtful) advocate of the interest of the Duke of Monmouth, the role of the Doctor and the Venetian Nobleman is for the most part to pose questions of the English Gentleman, who in response offers both an analysis of where and why the English constitution is no longer functioning properly, and a series of remedies that he believes would restore it to health and natural balance.

The language, the references, and the subject matter of these dialogues are, as the annotation to this edition repeatedly shows, full of extremely topical material. In one sense, therefore, *Plato Redivivus* is unquestionably a text of its moment. Yet the English Gentleman's analysis of how

46. Burnet, *History*, vol. 1, pp. 457–58.

and why the English government began to become unbalanced with the accession of Henry VII, as the ownership of landed property began to pass ever more substantially into the hands of the commons, is clearly derived from the thought of James Harrington; and there are many passages in *Plato Redivivus* (again pointed out in the annotation to this edition) in which the same historical and Biblical examples are made to perform the same argumentative tasks which had been previously set for them in works by Harrington. *Plato Redivivus* is an essay in repurposing the republican political theory of the late 1650s to the circumstances and opportunities created by the Exclusion Crisis.

The English Gentleman's Harringtonian analysis of what is wrong with the English government can be reduced to these heads. The protracted political tension and unrest of seventeenth-century England had been the natural and inescapable product of the growing discrepancy between the location of property and the location of political power. This transfer of land had been underway in England since the accession of Henry VII and the implementation of that king's policy of reducing the power and wealth of the aristocracy. Accordingly, a more natural and therefore more stable balance between property and power could be restored in one of two ways. Either the Crown and the aristocracy could acquire more property, or the Commons could be given more power. The former option is dismissed as impractical, leaving only the latter. To achieve that end, the Crown is to be induced to transfer certain of its prerogative powers to a group of councils made up of members of Parliament, elected from below rather than nominated from above, and regularly refreshed by rotation.

It will immediately be clear that *Plato Redivivus* takes advantage of the turmoil generated by the Exclusion Crisis but does not directly address the practical issues of religion and government which that crisis had set in motion. Neville's English Gentleman is massively untroubled by the alleged threat to England posed by Roman Catholicism; he ostentatiously shrinks from the damage to the principle of hereditary succession that would be inflicted by the successful exclusion of the Duke of York; and he fears that any attempt to legitimize the Duke of Monmouth would provoke a civil war. Moreover, he is careful to lavish compliments on Charles II. But this courtly suavity is deceptive. The English Gentleman's underlying but undeclared position is that the spectre of a Roman Catholic king would be much less alarming were the Crown itself to be shorn of some of its prerogative powers. For Neville, Parliament had been tackling the challenge posed by the religion of the Duke of York in an unintelligently direct way. In the end, what would the king's religion matter if the powers of the Crown could be trimmed, checked, and brought into line with the distribution of landed property in the kingdom?

The key to discerning Neville's intention in *Plato Redivivus* is contained in the revisions he made to the book for its second edition, published later in 1681. Revisions can be of two kinds. Some are the result of a change or inflection of authorial intention. Others, however, can emerge from the strengthening or deepening of an original intention. This second kind of revision shows an author cleaving more closely and with greater determination to an original purpose that, for some reason, had failed to have the desired impact in the form in which it first saw publication. The revisions Neville made for the second edition of *Plato Redivivus* are of this second kind.

Aside from a handful of smaller adjustments to wording, the variants in the second edition of *Plato Redivivus* are of two sorts. The first sort are additions to the text of the dialogues. Here we find substantial inserted passages, some strengthening the anticlerical character of the work, others expanding on the English Gentleman's reasons for not supporting the legitimizing of the Duke of Monmouth.[47] The second sort is the introduction of a completely new element to the book, the paratextual booklist of twelve "Political Discourses and Histories worth reading."[48] Is it possible to see these two aspects of the revisions Neville made for the second edition of *Plato Redivivus* as different aspects of a single authorial impulse?

---

47. See below, pp. 147–55 and 259–68, and, for full details, the "Textual Collation," below, pp. 448 and 464.

48. See below, pp. 51–53.

Insofar as scholars have hitherto bestowed any attention on Neville's booklist, they have tended to dismiss it as a publisher's list. However, it cannot be that. In the first place, not all the books it lists had the same publisher.[49] Secondly, it is placed in the wrong part of the book: publishers' lists are found at the end of a book, not inserted between the prefatory matter and the text proper, as Neville's booklist is. And finally, publishers' lists tend to be very long and very miscellaneous, as their function of advertising the full range of a publisher's wares required.[50] Neville's booklist, however, is short and tightly focused on recent European— importantly, *not* English—political history since the fifteenth century. Even the sole text in the list that seems not to conform to this pattern— Procopius's *Secret History*—does not in fact disrupt it as much as it might seem to at first glance. For although it is a text composed during late antiquity and describing events of the sixth century A.D., it was also a modern and topical text, as the manuscript had been discovered in the Vatican Library only recently, the *editio princeps* having been published in Lyon by Niccolò Alamanni in 1623.

The modern focus of the booklist is in keeping with the English Gentleman's insistence that medieval history and the ancient constitution can supply no guidance to Englishmen in their current predicament, while its exclusion of narrowly English material and its relocation of attention toward the Eastern Mediterranean chimes with his encouragement to his countrymen to look beyond their native political traditions for help in framing solutions to their present discontents.

A full analysis of how the booklist was shrewdly calculated to nudge Neville's first readers toward a better understanding of the deep, at points quite radical and vigorously republican, political doctrine of *Plato Redivivus*

---

49. Most of the books on the list were published by John Starkey, but two—the translation of Boccalini and the translation of Procopius's *Secret History*—were not.

50. For instance, the publisher's list included by Starkey in the 1675 translation of Machiavelli extends over five pages and includes seventy-seven items, divided under the headings "Divinity," "Physick," "Law," "History," "Poetry and Plays," and "Miscellanies." The list Starkey appended to Nani's *History of Europe* was only slightly shorter (seventy-one items), but was just as miscellaneous.

would require a book to itself.[51] But the outlines of such an argument can be briefly drawn.

In the first place, the exclusion of narrowly English material from the booklist sent a strong message that Englishmen needed to break free from the obsessive parochialism that had for the most part characterized English political thought since the accession of James I. Implicit here of course was a rejection of ancient constitutionalism, but hand in hand with that went something more positive: an invitation to consider the politics of Italy, of France, of the United Provinces, even of the Ottoman Empire, and to extract from their very different political experiences and the political models to which that experience had given birth valuable insights that might fruitfully be applied to England's current crisis.

Once the reader had begun to do that, in what direction would those insights lead him? In the first place, the writings of Machiavelli (and in particular the spurious "Vindication" that Neville had in all probability composed himself and then cheekily inserted into this volume of genuine translations) would draw the reader to reflect on how the removal of an explicitly Christian framework from the debate on government might change and extend the menu of political possibilities. Elsewhere in the booklist he would find material that suggested how intensely sacerdotal governments, like that of the emperor Justinian, could produce exotically despotic regimes; such was the lesson, in this context, taught by Procopius. From Commines, he could inspect the origins of early modern French absolutism and see how even the greatest of aristocratic magnates, the Duke of Burgundy, was maneuvered into forwarding precisely what he wished to resist. Aristocracy, it seemed, even in its most flamboyant and magnificent form, offered no bulwark against despotism—indeed, the very opposite had been true in fifteenth-century France. Venice's history and her institutions suggested that the pillars of a durable political settlement would be republican in nature and would embrace the devices of the ballot and the rota to suppress the growth of private interests. Rycaut's vivid (but also interestingly evenhanded) account of Ottoman institutions, and his retelling of the recent history of this monarchy which posed such a for-

---

51. See my *Henry Neville's Booklist*, forthcoming from Oxford University Press.

midable military threat to Christendom, would have provoked disquieting thoughts concerning the resilience of Western Europe, riven as she was by confessional divisions, against the Ottoman menace.[52]

When readers turned back to Neville's dialogues from perusing the titles included in the booklist, how might the resulting insights have guided and deepened their reading of the political doctrine embedded in the text? Those insights would have encouraged Neville's early readers to see past the language of courtly compliment with which Neville had disguised the radical tendency of his thought, and to have realized that *Plato Redivivus* was in fact an appeal to Englishmen to begin dismantling the apparatus and ideology, not just of Stuart monarchy, but of English monarchy *tout court*. Once the way in which the booklist interacts with the sentiments and language of the dialogues has been grasped, *Plato Redivivus* emerges as both audacious in doctrine and adventurous in technique, as both astute and intrepid.

Conclusion

Neville has existed in the shadow of the giants of seventeenth-century English political thought—Hobbes, Harrington, Locke—and has tended to play a supporting role in their stories rather than taking center stage himself. In one respect at least this is not a great injustice. His writings are much less systematic and analytic than those of Hobbes and Locke, and his prescriptions for England's body politic were not fleshed out or imagined with anything like Harrington's thoroughness or intensity.

More than any of those three greater political theorists, however, Neville was a practical politician, holding higher public office than any of them and, while he was a member of the Council of State, participating in public life at a pitch which none of them approached. He was, perhaps,

---

52. In 1681 the Ottomans were a clear and present military threat to the eastern fringes of Christendom. From 1648 until 1669 the Ottomans had besieged the Venetian-ruled city of Candia on Crete, finally taking it after twenty-one years and thereby gaining control of the whole island (which they would retain until 1897). In 1683 an Ottoman army of 150,000 would come close to taking Vienna before being routed by a combined German and Polish force.

too attuned to what might practically be possible to pursue very far either pure theory (in the manner of Hobbes or Locke) or political fantasy (in the manner of Harrington, however much Neville may have agreed with Harrington's diagnosis of England's political ailments and the powerful political generalizations upon which that diagnosis rested). Instead, Neville's writings give us something different. They are the products of an experienced political actor who united a practitioner's sense of possibility with literary flair and imagination as he struggled to achieve headway for his republican commitments in the deceptive waters of the late Stuart monarchy. It is this combination of fundamental staunch republicanism with the tactical acuity and flexibility of the politician which makes *Plato Redivivus* such a distinctive contribution to late seventeenth-century English political writing.

David Womersley
Munich, 2019

FURTHER READING

A: Modern Editions of Works by Neville

Bruce, Susan, ed. *Three Early Modern Utopias: "Utopia," "New Atlantis," and "The Isle of Pines."* Oxford: Oxford University Press, 1999.

Hughes, Derek, ed. *Versions of Blackness: Key Texts on Slavery from the Seventeenth Century.* Cambridge: Cambridge University Press, 2007.

Robbins, Caroline, ed. *Two English Republican Tracts.* Cambridge: Cambridge University Press, 1969.

Scheckter, John, ed. *The Isle of Pines, 1668: Henry Neville's Uncertain Utopia.* Farnham, England: Ashgate, 2011.

B: Secondary Works

Aldridge, A. O. "Polygamy in Early Fiction: Henry Neville and Denis Veiras." *Publications of the Modern Language Association of America*, 65, no. 4 (1950), pp. 464–72.

Beach, Adam R. "A Profound Pessimism about the Empire: *The Isle of Pines*, English Degeneracy and Dutch Supremacy." *The Eighteenth Century: Theory and Interpretation*, 41, no. 1 (2000), pp. 21–36.

Boesky, Amy. "Nation, Miscegenation: Membering Utopia in Henry Neville's *The Isle of Pines*." *Texas Studies in Literature and Language*, 37, no. 2 (1995), pp. 165–84.

Bond, W. H. *Thomas Hollis of Lincoln's Inn: A Whig and His Books*. Cambridge: Cambridge University Press, 1990.

Carey, Daniel. "Henry Neville's *Isle of Pines*: Travel, Forgery, and the Problem of Genre." *Angelaki*, 1 (1996), pp. 23–39.

———. "Henry Neville's *The Isle of Pines*: From Sexual Utopia to Political Dystopia." In *New Worlds Reflected: Travel and Utopia in the Early Modern Period*, edited by Chloë Houston and Andrew Hadfield, pp. 203–22. Farnham, England: Ashgate, 2010.

———. "Travel and Sexual Fantasy in the Early Modern Period." In *Writing and Fantasy*, edited by Ceri Sullivan and Barbara White, pp. 151–65. New York: Longman, 1999.

Cress, Lawrence Delbert. "Radical Whiggery on the Role of the Military: Ideological Roots of the American Revolutionary Militia." *Journal of the History of Ideas*, 40, no. 1 (1979), pp. 42–60.

Crino, A. M. *Fatti e Figure del Seicento Anglo-Toscano*. Florence: Olschki, 1957.

———. *Il Popish Plot*. Rome: Edizioni di storia e letteratura, 1954.

Davis, J. C. "Going Nowhere: Travelling to, through, and from Utopia." *Utopian Studies: Journal of the Society for Utopian Studies*, 19, no. 1 (2008), pp. 1–23.

Denbo, Seth. "Generating Regenerated Generations: Race, Kinship, and Sexuality on Henry Neville's *Isle of Pines* (1668)." In *Gender and Utopia in the Eighteenth Century: Essays in English and French Utopian Writing*, edited by Nicole Pohl and Brenda Tooley, pp. 147–61. Aldershot, England: Ashgate, 2007.

Dickinson, H. T. "The Eighteenth-Century Debate on the Sovereignty of Parliament." *Transactions of the Royal Historical Society*, 5, no. 26 (1976), pp. 189–210.

Fatovic, Clemment. "The Anti-Catholic Roots of Liberal and Republican Conceptions of Freedom in English Political Thought." *Journal of the History of Ideas*, 66, no. 1 (2005), pp. 37–58.

Fausett, David. *Writing the New World: Imaginary Voyages and Utopias of the Great Southern Land*. Syracuse, N.Y.: Syracuse University Press, 1993 (pp. 79–90).

Goodale, J. R. "J. G. A. Pocock's Neo-Harringtonians: A Reconsideration." *History of Political Thought*, 1, no. 2 (1980), pp. 237–59; and see also Pocock's reply, "A Reconsideration Impartially Considered," *History of Political Thought*, 1, no. 3 (1980), pp. 541–45.

Hardy, Nat. "Euphemizing Utopia: Repressing Sex and Violence in the *Isle of Pines'* Frontispiece." *Utopian Studies: Journal of the Society for Utopian Studies*, 17, no. 1 (2006), pp. 99–107.

Jones, Stephanie. "Colonial to Postcolonial Ethics." *Interventions*, 11, no. 2 (2009), pp. 212–34.

Loveman, Kate. *Reading Fictions, 1660–1740: Deception in English Literary and Political Culture*. Aldershot, England: Ashgate, 2008.

Mahlberg, Gaby. *Henry Neville and English Republican Culture in the Seventeenth Century: Dreaming of Another Game*. Manchester: Manchester University Press, 2009.

———. "The Publishing History of *The Isle of Pines*." *Utopian Studies: Journal of the Society for Utopian Studies*, 17, no. 1 (2006), pp. 111–29.

———. "Republicanism as Anti-Patriarchalism in Henry Neville's *The Isle of Pines* (1668)." In *Liberty, Authority, Formality: Political Ideas and Culture, 1600–1900: Essays in Honour of Colin Davis*, edited by John Morrow, pp. 131–52. Exeter, England: Imprint Academic, 2008.

Maltzahn, Nicholas von. "Neville, Henry (1620–1694)." *Oxford Dictionary of National Biography*. Oxford: Oxford University Press, 2004.

McDowell, Nicholas. *The English Radical Imagination: Culture, Religion, and Revolution, 1630–1660*. Oxford: Oxford University Press, 2003.

Norbrook, David. *Writing the English Republic: Poetry, Rhetoric, and Politics 1627–1660*. Cambridge: Cambridge University Press, 1999.

Patterson, Annabel. *Early Modern Liberalism*. Cambridge: Cambridge University Press, 1997.

Pocock, J. G. A. *The Machiavellian Moment: Florentine Political Thought and the Atlantic Republican Tradition*. Princeton, N.J.: Princeton University Press, 1975.

———. "A Reconsideration Impartially Considered." *History of Political Thought*, 1, no. 3 (1980), pp. 541–45.

Pohl, Nicole. "The Quest for Utopia in the Eighteenth Century." *Literature Compass*, 5, no. 4 (2008), pp. 685–706.

Poole, William. "Francis Godwin, Henry Neville, Margaret Cavendish, H. G. Wells: Some Utopian Debts." *ANQ: A Quarterly Journal of Short Articles, Notes, and Reviews*, 16, no. 3 (2003), pp. 12–18.

Quint, David. *Epic and Empire*. Princeton, N.J.: Princeton University Press, 1993.

Rahe, Paul A. *Against Throne and Altar: Machiavelli and Political Theory under the English Republic*. Cambridge: Cambridge University Press, 2008.

Richards, Judith, Lotte Mulligan, and John K. Graham. "'Property' and 'People': Political Usages of Locke and Some Contemporaries." *Journal of the History of Ideas*, 42, no. 1 (1981), pp. 29–51.

Robbins, Caroline. *The Eighteenth-Century Commonwealthman: Studies in the Transmission, Development, and Circumstance of English Liberal Thought from the Restoration of Charles II until the War with the Thirteen Colonies.* Cambridge, Mass.: Harvard University Press, 1959, repr. 1961.

Rothschild, Jeffrey M. "Renaissance Voices Echoed: The Emergence of the Narrator in English Prose." *College English*, 52, no. 1 (1990), pp. 21–35.

Sargent, Lyman Tower. "Themes in Utopian Fiction in English before Wells." *Science Fiction Studies*, 3, no. 3 (1976), pp. 275–82.

Smith, Nigel. *Literature and Revolution in England, 1640–1660.* New Haven, Conn.: Yale University Press, 1994.

Stillman, Peter G. "*The Isle of Pines*: Texts." *Utopian Studies: Journal of the Society for Utopian Studies*, 17, no. 1 (2006), pp. 11–88.

———. "Monarchy, Disorder, and Politics in *The Isle of Pines.*" *Utopian Studies: Journal of the Society for Utopian Studies*, 17, no. 1 (2006), pp. 147–75.

Sullivan, Vicki B. *Machiavelli, Hobbes, and the Formation of a Liberal Republicanism in England.* Cambridge: Cambridge University Press, 2004.

Weber, Harold. "Charles II, George Pines, and Mr. Dorimant: The Politics of Sexual Power in Restoration England." *Criticism*, 32, no. 2 (1990), pp. 193–219.

Williamson, Bethany. "English Republicanism and Global Slavery in Henry Neville's *The Isle of Pines.*" *Eighteenth-Century Fiction*, 27, no. 1 (2014), pp. 1–23.

Wiseman, Susan. "'Adam, the Father of All Flesh,' Porno-Political Rhetoric and Political Theory in and after the English Civil War." *Prose Studies*, 14, no. 3 (1991), pp. 134–57.

Wootton, David, ed. *Republicanism, Liberty, and Commercial Society, 1649–1776.* Stanford, Calif.: Stanford University Press, 1994.

Worden, Blair. *God's Instruments: Political Conduct in the England of Oliver Cromwell.* Oxford: Oxford University Press, 2012.

———. *Literature and Politics in Cromwellian England.* Oxford: Oxford University Press, 2007.

NOTE ON THE TEXTS

The publication history of both texts included in this edition is intricate and deserves comment.

The Isle of Pines

We have no information concerning when Neville began writing *The Isle of Pines*. The first printing of *The Isle of Pines, or A Late Discovery of a Fourth Island near Terra Australis, Incognita* was licensed on 27 June 1668. This first text comprised only the narrative of George Pine himself. It was quickly twice reprinted and was translated into Dutch, German, French, Danish, and Italian. The following month, on 22 July, *A New and Further Discovery of the Islle of Pines* was published. This was a more elaborate narrative, in which a *précis* of George Pine's narrative delivered by his descendant William Pine was framed within the narrative of Cornelius van Sloetton's rediscovery of the island in its populated condition, together with the paratextual addition of a postscript. Finally, on 27 July 1668 *The Isle of Pines, or A Late Discovery of a Fourth Island near Terra Australis, Incognita* was licensed. This third text was a conflation of the first two. George Pine's narrative was now placed within van Sloetton's account, and a further paratext of two prefatory letters from Abraham Keek was added. The copy text for this edition is this third and final text licensed on 27 July 1668. For fuller information, see Gaby Mahlberg, "The Publishing History of *The Isle of Pines*," *Utopian Studies*, 17, no. 1 (2006), pp. 93–98.

Plato Redivivus

It seems probable that most of *Plato Redivivus* was composed between the dissolution of the Habeas Corpus Parliament on 12 July 1679 and the assembly of the Exclusion Bill Parliament on 21 October 1680, although some details in the text suggest that at least parts of it may have been composed considerably earlier (see below, p. 167, n. 290, and p. 252, n. 495). This first edition was published probably in October 1680, although the title page bears the date 1681. A second edition, with important additions to the text of the dialogues and the transformative inclusion of the paratextual booklist, "*Political* Discourses *and* Histories *Worth Reading*," was published probably early in the following year, 1681. The copy text for this edition is the second, enlarged edition of 1681. A full collation of the two editions is included (see below, pp. 439–70).

ABBREVIATIONS

Aglionby, *United Provinces*	William Aglionby. *The Present State of the United Provinces.* Second edition. 1671.
Amelot de la Houssaie, *Venice*	Amelot de la Houssaie. *The History of the Government of Venice.* 1677.
Antidotum	*Antidotum Britannicum: Or, a Counter-Pest against the Destructive Principles of Plato Redivivus.* 1681.
Antimonarchical Authors	*Antimonarchical Authors.* 1699.
Armie's Dutie	Anon. *The Armie's Dutie.* 1659.
Aubrey, *Brief Lives*	John Aubrey. *Brief Lives.* Edited by Kate Bennett. 2 vols. Oxford: Oxford University Press, 2015.
Bacon, *Essayes*	Sir Francis Bacon. *The Essayes or Counsels, Civill and Morall.* Edited by Michael Kiernan. Oxford: Clarendon Press, 1985.
Bacon, *Henry VII*	Francis Bacon. *The Historie of the Raigne of King Henry the Seventh.* 1622.
Blackstone, *Commentaries*	William Blackstone. *Commentaries on the Laws of England.* 4 vols. 1765–69.

Boccalini, *Advertisements*

Trajano Bocalini [*sic*]. *I ragguagli di Parnasso: Or, Advertisements from Parnassus.* Translated by Henry Carey, Second Earl of Monmouth. Third edition. 1674.

Bodin, *Common-Weale*

Jean Bodin. *The Six Bookes of a Common-Weale.* Translated by Richard Knolles. 1606.

Brady, *History*

Robert Brady. *A Complete History of England.* 1685.

Bulstrode Papers

Richard Bulstrode. *The Bulstrode Papers.* 1897.

Burke, *Reflections*

Edmund Burke. *Reflections on the Revolution in France.* Edited by J. C. D. Clark. Stanford, Calif.: Stanford University Press, 2001.

Burnet, *History*

Bishop Burnet's History of His Own Time. 2 vols. 1724 and 1734.

Burton, *Diary*

Diary of Thomas Burton. Edited by John Towill Rutt. 4 vols. London: Henry Colbourn, 1828.

Carey, *Considerations*

Sir Nicholas Carey (or Carew). *Some Considerations upon the Question, Whether the Parliament Is Dissolved by It's Prorogation for 15 Months.* 1676.

Cato's Letters

John Trenchard and Thomas Gordon. *Cato's Letters or Essays on Liberty, Civil and Religious, and Other Important Subjects.* Edited by Ronald Hamowy. 2 vols. Indianapolis: Liberty Fund, 1995.

Champion, *Priestcraft*

J. A. I. Champion. *The Pillars of Priestcraft Shaken: The Church of England and Its Enemies 1660–1730.* Cambridge: Cambridge University Press, 1992.

CJ

Journals of the House of Commons. 51 vols. 1803.

Clarendon, *History*	*The History of the Rebellion and Civil Wars in England Begun in the Year 1641, by Edward, Earl of Clarendon*. Edited by W. Dunn Macray. 6 vols. Oxford: Clarendon Press, 1992.
Coke, *Detection*	Roger Coke. *A Detection of the Court and State of England*. 1697.
Coke, *Selected Writings*	*The Selected Writings of Sir Edward Coke*. Edited by Steve Sheppard. 3 vols. Indianapolis: Liberty Fund, 2003.
Commines, *Memoirs*	*The Memoirs of Philip of Comines*. 1674.
Contarini, *Venice*	*The Commonwealth and Government of Venice. Written by the Cardinall Gasper Contareno*. Translated by Lewes Lewkenor. 1599.
Copy of a Letter	Anonymous. *A Copy of a Letter from an Officer of the Army in Ireland, to His Highness the Lord Protector, concerning His Changing of the Government*. 1656.
Crino, *Fatti e figure*	A. M. Crino. *Fatti e figure del seicento Anglo-Toscano*. Florence: Olschki, 1957.
Crino, *Popish Plot*	A. M. Crino. *Il Popish Plot*. Rome: Edizioni di storia e letteratura, 1954.
Evelyn, *Diary*	*The Diary of John Evelyn*. Edited by E. S. de Beer. 6 vols. Oxford: Clarendon Press, 1955.
Filmer, *Patriarcha*	Sir Robert Filmer. *Patriarcha and Other Writings*. Edited by Johann P. Somerville. Cambridge: Cambridge University Press, 1991.
Gailhard, *Italy*	Jean Gailhard. *The Present State of the Princes and Republicks of Italy*. Second edition. 1671.
Gibbon, *Decline and Fall*	Edward Gibbon. *The History of the Decline and Fall of the Roman Empire*.

	Edited by David Womersley. 3 vols. London: Allen Lane, 1994.
Gibbon, *Letters*	*The Letters of Edward Gibbon.* Edited by J. E. Norton. 3 vols. London: Cassell, 1956.
Goddard, *Plato's Demon*	Thomas Goddard. *Plato's Demon: Or, the State-Physician Unmaskt; Being a Discourse in Answer to a Book Call'd "Plato Redivivus."* 1684.
Grey, *Debates*	Anchitell Grey. *Debates of the House of Commons, from the Year 1667 to the Year 1694.* 10 vols. 1763.
Grotius, *War and Peace*	Hugo Grotius. *The Rights of War and Peace.* Edited by Richard Tuck. 3 vols. Indianapolis: Liberty Fund, 2005.
Hay, *Policy*	Paul Hay du Chastelet. *The Policy and Government of the Venetians, Both in Civil and Military Affairs.* 1671.
Heylyn, *ΜΙΚΡΟΚΟΣΜΟΣ*	Peter Heylyn. *ΜΙΚΡΟΚΟΣΜΟΣ,* "Augmented and Reuised." 1625.
Hobbes, *Leviathan*	Thomas Hobbes. *Leviathan.* Edited by Richard Tuck. Cambridge: Cambridge University Press, 1996.
Hughes	*Versions of Blackness: Key Texts on Slavery from the Seventeenth Century.* Edited by Derek Hughes. Cambridge: Cambridge University Press, 2007.
Hume, *Essays*	David Hume. *Essays Moral, Political, and Literary.* Edited by Eugene F. Miller. Indianapolis: Liberty Fund, 1987.
James VI and I, *Political Writings*	King James VI and I. *Political Writings.* Edited by Johann P. Somerville. Cambridge: Cambridge University Press, 1994.
Janson, *Natural History of Latin*	Tore Janson. *A Natural History of Latin.* Oxford: Oxford University Press, 2004.

Jones, *Secret History*   David Jones. *The Secret History of White-Hall.* 1697.

Jones, *Theatre of Wars*   David Jones. *A Theatre of Wars between England and France.* 1698.

Jones, *Tragical History*   David Jones. *The Tragical History of the Stuarts.* 1697.

Kenyon, *Stuart Constitution*   J. P. Kenyon. *The Stuart Constitution 1603–1688: Documents and Commentary.* Cambridge: Cambridge University Press, 1966.

Knolles, *Turkes*   Richard Knolles. *The General Historie of the Turkes.* 1603.

Lee, *Popular Sovereignty*   Daniel Lee. *Popular Sovereignty in Early Modern Constitutional Thought.* Oxford: Oxford University Press, 2016.

Lives of the Poets   Samuel Johnson. *The Lives of the Poets.* Edited by Roger Lonsdale. 4 vols. Oxford: Clarendon Press, 2006.

Locke, *Two Treatises*   John Locke. *Two Treatises of Government.* Edited by Peter Laslett. Cambridge: Cambridge University Press, 1988.

Ludlow, *Memoirs*   Edmund Ludlow. *Memoirs of Edmund Ludlow, Esq.* 2 vols. Vevay, 1698.

Machiavelli, *Works*   *The Works of the Famous Nicholas Machiavel.* 1675.

Magalotti, *Relazioni*   Lorenzo Magalotti. *Relazioni d'Inghilterra 1668 e 1688.* Edited by Anna Maria Crino. Florence: Olschki, 1972.

Mahlberg   Gaby Mahlberg. *Henry Neville and English Republican Culture in the Seventeenth Century: Dreaming of Another Game.* Manchester: Manchester University Press, 2009.

Mandeville, *Fable of the Bees* Bernard Mandeville. *The Fable of the Bees.* Edited by F. B. Kaye. 2 vols.

	Oxford: Clarendon Press, 1924; Indianapolis: Liberty Fund, 1988.
Marvell, *Poems and Letters*	*The Poems and Letters of Andrew Marvell.* Edited by H. M. Margoliouth. Second edition. Oxford: Clarendon Press, 1952.
Marvell, *Prose Works*	*The Prose Works of Andrew Marvell.* Edited by M. Dzelzainis, Annabel Patterson, Nicholas von Maltzahn, and N. H. Keeble. 2 vols. New Haven, Conn.: Yale University Press, 2003.
May, *History*	Thomas May. *The History of the Parliament of England.* 1647.
Mayerne, *Spaine*	Lewis de Mayerne Turquet. *The Generall Historie of Spaine.* Translated by Edward Grimeston. 1612.
Morton, *Freedom*	A. L. Morton, ed. *Freedom in Arms: A Selection of Leveller Writings.* London: Lawrence and Wishart, 1975.
Nani, *Affairs of Europe*	Battista Nani. *The History of the Affairs of Europe in This Present Age.* 1673.
Neville, *Shufling*	Henry Neville. *Shufling, Cutting, and Dealing in a Game of Pickquet.* 1656.
ODNB	*Oxford Dictionary of National Biography*
OED	*Oxford English Dictionary*
Paine, *Rights of Man*	Thomas Paine. *Rights of Man.* Edited by Henry Collins. Harmondsworth, England: Penguin, 1983.
Pepys, *Diary*	*The Diary of Samuel Pepys.* Edited by Robert Latham and William Matthews. 11 vols. London: G. Bell and Sons, 1970–83.
Pocock, *Ancient Constitution*	J. G. A. Pocock. *The Ancient Constitution and the Feudal Law: A Study of English Historical Thought in the Seventeenth*

	Century. Cambridge: Cambridge University Press, 1957.
Pocock, *Harrington*	*The Political Works of James Harrington.* Edited by J. G. A. Pocock. Cambridge: Cambridge University Press, 1977.
Priolo, *History of France*	Benjamin Priolo. *The History of France under the Ministry of Cardinal Mazarine.* Translated by Christopher Wase. 1671.
Raab, *English Face*	Felix Raab. *The English Face of Machiavelli: A Changing Interpretation 1500–1700.* London: Routledge and Kegan Paul, 1964.
Rahe, *Throne and Altar*	Paul A. Rahe. *Against Throne and Altar: Machiavelli and Political Theory under the English Republic.* Cambridge: Cambridge University Press, 2008.
Ralegh, *History of the World*	Sir Walter Ralegh. *The History of the World.* 1617.
Redford, *Letters*	*The Letters of Samuel Johnson.* Edited by Bruce Redford. "The Hyde Edition." 5 vols. Oxford: Clarendon Press, 1992–94.
Robbins, *Commonwealthman*	Caroline Robbins. *The Eighteenth-Century Commonwealthman: Studies in the Transmission, Development, and Circumstance of English Liberal Thought from the Restoration of Charles II until the War with the Thirteen Colonies.* Cambridge, Mass.: Harvard University Press, 1961.
Robbins, *Republican Tracts*	Caroline Robbins. *Two Republican Tracts.* Cambridge: Cambridge University Press, 1969.
Rushworth, *Collections*	John Rushworth. *Historical Collections.* 1680.

Rycaut, *History* — Paul Rycaut. *The History of the Turkish Empire.* 1680.

Rycaut, *Present State* — Paul Rycaut. *The Present State of the Ottoman Empire.* Third edition. 1670.

Scheckter — John Scheckter. *The Isle of Pines, 1668: Henry Neville's Uncertain Utopia.* Farnham, England: Ashgate, 2011.

Schwoerer, *Armies* — Lois G. Schwoerer. *"No Standing Armies!": The Antiarmy Ideology in Seventeenth-Century England.* Baltimore: Johns Hopkins University Press, 1974.

Scott, *Commonwealth Principles* — Jonathan Scott. *Commonwealth Principles: Republican Writing of the English Revolution.* Cambridge: Cambridge University Press, 2004.

Sharpe, *Personal Rule* — Kevin Sharpe. *The Personal Rule of Charles I.* New Haven, Conn.: Yale University Press, 1992.

Sidney, *Court Maxims* — Algernon Sidney. *Court Maxims.* Edited by Hans W. Blom, Eco Haitsma Mulier, and Roland Janse. Cambridge: Cambridge University Press, 1996.

Sidney, *Discourses* — Algernon Sidney. *Discourses concerning Government.* Edited by Thomas G. West. Indianapolis: Liberty Fund, 1990.

Skinner, *Liberty* — Quentin Skinner. *Liberty before Liberalism.* Cambridge: Cambridge University Press, 1998.

Smith, *Republica* — Sir Thomas Smith. *De Republica Anglorum.* Edited by M. Dewar. Cambridge: Cambridge University Press, 1982.

State-Tracts — *State-Tracts: In Two Parts.* 2 vols. 1693.

Streater, *Glympse* — John Streater. *A Glympse of That Jewel.* 1653.

Stubbs, *Constitutional History*   William Stubbs. *The Constitutional History of England in Its Origin and Development.* Second edition. 3 vols. Oxford: Clarendon Press, 1875–78.

Swift, *Correspondence*   *The Correspondence of Jonathan Swift, D. D.* Edited by David Woolley. 5 vols. Frankfurt am Main: Peter Lang, 1999–2014.

Swift, *Gulliver's Travels*   Jonathan Swift. *Gulliver's Travels.* Edited by David Womersley. Cambridge: Cambridge University Press, 2012.

Swift, *Prose Writings*   *The Prose Writings of Jonathan Swift.* Edited by Herbert Davis et al. 14 vols. Oxford: Blackwell, 1939–68.

Sydney, *Letters*   *Letters of the Honourable Algernon Sydney, to the Honourable Henry Savile. Ambassador in France. In the Year 1679, &c.* 1742.

Toland, *Harrington*   *The Oceana of James Harrington and Other Works.* Edited by John Toland. 1700.

W&S   *The Writings and Speeches of Edmund Burke.* Edited by Paul Langford et al. 9 vols. Oxford: Clarendon Press, 1981–2016.

Wootton, *Divine Right*   David Wootton, ed. *Divine Right and Democracy: An Anthology of Political Writing in Stuart England.* Harmondsworth, England: Penguin, 1986.

Wootton, *Republicanism*   David Wootton, ed. *Republicanism, Liberty, and Commercial Society, 1649–1776.* Stanford, Calif.: Stanford University Press, 1994.

CHRONOLOGY OF THE LIFE
OF HENRY NEVILLE

1620   Born in Billingbear, near Windsor, Berkshire

1635   Enters Merton College, Oxford; translates to University College; leaves without obtaining his degree

1639   Marries Elizabeth Staverton

1641–45   Travels in Europe during the English Civil War, first to France, and then to Italy

1647   Publication of *The Parliament of Ladies*

Publication of *The Ladies, a Second Time, Assembled in Parliament*

1647–48   Appointed to the General Committee in Berkshire

1649   Elected recruiter MP at Abingdon, Berkshire

November—gains seat in the Committee of Goldsmiths' Hall

1650   March 4—added to the Committee for the Sequestrations in Berkshire

Publication of *Newes from the New Exchange, or, The Common-Wealth of Ladies*

1651   Elected to the Council of State

September 23—charged with preparing a draft bill "for calling a new Parliament"

1652   Fails to be reelected to Council of State

1653   April—dissolution of the Rump by Cromwell

1654   Banished from London by Cromwell

1655   Returns to London under a special license

1656   Summer—Parliament called by major-generals

        Fails to win a seat in Parliament when his election is blocked by the Cromwellian interest

        Sues the sheriff of Berkshire, resulting in the publication of *Nevill versus Strood: The State of the Case* and *A True and Perfect Relation of the Manner and Proceeding, Held by the Sheriffe for the County of Berk: At Redding, upon the 20th. of Aug. Last 1656.*

        Publishes *A Copy of a Letter from an Officer in the Army*

1658   Death of Oliver Cromwell

        Returns to Parliament to represent Reading

1659   Charged with atheism and blasphemy

        April—army pressures Richard Cromwell into dissolving Parliament and restoring the Rump

        Publication of *The Armies Dutie*

        Publication of *The Humble Petition of Divers Well-Affected Persons*

        Elected to the new Council of State

        Writes *Shufling, Cutting, and Dealing, in a Game at Pickquet: Being Acted from the Year, 1653 to 1658*

        Publication of *A Proposition in Order to the Proposing of a Commonwealth or Democracie*

        October—second expulsion of the Rump by the army

        December—restoration of the Rump

1660   March—fails to be reelected to the Convention Parliament at Christchurch

        Writes *Letter Sent to General Monk* to nominate a committee to prevent an oligarchic or monarchical outcome

1663   Arrested on suspicion of being involved in the "Yorkshire" or "Northern" Plot

1664   Petitions successfully for release from the Tower

1664–67 Returns to Italy; Clarendon requests him to promote English interests and to spy on Catholic groups

1668   Returns to England

Publishes *The Isle of Pines*

Publishes *A New and Further Discovery of the Isle of Pines*

1672   Charles II begins secret negotiations with Louis XIV

Declaration of Indulgence—penal laws against Catholics suspended

1675   Publication of the English translation of Machiavelli's *Works* by John Starkey

1679   Parliament is dissolved

Composes *Plato Redivivus*

1680   Publication of *Plato Redivivus*

1683   Suspected of involvement in the Rye House Plot

1694   Dies in Silver Street, Covent Garden; buried at Warfield, Berkshire

ACKNOWLEDGMENTS

My work on this edition has been greatly assisted by the following current or former colleagues at Oxford, who have either answered questions or made material available to me: Susan Brigden, Tom Keymer, David Parrott, Blair Worden, and Marcello Cattaneo. At a late stage Paul Seaward, of the History of Parliament Trust, very generously provided swift and full information concerning some stubbornly obscure patches of Carolean parliamentary history. My grateful thanks to them all.

The work for this edition was completed under ideal circumstances while I was living in Munich as a C. F. von Siemens Fellow at the C. F. von Siemens Stiftung. My sincere thanks go to the Stiftung for their most generous support of my work, to its director, Professor Heinrich Meier, and to the staff of the Stiftung: all of whom made my residence in Munich so productive and pleasant.

A DESCRIPTION OF Ẏ ISLE OF PINES

How they were cast away

gathering there Ship wracke

Pine Numbring his People

Ẏ Dutch ship taking Ẏ‑writing

The ISLE of
PINES,[1]
OR,
A late Discovery of a fourth ISLAND near
Terra Australis, Incognita[2]
BY
Henry Cornelius Van Sloetten.

Wherein is contained.

A True Relation of certain *English* persons, who in Queen *Elizabeths* time,[3] making a Voyage to the *East Indies*[4] were cast away, and wracked near to the Coast of *Terra Australis, Incognita*, and all drowned, except one Man and four Women. And now lately *Anno Dom.* 1667. a *Dutch* Ship making a Voyage to the *East Indies*, driven by foul weather there, by chance have found their Posterity, (speaking good *English*) to amount (as they suppose) to ten or twelve thousand persons.[5] The whole Relation (written, and left by the Man himself a little before his death, and delivered to the *Dutch* by his Grandchild) Is here annexed with the Longitude and Latitude of the Island, the scituation and felicity thereof, with other matter observable.

Licensed *July* 27. 1668.

LONDON, Printed for *Allen Banks* and *Charles Harper*
next door to the three Squerrills in *Fleet-street*, over against
St. *Dunstans* Church, 1668.

1. At first glance, this seems an innocuous reference to afforestation; but to pine is also to languish or weaken. The reader learns later that the island was named after its discoverer, George Pine (see below, p. 20). The frontispiece illustration to the copy-text (above, p. lvi) seems to show pine trees growing on the island, which perhaps indicates that the artist had little acquaintance with the text he was illustrating. On the inaccuracies and suppressions in this frontispiece, see Nat Hardy, "Euphemizing Utopia: Repressing Sex and Violence in *The Isle of Pines*' Frontispiece," *Utopian Studies*, 17, no. 1 (2006), pp. 99–107. It was pointed out as early as 1668 that "pines" is an anagram of "penis" (Mahlberg, p. 115; cf. Hughes, p. xi). There was, however, an actual Isla de Pinos off the coast of Cuba which had been mentioned in Francis Godwin's Lucianic and utopian *The Man in the Moone* (1638); see William Poole, "Francis Godwin, Henry Neville, Margaret Cavendish, H. G. Wells: Some Utopian Debts," *ANQ*, 13, no. 3 (2003), pp. 14–15. If Neville took the hint for the name of his island from this source, then (as Poole observes) this surely lessens, and perhaps eliminates, the importance of the anagram "pines/penis."

2. I.e., "the unknown land of the south." The assumption that there must be a large mass of land in the southern hemisphere to balance the land masses of the northern hemisphere was a favorite notion of early modern geographers. James Howell, for example, asserted that "in the opinion of the knowingst and most inquisitive Mathematicians, ther is towards the *southern* clime as much land yet undiscovered as may equal in dimension the late new world, in regard, as they hold ther must be of necessity such a portion of earth the balance the Centre on all sides" (*Epistolae Ho-elianae* [1650], vol. 2, p. 22). For some further examples, see also Sir William Temple, "An Essay upon the Ancient and Modern Learning" (1690) in *The Works of Sir William Temple*, 2 vols. (1720), vol. 1, p. 163; and Woodes Rogers, *A Cruising Voyage round the World*, second edition (1718), p. 325. Cf. Goddard, *Plato's Demon*, p. 114.

3. Elizabeth I reigned from 1558 to 1603. We learn later that George Pine's master's voyage began in April 1570 (see below, p. 12).

4. India and the adjacent regions of Southeast Asia.

5. For discussion and commentary, see Scheckter, pp. 111–19. One of Neville's fellow members of the Rota Club, Sir William Petty, would consider the question of the rate at which populations increase in his *An Essay concerning the Multiplication of Mankind* (1686). Algernon Sidney held it for a maxim that a people will always thrive and increase "in a good climate under a good government" (Sidney, *Discourses*, p. 210).

Two Letters concerning the Island of *Pines* to a Credible[6] person in *Covent Garden*[7]

Amsterdam, *June* the 29th 1668

It is written by the last Post from Rochel,[8] *to a Merchant in this City, that there was a French ship arrived, the Master and Company of which reports, that about 2 or 300 Leagues Northwest from* Cape Finis Terre,[9] *they fell in with an Island, where they went on shore, and found about* 2000[10] *English people without cloathes, only some small coverings about their middle, and that they related to them, that at their first coming to this Island (which was in Queen* Elizabeths *time) they were but five in number men and women, being*

6. An ambiguous word at this time, capable of bearing both its common current meaning of "trustworthy, reliable" (*OED*, s.v. "credible," A1a), and also "ready, willing, or inclined to believe; credulous" (A2).

7. An ambiguous word at this time, capable of bearing both its common current meaning of "trustworthy, reliable" (*OED*, s.v. "credible," A1a), and also "ready, willing, or inclined to believe; credulous" (A2).

8. I.e., La Rochelle, on the French Atlantic coast.

9. Given the prior mention of La Rochelle, it would be most natural to assume that this refers to the westernmost tip of Brittany. However, it is difficult to reconcile this with the supposed position of the Isle of Pines in the southern hemisphere. Note Abraham Keek's suspicion that there may be "some mistake in the number of the Leagues, as also of the exact point of the Compass" (p. 4)—a hint at the mock geography of the text.

10. Not the "ten or twelve thousand persons" mentioned on the title page.

cast on shore by distress or otherwise, and had there remained ever since, without having any correspondence with any other people, or any ship coming to them. This story seems very fabulous, yet the Letter is come to a known Merchant, and from a good hand in France, *so that I thought fit to mention it, it may be that there may be some mistake in the number of the Leagues, as also of the exact point of the Compass, from* Cape Finis Terre; *I shall enquire more particularly about it. Some* English *here suppose it may be the Island of* Brasile[11] *which have been so oft sought for, Southwest from* Ireland, *if true, we shall hear further about it; Your friend and Brother,*

Abraham Keek.

Amsterdam, *July* the 6th, 1668

It is said that the ship that discovered the Island, of which I hinted to you in my last, is departed from Rochel, *on her way to* Zealand,[12] *several persons here have writ thither to enquire for the said Vessel, to know the truth of this business. I was promised a Copy of the Letter that came from* France, *advising the discovery of the Island abovesaid, but it's not yet come to my hand; when it cometh, or any further news about this Island, I shall acquaint you with it,*

Your Friend and Brother,
A. Keek.

11. A reference to the old Irish tradition of a mythical island situated to the west, not to the country in South America (which had, however, been discovered and settled by this time).
12. A province of the Low Countries, situated in the extreme southwest.

The Isle of Pines,
Discovered

Near to the Coast of *Terra Australis Incognita*, by *Henry Cornelius Van Sloetten*,[13] in a Letter to a friend in *London*, declaring the truth of his Voyage to the East *Indies*.

SIR,

I received your Letter of this second instant,[14] wherein you desire me to give you a further account concerning the Land of *Pines*, on which we were driven by distress of Weather the last Summer,[15] I also perused the Printed Book thereof [16] you sent me, the Copy of which was surreptitiously taken out of my hands, else should I have given you a more fuller account upon what occasion we came thither, how we were entertained, with some other circumstances of note wherein that relation is defective. To satisfie therefore your desires, I shall briefly yet fully give you a particular

13. This name was possibly chosen for its flavor of sexual innuendo (Sloetten/ slut; Cornelius/*Lat.* cornus, "horn," the sign of a cuckold).

14. I.e., the second of the present month (*OED*, s.v. "instant," *adj.*, II2b).

15. I.e., the summer of 1667.

16. A version of the text, stripped of the framing narrative, had been published in June 1668. The full text including the framing narrative followed in either July or August 1668. See "Note on the Texts," above, pp. xxxix–xl.

account thereof, with a true Copy of the Relation it self; desiring you to bear with my blunt Phrases,[17] as being more a Seaman then a Scholler.

April the 26*th* 1667. We set sail from *Amsterdam*, intending for the *East-Indies*; our ship had to name the place from whence we came, the *Amsterdam* burthen 350. Tun, and having a fair gale of Wind, on the 27 of *May* following we had a sight of the high Peak of *Tenriffe*[18] belonging to the *Canaries*, we have touched at the Island *Palma*,[19] but having endeavoured it twice, and finding the winds contrary, we steered on our course by the Isles of *Cape Verd*,[20] or *Insulae Capitis Viridis*, where at St. *James's*[21] we took in fresh water, with some few Goats, and Hens, wherewith that Island doth plentifully abound.

17. The language of seafaring men was proverbially coarse and plain. William Dampier's comments on his own style are relevant: "As to my Stile, it cannot be expected, that a Seaman should affect Politeness; for were I able to do it, yet I think I should be little sollicitous about it, in a work of this Nature. I have frequently indeed, divested my self of Sea Phrases, to gratify the Land Reader; for which the Seamen will hardly forgive me: And yet, possibly, I shall not seem Complaisant enough to the other; because I still retain the use of so many Sea-terms. I confess I have not been at all scrupulous in this matter, either as to the one or the other of these; for I am perswaded, that if what I say be intelligible, it matters not greatly in what words it is express'd" (*A New Voyage Round the World* [1697], sig. A3ᵛ). Cf. for a literary parallel the character of Ben in William Congreve's *Love for Love* (1695).

18. One of the Canary Islands, formed by volcanic activity. The Peak of Teneriffe is the cone of Mount Teide, which rises to 3,718 meters above sea level. It was proverbial at this time for its height: e.g., William Shipton, *Dia* (1659), p. 26; Henry Foulis, *The History of the Wicked Plots and Conspiracies of Our Pretended Saints Representing the Beginning, Constitution, and Designs of the Jesuite* (1662), p. 145; Henry Power, *Experimental Philosophy* (1664), p. 106 ("deservedly famed for the highest Hill in the world"); John Milton, *Paradise Lost* (1667, 1674), 4.987; Richard Head, *Nugae Venales* (1675), p. 12; *The Country Club: A Poem* (1679), p. 27; Andrew Marvell, "Upon the Hill and Grove at Bilbrough," l. 28, in *Miscellaneous Poems* (1681), p. 74; Samuel Clarke, *A New Description of the World* (1689), p. 230. Thomas Sprat would include "A Relation of the Pico Teneriffe" in his *History of the Royal Society of London* (1667), pp. 200–13.

19. One of the Canary Islands, an archipelago sixty miles west of the coast of Morocco.

20. The Cape Verde islands, an archipelago of ten small volcanic islands approximately 350 miles off the western coast of Africa.

21. I.e., Santiago, the largest of the Cape Verde islands.

June the 14.[22] We had a sight of *Madagascar*, or the Island of St. *Laurence*,[23] an Island of 4000 miles in compass, and scituate under the Southern Tropick;[24] thither we steered our course, and trafficked with the inhabitants for Knives, Beads, Glasses and the like, having in exchange thereof Cloves and Silver. Departing from thence, we were incountred with a violent storm, and the winds holding contrary, for the space of a fortnight, brought us back almost as far as the Isle *Del Principe*;[25] during which time many of our men fell sick, and some dyed, but at the end of that time it pleased God the wind favoured us again, and we steered on our course merrily, for the space of ten days: when on a sudden we were encountered with such a violent storm, as if all the four winds together had conspired for our destruction, so that the stoutest spirit of us all quailed, expecting every hour to be devoured by that merciless element of water, sixteen dayes together did this storm continue, though not with such violence as at the first, the Weather being so dark all the while, and the Sea so rough, that we knew not in what place we were, at length all on a sudden the Wind ceased, and the Air cleared, the Clouds were all dispersed, and a very serene Sky followed, for which we gave hearty thanks to the Almighty, it being beyond our expectation that we should have escaped the violence of that storm.

At length one of our men mounting the Main-mast espyed fire, an evident sign of some Countrey near adjoyning, which presently after we apparently discovered, and steering our course more nigher, we saw

22. On the impossible internal chronology of the text and the conflict of this date with the date of 8 June (below, p. 31), see Peter G. Stillman, "Monarchy, Disorder, and Politics in *The Isle of Pines*," *Utopian Studies*, 17, no. 1 (2006), p. 150.

23. A large island in the Indian Ocean lying off the southeast coast of Africa, Madagascar was infamous for tempestuous weather (see, e.g., Sir Richard Blackmore, *Alfred* [1723], p. 429). It was also a center for the Portuguese slave trade, and unofficial British slavers also picked up cargo there, as the East India Company complained. Madagascar was also reputed to be a "Nest of Pyrates," with a complicated coastline of creeks and inlets which favored concealment. Defoe would speak of "*Madagascar* Men, *as we call'd them*; that is to say, Pyrates and Rogues" (*A Compleat Collection of Remarkable Tryals*, 4 vols. [1718–21], vol. 2, p. 8).

24. I.e., the Tropic of Capricorn. The position of Madagascar is accurately given.

25. A small island off the western coast of Africa in the Gulf of Guinea.

several persons promiscuously[26] running about the shore, as it were wondering and admiring at what they saw: Being now near to the Land, we manned out our long Boat with ten persons, who approaching the shore, asked them in our *Dutch* Tongue "Wat Eylant is dit?"[27] to which they returned this Answer in English, *That they knew not what we said.* One of our Company named *Jeremiah Hanzen* who understood *English* very well, hearing their words discourst to them in their own Language; so that in fine[28] we were very kindly invited on shore, great numbers of them flocking about us, admiring at our Cloaths which we did wear, as we on the other side did to find in such a strange place, so many that could speak *English*, and yet to go naked.

Four of our men returning back in the long Boat to our Ships company, could hardly make them believe the truth of what they had seen and heard, but when we had brought our ship into harbour, you would have blest your self to see how the naked Islanders flocked unto us, so wondering at our ship, as if it had been the greatest miracle of Nature in the whole World.

We were very courteously entertained by them, presenting us with such food as that Countrey afforded, which indeed was not to be despised; we ate of the Flesh both of Beasts, and Fowls, which they had cleanly drest, though with no great curiosity, as wanting materials, wherewithal to do it; and for bread we had the inside or Kernel of a great Nut as big as an Apple,[29] which was very wholsome, and sound for the body, and tasted to the Pallat very delicious.

Having refreshed our selves, they invited us to the Pallace of their Prince or chief Ruler, some two miles distant off from the place where we landed; which we found to be about the bigness of one of our ordinary village houses, it was supported with rough unhewn pieces of Timber,

26. Here meaning "without distinction, discrimination, or order; indiscriminately, at random" (*OED*, s.v. "promiscuous," 1a). The adjective "promiscuous" did not yet possess the meaning of "undiscriminating in sexual relations" (1c); the first usage recorded in the *OED* is in a letter of Coleridge's dated 1804.

27. I.e., "What island is this?" Neville's Dutch looks faulty but has been defended by Scheckter (p. 42 and n. 17).

28. I.e., in the end, at last (*OED*, s.v. "fine" *n. 1,* I1b).

29. I.e., a breadfruit.

and covered very artificially with boughs, so that it would keep out the greatest showers of Rain, the sides thereof were adorned with several sorts of Flowers, which the fragrant fields there do yield in great variety. The Prince himself (whose name was *William Pine* the Grandchild of *George Pine* that was first on shore in this Island) came to his Pallace door and saluted us very courteously, for though he had nothing of Majesty in him, yet had he a courteous noble and deboneyre[30] spirit, wherewith your English Nation (especially those of the Gentry) are very much indued.

Scarce had he done saluting us when his Lady or Wife, came likewise forth of their House or Pallace, attended on by two Maid-servants, she was a woman of an exquisite beauty, and had on her head as it were a Chaplet of Flowers, which being intermixt with several variety of colours became her admirably. Her privities[31] were hid with some pieces of old Garments, the Relicts of those Cloaths (I suppose) of them which first came hither, and yet being adorned with Flowers those very rags seemeth beautiful; and indeed modesty so far prevaileth over all the Female Sex of that Island, that with grass and flowers interwoven and made strong by the peelings of young Elms (which grow there in great plenty) they do plant together so many of them as serve to cover those parts which nature would have hidden.

We carried him as a present some few Knives, of which we thought they had great need, an Ax or Hatchet to fell Wood, which was very acceptable unto him, the Old one which was cast on shore at the first, and the only one that they ever had, being now so quite blunt[32] and dulled, that it would not cut at all, some few other things we also gave him, which he very thankfully accepted, inviting us into his House or Pallace, and causing us to sit down with him, where we refreshed our selves again, with some more Countrey viands which were no other then such we tasted of before; Prince and peasant here faring alike, nor is there any

---

30. "Of gentle disposition, mild, meek; gracious, kindly; courteous, affable" (*OED*, s.v. "debonair," *adj.* and *n.*, A. *adj.* a). This was a term at this time closely associated with Charles II, as for example by John Evelyn, who described him on his death as a "prince of many Virtues, & many greate Imperfections, Debonaire, Easy of accesse, not bloudy or Cruel" (Evelyn, *Diary*, vol. 4, p. 409).

31. I.e., genitals (*OED*, s.v. "privities," 4).

32. I.e., so completely blunt (*OED*, "quite," *adv.*, *adj.*, and *int.*, AI, 3a).

difference betwixt their drink, being only fresh sweet water, which the rivers yield them in great abundance.[33]

After some little pause, our Companion (who could speak *English*) by our request desired to know of him something concerning their Original and how that people speaking the Language of such a remote Countrey should come to inhabit there, having not, as we could see, any ships or Boats amongst them the means to bring them thither, and which was more, altogether ignorant and meer strangers to ships, or shipping, the main thing conducible to that means, to which request of ours, the courteous Prince thus replyed.

Friends (for so your actions declare you to be, and shall by ours find no less)[34] know that we are inhabitants of this Island of no great standing, my Grandfather being the first that ever set foot on this shore, whose native Countrey was a place called *England*, far distant from this our Land, as he let us to understand;[35] He came from that place upon the Waters,[36] in a thing called a Ship, of which no question but you may have heard; several other persons were in his company, not intending to

---

33. A common utopian trope evoking the simplicity, plenty, and equality associated with the Golden Age; the first of a number of such evocations (see below, pp. 16, n. 59; 21, n. 79; 24, n. 90; 25, n. 94; 26, nn. 95 and 96; 28, n. 101; and 37, n. 141). The phrase "prince and peasant," however, had a more somber currency in religious writing at this time, as an illustration of the impartial omnivorousness of death. See, e.g., Anthony Munday, *A Banquet of Daintie Conceits* (1588): "Death is not partiall, as the Prouerbe saies, the Prince and Peasant, both with him are one" (sig. E1ᵛ). For further examples, see Richard Turner, *The Garland of a Greene Witte* (1595), sig. D2ʳ ("On euery corner let Poets write these words, / Both Prince and Pesant death deuours"); John Preston, *A Sermon* (1619), p. 23; George Ballard, *The History of Susanna* (1638), sig. I1ᵛ; John Quarles, *Gods Love and Mans Unworthiness* (1651), p. 52; Joshua Clarke, *Two Sermons* (1655), p. 18; John Brinsley, *The Drinking of the Bitter Cup* (1660), p. 199; Thomas Hall, *The Beauty of Magistracy* (1660), p. 271; George Swinnock, *Men Are Gods* (1660), p. 271; James Howell, *Poems* (1663), p. 61. For a more neutral example of the use of the phrase, see Michael Drayton, *The Barrons Wars* (1603), fol. 70ᵛ.

34. I.e., "You will discover by our actions that we are just as friendly as you."

35. Sometimes amended to "led us to understand," but unnecessarily so, "let" possessing at this time the meaning of "to introduce to the knowledge of, make acquainted with, inform about" (*OED*, s.v., "let," 11a).

36. Note the Biblical resonance: cf. "And the Spirit of God moved upon the face of the waters" (Genesis 1:2). Cf. also Ecclesiastes 11:1.

have come hither (as he said) but to a place called *India*,[37] when tempestuous weather brought him and his company upon this Coast, where falling among the Rocks his ship split all in pieces; the whole company perishing in the Waters, saving only him and four women, which by means of a broken piece of that Ship, by Divine assistance got on Land.

What after passed (said he) during my Grandfathers life, I shall show you in a Relation thereof written by his own hand, which he delivered to my Father being his eldest Son, charging him to have a special care thereof, and assuring him that time would bring some people or other thither to whom he would have him to impart it, that the truth of our first planting here might not be quite lost, which his commands my Father dutifully obeyed; but no one coming, he at his death delivered the same with the like charge to me, and you being the first people, which (besides our selves) ever set footing in this Island, I shall therefore in obedience to my Grandfathers and Fathers commands, willingly impart the same unto you.

Then stepping into a kind of inner room, which as we conceived was his lodging Chamber, he brought forth two sheets of paper fairly written in *English*, (being the same Relation which you had Printed with you at *London*)[38] and very distinctly read the same over unto us, which we hearkened unto with great delight and admiration, freely proffering us a Copy of the same, which we afterward took and brought away along with us; which Copy hereafter followeth.

A way to the East *India's* being lately discovered by Sea, to the South of *Affrick* by certain *Portugals*, far more safe and profitable then had been heretofore; certain *English* Merchants encouraged by the great advantages arising from the Eastern Commodities,[39] to settle a Factory[40] there for

37. I.e., the East Indies.

38. See above, p. 5, n. 16.

39. In the late sixteenth and early seventeenth centuries trade with Southeast Asia was the object of sharp international rivalry between the Portuguese, the English, and the Dutch. The struggle for dominance of the lucrative trade in spices reached its peak in 1623, when agents of the Dutch East India Company tortured and murdered twenty English, Japanese, and Portuguese at Amboyna; this incident lingered long in English memories and was dramatized in 1673 by Dryden.

40. I.e., a trading station (*OED*, s.v. "factory," 2a).

the advantage of Trade. And having to that purpose obtained the Queens Royal Licence *Anno Dom.* 1569. 11. or 12. *Eliz.* furnisht out for those parts four ships, my Master being sent as Factor[41] to deal and Negotiate for them, and to settle there, took with him his whole Family, (that is to say) his Wife, and one Son of about twelve years of age, and one Daughter of about fourteen years, two Maidservants, one *Negro* female slave, and my Self, who went under him as his Book-keeper, with this company on Monday the third of *April* next following, (having all necessaries for Housekeeping when we should come there) we Embarqued our selves in the good ship called the *India Merchant*, of about four hundred and fifty Tuns burthen, and having a good wind, we on the fourteenth day of *May* had sight of the *Canaries*, and not long after of the Isles of *Cape Vert*, or *Verd*, where taking in such things as were necessary for our Voyage, and some fresh Provisions, we stearing our course South, and a point East, about the first of *August* came within sight of the Island of St. *Hellen*,[42] where we took in some fresh water, we then set our faces for the Cape of Good hope, where by Gods blessing after some sickness, whereof some of our company died, though none of our family;[43] and hitherto we had met with none but calm weather, yet so it pleased God, when we were almost in sight of St. *Laurence*, an Island so called, one of the greatest in the world, as Marriners say, we were overtaken and dispersed by a great storm of Wind,[44] which continued with such violence many days, that losing all hope of safety, being out of our own knowledge, and whether we should fall on Flats or Rocks, uncertain in the nights, not having the least benefit of the light, we feared most, always wishing for day, and then for Land, but it came too soon for our good; for about the first of *October*, our fears having made us forget how the time passed to a certainty; we about the break of day discerned Land (but what we knew not) the Land seemed high and Rockey, and the Sea continued still very

---

41. I.e., the manager of a trading station (*OED*, s.v. "factor," 1b).

42. I.e., St. Helena, not yet a British colony.

43. Here used in the now-archaic sense of a household rather than a group of blood relations (*OED*, s.v. "family," 1a).

44. Cf. above, p. 7, n. 23. Pine's experience will later be repeated by Van Sloetten.

stormy and tempestuous, insomuch as there seemed no hope of safety, but looked[45] suddenly to perish. As we grew near Land, perceiving no safety in the ship, which we looked would suddenly be beat in pieces: The Captain, my Master, and some others got into the long Boat, thinking by that means to save their lives, and presently after all the Seamen cast themselves overboard, thinking to save their lives by swimming, onely my self, my Masters Daughters,[46] the two Maids, and the *Negro* were left on board, for we could not swim, but those that left us, might as well have tarried with us, for we saw them, or most of them perish, ourselves now ready after to follow their fortune, but God was pleased to spare our lives, as it were by miracle, though to further sorrow; for when we came against the Rocks, our ship having endured two or three blows against the Rocks, (being now broken and quite foundred in the Waters), we having with much ado gotten our selves on the Bowspright, which being broken off, was driven by the Waves into a small Creek, wherein fell a little River, which being encompassed by the Rocks, was sheltered from the Wind, so that we had opportunity to land ourselves, (though almost drowned) in all four persons, besides the *Negro*: when we were got upon the Rock, we could perceive the miserable Wrack to our great terrour, I had in my pocket a little Tinder-box and Steel, and Flint to strike fire at any time upon occasion, which served now to good Purpose, for its being so close,[47] preserved the Tinder dry. With this, and the help of some old rotten Wood which we got together, we kindled a fire and dryed ourselves, which done, I left my female company, and went to see, if I could find any of our Ships company, that were escaped, but could hear of none, though I hooted and made all the noise I could; neither could I perceive the footsteps of any living Creature (save a few Birds, and other Fowls). At length it drawing towards the Evening, I went back to my company, who were very much troubled for want of me. I being

45. I.e., expected (*OED*, s.v. "looked," 8a).

46. Cf. above, p. 12, where Pine's master is said to have "one Son of about twelve years of age, and one Daughter of about fourteen years."

47. I.e., close-fitting, and therefore watertight (*OED*, s.v. "close," *adj.* and *adv.*, B4).

now all their stay[48] in this lost condition, we were at first affraid that the wild people of the Countrey might find us out, although we saw no footsteps of any not so much as a Path; the Woods round about being full of Briers and Brambles, we also stood in fear of wild Beasts, of such also we saw none, nor sign of any: But above all, and that we had greatest reason to fear, was to be starved to death for want of Food, but God had otherwise provided for us as you shall know hereafter; this done, we spent our time in getting some broken pieces of Boards, and Planks, and some of the Sails and Rigging on shore for shelter; I set up two or three Poles, and drew two or three of the Cords and Lines[49] from Tree to Tree, over which throwing some Sailcloathes and having gotten Wood by us, and three or four Sea-gowns,[50] which we had dryed, we took up our Lodging for that night altogether (the *Blackmoor* being less sensible[51] then the rest we made our Centry). We slept soundly that night, as having not slept in three or four nights before (our fears of what happened preventing us) neither could our hard lodging, fear, and danger hinder us we were so over watcht.[52]

On the morrow, being well refresht with sleep, the winde ceased, and the weather was very warm; we went down the Rocks on the sands at low water, where we found great part of our lading,[53] either on shore or floating near it. I by the help of my company, dragged most of it on shore; what was too heavy for us broke,[54] and we unbound the Casks and Chests, and, taking out the goods, secured all; so that we wanted no clothes, nor any other provision necessary for Housekeeping, to furnish a better house than any we were like to have; but no victuals (the last water[55] having spoiled all) only one Cask of bisket, being lighter than the rest was dry;

48. A thing or a person that affords support; an object of reliance (*OED*, s.v. "stay," *n. 2*, 1b).

49. A nautical term for ropes (*OED*, s.v. "line," *n. 2*, 1a).

50. Sea cloaks for use at night or in bad weather; cf. *Hamlet*, 5.2.14.

51. I.e., less sensitive, and possessing therefore greater powers of endurance (*OED*, s.v. "sensible," 8a).

52. I.e., tired from too much watching, from remaining awake too long.

53. I.e., cargo (*OED*, s.v. "lading," 2).

54. I.e., "we broke."

55. I.e., the last tide (*OED*, s.v. "water," *n.*, 14a).

this served for bread a while, and we found on Land a sort of fowl about the bigness of a Swan, very heavie and fat, that by reason of their weight could not fly, of these we found little difficulty to kill, so that was our present food; we carried out of *England* certain Hens and Cocks to eat by the way, some of these when the ship was broken, by some means got to land, & bred exceedingly, so that in the future they were a great help unto us; we found also, by a little River, in the flags,[56] store of eggs, of a sort of foul much like our Ducks, which were very good meat, so that we wanted nothing to keep us alive.

On the morrow, which was the third day, as soon as it was morning, seeing nothing to disturb us, I lookt out a convenient place to dwell in, that we might build us a Hut to shelter us from the weather, and from any other danger of annoyance, from wild beasts (if any should finde us out). So closse by a large spring which rose out of a high hill over-looking the Sea, on the side of a wood, having a prospect towards the Sea, by the help of an Ax and some other implements (for we had all necessaries, the working of the Sea, having cast up most of our goods) I cut down all the straightest poles I could find, and which were enough for my purpose, by the help of my company (necessity being our Master) I digged holes in the earth setting my poles at an equal distance, and nailing the broken boards of the Caskes, Chests, and Cabins, and such like to them, making my door to the Seaward, and having covered the top, with sailclothes strain'd,[57] and nail'd, I in the space of a week had made a large Cabbin big enough to hold all our goods and our selves in it, I also placed our Hamocks for lodging, purposing (if it pleased God to send any Ship that way) we might be transported home, but it never came to pass, the place, wherein we were (as I conceived) being much out of the way.

We having now lived in this manner full four months, and not so much as seeing or hearing of any wild people, or of any of our own company, more then our selves (they being found now by experience to be all drowned) and the place as we after found, being a large Island, and disjoyned, and

56. A kind of coarse grass growing in damp places (*OED*, s.v. "flag," *n. 1*, 1c).
57. I.e., stretched (*OED*, s.v. "strain," *v. 1*, II10c); a usage with nautical connotations.

out of sight of any other Land, was wholly uninhabited by any people, neither was there any hurtful beast to annoy us: But on the contrary the countrey so very pleasant, being always clothed with green, and full of pleasant fruits, and variety of birds, ever warm, and never colder then in *England* in *September*: So that this place (had it the culture,[58] that skilful people might bestow on it) would prove a *Paradise*.[59]

The Woods afforded us a sort of Nuts,[60] as big as a large Apple, whose kernel being pleasant and dry, we made use of instead of bread, that fowl before mentioned, and a sort of water-fowl like Ducks, and their eggs, and a beast about the size of a Goat, and almost such a like creature,[61] which brought two young ones at a time, and that twice a year, of which the Low Lands and Woods, were very full, being a very harmless creature and tame, so that we could easily take and kill them: Fish, also, especially Shell-fish (which we could best come by) we had great store of, so that in effect as to Food we wanted nothing; and thus, and by such like helps, we continued six moneths, without any disturbance or want.

Idleness and Fulness of every thing begot in me a desire of enjoying the women, beginning now to grow more familiar, I had perswaded the two Maids to let me lie with them, which I did at first in private, but after, custome taking away shame (there being none but us) we did it more openly, as our Lusts gave us liberty; afterwards my Masters Daughter was content also to do as we did; the truth is, they were all handsome Women when they had Cloathes, and well shaped, feeding well. For we wanted no Food, and living idlely, and seeing us at Liberty to do our wills, without hope of ever returning home made us thus bold: One of the first of my Consorts with whom I first accompanied[62] (the tallest and handsomest) proved presently with child, the second was my Masters Daughter, and the other also not long after fell into the same condition: none now remaining but

58. I.e., the cultivation of the soil or tillage (*OED*, s.v. "culture," I1a).
59. The absence of seasonality is another characteristic of the mythological Golden Age: see, e.g., Hesiod, *Works and Days*, ll. 109–26. In *Paradise Lost* the "change / Of seasons to each clime" is a consequence of the Fall (10.651–707).
60. Cf. above, p. 8, n. 29.
61. I.e., "so similar a creature."
62. I.e., had sex with (*OED*, s.v. "accompany," 3a).

my *Negro*, who seeing what we did, longed also for her share; one Night, I being asleep, my *Negro*, (with the consent of the others) got closse to me, thinking it being dark, to beguile me, but I awaking and feeling her, and perceiving who it was, yet willing to try the difference, satisfied my self with her, as well as with one of the rest: that night, although the first time, she proved also with child, so that in the year of our being here, all my women were with child by me, and they all coming at different seasons, were a great help to one another.

The first brought me a brave Boy, my Masters Daughter was the youngest, she brought me a Girl, so did the other Maid, who being something fat sped worse at her labour: the *Negro* had no pain at all, brought me a fine white Girl, so I had one Boy and three Girls, the Women were soon well again, and the two first with child again before the two last were brought to bed, my custome being not to lie with any of them after they were with child,[63] till others were so likewise, and not with the black at all after she was with child, which commonly was at the first time I lay with her, which was in the night and not else, my stomach would not serve me,[64] although she was one of the handsomest Blacks I had seen, and her children as comly as any of the rest; we had no clothes for them,[65] and therefore when they had suckt, we laid them in Mosse to sleep, and took no further care of them, for we knew, when they were gone more would come, the Women never failing once a year at least, and none of the Children (for all the hardship we put them to) were ever sick; so that wanting now nothing but Cloathes, nor them much neither, other then for decency, the warmth of the Countrey and Custome supplying that Defect, we were now well satisfied with our condition, our Family beginning to grow large, there being nothing to hurt us, we many times lay

63. Intercourse during pregnancy was discouraged in the sex manuals of the period, e.g., *Aristotle's Compleat Master-Piece*, 11th ed. (1715?), p. 55; and *Aristotle's Compleat and Experienc'd Midwife*, 2nd ed. (1711), p. 31. Intercourse during pregnancy is not, however, prohibited in Leviticus.

64. In ancient medicine the stomach was thought to be the seat of lust and passion (*OED*, s.v. "stomach," 1g and 6a). In consequence the word had acquired the metaphorical sense of relish, inclination, or desire (5b). This is the sense that is uppermost here.

65. I.e., bedding (*OED*, s.v. "clothes," *n.*, 3).

abroad on Mossey Banks,[66] under the shelter of some Trees, or such like (for having nothing else to do) I had made me several Arbors to sleep in with my Women in the heat of the day, in these I and my women passed the time away, they being never willing to be out of my company.

And having now no thought of ever returning home, as having resolved and sworn each to other, never to part or leave one another, or the place; having by my several wives, forty seven Children,[67] Boys and Girls, but most Girls, and growing up apace, we were all of us very fleshly,[68] the Country so well agreeing with us, that we never ailed any thing; my *Negro* having had twelve, was the first that left bearing, so I never medled with her more: My Masters Daughter (by whom I had most children, being the youngest and handsomest) was most fond of me, and I of her. Thus we lived for sixteen years, till perceiving my eldest Boy to mind the ordinary work of Nature, by seeing what we did, I gave him a Mate, and so I did to all the rest, as fast as they grew up, and were capable: My Wives having left bearing, my children began to breed apace, so we were like to be a multitude; My first Wife brought me thirteen children, my second seven, my Masters Daughter fifteen, and the *Negro* twelve, in all forty seven.

After we had lived there twenty two years,[69] my *Negro* died suddenly, but I could not perceive any thing that ailed her; most of my children being grown, as fast as we married them, I sent them and placed them over the River by themselves severally, because we would not pester one an-

66. Another paradisiac or utopian touch: cf. Marvell, "Upon Appleton House": "Then, languishing with ease, I toss / On Pallets swoln of Velvet Moss; / While the Wind, cooling through the Boughs, / Flatters with Air my panting Brows" (ll. 593–96). William Browne had described the abode of the Muses as "the mossie bankes / Of drisling *Hellicon*" (*Britannia's Pastorals* [1625], p. 92). In Thomas Carew's "A Pastorall Dialogue" the lovers sleep on a "mossie bank" (*Poems* [1651], p. 59). For a more general parallel, cf. Milton's description of Adam and Eve's "blissful Bower" (*Paradise Lost*, 4.689–719) in which a profusion of plants collaborate to supply the productions of art, thus inverting Spenser's "Bowre of Blisse" in which art imitates nature (*The Faerie Queene*, 2.12.42–80).

67. With four partners, and assuming that Pine was able to impregnate them all as soon as they had given birth, it must have taken him and his women at least eight years to produce forty-seven children. Therefore, at this point in the narrative the date is at least 1578.

68. A complicated word, meaning well-fed, fat, or plump (*OED*, s.v. "fleshly," 6), but also with possibly pejorative overtones of lascivious or sensually inclined (1a).

69. I.e., in 1592.

other; and now they being all grown up, and gone, and married after our manner (except some two or three of the youngest) for (growing my self into years) I liked not the wanton annoyance of young company.

Thus having lived to the sixtieth year of my age, and the fortieth of my coming thither,[70] at which time I sent for all of them to bring their children, and there were in number descended from me by these four Women, of my Children, Grand-children, and great Grand-children, five hundred sixty five of both sorts, I took off the Males of one Family, and married them to the Females of another, not letting any to marry their sisters,[71] as we did formerly out of necessity, so blessing God for his Providence and goodness, I dismist them, I having taught some of my children to read formerly, for I had left still the Bible, I charged it should be read once a moneth at a general meeting: At last one of my Wives died being sixty eight years of age, which I buried in a place, set out on purpose, and within a year after another, so I had none now left but my Masters Daughter, and we lived together twelve years longer, at length she died also, so I buried her also next the place where I purposed to be buried my self, and the tall Maid my first Wife next me on the other side, the *Negro* next without her, and the other Maid next my Masters Daughter. I had now nothing to mind, but the place whether I was to go, being very old, almost eighty years,[72] I gave my Cabin and Furniture that was left to my eldest son after my decease, who had married my eldest Daughter by my beloved Wife,[73] whom I made King and Governour of all the rest: I informed them of the Manners of *Europe*, and charged them to remember the Christian Religion, after the manner of them that spake the same Language,[74] and to admit no other, if hereafter any should come and find them out.

70. I.e., 1610; so Pine was born in 1550 and was twenty when the voyage began.
71. Cf. Leviticus 18:9. The "Table of Kindred and Affinity, wherein whosoever are related, are forbidden in Scripture and Our Laws to Marry together" was printed at the end of the *Book of Common Prayer*, and its variants served to define the fluctuating boundary separating incest from lawful sexual union.
72. I.e., the date is nearly 1630.
73. Presumably Pine's master's daughter, who bore him his first daughter (see above, p. 17).
74. I.e., the form of moderate Protestantism instituted by Elizabeth in the early years of her reign.

And now once for all, I summoned them to come to me, that I might number them,[75] which I did, and found the estimate to contain in or about the eightieth year of my age, and the fifty ninth of my coming there;[76] in all, of all sorts, one thousand seven hundred eighty and nine. Thus praying God to multiply them, and send them the true light of the Gospel, I last of all dismist them: For, being now very old, and my sight decayed, I could not expect to live long. I gave this Narration (written with my own hand) to my eldest Son, who now lived with me, commanding him to keep it, and if any strangers should come hither by chance; to let them see it, and take a Copy of it if they would, that our name be not lost from off the earth.[77] I gave this people (descended from me) the name of the *ENGLISH PINES*, *George Pine* being my name, and my Masters Daughters name *Sarah English*, my two other Wives were *Mary Sparkes*, and *Elizabeth Trevor*, so their severall Descendants are called the *ENGLISH*, the *SPARKS*, and the *TREVORS*, and the *PHILLS*, from the Christian Name of the Negro, which was *Philippa*, she having no surname: And the general name of the whole the *ENGLISH PINES*; whom God bless with the dew of Heaven, and the fat of the Earth,[78] AMEN.

After the reading and delivering unto us a Coppy of this Relation, then proceeded he on in his discourse.

My Grandfather when he wrote this, was as you hear eighty yeares of age, there proceeding from his Loyns one thousand seven hundred eighty nine children, which he had by them four women aforesaid: My Father was his eldest son, and was named *Henry*, begotten of his wife *Mary Sparkes*, whom he appointed chief Governour and Ruler over the rest; and having given him a charge not to exercise tyranny over them, seeing they were his fellow brethren by Fathers side (of which there could be no doubt

---

75. A phrase with Biblical overtones. Cf. Numbers 1:1–3.

76. I.e., in 1629.

77. Another phrase with Biblical overtones. Cf. Genesis 7:23; Exodus 9:15; Joshua 7:9; Psalms 109:15; Proverbs 2:22; Nahum 2:13.

78. An allusion to Genesis 27:28: "God give thee of the dew of heaven, / And the fatness of the earth, and plenty of corn and wine" (cf. 27:39 and Daniel 4:15, 23, and 25).

made of double dealing therein) exhorting him to use justice and sincerity amongst them, and not to let Religion die with him, but to observe and keep those Precepts which he had taught them he quietly surrendred up his soul, and was buried with great lamentation of all his children.

My father coming to rule, and the people growing more populous, made them to range further in the discovery of the Countrey, which they found answerable to their desires, full both of Fowls and Beasts, and those too not hurtful to mankinde, as if this Country (on which we were by providence cast without arms or other weapons to defend ourselves, or offend others,) should by the same providence be so inhabited as not to have any need of such like weapons of destruction wherewith to preserve our lives.[79]

But as it is impossible, but that in multitudes disorders will grow, the stronger seeking to oppress the weaker; no tye of Religion being strong enough to chain up the depraved nature of mankinde, even so amongst them mischiefs began to rise, and they soon fell from those good orders prescribed them by my Grandfather. The source from whence those mischiefs spring, was at first, I conceive, the neglect of hearing the Bible read, which (according to my Grandfathers proscription) was once a moneth at a general meeting, but now many of them wandring far up into the Country, they quite neglected the coming to it, with all other means of Christian instruction, whereby the sence of sin being quite lost in them, they fell to whoredoms, incests, and adulteries; so that what my Grand-father was forced to do for necessity, they did for wantonness; nay not confining themselves within the bound of any modesty, but brother and sister lay openly together; those who would not yeild to their lewd embraces, were by force ravished, yea many times endangered of their lives.[80] To redress those enormities, my father assembled all the Company near unto him, to whom he declared the wickedness of those their brethren; who all with one consent agreed that they should be severely punished; and so arming themselves with boughs, stones, and such like weapons, they marched against them, who having notice of their coming, and fearing their deserved punishment, some of them fled into

79. Another evocation of the Golden Age; cf. above, p. 10, n. 33.
80. Cf. above, p. 19, n. 71.

woods, others passed over a great River, which runneth through the heart of our Countrey, hazarding drowning to escape punishment; But the grandest offender of them all was taken, whose name was *John Phill*, the second son of the *Negro-woman* that came with my Grandfather into this Island. He being proved guilty of divers ravishings & tyrannies committed by him, was adjudged guilty of death, and accordingly was thrown down from a high Rock[81] into the Sea, where he perished in the waters. Execution being done upon him, the rest were pardoned for what was past, which being notified abroad, they returned from those Desart and Obscure places, wherein they were hidden.

Now as Seed being cast into stinking Dung produceth good and wholesome Corn for the sustentation[82] of mans life, so bad manners produceth good and wholesome Laws for the preservation of Humane Society. Soon after my Father with the advice of some few others of his Counsel, ordained and set forth these Laws to be observed by them.[83]

1. That whosoever should blaspheme or talk irreverently of the name of God should be put to death.

2. That who should be absent from the monethly assembly to hear the Bible read, without sufficient cause shown to the contrary, should for the first default be kept without any victuals or drink, for the space of four days, and if he offend therein again, then to suffer death.

3. That who should force or ravish any Maid or Woman should be burnt to death, the party so ravished putting fire to the wood that should burn him.

4. Whosoever shall commit adultery, for the first crime the Male shall lose his Privities, and the Woman have her right eye bored out, if after that she was again taken in the act, she should die without mercy.

5. That who so injured his Neighbour, by laming of his Limbs, or taking any thing away which he possesseth, shall suffer in the same kind

---

81. In ancient Rome condemned criminals were executed by being thrown from the Tarpeian rock, at the southwest corner of the Capitoline Hill.

82. I.e., sustenance, food, nourishment (*OED*, s.v. "sustentation," 5).

83. Cf. Exodus 20–22.

himself by loss of Limb; and for defrauding his Neighbour, to become servant to him, whil'st he had made him double satisfaction.

6. That who should defame or speak evil of the Governour, or refuse to come before him upon Summons, should receive a punishment by whipping with Rods, and afterwards be exploded[84] from the society of all the rest of the inhabitants.

Having set forth these Laws, he chose four several persons under him to see them put in Execution, whereof one was of the *Englishes*, the Off-spring of *Sarah English*; another of his own Tribe, the *Sparks*; a third of the *Trevors*, and the fourth of the *Phills*; appointing them every year at a certain time to appear before him, and give an account of what they had done in the prosecution of those Laws.

The Countrey being thus settled, my Father lived quiet and peaceable till he attained to the age of ninety and four years,[85] when dying, I succeeded in his place, in which I have continued peaceably and quietly till this very present time.[86]

He having ended his Speech, we gave him very heartily thanks for our information, assuring him we should not be wanting to him in any thing which lay in our powers, wherewith we could pleasure him in what he should desire; and thereupon proferred[87] to depart, but before our going away, he would needs engage us to see him, the next day, when was to be their great assembly or monethly meeting for the celebration of their Religious Exercises.

Accordingly the next day we came thither again, and were courteously entertained as before. In a short space there was gathered such a multitude of people together as made us to admire; and first there was several Weddings celebrated, the manner whereof was thus. The Bridegroom and Bride appeared before him who was their Priest or Reader of the Bible, together with the Parents of each party, or if any of their Parents were dead, then the next relation unto them, without whose consent as well as the parties to

---

84. I.e., banished (*OED*, s.v. "explode," 2a).
85. If Henry Pine had been born in 1571, he therefore died in 1665.
86. I.e., 1667.
87. I.e., attempted or offered (*OED*, s.v. "profer," 1).

be married, the Priest will not joyn them together: but being satisfied in those particulars, after some short Oraizons,[88] and joyning of hands together, he pronounces them to be man and wife: and with exhortations to them to live lovingly towards each other, and quietly towards their neighbors, he concludes with some prayers, and so dismisses them.

The Weddings being finished, all the people took their places to hear the Word read, the new married persons having the honour to be next unto the Priest that day, after he had read three or four Chapters he fell to expounding the most difficult places therein, the people being very attentive all that while, this exercise continued for two or three hours, which being done, with some few prayers he concluded, but all the rest of that day was by the people kept very strictly, abstaining from all manner of playing or pastimes,[89] with which on other dayes they use to pass their time away, as having need of nothing but victuals, and that they have in such plenty as almost provided to their hands.[90]

88. I.e., either prayers (*OED*, s.v. "orison," 1a) or, more neutrally, speeches (2).

89. In the controversial declaration referred to as the *Book of Sports* (1618), James I had explicitly encouraged his subjects to engage in customary pastimes and rural diversions after attending church: *"And as for Our good peoples lawfull Recreation, Our pleasure likewise is, That after the end of Diuine Seruice, Our good people be not disturbed, letted, or discouraged from any lawfull Recreation; Such as dauncing, either men or women, Archerie for men, leaping, vaulting, or any other such harmlesse Recreation, nor from hauing of May-Games, Whitson Ales, and Morris-dances, and the setting vp of Maypoles and other sports therewith vsed, so as the same be had in due and conuenient time, without impediment or neglect of diuine Seruice"* (pp. 6–7). The *Book of Sports* had been reissued by Charles I in 1633 to reinforce the tendency of Archbishop Laud's reforms of the Church of England. This gave rise to what Leah Marcus has referred to as a "paradox of state," in which "festival freedom was seen as a sign of submission to royal power" (*The Politics of Mirth* [Chicago: University of Chicago Press, 1986], pp. 7–8). These customary pastimes and rural sports, so closely associated with Stuart rule, had been suppressed by Parliament during the Civil War, which had also ordered the *Book of Sports* to be burned by the common hangman. The resolutions of the House of Commons on ecclesiastical innovations of 1 September 1641 provided, inter alia, that "the Lord's Day shall be duly observed and sanctified; all dancing, or other sports, either before or after divine service, be forborne and restrained" (Kenyon, *Stuart Constitution*, pp. 258–59).

90. Another detail reminiscent of the Golden Age, as is the absence of commerce. Cf. Theocritus, *Idylls*, 7.143–46, and, more recently, Andrew Marvell, "The Garden": "What wondrous life is this I lead! / Ripe apples drop about my head; / the luscious clusters of the vine / Upon my mouth do crush their wine; / The nectarene, and curious peach, / Into my hands themselves do reach" (ll. 33–38).

Their exercises of Religion being over, we returned again to our Ship, and the next day, taking with us two or three Fowling-pieces,[91] leaving half our Company to guard the Ship, the rest of us resolved to go up higher into the Country for a further discovery: All the way as we passed the first morning, we saw abundance of little Cabbins or Huts of these inhabitants, made under Trees, and fashioned up with boughs, grass, and such like stuffe to defend them from the Sun and Rain; and as we went along, they came out of them much wondering at our Attire, and standing aloof off from us as if they were afraid, but our companion that spake English, calling to them in their own Tongue, and giving them good words, they drew nigher, some of them freely proffering to go along with us, which we willingly accepted; but having passed some few miles, one of our company espying a Beast like unto a Goat come gazing on him, he discharged his Peece,[92] sending a brace of Bullets into his belly, which brought him dead upon the ground; these poor naked unarmed people hearing the noise of the Peece, and seeing the Beast lie tumbling in his gore, without speaking any words betook them to their heels, running back again as fast as they could drive, nor could the perswasions of our Company, assuring them they should have no hurt,[93] prevail any thing at all with them, so that we were forced to pass along without their company: all the way that we went we heard the delightful harmony of singing Birds, the ground very fertile in Trees, Grass, and such flowers, as grow by the production of Nature, without the help of Art;[94] many and several sorts of Beasts we saw, who

91. I.e., light guns for shooting wild fowl (*OED*, s.v. "fowling piece," 1).
92. I.e., his gun.
93. The first encounter between savages and firearms is a recurrent *topos* in early modern travel literature, the common Eurocentric and colonialist implications of which have been drawn out by Stephen Greenblatt ("Invisible Bullets," in his *Shakespearean Negotiations* [Oxford: Clarendon Press, 1988], pp. 21–65). A later relevant parallel occurs in *Robinson Crusoe* when Crusoe opens fire on the cannibals: "As I came nearer, I perceiv'd presently, he had a Bow and Arrow, and was fitting it to shoot at me; so I was then necessitated to shoot at him first, which I did, and kill'd him at the first Shoot; the poor Savage who fled [Friday], but had stopp'd; though he saw both his Enemies fallen, and kill'd, as he thought; yet was so frighted with the Fire, and Noise of my Piece, that he stood Stock still, and neither came forward or went backward" (Daniel Defoe, *Robinson Crusoe*, ed. Tom Keymer [Oxford: Oxford University Press, 2007], p. 171).
94. Another detail reminiscent of the Golden Age.

were not so much wild as in other Countries;[95] whether it were as having enough to satiate themselves without ravening upon others, or that they never before saw the sight of man, nor heard the report of murdering Guns, I leave it to others to determine. Some Trees bearing wild Fruits we also saw, and of those some whereof we tasted, which were neither unwholsome nor distastful to the Pallate, and no question had but Nature here the benefit of Art added unto it, it would equal, if not exceed many of our *Europian* Countries; the Vallyes were every where intermixt with running streams, and no question but the earth hath in it rich veins of Minerals, enough to satisfie the desires of the most covetous.

It was very strange to us, to see that in such a fertile Countrey which was as yet never inhabited, there should be notwithstanding such a free and clear passage to us, without the hinderance of Bushes, Thorns, and such like stuff,[96] wherewith most Islands of the like nature are pestered: the length of the Grass (which yet was very much intermixt with flowers) being the only impediment that we found.

Six dayes together did we thus travel, setting several marks in our way as we went for our better return, not knowing whether we should have the benefit of the Stars for our guidance in our going back, which we made use of in our passage: at last we came to the vast Ocean on the other side of the Island, and by our coasting it, conceive it to be of an oval form, only here and there shooting forth with some Promontories. I conceive it hath but few good Harbours belonging to it, the Rocks in most places making it inaccessible. The length of it may be about two hundred, and breadth one hundred miles, the whole in circumference about five hundred miles.

It lyeth about seventy six degrees of Longitude, and twenty of Latitude, being scituate under the third Climate,[97] the longest day being about

95. Another detail reminiscent of the Golden Age. In *Paradise Lost* before the Fall, the animals in Eden are tame (8.349–54). Thereafter they become feral: "Beast now with beast gan war, and fowl with fowl, / And fish with fish; to graze the herb all leaving, / Devour'd each other; nor stood much in awe / Of man, but fled him, or with count'nance grim / Glared on him passing" (10.710–14).

96. The absence of harmful plants again recalls the Golden Age. Cf. Milton's description of the flora of prelapsarian Eden (*Paradise Lost*, 4.625–33).

97. "Climate" is here being used as in ancient and medieval geography to refer to the bands or belts of the earth's surface stretching from west to east and associ-

thirteen hours and fourty five minutes. The weather as in all Southern Countries, is far more hot than with us in *Europe*; but what is by the Sun parched in the day, the night again refreshes with cool pearly dews.[98] The Air is found to be very healthful by the long lives of the present inhabitants, few dying there till such time as they come to good years of maturity, many of them arriving to the extremity of old age.

And now speaking concerning the length of their Lives, I think it will not be amisse in this place to speak something of their Burials, which they used to do thus.

When the party was dead, they stuck his Carkass all over with flowers, and after carried him to the place appointed for Burial, where setting him down, (the Priest having given some godly Exhortations concerning the frailty of life) then do they take stones (a heap being provided there for that purpose) and the nearest of the kin begins to lay the first stone upon him, afterwards the rest follows, they never leaving till they have covered the body deep in stones, so that no Beast can possibly come to him, and this shift were they forced to make, having no Spades or Shovels wherewith to dig them Graves; which want of theirs we espying, bestowed a Pick-ax and two Shovels upon them.

Here might I add their way of Christening Children, but that being little different from yours in *ENGLAND*, and taught them by *GEORGE PINES* at first which they have since continued, I shall therefore forbear to speak thereof.

---

ated with specific parallels of latitude (*OED*, s.v. "climate," 1a). The third climate corresponded to the latitude of the Canary Islands, i.e., between the latitudes of 25 and 30 degrees north.

98. A very common poeticism, and in origin an embellishment of Psalm 133; see, e.g., Edmund Spenser, *The Faerie Queene* (1596), 4.5.45, l.5; Robert Albott, *Englands Parnassus* (1600), pp. 329 and 334; George Wither, *Prince Henries Obsequies* (1612), elegy 33; William Barton, *The Book of Psalms in Metre* (1644), p. 275; Richard Crashaw, "To the Morning: Satisfaction for Sleepe," in *Steps to the Temple* (1646), p. 48; Robert Heath, *Clarestella* (1650), p. 16; Sir John Mennes, *Musarum Deliciae* (1655), p. 27; John Gamble, *Ayres and Dialogues* (1659), p. 29; Abraham Cowley, "The Complaint," in *Verses, Written upon Several Occasions* (1663), p. 55; and Richard Walden, *Parnassus Aboriens* (1664), p. 12.

After our return back from the discovery of the Countrey, the Wind not being fit for our purpose, and our men also willing thereto, we got all our cutting Instruments on Land, and fell to hewing down of Trees, with which, in a little time, (many hands making light work) we built up a Pallace for this *William Pines* the Lord of that Countrey. Which, though much inferiour to the houses of your Gentry in *England*, yet to them which never had seen better, it appeared a very Lordly Place. This deed of ours was beyond expression acceptable unto him, loading us with thanks for so great a benefit, of which he said he should never be able to make a requital.

And now acquainting him, that upon the first opportunity we were resolved to leave the Island, as also how that we were near Neighbours to the Countrey of *England*, from whence his Ancestors came; he seemed upon the news to be much discontented that we would leave him, desiring, if it might stand with our commodity [99] to continue still with him, but seeing he could not prevail, he invited us to dine with him the next day, which we promised to do, against which time he provided, very sumptuously (according to his estate) [100] for us, and now was he attended after a more Royal manner then ever we saw him before, both for number of Servants, and multiplicity of Meat, on which we fed very heartily; but he having no other Beverage for us to drink, then water, we fetched from our Ship a Case of Brandy, presenting some of it to him to drink, but when he had tasted of it, he would by no means be perswaded to touch thereof again, preferring (as he said) his own Countrey Water before all such Liquors whatsoever. [101]

After we had Dined, we were invited out into the Fields to behold their Country Dauncing, which they did with great agility of body; and though they had no other then only Vocal Musick (several of them singing all that while) yet did they trip it [102] very neatly, giving sufficient satisfaction to all that beheld them.

99. I.e., "accord with our convenience, advantage, benefit, or interest" (*OED*, s.v. "commodity," *n.*, 3).

100. I.e., means or ability (*OED*, s.v. "estate," 2a).

101. A preference for water over alcohol is another frequent characteristic of the inhabitants of utopias (Ovid, *Metamorphoses*, 1.111–12; Sir Thomas More, *Utopia*, ed. G. M. Logan and Robert M. Adams [Cambridge: Cambridge University Press, 2002], p. 44). In the Golden Age, alcohol was unknown.

102. I.e., dance (*OED*, s.v. "trip," *v.*, 1a).

The next day we invited the Prince *William Pines* aboard our Ship, where was nothing wanting in what we could to entertain him, he had about a dozen of Servants to attend on him he much admired at the Tacklings of our Ship, but when we came to discharge a piece or two of Ordnance, it struck him into a wonder and amazement to behold the strange effects of Powder; he was very sparing in his Diet, neither could he, or any of his followers be induced to drink any thing but Water: We there presented him with several things, as much as we could spare, which we thought would any wayes conduce to their benefit, all which he very gratefully received, assuring us of his real love and good will, whensoever we should come thither again.

And now we intended the next day to take our leaves, the Wind standing fair, blowing with a gentle Gale *South* and by *East*, but as we were hoising of our Sails, and weighing Anchor, we were suddenly Allarm'd with a noise from the shore, the Prince, *W. Pines* imploring our assistance in an Insurrection which had happened amongst them, of which this was the cause.

Henry Phil, the chief Ruler of the Tribe or Family of the *Phils*, being the Off-spring of *George Pines* which he had by the *Negro*-woman; this man had ravished the Wife of one of the principal[103] of the Family of the *Trevors*, which act being made known, the *Trevors* assembled themselves all together to bring the offender unto Justice: But he knowing his crime to be so great, as extended to the loss of life: sought to defend that by force, which he had as unlawfully committed, whereupon the whole Island was in a great hurly burly, they being two[104] great Potent Factions, the bandying[105] of which against each other, threatned a general ruin to the whole State.

The Governour[106] *William Pines* had interposed in the matter, but found his Authority too weak to repress such Disorders; for where the Hedge of Government is once broken down, the most vile bear the greatest rule,[107]

---

103. I.e., chief or man of high rank (*OED*, s.v. "principal," 2b).

104. Here corrected from the copy-text's "too," although it should be noted that the uncorrected reading, with its sense of excessive power, relates significantly to the politics of the text, in particular to its concern with tyranny.

105. I.e., to league or confederate (*OED*, s.v. "bandy," II7a).

106. A possibly significant change of title from the earlier "Prince."

107. Cf. Ecclesiastes 10:8: "He that diggeth a pit shall fall into it; and whoso breaketh an hedge, a serpent shall bite him." This passage of Scripture was frequently applied during the seventeenth century to the subject of government, and in particu-

whereupon he desir'd our assistance, to which we readily condescended, and arming out twelve of us went on Shore, rather as to a surprize then fight,[108] for what could nakedness do to encounter with Arms. Being conducted by him to the force of our Enemy, we first entered into parley, seeking to gain them rather by fair means then force, but that not prevailing, we were necessitated to use violence, for this *Henry Phill* being of an undaunted resolution, and having armed his fellows with Clubs and Stones, they sent such a Peal[109] amongst us, as made us at the first to give back, which encouraged them to follow us on with great violence, but we discharging off three or four Guns, when they saw some of themselves wounded, and heard the terrible reports which they gave, they ran away with greater speed then they came. The Band of the *Trevors* who were joyned with us, hotly pursued them, and having taken their Captain, returned with great triumph to their Governour, who sitting in Judgment upon him, he was adjudged to death, and thrown off a steep Rock into the Sea, the only way they have of punishing any by death, except burning.

------

lar connection with the upheavals of the Civil Wars—e.g., John Price, *A Sermon Preached before the Honourable House of Commons* (1660): "Lets confesse that we have digg'd a pit and we have fallen into it; We have broken the hedge and a Serpent hath bit us, *Eccles.* 10.8. We have broken the hedge of government. A serpent hath a two-forked tongue, and we have felt its sting, oppression in our gates, schismes and divided opinions amongst our selves" (p. 27). See other examples: Philip Hunton, *A Vindication of the Treatise of Monarchy* (1644), p. 65; John Collinges, *The Spouses Hidden Glory* (1646), p. 3; Richard Baxter, *The Saints Everlasting Rest* (1650), p. 520; Samuel Gardiner, *Moses and Aaron Brethren* (1653), p. 5 ("*Government* a singular mercy: for as it directs men where they are apt to erre, provides for such as are most exposed to want; so it protects all in what they enjoy. Pluck up the hedge of *Government,* and all things are common"); Thomas Hall, *The Beauty of Magistracy* (1660), p. 231 ("These four proverbial expressions speak the danger of them that go about to supplant their Rulers. Whilest they are digging pits to catch others, the earth falleth on them, and murdereth themselves. When they are breaking up the old hedge of Government, Serpents and Adders which use to harbour in old walls and hedges will sting them. God will make men know that it is a dangerous thing to confound rule and subjection, and to break down the partition wall which he hath set up between Magistrates and people"); Francis Smith, *Symptoms of Growth and Decay* (1660), p. 106; George Swinnock, *Men Are Gods* (1660), p. 231; Adam Littleton, *Solomons Gate* (1662), p. 352.

108. I.e., to an ambush (*OED*, s.v. "surprize," *n.,* 1 and 2a) rather than to a formal battle.

109. Either a volley of stones (*OED*, s.v. "peal," 2) or a loud shout or war cry (3).

And now at last we took our solemn leaves of the Governour, and departed from thence, having been there in all, the space of three weeks and two dayes, we took with us good store of the flesh of a Beast which they call there *Reval*, being in tast different either from Beef or Swines-flesh, yet very delightful to the Pallate, and exceeding nutrimental. We took also with us alive, divers Fowls which they call *Marde*, about the bigness of a Pullet,[110] and not different in taste, they are very swift of flight, and yet so fearless of danger, that they will stand still till such time as you catch them: We had also sent us in by the Governour about two bushels of eggs, which as I conjecture were the *Mards* eggs, very lussious in taste, and strengthening to the body.

June 8. We had a sight of *Cambaia*,[111] a part of the *East Indies*, but under the Government of the great *Cham* of *Tartary*;[112] here our Vessel springing a leak, we were forced to put to shore, receiving much damage in some of our Commodities; we were forced to ply the Pump for eighteen hours together, which, had that miscarried, we had inevitably have perished; here we stai'd five dayes mending our Ship, and drying some of our Goods, and then hoising[113] Sail, in four days time more we came to *Calecute*.[114]

---

110. I.e., a young hen (*OED*, s.v. "pullet," 1).

111. Modern-day Khambhat, on the western coast of India. Now silted up, it was at this time an important trading port. According to Peter Heylyn, who is apparently Neville's source for the trade, anthropology, and geography of India, it was "a mighty City . . . containing 800000 persons" (Heylyn, ΜΙΚΡΟΚΟΣΜΟΣ, p. 681). Heylyn had written a biography of Laud, was (according to Algernon Sidney) an apologist for absolutism, and in the late 1650s had crossed swords with Neville's friend and associate James Harrington (Scott, *Commonwealth Principles*, p. 125; Pocock, *Harrington*, pp. 96–97).

112. The ruler of the Tartars and Mongols.

113. I.e., to raise aloft by means of rope or pulley and tackle (*OED*, s.v. "hoise," 1a).

114. I.e., Calcutta, a port on the western coast of India and important for the trade in spices with Europe. Neville here is closely following Heylyn, ΜΙΚΡΟΚΟΣΜΟΣ, p. 680. For Heylyn's polemical involvement in the circles surrounding Neville, see Pocock, *Harrington*, pp. 96–97.

This *Calecute* is the chief Mart Town[115] and Staple[116] of all the *Indian Traffique*, it is very populous, and frequented by Merchants of all Nations. Here we unladed a great part of our Goods, and taking in others, which caused us to stay there a full Moneth, during which space, at leisure times I went abroad to take a survey of the City, which I found to be large and populous, lying for three miles together upon the Sea-shore. Here is a great many of those persons whom they call *Brachmans*,[117] being their Priests or Teachers whom they much reverence. It is a custome here for the King to give to some of those *Brachmain*, the hanselling[118] of his Nuptial Bed; for which cause, not the Kings, but the Kings sisters sons succeed in the King-dom, as being more certainly known to be of the true Royal blood:[119] And these sisters of his choose what Gentleman they please, on whom to bestow their Virginities; and if they prove not in a certain time to be with child, they betake themselves to these *Brachman Stalions*,[120] who never fail of doing their work.[121]

115. I.e., market town or center of trade (*OED*, s.v. "mart," 3a and b).

116. I.e., a town or country which is the principal market or entrepôt for some particular class of merchandise (*OED*, s.v. "staple," 1b).

117. I.e., the highest priestly caste among the Hindus.

118. I.e., to offer the gift or first use of something in order to secure good fortune (*OED*, s.v. "handsel," 1, 2, 3, and 4).

119. Contrary to the case on the Island of Pines, as noted above (p. 19).

120. In the Laudian Peter Heylyn's ΜΙΚΡΟΚΟΣΜΟΣ this is presumably a satiric touch intended to distinguish the carnality of pagan priesthoods from the chastity and purity of life of their Christian counterparts. Transposed into Neville's text, however, the observation acquires a more comprehensive anticlerical vigor. The association between the clerical character and clandestine sexual potency and appetite had already amused Neville in *A Parliament of Ladies* (1647), where the final demand in the "*chiefe Heads of the Ladies Lawes*" is that "*if any Iesuite returne into our Land againe, being once banished, that he shall be gelt or libb'd, to avoid jealousies of our husbands*" (sig. B3v; cf. *The Ladies, A Second Time, Assembled in Parliament* [1647], sigs. A3r and B3v; and *Newes from the New Exchange, or the Commonwealth of Ladies* [1650], p. 5). It was a joke with some staying power. In Swift's *Argument against Abolishing Christianity* (1711) the persona (though not without a detectable degree of Swiftian participation) comments on how fortunate it is that the clergy, "reduced by the wise Regulations of *Henry* the Eighth, to the Necessity of a low Diet, and moderate Exercise," can become the "only great Restorers of our Breed" by taking the place of the "scrophulous consumptive Productions furnished by our Men of Wit and Pleasure" (Swift, *Prose Writings*, vol. 2, pp. 30–31).

121. A passage copied verbatim from Heylyn, ΜΙΚΡΟΚΟΣΜΟΣ, p. 680.

The people are indifferently[122] civil and ingenious, both men and women imitate a Majesty in their Train and Apparel, which they sweeten with Oyles and Perfumes: adorning themselves with Jewels and other Ornaments befitting each Rank and Quality of them.

They have many odd Customs amongst them which they observe very strictly; as first, not knowing their Wives after they have born them two children: Secondly, not accompanying them, if after five years cohabition they can raise no issue by them, but taking others in their rooms: Thirdly, never being rewarded for any Military exploit, unless they bring with them an enemies Head in their Hand, but that which is strangest, and indeed most barbarous, is that when any of their friends falls sick, they will rather chuse to kill him, then that he should be withered by sickness.

Thus you see there is little employment there for Doctors, when to be sick, is the next way for to be slain, or perhaps the people may be of the mind rather to kill themselves, then to let the Doctors do it.[123]

Having dispatched our business, and fraighted[124] again our Ship, we left *Calecute*, and put forth to Sea, and coasted along several of the Islands belonging to *India*, at *Camboia*[125] I met with our old friend Mr. *David Prire*, who was overjoyed to see me, to whom I related our Discovery of the Island of *Pines*, in the same manner as I have related it to you; he was then but newly recovered of a Feaver, the Air of that place not being agreeable to him; here we took in good store of Aloes,[126] and some other Commodities, and victualled our Ship for our return home.

After four dayes sailing, we met with two *Portugal* Ships which came from *Lisbon*, one whereof had in a storm lost its Top-mast, and was forced in part to be towed by the other. We had no bad weather in eleven dayes space, but then a sudden storm of Wind did us much harm in our Tacklings, and swept away one of our Sailors off from the Fore Castle.

122. I.e., impartially (*OED*, s.v. "indifferent," 2).

123. The tendency of doctors to kill their patients is a familiar trope in anti-medical satire: cf. Mandeville, *Fable of the Bees*, vol. 1, pp. 20–21; and Swift, *Gulliver's Travels*, part 4, chapter 6, pp. 376–81.

124. I.e., loaded.

125. See above, p. 31, n. 111.

126. I.e., the resin or decaying heartwood of any of several Southeast Asian trees of the genus *Aquilaria* (family *Thymelaeaceae*), burnt or used as incense (*OED*, s.v. "aloe," 1).

November the sixth had like to have been a fatal day unto us, our Ship striking twice upon a Rock, and at night was in danger of being fired by the negligence of a Boy, leaving a Candle carelesly in the Gun-room; the next day we were chased by a Pyrate of *Argiere*,[127] but by the swiftness of our Sails we out ran him. *December* the first we came again to *Madagascar*, where we put in for a fresh recruit[128] of Victuals and Water.

During our abode here, there hapned a very great Earthquake, which tumbled down many Houses; The people of themselves are very Unhospitable and Treacherous, hardly to be drawn to Traffique with any people; and now, this calamitie happening upon them, so enraged them against the Christians, imputing all such calamities to the cause of them, that they fell upon some *Portugals* and wounded them, and we seeing their mischievous Actions, with all the speed we could put forth to Sea again, and sailed to the Island of St. *Hellens*.

Here we stayed all the *Christmas Holy-dayes*, which was very much celebrated by the Governour there under the King of *Spain*: Here we furnished our selves with all necessaries which we wanted; but upon our departure, our old acquaintance Mr. *Petrus Ramazina*, coming in a Skiff[129] out of the Isle *del Principe*,[130] or the Princes Island, retarded our going for the space of two dayes, for both my self and our Purser[131] had Emergent[132] business with him, he being concerned in those Affairs of which I wrote to you in *April* last: Indeed we cannot but acknowledge his Courtesies unto us, of which you know he is never sparing. *January* the first, we again hoised Sail, having a fair and prosperous gail of Wind, we touched at the *Canaries*, but made no tarriance,[133] desirous now to see our Native Countrey; but the Winds was very cross unto us for the space of a

127. I.e., Algiers. In the seventeenth century the North African coast was infested with pirates, or corsairs, who preyed on European shipping.

128. I.e., replenishment (*OED*, s.v. "recruit," 3b).

129. I.e., a small seagoing boat adapted for both rowing and sailing (*OED*, s.v. "skiff," 1).

130. See above, p. 7, n. 25.

131. I.e., the shipboard officer responsible for provisions and keeping accounts (*OED*, s.v. "purser," 2a).

132. I.e., pressing (*OED*, s.v. "emergent," 5b).

133. I.e., delay or temporary residence (*OED*, s.v. "terriance," 1, 2).

week, at last we were favoured with a gentle Gale, which brought us on merrily; though we were on a sudden stricken again into a dump;[134] a Sailor from the main Mast discovering five Ships, which put us all in a great fear, we being Richly Laden, and not very well provided for Defence; but they bearing up to us, we found them to be *Zealanders* and our Friends; after many other passages concerning us, not so much worthy of Note, we at last safely arrived at home, *May* 26. 1668.

Thus Sir, have I given you a brief, but true Relation of our Voyage, Which I was the more willing to do, to prevent false Copies[135] which might be spread of this nature: As for the Island of *Pines* it self, which caused me to Write this Relation, I suppose it is a thing so strange as will hardly be credited by some, although perhaps knowing persons, especially considering our last age being so full of Discoveries, that this Place should lie Dormant[136] for so long a space of time; Others I know, such Nullifidians[137] as will believe nothing but what they see, applying that Proverb unto us, *That Travelors may lye by authority.*[138] But Sir, in writing to you, I question not but to give Credence, you knowing my disposition so hateful to divulge Falsities; I shall request you to impart

---

134. I.e., "cast into perplexity or dejection" (*OED*, s.v. "dump," *n. 1,* 1, 2).

135. Perhaps another reference to the prior publication of George Pine's narration; see "Note on the Texts."

136. I.e., in a state of inactivity (*OED*, s.v. "dormant," 2a).

137. I.e., skeptics or disbelievers (*OED*, s.v. "nullifidian," 2).

138. The syntax of this sentence is clearly corrupt. The probable sense may be restored if the phrase "will not disbelieve" is supplied before "that this Place," since Neville seems to be contrasting "knowing persons" (who are not automatically skeptical) with the vulgar "Nullifidians" who disbelieve travellers' accounts if they relate things outside their experience without seriously examining them. In *An Essay concerning Human Understanding* (1689), John Locke illustrates how our sense of probability is conditioned by the extent of our experience: "To a Man, whose Experience has been always quite contrary, and has never heard of any thing like it, the most untainted Credit of a Witness will scarce be able to find belief. As it happened to a Dutch Ambassadour, who entertaining the King of *Siam* with the particularities of *Holland*, which he was inquisitive after, amongst other things told him, that the Water in his Country, would sometimes, in cold weather, be so hard that Men walked upon it, and that it would bear an Elephant, if he were there. To which the King replied, *Hitherto I have believed the strange Things you have told me, because I look upon you as a sober fair Man, but now I am sure you lye*" (4.15.5).

this my Relation to Mr. *W. W.* and Mr. *P. L.* remembring me very kindly unto them, not forgetting my old acquaintance Mr. *J. P.* and Mr. *J. B.* no more at present, but only my best respects to you and your second self,[139] I rest

Yours in the best of friendship,

July 22. 1668.   *Henry Cornelius Van Sloetten.*

---

139. A periphrasis for "wife": "Without doubt, the uniting of Hearts in holy Wedlock, is of all conditions the happiest; for then a Man has a second self to whom he can unravel his Thoughts, as well as a sweet Companion in his Labour; he has one in whose Breast, as in a safe Cabinet, he may repose his inmost Secrets, especially where Reciprocal Love, and inviolate Faith is centered; for there no cares, fears, jealousies, mistrust or hatred, can ever interpose; for what Man, ever hated his own Flesh?" (Anonymous, *Aristotle's Master-Piece Compleated* [1697], p. 43; cf., e.g., William Annand, *Pater Noster* [1670], p. 339). *OED* also gives as a possible meaning the less specific "a friend who agrees absolutely with one's tastes and opinions, or for whose welfare one cares as much as for one's own" (*OED*, s.v. "second," *adj.* and *n.*, 2, 4c).

Post-Script.

One thing concerning the Isle of *Pines*, I had almost quite forgot, we had with us an *Irish* man named *Dermot Conelly* who had formerly been in *England*, and had learned there to play on the Bag-pipes, which he carried to Sea with him; yet so un-Englished he was, that he had quite forgotten your Language, but still retained his Art of Bagpipe-playing, in which he took extraordinary delight; being one day on Land in the Isle of *Pines*, he played on them, but to see the admiration of those naked people concerning them, would have striken you into admiration; long time it was before we could perswade them that it was not a living creature, although they were permitted to touch and feel it, and yet are the people very intelligible,[140] retaining a great part of the Ingenuity and Gallantry of the *English* Nation, though they have not that happy means to express themselves; in this respect we may account them fortunate, in that possessing little, they enjoy all things,[141] as being contented with what they have, wanting those alurements to mischief, which our *European* Countries are enriched with. I shall not dilate any further, no question but time will make this Island known better to the world; all that I shall ever

---

140. I.e., intelligent (*OED*, s.v. "intelligible," 1).
141. Another evocation of the Golden Age.

say of it is, that it is a place enriched with Natures abundance, deficient in nothing conducible to the sustentation[142] of mans life, which were it Ma-nured by Agri-culture and Gardening, as other of our *European* Coun-tries are, no question but it would equal, if not exceed many which now pass for praise worthy.

FINIS.

---

142. I.e., sustenance (*OED*, s.v. "sustentation," 5).

PLATO

REDIVIVUS:[1]

OR, A

DIALOGUE

CONCERNING

Government,

Wherein, by Observations drawn from other
KINGDOMS and STATES both Ancient and
Modern, an Endeavour is used to discover the
present POLITICK DISTEMPER of our OWN,
with the CAUSES, and REMEDIES.

Non Ego sum Vates, sed Prisci conscius aevi.
Pluribus exemplis haec tibi Mysta Cano.
Res nolunt male administrari.[2]

The Second Edition, with Additions.

LONDON,
Printed for *S. I.* and Sold by *R. Dew*, 1681.

1. Literally "Plato brought back to life," but with an undertone also of "renewed" or "refurbished." The anonymous "worthy Friend of mine" whom the publisher consults about the significance of the title sees in the title nothing more than a hint about the book's imitation of the Platonic dialogue form (below, p. 47). However, for speculations about the possible broader and more esoteric resonances of Neville's invocation of Plato, see the introduction (above, pp. xxvi–xxxiii). Toland had also detected an element of Platonic imitation in Harrington's *Oceana*, which "is written after the manner of a Romance, in imitation of Plato's *Atlantic Story*," and further notes that this is "a method ordinarily follow'd by Lawgivers" (Toland, *Harrington*, p. xxi; cf. Pocock, *Harrington*, p. 121). Men's thoughts might naturally turn toward Plato in the speculation about political innovation fostered by the Exclusion Crisis: "As *Plato* phansi'd his *Community*, and Sir *Thomas Moor* his *Utopia;* so are these people bigg with hopes of a *Relation;* thereby to reassume their Idoliz'd *Model* of a *Commonwealth*, out of the scatter'd *Gentry*, in the nature of a *House of Commons*" (Anonymous, *The Interest of the Three Kingdoms* [1680], p. 8). For a wide-ranging consideration of the importance of Plato and Platonic doctrine to English seventeenth-century republicanism, see Scott, *Commonwealth Principles*, pp. 19–40.

2. "I am no prophet, but I am aware of the past, and as a priest of those secret rites I sing to you of many examples. A bad government cannot last" (untraced, and not a fragment of classical Latin). The final line of the epigraph, however, was a proverbial political maxim, current in English since the Venerable Bede: see Thomas Barlow, *Genuine Remains* (1693), pp. 235–36. A distant and speculative source for the idea has been suggested in Aristotle, *Metaphysics*, 12.10.14: "οὐ βούλεται πολιτεύεσθαι κακῶς," "The world must not be governed badly"; cf. Sir Peter Pett, *The Happy Future State of England* (1688), p. 250; and Cicero, *De Inventione*, 1.34. The maxim was frequently cited in the later seventeenth century: Sir William Petty, *A Treatise of Taxes* (1662), sig. A3ᵛ, and *A Discourse Made before the Royal Society* (1674), "The Epistle Dedicatory"; William Payne, *The Unlawfulness of Stretching Forth the Hand* (1683), p. 31; William Penn, *A Perswasive to Moderation* (1685), p. 42. Walter Moyle reported that the maxim was a favorite of Robert Harley, Earl of Oxford (Walter Moyle, "An Essay on the Lacedaemonian Government," in his *Whole Works* [1727], p. 60). By 1729, however, when Swift quoted it in a letter to Bolingbroke, it had evidently become trite: "Pray will you please to take your pen and blot me out that political maxim from whatever book it is in: that *Res nolunt diu male administrari;* the commonness makes me not know who is the author, but sure he must be some Modern" (Swift, *Correspondence*, vol. 3, p. 230; cf. vol. 2, p. 78; and Swift, *Prose Writings*, vol. 8, p. 180, and vol. 12, p. 309). Taken as a whole, however, the epigraph contains two important hints. It alerts the reader to the importance of historical example in the text that follows ("Prisci . . . aevi"), thus corroborating the implications of the book list (see the introduction, above, pp. xxx–xxxiii). And in its playful (but not entirely ironic) characterization of the author as a "Mysta," a priest who has been initiated into secret doctrine, it also warns the reader to expect covert or sub-superficial meanings—a hint further strengthened by the fact that the word "conscius" can refer to the secret knowledge possessed by a conspirator.

The Publisher to the Reader

Courteous Reader,

All the Account I can give thee of this Piece is; that about the middle of October last it was sent to me, accompanied with a Letter without a Name, and written in a Hand altogether unknown to me,[3] though different from the Character of the Dialogue it self, and the Argument. The Letter was very short; and contained only, that the Writer having the fortune to meet with this Discourse (of which he denied to be the Author) he thought it very fit to be sent to me, to the end if I thought it could be of any advantage to me, and no prejudice, I might publish it if I pleased, and make my best of it. When I had opened it, and perceived that it treated of Government, and of the present Times; I supposing it to be something of the nature of those scurrulous Libels which the Press spawns every day, was ex-treamly displeased with my Servant, for receiving in my absence, and in these dangerous days,[4] such a Pacquet, without taking any account or notice of the

---

3. A protective disclaimer concerning the authorship of the text. These gestures may seem alarmist, but on 7 December 1683 Algernon Sidney would be executed for exploring politically heterodox ideas in a private manuscript written in his own hand.

4. *Plato Redivivus* was published in 1681, and the manuscript was delivered to the publisher about "*the middle of* October *last*," i.e., October 1680. It is thus likely that the text was composed, as Caroline Robbins suggests, "between the dissolution of the Habeas Corpus Parliament [also known as the first Exclusion Parliament;

Messenger who brought it: 'till he, to appease me, assured me, that the Bearer did look like a Gentleman, and had a very unsuitable Garb to a Trapan;[5] and that he did believe he had seen him often at my Shop, and that I knew him well. When I had begun to read it, and found no harm, I was resolved to peruse it in the Company of a Gentleman, a worthy Friend of mine; who, to his exact Skill and Learning in the Laws of his Country, hath added a very profound Knowledge in all other Literature; and particularly, the excellence of Platonick *Philosophy. When we had joyntly gone through it, he was clearly of Opinion, That although some might be angry with certain passages in it, yet the Discourse reflecting upon*

---

dissolved on 12 July 1679] and the meeting of the next, the Westminster or second Exclusion Parliament, on 21 October 1680" (Robbins, *Republican Tracts*, p. 16). If so, Neville was conforming to a familiar rhythm for the publication of political texts timed to the sittings of Parliament, as Marvell had observed in *Mr. Smirke, or The Divine in Mode* (1676): "For nothing is more usual than to Print and present to them [MPs] Proposals of Revenue, Matters of Trade, or any thing of publick Convenience" immediately in advance of a sitting (Marvell, *Prose Works*, vol. 2, pp. 50–51). This period of composition coincided with the climax of the Exclusion Crisis, in which moves were made in Parliament and agitation was pursued out of doors to exclude the heir apparent to the throne, Charles II's brother James, Duke of York, from the succession on the grounds of his Roman Catholicism (he had been received into the Roman Catholic Church in the spring of 1672). On the Exclusion Crisis, see, still, J. R. Jones, *The First Whigs: The Politics of the Exclusion Crisis 1678–1683* (London: Oxford University Press, 1961). As Gilbert Burnet would explain, the Exclusion Crisis involved the most fundamental ideas of government, setting in opposition those on the one hand who believed that "Government was appointed for those that were to be governed, and not for the sake of the Governors themselves" and those on the other who held that "Law could not alter what God had settled" (Burnet, *History*, vol. 1, pp. 457 and 458).

5. I.e., a person who entraps or decoys others into actions or positions which may be to his advantage and to their ruin or loss (*OED*, s.v. "trapan," *n.* 2, 1). In 1681 "trapan" was virtually a neologism. *OED* gives the earliest use of the noun (it could be used also as a verb) in 1653, and Marvell had used it as a verb in *The Rehearsal Transpros'd* of 1672 (Marvell, *Prose Works*, vol. 1, p. 99). In chapter 2, section 12, of his *Discourses concerning Government*, composed between 1681 and 1683, Algernon Sidney referred to "Trepanners" as "a new coin'd word" (Sidney, *Discourses*, p. 146), although he himself had used it repeatedly some years earlier in his *Court Maxims* of 1664–65 (e.g., Sidney, *Court Maxims*, pp. 115 and 161). For a significant early use of the word emanating from the circles surrounding Neville and dropping from the lips of the Lord Protector in 1656, see Toland, *Harrington*, p. xx. See also, e.g., Samuel Butler, *Hudibras*, 3.2.351–58, 831, 1055, 1145, and 1179; John Trenchard, *A Short History of Standing Armies* (1698), p. 12; and Jonathan Swift, *A Tale of a Tub*, section 11, in Swift, *Prose Writings*, vol. 1, p. 131.

no particular person, was very uncapable of bringing me into any danger for pub-
lishing it; either from the State, or from any private Man. When I had secured my
self against Damnum Emergens,[6] *we went about the Consideration of the other*
part of the distinction of the Schools, which is Lucrum cessans,[7] *And I made some*
Objections against the probability of vending this Dialogue to Profit; which, in
things of my Trade, is always my design, as it ought to be. My first Fear in that
behalf was, that this Author would disgust the Reader, in being too confident and
positive in matters of so high a Speculation. My Friend replied, that the Assurance
he shewed was void of all Sawciness, and expressed with great Modesty: and that
he verily believed that he meant very faithfully and sincerely towards the Interest
of England. *My next doubt was, that a considerable part of this Treatise being a*
Repetition of a great many Principles and Positions out of Oceana,[8] *the Author*
would be discredited for borrowing from another, and the Sale of the Book hin-
dred. To that my Friend made answer, that before ever Oceana *came out, there*
were very many Treatises and Pamphlets, which alledged the Political Principle,
That Empire was founded in Property,[9] *and discoursed rationally upon it:*

6. I.e., direct loss. A technical legal phrase.

7. I.e., the loss or interruption of expected profits. A technical legal phrase.

8. James Harrington, *The Commonwealth of Oceana* (1656). According to John Aubrey, Neville was Harrington's "great familiar and Confident friend," and Thomas Hobbes went so far as to claim that Neville had contributed to the composition of *Oceana* (Aubrey, *Brief Lives*, pp. 318 and 322; Robbins, *Republican Tracts*, p. 7 and n. 4; Rahe, *Throne and Altar*, p. 322).

9. This is possibly deliberately misleading. Toland was adamant that Harrington was the sole author of this political insight: "THAT *Empire follows the Balance of Property,* whether lodg'd in one, in a few, or in many hands, he was the first that ever made out; and is a noble Discovery, wherof the Honor solely belongs to him, as much as those of the Circulation of the Blood, of Printing, of Guns, of the Compass, or of Optic Glasses, to their several Authors. 'Tis incredible to think what gross and numberless Errors were committed by all the Writers before him, even by the best of them, for want of understanding this plain Truth, which is the foundation of all Politics" (Toland, *Harrington*, p. xviii). In the next century, however, Hume would pause in (perhaps feigned) perplexity over the equation of political power and the possession of property, as something he was prepared to believe true in theory but which undeniably had not always occurred in practice: "A noted author has made property the foundation of all government; and most of our political writers seem inclined to follow him in that particular. This is carrying the matter too far; but still it must be owned, that the opinion of right to property has a great influence in this subject. . . . A Government may endure for several ages, though the balance of power, and the balance of property do not coincide. This chiefly happens, where any rank or order of the state has acquired a

Amongst the rest, one entituled A Letter from an Officer in *Ireland,* to His Highness the Lord Protector, *(which he then shewed me) printed in* 1653.[10] *as I*

---

large share in the property; but from the original constitution of the government, has no share in the power. Under what pretence would any individual of that order assume authority in public affairs? As men are commonly much attached to their ancient government, it is not to be expected, that the public would ever favour such usurpations. But where the original constitution allows any share of power, though small, to an order of men, who possess a large share of the property, it is easy for them gradually to stretch their authority, and bring the balance of power to coincide with that of property. This has been the case with the house of commons in England" (Hume, *Essays,* pp. 33–34 and 35; cf. the first paragraph of "Whether the British Government Inclines More to Absolute Monarchy or to a Republic," ibid., pp. 47–48; and "Idea of a Perfect Commonwealth," ibid., pp. 514–16). For Burke, writing his *Second Letter on a Regicide Peace* in 1796, a particular deformity of the revolutionary government of France was that it had contrived to separate government from property: "We have not considered as we ought the dreadful energy of a State, in which the property has nothing to do with the Government. Reflect, my dear Sir, reflect again and again on a Government, in which the property is in complete subjection, and where nothing rules but the mind of desperate men. The condition of a commonwealth not governed by it's property was a combination of things, which the learned and ingenious speculator Harrington, who has tossed about society into all forms, never could imagine to be possible" (*W&S,* vol. 9, p. 289). Cf. his comments in the *Third Letter on a Regicide Peace* (1797): "The present war is, above all others, (of which we have heard or read) a war against landed property. That description of property is in it's nature the firm base of every stable government; and has been so considered, by all the wisest writers of the old philosophy, from the time of the Stagyrite, who observes that the agricultural class of all others is the least inclined to sedition" (*W&S,* vol. 9, p. 374). Harrington had referred to this opinion of Aristotle's in *Oceana,* using language close to that later used by Burke (Pocock, *Harrington,* p. 158).

10. The pamphlet is dated from Waterford on 24 June 1654, but it is usually thought to have been published in June 1656; the postscript extenuates the lapse of time between composition and publication. It has been attributed, in whole or part, to Henry Neville himself (Robbins, *Republican Tracts,* p. 7). For further information on authorship and date, see Pocock, *Harrington,* pp. 10–12; and Rahe, *Throne and Altar,* pp. 226–27 and n. 31. Toland maintains that this text was the result of anticipatory plagiarism by a friend of Harrington's: "He no sooner discours'd publicly of this new Doctrin, being a man of universal acquaintance, but it ingag'd all sorts of people to busy themselves about it as they were variously affected. Som, because they understood him, despis'd it, alleging it was plain to every man's capacity, as if his highest merit did not consist in making it so. Others, and those in number the fewest, disputed with him about it, merely to be better inform'd; with which he was well pleas'd, as reckoning a pertinent Objection of greater advantage to the discovery of Truth (which was his aim) than a complaisant applause or approbation.

remember; which was more than three years[11] *before* Oceana *was written: and yet, said he, no Man will aver that the Learned Gentleman who writ that Book had stollen from that Pamphlet. For whosoever sets himself to study Politicks, must do it by reading History, and observing in it the several Turns and Revolutions of Government: and then the Cause of such Change will be so visible and obvious, that we need not impute Theft to any Man that finds it out: it being as lawful,*

But a third sort, of which there never wants in all places a numerous company, did out of pure envy strive all they could to lessen or defame him; and one of 'em (since they could not find any precedent Writer out of whose Works they might make him a Plagiary) did indeavor, after a very singular manner, to rob him of the Glory of this Invention: for our Author having friendly lent him a part of his Papers, he publish'd a small piece to the same purpose, intitl'd, *A Letter from an Officer of the Army in* Ireland, &c. Major WILDMAN was then reputed the Author by som, and HENRY NEVIL by others; which latter, by reason of this thing, and his great intimacy with HARRINGTON, was by his detractors reported to be the Author of his Works, or that at least he had a principal hand in the composing of them. Notwithstanding which provocations, so true was he to the Friendship he profest to NEVIL and WILDMAN, that he avoided all harsh Expressions or public Censures on this occasion, contenting himself with the Justice which the World was soon oblig'd to yield to him by reason of his other Writings, where no such clubbing of Brains could be reasonably suspected" (Toland, *Harrington*, p. xviii). The text of the pamphlet is reprinted in appendix A.

11. It was certainly three years before the publication of *Oceana* in the late autumn and early winter of 1656. However, the possibly spurious document published by John Toland as "The Examination of James Harrington" suggests that the composition of *Oceana* had begun about two years beforehand, around 1654, in response to discussions between Cromwell and some of his senior officers about the nature of a commonwealth: "He [i.e., Cromwell] having started up into the Throne, his Officers (as pretending to be for a Commonwealth) kept a murmuring, at which he told them that he knew not what they meant, nor themselves; but let any of them shew him what they meant by a Commonwealth (or that there was any such thing) they should see that he sought not himself: the Lord knew he sought not himself, but to make good the Cause. Upon this som sober men came to me and told me, if any man in *England* could shew what a Commonwealth was, it was my self. Upon this persuasion I wrote; and after I had written, OLIVER never answer'd his Officers as he had don before, therfore I wrote not against the King's Government. And for the Law, if the Law could have punish'd me, OLIVER had don it; therfore my Writing was not obnoxious to the Law. After OLIVER the Parlament said they were a Commonwealth; I said they were not, and prov'd it" (Toland, *Harrington*, p. xxxiv; cf. Rahe, *Throne and Altar*, p. 321). In the "Epistle to the Reader" prefacing the first edition of *Oceana*, Harrington claimed that he had "not been yet two years" busy in the composition of the text (Pocock, *Harrington*, p. 156).

and as easie for any Person, as well as for the Author *of* Oceana, *or that Pamphlet, to read* Thucidides, Polybius, Livy *or* Plutarch: *and if he do so with attentiveness, he shall be sure to find the same things there that they have found.*[12] *And if this were not Lawful, when that any one Person has written in any Science, no Man must write after him: for in* Polity, *the Orders of* Government; *in* Architecture, *the several Orders of* Pillars, Arches, Architraves, Cornishes,[13] &c. *In* Physick,[14] *the* Causes, Prognosticks[15] *and* Crisis *of* Diseases, *are so exactly the same in all Writers, that we may as well accuse all subsequent Authors to have been but Plagiaries of the Antecedent. Besides this, the Learned Gentleman added, that* Oceana *was written (it being thought Lawful so to do in those times) to evince out*[16] *of these Principles, that* England *was not capable of any other* Government *than a* Democracy. *And this Author out of the same* Maxims,[17] *or Aphorisms of Politicks, endeavours to prove that they may be applied*

---

12. Thucydides (c. 460–c. 400 B.C.): Athenian historian, soldier, and statesman; historian of the Peloponnesian War (459–446 B.C.). Polybius (c. 202–120 B.C.): Greek historian who extolled and analyzed Roman supremacy in the Mediterranean. Titus Livius (59 B.C.–A.D. 17): Roman historian who composed the history of the city from its foundation until 9 B.C., not all of which has survived. Plutarch (46–c. 120 A.D.): Greek biographer and moral philosopher, most celebrated for his *Parallel Lives*, in which the biographies of notable political and military figures from Greek and Roman antiquity are placed in revealing juxtaposition. Neville draws heavily and frequently on these biographies in *Plato Redivivus*.

13. There were three orders of Greek architecture, each of which comprised distinctive elements and adopted different proportions: the *Doric*, the most ancient and least decorated; the *Ionic*, less massive and more decorated; and the *Corinthian*, the most decorated of all, in which the capitals of columns were carved into intricate representations of acanthus leaves. *Architraves* are the main beams which rest immediately on the capitals of the columns of a building; also known as the epistyle (*OED*, s.v. "architrave," *n.* 1). *Cornishes* (now normally spelled "cornices") are moldings which crown or finish off the entablature of a building (*OED*, s.v. "cornice," 1a).

14. I.e., medicine.

15. I.e., symptoms upon which a prognosis (a prediction of the likely course and outcome of a disease) are based (*OED*, s.v. "prognosticks," 1).

16. I.e., to prove by argument or evidence; to establish (*OED*, s.v. "evince," 4b).

17. I.e., pithily worded expressions of general truth (*OED*, s.v. "maxim," 2b), but at this time possessing connotations of amorality and cynicism (as in Algernon Sidney's *Court Maxims*). See, e.g., Juan de Santa Mariá, *Policie Vnveiled, or, Maximes, and Reasons of State* (1637); "Sir Walter Raleigh," *The Prince, or, Maxims of*

naturally and fitly, to the redressing and supporting one of the best Monarchies *in the* World, *which is that of* England. *I had but one Doubt more, and that was an Objection against the Title, which I resolved at the first not to mention, because I could salve* [18] *it by altering the Title Page. But since I had opportunity, I acquainted the Gentleman with it: And it was, That certainly no Man would ever buy a Book that had in Front of it so insolent and presumptuous a Motto as* Plato Redivivus; *for that he must needs be thought not only vain in the highest degree, but void of Sence and Judgement too, who compares himself with* Plato, *the greatest* Philosopher, *the greatest* Politician *(I had almost said the greatest* Divine *too) that ever lived. My* Counsellor *told me that he had as great a resentment of any injury done to* Plato *as I, or any Man could have. But that he was hard to believe that this Man intended to compare himself to* Plato, *either in Natural Parts or Learning; but only to shew that he did imitate his way of Writing, as to the manner of it; (though not the matter) as he hath done exactly. For* Plato *ever writ these high Matters in easie and familiar Dialogues, and made the great Philosophers, and learned men of that Age; as* Simias, Cebes, Timaeus, Callias, Phaedon, &c. yea and Socrates himself,* [19] *the* Interlocutors, *although they never heard any thing of it till the Book came out. And although talking of* State *Affairs in a* Monarchy *must needs be more offensive than it was in the* Democracy *where* Plato *lived, and therefore our Author has forborn the naming the Persons who constitute this* Dialogue; *yet he does make a pretty near*

State (1642); Anonymous, *Maximes Unfolded* (1643); Hugo Grotius, *Politick Maxims* (1654); William Ball, *State-Maxims* (1656); Paulo Paruta, *Maximes of State and Government* (1667); Anonymous, *The Present Policies of France and the Maxims of Lewis XIV* (1689). Note also the full titles of the works on the Ottoman Empire by Sir Paul Rycaut included in the booklist.

18. I.e., heal or remedy (*OED*, s.v. "salve," 2a).

19. Simias: Simmias of Thebes, a speaker in Plato's *Phaedo*, and mentioned in the *Crito* and the *Phaedrus*. Cebes: a Pythagorean philosopher, a speaker in Plato's *Phaedoi*, and mentioned in the *Crito* and in passages of Lucian. Timaeus: a Pythagorean philosopher and a speaker in Plato's dialogue of the same name, where he expounds the origin and system of the universe; also a speaker in the *Critias*. Callias: a wealthy Athenian statesman and aristocrat, in whose house Plato set the *Protagoras*. Phaedon: Phaedo of Elis, a disciple of Socrates, who in Plato's *Phaedo* relates the conversation of Socrates and his followers in the last hour of his life.

Representation and Character[20] *of some Persons, who, I dare swear never heard of this Discourse, nor of the Author's Design. This convinced me, and made me suffer the Title to pass. So that I have nothing more to say to thee, Courteous Reader, but to desire thee to pardon the Faults in Printing,*[21] *and also the plainness and easiness of the Style, and some Tautologies: which latter I could easily have*

20. "The Characters of the Persons engaged in those Dialogues [i.e., *Plato Redivivus*] are real. The Stranger, was a Nobleman of Venice, who had gone through several offices in that State; the English Gentleman is Harry Neville himself; and the Physician his great friend the celebrated Doctor Lower" (Thomas Hollis, "SOME ACCOVNT OF H. NEVILLE," below, p. 432; see also, for confirmation of the identification of Lower from a hostile quarter, *Antimonarchical Authors*, p. 147). Richard Lower (1631–91) was royal physician from 1675; an eminent physician and physiologist; an associate of William Harvey, Robert Boyle, and Thomas Willis; a Fellow of the Royal Society; and the first man to perform a successful blood transfusion. Lower figures in Lorenzo Magalotti's list of "Uomini celebri per lettura in Inghilterra," where he is praised as "de migliori anotomisti d'Inghilterra" (Magalotti, *Relazioni*, p. 146). As well as enjoying a lucrative medical practice (Anthony à Wood praised Lower as "the most noted physician in Westminster and London"), Lower made important discoveries in the fields of neuroanatomy, pulmonary circulation, and cardiorespiratory function, his most important publication being the *Tractatus de corde* (1669). "Eventually, however, Lower's strongly held political opinions adversely affected his medical career, as his protestant religious beliefs and close affiliation with the whig party led to his loss of court appointments and a considerable decline in his reputation and practice. Lower actively opposed the policies of James II, who once remarked that he 'did him more mischief than a troop of horse,' although Lower seems to have spent much of his time in Cornwall while James was in power" (*ODNB*). For Algernon Sidney's praise of Lower, see Sidney, *Discourses*, p. 13. If Neville means that the Venetian Nobleman's near relation was ambassador to the French court in 1680 (when the dialogues are set), then he would have been a relative of either Domenico Contarini or Sebastiano Foscarini (see below, p. 56, n. 24). Not all of Neville's first readers were prepared to accept the fiction of three speakers: see Goddard, *Plato's Demon*, p. 53.

21. Both the first and second editions of *Plato Redivivus* are in some respects poorly printed books, with localized areas of frequent error, as can be deduced from the list of corrections to the copy-text (below, pp. 435–38). These patches of concentrated error may suggest that the typesetting of the book was divided between a number of different printers, a practice favored at the time on grounds of both speed and secrecy (since no one printer would have possessed a full text of the work). Note that Harrington says of *Oceana* that the text of the first edition "was dispersed into three Presses," that this resulted in irremediable errors, and that the reason for this expedient of divided typesetting was a "Spanell questing"—by which he means presumably an agent of the present government trying to interfere with the printing (Pocock, *Harrington*, pp. 156 and 6–7; cf. the contempt for "beagles [employed] to hunt after books" in *The English Souldiers Standard*, in Morton, *Freedom*, p. 233).

mended, but that I thought the Author did not let them pass out of neglect, but design: and intended that both they, and the familiarity of the words and expressions, suited better with his purpose of disposing this matter to be treated in ordinary Conversation amongst private Friends, than full Periods [22] and starch'd Language would have done; which might have been Impropriety. The next Request I have to thee is, that if thou dost believe this Discourse to be a very foolish one, as it may be for ought I know (for I am no fit Judge of such matters) that thou wilt yet vouchsafe to suspend thy Censure of it for a while, till the whole Impression is vended: that so, although neither the Publick nor thy self may ever reap any Benefit or Profit by it, I may be yet so fortunate by thy favour as to do it. Which will make me study thy Content hereafter in something better; and in the mean time remain,

Thy Friend and Servant

22. An elevated, formal, and verbose style.

Political Discourses and
Histories Worth Reading

1. The *Works* of the famous *Nicholas Machiavel*, Citizen and Secretary of *Florence*, containing, 1. The *History* of *Florence*. 2. The *Prince*. 3. The Original of the *Guelf* and *Ghibilin* Factions. 4. The Life of *Castruccio Castracani*. 5. The Murther of *Vitelli*, &c. by Duke *Valentino*. 6. The State of *France*. 7. The State of *Germany*. 8. The Discourses on *Titus Livius*. 9. The Art of *War*. 10. The Marriage of *Belphegor*, a Novel. 11. *Nicholas Machiavel's* Letter, in Vindication of *himself* and his *writings*: All written in *Italian*, and from thence newly and faithfully Translated into *English*. In Folio, *Price Bound*, 16 *s*.

2. *I Ragguagli di Parnasso*; or Advertisements from *Parnassus*, in two Centuries, with the *Politick Touchstone*, written Originally in *Italian*, By that Noble Roman *Trajano Boccalini*. Englished by the *Earl* of *Monmouth*: In Folio *Price bound* 8 *s*.

3. The *History* of the Affairs of *Europe*, in this present age, but more particularly of the *Republick of Venice*, written in *Italian*, by *Battista Nani*, Cavalier and Procurator of St. *Mark*: Englished by Sir *Robert Honiwood*, Knight; in Folio, *price bound* 12 *s*.

For a discussion of this booklist and its relation to the text of *Plato Redivivus*, see the introduction, above, pp. xxx–xxxiii.

4. The *History* of the *Government* of *Venice*, wherein the *Policies, Councils, Magistrates,* and *Laws* of that *State* are fully related, and the use of the *Balloting Box,* exactly described: Written in the Year 1675, in Octav. *Price bound* 3 *s.*

5. The *History* of the *Turkish Empire,* from the year 1623, to the year 1677, containing the Reigns of the *three* last Emperours, *viz. Sultan Morat,* Sultan *Ibrahim,* and Sultan *Mahomet* 4th, his Son, the 13th *Emperour* now Reigning: By *Paul Rycaut,* Esq; late Consul of *Smyrna.* In Folio, *Price bound* 14 *s.*

6. The present *State* of the *Ottoman Empire* in 3 Books, containing the *Maximes* of the *Turkish Polity,* their *Religion* and *Military Discipline,* Illustrated with divers Figures. Written by *Paul Rycaut,* Esq; late Secretary to the *English* Ambassadour there, and since *Consul* of *Smyrna.* The Fourth Edition, in Octavo, *Price bound* 5 *s.*

7. The *Memoires* of *Philip de Commines* Lord of *Argenton,* containing the History of *Lewis* XI. and *Charles* VIII, Kings of *France,* with the most remarkable occurrences in their particular *Reigns,* from the Year 1464, to 1498, Revised and Corrected by *Denis Godfrey,* Councellour and Historiographer to the *French* King, and from his Edition lately Printed at *Paris,* newly Translated into *English,* in Octav. *Price bound* 5 *s.*

8. The *History* of *France,* under the Ministry of Cardinal *Mazarine,* viz. from the Death of King *Lewes* XIII, to the year 1664, wherein all the Affairs of *State* to that time are exactly Related: By *Benjamine Priolo,* and faithfully Englished, by *Christopher Wase,* Gent. in Octav. *Price bound* 4 *s.*

9. The Present *State* of the *United Provinces* of the *Low Countries,* as to the *Government, Laws, Forces, Riches, Manners, Customes, Revenue,* and *Territory* of the *Dutch;* Collected out of divers Authors: By *W. A.* Fellow of the *Royal* Society, the Second Edition in twelves: *Price bound* 2 *s.* 6 *d.*

10. The Present *State* of the *Princes* and *Republicks* of *Italy,* the Second Edition enlarged, with the manner of *Election* of *Popes,* and a *Character* of *Spain.* Written Originally in *English* by *J. Gailhard,* Gent. in twelves. *Price bound* 1 *s.* 6 *d.*

11. The *Policy* and *Government* of the *Venetians*, both in *Civil* and *Military* Affairs: Written in *French* by the *Sieur de la Hay*, and faithfully *Englished*, in 12s. *Price bound* 1 *s.*

12. The *Secret History* of the *Court* of the *Emperour Justinian*, giving a true account of the *Debaucheries thereof:* Written in *Greek*, by *Procopius* of *Caesaria*; faithfully *Englished*, in Octav. *Price bound* 1 *s.* 6 *d.*

The Argument

A Noble Venetian, *not one of the young Fry,*[23] *but a grave sober person, who had born Office and Magistracy in his own Commonwealth, having been some years since in* France *with a near Relation of his who was Ambassadour at that*

23. I.e., immature offspring (*OED*, s.v. "fry," 4). Several of the books in the booklist comment on the wisdom of the Venetian practice whereby men came to hold high office only in later life after having served in a wide range of lesser stations. See, e.g., Battista Nani's comments on the election of Giovanni Bembo as Doge: "In the very end of the year past, *Marco Anthonio Memo*, Duke of *Venice*, dying, *Giovanni Bembo* gave happy presages to the Commonwealth, being taken up from the Procuratorship of St. *Marco* into the highest dignity, after having gone through considerable Imployments, and the Command of the Sea; a person of much vertue and a decrepit age, as is usual in the Government, in which men rise to the height by long steps of merit, and not by the favorable wings of Fortune" (Nani, *Affairs of Europe*, p. 59). A similar point is placed in the mouth of Aretino by Boccalini in the Fifth Advertisement from Parnassus: "That excellent custom of the State of *Venice*, in not conferring places upon her Nobility by skips and leaps, but by degrees and gradation, was that sound Basis whereon the greatness and eternity of such Liberty was grounded; and that it was an excellent Rule, that whatsoever Noble man would arrive at the Supreme Dignities, he must even from his youth begin at the meanest Magistracies: A wholsome Custom which produceth the important effect of maintaining that true and essential equality amongst the Nobles of an Aristocrasie, which makes Liberty long-liv'd: for with those that understand State-affairs, the parity of wealth is not that which equals Senators in a Common-wealth; but the making all the Nobles march on towards the Grandeur of the highest Dignities, beginning at the meanest Employments" (Boccalini, *Advertisements*, p. 8; cf. p. 54, Advertisement 41; on the importance of Boccalini to Harrington, see Pocock,

Court,[24] *and finding himself out of Employment, resolved to divert himself by*
visiting some part of the World which he had never seen; and so passing through
Germany, Flanders, *and* Holland, *arrived in* England *about the beginning of*
May *last,*[25] *bringing Letters of recommendation to several* English *Gentlemen,*
who had been Travellers, and made Friendship in his Countrey.[26] *A Custom*

Harrington, pp. 74–75). Cf. Amelot de la Houssaie, *Venice,* p. 19; and Hay, *Policy,*
pp. 14 and 21. Machiavelli, however, insists that in the Roman Republic no attention
was paid to the age of a candidate for high office; the sole criterion was virtue (*Discourses,* 1.60). In *Oceana* Harrington makes the Lord Archon approve the Venetian
practice and censure that of Rome (Pocock, *Harrington,* pp. 311–12). Harrington's
mouthpiece, Publicola, argues similarly in favor of an age qualification for office
holders in *Valerius and Publicola* (ibid., p. 792).

24. Giovanni Battista Nani (the historian whose history of Europe Neville included in the booklist) had been Venetian ambassador to France from 1643 to 1668,
Giovanni Morosini from 1668 to 1674, Francesco Michiel from 1670 to 1674, Ascanio II Giustinian from 1673 to 1676, Domenico Contarini from 1676 to 1686, and
Sebastiano Foscarini from 1678 to 1683.

25. I.e., May 1680.

26. Neville lived in Italy for extended periods twice in his life. The first period of
residence was in the early 1640s: "Soon after [May 1641], he made an extended tour on
the continent, especially of Italy, which his older brother, Richard (1615–1676), seems
already to have visited in 1636 in the company of James Harrington. He stayed chiefly
in Florence and Rome during 1643–4, and made a further visit to Venice. Among his
friends dating from this trip were the Florentine lawyer Ferrante Capponi and Bernardo Guasconi (Bernard Gascoigne); Guasconi later fought in Neville's brother's
royalist regiment of horse in 1644. In 1645 Neville returned to England" (*ODNB*).
The second was in the mid-1660s: "Having maintained his Italian connections in the
two decades since his first visit, he now [May 1664] returned there for three years,
during which time his correspondence shows him to have been chiefly in Florence, at
the court of Ferdinand II of Tuscany, and Rome, where his brother was still writing
to him in June 1667" (*ODNB*). In his copy of *Plato Redivivus* Thomas Brand inscribed
a list of Englishmen who "were in Italy, together, or within a few years of each other,
culling elegance & knowlege [*sic*], & who afterwards espoused the Cause of Liberty
and the Parliament and died or suffered for it" (British Library, 8025.f.62, second
front free end-paper, recto). As well as Neville, Brand's list comprises John Hamden,
Henry Marten, Thomas Chaloner, John Milton, James Harrington, Andrew Marvell, Algernon Sydney, and John Pym (ibid., second front free end-paper, verso). On
this group of cosmopolitan republicans, see in particular Blair Worden's "Marchamont Nedham and the Beginnings of English Republicanism, 1649–1656": "To grasp
those principles [i.e., the timeless principles of political wisdom], republicans believed, Englishmen must look beyond their own histories. They must seek their lessons in the histories, ancient and modern, of foreign lands, and in the political
thought to which those histories had given rise" (Wootton, *Republicanism,* p. 50).

usually practised amongst such who travel into any part where they have no hab-itude[27] *or acquaintance. Amongst the rest, he was addressed to one of the Gentle-men who acts a part in this Dialogue: Who after he had waited upon him, and served him*[28] *for near two Moneths, had certain necessary occasions, which called him for some time into the Country. Where he had not been above three Weeks, before he heard, by meer accident, that the Gentleman of* Venice *was fallen dangerous sick of a malignant Feaver. Which made him post away immediately to* London, *to assist and serve him in what he might. But he found him almost perfectly restored to his health by an eminent Physician of our Nation,*[29] *as renowned for his Skill and Cures at home; as for his Writings both here and abroad: And who besides his profound knowledge in all Learning, as well in other Professions as his own, had particularly arriv'd to so exact and perfect a discovery of the formerly hidden parts of human Bodies,*[30] *that every one who can but understand Latine, may by his means know more of Anatomy than either* Hypocrates,[31] *or any of the Ancients or Moderns did, or do perceive. And if he had lived in the days of* Solomon, *that great Philosopher would never have said,* Cor hominis inscrutabile.[32] *This excellent Doctor being in the sick mans Chamber, when the other* English *Gentleman, newly alighted, came to visit him. After some Compliments and Conversation of course, they begun to talk of Political Matters, as you will better understand by the Introduction, and by the Discourse it self.*

27. I.e., associates or friends (*OED*, s.v. "habitude," 3b).

28. I.e., attended upon him (without any implication of subservience).

29. I.e., Richard Lower; see above, p. 48, n. 20.

30. Lower was an extremely accomplished dissectionist: "In the preface to *Cerebri anatome*, [Thomas] Willis praised Lower as 'an anatomist of supreme skill' whose 'most skillful dissecting hand' and 'indefatigable Industry, and unwearied Labour' had provided Willis with the data needed to describe the 'structure and function of bodies, whose secrets were previously concealed'" (*ODNB*).

31. Hippocrates (b. c. 460 B.C.), preeminent Greek physician.

32. "The heart of man is unsearchable." The closest Biblical text is Jeremiah 17:9, "The heart is deceitful above all things"; in the Vulgate, "Pravum est cor omnium et inscrutabile" (some versions of the Vulgate read "hominis" or "hominum" for "omnium"). However, Jeremiah is not a Solomonic book. But cf. Proverbs 25:3, "The heart of kings is unsearchable"; in the Vulgate, "Cor regum inscrutabile." Neville's substitution of "hominis" for "regum" is significant and perhaps supplies a hint concerning his attitude toward monarchy. Cf. *Antimonarchical Authors*, pp. 147–48.

The First Day.

The Introduction

English Gentleman. The sudden news I had of your sad distemper,[33] and the danger you were in, has been the cause of a great deal of affliction to me, as well as of my present and speedy repair to *London*, some Weeks sooner than I intended: I must confess I received some comfort to hear at my arrival of your amendment, and do take much more now to find you up, and as I hope recover'd; which I knew would be a necessary consequence of your sending for this excellent Physician, the *Esculapius*[34] of our Age, it being the first request I had to make to you, if by seeing him here in your Chamber I had not found it needless. For the Destiny of us *English*-men depends upon him, and we either live or dye Infallibly, according to the Judgment or good Fortune we have, when we are sick, either to call or not call him to our assistance.

Noble Venetian. I am Infinitely obliged to you, for your care of me, but am sorry it has been so inconvenient to you, as to make you leave your Affairs in the Countrey sooner than you proposed to your self to do: I wish

33. I.e., disease (*OED*, s.v. "distemper," 4a).
34. The Latin form of Asclepius, in Greek mythology the son of Apollo and the god of medicine.

I might be so fortunate in the course of my Life, as to find an opportunity of making some part of an acknowledgment, for this and all the rest of your favours, but shall pray God it may not be in the same kind; but that your health may ever be so entire, that you never need so transcendent a Charity, as I now receive from your Goodness: And as to this incomparable Doctor; although, I must confess, that all the good which has happen'd to me in this Country, as well as the knowledge I have received of Persons and Things, does derive from you; yet I must make an exception, as to this one point; for if I can either read, or hear, this Gentleman's excellent Writings, and the Fame he worthily injoys in my Country, would have made it inexcusable in me, to implore the help of any other; and I do assure you, that, before I left *England*, it was in my Ambition to beg your Mediation towards the bringing me into the acquaintance and favour of this Learned Person, even before I had any thoughts of becoming the Object of his Care and Skill, as now I am the Trophy[35] of both.

Doctor. Well, Gentlemen, you are both too great to be Flatterers, and I too little to be flattered, and therefore I will impute this fine discourse you both make about me, to the overflowing of your Wit, and the having no Object near you to vent[36] it upon but me. And for you, Sir, if my Art fail me not, the voiding this Mirth, is a very good sign that you are in a fair way to a perfect recovery. And for my Countryman here: I hope whilst he has this vent, that his Hypocondriack distemper will be at quiet, and that neither his own thoughts, nor the ill posture of our Publick Affairs[37] will make him hang himself, for at least this twelve Months: Only, Gentlemen, pray take notice, that this does not pass upon me, nor do I drink it like Milk (as the *French* phrase it)[38] being mindful of what a grave Gentleman at *Florence* replyed to a young Esquire, who answered

---

35. I.e., a token or evidence of victory, courage, skill, or success (*OED*, s.v. "trophy," 4a).

36. I.e., to relieve or unburden oneself of something (*OED*, s.v. "vent," I1b).

37. Cf. above, p. 41, n. 4.

38. In French, "to drink milk" ("boire du lait" or "boire du petit-lait") means to feel pleasure on being flattered.

his Compliments with, *Oh, Sir, you flatter me, i prencipi s'adulano i pari vostri si coglionono*;[39] That last word I cannot render well into *Latin*.[40]

English Gentleman. Well, Doctor, we will not offend your Modesty:[41] The next time we do you Justice, it shall be behind your back, since you are so severe upon us. But you may assure your self that my intention of recommending you to this Gentleman, was for his own sake, and not for yours: For you have too many Patients already, and it were much better, both for you and us, that you had but half so many: For then we should have more of your Writings,[42] and sometimes enjoy your good Conversation; which is worth our being sick on purpose for. And I am resolved to put my self sometimes into my Bed, and send for you, since you have done coming to our Coffee-House.[43]

39. "The principle of flattery is if your equals understand you"—perhaps a further hint that the text may contain covert meanings. For mockery of this flourish of Italian, see Goddard, *Plato's Demon*, p. 55.

40. The Doctor is speaking in Latin, still at the end of the seventeenth century the learned language of Europe, and one especially favored by physicians: "Until the eighteenth century it was very common for doctors to speak Latin to each other" (Janson, *Natural History of Latin*, p. 151). As late as 1782 Samuel Johnson deferred to the established linguistic customs of the medical profession and corresponded with his physician Thomas Lawrence in Latin (Redford, *Letters*, vol. 4, pp. 24–25 and 34). However, the Englishman and the Venetian are speaking Italian; see below, p. 66.

41. I.e., by praising you to your face.

42. Richard Lower's principal publications are *Diatribae Thomae Willisi de febribus vindicatio* (1665), *A Brief Account of the Virtues of the Famous Well of Astrop* (1668), *Tractatus de corde* (1669), *Bromographia* (1669), and *Dissertatio de origine catarrhi* (1670).

43. Neville was an *habitué* at different times of various London coffeehouses. The Rota Club, of which Neville was an important member, met during the winter of 1659 at the Turk's Head, or Miles's Coffee House, as Thomas Hollis reports (below, p. 430; cf. Rahe, *Throne and Altar*, pp. 350–51). Later in life Neville frequented the Grecian coffeehouse, where Richard Lower was also to be found (Wootton, *Republicanism*, p. 175), and also perhaps Will's in Covent Garden, close to his lodgings (Champion, *Priestcraft*, p. 187). For the social role and cultural significance of the coffeehouse at this time, see Markman Ellis, *The Coffee House: A Cultural History* (London: Weidenfeld and Nicolson, 2004).

But to leave this Subject now, I hear you say, that this Gentleman is in a perfect way of recovery; pray is he well enough to hear, without any prejudice to his convalescence, a reprehension I have to make him?

Doctor. Yes, yes; you may say what you will to him, for your Repremands will rather divert than trouble him, and prove more a Cordial than a Corrosive.[44]

English Gentleman. Then, Sir, pray consider what satisfaction you can ever make me, for the hard measure you have used towards me, in letting me learn from common Fame and Fortune, the news of your Sickness, and that not till your recovery; and for depriving me of the opportunity of paying the debt I owe to your own merit, and to the recommendation of those worthy Persons in *Italy*,[45] who did me the honour to address you to me. And this injury is much aggravated by the splendour of your Condition, and greatness of your Fortune, which makes it impossible for me ever to hope for any other occasion to express my faithful service to you, or satisfie any part of the duty I have to be at your devotion. To be sick in a strange Country, and to distrust the sincerity and obedience of—

Noble Venetian. Pray, Sir, give me leave to interrupt you, and to assure you, that it was not any distrust of your goodness to me, of which I have had sufficient experience; nor any insensibleness how much your care might advantage me; much less any scruple I had of being more in your debt; which if it had been possible for me to entertain, it must have been thought of long since, before I had received those great Obligations, which I never made any difficulty to accept of. It was not, I say, any of these Considerations, which hindred me from advertising you of my Distemper; but the Condition and Nature of it, which in a moment

44. I.e., a restorative medicine (*OED*, s.v. "cordial," 2a) and a caustic or escharotic medicine (*OED*, s.v. "corrosive," 2b), respectively.

45. For Neville's periods of residence in Italy, the persons we know he met there, and discussion of the significance of the years spent in Italy for his intellectual development, see the introduction (above, pp. x and xv–xvi), and p. 56, n. 26, above.

depriv'd me of the exercise of those Faculties which might give me a Capacity of helping my self in any thing. But otherwise I assure you that no day of my life shall pass, wherein I will not express a sence of your Favours, and—

Doctor. Pray now, Sir, permit me to interrupt you; for this Gentleman, I dare say, looks for no Compliments; but that which I have to say, is; That the desire you signified to me, to give you some account of our Affairs here, and the turbulency of our present State, will be much better placed, if you please to address it to this Gentleman whose Parts and Studies have fitted him for such an Employment; besides his having had a great share in the managing Affairs of State here, in other times:[46] And really no man understands the Government of *England* better than he.

English Gentleman. Now, Doctor, I should tell you, *i pari miei si coglionono*,[47] for so you your self have baptized this kind of Civility; But however, this is a Province that I cannot be reasonably prest to take upon me, whilst you are present, who are very well known to be as skillful in the Nature and Distemper of the Body Politick,[48] as the whole Nation

46. For a brief account of Neville's career in public life and government, see the introduction (above, pp. x–xv).

47. "My equals understand me"; cf. above, p. 61, n. 39.

48. The discussion of politics in terms drawn from Hippocratic medicine goes back to Plato and Aristotle and had been revived by Thomas Aquinas, Savonarola, and Machiavelli (Rahe, *Throne and Altar,* p. 49); cf. Hobbes, *Leviathan,* p. 9. However, the imaginative proximity between medicine and politics that was widespread in Neville's circle had been reenergized by contemporary medical breakthroughs. Just as discoveries were being made about the previously hidden mechanisms and systems of the body—and one of the speakers in *Plato Redivivus* was a leader in that area—so the hope was that similar, previously hidden, but natural and efficient systems might be discovered in the realms of politics and government: "Government is political, as a human body is natural, mechanism: both have proper springs, wheels, and a peculiar organization to qualify them for suitable motions . . . and though neither of them ought to be murdered, yet, when they are dead, they ought to be interred" (*Cato's Letters,* p. 607, no. 84, 7 July 1722). Hence Harrington had likened the principle of rotation to the circulation of the blood (Pocock, *Harrington,* p. 69; cf. Scott, *Commonwealth Principles,* pp. 164–66 and pp. 179–80, for a parallel instance in John Streater's *Observations,* no. 4, p. 22),

confesses you to be in the concerns of the Natural. And you would have good store of Practice in your former Capacity, if the wise Custom amongst the Ancient *Greeks* were not totally out of use. For they, when they found any Craziness or indisposition in their several Governments, before it broke out into a Disease, did repair to the Physicians of State (who, from their Profession, were called the Seven Wise Men of *Greece*)[49] and obtain'd from them some good *Recipes* to prevent those seeds of distemper from taking root, and destroying the publique Peace. But in our days, these Signes or Forerunners of Diseases in State are not foreseen, till the whole Mass is corrupted, and that the Patient is incurable, but by violent Remedies. And if we could have perceived the first Symptoms of

---

and in the preface to *The Art of Lawgiving* Harrington had further explored the affinities between physical and political anatomy: "But the fearful and wonderful making, the admirable structure and great variety of the parts of man's body, in which the discourses of anatomists are altogether conversant, are understood by so few that I may say they are not understood by any. Certain it is that the delivery of a model of government (which must either be of none effect, or embrace all those muscles, nerves, arteries and bones, which are necessary unto any function of a well-ordered commonwealth) is no less than political anatomy" (Pocock, *Harrington*, p. 656; cf. p. 854). Such language might sometimes be heard also in Parliament. In 1678 John Birch (1615–91) had said, "In the body [politic] 'tis as in the body natural. If the money does not circulate, all will fly to the head, like the blood, and kill presently. If those at the helm do not consider to bring the blood round again, the many consequences will be fatal" (Grey, *Debates*, vol. 5, pp. 182–83). "This Harringtonian description of the organic nature of the body politic provided the intrinsic conceptual backcloth for the analysis of society proposed by such men as Henry Neville, Robert Molesworth, Walter Moyle and Toland" (Champion, *Priestcraft*, p. 203). James I, however, had been sharp-sighted enough to realize in *The Trew Law of Free Monarchies* (1598) that medicinal metaphors, when applied to politics, tended to support arguments for resistance to princes and covert republicanism (Wootton, *Divine Right*, p. 100; James VI and I, *Political Writings*, p. 78). Cf. Skinner, *Liberty*, pp. 24–25.

49. The name traditionally given to seven men of practical political wisdom who lived between 620 and 550 B.C. There are various lists, but four names are common to them all: Solon, Thales, Pittacus of Mitylene, and Bias of Priene. Some lists also include the tyrants Periander of Corinth and Cleobulus of Rhodes. Their teaching was handed down in the form of aphorisms, such as "Know thyself" and "Nothing in excess." Cf. Boccalini, *Advertisements*, pp. 94–104, no. 77, where the Seven Wise Men of Greece are unable to settle on a cure for the ineradicable vices of modern Europe.

our Distemper, and used good Alteratives,[50] the curiosity of this worthy Gentleman had been spared, as also his command to you, to give him some light into our matters; and we unfortunate *English-men* had reposed in that quiet, ease, and security, which we enjoy'd three hundred years since.[51] But let us leave the contest who shall inform this Gentleman, lest we spend the time we should do it in unprofitably, and let each of us take his part; for if one speak all, it will look like a studied discourse fitted for the Press, and not a familiar Dialogue. For it ought to be in private Conversation, as it was originally in the planting the Gospel, when there were two sorts of preaching;[52] the one Concionary, which was used by the Apostles and other Missionaries, when they spoke to those who had never heard of the Mysteries of Christian Religion, possibly not so much as of the Jewish Law, or the History of Christ. The duty of those was to hear, and not reply, or any way interrupt the harrangue: But when the Believers (called the Church) assembled together, it was the Custom of such of the Auditors, to whom any thing occurred, or (as S. *Paul* calls it)[53] was revealed, to interpose and desire to be heard, which was called an Interlocutory Preaching, or Religious Conversation; and served very

50. I.e., medicines that work by altering bodily processes, as opposed to those that work by stimulating excretion or evacuation (*OED*, s.v. "alterative," B1).

51. I.e., during the reign of Edward III (reigned 1327–77). Nostalgic medievalism is an interesting thread in Neville's argument. Note the later praise of Edward III (below, pp. 166 and 278). These moments of nostalgia should not be confused with ancient constitutionalism, however (pace Pocock, *Harrington*, p. 134). Neville has no desire to refurbish England's medieval constitution, ill adapted as it would be to the underlying economic realities of the late seventeenth century. As he had said in Parliament on 18 February 1659: "We are upon alterations, and no thought now is to be taken of what was done by John of Gaunt, and such fellows" (Burton, *Diary*, vol. 3, p. 331).

52. This is an early stroke in Neville's attempts to present his speaker as a defender of pure and primitive Christianity but no friend to church establishments and priesthoods, which he will shortly denounce as later, human corruptions (below, pp. 147–55). "Concionary preaching" (from the Latin *contionarius*, meaning "belonging to an assembly") refers to preaching in which an argument is developed by a single speaker. "Interlocutory preaching" refers to discussions on religious subjects in which a number of speakers take part.

53. "If anything be revealed to another that sitteth by, let the first hold his peace. For ye may all prophesy one by one, that all may learn, and all may be comforted" (1 Corinthians 14:30–31).

much to the instructing and edifying those who had long believed in Christ, and possibly knew as much of him as their Pastor himself; and this is used still amongst many of our Independent Congregations.[54]

Doctor. I have (besides the reason I alledged before, and which I still insist upon) some other cause to beg that you will please to give your self the trouble of answering this Gentleman's Queries; which is, that I am very defective in my Expressions in the *Italian* Language; which though I understand perfectly, and so comprehend all that either of you deliver, yet I find not words at hand to signifie my own meaning, and am therefore necessitated to deliver my self in Latin, as you see. And I fear that our pronunciation[55] being so different from that which is used in *Italy*, this worthy person may not so easily comprehend what I intend, and so be disappointed in the desire he hath to be perfectly instructed in our Affairs.

Noble Venetian. Really, Sir, that is not all; for besides that, I confess your pronunciation of the Latin Tongue to be very new to me, and for that reason I have been forced to be troublesom to you, in making you repeat things twice, or thrice. I say besides that your Latinity, as your Writings shew, and all the world knows, is very pure and elegant, which it is noto-

---

54. E.g., the Quakers.

55. On the variations in the pronunciation of Latin in different countries of Western Europe from the medieval period onward, see Janson, *Natural History of Latin*, pp. 107–15. As Janson says, "The Italian pronunciation of Latin has always had the greatest prestige" (p. 113). In his "Life of Milton," Johnson records that the blind Milton required Elwood, the Quaker retained to read Latin to him, to "learn and practise the Italian pronunciation, which, he said, was necessary, if he would talk with foreigners." Johnson, always ready to disagree with Milton, will have none of it: "This seems to have been a task troublesome without use. There is little reason for preferring the Italian pronunciation to our own, except that it is more general; and to teach it to an Englishman is only to make him a foreigner at home. He who travels, if he speaks Latin, may so soon learn the sounds which every native gives it, that he need make no provision before his journey; and if strangers visit us, it is their business to practise such conformity to our modes as they expect from us in their own countries" (*Lives of the Poets*, vol. 1, pp. 264–65, §107). The classic text on the subject of Latin pronunciation is Erasmus's *De recta Latini Graecique sermonis pronuntiatione* (1528).

rious to all, that we in *Italy* scarce understand: Gentlemen there never Learning more Latin, than what is necessary to call for Meat and Drink, in *Germany* or *Holland*, where most of the Hosts speak a certain *Franck*,[56] compounded of *Dutch, Latin*, and *Italian*. And though some of us have *Latin* enough to understand a good Author, (as you have of our Language) yet we seldom arrive to speak any better than this *Franck*, or can without study comprehend good *Latin*, when we meet with it in discourse. And therefore it is your perfection in that Tongue, and my ignorance in it, that makes me concur with you, in desiring this Gentleman, to take the pains of instructing my Curiosity in *Italian*.

English Gentleman. I shall obey you in this, and all things else, upon this condition, that both you and the Doctor will vouchsafe to interrogate me, and by that means give me the Method of serving you in this: And then that you will both please to interrupt and contradict me, when you think I say any thing amiss, or that either of you are of a different Opinion, and to give me a good occasion of explaining my self, and possibly of being convinced by you, which I shall easily confess; for I hate nothing more than to hear disputes amongst Gentlemen, and men of sence, wherein the Speakers seem (like Sophisters in a Colledge) to dispute rather for Victory, than to discover and find out the Truth.

Doctor. Well, all this I believe will be granted you; so that we have nothing to do now, but to adjourn, and name a time when to meet again. Which I, being this Gentlemans Physician, will take upon me to appoint, and it shall be to morrow morning about nine of the Clock, after he has slept well, as I hope he will, by means of a Cordial I intend to send him immediately. In the mean time, not to weary him too much, we will take our leaves of him for this Night.

Noble Venetian. I shall expect your return with great impatience, and if your Cordial be not very potent, I believe the desire of seeing you will

56. I.e., a lingua franca, or mixed language (*OED*, s.v. "franck," 3, citing this passage).

make me wake much sooner than the hour you appoint. And I am very confident, that my mind as well as my body, will be sufficiently improved by such Visits. It begins to be darkish, Boy light your Torch, and wait on these Gentlemen down.

Both. Sir, we wish you all good rest and health.

Noble Venetian. And I, with a thousand thanks, the like to you.

The Second Day.

Doctor. Well, Sir, how is it? Have you rested well to Night? I fear we come too early.

Noble Venetian. Dear Doctor, I find my self very well, thanks to your Care and Skill, and have been up above these two hours, in expectation of the favour you and this Gentleman promist me.

Doctor. Well, then pray let us leave off Compliments and Repartees, of which we had a great deal too much yesterday, and fall to our business, and be pleas'd to interrogate this Gentleman what you think fit.

Noble Venetian. Then, Sir, my first request to you, is, That you will vouchsafe to acquaint me for what Reasons this Nation, which hath ever been esteemed (and very justly) one of the most considerable People of the World, and made the best Figure both in Peace, Treaties, War, and Trade, is now of so small regard,[57] and signifies so little abroad? Pardon

---

57. The poor figure cut by England and its monarch on the stage of early seventeenth-century European politics is something on which Battista Nani repeatedly comments: "*James* King of *England*, hiding the intern weakness of his Kingdom under a great Cloak of Authority, and honouring his own quiet with the name of Studies and Learning, contributes nothing but his good offices"; "The

the freedom I take, for I assure you it is not out of disrespect, much less of contempt that I speak it: For since I arrived in *England*, I find it one of the most flourishing Kingdoms in *Europe*, full of splendid Nobility and Gentry; the comliest persons alive, Valiant, Courteous, Knowing and Bountiful; and as well stored with Commoners, Honest, Industrious, fitted for Business, Merchandise, Arts, or Arms; as their several Educations lead them. Those who apply themselves to study, prodigious for Learning, and succeeding to admiration in the perfection of all Sciences: All this makes the Riddle impossible to be solved; but by some skillful *Sphynx*,[58] such as you are; whose pains I will yet so far spare, as to acknowledge, that I do in that little time I have spent here, perceive that

---

eyes of the whole Empire were now turned towards the King of *England*, because being so nearly allied to the *Palatine*, and in all affairs endeavouring to thwart the advantages of the *Austrians*, it seemed that it would be difficult for him not to ingage in Arms. But in that Prince *decorum* and want of power were commonly opposites. He being *Scotch* by birth, and come to the Crown by inheritance, was the first that governed the two Nations, by natural Antipathy and ancient emulation Enemies, and designing to reclaim the fierceness of those people with ease and idleness, had set up his rest in Peace, and avoided as much as possible the calling of Parliaments, without which having not the power to impose Contributions, nor levy Money, he contented himself rather to struggle with many straights and difficulties, than see them meet with a jealousie of them, or being met, be obliged to separate them with the disgust of the people, or with a satisfaction of prejudice to the Supreme Power. These Novelties of *Germany* coming to his knowledge, he first disapproves the resolution of his Son-in-law to accept the Crown; afterwards publishes at last that he would assist him, and dispatching an Ambassadour to *Vienna*, demands impossible Conditions of Peace, proposing that *Bohemia* should remain to the *Palatine*; whereupon from measures so fickle and ambiguous, the opinion was universally confirmed, that he inclined more to foment the flames of the Empire, than to extinguish them"; "*And we see* England, *that having nothing great but the name, hath a King always in fear to be constrained to a War, and his Ministers to continue Peace in Holland, fixed in the same reasons which induced them to procure it*"; "The offices of *James* were discredited by the weakness wherewith he accompanied his force"; "the King of *England*, . . . laught at by the World" (Nani, *Affairs of Europe*, pp. 46, 137–38, 144, 177, and 188).

58. In Greek mythology, a hybrid monster represented with a woman's breasts on the winged body of a lion. "Sphinx" is derived from the Greek word for "strangler" or "throttler," the etymology being a reference to the challenging riddles posed by the sphinx (as in the story of Oedipus). Neville is using the word in an extended sense to refer to someone who can solve rather than pose riddles (see *OED*, s.v. "sphinx," 1b).

the immediate cause of all this, is the Dis-union of the People and the Governours; the Discontentment of the Gentry, and Turbulency of the Commonalty; although without all Violence or Tumult, which is Miraculous. So that what I now request of you, is, That you will please to deduce particularly to me, the Causes of this Division, that when they are laid open, I may proceed (if you think fit to permit it) from the Disease, when known, to enquire out the Remedies.

English Gentleman. Before I come to make you any Answer, I must thank you for the Worthy and Honourable Character you give of our Nation, and shall add to it, That I do verily believe, that there are not a more Loyal and Faithful People to their Prince in the whole world, than ours are; nor that fear more to fall into that State of Confusion, in which we were twenty years since;[59] and that, not only this Parliament, which consists of the most Eminent Men of the Kingdom, both for Estates and Parts; but all the Inhabitants of this Isle in general; even those (so many of them as have their understandings yet entire) which were of the Antiroyal Party, in our late Troubles,[60] have all of them the greatest horrour imaginable, to think of doing any thing, that may bring this poor Country into those Dangers and Uncertainties, which then did threaten our Ruin; and the rather for this Consideration; that neither the Wisdom of some, who were engaged in those Affairs, which I must aver to have been very great, nor the success of their Contest, which ended in an absolute Victory, could prevail, so as to give this Kingdom any advantage; nay, not so much as any settlement, in Satisfaction and Requital of all the Blood it had lost, Mony it had spent, and Hazzard it had run. A clear Argument why we must totally exclude a Civil War from being any of the Remedies, when we come to that point. I must add further, That as we have as loyal subjects as are any where to be found, so we have as gracious and good a Prince: I never having yet heard that he did, or attempted to do, any the least Act of Arbitrary Power, in any publick Concern; nor did ever take, or endeavour to take from any particular person the benefit of

---

59. I.e., immediately before the Restoration of Charles II in 1660.
60. I.e., the English Civil Wars (1642–49).

the Law. And for his only Brother[61] (although accidentally he cannot be denied to be a great motive of the Peoples unquietness) all men must acknowledge him to be a most Glorious and Honourable Prince; one who has exposed his life several times[62] for the Safety and Glory of this Nation; one who pays justly and punctually his Debts, and manages his own Fortune discreetly; and yet keeps the best Court and Equipage of any Subject in Christendom;[63] is Courteous and Affable to all; and in fine, has nothing in his whole Conduct to be excepted against, much less dreaded; excepting, that he is believed to be of a Religion contrary to the Honour of God, and the Safety and interest of this People, which gives them just Apprehensions of their Future Condition: But of this matter, we shall have occasion to Speculate hereafter; in the mean time, since we have such a Prince, and such Subjects, we must needs want the ordinary cause of Distrust and Division, and therefore must seek higher to find out the Original of this turbulent posture we are in.

Doctor. Truly you had need seek higher or lower to satisfie us, for hitherto you have but enforced the Gentleman's Question, and made us more admire what the Solution will be.

---

61. I.e., James, Duke of York (1633–1701), later James II. James's reception into the Roman Catholic Church in 1672 was the primary reason why the likelihood of his succeeding Charles II gave rise to what Neville calls "the Peoples unquietness."

62. In the 1650s James had served with distinction in the French army under Turenne, where his conduct had drawn from no less a judge than Condé the praise that "if ever there was a Man in the World without Fear, it was the Duke of *York*" (Francis Brettonneau, *An Abridgment of the Life of James II* [1704], p. 7). After the Restoration, James served as Lord Admiral. He commanded in person at the Battle of Lowestoft, where a Dutch fleet was defeated and where Pepys reports that James had been in the thick of the action: "The Earl of Falmouth, Muskery, and Mr. Rd. Boyle killed on board the Dukes ship, the Royall Charles, with one shot. Their blood and brains flying in the Duke's face—and the head of Mr. Boyle striking down the Duke, as some say" (Pepys, *Diary*, vol. 6, p. 122). Marvell's response to these reports was both witty and unimpressed: "His shatter'd head the fearless Duke distains, / And gave the last first proof that he had Brains" ("Second Advice to a Painter," ll. 187–88).

63. A judgment confirmed by Gilbert Burnet, who said of James that he "was a frugal Prince, and brought his Court into method and magnificence" (Burnet, *History*, vol. 1, p. 170).

English Gentleman. Gentlemen, then I shall delay you no longer: The *Evil Counsellors*, the *Pensioner-Parliament*,[64] the *Thorowpac'd Judges*,[65] the *Flattering Divines*, the *Busie* and *Designing Papists*, the *French Counsels*,[66] are not the *Causes* of our *Misfortunes*, they are but the *Effects* (as our present

64. The contemptuous name given to the long Parliament of Charles II (1661–79), so called because of the many officeholders under the Crown who sat in it and who were, at least at the outset, docile to the wishes of the king, before eventually turning "short upon the Court": "For it is too notorious to be concealed, that near a third part of the House have beneficial Offices under his Majesty, in the Privy Councill, the Army, the Navy, the Law, the Household, the Revenue both in England and Ireland, or in attendance on his Majesties person. These are all of them indeed to be esteemed Gentlemen of Honor, but more or less according to the quality of their several imployments under his Majesty, and it is to be presumed that they brought along with them some Honour of their own into his service, at first to set up with" (Marvell, *Prose Works*, vol. 2, p. 299; cf. Robbins, *Commonwealthman*, p. 53, and Sidney, *Discourses*, pp. 571–72, for a similar analysis of how Charles II and his advisers had corrupted Parliament). Cf. Grey, *Debates*, vol. 3, pp. 53–58 and 370, and vol. 7, p. 23. The matter had flared up in 1679 in the Commons, particularly during the examination of Sir Stephen Fox concerning his accounts and payments made (Grey, *Debates*, vol. 7, pp. 316–36). For a defense of pensions bestowed on MPs, see Goddard, *Plato's Demon*, p. 63. The anonymous but surely Jacobite author of *Antimonarchical Authors* defended "*That Parliament which they Libelled, Publisht for Pensionary; only because it would not take pay of the People, where perhaps, they would have been truly paid*" (*Antimonarchical Authors*, sig. B2r). According to John Pocock it was concern about this use of Crown patronage by the Earl of Danby to corrupt Parliament by building up a strong government interest in the House of Commons that had provided the setting for "the neo-Harringtonian revival" (Pocock, *Harrington*, p. 130).

65. I.e., thoroughly trained; a term used literally of horses (*OED*, s.v. "thorough-paced," *adj. 1*) but here applied to judges with connotations of a culpable lack of independence. Cf. "The Crown [the legal Prerogative I mean] could do no wrong, but the Head that wore it hath done a World of mischief. The Judges did not obey the Crown [the Rightful Sovereignty] when they illegally destroyed Charters; nor were those vile Varlets that suborned Witnesses, truly Loyal; or those Mercenary Judges, Council and Jury, who (in contradiction to their own Consciences) seemed to believe those State-hired-Hackney-thorough-paced-perjured-Caitifs, who judicially murdered Men" (Laurence Braddon, *Innocency and Truth Vindicated* [1689], p. 65); cf. also Marvell, *Prose Works*, vol. 2, p. 150. Cf. Burke on the mutations of the Whigs from a party of revolution to a party of administration: "Almost all the high-bred republicans of my time have, after a short space, become the most decided, thorough-paced courtiers" (Burke, *Reflections*, p. 222).

66. On 22 May 1670 Charles had signed the secret Treaty of Dover with France, under the terms of which he received payments from Louis XIV in return for

Distractions are) of one *Primary Cause*; which is *the Breach and Ruin of our Government*; which having been decaying for near two hundred years,[67] is in our Age brought so near to Expiration, that it lyes agonizing, and can no longer perform the Functions of a *Political* Life, nor carry on the work of Ordering and Preserving Mankind: So that the Shifts that our *Courtiers* have within some years used, are but so many Tricks, or Conclusions which they are trying to hold Life and Soul together a while longer; and have played Handy-Dandy[68] with *Parliaments*, and especially with the *House of Commons*, (the only part which is now left entire of the old Constitution) by *Adjourning*, and *Proroguing*, and *Dissolving*[69] them (contrary to the true

---

military help against the Dutch and a public declaration of his conversion to Roman Catholicism. See Jones, *Secret History*, p. 55.

67. I.e., since the accession of Henry VII in 1485. For Harrington too, the reign of Henry VII marked the watershed between a preceding period when power had been broadly aligned with property, and a subsequent period when property had migrated toward fractions of society excluded from a say in government: "Henry the Seventh . . . was the richest in money of English princes. Nevertheless this accession of revenue did not at all preponderate on the king's part, nor change the balance. But while, making farms of a standard, he increased the yeomanry and, cutting off retainers, he abased the nobility, he began that breach in the balance of land, which proceeding, hath ruined the nobility and in them that government" (*The Prerogative of Popular Government*, in Pocock, *Harrington*, p. 408 and cf. also p. 436; cf. *The Art of Lawgiving* [1659], in ibid., pp. 606 and 659; and *The Prologue in Answer to Mr. Wren's Preface*, in ibid., p. 709). Neville had sketched this periodization of English political history in Parliament on 8 February 1659: "The Barons got a great share, and having a considerable part of the land, and not part in the Government, they began to stir and ruffle with the King; and in fine got authority, and gave laws both to King and Commons, until King Henry VII's time. He designed to weaken the hands of the nobility and their power" (Burton, *Diary*, vol. 3, p. 133).

68. I.e., to frustrate or subvert by frequent alteration (*OED*, s.v. "handy dandy," 2b). Cf. "Frequent Dissolutions of Parliament have always been esteemed prejudicial to the People; for when Kings play at Handy dandy with Parliaments, they design to play a Game without them" (*Observator*, 4 July 1702).

69. *Adjourn*: to postpone, defer, or suspend a sitting of Parliament; *prorogue*: to discontinue a sitting of Parliament without however dissolving it; *dissolve*: to terminate a Parliament. Charles II had recently employed all these stratagems. For instance, the "Exclusion Bill Parliament" had been summoned 24 July 1679, prorogued until 21 October 1680, and dissolved on 18 January 1681. See Grey, *Debates*, vol. 7, pp. 345–46 and 446. The author of *A Copy of a Letter* had identified frequent recourse to dissolutions as a deplorable feature of the Stuart monarchy that had damaged public trust (p. 10).

meaning of the *Law*) as well in the Reign of our *late King*,[70] as during his *Majesties* that *now is*. Whereas indeed our *Counsellors* (perceiving the decay of the *Foundation*, as they must, if they can see but one Inch into the *Politicks*) ought to have Addrest themselves to the *King* to call a *Parliament*, the true Physician, and to lay open the Distemper there, and so have endeavour'd a Cure, before it had been too late, as I fear it now is: I mean the piecing and patching up the Old Government. It is true, as the Divine *Machiavil* says, That Diseases in Government are like a *Marasmus*[71] in the Body Natural, which is very hard to be discovered whilst it is Curable; and after it comes to be easie to discern, difficult if not impossible to be Remedy'd; yet it is to be supposed that the *Counsellors* are, or ought to be skilful Physicians, and to foresee the Seeds of State-Distempers, time enough to prevent the Death of the Patient; else they ought in Conscience to excuse themselves from that sublime Employment, and betake themselves to Callings more suitable to their Capacities. So that although for this Reason the *Ministers of State* here are inexcusable, and deserve all the Fury which must one time or other be let loose against them, (except they shall suddenly fly from the wrath to come, by finding out in time, and advising the true means of setting

70. I.e., Charles I (1600–1649).

71. A marasmus is a wasting sickness. Neville probably has in mind the following passage from chapter 3 of *The Prince*: "And it falls out in this case, as the Physitians say of an Hectick Feaver ['dell'etico']; that at first it is easily cur'd, and hard to be known, but in process of time, not being observ'd, or resisted in the beginning, it becomes easie to be known, but very difficult to be cur'd: So is it in matters of State, things which are discover'd at a distance (which is done only by prudent men) produce little mischief, but what is easily averted: But when thorow ignorance or inadevertency, they come to that height that every one discerns them, there is no room for any remedy, and the disease is incurable" (Machiavelli, *Works*, p. 201). Cf. chapter 13: "But the imprudence of Man begins many things, which savouring of present good, conceal the poyson that is latent, (as I said before of the Hectick Feaver) wherefore if he who is rais'd to any Soveraignty, foresees not a mischief till it falls upon his head, he is not to be reckoned a wise Prince, and truly that is a particular blessing of God, bestowed upon few people" (Machiavelli, *Works*, p. 218). There is a similar sentiment in the *Discourses*, 1.33 (albeit without the metaphor of disease): "which error, if suffered to run on, will be more dangerous to oppose than to comply with; for it is so much the harder to find out these inconveniences in the beginning" (Machiavelli, *Works*, p. 302). The phrase irritated Neville's critics: see Goddard, *Plato's Demon*, p. 54, and *Antimonarchical Authors*, p. 149.

themselves to rights) yet neither *Prince* nor *People* are in the mean time to be blamed for not being able to Conduct things better. No more than the Waggoner is to answer for his ill guiding, or the Oxen for their ill drawing the Waggon, when it is with Age and ill usage broken, and the Wheels unserviceable: Or the Pilot and Marriners, for not weathring out a Storm, when the Ship hath sprung a planck.[72] And as in the body of Man, sometimes the Head and all the Members are in good Order, nay, the Vital Parts are sound and entire; yet if there be a Considerable Putrifaction in the humors,[73] much more, if the Blood (which the Scripture calls the life) be Impure and Corrupted; the Patient ceases not to be in great Danger, and oftentimes dies without some skillful Physician: And in the mean time the Head and all the parts suffer, and are unquiet, full as much, as if they were all immediately affected. So it is in every respect with the Body Politick, or Commonwealth, when their Foundations are moulder'd: And although in both these Cases, the Patients cannot (though the Distemper be in their own Bodies) know what they ail, but are forced to send for some Artist to tell them; yet they cease not to be extreamly uneasie and impatient, and lay hold oftentimes upon unsuitable Remedies, and impute their Malady to wrong and ridiculous Causes. As some people do here, who think that *the growth of Popery*[74] is our only Evil, and that if we were secure against that,

72. I.e., the splitting or cracking of a ship's wooden hull (*OED*, s.v. "planck," 4a).

73. In the Hippocratic and Galenic medicine of antiquity, which retained authority in Europe until the nineteenth century, the health of the body depended upon the correct balance between the four humors of black bile, yellow bile, phlegm, and blood.

74. An "Address, for preventing the Growth of Popery" had been introduced into Parliament by Henry Powle (1630–92) on 3 March 1673 (Grey, *Debates*, vol. 2, pp. 78–79). On 12 March it passed the Commons with amendments as "An Act for Preventing Dangers that May Happen by Popish Recusants" (Grey, *Debates*, vol. 2, p. 100), eventually receiving the royal assent and reaching the statute book as the Test Act on 29 March. Powle, like Neville, belonged to the Berkshire gentry and in the Cavalier and Exclusion Parliaments would show himself to be a leading critic of royal policy (although, again like Neville, he did not support Exclusion). Powle would go on to preside as the Speaker of the Convention of 1689. The phrase "growth of Popery" also recurs in the title of a tract by Andrew Marvell published in 1677, *An Account of the Growth of Popery and Arbitrary Government*. As Nicholas von Maltzahn has suggested, Marvell was close to Neville in being relatively untroubled by Roman

our Peace and Settlement were obtain'd, and that our Disease needed no other Cure. But of this more when we come to the Cure.

Noble Venetian. Against this Discourse, certainly we have nothing to reply: but must grant, that when any Government is decay'd, it must be mended, or all will Ruine. But now we must Request you to declare to us, how the Government of *England* is decay'd, and how it comes to be so. For I am one of those Unskilful Persons, that cannot discern a State *Marasmus*, when the danger is so far off.

English Gentleman. Then no man living can: for your Government is this day the only School in the World, that breeds such Physicians,[75] and you

---

Catholicism as a religion (Anna Maria Crino even going so far as to claim, on the basis of a letter of 1672, that Neville was "simpatizzante per i Cattolici": Crino, *Fatti e figure*, p. 197; cf. p. 203). It was rather the absolutist mode of government with which Roman Catholicism was associated and which it had tended to produce, particularly in France, that alarmed him (Marvell, *Prose Works*, vol. 2, pp. 181–82 and n. 6). As Richard Hampden (1631–95) had said in the House of Commons on 4 November 1680, arguing for the Exclusion of the Duke of York, "not so much as a Papist, but because of the inseparable principles of that Religion, in which it is impossible the nation should be safe" (Grey, *Debates*, vol. 7, p. 421). On 27 November he made a similar point: "Popery will bring in Arbitrary Power, and Arbitrary Power Popery" (Grey, *Debates*, vol. 8, p. 100). In the House of Commons in 1679, Sir Henry Capel had pithily sketched the natural history of popery and absolutism: "From Popery came the notion of a standing Army and arbitrary power. . . . Lay Popery flat, and there's an end of arbitrary Government and Power. It is a meer chimaera, or notion, without Popery" (Grey, *Debates*, vol. 7, p. 149). Shaftesbury had made a similar point in the House of Lords on 25 March 1679: "*Popery* and *Slavery*, like two Sisters, go hand in hand, sometimes one goes first, sometimes the other in a doors, but the other is always following close at hand" (*State-Tracts*, vol. 2, p. 71). In the Commons debate on ways and means to resist popery and arbitrary power on 15 December 1680, Hampden had returned to the charge and asserted, "Popery, in a great measure, is set up for Arbitrary Power's sake; they are not so forward for Religion" (Grey, *Debates*, vol. 8, p. 158). Cf. Edward Vaughan's remarks in Parliament on 23 December 1680: "It has been long contended, whether Popery comes before Arbitrary Government, or Arbitrary Government before Popery; but now they are *pari gradu*" (Grey, *Debates*, vol. 8, p. 205).

75. Cf., e.g., Benjamin Priolo's praise of Venice: "*After that I Travelled to* Venice, *the joy and darling of Heaven, the Shop of Policy, the School of Wisdom; where I searched into the Mystery of your Government. . . . A Republick happy in its Orders, with which,*

are esteemed one of the ablest amongst them: And it would be manifest to all the World for Truth; although there were no argument for it, but the admirable Stability and Durableness of your Government, which hath lasted above twelve hundred years entire and perfect;[76] whilst all the rest of the Countreys in *Europe*, have not only changed Masters very frequently in a quarter of that time, but have varied and altered their Polities very often. Which manifests that you must needs have ever enjoy'd a Succession of wise Citizens, that have had skill and Ability to forwarn you betimes of those Rocks against which your excellently-built Vessel might in time split.

Noble Venetian. Sir, you over-value, not only me, but the Wisdom of my Fellow Citizens; for we have none of these high Speculations, nor hath

---

as with Ligatures, it stands unshaken without fear of fall; boasting of its duration for 1300 *years. . . . Laws you have few and good; as Medicines, which should neither be many nor divers"* (Priolo, *History of France*, sigs. A8ʳ⁻ᵛ). At the moment of publication of *Plato Redivivus* such metaphors were used in Parliament in debates on Exclusion: see, e.g., Grey, *Debates*, vol. 8, p. 134. But it was metaphor with lasting appeal: cf., e.g., Burke, on the medicinal metaphor as applied to politics: "The physician of the state, who, not satisfied with the cure of distempers, undertakes to regenerate constitutions, ought to shew uncommon powers" (Burke, *Reflections*, p. 343).

76. The republic of Venice took its rise from the invasion of Italy by Attila the Hun in 452, when the inhabitants of the large northern Italian province of Venetia took refuge from the barbarians on the islands and marshes of the northern Adriatic (Nani, *Affairs of Europe*, p. 1; Hay, *Policy*, pp. 1–4). The durability of the Venetian Republic was proverbial, being "equally durable and wonderful" (Nani, *Affairs of Europe*, p. 2), "a miracle of Nature, and a Prodigy of Art" (Gailhard, *Italy*, p. 120). Even Amelot de la Houssaie, despite his critical view of Venice, acknowledged as much: "*Venice* has this advantage, she has maintain'd her self longer than all the famous *Republicks* of the *Ancients* . . . a strong presumption of the excellence of the *Venetian Common-wealth*, whose present State and Condition is the only thing I design to represent in this Book." However, Amelot de la Houssaie insists that the Venetian constitution had changed dramatically over the course of its history (Amelot de la Houssaie, *Venice*, pp. 2–5; cf. Priolo, *History of France*, sigs. A8ʳ⁻ᵛ). In 1708 Swift would diagnose the imminent demise of the Venetian Republic, "which, founded upon the wisest Maxims, and digested by a great Length of Time, hath, in our Age, admitted so many Abuses, through the Degeneracy of the Nobles, that the Period of its Duration seems to approach" (Swift, *Prose Writings*, vol. 2, p. 14).

scarce any of our Body read *Aristotle, Plato,* or *Cicero,*[77] or any of those great Artists, Ancient or Modern, who teach that great Science of the Governing and Increasing great States and Cities; without studying which Science no man can be fit to discourse pertinently of these matters; much less to found or mend a Government, or so much as find the defects of it. We only study our own Government, and that too Chiefly to be fit for advantagious Employments, rather than to foresee our dangers. Which yet I must needs confess some amongst us are pretty good at, and will in a Harangue made upon passing a Law, venture to tell us what will be the Consequence of it two hundred years hence. But of these things I shall be very prodigal in my discourse, when you have Leisure and Patience to command me to say any thing of our Polity; in the mean time pray be pleased to go on with your Edifying Instruction.

English Gentleman. Before I can tell you how the Government of *England* came to be decayed, I must tell you what that Government was, and what it now is: And I should say something too of Government in General, but that I am afraid of talking of that Subject, before you who are so exact a Judge of it.

Noble Venetian. I thought you had been pleased to have done with this Discourse,[78] I assure you, Sir, if I had more skill in that matter than ever I can pretend to, it would but serve to make me the fitter Auditor of what you shall say on that Subject.

English Gentleman. Sir, in the Course of my Reasoning upon this Point, I shall have occasion to insist and expatiate upon many things, which both my

77. Aristotle (384–322 B.C.): ancient Greek philosopher. Plato (c. 427–348 B.C.): ancient Greek philosopher. Cicero (106–43 B.C.): Roman orator, statesman, and man of letters.

78. I.e., ceasing to indulge in compliments and courtesies, as the Doctor has recently encouraged them to do: "Pray let us leave off Compliments and Repartees, of which we had a great deal too much yesterday, and fall to our business" (above, p. 69).

self and others have Publish'd in former times.[79] For which I will only make this excuse, that the Repetition of such matters is the more pardonable, because they will be at least new to you, who are a stranger to our Affairs and Writings. And the rather because those discourses shall be apply'd to our present condition, and suited to our present occasions. But I will say no more, but obey you, and proceed. I will not take upon me to say, or so much as Conjecture, how and when Government began in the World, or what Government is most Ancient: History must needs be silent in that point, for that Government is more Ancient than History. And there was never any Writer, but was bred under some Government, which is necessarily supposed to be the Parent of all Arts and Sciences, and to have produced them. And therefore it would be as hard for a man to Write an account of the beginning of the Laws and Polity of any Countrey, except there were memory of it, (which cannot be before the first Historiographer) as it would be to any person without Records to tell the particular History of his own Birth.[80]

Doctor. Sir, I cannot comprehend you, may not Historians Write a History of Matters done before they were born? If it were so, no man could Write but of his own times.

English Gentleman. My meaning is, Where there are not Stories, or Records, extant; for as for Oral Tradition, it lasts but for one Age, and then degenerates into Fable: I call any thing in Writing, whereby the account of the Passages or Occurrences of former times is derived to our knowledge, a History, although it be not pend Methodically, so as to make the Author

79. Principally a reference to Harrington's *Oceana* (1656), to which Neville is supposed by Hobbes to have contributed (Aubrey, *Brief Lives*, vol. 1, p. 318).
80. Cf. Locke on the historiographical silence which surrounds the origin of government: "Government is every where antecedent to Records, and Letters seldome come in amongst a People, till a long continuation of Civil Society has, by other more necessary Arts provided for their Safety, Ease, and Plenty. . . . For 'tis with *Common-wealths* as with particular Persons, they are commonly *ignorant of their own Births* and *Infancies*" (Locke, *Two Treatises*, "Second Treatise," chapter 8, "Of the Beginning of Political Societies," §101, p. 318). Cf. Adam in conversation with Raphael: "For Man to tell how human Life began / Is hard: for who himself beginning knew?" (*Paradise Lost*, 8.250–51).

pass for a Wit: And had rather read the Authentick Records of any Country, that is a Collection of their Laws and Letters concerning Transactions of State, and the like, than the most Eloquent and Judicious Narrative that can be made.

Noble Venetian. Methinks, Sir, your discourse seems to imply, that we have no account extant of the beginning of Governments; pray what do you think of the Books of *Moses*, which seem to be pend on purpose to inform us how he, by Gods Command, led that People out of *Egypt* into another Land, and in the way made them a Government? Besides, does not *Plutarch* tell us,[81] how *Theseus* gathered together the dispersed Inhabitants of *Attica*, brought them into one City, and under one Government of his own making? The like did *Romulus* in *Italy*, and many others in divers Countries.

English Gentleman. I never said that we had not sufficient knowledge of the Original of particular Governments; but it is evident, that these great Legislators had seen, and lived under other Administrations, and had the help of Learned Law-givers and Philosophers, excepting the first who had the Aid of God himself. So that it remains undiscovered yet, how the first Regulation of man-kind began: And therefore I will take for granted that which all the Politicians conclude: Which is, That Necessity made the first Government.[82] For every man by the first Law of

81. "After the death of Aegeus, Theseus conceived a wonderful design, and settled all the residents of Attica in one city, thus making one people of one city out of those who up to that time had been scattered about and were not easily called together for the common interests of all, nay, they sometimes actually quarrelled and fought with each other. He visited them, then, and tried to win them over to his project township by township and clan by clan. The common folk and the poor quickly answered to his summons; to the powerful he promised government without a king and a democracy, in which he should only be commander in war and guardian of the laws, while in all else everyone should be on an equal footing" (Plutarch, "Theseus," 24).

82. Aristotle (*Politics*, 1.1, 1252a) identifies necessity (ἀνάγκη) as the impulse to the creation of political societies; cf. Lucretius, 5.1143–50. Among seventeenth-century theorists, see Hobbes, *Elements of Law*, part 1, "Human Nature," chapter 19, "Of the Necessity and Definition of a Body Politic"; *De Cive*, chapter 5, "Of the

Nature (which is common to us and brutes) had, like Beasts in a Pasture, right to every thing, and there being no Property, each Individual, if he were the stronger, might seize whatever any other had possessed himself of before, which made a State of perpetual War.[83] To Remedy which, and the fear that nothing should be long enjoyed by any particular person (neither was any mans Life in safety) every man consented to be debar'd of that Universal Right to all things, and confine himself to a quiet and secure enjoyment of such a part as should be allotted him: Thence came in Ownership, or Property; to maintain which it was necessary to consent to Laws, and a Government to put them in Execution. Which of the Governments now extant, or that have been formerly, was first, is not possible now to be known; but I think this must be taken for granted, that whatsoever the Frame or Constitution was first, it was made by the Perswasion and Meditation of some Wise and vertuous Person,[84] and

---

Causes and First Original of Civil Government"; and *Leviathan*, part 2, chapter 17, "Of the Causes, Generation, and Definition of a Commonwealth." Cf. Sidney, *Discourses*, chapter 2, section 5, p. 100. Locke's almost contemporary formulation on the question of the origin of government is particularly close in wording to Neville's: "God having made Man such a Creature, that, in his own Judgment, it was not good for him to be alone, put him under strong Obligations of Necessity, Convenience, and Inclination to drive him into Society, as well as fitted him with Understanding and Language to continue and enjoy it" (Locke, *Two Treatises*, "Second Treatise," chapter 7, "Of Political or Civil Society," §77, p. 318). Cf. also James Tyrrell, *Bibliotheca Politica* (1694), p. 63: "In all Nations, where there is any property either in Lands or Goods, there is a necessity of some Civil Government to maintain it."

83. Neville's language here recalls Hobbes's characterization of the state of nature: "During the time men live without a common Power to keep them all in awe, they are in that condition which is called Warre; and such a warre, as is of every man, against every man" (Hobbes, *Leviathan*, chapter 13, "Of the Naturall Condition of Mankind," p. 88). Locke would depart from Hobbes by asserting that the "*State of Nature* has a Law of Nature to govern it, which obliges every one: And Reason, which is that Law, teaches all Mankind, who will but consult it, that being all equal and independent, no one ought to harm another in his Life, Health, Liberty, or Possessions" (Locke, *Two Treatises*, "Second Treatise," chapter 2, "Of the State of Nature," §6, p. 271).

84. The political mythology of antiquity offers many examples of the preternaturally wise founders of states. Examples of such heroic figures include Lycurgus, the architect of the Spartan constitution; Solon, who reformed the constitution of Athens; and Numa, who prescribed laws and religious rituals to the early

consented to by the whole Number. And then, that it was instituted for the good and Preservation of the Governed, and not for the Exaltation and greatness of the Person or Persons appointed to Govern:[85] The

---

Romans. Harrington's attention, guided no doubt by Machiavelli's view that the reformation of a republic must be the work of a single man, had been caught by these examples: "We are not to think it hath been for nothing that the wisest nations have, in the formation of government, as much relied upon the invention of some one man as upon themselves; for whereas it cannot be too often inculcated that reason consisteth of two parts, the one invention, the other judgment, a people or an assembly are not more eminent in the matter of judgment than void of invention" (*The Art of Lawgiving* [1659], in Pocock, *Harrington*, pp. 658–59; see also "Epistle to the Reader" in *The Prerogative of Popular Government*: "Invention is a solitary thing. . . . A sole legislator is of absolute necessity," ibid., p. 391; cf. p. 598 and p. 777: "Invention is most perfect in one man" and "the wisest assemblies, in the formation or reformation of government, have pitched upon a sole legislator"; cf. Machiavelli, *Discourses*, book 1, chapter 9, and Sidney, introduction to *Discourses*, pp. 5–6). In *Oceana* the Lord Archon is praised as "from Moses and Lycurgus, the first legislator that hitherto is found in story to have introduced or erected an entire commonwealth at once" (Pocock, *Harrington*, p. 210). There are hints that, in the great crisis of 1659, Harrington may even have wanted to cast himself in this role (Pocock, *Harrington*, p. 114; and note how Harrington associates himself with Solon and Lycurgus in *Politicaster*, ibid., p. 719; cf. also Harrington's comments on the *punctum saliens* in *A System of Politics*, ibid., pp. 839–40). For discussion of precisely why civic humanism had thrown these heroic legislators into prominence, and of the role they had assumed in that political framework, see Pocock, *Harrington*, p. 23. Locke insisted, however, that the origin of government in the inspired provisions of an individual holds no implications for the form that a mature government should take: "And therefore, though perhaps at first, . . . some one good and excellent Man, having got a Preheminency amongst the rest, had this Deference paid to his Goodness and Vertue, as to a kind of Natural Authority, . . . yet when time, giving Authority, and (as some Men would perswade us) Sacredness to Customs, which the negligent, and unforeseeing Innocence of the first Ages began, had brought in Successors of another Stamp, the People finding their Properties not secure under the Government, as then it was, (whereas Government has no other end but the preservation of Property) could never be safe nor at rest, *nor think themselves in Civil Society*, till the Legislature was placed in collective Bodies of Men, call them Senate, Parliament, or what you please" (Locke, *Two Treatises*, "Second Treatise," chapter 7, "Of Political or Civil Society," §94, pp. 329–30).

85. Hobbes supposed that the "finall Cause, End, or Designe of men . . . in the introduction of that restraint upon themselves [i.e., government] . . . is the foresight of their own preservation, and of a more contented life thereby; that is to say, of getting themselves out from that miserable condition of Warre" (Hobbes,

Reason why I beg this Concession is, That it seems very improbable, not to say impossible, that a vast number of people should ever be brought to consent to put themselves under the Power of others, but for the ends abovesaid, and so lose their Liberty without advantaging themselves in any thing. And it is full as impossible that any person (or persons so inconsiderable in number as Magistrates and Rulers are) should by force get an Empire to themselves. Though I am not ignorant that a whole people have in imminent Dangers, either from the Invasion of a powerful Enemy, or from Civil Distractions, put themselves wholly into the hands of one Illustrious Person[86] for a time, and that with good Success, under the best Forms of Government: But this is nothing to the Original of States.

Noble Venetian. Sir, I wonder how you come to pass over the Consideration of Paternal Government,[87] which is held to have been the beginning of Monarchies?

Leviathan, chapter 17, p. 117). Locke specifies the end of government as "the mutual *Preservation* of their Lives, Liberties and Estates, which I call by the general Name, *Property*" and "the publick good and preservation of Property" (Locke, *Two Treatises*, "Second Treatise," chapter 9, "Of the Ends of Political Society and Government," §123, p. 350; and chapter 19, "Of the Dissolution of Government," §239, p. 424). Notwithstanding the word and concept of "preservation" found in both Hobbes and Locke, Neville's formulation seems more Lockean than Hobbesian in its explicit subordination of the interests of the magistrate to those of the subject.

86. Most immediately and obviously a reference to the Roman dictator, a magistrate who in grave emergencies and on the nomination of the consuls might be entrusted with supreme military and judicial power for a period of six months. The office was abolished after the assassination of Julius Caesar. The Roman dictatorship was occasionally recalled in contemporary political writing, e.g., Aglionby, *United Provinces*, p. 110; and also in debates in the House of Commons, e.g., Grey, *Debates*, vol. 9, p. 274.

87. The derivation of political authority from the authority enjoyed by a father in a family was at this time associated most closely with Sir Robert Filmer (1588–1653), whose fullest statement of the doctrine, *Patriarcha*, had been composed probably during the English Civil War and first published in 1680. In that work, Filmer contended that because it is impossible to imagine "how the children of Adam, or of any man else, can be free from subjection to their parents," it follows that "this subjection of children is the only fountain of all regal authority, by the ordination of God himself" (Filmer, *Patriarcha*, p. 7). Locke's *First Treatise of Gov-*

English Gentleman. Really I did not think it worth the taking notice of, for though it be not easie to prove a Negative, yet I believe if we could trace all Foundations of Polities that now are, or ever came to our knowledge since the World began; we shall find none of them to have descended from Paternal Power; we know nothing of *Adam's* leaving the Empire to *Cain*, or *Seth*: It was impossible for *Noah* to retain any Jurisdiction over his own three Sons; who were dispersed into three parts of the World, if our Antiquaries Calculate right;[88] and as for *Abraham*, whilst he lived, as also his Son *Isaac*, they were but ordinary Fathers of Families, and no question governed their own Houshold as all others do; but when *Jacob* upon his Death-bed[89] did relate to his Children, the Promise Almighty God had made his Grandfather, to make him a great Nation, and give his Posterity a fruitful Territory, he speaks not one word of the Empire of *Reuben* his first-born, but supposes them all equal: And so they were taken to be by *Moses*, when he divided the Land to them by Lot;[90] and by Gods command made them a *Commonwealth*. So that I believe this fancy to have been first started, not by the solid Judgement of

---

ernment is an extended critique of Filmer's doctrine, and Algernon Sidney's *Discourses concerning Government* was also provoked by a reading of Filmer (Sidney, *Discourses*, p. 5). For Neville's attitude toward patriarchalism, see Mahlberg, pp. 83–138; for his early mockery of it, see especially p. 84.

88. "And the sons of Noah, that went forth of the ark, were Shem, and Ham, and Japheth: and Ham is the father of Canaan. These are the three sons of Noah: and of them was the whole earth overspread" (Genesis 9:18–19); for the detail of how the sons of Noah populated the earth, see Genesis 10:1–32. Seventeenth-century antiquarians had expended much ingenuity in tracing the peoples of Europe back to the individual sons of Noah from whom they sprang. Geoffrey Keating (1570?–1644?) traced the Irish back to Japheth in his posthumously published *History of Ireland* (1723). Olaus Rudbeck the Elder (1630–1702) in his *Atlantica* (4 vols., Uppsala, 1679–1702) argued that Sweden was the Atlantis of ancient mythology and that it had been peopled by the descendants of Askenaz, the son of Gomer, the son of Japheth. Abulghazi Bahadur Khan (1603–63) in his *Genealogical History of the Tatars* (English translation, 2 vols., 1730) similarly traced the origin of his people back to the Noachic diaspora. Filmer had also cited the Noachic diaspora in tracing the Biblical roots of his patriarchal political theory (Filmer, *Patriarcha*, pp. 7–9).

89. Genesis 49:1–33.

90. Numbers 26:55, 33:54, and 34:13; Joshua 13:6; Ezekiel 47:22 and 48:29.

any man, but to flatter some Prince, and to assert, for want of better Arguments, the *jus Divinum* of Monarchy.[91]

Noble Venetian. I have been impertinent in interrupting you, but yet now I cannot repent of it, since your Answer hath given me so much satisfaction; but if it be so as you say, that Government was at first Instituted for the Interest and Preservation of Mankind, how comes it to pass, That there are and have been so many absolute Monarchies in the World, in which it seems that nothing is provided for, but the Greatness and Power of the Prince.

English Gentleman. I have presumed to give you already my Reason, why I take for granted, that such a Power could never be given by the Consent of any People, for a perpetuity; for though the People of *Israel* did against the will of *Samuel*, and indeed of God himself demand, and afterwards chuse themselves a King;[92] yet he was never such a King as we speak of; for that all the Orders of their Commonwealth the Sanhedrim, the Congregation of the People, the Princes of the Tribes, *&c.* did still remain in being, as hath been excellently proved by a learned Gentleman of our Nation,[93] to whom I refer you; it may then be enquired into, how these Monarchies at first did arise. History being in this point silent, as to the

91. On the doctrine of the "ius divinum," or divine right of kings, see J. N. Figgis, *The Divine Right of Kings*, 2nd ed. (Cambridge: Cambridge University Press, 1914). It began as "a doctrine of the right of secular governments to be free from clerical interference," but it became a foundation of monarchical absolutism (Figgis, *Divine Right*, p. 160). In an English context it was a doctrine closely associated with Stuart kingship. James I's *The Trew Law of Free Monarchies*, published in 1598 when he was still merely James VI of Scotland, gives a full statement of the doctrine.

92. 1 Samuel 8:1–22. This Biblical passage is also cited by Harrington in *The Prerogative of Popular Government* (1658) (Pocock, *Harrington*, pp. 462–63).

93. John Selden (1584–1654), whose account of the commonwealth of Israel, *De Synedriis et Praefecturis Juridicis Veterum Ebraeorum* (1650), had also been drawn upon by Harrington in composing *Oceana* (1656) and *The Prerogative of Popular Government* (1658). Note, however, Harrington's slight dissembling of this reliance on Selden in *The Prerogative of Popular Government*: "Nor am I wedded unto Grotius or Selden, whom sometimes I follow and sometimes I leave, making use of their learning but of my own reason" (Pocock, *Harrington*, p. 520).

Ancient Principalities, we will Conjecture, that some of them might very well proceed from the Corruption of better Governments, which must necessarily cause a Depravation in manners (as nothing is more certain than that Politick defects breed Moral ones, as our Nation is a pregnant Example) this Debauchery of manners might blind the understandings of a great many, destroy the Fortunes of others, and make them indigent, infuse into very many a neglect and carelesness of the publick good (which in all setled States is very much regarded) so that it might easily come into the Ambition of some bold aspiring Person to affect Empire, and as easily into his Power, by fair pretences with some, and promises of advantages with others, to procure Followers, and gain a numerous Party, either to Usurp Tyranny over his own Countrey, or to lead men forth to Conquer and Subdue another. Thus it is supposed that *Nimrod* got his Kingdom;[94] who in Scripture is called a Great Hunter before God, which

94. "And Cush begat Nimrod: he began to be a mighty one in the earth. He was a mighty hunter before the Lord: wherefore it is said, Even as Nimrod the mighty hunter before the Lord. And the beginning of his kingdom was Babel, and Erech, and Accad, and Calneh, in the land of Shinar" (Genesis 10:8–10). For Bodin, Nimrod was indeed the first sovereign, but he had acquired his power by rapine: "The first Monarchie was established in *Assiria,* vnder the power of *Nemrod,* whom the holie scripture calleth the great hunter; which is a common phrase of speach amongst the *Hebrewes,* by which word they signifie a theefe, or robber. . . . For before the time of *Nemrod* no man is found to haue had power and rule one ouer an other, all men liuing in like libertie; he being the first that tooke vpon him the soueraigntie, and that caused free borne men to serue: whose name seemeth to haue beene giuen him according vnto his qualitie, for asmuch as *Nemrod* signifieth a terrible lord. Soone after the world was seene full of slaues" (Bodin, *Common-Weale,* book 2, chapter 2, p. 200). Ralegh agreed that Nimrod was the "first of all that raigned as Soueraigne Lord after the Floud," but defended his rule as "by iust authoritie" (Ralegh, *History of the World,* pp. 185–86). During the later seventeenth century Nimrod was appealed to by defenders of monarchy (e.g., Michael Hawke, *The Right of Dominion* [1655], pp. 35, 46–47, 52, and 70; Sir Robert Poyntz, *A Vindication of Monarchy* [1661], p. 113; John Nalson, *The Common Interest of King and People* [1677], pp. 7 and 77; John Wilson, *A Discourse of Monarchy* [1684], p. 29; Nathaniel Johnston, *The Excellency of Monarchical Government* [1686], p. 110), but also cited by monarchy's detractors (e.g., John Cook, *Monarchy, No Creature of God's Making* [1651], pp. 6 and 15; Streater, *Glympse,* sig. A3v; John Spittlehouse, *An Answer to One Part of the Lord Protector's Speech* [1654], p. 14; William Sprigg, *A Modest Plea for an Equal Common-wealth against Monarchy* [1659], p. 8; John Streater, *Government Described* [1659], sig. A1v). Filmer followed Bodin in seeing

Expositers interpret, A great Tyrant. The Modern Despotical Powers have been acquired by one of these two ways, either by pretending by the first Founder thereof, that he had a Divine Mission and so gaining not only Followers, but even easie Access in some places without Force to Empire, and afterwards dilateing their Power by great Conquests. Thus *Mahomet*[95] and *Cingis Can*[96] began, and established the *Sarazen* and *Tartarian* Kingdoms; or by a long Series of Wisdom in a Prince, or chief Magistrate of a mixt Monarchy, and his Council, who by reason of the Sleepiness and Inadvertency of the People, have been able to extinguish the great Nobility, or render them Inconsiderable; and so by degrees taking away from the People their Protectors, render them Slaves. So the Monarchies of *France*, and some other Countries, have grown to what they are at this day; there being left but a Shadow of the three States in any of these Monarchies, and so no bounds remaining to the Regal Power; but since Property remains still to the Subjects, these Governments may be said to be changed, but not founded or established; for

---

Nimrod as "the author and first founder of monarchy," even though he grasped political (as opposed to patriarchal) power "by tyranny or usurpation" (Filmer, *Patriarcha*, p. 8; cf. James Tyrrell, *Patriarcha Non Monarcha* [1681], p. 5). In his *Politicaster* (1659) Harrington challenged the interpretation of this Biblical text as indicating that monarchy is the most ancient form of government (Pocock, *Harrington*, p. 712), and Milton would in 1667 memorably characterize Nimrod as the archetype of usurped and therefore unjustified monarchy (*Paradise Lost*, 12.24–37). Nimrod might occasionally be referred to in Parliament: see, e.g., Burton, *Diary*, vol. 3, p. 266. The association of Nimrod with tyranny would persist into the next century, when it might be retorted on Whigs by Tories when glancing at William III via the Norman kings who shared his name; cf. Alexander Pope, "Windsor-Forest," ll. 61–62. Rycaut had referred to the grand signior and the emperor as "those two great *Nimrods* of the East and West" (Rycaut, *History*, p. 24; cf. also Rycaut's comparisons of Mahomet IV to Nimrod, sigs. M4ᵛ and Nn4ᵛ). For an illuminating discussion of why, at midcentury, men's minds might have been preoccupied with the example of Nimrod and what it represented, see Pocock, *Harrington*, pp. 23–24.

95. Mahomet (c. 570–632), prophet and founder of Islam. In 629 Mahomet conquered Mecca, and after his death Islamic forces established their authority over the Middle East, North Africa, and parts of Southern Europe.

96. Genghis Khan (c. 1162–1227), founder of the Mongol Empire (who, however, did not claim any divine mission and who practiced a measure of religious toleration).

there is no Maxim more Infallible and Holding in any Science, than this
is in the Politicks, *That Empire is founded in Property.*[97] Force or Fraud
may alter a Government; but it is Property that must Found and Eternise
it: Upon this undeniable *Aphorisme* we are to build most of our subsequent Reasoning, in the mean time we may suppose, that hereafter the
great power of the *King* of *France* may diminish much, when his enraged
and oppressed Subjects come to be commanded by a Prince of less Courage, Wisdom, and Military Vertue, when it will be very hard for any such
King to Govern Tyrannically a Country which is not entirely his own.[98]

Doctor. Pray, Sir, give me leave to ask you by the way, what is the Reason
that here in our Country, where the Peerage is lessened sufficiently, the

97. The grounding of political authority in the possession of real property
was a principle that had been deployed by Henry Ireton against the Levellers in
the Putney Debates of 1647 (Pocock, *Harrington*, pp. 26–27). It had been adopted
by Harrington in *Oceana* (1656) as the cornerstone of his political philosophy
(Pocock, *Harrington*, pp. 163–65). As a principle it was vigorously opposed by
those who believed that, on the contrary, government was the origin of property
(see, e.g., George Dawson, *Origo Legum* [1694], p. 70). See also above, p. 43 and
n. 9.

98. The present king of France was Louis XIV (1638–1715). His vicious and in-
dolent successor, Louis XV (1710–74) enjoyed a long and quiet reign. The political
whirlwind predicted by Neville was in fact reaped by his successor, Louis XVI
(1754–93), of whom Gibbon wrote on 15 December 1789: "The abuses of the court
and government called aloud for reformation and it has happened as it will always
happen, that an innocent well-disposed prince pays the forfeit of the sins of his
predecessors" (Gibbon, *Letters*, vol. 3, p. 183). Cf. Algernon Sidney's disenchanted
assessment of contemporary French greatness: "The beauty of it [i.e., the France of
Louis XIV] is false and painted. There is a rich and haughty king who is blessed
with such neighbours as are not likely to disturb him, and has nothing to fear from
his miserable subjects; but the whole body of that state is full of boils, and wounds,
and putrid sores: there is no real strength in it" (Sidney, *Discourses*, p. 216). The
phrase "King of France" perhaps carries a latent anti-Stuart implication, in that it
seems to discount the still-current English claim to the French crown. On 2 November 1675 Sir Winston Churchill had been rebuked in the House of Commons
for carelessly referring to the "King of France," rather than to the "French King"
(Grey, *Debates*, vol. 3, p. 376; see also p. 458; cf. vol. 4, pp. 107–9 and 369–70). In
1689 France was deliberately included in the royal style of William and Mary
(Grey, *Debates*, vol. 9, pp. 76–77 and 83).

King has not gotten as great an Addition of Power as accrews to the Crown in *France?*

English Gentleman. You will understand that, Doctor, before I have finisht this discourse; but to stay your Stomach till then, you may please to know that in *France* the greatness of the Nobility which has been lately taken from them, did not consist in vast Riches and Revenues, but in great Priviledges, and Jurisdictions, which obliged the People to obey them; whereas our great Peers in former times had not only the same great Dependences, but very Considerable Revenues besides, in Demesnes, and otherwise: This Vassallage over the People, which the Peers of *France* had, being abolisht, the Power over those Tenants, which before was in their Lords, fell naturally and of course into the Crown, although the Lands and possessions divested of those Dependences did and do still remain to the Owners; whereas here in *England,* though the Services are for the most part worn out, and insignificant; yet for want of Providence and Policy in former Kings, who could not foresee the danger a-far off, Entails[99] have been suffered to be cut off; and so two parts in ten of all those vast Estates, as well Mannours as Demesnes, by the Luxury and Folly of the Owners, have been within these two hundred years

99. The settlement of the succession of a landed estate, so that it cannot be bequeathed at pleasure by any one possessor (*OED,* s.v. "entail," *n.* 2, 1). In fact, and notwithstanding Neville's gloomy analysis, entails continued to protect many large English estates until the passage of the Settled Land Act (1882); see John Habakkuk, *Marriage, Debt, and the Estates System: English Landownership, 1650–1950* (Oxford: Clarendon Press, 1994). It is worth remarking that Harrington in *Oceana* proposed that estates should be divided among the sons, rather than preserved entire by means of an entail for the eldest (Pocock, *Harrington,* p. 237). The author of *A Copy of a Letter* had also seen political importance in the erosion of entails: "This was the first time [the dissolution of the monasteries] they [i.e., the Commons] began to bear up with the Lords, who since have been abased and impoverished by manie accidents, as by finding a means to cut off Intailes, whereby it came to be in the power of those who were in present possession, to sell their posteritie and revenues, and so to ruine the Lords who succeeded them, (which estates too) being most what spent in Court vices and luxurie, lost the interest of the Peers in their Countries, and made them contemptible to the whole Nation, and slaves to the Citizens, who by their prodigalities grew into great wealth, and possest their lands" (p. 9).

purchased by the lesser Gentry and the Commons; which has been so far
from advantaging the Crown, that it has made the Country scarce gov-
ernable by Monarchy: But if you please, I will go on with my discourse
about Government, and come to this again hereafter?

Noble Venetian. I beseech you, Sir, do.

English Gentleman. I cannot find by the small reading I have, that there
were any other Governments in the World Anciently than these three,
Monarchy, Aristocracy, and *Democracy.*[100] For the first, I have no light out

---

100. This three-way division of states into different kinds by reference to the
location and distribution of sovereignty within them is a legacy of the political
thought of antiquity: see Aristotle, *Politics*, 3.5.1, and Polybius, 6.2.3. In the civic
humanist tradition, the republic was typically presented as a mixture of the one,
the few, and the many (Pocock, *Harrington*, pp. 16–17; Scott, *Commonwealth
Principles*, pp. 133–35). This three-way division had been restated by Machiavelli in
the opening pages of the *Discourses*: "It is convenient to premise (what has been
asserted by several Authors) that there are but three sorts of Governments *Monarchy, Aristocracy,* and *Democracy,* to either of which who-ever intends to erect a
Government, may apply as he pleases" (Machiavelli, *Discourses*, 1.2, in Machiavelli, *Works*, p. 270). But note also the opening words of chapter 1 of *The Prince*:
"There never was, nor is at this day any Government in the World, by which one
Man has rule and dominion over another, but it is either a Commonwealth, or a
Monarchy" (Machiavelli, *Works*, p. 199). In an early modern English context, Sir
Thomas Smith had begun his treatise on English government, *De Republica An-
glorum*, with this point (Smith, *Republica*, p. 49); cf. *The King's Answer to the Nineteen Propositions* (1642), in Kenyon, *Stuart Constitution*, p. 21; and Philip Hunton, *A
Treatise of Monarchy* (1643), in Wootton, *Divine Right*, p. 191. More recently, James
Harrington also restated it in the opening pages of *Oceana* (1656) and in *The Prerogative of Popular Government* (1658) (Pocock, *Harrington*, pp. 162 and 441), but
perhaps most vividly in *A Discourse* (1659): "In all the circle of government, there
are but three spirits: the spirit of a prince, the spirit of the oligarchy, and the spirit
of a free people" (Pocock, *Harrington*, p. 736; cf. *Valerius and Publicola*, ibid.,
p. 785). This tripartite political typology had been frequently mentioned in Parliament during the constitutional debates of 1659, in which Neville participated: e.g.,
Burton, *Diary*, vol. 3, p. 555. It is also invoked in *The Armies Dutie* (1659), p. 25 (see
below, appendix C, pp. 364–69). The United Provinces had been produced by
William Aglionby as a modern-day example of the same virtuous union of the three
basic types of government that Polybius had previously identified as the foundation
of Rome's greatness (Aglionby, *United Provinces*, pp. 187–88). Algernon Sidney asserted that "there never was a good government in the world, that did not consist

of Antiquity to convince me, that there were in old times any other *Monarchies*, but such as were absolutely *Despotical*; all Kingdoms then, as well in *Greece* (as *Macedon*, *Epirus*, and the like; and where it is said, the Princes exercised their Power moderately) as in *Asia*, being altogether unlimited by any Laws, or any Assemblies of Nobility or People. Yet I must confess, *Aristotle*, when he reckons up the Corruptions of these three Governments,[101] calls Tyranny the Corruption of Monarchy; which if he means a Change of Government, (as it is in the Corruptions of the other two) then it must follow, that the Philosopher knew of some other Monarchy at the first, which afterwards degenerated into Tyranny, that is, into Arbitrary Power; for so the Word Tyranny is most commonly taken, though in modern Languages it signifies the ill Exercise of Power; for certainly Arbitrary Government cannot be called Tyranny, where the whole Property is in the Prince (as we reasonably suppose it to have been in those Monarchies) no more than it is Tyranny for you to govern your own House and Estate as you please: But it is possible *Aristotle* might not in this speak so according to Terms of Art, but might mean, that the ill Government of a Kingdom or Family is Tyranny. However we have one Example, that puzzles Politicians, and that is *Egypt*, where *Pharaoh* is called King;[102] and yet we see, that till *Joseph's* time he had not the whole Property; for the Wisdom of that Patriarch taught his Master a way to make a new use of that Famine, by telling him, that if they would buy their Lives, and sell their Estates (as they did afterwards, and preserve themselves by the Kings Bread) they shall serve *Pharaoh*; which shews that *Joseph* knew well, that *Empire was founded in Property*:[103] But most of

---

of the three simple species of monarchy, aristocracy and democracy" (Sidney, *Discourses*, p. 166). For further commentary, see Scott, *Commonwealth Principles*, pp. 19–40, especially pp. 22–24.

101. Aristotle, *Politics*, 3.5.

102. Genesis 40:1.

103. Genesis 47:13–26. Harrington had used this same Biblical example in *The Art of Lawgiving* (1659) (Pocock, *Harrington*, p. 604). Neville, if he was indeed one of the authors of *The Armie's Dutie* (1659), had also already cited this passage of Biblical history: "so *Joseph* that new moulded the *Egyptian* Monarchy, devised a way for the King to get all the possessions into his hands, that so the people might serve *Pharaoh*, which was a necessary consequence" (*Armie's Dutie*, p. 17).

the Modern Writers in Polity, are of Opinion, that *Egypt* was not a Monarchy till then, though the Prince might have the Title of King, as the *Heraclides*[104] had in *Sparta*, and *Romulus* and the other Kings had in *Rome*; both which *States* were Instituted *Common-Wealths*. They give good Conjectures for this their Opinion, too many to be here mentioned; only one is, That Originally (as they go about to prove) all Arts and Sciences had their Rise in *Egypt*, which they think very improbable to have been under a Monarchy. But this Position, That all Kings in former times were absolute, is not so Essential to the intent I have in this Discourse, which is to prove, That in all States, of what kind soever, this Aphorisme takes place: *Imperium fundatur in Dominio.*[105] So that if there were mixed Monarchies, then the King had not all the Property; but those who shared with him in the Administration of the Soveraignty, had their part, whether it were the Senate, the People, or both; or if he had no Companions in the Soveraign Power, he had no Sharers likewise in the Dominion or Possession of the Land. For that is all we mean by Property, in all this Discourse; for as for Personal Estate, the Subjects may enjoy it in the largest Proportion, without being able to invade the Empire: The Prince may when he pleases take away their Goods, by his Tenants and Vassals (without an Army) which are his Ordinary Force, and answers to our *Posse Comitatus.*[106] But the Subjects with their Money cannot invade his Crown.[107] So that all the Description we need make of

104. The Heraclides are the children or descendants of Hercules, who in Greek mythology overran Greece and established various monarchies.

105. "Power is founded in property" (see above, p. 43, n. 9)—apparently a Latin phrase composed by Neville himself. It became mildly notorious: cf. Thomas Goddard, *Plato's Demon* (1684), p. 112; and George Dawson, *Origo Legum* (1694), p. 70. Neville had himself used the phrase in Parliament on 8 February 1659 (Burton, *Diary*, vol. 3, p. 133). Captain Baynes in the same debate had also adopted the principle and its associated Harringtonian language (ibid., pp. 146–48).

106. The population of able-bodied men above the age of fifteen in a county whom the sheriff may summon to repress a riot, pursue felons, etc.; a body of men so raised and commanded by the sheriff (*OED*, s.v. "posse comitatus").

107. It would not be long, however, before Tory satirists and propagandists such as Swift were wringing their hands over precisely the eventuality that Neville had airily dismissed as an impossibility: "Let any Man observe the Equipages in this Town; he shall find the greater Number of those who make a Figure, to be a

this Kind or Form of Government, is, That the whole possession of the Country, and the whole power lies in the Hands and Breast of one man; he can make Laws, break and repeal them when he pleases, or dispense with them in the mean time when he thinks fit; interpose in all Judicatories, in behalf of his *Favourites*, take away any particular mans personal Estate, and his Life too, without the formality of a Criminal Process, or Trial; send a Dagger, or a Halter to his chief Ministers, and command them to make themselves away; and in fine, do all that his Will or his Interest suggests to him.[108]

Doctor. You have dwelt long here upon an Argumentation, That the Ancients had no Monarchies, but what were Arbitrary.

English Gentleman. Pray give me leave to save your Objections to that point, and to assure you first, That I will not take upon me to be so positive in that; for that I cannot pretend to have read all the Historians and Antiquaries that ever writ; nor have I so perfect a memory as to remember, or make use of, in a Verbal and Transient[109] Reasoning, all that I have ever read; And then to assure you again, that I build nothing upon that Assertion, and so your Objection will be needless, and only take up time.

Doctor. You mistake me, I had no intent to use any Argument or Example against your Opinion in that; but am very willing to believe that it

---

Species of Men quite different from any that were ever known before the Revolution [of 1688]; consisting either of Generals and Colonels, or of such whose whole Fortunes lie in Funds and Stocks: So that *Power*, which, according to the old Maxim, was used to follow *Land*, is now gone over to *Money*" (*The Examiner*, 13, 2 November 1710; in Swift, *Prose Writings*, vol. 3, p. 5).

108. Cf. Harrington's *Oceana*: "If one man be sole landlord of a territory, or overbalance the people, for example, three parts in four, he is grand signor, for so the Turk is called from his property; and his empire is absolute monarchy" (Pocock, *Harrington*, p. 163). It was an idea adopted by Defoe, who in book 5 of *Jure Divino* would fantasize about the power possessed by a sole freeholder: "The Nation's all *his House*, his People lie, / Within the *Limits of his Family*; / They're *his Domesticks*, in his Service bred, / His Slaves by Birth, and *he by Birth's their Head*" (Defoe, *Jure Divino* [1706], book 5, pp. 9-10).

109. I.e., brief (*OED*, s.v. "transient," 1a).

may be so. What I was going to say was this, that you have insisted much upon the point of Monarchy, and made a strange description of it, whereas many of the Ancients, and almost all the Modern Writers, magnifie it to be the best of Governments.[110]

English Gentleman. I have said nothing to the contrary. I have told you *de facto* what it is, which I believe none will deny. The Philosophers[111] said it was the best Government; but with this restriction, *ubi Philosophi regnant*,[112] and they had an Example of it, in some few *Roman* Emperours;[113] but in the most turbulent times of the Commonwealth, and Factions between the Nobility and the People, *Rome* was much more full of Vertuous and Heroick Citizens,[114] than ever it was under *Aurelius* or *Antoninus*:[115] For the Moderns that are of that Judgement, they are most of

---

110. Aristotle believed monarchy to be, in theory, the best form of government, although he recognized that it was liable to corruption (*Politics*, 3). Among modern theorists, Bodin had extolled monarchy in his *Six livres de la république* (1576). James I had opened his *Trew Law of Free Monarchies* (1598) with the strong claim that monarchy was "the forme of gouernment, as resembling the Diuinitie, [which] approcheth nearest to perfection, as all the learned and wise men from the beginning haue agreed vpon; Vnitie being the perfection of all things" (James VI and I, *Political Writings*, p. 63). Although in *Leviathan* (1651) Hobbes is clear that sovereign power can be wielded either by an individual or by an assembly of men, the tendency of his political thought is toward a defense of monarchy, albeit a defense resting on unconventional grounds (Hobbes, *Leviathan*, p. 121; 2.18).

111. I.e., principally Plato. Hobbes had made the same point in chapter 31 of *Leviathan*: "I am at the point of believing this my labour, as uselesse, as the Common-wealth of *Plato*; For he also is of opinion that it is impossible for the disorders of State, and change of Governments by Civill Warre, ever to be taken away, till Soveraigns be Philosophers" (Hobbes, *Leviathan*, p. 254).

112. "Where the kings are philosophers": a Latin version of Socrates's formulation of what is necessary for the creation of the just city; see Plato, *Republic*, 5, 473d. In book 6 of *The Republic* Socrates sets out at length his reasons for believing that kings should be philosophers.

113. Notably Marcus Aurelius Antoninus, who ruled as emperor from A.D. 161 to 180 and whose *Meditations* express his Stoic philosophy.

114. A *précis* of the argument of Machiavelli's *Discourses*, book 1, chapter 4, that the turbulence of the Roman Republic had aroused the virtue of its citizens.

115. Marcus Aurelius Antoninus (see above, n. 113). Antoninus Pius (A.D. 86–161), emperor of Rome from A.D. 138 to 161. The reading of "Antonius" in the

them Divines,[116] not Politicians, and something may be said in their be-
half, when by their good Preaching, they can infuse into their imaginary
Prince (who seems already to have an Image of the Power of God) the
Justice, Wisdom, and Goodness too of the Deity.

Noble Venetian. We are well satisfied with the Progress you have hitherto
made in this matter; pray go on to the two other Forms used amongst the
Ancients, and their Corruptions, that so we may come to the Modern
Governments, and see how *England* stands, and how it came to decay,
and what must Rebuild it.

English Gentleman. You have very good Reason to hasten me to that; for
indeed, all that has been said yet, is but as it were a Preliminary discourse
to the knowledge of the Government of *England,* and its decay: when it
comes to the Cure, I hope you will both help me, for both your self and
the Doctor are a thousand times better than I at Remedies. But I shall
dispatch the other two Governments. *Aristocracy,* or *Optimacy,* is a Commonwealth, where the better sort, that is, the Eminent and Rich men,
have the chief Administration of the Government: I say, the chief,
because there are very few ancient *Optimacies,* but the People had some
share, as in *Sparta,* where they had power to Vote, but not Debate; for so
the Oracle of *Apollo,* brought by *Lycurgus* from *Delphos,* settles it;[117] But

---

copy-text is clearly a slip. Note, however, that exactly the same mistake is made in
A Copy of a Letter (1656), p. 4 (appendix A, below, p. 320).

116. "Most of the clergy continued to preach the doctrines of divine right and
passive obedience throughout the reigns of William III and Anne, and beyond,
whether from Whig commitment or in hope of better times. Abednego Seller's
influential *History of Passive Obedience since the Reformation* (1689–90), for example,
was designed to show that the theories were not innovations of clever Stuart policy, but had been basic tenets of the Church from its beginnings, designed to
counter the claimed deposing power of the Pope and the pretended right of popular deposition" (J. C. D. Clark, *English Society 1688–1832* [Cambridge: Cambridge
University Press, 1985], p. 123). It remained a sensitive issue in the Convention
Parliament: see, e.g., Grey, *Debates,* vol. 9, p. 37.

117. "τοῦ δὲ πλήθους ἀθροισθέντος εἰπεῖν μὲν οὐδενὶ γνώμην τῶν ἄλλων
ἐφεῖτο, τὴν δ᾽ ὑπὸ τῶν γερόντων καὶ τῶν βασιλέων προτεθεῖσαν ἐπικρῖναι
κύριος ἦν ὁ δῆμος": "When the multitude was thus assembled, no one of them was

the truth is, these people were the natural *Spartans*. For *Lycurgus* divided
the Country[118] or Territory of *Laconia* into 39000 Shares; whereof Nine
thousand only of these Owners were Inhabitants of *Sparta*; the rest lived
in the Country: so that although *Thucidides*[119] call it an Aristocracy, and
so I follow him, yet it was none of those Aristocracies usually described
by the Politicians, where the Lands of the Territory were in a great deal
fewer Hands. But call it what you will, where ever there was an Aristocracy, there the Property, or very much the Over-ballance of it, was in the
hands of the *Aristoi*,[120] or Governours, be they more or fewer; for if the
People have the greatest interest in the Property, they will, and must
have it in the Empire: A notable example of it is *Rome*, the best and most
glorious Government that ever the Sun saw; where the Lands being
equally divided amongst the Tribes, that is the People; it was impossible
for the *Patricii* to keep them quiet, till they yielded to their desires, not
only to have their *Tribunes*, to see that nothing passed into a Law without
their consent, but also to have it declared, that both the *Consuls* should
not only be chosen by the people (as they ever were, and the Kings too
before them) but that they might be elected too, when the people pleased,
out of *Plebeian* Families.[121] So that now I am come to *Democracy*. Which

---

permitted to make a motion, but the motion laid before them by the senators and
kings could be accepted or rejected by the people" (Plutarch, *Lycurgus*, 6).

118. "Ἐπάγων δὲ τῷ λόγῳ τὸ ἔργον ἔνειμε τὴν μὲν ἄλλην τοῖς περιοίκοις
Λακωνικὴν τρισμυρίους κλήρους, τὴν δὲ εἰς τὸ ἄστυ τὴν Σπάρτην συντελοῦσαν
ἐνακισχιλίους": "Suiting the deed to the word, he distributed the rest of the Laco-
nian land among the 'perioeci,' or free provincials, in thirty thousand lots, and that
which belonged to the city of Sparta, in nine thousand lots, to as many genuine
Spartans" (Plutarch, *Lycurgus*, 8).

119. "Καὶ οἱ μὲν Λακεδαιμόνιοι οὐχ ὑποτελεῖς ἔχοντες φόρου τοὺς ξυμμάχους
ἡγοῦντο, κατ' ὀλιγαρχίαν δὲ σφίσιν αὐτοῖς μόνον ἐπιτηδείως ὅπως πολιτεύσουσι
θεραπεύοντες": "The Lacedaemonians maintained their hegemony without keeping their allies tributary to them, but took care that these should have an oligarchical form of government conformably to the sole interest of Sparta" (Thucydides,
1.19).

120. A transliteration of the Greek αριστοι, meaning "the best."

121. *Patricii*: members of certain distinguished families at Rome, the privileged
or aristocratic class; *Tribunes*: more fully, *tribuni plebis*, the tribunes of the people,
originally two in number, magistrates of free plebeian birth charged with the protection of the people and to that end possessing the right of veto; *Consuls*: the two

you see is a Government where the chief part of the Sovereign Power, and the exercise of it, resides in the *People*; and where the Style is, *Iussu populi authoritate patrum*.[122] And it doth consist of three fundamental Orders. The Senate proposing, the People resolving, and the Magistrates executing. This Government is much more Powerful than an *Aristocracy*, because the latter cannot arm the People, for fear they should seize upon the Government, and therefore are fain to make use of none but Strangers and Mercinaries for Souldiers; which, as the Divine *Machiavil* says,[123] has hindred your Commonwealth of *Venice* from mounting up to Heaven, whither those incomparable Orders, and that venerable Wisdom used by your Citizens in keeping to them, would have carried you, if in all your Wars you had not been ill served.

Doctor. Well, Sir, pray let me ask you one thing concerning *Venice*: How do you make out your *Imperium fundatur in dominio* there? Have the Gentlemen there, who are the Party governing, the possession of the whole Territory? Does not property remain entire to the Gentlemen, and other Inhabitants in the several Countries of *Padua, Brescia, Vicenza, Verona, Bergamo, Creman, Trevisi,* and *Friuli,* as also in the *Ultramarine* Provinces, and *Islands?*[124] And yet I believe you will not deny, but that the Government of *Venice* is as well founded, and hath been of as long continuance as any that now is, or ever was in the World.

---

senior magistrates in the Roman Republic, elected annually by the people, and to whom on the expulsion of the kings military and judicial authority (*imperium*) had been entrusted; *Plebeian*: Roman burgesses other than the patricians, the common citizens.

122. "By the order of the people and by the authority of the fathers [i.e., senators]."

123. In *The Prince*, chapter 12: "If the progress of the *Venetians* be considered, they will be found to have acted securely, and honorably whilst their affairs were managed by their own forces (which was before they attempted any thing upon the *terra firma*) then all was done by the Gentlemen and Common People of that City, and they did very great things; but when they began to enterprize at land, they began to abate of their old reputation and discipline, and to degenerate into the customs of *Italy* [i.e., by using mercenaries]" (Machiavelli, *Works,* pp. 215–16).

124. All were territories under Venetian rule in the later seventeenth century.

English Gentleman. Doctor, I shall not answer you in this, because I am sure it will be better done by this Gentleman, who is a worthy Son of that honourable Mother.

Noble Venetian. I thought you had said, Sir, that we should have done Complimenting; but since you do Command me to clear the Objection made by our learned Doctor, I shall presume to tell you, first how our City began. The *Goths, Huns,* and *Lombards* coming with all the Violence and Cruelty immaginable, to invade that part of *Italy* which we now call *Terra firma,* and where our Ancestors did then inhabit, forced them in great numbers to seek a shelter amongst a great many little Rocks, or *Islands,* which stood very thick in a vast Lake, or rather Marsh, which is made by the *Adriatique* Sea, we call it *Laguna;* here they began to build, and getting Boats, made themselves Provisions of all kind from the Land; from whence innumerable people began to come to them, finding that they could subsist, and that the barbarous people had no Boats to attack them, nor that they could be invaded either by Horse or Foot without them.[125] Our first Government, and which lasted for many years, was no more than what is practised in many Country Parishes in *Italy,* and possibly here too, where the Clerk, or any other person, calls together the chief of the Inhabitants to consider of Parish-business, as chusing of Officers, making of Rates, and the like. So in

125. The Goths, Huns, and Lombards were all tribes of barbarians from the north and east of the Roman Empire who overran its territories in the fourth and fifth centuries A.D. *Venetia* originally denoted a rich and densely populated province in northern Italy, extending from the border with Pannonia to the river Addua, and from the river Po to the Rhaetian and Julian Alps. The invasion of Attila and the Huns in A.D. 452 drove the populace of Venetia to seek refuge in the marshy islands at the northern end of the Adriatic, where they established settlements that would become the city of Venice. The history of the founding of the city was related in a number of the books listed by Neville in the second edition of *Plato Redivivus:* see, e.g., Hay, *Policy,* pp. 1–4 and Machiavelli, *Works,* p. 268 (*Discourses,* 1.1). Cf. Contarini, *Venice,* pp. 3–4. Neville's phrasing is close to that of Harrington in *Oceana,* "The Preliminaries": "those inundations of Huns, Goths, Vandals, Lombards, Saxons which, breaking the Roman Empire, deformed the whole face of the world with those ill features of government which at this time are become far worse in these western parts, except Venice which, escaping the hands of the barbarians by virtue of her impregnable situation, hath had her eye fixed upon ancient prudence and is attained to a perfection even beyond her copy" (Pocock, *Harrington,* p. 161).

Venice, when there was any publick provision to be made by way of law, or otherwise, some Officers went about to persons of the greatest Wealth and Credit, to intreat them to meet and consult; from whence our Senate is called to this day *Consiglio de pregadi*, which in our Barbarous Idiom is as much as *Pregati*[126] in *Tuscan* Language: Our security increased daily, and so by consequence our Number and our Riches; for by this time there began to be another inundation of *Sarazens* upon *Asia* Minor,[127] which forced a great many of the poor people of *Greece* to fly to us for protection, giving us the possession of some Islands, and other places upon the Continent: This opened us a Trade, and gave a beginning to our greatness; but chiefly made us consider what Government was fittest to conserve our selves, and keep our Wealth (for we did not then much dream of Conquests, else without doubt we must have made a popular Government).[128] We pitcht upon an

126. "The council of those who have been entreated [i.e., to attend]." "There are *three* principal *Councils* in *Venice*; that is to say, the *Grand Council*, which comprehends the whole body of the *Nobles*: the *Pregadi*, which is the *Senate*; and the *Colledg* where *Embassadors* have their audience" (Amelot de la Houssaie, *Venice*, p. 5). Cf. Pocock, *Harrington*, pp. 177 and 482–86 (a more extended consideration by Harrington of the orders and institutions of the Venetian Republic). In *Aphorisms Political*, Harrington had given a potted account of the origin of this council and of the vital role it had played in the formation of the Venetian constitution: "The Venetians, having slain divers of their dukes for their tyranny, and being assembled by such numbers in their great council as were naturally incapable of debate, pitched upon thirty gentlemen who were called *pregati*, in that they were prayed to go apart and, debating upon the exigence of the commonwealth, to propose as they thought good unto the great council; and from thence first arose the senate of Venice, to this day called the *pregati*, and the great council: that is, the senate and the popular assembly of Venice; and from these two arose all those admirable orders of that commonwealth" (Pocock, *Harrington*, p. 772).

127. Perhaps a reference to the Saracen incursions into the Byzantine Empire in A.D. 668–75 and 716–18, both of which resulted in Constantinople being besieged and large parts of Asia Minor being overrun.

128. A précis of Machiavelli, *Discourses*, 1.6: "He then who would set up a new Common-wealth, should consider whether he would have it (like *Rome*) extend its Dominion and Soveraignty; or keep it self within its own bounds without any dilatation. In the first case it is necessary to imitate the *Romans*, and give way to the tumults and publick dissentions as well as he can; for without his Citizens be numerous, and well disciplin'd and arm'd, he can never extend his Dominion; and if he could, it would be impossible to keep it. In the second, he is to frame to the Model of the *Spartans*, and *Venetians*; but because augmentation of Empire, is

Aristocracy, by ordering that those who had been called to Council for that present year, and for four years before, should have the Government in their hands, and all their Posterity after them for ever, which made first the distinction between Gentlemen and Citizens; the People, who consisted of divers Nations, most of them newly come to inhabit there, and generally seeking nothing but safety and ease, willingly consented to this change, and so this *State* hath continued to this day;[129] though the several Orders and Counsels have been brought in since, by degrees, as our Nobility encreased, and for other causes. Under this Government we have made some Conquests in *Italy*, and *Greece*, for our City stood like a Wall between the two great Torrents of *Goths* and *Sarazens*; and as either of their Empires declin'd, it was easie for us, without being very Warlike, to pick up some pieces of each side; as for the Government of these Conquests, we did not think fit to divide the Land amongst our Nobility, for fear of envy, and the

commonly the destruction of such Common-wealths, they are always destructive and pernicious, as Experience has shown in the Examples of *Sparta* and *Venice*" (Machiavelli, *Works*, p. 276; cf. Sidney, *Court Maxims*, p. 16).

129. Once again a précis of a passage which comes slightly earlier in Machiavelli, *Discourses*, 1.6: "*Venice* did not divide the Government into distinct Names; but all who were admitted to the administration were called *Gentlemen* under one common appellation; and that, more by accident, than any prudence in the Legislator; for when to those Rocks upon which that City is now seated, many people did repair for the reasons abovesaid, in process of time their number encreasing so fast, that they could not live peaceably without Laws, they resolved to put themselves under some form, and meeting often together to deliberate upon what, when they found they were numerous enough to subsist by themselves, they made a Law to praeclude all new comers from the Government: and finding afterwards their numbers encrease, and that there were multitudes of Inhabitants incapable of publick administration; in honour to the Governors they called them *Gentlemen* of *Venice*, and the others but *Citizens*; and this distinction might not only be instituted, but continued without tumult, because when first introduced, all the Inhabitants participating of the Government, no body could complain, and they who came after, finding it firm and established, had no reason, nor opportunity to disturb it; They had no reason, because no injury was done them; they had no opportunity, because the Government restrained them, and they were not employed in any thing that might furnish them with authority: besides those who came after were not in number disproportionable to the Governors, the latter being equally, if not more numerous than they; for which reasons the *Venetians* were able not only to erect, but maintain their Government a long time, without any revolution" (Machiavelli, *Works*, p. 275).

effects of it: much less did we think it adviseable to plant Colonies of our People, which would have given the Power into their hands, but we thought it the best way for our Government to leave the People their Property, tax them what we thought fit, & keep them under by Governours and Citadels, and so in short make them a Province.[130] So that now the Doctors Riddle is solved; for I suppose this Gentleman did not mean that his Maxime should reach to Provincial Governments.

English Gentleman. No, Sir, so far from that, that it is just contrary; for as in National or Domestick Government, where a Nation is Governed either by its own People or its own Prince, there can be no settled Government, except they have the Rule who possess the Country. So in Provincial Governments, if they be wisely ordered, no man must have any the least share in the managing Affairs of State, but strangers, or such as have no share or part in the possessions there, for else they will have a very good opportunity of shaking off their Yoak.

Doctor. That is true; and we are so wise here (I mean our Ancestors were) as to have made a Law, That no Native in *Ireland* can be *Deputy* there:[131] But, Sir, being fully satisfied in my demand, by this Gentleman; I beseech you to go on to what you have to say, before you come to *England.*

---

130. Cf. Machiavelli's comments on the unhappy consequences of this enlargement of Venetian power in chapter 12 of *The Prince*: "If the progress of the *Venetians* be considered, they will be found to have acted securely, and honorably whilst their affairs were managed by their own forces (which was before they attempted any thing upon the *terra firma*) then all was done by the Gentlemen and Common People of that City, and they did very great things; but when they began to enterprize at land, they began to abate of their old reputation and discipline, and to degenerate into the customs of *Italy*" (Machiavelli, *Works*, pp. 215–16).

131. As a result of the Commission of 1622 on the governance of Ireland it had become a maxim of English policy that only those of English birth could occupy the position of chief governor in Ireland. Only such men were thought to be, on the one hand, able to uphold the interest of the crown, and on the other, able to arbitrate between conflicting groups among the native Irish. See Nicholas Canny, *Making Ireland British 1580–1650* (Oxford: Oxford University Press, 2001), p. 246.

English Gentleman. I shall then offer two things to your observation; the first is, That in all times and places, where any great Heroes or Legislators, have founded a Government, by gathering people together to build a City, or to invade any Countrey to possess it, before they came to dividing the conquered Lands, they did always very maturely deliberate under what Form or Model of Government they meant to live, and accordingly made the Partition of the Possessions; *Moses, Theseus,* and *Romulus,* Founders of *Democracies,* divided the Land equally:[132] *Licurgus* who meant an *Optimacy,* made a certain number of Shares, which he intended to be in the hands of the People of *Laconia.*[133] *Cyrus,* and other conquering Monarchs before him, took all for themselves and Successors, which is observed in those Eastern Countries to this day, and which has made those Countries continue ever since under the same Government, though Conquered and possessed very often by several Nations:[134] This brings me to the second thing to be observed, which is, *That wherever this apportionment of Lands came to be changed in any kind, the Government either changed with it, or was wholly in a state of confusion:* And for this reason *Licurgus,* the greatest Politician that ever Founded any Government, took a sure way to fix Property by Confounding it, and bringing all into Common: And so the whole number of the Natural *Spartans,* who inhabited the City of *Lacedemon,* eat and drank in their several *convives*[135] together:[136] And as long as they continued so to do, they did not only

---

132. *Moses*: Numbers 33:54. The authors of *The Armie's Dutie* (1659), of which Neville may have been one, had also cited this example: "When God himself formed the people of Israel, by *Moses* hand, into a free Common-wealth, there was not only a suitable division of the lands at the first, but a perpetuall law of Jubilee, to prevent alienation of lands, and the growth of any to such unequall interest, as his power might be dangerous to the government" (*Armie's Dutie,* p. 19). *Theseus*: Plutarch, *Theseus,* 24–25; cf. Machiavelli, *Works,* p. 268. *Romulus*: Plutarch, *Romulus,* 27. Machiavelli praises Moses, Cyrus, Romulus, and Theseus as the greatest founding legislators in chapter 6 of *The Prince* (Machiavelli, *Works,* p. 205).

133. See above, p. 97, n. 118.

134. Cyrus the Great, of the Persian family of the Achaemenids, the founder of the Persian Empire, d. 529 B.C. See Xenophon, *Cyropaedia,* passim and esp. 1.1.4–6.

135. I.e., banquets or feasts (*OED,* s.v. "convive"); archaic by 1681.

136. Plutarch, *Lycurgus,* 10–12.

preserve their Government entire, and that for a longer time than we can read of any Common-Wealth that ever lasted amongst the Ancients, but held as it were the principality of *Greece*. The *Athenians*, for want of some Constitutions to fix Property, as *Theseus* placed it, were in danger of utter ruine, which they had certainly encounter'd, if the good Genius (as they then call'd it) of that People, had not raised them up a second Founder, more than six hundred years after the first, which was *Solon*:[137] And because the History of this matter will very much conduce to the illustrating of this Aphorisme we have laid down, I will presume so much upon your patience as to make a short recital of it, leaving you to see it more at large in *Plutarch* and other Authors.[138] The Lands in the Territory of *Attica* which were in the possession of the Common People, (for what reason History is silent) were for Debt all Mortgaged to the great Men of the City of *Athens*, and the Owners having no possibility of Redeeming their Estates, were treating to Compound with their Creditors, and deliver up their Lands to them: *Solon* (who was one of those State Physicians we spake of,)[139] was much troubled at this, and harangued daily to the Nobility and People against it, telling them first, that it was impossible for the *Grecians* to resist the *Medes* (who were then growing up to a powerful Monarchy) except *Athens* the second City of *Greece* did continue a Democracy; That it was as Impossible the People could keep their Empire, except they kept their Lands, nothing being more contrary to Nature, than that those who possess nothing in a Country can pretend to Govern it. They were all sensible of his Reasons, and of their own Danger, but the only Remedy (which was, that the great Men should forgive the Common People their Debts) would not at all be digested; so that the whole City now fully understanding their condition, were con-

---

137. Solon (c. 640–c. 558 B.C.): Athenian aristocrat and statesman; made archon c. 594 B.C., at which point he reformed the Athenian constitution in the way Neville describes. This comparison between Lycurgus and Solon follows closely the similar comparison drawn by Machiavelli in *Discourses*, 1.2 (Machiavelli, *Works*, p. 271). Solon was particularly admired by Marchamont Nedham (Scott, *Commonwealth Principles*, pp. 137–38).

138. Plutarch composed a life of Solon.

139. See above, p. 64.

tinually in an uproar, and the People flock'd about *Solon*, whenever he came abroad, desiring him to take upon him the Government, and be their Prince, and they would make choice of him the next time they assembled. He told them no, he would never be a Tyrant, especially in his own Country; meaning, that he who had no more share than other of the Nobles, could not Govern the rest, without being an Usurper or Tyrant: But this he did to oblige his Citizens, he frankly forgave all the Debts that any of the People owed to him, and released their Lands immediately; and this amounted to fifteen *Attick* Talents of Gold, a vast sum in those days; and betook himself to a voluntary Exile, in which he visited *Thales*, and went to the Oracle of *Delphos*,[140] and offer up his Prayers to *Apollo* for the preservation of his City: In return of which (as the People then believed) the hearts of the great ones were so changed and inlarged, that they readily agreed to remit all their Debts to the People, upon Condition that *Solon* would take the pains to make them a New Model of Government, and Laws suitable to a Democracy, which he as readily accepted and performed; by vertue of which that City grew and continued long the greatest, the Justest, the most Vertuous, Learned and Renowned of all that Age; drove the *Persians* afterwards out of *Greece*, defeated them both by Sea and Land, with a quarter of their number of Ships and Men; and produced the greatest Wits and Philosophers that ever lived upon Earth. The City of *Athens* Instituted a Solemn Feast in Commemoration of that great Generosity and Self-denial of the Nobility; who Sacrificed their own Interest to the preservation of their Country: which Feast was called the Solemnity of the *Seisactheia*,[141] which signifies recision or abolition of Debts, and was observed with Processions, Sacrifices and Games, till the time of the *Romans'* Dominion over them (who encouraged it,) and ever till the change of Religion in *Greece*, and Invasion of the *Sarazens*. The *Romans* having omitted in their Institution to provide for the fixing of Property, and so the Nobility called *Patricii*, beginning

140. The oracular shrine of Apollo at Delphi on Mount Parnassus, where the priestess of the god (the Pythia) gave cryptic answers to the questions of suppliants.

141. Literally, "shaking off the burden." Harrington also referred to this Athenian cancelling of debts: see Pocock, *Harrington*, pp. 241 and 439.

to take to themselves a greater share in the conquer'd Lands than had been usual (for in the first times of the Commonwealth under *Romulus*, and ever after, it was always practised to divide the Lands equally amongst the Tribes) this Innovation stirred up *Licinius Stolo*,[142] then Tribune of the People, to propose a Law; which, although it met with much difficulty, yet at last was consented to; by which it was provided, that no *Roman* Citizen, of what degree soever, should possess above five hundred Acres of Land; and for the remaining part of the Lands which should be Conquer'd, it was Ordered to be equally divided, as formerly, amongst the Tribes: This found admittance, after much opposition, because it did provide but for the future, no Man at that time being owner of more Lands than what was lawful for him to possess; and if this law had been strictly observed to the last, that glorious Commonwealth might have subsisted to this day,[143] for aught we know.

Doctor. Some other Cause would have been the Ruine of it, what think you of a Foreign Conquest?

English Gentleman. Oh *Doctor*, if they had kept their Poverty they had kept their Government and their Vertue too, and then it had not been an easie matter to subdue them, *Quos vult perdere Jupiter dementat*;[144] Breach of Rules and Order causes Division, and Division when it comes to be Incurable, exposes a Nation almost as much as a Tyrannical Government does. The *Goths* and *Vandals*, had they Invaded in those days, had met with the

142. Gaius Licinius Calvus Stolo: tribune of the plebs, 376–367 B.C.; eventually prosecuted and fined for breaking his own agrarian laws concerning the maximum amount of land a Roman might possess; see Livy, 6.32–34, 36, and 38.

143. Cf. Machiavelli's similar comment about Florence at the end of the thirteenth century: "And had not this tranquillity been at length interrupted by dissention within, it had been in no danger from abroad; . . . that disease from which *ab extra* it was secure, was ingendred in its own bowels" (Machiavelli, *Works*, p. 30).

144. "Those whom Jupiter wishes to destroy he first makes mad." This famous saying is often attributed (wrongly) to Euripides. Neville's probable source is James Duport, *Gnomologia Homerica* (1660), p. 262, but it had become proverbial.

same success which befell the *Cymbri*, and the *Teutones*.[145] I must confess, a Foreign Invasion is a Formidable thing, when a Commonwealth is weak in Territory and Inhabitants, and that the Invader is numerous and Warlike: And so we see the *Romans* were in danger of utter ruine when they were first attacqued by the *Gauls* under *Brennus*:[146] The like hazzard may be fear'd, when a Commonwealth is assaulted by another of equal Vertue, and a Commander of equal Address and Valour to any of themselves. Thus the *Romans* ran the risk of their Liberty and Empire, in the War of *Hannibal*;[147] but their Power and their Vertue grew to that heighth in that contest, that when it was ended, I believe, that if they had preserved the Foundation of their Government entire, they had been Invincible: And if I were alone of this Opinion, I might be ashamed; but I am backt by the Judgement of your Incomparable Country-man *Machiavil*;[148] and no Man will condemn either of us of rashness, if he first consider, what small States, that have stood upon right bottoms, have done to defend their Liberty against great Monarchs; as is to be seen in the example of the little Commonwealth of *Athens*, which destroyed the Fleet of *Xerxes*, consisting of a thousand Vessels, in the Streights of *Salamis*, and before the land army of *Darius* of three hundred thousand in the Plains of *Marathon*,[149] and drove them out of *Greece*; for though the whole Confederates were present at the

145. Ancient tribes that fought the Roman Republic from 113 to 101 B.C., when they were defeated by Gaius Marius.

146. Brennus led a Gallic army that defeated the Romans at the Allia and occupied Rome in 390 B.C. but failed to capture the Capitol.

147. I.e., the Second Punic War (218–202 B.C.).

148. In the *Discourses*, 3.24, Machiavelli attributed the decline of the Roman Republic to two causes: disputes about the Agrarian law, and the prolongation of military commands, an innovation required to pursue wars in several theaters over many years, such as the Punic Wars. "If it be objected, that their great affairs could not have been managed at so great a distance, without the prolongation of commands; I answer, That 'tis possible their Empire might have been longer before it came to that height; but then it would have been more lasting, for the adversary would never have been able to have erected a Monarchy, and destroyed their liberty so soon" (Machiavelli, *Works*, p. 410).

149. Salamis was the great naval battle fought in 480 B.C. off the coast of Athens, in which the Greeks defeated the fleet of the Persian monarch Xerxes. On the plain of Marathon, twenty-two miles northeast of Athens, in 490 B.C. an Athenian army under the command of Miltiades had defeated the invading Persians.

Battel of *Plataea*, yet the *Athenian* Army singly under their General *Milti-ades*, gain'd that renowned Battel of *Marathon*.

Noble Venetian. I beseech you, Sir, how was it possible, or practicable, that the *Romans* Conquering so many and so remote Provinces, should yet have been able to preserve their Agrarian Law, and divide all those Lands equally to their Citizens; Or if it had been possible, yet it would have ruin'd their City, by sending all their Inhabitants away; and by tak-ing in Strangers in their room, they must necessarily have had people less Vertuous and less Warlike, and so both their Government and their Mil-itary Discipline must have been Corrupted; for it is not to be imagined, but that the People would have gone with their Families to the place where their Lands lay: So that it appears that the *Romans* did not pro-vide, in the making and framing their first Polity, for so great Conquests as they afterwards made.

English Gentleman. Yes, surely they did; from their first beginning they were Founded in War, and had neither Land nor Wives but what they fought for;[150] but yet what you object were very weighty, if there had not been a consideration of that early: For as soon as that great and wise People had subdued the *Samnites*[151] on the *East*, and brought their Arms as far as the *Greek* Plantations,[152] in that part of *Italy* which is now called the Kingdom of *Naples*; and Westward, had reduced all the *Tuscans* under their Obedience, as far as the River *Arnus*,[153] they made that and

150. For the early conquests of neighboring territories by the first Romans, see Livy, 1.1. For the story of the rape of the Sabine women, see Livy, 1.1.9–13, and Plutarch, *Romulus*, 14–19. Cf. Machiavelli, *Discourses*, 1.40.

151. The Samnites were an ancient Italian tribe dwelling to the south of Rome. The Romans fought three Samnite wars: 343–341 B.C., 326–304 B.C., and 298–290 B.C. In the *Discourses* Machiavelli refers frequently to these wars of the young re-public: e.g., 1.14, 1.15, 1.31, 2.1, 2.2, 2.6, 2.9, 2.11, 2.13, 2.23, 3.38, 3.39, 3.41–42, 3.47.

152. I.e., Greek colonies.

153. The Romans fought a series of wars with the Etruscans to the north and west of Rome from the very earliest years of the foundation of the city until the two Roman victories at Lake Vadimo (310 and 283 B.C.), after which the Etruscans were assimilated into Rome. Again, Machiavelli comments frequently on these wars in the *Discourses*: e.g., 1.15, 1.26, 2.1, 2.4–6, 2.12, 2.25–26, 2.33, 3.30–31.

the River *Volturnus* (which runs by the Walls of *Capua*) the two Bound-aries of their Empire, which was called *Domicilium Imperii*.[154] These were the *ne plus ultra*,[155] for what they Conquered between these two Rivers, was all confiscated and divided amongst the Tribes; the *Rustick* Tribes being twenty seven, and the *Urbane* Tribes nine, which made thirty six in all. The City Tribes were like our Companies in *London*, consisting of Tradesmen. The Country Tribes were divided like Shires, and there was scarce any Landed Man, who Inhabited in the City, but he was written in that Tribe where his Estate lay; so that the *Rustick* Tribes (though they had all equal Voices) were of far more Credit and Reputa-tion than the *Urbane*. Upon the days of the *Comitia*,[156] which were very well known, as many as thought fit amongst the Country Tribes, came to give their Voices, though every Tribe was very numerous of Inhabitants that lived in the City. Now the *Agrarian*[157] did not extend to any Lands

154. Literally, "the abode of empire."

155. I.e., the utmost limit (*OED*, s.v. "ne plus ultra"). Cf. Rycaut, *History*, sig. Ee3ᵛ; Rycaut, *Present State*, p. 69; and Overton, *The Baiting of the Great Bull of Bashan* (1649), in Morton, *Freedom*, p. 285.

156. There were three types of *comitia*, or assembly, in the Roman Republic, each of which had a distinctive composition and function. The *comitia centuriata* was the assembly of the Roman people in "hundreds," a military division created by Servius Tullius. The *comitia curiata* was the assembly of the wards, or curiae, at Rome. The *comitia tributa* was the assembly of the Roman people collected in their tribes. In 1565 Sir Thomas Smith had compared the *comitia centuriata* to the English Parliament (Smith, *Republica*, pp. 78–79). The functions of the Roman *comitia* had engaged the attention of earlier seventeenth-century theorists of popular sovereignty (both for and against) such as Sir Robert Filmer: see Lee, *Popular Sovereignty*, pp. 308–9. Harrington had described their operation in *Oceana* (Pocock, *Harrington*, pp. 211–12).

157. I.e., the agrarian laws governing the distribution of conquered lands. These were initiated by Gaius Licinius Calvus Stolo (above, p. 106, n. 142). They were revived by the Gracchi brothers, Tiberius Sempronius Gracchus and Gaius Sem-pronius Gracchus (see below, p. 110, n. 159). For Machiavelli's comments on the Roman agrarian law and its consequences, see *Discourses*, 1.37 (Machiavelli, *Works*, pp. 305–7). For Harrington, agrarian laws were the key to his understanding of how expansive Roman and durable Venetian qualities could be combined in a sin-gle commonwealth. A vigorously enforced agrarian law would allow a state to ex-pand as Rome had done, but without succumbing to corruption. It might therefore hope to be stable—even, perhaps, immortal—in the manner of Venice: "An equal agrarian is a perpetual law establishing and preserving the balance of dominion,

conquered beyond this Precinct, but they were left to the Inhabitants, they paying a Revenue to the Commonwealth; all but those which were thought fit to be set out to maintain a *Roman* Colony, which was a good number of *Roman* Citizens, sent thither, and provided of Lands and Habitations, which being Armed, did serve in the nature of a Citadel and Garison to keep the Province in Obedience, and a *Roman* Praetor, Proconsul,[158] or other Governour, was sent yearly to Head them, and brought Forces with him besides. Now it was ever lawful for any *Roman* Citizen to purchase what Lands he pleased in any of these Provinces; it not being dangerous to a City to have their People rich, but to have such a Power in the Governing part of the Empire, as should make those who managed the Affairs of the Commonwealth depend upon them; which came afterwards to be that which ruined their Liberty, and which the *Gracchi*[159] endeavoured to prevent when it was too late; For those Illustri-

---

by such a distribution that no one man or number of men within the compass of the few or aristocracy can come to overpower the whole people by their possessions in lands" (Pocock, *Harrington*, p. 181; cf. pp. 70–71, 664–65). It had been the neglect of the agrarian by the Romans that had "let in the sink of luxury, and forfeited the inestimable treasure of liberty for themselves and posterity" (p. 188; cf. p. 689). As the Lord Archon explains, "For want of this fixation [i.e., an agrarian], potent monarchies and commonwealths have fallen upon the heads of the people, and accompanied their own sad ruins with vast effusions of innocent blood" (Pocock, *Harrington*, p. 235; cf. p. 352). Nevertheless, Harrington had recognized that people were wary of agrarian laws: "Agrarian laws of all others have ever been the greatest bugbears, and so in the institution were these [of Oceana]; at which time it was ridiculous to see how strange a fear appeared in everybody of that which, being good for all, could hurt nobody" (Pocock, *Harrington*, p. 231).

158. *Praetor*: originally the generic term for holders of executive authority, or *imperium*, in the Roman Republic; later and more narrowly the title of the magistrate who administered justice. *Proconsul*: the title given to a consul in the Roman Republic whose authority had been prolonged beyond the normal year of office to enable him to complete a military campaign or to govern a province.

159. Tiberius Sempronius Gracchus (d. 133 B.C.) and Gaius Sempronius Gracchus (d. 121 B.C.): Roman politicians whose attempt to solve the economic problems arising from the immense landholdings of the wealthy led to their assassinations at the hands of their fellow patricians. Plutarch composed lives of the two Gracchi. Cf. Machiavelli, *Discourses*, 1.37 (Machiavelli, *Works*, p. 306). In *The Art of War* Machiavelli makes Fabritio say that Rome was well governed "till the time of the *Gracchi*" (Machiavelli, *Works*, p. 439). For Harrington the Gracchi had illustrated the point of balance in the constitution of the Roman Republic (Pocock,

ous persons, seeing the disorder that was then in the Commonwealth, and rightly comprehending the Reason, which was the intermission of the *Agrarian*, and by consequence the great Purchases which were made by the Men of *Rome* (who had inriched themselves in *Asia* and the other Provinces) in that part of *Italy* which was between the two Rivers, before mentioned, began to harrangue the People, in hopes to perswade them to admit of the right Remedy, which was to confirm the *Agrarian* Law with a Retrospect; which although they carried, yet the difficulties in the Execution proved so great, that it never took effect, by reason that the Common People, whose Interest it was to have their Lands restored; yet having long lived as Clients, and Dependents of the great ones, chose rather to depend still upon their Patrons, than to hazard all for an Imaginary deliverance, by which supineness in them, they were prevail'd with rather to joyne (for the most part) with the Oppressors of themselves and their Countrey, and to cut the throats of their redeemers, than to employ their just resentment against the covetous Violators of their Government and Property. So perished the two renowned *Gracchi*, one soon after the other, not for any crime, but for having endeavoured to preserve and restore their Commonwealth; for which (if they had lived in times suitable to such an Heroick undertaking, and that the vertue of their Ancestors had been yet in any kind remaining) they would have merited and enjoyed a Reputation equal to that of *Lycurgus*, or *Solon*,[160] whereas as it happen'd they were sometime after branded with the name of Sedition, by certain Wits,[161] who prostituted the noble flame of Poetry (which before had wont to be employed in magnifying Heroick Actions) to flatter the Lust and Ambition of the *Roman* Tyrants.

Harrington, p. 607). Cf. *Copy of a Letter*, p. 7. In the late 1650s, after the death of Oliver Cromwell but before the Restoration, the Gracchi might be cited as predecessors of the Levellers (Scott, *Commonwealth Principles*, p. 300).

160. See above, pp. 103–4 and n. 137.

161. An allusion to Juvenal's illustration of intolerable hypocrisy, "Quis tulerit Gracchos de seditione querentes?," "Who could endure the Gracchi complaining about sedition?" (2.24). However, Juvenal was so little a flatterer of authority that he was temporarily banished from Rome for insulting Paris, the favorite actor of the emperor Domitian. This Juvenalian tag had also been quoted by Sidney in his *Court Maxims* (Sidney, *Court Maxims*, p. 103).

Noble Venetian. Sir, I approve what you say in all things, and in Confirmation of it, shall further alledge the two famous Princes of *Sparta, Agis,* and *Cleomines,* which I couple together, since *Plutarch*[162] does so; These finding the Corruption of their Commonwealth, and the Decay of their ancient Vertue, to proceed from the neglect and inobservance of their Founders Rules, and a breach of that Equality which was first instituted; endeavoured to restore the Laws of *Lycurgus,* and divide the Territory anew; their Victory in the *Peloponnesian* War,[163] and the Riches and Luxury brought into their City by *Lisander,*[164] having long before broken all the Orders of their Commonwealth, and destroyed the Proportions of Land allotted to each of the Natural *Spartans*: But the first of these two excellent Patriots perished by Treachery in the beginning of his Enterprize, the other began and went on with incomparable Prudence and Resolution, but miscarried afterwards by the Iniquity of the times, and baseness and wickedness of the People;[165] so

162. *Agis*: Agis IV (c. 265–241 B.C.), king of Sparta, whose attempt to restore the constitution of Lycurgus led to his condemnation by the ephors and execution by strangulation. *Cleomines*: Cleomenes III (c. 265–219 B.C.), king of Sparta; another reforming king who followed Agis IV in restoring the constitution of Lycurgus. *Plutarch*: Plutarch (c. A.D. 46–120), Greek biographer and moral philosopher. Agis had been an important figure for Harrington, illustrating the point of balance in the Spartan constitution (Pocock, *Harrington*, p. 607). Cf. *Copy of a Letter*, p. 7.

163. The struggle for dominance in Greece from 431 to 404 B.C. between the democratic sea power of Athens and an alliance of most of the states of the Peloponnese under the leadership of the oligarchical Spartans, who possessed the most formidable land force of the day. Athens was eventually reduced to the condition of a subject-ally of the Spartans. Our principal sources for this war are the history of Thucydides and the *Hellenica* of Xenophon.

164. Lysander (d. 395 B.C.), a Spartan naval commander in the latter part of the Peloponnesian War, who established the Thirty Tyrants (see below, p. 114, n. 168) in Athens. Biographies of him by Nepos and Plutarch have survived.

165. Cf. Machiavelli, *Discourses*, 1.9: "*Agis* King of *Sparta* observing his Citizens had lost much of their ancient virtue, and by consequence were decayed both in their power and Empire, imputing it in part to their deviation from the Laws of *Lycurgus*, desired very earnestly to reduce them again, but before he could bring it to perfection he was slain by the Spartan *Ephori*, as one who designed to make himself absolute; but *Cleomenes* succeeding him in the Government, having the same inclination, and perceiving by some Records and Writings which *Agis* had left behind, what was his intention, he found that he could not do his Country that service any way, but by making himself absolute: for by the ambition of some persons, he found that he could not do the good which he designed to the general-

infallibly true it is, That where the Policy is corrupted, there must necessarily be also a corruption and depravation of Manners, and an utter abolition of all Faith, Justice, Honour, and Morality; but I forget my self, and intrench upon your Province: there is nothing now remains to keep you from the Modern Policies, but that you please to shut up this Discourse of the Ancient Governments, with saying something of the Corruptions of *Aristocracy* and *Democracy*; for I believe both of us are satisfied that you have abundantly proved your Assertion, and that when we have leisure to examine all the States or Policies that ever were, we shall find all their Changes to have turn'd upon this Hinge of Property, and that the fixing of that with good lawes in the beginning or first Institution of a state, and the holding to those Lawes afterwards, is the only way to make a Commonwealth Immortal.

English Gentleman. I think you are very right; but I shall obey you, and do presume to differ from *Aristotle*, in thinking that he has not fitly called those extreams (for so I will stile them) of *Aristocracy* and *Democracy*, Corruptions;[166] for that they do not proceed from the alteration of Property, which is the *Unica corruptio politica:*[167] For Example, I do not find that Oligarchy, or Government of a few, which is the Extream of an Optimacy, ever did arise from a few Mens getting into their hands the Estates of all the rest of the Nobility: For had it began so, it might have lasted, which I never read of any that did. I will therefore conclude, that they were all Tyrannies; for so the *Greeks* called all Usurpations, whether of one or more persons, and all those that I ever read of, as they came in either by Craft or violence, as the

---

ity, by reason of the malevolence of a few, wherefore he caused the *Ephori*, and who-ever else he thought likely to obstruct him, to be killed, and revived the Laws of *Lycurgus*, which noble act might have recovered that State, and have made *Cleomenes* as venerable as *Lycurgus* himself, had it not been for the power of *Macedon*" (Machiavelli, *Works*, p. 280).

166. παρεκβάσις, meaning "a deviation," is the term used by Aristotle (*Politics*, 3.5).

167. "The sole source of political corruption." "Unica" can have a strongly pejorative connotation. The phrase is apparently Neville's own coinage. It does not occur in classical Latin. It was mocked by his critics: see, e.g., Goddard, *Plato's Demon*, p. 261.

Thirty Tyrants of *Athens*,[168] the Fifteen of *Thebes*,[169] and the *Decemviri* of *Rome*[170] (though these at first came in lawfully) so they were soon driven out; and ever, were either assassinated, or dyed by the Sword of Justice; and therefore I shall say no more of them, not thinking them worth the name of a Government. As for the Extream of *Democracy*, which is *Anarchy*, it is not so: for many Commonwealths have lasted for a good time under that Administration (if I may so call a State so full of Confusion.) An *Anarchy* then is, when the People not contented with their Share in the Administration of the Government, (which is the right of Approving, or Disapproving of Lawes, of Leagues, and of making of War and Peace, of Judging in all Causes upon an Appeal to them, and chusing all manner of Officers) will take upon themselves the Office of the *Senate* too, in manageing Subordinate Matters of State, Proposing Lawes Originally, and assuming Debate in the Market place,[171] making their Orators their Leaders; nay, not content with this, will take upon them to alter all the Orders of the Government when they please; as was frequently practised in *Athens*, and in the Modern State of *Florence*.[172] In both these Cities, when ever any great person who

168. Following the defeat of Athens in the Pelopponesian War in 404 B.C., the Athenian oligarchs, supported by the Spartan commander Lysander, nominated a body of thirty who ruled the state and set about drawing up a new and undemocratic constitution. Their rule was short-lived, however, the old democracy being restored in 403 B.C. after the intervention of the Spartan king Pausanias.

169. A reference to the oligarchy established in Thebes by Sparta after the defeat of the Persians at Plataea (479 B.C.) and the ensuing aggression by Athens. This change of government in Thebes is mentioned several times by Machiavelli: see *Discourses*, 3.6, and *The Prince*, chapters 5 and 12.

170. The "decemviri" were ten-man commissions to whom the Roman Republic turned for the composition of laws. There were several such commissions during the period of the republic, but the most notorious (because most despotic in inclination) was that of 450 B.C. Machiavelli devoted several chapters of the *Discourses* to the subject of the decemviri (1.40–45). For Harrington's censure of the decemviri as an oligarchy lacking balance, see Pocock, *Harrington*, pp. 206 and 696. The decemviri were occasionally mentioned in Parliament: see, e.g., Burton, *Diary*, vol. 3, p. 112.

171. The agora in ancient Athens and the forum in ancient Rome were both marketplaces in which political business was also transacted.

172. In his *History of Florence* Machiavelli recounts a number of episodes when the Florentine people "thought fit to re-order the Government": see, e.g., Machiavelli, *Works*, pp. 26, 28, 30, 38, 47, 50–53, 56, 59–60, 64; quotation on p. 30.

could lead the People, had a mind to alter the Government, he call'd them together, and made them Vote a Change. In *Florence* they call'd it, *Chiamar il popolo a Parlamento e ripigliar lo Stato*,[173] which is summoning the People into the Market-place to resume the Government, and did then presently Institute a new one, with new Orders, new Magistracies, and the like. Now that which originally causes this Disorder, is the admitting (in the beginning of a Government, or afterwards) the meaner sort of People,[174] who have no Share in the Territory, into an equal part of Ordering the Commonwealth; these being less sober, less considering, and less careful of the Publick Concerns; and being commonly the Major part, are made the Instruments oft-times of the Ambition of the great ones, and very apt to kindle into Faction: but notwithstanding all the Confusion which we see under an Anarchy, (where the wisdom of the better sort is made useless by the fury of the People) yet many Cities have subsisted hundreds of years in this condition; and have been more considerable, and performed greater Actions, than ever any Government of equal Extent did, except it were a well-regulated *Democracy*; But it is true, they ruine in the end, and that never by Cowardize or baseness, but by too much boldness and temerarious undertakings, as both *Athens* and *Florence* did;[175] The first undertaking the Invasion of *Sicily*, when their Affairs went ill elsewhere; and the other by provoking the *Spaniard* and the *Pope*. But I have done now, and shal pass to say something of the Modern Policies.

173. I.e., to call the people to a parliament and to reform the state.

174. A clear example of Neville's opposition to populism and democracy, and of his adherence to aristocracy. This need not have been simply a matter of class solidarity on Neville's part. In the later 1670s, the constitutional importance of an aristocracy had come into greater prominence. A monarchy could support itself by either a standing army or a peerage, and of these the latter was greatly preferable, as Shaftesbury repeatedly insisted (*State-Tracts* [1693], pp. 55 and 56–60). In *Oceana* Harrington had maintained that "a nobility or gentry in a popular government, not overbalancing it, is the very life and soul of it" (Pocock, *Harrington*, p. 167).

175. The Athenian invasion of Sicily in 415 B.C., which ended in the destruction of the Athenian fleet and army, was a turning point in the Pelopponesian War. The Treaty of Barcelona (19 January 1493), to which Clement VII (the former Cardinal Giulio de Medici) and the emperor and king of Spain Charles V were signatories, led to the invasion of Florence and the restoration of the Medici.

Noble Venetian. Before you come to that, Sir, pray satisfie me in a Point which I should have moved before, but that I was unwilling to interrupt your rational Discourse; How came you to take it for granted, that *Moses, Theseus,* and *Romulus* were Founders of Popular Governments? As for *Moses,* we have his Story written by an Infallible Pen; *Theseus* was ever called King of *Athens,* though he liv'd so long since, that what is written of him is justly esteem'd fabulous; but *Romulus* certainly was a King, and that Government continued a Monarchy, though Elective, under seven Princes.

English Gentleman. I will be very short in my Answer, and say nothing of *Theseus,* for the reason you are pleased to alledge: But for *Moses,* you may read in Holy Writ,[176] that when, by God's Command, he had brought the *Israelites* out of *Egypt,* he did at first manage them by acquainting the People with the Estate of their Government, which People were called together with the sound of a Trumpet, and are termed in Scripture, the Congregation of the Lord; this Government he thought might serve their turn in their passage, and that it would be time enough to make them a better when they were in possession of the Land of *Canaan;* Especially having made them Judges and Magistrates at the instance of his Father-in-law,[177] which are called in Authors, *Praefecti Jethroniani;*[178] but finding that this

176. Exodus 18:1–24, 19:16, and 20:18.

177. I.e., Jethro.

178. The Jethronian magistracy. This was a Biblical topic of great political moment in mid-seventeenth-century England, although by the mid-eighteenth century it had become of only antiquarian interest (e.g., Moses Lowman, *A Dissertation on the Civil Government of the Hebrews* [1740], pp. 163–64). In *Oceana* Harrington, following the line taken by Hobbes in book 3 of *Leviathan* (Pocock, *Harrington,* p. 79) and guided in Hebraic and Talmudic learning by John Selden's *De Synedriis* (1652–54), had emphasized that "the republic of Israel was established less through divine revelations made to Moses, than through human reason in the advice given to Moses by Jethro the Midianite" (Pocock, *Harrington,* p. 47; for examples from *Oceana,* see pp. 177, 209, 305; for examples from *The Prerogative of Popular Government,* see pp. 411, 485, 496, 532–33, 547, 572–73). The significance of this interpretation of chapter 18 of Exodus is that, by insisting that the constitutional design of the republic of Israel had been the handiwork of Jethro the Midianite—who was a Gentile and a heathen—it destroys the argument that the political institutions of the republic of Israel possessed a divine sanction. On the contrary, they emerge as purely human contrivances. Conversely, if it can be assumed that God worked through Jethro the Midianite, that might open a path toward the reconciliation of divine providence

Provision was not sufficient, complained to God of the difficulty he had, to make that State of Affairs hold together; God was pleased to order him to let seventy Elders be appointed for a Senate, but yet the Congregation of the Lord continued still and acted: And by the severall soundings of the Trumpets, either the Senate or popular Assembly were called together, or both; so that this Government was the same with all other *Democracies*, consisting of a Principal Magistrate, a Senate, and a People Assembled together, not by Representation, but in a body. Now for *Romulus*, it is very plain, that he was no more then the first Officer of the Commonwealth, whatever he was called, and that he was chosen (as your *Doge* is) [179] for Life; and when the last of those seven Kings [180] usurpt the place, that is, did reign *injussu Populi*,[181] and excercise the Government Tyrannically, the People

---

and human prudential wisdom. Note one of the questions Harrington posed to the "godly man" at the end of book I of *The Prerogative of Popular Government*: "Whether human prudence be not a creature of God, and to what end God made this creature?" (Pocock, *Harrington*, p. 496). Harrington had crossed swords with Ferne on precisely this point: see *Pian Piano* (ibid., pp. 373–78, 387), and note especially the following passage, referring to and quoting from Exodus 18:17–24, which is particularly close to Neville's wording: "Moses in that of Exodus *hearkens unto the voice of his father-in-law*, Jethro the priest of Midian; *making able men out of Israel heads over the people, rulers of thousands, rulers of hundreds, rulers of fifties, and rulers of tens. And they judged the people at all seasons: the hard causes they brought unto Moses, but every small matter they judged themselves.* These were the Jethronian prefectures, or the courts, afterwards consisting of twenty-three judges, that sat in the gates of every city" (pp. 375–76; cf. *The Art of Lawgiving*, ibid., pp. 628–29 and 652–53). Cf. also Peter Heylyn, *Certamen Epistolare* (1659), pp. 222–23, 265, 287, 290–93, and Sir Henry Vane, *A Needful Corrective* (1659). In the preface to *Observations upon Aristotle's Politiques* (1652), however, Filmer had roundly asserted that we "nowhere find any supreme power given to the people, or to a multitude, in scripture, or ever exercised by them" (Wootton, *Divine Right*, p. 111).

179. "They make him Duke for his life, to render him more Majestick, and like to the Crowned Heads, among whom they are willing he should be reckoned; as also to coax him for the little Power he has, by the Duration of his Dignity: but they choose him always antient, that other pretenders may have hopes to succeed. Besides, old age wanting the Vigor of youth, is not so bold and undertaking" (Amelot de la Houssaie, *Venice*, p. 131).

180. The seven Roman kings were Romulus, Numa Pompilius, Tullus Hostilius, Ancus Marcius, Tarquinius Priscus, Servius Tullius, and Tarquinius Superbus. The Roman monarchy came to an end in 510 B.C., when Tarquinius Superbus and his family were expelled.

181. I.e., without the sanction or authorization of the people.

drove him out[182] (as all People in the World that have Property will do in the like Case, except some extraordinary qualifications in the Prince preserve him for one Age) and afterwards appointed in his room two Magistrates,[183] and made them Annual, which two had the same Command, as well in their Armies as in their Cities, and did not make the least alteration besides, excepting that they chose an Officer that was to perform the Kings Function in certain Sacrifices (which *Numa* appointed to be performed by the King) lest the People should think their Religion were changed: This Officer was called *Rex Sacrificulus*.[184] If you are satisfied, I will go on to the consideration of our Modern States.

Noble Venetian. I am fully answered, and besides am clearly of Opinion, that no Government, whether mixt Monarchy or Commonwealth, can subsist without a Senate,[185] as well from the turbulent State of the *Israel-*

---

182. According to Roman legend, in 510 B.C. Lucius Junius Brutus exploited the rape of Lucretia at the hands of Sextus, the son of the Roman monarch Tarquinius Superbus, to expel the Tarquins and introduce a republic.

183. I.e., the consuls. Following the expulsion of the Tarquins, the military and judicial (but not religious) authority previously wielded by the kings was placed in the hands of the two consuls, elected annually by the people. Cf. Machiavelli, *Discourses*, 1.9: "After the expulsion of the *Tarquins*, there being nothing innovated or altred by the *Romans*, only instead of one perpetual King, they created two annual Consuls" (Machiavelli, *Works*, p. 280).

184. More commonly and correctly, *rex sacrorum*; after the expulsion of the kings, this was the priest whose duty it was to perform some of the king's religious functions (others were assumed by the *pontifex maximus*), particularly certain state sacrifices. In *Discourses* 1.25 Machiavelli had cited the creation of this office following the expulsion of the Tarquins as an example of Roman political wisdom in preserving the shadow and appearance of the old ways when embarking on political reform: "There was an anniversary Sacrifice in *Rome*, in which the Ministry of the King was of necessity required: To salve that defect, the *Romans* created a chief of the said Sacrifice with the Title of Royal Priest (but with subordination to the High Priest) by which Artifice the people were satisfied with their Sacrifice, and took no occasion to complain for the expulsion of their King" (Machiavelli, *Works*, p. 296). This Roman office had also attracted the attention of Harrington in *The Prerogative of Popular Government* (Pocock, *Harrington*, p. 519).

185. Cf. Harrington, *Valerius and Publicola*: "There must be a senate, which amounts to thus much: without a senate there can be no commonwealth; and with a senate there will always be practising upon the liberty of the people" (Pocock, *Harrington*, p. 790). The same stipulation is made in *Aphorisms Political*: "A popular assembly without a senate cannot be wise" (ibid., p. 771).

ites under *Moses* till the *Sanhedrin*[186] was instituted, as from a certain Kingdom of the *Vandals* in *Africa*; where after their Conquest of the Natives, they appointed a Government consisting of a Prince and a Popular Assembly, which latter, within half a year, beat the Kings brains out, he having no bulwark of Nobility or Senate to defend him from them.[187] But I will divert you no longer.

English Gentleman. Sir, you are very right, and we should have spoken something of that before, if it had been the business of this Meeting to Discourse of the particular Models of Government; but intending only to say so much of the Ancient Policy as to shew what Government in General is, and upon what Basis it stands, I think I have done it sufficiently to make

186. Or "sanhedrim"; among the Hebrews, the highest court of justice and the supreme council in Jerusalem. In equating the sanhedrin with a senate, Neville was again following Harrington's *Oceana*: "The senate of Israel, called in the Old Testament the seventy elders and in the New the Sanhedrim, which word is usually translated the Council, was appointed by God and consisted of seventy elders besides Moses (Numbers, 11), which were at the first elected by the people (Deuteronomy, 1), but in what manner is rather intimated (Numbers, 11) than shown" (Pocock, *Harrington*, p. 176; cf. pp. 184–85, 189, 260, 287, 294, 376–78, 421, 496, 500, 519–23, 535–38, 547, 573–77, 616, 618, 620, 628–30, 638, 645–52, 675, 730–31, 742). Harrington's repeated equation of the sanhedrin with a senate is an aspect of his denial that the political institutions of the kingdom of Israel shared in the authority of divine revelation (Pocock, *Harrington*, p. 80).

187. An example drawn most immediately from *Oceana*, where Harrington had also been struck by the evidence it supplied for the necessity of a senate, or aristocratic element, even in a monarchy: "For if there have been anciently some governments called kingdoms—as one of the Goths in Spain, and another of the Vandals in Africa—where the king ruled without a nobility, and by a council of the people only, it is expressly said by the authors that mention them that the kings were but the captains, and that the people not only gave them laws, but deposed them as often as they pleased; nor is it possible in reason that it should be otherwise in like cases, wherefore these were either no monarchies, or had greater flaws in them than any other" (Pocock, *Harrington*, p. 179, cf. p. 201; although see also pp. 438 and 459 for historical examples which seem to point in the opposite direction). Rycaut traces the notion that an aristocracy serves the function of preventing a monarchy from lapsing into despotism back to Bacon's *Essayes*: Rycaut, *Present State*, p. 69, and Bacon, *Essayes*, p. 41, "Of Nobility." Shaftesbury had made the same point in the House of Lords on 20 October 1675: "There is no *Prince* that every Govern'd without *Nobility* or an *Army*: If you will not have one, you must have t'other, or the *Monarchy* cannot long support, or keep it self from tumbling into a *Democratical Republique*" (*State-Tracts*, vol. 1, p. 59).

way for the understanding of our own, at least when I have said something
of the Policies which are now extant; and that with your favour I will do. I
shall need say little now of those Commonwealths, which however they
came by their Liberty, either by Arms or Purchase, are now much-what[188]
under the same kind of Policy as the Ancients were. In *Germany*, the Free
Towns, and many Princes make up the Body of a Commonwealth called
the Empire, of which the Emperour is Head; this General Union hath its
Diets or Parliaments, where they are all represented, and where all things
concerning the Safety and Interest of *Germany* in General, or that belong to
Peace and War, are Transacted; these Diets never intermeddle with the
particular Concerns or Policies of those Princes or States that make it up,
leaving to them their particular Soveraignties: The several Imperial Cities,
or Commonwealths, are divided into two kinds, *Lubeck's* Law, and *Collen's*
Law,[189] which being the same exactly with the ancient *Democracies* and *Optimacies*, I will say no more of them.[190] The Government of *Swizerland*,[191]

188. I.e., pretty much, pretty well, to a considerable degree (*OED*, s.v. "much-
what," B).

189. Mercantile codes linked to Lübeck and Cologne.

190. Cf. Harrington's disparaging comments on the German constitution in *The
Prerogative of Popular Government* (Pocock, *Harrington*, p. 456). Harrington speaks
of the German and Swiss constitutions together in *A System of Politics* (Pocock,
Harrington, pp. 840–41). Both Harrington and Neville were following Machiavelli,
who had written in similar terms in *Discourses*, 2.19: "That part of *Germany* of which
I now speak . . . was subject to the Empire of the *Romans*: But when afterwards
that Empire began to decline, and the title of the Empire was removed into that
Province, Those that were the wealthiest and most powerful of the Cities (taking
advantage of the pusillanimity or distresses of their Emperors) made themselves
free, paying only a small annual Rent for the redemption of their liberties; which
being permitted, by degrees all those Cities which held immediately of the Emperour, and had no dependance upon any body else, redeemed themselves in that manner" (Machiavelli, *Works*, pp. 357–58; quotation on p. 358). Machiavelli's comments
in chapter 10 of *The Prince* are also apposite: "The Towns in *Germany* are many of
them free; though their Country and district be but small, yet they obey the Emperor but when they please, and are in no awe, either of him, or any other Prince of
the Empire, because they are all so well fortified, every one looks upon the taking
of any one of them as a work of great difficulty and time" (Machiavelli, *Works*,
p. 213). Cf. also "The State of Germany" ("Rapporto delle cose dell'Alemagna"), a
short text written in 1508 (Machiavelli, *Works*, pp. 265–67).

191. In 1681, Switzerland was an example of a commonwealth or republic in that
it consisted of a confederacy of the valley communities, or cantons, of the central

and the Seven Provinces of the *Low-Countries*[192] were made up in haste, to Unite them against Persecution and Oppression, and to help to defend themselves the better, which they both have done very gallantly and successfully: They seem to have taken their Pattern from the *Grecians*, who when their Greatness began to decline, and the several Tyrants[193] who succeeded *Alexander* began to press hard upon them, were forced to League themselves (yet in severall Confederacies, as that of the *Etolians*, that of the *Achaians*,[194] &c.) for their mutual defence. The *Swisses* consist of Thirteen Soveraignties; some Cities which are most *Aristocraticall*, and some Provinces which have but a Village for their head Township. These are all *Democracies*, and are Govern'd all by the Owners of Land, who Assemble as our Free-Holders do at the County-Court. These have their General Diets, as in *Germany*. The Government of the United Provinces has for its Foundation the Union of *Utrecht*, made in the beginning of their standing upon their Guard against the Cruelty and Oppression of the *Spaniard*,[195]

Alps. This constitution lasted until 1798, when the revolutionary French government conquered Switzerland and suppressed its constitution.

192. Another contemporary example of republican government. William Aglionby's *The Present State of the United Provinces* (1671), which Neville had included in his booklist, had described the constitution of the Low Countries in detail. In *Oceana* Harrington had also linked the constitutions of Switzerland and the Low Countries (Pocock, *Harrington*, pp. 177–78).

193. I.e., the so-called "Diadochi," the rulers who succeeded to various parts of the empire of Alexander the Great. Conspicuous among them were Craterus and Antipater. The surprising security of tenure enjoyed by the successors of Alexander after his death is the subject of chapter 4 of *The Prince* (Machiavelli, *Works*, pp. 203–4).

194. The Aetolian League was a confederacy of the cities of Aetolia set up after the death of Alexander the Great in 323 B.C., which in time emerged as the chief rival to Macedonia. The Achaean League comprised the cities of Achaea in the Peloponnese that had seceded from Macedonia in 275 B.C. After a period of increasing power and influence on the Peloponnese, it was finally dissolved by the Romans in 146 B.C. For Machiavelli's comparisons of the Swiss with the Aetolian and Achaean Leagues, see *Discourses*, 2.4 (Machiavelli, *Works*, pp. 338–39).

195. The Union of Utrecht was signed on 23 January 1579 by the four northern provinces of the Low Countries (Holland, Zeeland, Utrecht, and Groningen), and signalled their determination to resist the oppressive government of Hapsburg Spain. For commentary and analysis, see Aglionby, *United Provinces*, pp. 60–70. The treaty was notable for its endorsement of religious toleration.

and patcht up in haste; and seeming to be compos'd only for necessity, as a state of War, has made Modern Statesmen Conjecture[196] that it will not be very practicable in time of Peace, and Security. At their General Diet, which is called the States General, do intervene the Deputies of the Seven Provinces, in what number their Principals please; but all of them have but one Vote, which are by consequence Seven, and every one of the Seven hath a Negative; so that nothing can pass without the Concurrence of the whole Seven. Every one of these Provinces have a Counsel or Assembly of their own, called the States Provincial, who send and Instruct their Deputies to the States-General, and perform other Offices belonging to the Peace and Quiet of the Province. These Deputies to the States Provincial, are sent by several Cities of which every Province consists, and by the Nobility of the Province, which hath one Voice only: The Basis of the Government lies in these Cities, which are every of them a distinct Soveraignty; neither can the States of the Province, much less the States General, intrench in the least upon their Rights, nor so much as intermeddle with the Government of their Cities, or Administration of Justice, but only treat of what concerns their mutual Defence, and their Payments towards it. Every one of these Cities is a Soveraignty, governed by an *Optimacy*, consisting of the chief Citizens, which upon death are supplyed by new ones Elected by themselves; these are called the *Urnuscaperie* or *Herne*,[197] which Council has continued to Govern those Towns, time out of mind; even in the times of their Princes, who were then the Soveraigns; for without the consent of him, or his Deputy, called State Holder,[198] nothing could be concluded in those days. Since they have Instituted an artificial Minister of their own, whom they still call State-Holder, and make choice of him in their Provincial As-

196. Aglionby, *United Provinces*, pp. 174–78, attributes such a gloomy prognostication concerning the durability of the government of the United Provinces to Cardinal Giulio Bentivoglio (1577–1644), whose history of the wars in Flanders, *Della guerra di Fiandra* (1632–39), had been translated by Henry, Earl of Monmouth, in 1652. Aglionby himself took a more positive view: "'Tis certainly a great vanity to go about to dispute about futures; yet the Form and Government, and present felicity of a State, may give us leave to give a guess at its future happiness" (p. 174).

197. On the oligarchic nature of the urban government of the United Provinces, see Aglionby, *United Provinces*, pp. 136–40.

198. I.e., Stadtholder, the governor-general of the United Provinces; cf. Aglionby, *United Provinces*, pp. 100–111.

semblies, and for Form sake defer something to him, as the Approbation of their Skepen[199] and other Magistrates, and some other Matters: This has been continued in the Province of *Holland*, which is the chief Province in the Succession of the Princes of *Orange*, and in the most of the others too: The rest have likewise chosen some other of the House of *Nassaw*.[200] This Government (so oddly set together, and so compos'd of a State, intended for a Monarchy, and which, as Almanacks Calculated for one Meridian, are made in some sort to serve for another, is by them continued in these several *Aristocracies*) may last for a time, till Peace and Security, together with the abuse which is like to happen in the choice of the *Herne*, when they shall Elect persons of small note into their Body, upon Vacancies, for Kindred or Relation, rather than such as are of Estate and eminency, or that otherwise abuse their power in the execution of it, and then it is believed, and reasonably enough, that those People (great in wealth, and very acute in the knowledge of their own Interest) will find out a better Form of Government, or make themselves a prey to some great Neighbour-Prince in the attempting it; and this in case they in the mean time escape Conquest from this great and powerfull King of *France*,[201] who at this time gives Law to Christendom. I have nothing now left to keep me from the Modern Monarchies, but the most famous Commonwealth of *Venice*, of which it would be presumption for me to say any thing whilst you are present.

Noble Venetian. You may very safely go on if you please; for I believe Strangers understand the Speculative part of our Government, better than we do; and the Doctrine of the Ballat [202] which is our chiefe excellency:

199. Or "schepen"; a Dutch alderman or petty magistrate (*OED*, s.v. "schepen," quoting this passage).

200. The dominant aristocratic family of the United Provinces.

201. I.e., Louis XIV. In the Franco-Dutch War of 1672–78 France had made some gains of territory on its northern borders but had also been required to return some of its conquests to the Dutch. This war had established France for the time being as the dominant military power on the continent.

202. A celebrated feature of the Venetian constitution, designed to safeguard the election of magistrates from the distorting effects of faction: "The ballot as it is used in Venice consists of a lot, whence derives the right of proposing, and of an unseen way of suffrage or resolving" (Harrington, *The Art of Lawgiving* [1659], in Pocock, *Harrington*, p. 612). "The elaborate devices of indirect elections, through the use of ballot-boxes which combined selection with sortition, were intended to ensure a

For I have read many Descriptions of our Frame, which have taught me something in it which I knew not before; particularly, *Donato Gianotti* the *Florentine*,[203] to whom I refer those who are curious to know more of our Orders, for we that manage the Mechanical part of the Government are like Horses who know their Track well enough, without considering *East* or *West*, or what business they go about. Besides, it would be very tedious, and very needless, to make any Relation of our Model, with the several Counsels that make it up, and would be that which you have not done in Treating of any other Government: what we have said is enough to shew what beginning we had, and that serves your turn, for we who are called Nobility, and who manage the State, are the Descendents of

---

number of goals. They integrated the leadership of the Few with the evaluation of the Many; they prevented the formation of interest groups and factions by obliging the individual to cast his vote in privacy and in ignorance of the votes of others, as ignorant of his and chosen partly at random. He was to be compelled to address himself solely to the common good, and these were mechanisms intended to ensure that even his selfish and irrational actions were cancelled out and brought to operate to that end" (Pocock, *Harrington*, p. 68). Neville's friend James Harrington had specified balloting in *Oceana* and wrote a short description of the Venetian institution of the ballot (Pocock, *Harrington*, pp. 241–50 and 361–67). For praise of the institution, see Hay, *Policy*, pp. 60–61. For a more disenchanted account, see Amelot de la Houssaie, *Venice*, pp. 7–17, especially "They pretend to do all by Lots; but it is not with little balls of white stuff, but with large presents quite contrary to their promises" (p. 17).

203. Donato Giannotti (1492–1573), republican Italian political writer and playwright; one of the leaders of the Florentine Republic of 1527; author of *Libro de la republica de Vinitiani* (Rome, 1540); admired by Harrington (Pocock, *Harrington*, p. 161). Lewes Lewkenor had supplemented his translation of Contarini with material taken from Giannotti (Contarini, *Venice*, p. 150). Like Harrington and Neville himself, Giannotti had turned his mind to the post-Machiavellian problem of how a Venetian constitutional architecture might be adapted to a popular government with a citizen militia, although his "Della Repubblica Fiorentina" would not be published until 1721 (Pocock, *Harrington*, p. 70 and n. 3). It was from Giannotti that Harrington seems to have derived his understanding of the periodization of ancient and modern prudence: "These two times (that of ancient and that of modern prudence), the one, as is computed by Giannotti, ending with the liberty of Rome, the other beginning with the arms of Caesar (which, extinguishing liberty, became the translation of ancient into modern prudence, introduced into the Roman Empire by the Goths and Vandals)" (Pocock, *Harrington*, p. 401; cf. pp. 711–12). For Harrington's understanding of the changes in Roman land tenure which had allowed the Goths and Vandals to gain purchase on the empire, see Pocock, *Harrington*, p. 580.

the first Inhabitants, and had therefore been a *Democracy*, if a numerous Flock of Strangers (who are contented to come and live amongst us as Subjects) had not swelled our City, and made the Governing party seem but a handfull; so that we have the same foundations that all other *Aristocracies* have, who govern but one City, and have no Territory but what they Govern Provincially; and our People not knowing where to have better Justice, are very well contented to live amongst us, without any share in the Managing of Affairs; yet we have power to Adopt whom we please into our Nobility, and I believe that in the time of the *Roman* greatness, there were five for one of the Inhabitants who were written in no Tribe,[204] but look'd upon as Strangers, and yet that did not vitiate their *Democracy*, no more than our Citizens and Common People can hurt our *Optimacy*; all the difficulty in our Administration, hath been to regulate our own Nobility, and to bridle their faction and ambition, which can alone breed a Disease in the Vital part of our Government, and this we do by most severe Laws, and a very rigorous execution of them.

Doctor. Sir, I was thinking to Interpose concerning the Propriety of Lands in the Territory of *Padua*,[205] which I hear is wholly in the possession of the Nobility of *Venice.*

204. A reference to the institution of the early Roman Republic created by Servius Tullius, who divided the population of Rome into originally twenty and eventually thirty-five tribes or territorial districts, which were the basis of the rights and duties of citizenship.

205. Padua was under virtually constant Venetian rule from 1405 until 1797 and was clearly a restive city, as John Evelyn had found in 1645: "From hence I return'd to *Padoa*, when that Towne was so infested with Souldiers, that many houses were broken open in the night, some Murders committed; The *Nunns* next our lodging disturb'd, so as we were forc'd to be upon our guard, with *Pistols*, & other fire armes to defend our doores: And indeede the students themselves take a barbarous liberty in the Evenings, when they go to their strumpets, to stop all that go by the house, where any of their Companions in folly, are with them: This costome they call *Chi va li*; so as the streetes are very dangerous, when the Evenings grow dark; nor is it easy to reforme an intollerable usage, where there are so many strangers, of severall Nations" (Evelyn, *Diary*, vol. 2, pp. 471–72). The soldiers infesting the town had presumably been raised to serve in the war with the Turks: see below. In 1676 Padua had figured in an English context as the place of confinement of the lunatic Thomas Howard (1627–77), Duke of Norfolk (Grey, *Debates*, vol. 4, pp. 98–101, 217–23, 253–55, 342–43).

Noble Venetian. Our Members have very good Estates there, yet nothing but what they have paid very well for, no part of that Country, or of any other Province, having been shar'd amongst us as in other Conquests: 'Tis true, that the *Paduans* having ever been the most revengeful People of *Italy*, could not be deterr'd from those execrable and treacherous Murders which were every day committed, but by a severe Execution of the Laws as well against their Lives as Estates: And as many of their Estates as were Confiscated, were (during our necessities in the last War with the *Turks*)[206] exposed to sale, and sold to them that offered most, without any consideration of the persons purchasing; But it is very true that most of them came into the hands of our Nobility, they offering more than any other, by reason that their sober and frugal living, and their being forbidden all manner of Traffick, makes them have no way of employing the Money which proceeds from their Parsimony, and so they can afford to give more than others who may employ their Advance to better profit elsewhere. But I perceive, *Doctor*, by this Question, that you have studied at *Padua*.

Doctor. No really, Sir, the small learning I have was acquired in our own University of *Oxford*, nor was I ever out of this Island.[207]

Noble Venetian. I would you had, Sir, for it would have been a great honour to our Country to have contributed any thing towards so vast a knowledge as you are Possessor of: But I wish that it were your Countrey, or at least the place of your Habitation, that so we might partake not only of your excellent Discourse sometimes, but be the better for your skill, which would make us Immortal.

Doctor. I am glad to see you so well that you can make yourself so merry, but I assure you I am very well here; *England* is a good wholsome Climate for a Physician: But, pray let our Friend go on to his Modern Monarchies.

206. The history of tense relations between Venice and the Ottoman Empire leading up to this war (1645–69) had been circumstantially narrated in Nani, *Affairs of Europe*, passim. The events of the war itself, culminating in the siege and capture of Candia, had been narrated in Rycaut, *History*, pp. 20–281.

207. Both assertions are true of Richard Lower, the acquaintance of Neville's upon whom the character of the Doctor in the dialogue is modelled.

English Gentleman. That is all I have now to do: Those Monarchies are two, Absolute, and Mixt; for the first kind, all that we have knowledge of, except the Empire of the *Turks*, differ so little from the ancient Monarchies of the *Assyrians* and *Persians*, that having given a short Description of them before, it will be needless to say any more of the *Persian*, the *Mogull*, the King of *Pegu*,[208] *China*, *Prestor-John*,[209] or any other the great Men under those Princes, as the *Satrapes*[210] of old; being made so only by their being employed and put into great places and Governments by the Soveraign; But the Monarchy of the Grand Seignior[211] is somthing different;[212] they both agree in this, that the Prince

208. I.e., Burma, or Myanmar. During the seventeenth century Pegu figured prominently in geographical works such as Heylyn's *Cosmographie* (1652), which we know Neville had read: see above, p. 31, nn. 111 and 114, and p. 32, nn. 120 and 121. It was also associated with Dutch trade and the excesses that occasionally attended it: see Dryden, *Amboyna* (1673), p. 22. Harrington had cited an episode from the history of Pegu as an example of the vulnerability to military coups of polities that rejected the principle of rotation (James Harrington, *The Prerogative of Popular Government* [1657], pp. 129–30).

209. A legendary Christian patriarch supposed to rule over a vast kingdom, sometimes located in the Far East, sometimes in Ethiopia. He was associated at this time with immense wealth and the exorbitant desires of despotic rulers; cf. Priolo, *History of France*, p. 78.

210. I.e., the governors of provinces under the ancient Persian monarchy; frequently with a connotation of tyranny or ostentatious splendor (*OED*, s.v. "satrap," 1 and 2).

211. I.e., the Ottoman Sultan; also known as the Great Turk or the Mogul; for a roughly contemporary definition, see Henry Curzon, *The Universal Library*, 2 vols. (1712), vol. 1, p. 194. At this time in England "Grand Seignior" was a byword for despotic, autocratic rule and had recently been specified as such by John Locke in his *Second Treatise*, §91 (Locke, *Two Treatises*, p. 326). It was with these connotations in mind that Charles II had assured the Earl of Essex in 1673 that "he did not wish to be like a Grand Signior, with some mutes about him, and bags of bowstrings to strangle men, as he had a mind to it" (Burnet, *History*, vol. 1, p. 345). Cf. "The Constitution of our English Government (the best in the World) is no Arbitrary *Tyranny*, like the Turkish Grand Seignior's, or the French King's, whose Wills (or rather *Lusts*) dispose of the Lives and Fortunes of their unhappy Subjects" (Henry Care, *English Liberties* [1680], p. 1; see also p. 149; cf. Sidney, *Discourses*, p. 58). In Parliament on 14 May 1689 Sir Robert Cotton, speaking of the reprisals that had followed Monmouth's rebellion in 1685, would say that those "in the *West* did see such a Shambles, as made them think they had a *Turk*, rather than a Christian, to their King" (Grey, *Debates*, vol. 9, p. 246).

212. Neville here echoes the subtitle of the opening chapter of Rycaut, *Present State*: "*The Constitution of the* Turkish Government *being different from most others*

is in both absolute Proprietor of all the Lands, (excepting in the Kingdom of *Egypt*, of which I shall say somthing anon) but the diversity lies
in the Administration of the Property; the other Emperours as well
Ancient as Modern using to manage the Revenue of the several Towns,
and Parishes, as our Kings, or the Kings of *France* do; that is, keep it in
their hands, and Administer it by Officers: And so you may read that
Xerxes King of *Persia* allowed the Revenue of so many Villages to
Themistocles,[213] which Assignations are practiced at this day, both to
publick and to private uses, by the present Monarchs. But the *Turks*,
when they invaded the broken Empire of the *Arabians*,[214] did not at first

---

in the World, hath need of peculiar Maxims, and Rules, whereon to establish and conform it self" (Rycaut, *Present State*, p. 1). The exceptional nature of the political
institutions of the Ottoman Empire had also been remarked by Machiavelli in *The
Prince*, chapter 19: "This Government of the *Soldans* is different from all other
Monarchies" (Machiavelli, *Works*, p. 227). Harrington too had been fascinated by
the politics of the Ottoman Empire, finding that "the policy or superstructures of
all absolute monarchs, more particularly of the eastern empires, are not only contained but meliorated in the Turkish government" (*The Art of Lawgiving* [1659], in
Pocock, *Harrington*, p. 610). For Harrington the Turks do not provide a model for
the English to follow, but rather illustrate the different mode of government which
arises from a different distribution of property. Harrington had also anticipated
Neville in relating the character of Turkish absolutism to the different kinds of
military force available to the Sultan.

213. Themistocles (c. 524–459 B.C.), Athenian statesman and soldier, who fought
at Marathon (490 B.C.) and was the architect of the great Athenian sea victory at
Salamis (480 B.C.). Themistocles was ostracized c. 471 B.C. and sought refuge in Persia, where either Xerxes or his son Artaxerxes I was on the throne (for the uncertainty, see Plutarch, "Themistocles," 27). Thucydides specifies the grants of land and
revenue made to Themistocles by the Persians, to which Neville here refers:
"μνημεῖον μὲν οὖν αὐτοῦ ἐν Μαγνησίᾳ ἐστὶ τῇ Ἀσιανῇ ἐν τῇ ἀγορᾷ· ταύτης γὰρ
ἦρχε τῆς χώρας, δόντος βασιλέως αὐτῷ Μαγνησίαν μὲν ἄρτον, ἣ προσέφερε
πεντήκοντα τάλαντα τοῦ ἐνιαυτοῦ, Λάμψακον δὲ οἶνον (ἐδόκει γὰρ πολυοινότατον
τῶν τότε εἶναι), Μυοῦντα δὲ ὄψον"; "There is a monument to him [i.e., Themisto-
cles] at Magnesia in Asia, in the marketplace; for he was governor of this country,
the King having given him, for bread, Magnesia, which brought in a revenue of fifty
talents a year, for wine, Lampsacus, reputed to be the best wine country of all places
at that time; and Myus for meat" (Thucydides, *Peloponnesian War*, 1.138).

214. The Turks originated beyond the Caspian Sea and conquered Persia in 1038.
"This wandring and vnregarded people, but now the terrour of the world, thus first
seated in ARMENIA: long time there liued in that wide countrey, after their rude
and woonted manner (from which the Turcoman nation their posteritie in that

make any great alteration in their Policy, till the House of *Ottoman* the present Royal Family did make great Conquests in *Asia*, and afterwards in *Greece*;[215] whence they might possibly take their present way of dividing their conquered Territories; for they took the same course which the *Goths* and other Modern People had used with their Conquered Lands in *Europe*, upon which they planted Military Colonies, by dividing them amongst the Souldiers for their pay or maintenance.[216] These Shares were called by them *Timarr's*, which signifies *Benefices*, but differ'd in this only from the *European* Knights-Fees, that these last Originally were Hereditary, and so Property was maintained, whereas amongst the *Ottomans*, they were meerly at will; and they enjoyed their shares whilst they remained the *Sultan's* Souldiers, and no longer; being turn'd out both of his Service, and of their *Timarr's*, when he pleases.[217]

---

place, euen at this day as we said much differeth not) and not onely notably defended the countrey thus by them at the first possessed, but still incroching farther and farther, and gaining by other mens harmes, became at length dreadfull vnto their neighbours, and of some fame also farther off: whereunto the effeminat cowardise of those delicate people of ASIA, with whom they had to do gaue no lesse furtherance, than their owne valour; being neuerthelesse an hardie rough people, though not much skilfull or trained vp in the feats of war" (Knolles, *Turkes*, p. 3).

215. The dynasty of the Ottomans was founded by Othman, who reigned from 1299 to 1326. Between 1299 (the invasion of Nicomedia) and 1341, when they first passed into Europe, the Turks made wide and rapid conquests in Asia Minor. The Turkish conquest of Greece—apart from the city of Constantinople—was substantially complete by the end of the fourteenth century. Neville is here presumably relying upon Richard Knolles, since Rycaut's volumes do not address Turkish history before 1623.

216. Neville here describes the feudal system, in which subjects held land in return for military service. A few years later Andrew Fletcher would describe what he saw as the liberal advantages of feudalism: *"This constitution of government put the sword into the hands of the subject, because the vassals depended more immediately on the barons than on the king, which effectually secured the freedom of those governments. For the barons could not make use of their power to destroy those limited monarchies, without destroying their own grandeur; nor could the king invade their privileges, having no other forces than the vassals of his own demesnes to rely upon for his support in such an attempt"* (Andrew Fletcher, *Discourse of Government* [1698], pp. 7–8).

217. Cf. Rycaut, *Present State*, pp. 172–82, which provides a very detailed account of the timariots: "The whole Turkish Militia then is of two sorts; one that receives maintenance from certain Lands or Farms bestowed on them by the Grand Signior; others that receive their constant pay in ready mony. The great

This doubtless had been the best and firmest Monarchy in the World, if they could have stayed here, and not had a Mercenary Army [218] be-

---

nerve or sinew of the Turkish Empire is that of the first rank, which are of two sorts, viz. Zaims, which are like Barons in some Countries; and Timariots, who may be compared to the Decumani amongst the Romans. Those of the second sort, paid out of the Grand Signiors Treasury, are Spahees, Janizaries, Armoures Gunners, and Sea-Souldiers called Levens, who have no pay for life, or are enrolled amongst the military Orders; but only make an Agreement for five or six thousand Aspers for their voyage, which being ended, they are disbanded" (Rycaut, Present State, p. 172). On the tenure of the timariots, see Rycaut, Present State, p. 174. This feature of the Ottoman political and military establishment had been applied to European feudalism since the sixteenth century: Pocock, Harrington, p. 48.

218. I.e., the Janissaries, an elite corps in the army of the Ottoman Empire from the late fourteenth to the early nineteenth century: "About this time [1360] . . . Zinderlu Chelil, then Cadilesher or chiefe Iustice amongst the Turks, but afterwards better knowne by the name of Cairadin Bassa; by the commaundement of Amurath, tooke order that euerie fifth captiue of the Christians, being aboue fifteen yeeres old, should bee taken vp for the king, as by law due vnto him: and if the number were vnder fiue, then to pay vnto the king for euerie head 25 aspers, by way of tribute: appointing officers for collecting both of such captiues and tribute mony, of whom the aforesaid Cara Rustemes himselfe was chiefe, as first deuiser of the matter. By which meanes great numbers of Christian youths were brought to the court as the kings captiues, which by the counsel of the same Zinderlu Chelil, were distributed amongst the Turkish husbandmen in ASIA, there to learne the Turkish language, religion, and manners: where after they had been brought vp in all painefull labour and trauaile by the space of two or three yeeres, they were called vnto the court, and choice made of the better sort of them to attend vpon the person of the prince, or to serue him in his warres: where they dayly practising all feats of actiuitie, are called by the name of Ianizars (that is to say, new souldiers.) This was the first beginning of the Ianizars vnder this Sultan Amurath the first, . . . so that in processe of time they be grown to that greatnes as that they are oftentimes right dreadfull vnto the great Turke himselfe: after whose death, they haue sometimes preferred to the empire such of the emperours sonnes as they best liked, without respect of prerogatiue of age, contrarie to the will of the great Sultan himselfe" (Knolles, Turkes, p. 191; cf. Rycaut, Present State, pp. 190–99). In the seventeenth century the Janissaries were notorious for frequently taking a lead in palace coups (see, e.g., Harrington, Oceana, p. 31; cf. pp. 98 and 278; and Sidney, Discourses, p. 155). In 1628, in debates preceding the Petition of Right, deputy-lieutenants were compared to "janizaries" (Schwoerer, Armies, p. 26). "Janisary" (as it was commonly spelled) was a frequent term of abuse for the army during the Civil Wars, from both Royalists and more radical fringes of the Parliamentarians themselves: William Thompson, Englands Freedome, Souldiers Rights (1647), p. 6; Anonymous, Westminster Projects (1648), p. 4 ("their Grandee Janisaries, to wit Sul-

sides, which have often (like the Praetorians [219] in the time of the *Roman Tyrants*) made the Palace and the Serraglio the Shambles of their

---

tan *Cromwell*, Bashaw *Ireton*, &c"); John Lilburne, *A Whip* (1648), p. 25; Charles Collins, *An Outcry of the Young Men and Apprentices of London* (1649), p. 3; Anonymous, *A Parliamenters Petition to the Army* (1659), p. 6; Anonymous, *The Dignity of Kingship Asserted* (1660), p. 148 ("This God brought upon us for our great *sins*, one while giving up the whole *Nation*, the *Lords* and *majority* of the *Commons*, to the *odious servitude* of a *perjur'd Rump*, under whom, besides *monstrous Taxes*, [which they extorted to maintain their *Janisaries* the *Apostate Souldiers*, by whose *mutiny* and *rebellion*, they were first *constituted*, and by their *assistance* kept up (in *name* and *notion*) as the *Supreme Authority* of *England*]"); John Gauden, *A Sermon* (1660), p. 23; Francis Gregory, *The Last Counsel* (1660), p. 1; Samuel Butler, *Another Ballad Called the Libertines Lampoone* (1674), p. 1 ("*Cromwel and his* Janisaries"); cf. Pocock, *Harrington*, p. 10, for the occurrence of this language in *A Copy of a Letter* (1656) (and see below, appendix A, p. 327). This mid-century language of abuse had been revived in the late 1680s and thereafter: see Gilbert Burnet, *The Ill Effects of Animosities among Protestants* (1688), p. 11; Anonymous, *The Mystery of Iniquity* (1689), p. 18; Sir Roger Manley, *The History of the Rebellions* (1691), p. 155; John Tutchin, *A New Martyrology* (1693).

219. The Praetorians were the personal bodyguards of the Roman emperors and consisted of picked veterans who enjoyed better pay and conditions than ordinary legionaries. The Praetorians had been created by Augustus and originally comprised nine cohorts each of 1,000 men. At first stationed in different parts of Italy, the Praetorians were eventually concentrated by Sejanus into a single camp on the north side of Rome, which increased their effectiveness as an instrument of internal intimidation. In chapter 4 of book 1 of *The Art of War* Machiavelli had identified the creation of the Praetorian corps as a turning point in the trajectory of Roman decline: "For *Octavian* first, and afterwards *Tiberius* (preferring their private power before the profit of the publick) began to disarm the people (that thereby they might have them more easily at command) and to keep standing Armies upon the Frontiers of their Empire. But because they thought them insufficient to curb the people, and awe the Senate of Rome; they established another Army (which they called the *Pretorian*) which was quartered always about the City, and intended as a guard. But when afterwards the Emperors permitted them who were listed in those Bands, to lay aside all other professions, and devote themselves to War, they grew insolent immediately, and became not only terrible to the Senate, but pernicious to the Emperors, insomuch that many of them were put to death by the fury and insolence of those Soldiers, who created, and deposed their Emperors as they pleased; and sometimes it fell out that at the same time several Emperors were created by the several Armies, which occasioned the division first, and by degrees the destruction of the Empire" (Machiavelli, *Works*, p. 440; cf. *Discourses*, 1.10, in ibid., p. 281). Cf. Harrington, *Oceana*, p. 45; *Copy of a Letter*, p. 3; and Sidney, *Discourses*, p. 155, and pp. 455 and 508 (on the sufferings of the Romans under the sway of a "mad corrupted soldiery"). These episodes of

Princes; whereas if the *Timariots*, as well *Spahis* [220] or Horse, as Foot, had been brought together to Guard the Prince by Courses [221] (as they used to do King *David*) as well as they are to fight for the Empire; this horrid flaw and inconvenience in their Government had been wholly avoided. For though these are not planted upon entire Property as *David's* were, [222] (those being in the nature of Trained-Bands) yet the remoteness of their Habitations from the Court, and the Factions of the great City, and their desire to repair home, and to find all things quiet at their return, would have easily kept them from being infected with that cursed Disease of Rebellion against their Soveraign, upon whose favour they depend for the continuance of their livelihood: Whereas the *Janizaries* are for life, and are sure to be in the same Employment under the next Successor; so sure, that no Grand Seignior can, or dares go about to Disband them, the suspicion of intending such a thing having caused the death of more than one of their Emperours. [223] But I shall go to the limited Monarchies.

---

ancient history might occasionally be recalled in parliamentary debate (see, e.g., Grey, *Debates*, vol. 2, pp. 221 and 397).

220. Spahis were paid troops who "receive their constant pay from the Grand Signiors Treasury. . . . [They] may not improperly be termed the Gentry of the *Ottoman* Empire, because they are commonly better educated, courteous and refined, than the other sort of Turks" (Rycaut, *Present State*, p. 184).

221. I.e., a set of persons appointed to serve in their turn along with another set or sets (*OED*, s.v. "course," 32). At this time it was a word often used in connection with the political principle of rotation, as in Harrington's *The Prerogative of Popular Government* (1657), pp. 81, 103, 104, 107, and 131.

222. 1 Chronicles 27:1. The same Biblical text had been cited by Harrington in *The Prerogative of Popular Government* (1657), p. 104.

223. Rycaut had provided a careful analysis of the reasons why the Janizaries were now a source of instability in the Ottoman Empire: "But as there is no question but a standing Army of veterane and well-disciplin'd Souldiers must be always useful and advantageous to the Interest of a Prince; so, on the contrary, negligence in the Officers, and remissness of Government, produces that licentiousness and wrestiness in the Souldiery, as betrays them to all the disorders which are dangerous, and of evill consequence to the welfare of a State. And so it hath fared with the *Ottoman* Empire, which rising only by the power of Arms, and established on the blood of many valiant and daring Captains, gave Priviledges, Honours, and Riches to the Militia, and at all times encouraged their Prowess and forwardness by Rewards, and connivance at their Crimes; by which indulgence

Doctor. But pray, before you do so, Inform us something of the *Roman* Emperours: Had they the whole Dominion or Property of the Lands of *Italy?*

English Gentleman. The *Roman* Emperours I reckon amongst the Tyrants, for so amongst the *Greeks* were called those Citizens who usurpt the Governments of their Commonwealths, and maintain'd it by force, without endeavouring to Found or Establish it, by altering the Property of Lands, as not imagining that their Children could ever hold it after them, in which they were not deceived: So that it is plain that the *Roman* Empire was not a natural but a violent Government. The reasons why it lasted longer than ordinarily Tyrannies do, are many; First, because *Augustus* the first Emperour kept up the Senate, and so for his time cajold them with this bait of Imaginary Power, which might not have sufficed neither to have kept him from the fate of his Uncle, but that there had been so many Revolutions and bloody wars between, that all Mankind was glad to repose and take breath for a while under any Government that could protect them.[224] And he gain'd the service of these Senators

---

and impunity, these men ill-principled in rules of Virtue, and unequally bearing prosperity, and the favour of the Prince, have for a long time been gathering a flock of ill humours ready to receive any contagion of seditious design, and to maintain it with an impudence constant to the *Janizaries* for some ages, which may equal the levity of the Roman Souldiery, untill they shamelessly set their Empire to sale, and forgot both their old obedience to the Senate, and reverence to their new Emperors" (Rycaut, *Present State*, pp. 196–97). Cf. *Copy of a Letter*, pp. 3 and 11.

224. Caius Julius Caesar Augustus (63 B.C.–A.D. 14), adopted son of Julius Caesar and the first *princeps* of Rome. The strategy Neville here imputes to Augustus, whereby republican forms and language were used to camouflage an underlying despotism, is expressed in general terms in Machiavelli's *Discourses*, 1.25: "He who desires to set up a new form of Government in a Common-wealth, that shall be lasting, and acceptable to the people, is with great caution to preserve at least some shadow and resemblance of the old, That the people may (if possible) be insensible of the innovation; for the generality of Mankind do not penetrate so far into things, but that outward appearance, is as acceptable to them as verity it self" (Machiavelli, *Works*, p. 296; cf. Tacitus, *Annals*, 1.2, where such a policy is implicitly attributed to Augustus). Similar sentiments are to be found in *The Prince*, chapter 3, and particularly chapter 5: "There is nothing more difficult to undertake, more

the rather, because he suffered none to be so but those who had followed his Fortune in the several Civil Wars,[225] and so were engaged to support him for their own preservation; Besides, he confiscated all those who had at any time been proscribed,[226] or sided in any Encounter against him;

---

uncertain to succeed, and more dangerous to manage, than to make ones self Prince, and prescribe new Laws: Because he who innovates in that manner has for his Enemies all those who made any advantage by the Old Laws; and those who expect benefit by the new, will be but cool and luke-warm in his defence; which luke-warmness proceeds from a certain aw for their adversaries who have their old Laws on their side, and partly from a natural incredulity in mankind, which gives credit but slowly to any new thing, unless recommended first by the experiment of success" (Machiavelli, *Works*, p. 200 and pp. 205–6). The explicit application of this Machiavellian insight to Augustus had been made by Hobbes in his *Horae Subsecivae* (1620), pp. 240–41: "This was one occasion which *Augustus* laid hold of to establish the Monarchy, they were weary, their strength abated, and their courages foyled. Yet he would not presently take vnto him the Title belonging to Monarchy, especially not the name of King, but [*nomine Principis sub imperium accepit.*] Euery man that hath an office of command, though neuer so meane, desireth a name that may expresse the full vertue of his place, and most men receiue as great content from Title, as substance. Of this humour *Augustus* retained onely thus much at this time, that hee tooke a title which signified not authoritie, but dignitie before all the rest: as if the people of *Rome* had beene to be numbred one by one, hee thought himselfe worthy that they should begin with him. Also hee knew that the multitude was not stirred to sedition so much, with extraordinarie power, as insolent Titles, which might put them to consider of that power, and of the losse of their libertie. And therefore hee would not at the first take any offensiue Title, as that of *King* or *Dictator,* which for the abuses before done, were become odious to the people. And in a multitude, seeming things, rather then substantiall, make impression. But hauing gotten the mayne thing that he aspired vnto, to giue them then content in words, which cost him neither money, nor labour, hee thought no deare bargaine." In the eighteenth century this interpretation of Augustus's statecraft would be adopted and refined by Gibbon: "To resume, in a few words, the system of the Imperial government: as it was instituted by Augustus, and maintained by those princes who understood their own interest and that of the people, it may be defined an absolute monarchy disguised by the forms of a commonwealth" (Gibbon, *Decline and Fall*, vol. 1, p. 93).

225. For the final hundred years of its existence before it was transformed into a principate by Augustus, the Roman Republic suffered from endemic civil war. Neville here refers to the four civil wars that followed the assassination of Julius Caesar in 44 B.C.: the Liberators' civil war (44–42 B.C.), the Sicilian revolt (44–36 B.C.), the Perusine war (41–40 B.C.), and the final war of the Roman Republic (32–31 B.C.).

226. I.e., to publish or announce publicly the name of a person as condemned to death, and the confiscation of that person's property (*OED*, s.v. "proscribe," 1a).

which, considering in how few hands the Lands of *Italy* then were, might be an over-ballance of the Property in his hands. But this is certain, that what ever he had not in his own possession, he disposed of at his pleasure, taking it away, as also the lives of his people, without any judicial proceedings, when he pleased: That the Confiscations were great, we may see by his planting above sixty thousand Souldiers upon Lands in *Lombardy*; That is, erecting so many *Beneficia*,[227] or *Timarr*'s, and, if any Man's Lands lay in the way, he took them in for Neighbourhood, without any delinquency. *Mantua vae miserae nimium vicina Cremonae.*[228] And it is very evident that if these *Beneficia* had not afterwards been made Hereditary, that Empire might have had a stabler Foundation, and so a more quiet and orderly progress than it after had; for the Court Guards, call'd the Praetorians,[229] did make such havock of their Princes, and change them so often,[230] that this (though it may seem a Paradox) is another reason why this Tyranny was not ruin'd sooner; for the People, who had really an Interest to endeavour a change of Government, were so prevented by seeing the Prince, whom they designed to supplant, removed to their hand,[231] that they were puzled what to do, taking in the mean time great recreation to see those wild Beasts hunted down themselves, who had so often prey'd upon their Lives and Estates; besides that, most commonly the frequent removes of their Masters, made them scarce have time to do any mischief to their poor oppressed Subjects in particular, though they were all Slaves in general. This Government of

---

The practice of proscription had been initiated by Sulla in 82 B.C. and was a feature of the later civil wars of the republic.

227. I.e., grants of land as a recompense for military service.

228. "Mantua, unfortunately, was much too near Cremona" (Virgil, *Eclogues*, 9.28). There is a tradition that Virgil's family property near Mantua was confiscated by Octavian after the Battle of Philippi in 42 B.C. in order to reward his soldiers. Mantua was "much too near Cremona" because the boundary commissioner in charge of administering the sequestrations, Octavius Musa, having used up all the land around Cremona, extended the scope of the sequestrations to neighboring Mantua, and Virgil's property was seized as a result of this enlargement.

229. See above, p. 131, n. 219.

230. Cf. Machiavelli, *The Prince*, chapter 19 (Machiavelli, *Works*, pp. 225–27).

231. I.e., taken out of their power (*OED*, s.v. "hand," *n.*, 2).

the later *Romans* is a clear Example of the truth and efficacy of these Politick Principles we have been discoursing of. First, that any Government (be it the most unlimited and arbitrary Monarchy) that is placed upon a right Basis of Property, is better both for Prince and People, than to leave them a seeming Property, still at his devotion, and then for want of fixing the Foundation, expose their Lives to those dangers and hazzards with which so many Tumults and Insurrections, which must necessarily happen, will threaten them daily: And in the next place, that any violent constraining of mankind to a subjection, is not to be called a Government, nor does salve either the Politick or Moral ends, which those eminent Legislators amongst the Ancients proposed to themselves, when they set Rules to preserve the quiet and peace, as well as the plenty, prosperity, and greatness of the People; but that the Politicks or Art of Governing is a Science [232] to be learned and studied by Counsellors and

232. The view that politics was an art to be practiced only by insiders who understood what Tacitus had called the "arcana imperii" (*Histories*, 1.4), the secrets of power, reached back to the Roman empire. It was reinforced and given a new twist in the early seventeenth century by works produced in the "reason of state" or "ragion di stato" tradition, in which the amoral workings of the political world were described and occasionally approved (see Pocock, *Harrington*, pp. 851–54). However, against it arose a countervailing tendency of commentary, in which Hobbes and Harrington were central figures, that aimed to supplant this essentially prudential tradition of politics with something that could properly be called scientific because of the greater certainty, universality, and definiteness of its propositions. Accordingly, in the preface to book 1 of *The Prerogative of Popular Government*, Harrington had denied that politics was the preserve of insiders and practitioners: "To say that a man may not write of government except he be a magistrate, is as absurd as to say that a man may not make a sea-card unless he be a pilot" (Pocock, *Harrington*, p. 395). He would return to this point in *Politicaster*: "Are not they [i.e., Pierre du Moulin and Robert Sanderson] clearly on my side then, that there may be demonstration and yet not mathematical? Why, sure there may, sir; nay, and such a demonstration may be every whit as valid and convincing as if it were mathematical. For this I appeal to Mr. Hobbes: 'All true ratiocination (saith he) which taketh its beginning from true principles, produceth science, and is true demonstration.' This afterwards he declares 'in all sorts of doctrines' or arts, and consequently in the politics, to be holding" (Pocock, *Harrington*, p. 722). In particular, this scientific politics aspired to defend the necessity of government (against anarchists and utopians), and to identify and describe the features and functions that a true government ought to possess. See Noel Malcolm, *Reason of State, Propaganda, and the Thirty Years' War: An Unknown Translation by Thomas Hobbes*

Statesmen be they never so great; or else Mankind will have a very sad condition under them, and they themselves a very perplexed and turbulent life, and probably a very destructive and precipitous end of it.

Doctor. I am very glad I gave occasion to make this Discourse: now I beseech you, before you go to the mixt Monarchies, not to forget *Egypt*.

English Gentleman. 'Twas that I was coming to, before you were pleased to interrogate me concerning the *Roman* Empire. The *Egyptians* are this day, for aught I know, the only People that enjoy Property, and are Governed as a Province by any of the Eastern absolute Princes. For whereas *Damasco, Aleppo,* and most of the other Cities and Provinces of that Empire, whose Territory is divided into *Timarr's*, are Governed by a Bashaw,[233] who for his Guards has some small number of Janizaries or Souldiers; the Bashaw of *Egypt*, or of Grand *Cairo*, has ever an Army with him; and divers Forts are erected, which is the way *European* Princes use in Governing their Provinces, and must be so where Property is left entire, except they plant Colonies[234] as the *Romans* did. The reason why *Selim*, who broke the Empire of the *Mamalukes*, and conquered *Egypt*,

---

(Oxford: Clarendon Press, 2007). Neville here associates himself with this emergent school of political philosophy. David Hume's essay "That Politics May Be Reduced to a Science" is a late contribution to this tradition: "So great is the force of laws, and of particular forms of government, and so little dependence have they on the humours and tempers of men, that consequences almost as general and certain may sometimes be deduced from them, as any which the mathematical sciences afford us" (Hume, *Essays*, pp. 14–31; quotation on p. 16). The view that politics was a science influenced the American Founders, e.g., John Adams, whose thought has a clear Harringtonian cast: "The balance of dominion in land is the natural cause of empire; and this is the principle which makes politics a science undeniable throughout, and the most demonstrable of any" (*A Defence of the Constitutions of Government of the United States of America* [London, 1787], p. 165).

233. I.e., pasha, a high-ranking Turkish military commander or provincial governor (*OED*, s.v. "pasha"), with at this time connotations of haughtiness.

234. Cf. Machiavelli, *The Prince*, chapter 3: "There is another Remedy, rather better than worse, and that is, to plant Colonies in one or two places, which may be as it were the Keys of that State" (Machiavelli, *Works*, p. 201). Cf. also the opening of book 2 of the *History of Florence*: "Among the great and admirable orders of former Kingdoms and Common-wealths (though in our times it is discontinued

did not plant *Timarr's* upon it, was the Laziness and Cowardliness of the People, and the great Fruitfulness of the Soil, and Deliciousness of the Country, which has mollifi'd and rendred effeminate all the Nations that ever did Inhabit it.[235] So that a resolution was taken to impose upon

––––––––

and lost) it was the Custom upon every occasion to build new Towns and Cities, and indeed nothing is more worthy and becoming an excellent Prince, a well-disposed Common-wealth, nor more for the interest and advantage of a Province, than to erect new Towns, where men may cohabit with more Convenience, both for Agriculture, and Defence . . . in a new Conquer'd Countrey, a Colony placed by Authority, is a Fortress and a Guard to keep the Natives in obedience. . . . But the Custom of sending Colonies being laid aside, new Conquests are not so easily kept, void places not so easily supply'd, nor full and exuberant places so easily evacuated" (Machiavelli, *Works*, p. 22). In *Oceana* Harrington too had endorsed colonies as a means for a commonwealth to increase (Pocock, *Harrington*, pp. 324–25).

235. Egypt had been conquered by Selim I in 1517 (cf. Rycaut, *Present State*, p. 74). Cf. Machiavelli, *Discourses*, 1.1: "And who-ever would consider the Government of the *Soldan*, the discipline of the *Mamalukes*, and the rest of their Militia before they were extirpated by *Selimus* the Turk, might find their great prudence and caution in exercising their Souldiers, and preventing that softness and effeminacy to which the felicity of their soil did so naturally incline them" (Machiavelli, *Works*, p. 269). Rycaut's view of the military establishment of Egypt under the Ottomans differs from that of Neville: "THE Guard and protection of the Kingdom of *Egypt* is committed to the charge of twelve *Begs*, some of which are of the ancient Race of the *Mamalukes*, confirmed by *Sultan Selin* upon the taking of *Cairo*; these have the command of the whole Militia in their hands, whereby they are grown proud, powerful, and ready upon every discontent to rise in Rebellion; every one of these maintains 500 fighting men, well appointed for War, and exercised in Arms, which serve but as their Guard, and for Servants of their Court; with which they go attended in journeys, in their huntings, and publick appearances; under the command of these twelve Captains are twenty thousand Horse, paid at the charge of the Country, whose Office is by turns to convey yearly the Pilgrims to *Mecha*, and the annual Tribute of 600000 *Zechins* to the *Ottoman* Court, whether it be judged requisite to send it either by Land or Sea; these are the standing Militia of the Country, out of which, unless upon the foregoing occasions, they are not obliged to other service; their principal duty being, to prevent the invasion of the *African* Montaneers, who often make incursions from their barren Rocks, into the fat and fruitful Soyls of *Egypt*. Besides this Militia, are computed eighty thousand *Timariots*, out of which they yearly transport about 2500, or 3000 men to the Wars of *Candy*; but to more remote Countries, or the late Wars of *Hungary*, I did not hear that this Souldiery hath usually been called" (Rycaut, *Present State*, pp. 182–83). Rycaut's view of the government of Egypt under the Ottomans also diverges from that of Neville: "For indeed the Government of

them, first the maintaining an Army by a Tax, and then to pay a full half of all the Fruits and product of their Lands (to the Grand Seignior) which they are to Cultivate and improve: This is well managed by the Bashaws and their Officers, and comes to an incredible sum; the goods being sold, the Money is conveyed *in specie* to the Port,[236] and is the greatest part of that Prince's Revenue. And it is believed, that if all the Lands had been entirely confiscated, and that the Grand Seignior had managed them by his Officers, he would not have made a third part so much of the whole, as he receives now annually for one half: not only because those People are extreamly industrious where their own profit is concerned: but for that, it is clear, if they had been totally divested of their Estates, they would have left their Country, and made that which is now the most populous Kingdom of the World, a Desart, as is all the rest of the *Turkish* Dominions, except some Cities. And if the People had removed as they did elsewhere, there would not only have wanted hands to have Cultivated and Improved the Lands, but mouths to consume the product of it; so that the Princes Revenue by the cheapness of Victual, and the want of Labourers, would have almost fallen to nothing.

Noble Venetian. Pray God this be not the reason that this King of *France* leaves Property to his Subjects; for certainly he hath taken example by this Province of *Egypt*, his Subjects having a Tax (which for the continuance of it, I must call a Rent or Tribute) Impos'd upon them to the value of one full half of their Estates, which must ever increase as the Lands improve.

English Gentleman. I believe, Sir, there is another reason; For the Property there, being in the Nobility and Gentry, which are the hands by

---

Egypt, if well considered, is rather Aristocratical than Monarchical; for though they acknowledge the Sultan to be their Head, and accept his Pasha for Ruler, and pay a yearly Tribute, yet the Beghs which are great Lords in their respective Countries, carry the sway and Dominion in all other matters, and will endure nothing which savours of oppression or innovation" (Rycaut, *History*, p. 330). For the mamalukes, see below, p. 284, n. 573.

236. I.e., the Turkish court in Constantinople; known since 1536 and the alliance between Sultan Suleiman and Francis I of France as the "Sublime Porte."

which he manages his Force both at home and abroad, it would not have been easie or safe for him to take away their Estates. But I come to the limited Monarchies. They were first Introduced (as was said before) by the *Goths*,[237] and other Northern People. Whence those great swarms came, as it was unknown to *Procopius*[238] himself, who liv'd in the time of their Invasion, and who was a diligent searcher into all the circumstances of their concernments, so it is very needless for us to make any enquiry into it, thus much being clear, That they came Man, Woman, and Child, and conquer'd and possest all these parts of the World, which were then subject to the *Roman* Empire, and since Christianity came in have been so to the Latin Church, till honest *John Calvin*[239] taught some of us the

237. The manhood of the German nations, including the Goths, had long been used by the Roman emperors as military auxiliaries, increasingly so once the northern border of the empire had been stabilized by the campaigns of Marcus Aurelius Antoninus (A.D. 166–180); for Harrington's awareness of this development, see Pocock, *Harrington*, p. 190. However, in 376 pressure on their own eastern borders exerted by the Huns had induced the Goths to seek a settlement south of the Danube on the territories of the empire. Permission was granted, but the situation deteriorated rapidly and for the next ten years the Goths ravaged Thrace and its adjacent provinces. Although the Goths were eventually pacified, the Gothic settlements south of the Danube were now permanent. In 395 a revolt of the Goths set in train a mass emigration from the north that in less than fifty years would lead to the Gothic conquests of Gaul, Italy, Spain, and North Africa. Machiavelli had begun his *History of Florence* with a summary account of the incursions made by the Goths into the western provinces of the Roman Empire (Machiavelli, *Works*, pp. 1–7: cf. *Discourses*, 2.8, in Machiavelli, *Works*, pp. 342–43, on the pernicious character of the wars arising from such *Völkerwanderungen*).

238. Procopius of Caesarea (c. 500–c. 554), secretary to the great military commander Belisarius who served under the emperor Justinian. In his capacity as secretary, Procopius had accompanied Belisarius in his campaigns against the Vandal kingdom of North Africa (533) and against the Ostrogothic kingdom in Italy (538–40), witnessing both the Gothic siege of Rome (538) and Belisarius's triumphant entry into Ravenna (540). He wrote a Greek history of the wars of Justinian, Ὑπὲρ τῶν πολέμων λόγοι ("History of the Wars"), which includes narratives of the Vandalic and Gothic campaigns. Note the presence of Procopius's *Anecdota*, his scandalous secret history of the court of Justinian, in Neville's booklist (above, p. 53). Procopius speculates concerning the geographical origins of the Germanic tribes in *History of the Wars*, 3.2.

239. Jean Calvin (1509–64), Protestant theologian and founder of the theological system known as Calvinism. In "Nicholas Machiavel's Letter to Zanobius Buondelmontius in Vindication of Himself and His Writings," Neville makes Machi-

way how to deliver ourselves from the Tyrannical Yoak,[240] which neither we nor our Forefathers were able to bear. Whence those People had the Government they Establisht in these parts after their Conquest, that is, whether they brought it from their own Country, or made it themselves, must needs be uncertain, since their Original is wholly so; but it seems very probable that they had some excellent persons among them, though the ignorance and want of learning in that Age hath not suffered any thing to remain that may give us any great light; for it is plain, that the Government they setled, was both according to the exact Rules of the Politicks, and very natural and suitable to that Division they made of their several Territories. Whenever then these Invaders had quieted any Province, and that the People were driven out or subdued, they divided the Lands, and to the Prince they gave usually a tenth part, or thereabouts; to the great Men, or *Comites Regis* (as it was translated into Latine) every one (as near as they could) an equal share. These were to enjoy an Hereditary right in their Estates, as the King did in his part and in the Crown; but neither he, nor his Peers or Companions, were to have the absolute disposal of the Lands so allotted them, but were to keep a certain proportion to themselves for their use: and the rest was ordered to be divided amongst the Free-men, who came with them to Conquer. What they kept to themselves was called *Demesnes* in *English* and *French*, and in *Italian, Beni Allodiali*. The other part which they granted to the Free-men, was called a *Feud*: and all these Estates were held of these Lords Hereditarily, only the Tenants were to pay a small Rent annually, and at every Death or Change an acknowledgment in Money, and in some Tenures the best Beast besides: But the chief condition of the *Feud* or Grant, was, that the Tenant should perform certain Services to the Lord, of which one (in all Tenures of Free-men) was to follow him Armed to the Wars for the Service of the Prince and Defence of the

---

avelli praise Calvin as "that famous reformer, fled some years since out of *Picardy* to *Geneva*, who is of so great renown for learning and parts, and who promises us so perfect a reformation" (Machiavelli, *Works*, sig. ***3r). This spurious letter is dated 1537; Calvin had fled to Geneva in 1536; the real Machiavelli had died in 1527.

240. I.e., the temporal government of the popes.

Land. And upon their admittance to their *Feuds*, they take an Oath to be
true Vassals and Tenants to their Lords, and to pay their Rents, and perform their Services, and upon failure to forfeit their Estates; and these
Tenants were divided according to their Habitations into several Mannors,
in every one of which there was a Court kept twice every year, where
they all were to appear, and to be admitted to their several Estates, and to
take the Oath above mentioned. All these Peers did likewise hold all
their Demesnes, as also all their Mannors, of the Prince; to whom they
swore Allegiance and Fealty: There were besides these Freemen or
Francklins, other Tenants to every Lord, who were called Villains, who
were to perform all servile Offices and their Estates were all at the Lords
disposal when he pleased; these consisted mostly of such of the former
Inhabitants of these Countries, as were not either destroyed or driven
out, and possibly of others who were Servants amongst them, before they
came from their own Countries. Perhaps thus much might have been unnecessary to be said, considering that these Lords, Tenants, and Courts,
are yet extant in all the Kingdoms in *Europe*; but that to a Gentleman of
Venice, where there are none of these things, and where the *Goths* never
were,[241] something may be said in excuse for me.[242]

241. As the Noble Venetian has explained in his account of the origin of the
Venetian state (see above, pp. 99–102). This had been a circumstance of importance for Harrington in *Oceana*, explaining as it did how Venice had escaped con-
tamination with "those ill features of government which at this time are become
far worse in these western parts, except Venice which, escaping the hands of the
barbarians by virtue of her impregnable situation, hath had her eye fixed upon
ancient prudence and is attained to a perfection even beyond her copy" (Pocock,
Harrington, p. 161).

242. Neville here describes the leading features of the feudal form of government
instituted by the Germanic nations in the lands they conquered from the Romans
after the fall of the Roman Empire in the West. The early modern recognition that
feudal institutions, although barbaric in origin, nevertheless demanded and deserved study, arose in the south of France during the mid-sixteenth century, with
legal scholars such as Jacques Cujas and François Hotman assuming prominent
roles, and with a need to clarify the origins of the French monarchy and the nature
of its sovereignty (imperial or conciliar) acting as the spur. In England, Sir Henry
Spelman would arrive at the crucial insight that English feudal institutions derived
from, and were associated with, the similar features of other Western European nations: they had been imported into England at the time of the Conquest and in
consequence had been unknown to the Saxons (*Treatise of Feuds and Tenures* [comp.

Noble Venetian. 'Tis true, Sir, we fled from the *Goths* betimes, but yet in those Countries which we recovered since in *Terra firma*, we found the Footsteps of these Lords, and Tenures, and their Titles of Counts; though being now Provinces to us, they have no influence upon the Government, as I suppose you are about to prove they have in these parts.

English Gentleman. You are right, Sir; for the Governments of *France*, *Spain*, *England*, and all other Countries where these People setled, were

---

1639; first pub., 1698). Spelman's was an explosive insight, because it meant that in England, unlike in France, feudal institutions supported rather than undermined arguments for monarchical absolutism; the absolutist implications of this transformative perception were later pursued energetically by Robert Brady (*A Full and Clear Answer* [1681]). Neville dissociates himself from this more scholarly and royalist interpretation of feudalism (assuming he was aware of it in writing *Plato Redivivus*; he might have been, given that Brady's book was published in the same year as Neville's). He cleaves instead to the older, vaguer creed of an ancient constitution that had been bequeathed immemorially to the native English from the freedom-loving peoples of the Hercynian forest that had preceded royal grants and charters, and that was therefore intrinsically libertarian—a creed which had received a transfusion of scholarly credibility from John Selden's *Titles of Honour* (1614) (for a similar view, cf. Philip Hunton, *A Treatise of Monarchy* [1643], in Wootton, *Divine Right*, pp. 197–98). The authors of *The Armie's Dutie* (1659) had made a similar point: "The *Northern* people, who divided a land, when conquered, into so many parcels, as they had great Officers, leaving the choice of the best and largest share to their Prince or leader, he becoming their King, and the chief Officers, holding their large shares on him by some small acknowledgements, became his Dukes, Counts, and Earls; and the common souldiers (who came indeed to seek a countrey to inhabit) holding together with the poor natives some small parcels of land under those great men upon such conditions as made them wholly dependant upon their Landlords, and thus these Dukes and Earls paying homage and fealty and small acknowledgements to the Prince, became princes in their own divisions, and thus the interest of the King and his Peers over-weighed the properties of all other Inhabitants, whereupon the power of our ancient Monarchy was founded, and the Kings chief Officers were the tenants and vassalls of his Peers, to whome he sent upon occasion of trouble forreign or domestick to leavy arms, who gathered their vassalls together, and either assisted the King, or fought against him as they liked the quarrell, their souldiers never daring to dispute their Lords commands knowing no immediate Lord but them" (*Armie's Dutie*, pp. 19–20). For commentary on the general issue of feudalism and its deployment in political argument in England at this time, see J. G. A. Pocock, *The Ancient Constitution and the Feudal Law: A Study of English Historical Thought in the Seventeenth Century* (Cambridge: Cambridge University Press, 1957).

fram'd accordingly.[243] It is not my business to describe particularly the distinct Forms of the several Governments in *Europe*, which do derive from these People (for they may differ in some of their Orders and Laws, though the Foundation be in them all the same) this would be unnecessary, they being all extant, and so well known; and besides, little to my purpose, excepting to shew where they have declined from their first Institution, and admitted of some change. *France*, and *Poland*, have not, nor as I can learn, ever had any Free-men below the Nobility; that is, had no Yeomen; but all are either Noble, or Villains, therefore the Lands must have been Originally given, as they now remain, into the hands of these Nobles. But I will come to the Administration of the Government in these Countries, and first say wherein they all agree, or did at least in their Institution, which is, That the Soveraign power is in the States assembled together by the Prince, in which he presides; these make Laws, Levy Money, Redress Grievances, punish great Officers, and the like. These States consist in some places of the Prince and Nobility onely, as in *Poland*, and anciently in *France* (before certain Towns, for the encouraging of Trade, procured Priviledges to send Deputies; which Deputies are now called the third Estate) and in others, consist of the Nobility and Commonalty, which latter had and still have the same right to Intervene and Vote, as the great ones have both in *England, Spain*, and other Kingdomes.

Doctor. But you say nothing of the Clergy; I see you are no great friend to them, to leave them out of your Politicks.

English Gentleman. The truth is, *Doctor,* I could wish there had never been any: the purity of Christian Religion, as also the good and orderly Government of the World, had been much better provided for without them, as it was in the Apostolical time, when we heard nothing of Clergy. But my omitting their Reverend Lordships was no neglect, for I meant to come to them in order; for you know that the Northern People did not bring Christianity into these parts, but found it here, and were in time

243. An indication of Neville's dissociation of himself from the royalist opinions of Spelman and Brady.

converted to it,[244] so that there could be no Clergy at the first: but if I had said nothing at all of this Race, yet I had committed no Solecism in the Politicks; for the Bishops and great Abbots intervened in the States here, upon the same Foundation that the other Peers do, *viz.* for their great possessions, and the dependence their Tenants and Vassals have upon them; although they being a People of that great sanctity and knowledg, scorn to intermix so much as Titles with us profane Lay-Ideots, and therefore will be called Lords Spiritual. But you will have a very venerable opinion of them, if you do but consider how they came by these great possessions, which made them claim a third part of the Government.[245] And truely not unjustly by my rule, for I believe they had no less (at one time) than a third part of the Lands in most of these Countries.

244. The Goths were converted to Christianity by the bishop and apostle Ulphilas in approximately A.D. 360. By about A.D. 400 almost all the northern barbarians had embraced the new religion, albeit in a heterodox, Arian form.

245. Neville alludes to the fact that the bishops were one of the three estates of which Parliament was composed (the others being the Lords and the Commons). It was by no means a dormant issue in 1681. The political role of the bishops sitting in the House of Lords had become freshly controversial in 1679 in the context of the impeachment of the Earl of Danby: "Upon this [Danby's impeachment] a famous debate arose, concerning the Bishops right of voting in any part of a trial for treason. It was said, that, tho' the bishops did not vote in the final judgment, yet they had a right to vote in all preliminaries. . . . Many books were writ on both sides. . . . The truth was, they [i.e., the bishops] desired to have withdrawn, but the King would not suffer it. He was so set on maintaining the pardon [he had sealed for Danby], that he would not venture such a point on the votes of the temporal Lords. And he told the Bishops, they must stick to him, and to his prerogative, as they would expect that he should stick to them, if they came to be push'd at. By this means they were exposed to the popular fury" (Burnet, *History*, vol. 1, p. 460; cf. pp. 462–65, for Burnet's précis of the arguments deployed by both sides in the debate; Sydney, *Letters*, pp. 70–71; and Grey, *Debates*, vol. 7, p. 303; John Brydall, *A New-Years-Gift* [1682]; the same issue had arisen in relation to the trial of Strafford in 1641. Cf. particularly Denzil Holles, *Letter of a Gentleman to His Friend Shewing That Bishops Are Not to Be Judges in Parliament in Cases Capital* (1679), and Edward Stillingfleet, *The Grand Question, concerning the Bishops Right to Vote in Parliament* (1680). Clause III of the Act of Settlement (1701), mindful of Danby's escape, declared that "no pardon under the great seal of England should be pleadable to an impeachment by the commons in parliament." This resolved a point of uncertainty concerning the scope of the royal pardon which had emerged in 1679 in relation to Danby: see Sydney, *Letters*, pp. 40 and 71, and Grey, *Debates*, vol. 7, pp. 20–30, 57–63, 134–37, 152–57, 175–87, 299–300, 324–25.

Noble Venetian. Pray, how did they acquire these Lands? was it not here by the Charitable donation of pious Christians, as it was elsewhere?

English Gentleman. Yes, certainly, very pious men; some of them might be well meaning people, but still such as were cheated by these holy men,[246] who told them perpetually, both in publick and private, *that they represented God upon Earth, being Ordained by Authority from him who was his Viceroy here, and that what was given to them was given to God, and he would repay it largely both in this World and the next.* This wheedle[247] made our barbarous Ancestors, newly Instructed in the Christian Faith (if this Religion may be called so, and sucking in this foolish Doctrine more than the Doctrine of Christ) so zealous to these Vipers, that they would have pluckt out their eyes to serve them, much more bestow, as they did, the fruitfullest and best situate of their possessions upon them: Nay, some they perswaded to take upon them their Callings, vow Chastity, and give all they had to them, and become one of them, amongst whom, I believe, they found no more sanctity than they left in the World. But this is nothing to another trick they had, which was to insinuate into the most notorious and execrable Villains, with which that Age abounded; Men, who being *Princes*, and *other great Men* (for such were the Tools they work'd with) had treacherously poisoned, or otherwise murdered their nearest Relations, Fathers, Brothers, Wives, to reign, or enjoy their Estates; These they did perswade into a belief, *that if they had a desire to be sav'd, notwithstanding their execrable Villanies, they need but part with some of those great possessions*[248] (which they had acquired by those acts) *to their*

246. Neville's anticlericalism here emerges clearly. For commentary on the general subject of the resistance to priestly power, see J. A. I. Champion, *The Pillars of Priestcraft Shaken: The Church of England and Its Enemies 1660–1730* (Cambridge: Cambridge University Press, 1992): "Rather than deny God, . . . the radicals were concerned to debunk the false authority of the Church" (p. 9).

247. I.e., a piece of insinuating flattery or cajolery (*OED*, s.v. "wheedle," 1).

248. In the spurious "Nicholas Machiavel's Letter to Zanobius Buondelmontius in Vindication of Himself and His Writings," Neville makes Machiavelli express indignation at the scale of the Roman Catholic Church's landholdings: "I shall conclude this discourse after I have said a word of the most Hellish of all the innovations brought in by the *Popes*, which is the *Clergy*; these are a sort of men

Bishopricks or Monasteries, and they would pray for their Souls, and they were so holy and acceptable to God, that he would deny them nothing; which they immediately performed, so great was the ignorance and blindness of that Age;[249] and you shall hardly find in the story of those times, any great *Monastery*, *Abbey*, or other *Religious House* in any of these Countries (I speak confidently, as to what concerns our own *Saxons*) that had not its Foundation from some such Original.

Doctor. A worthy beginning of a worthy Race!

Noble Venetian. Sir, you maintain a strange Position here, That it had been better there had been no *Clergy*: Would you have had no *Gospel* preached, no *Sacraments*, no continuance of *Christian Religion* in the World? or do you think that these things could have been without a *Succession* of the true *Priesthood*, or (as you call it, of true *Ministry*) by means of *Ordination?* do's not your own *Church*[250] hold the same?

---

under pretence of ministring to the people in holy things, set a part and separated from the rest of mankind . . . by a humane Ceremony called by a divine name, *viz.* Ordination, these wherever they are found . . . make a Band which may be called the *Janizaries of the Papacy*, these have been the causers of all the Soloecisms and Immoralities in Government, and of all the impieties and abominations in Religion, and by consequence of all the disorder, villany, and corruption we suffer under in this detestable Age; these men by the Bishop of *Rome*'s help, have crept into all the Governments in *Christendom*, where there is any mixture of *Monarchy*, and made themselves a third estate; that is, have, by their temporalities (which are almost a third part of all the Lands in *Europe* given them by the blind zeal, or rather folly of the *Northern* people, who over-ran this part of the world) stept into the throne, and what they cannot perform by these secular helps, and by the dependancy their vassals have upon them, they fail not to claim and to usurp, by the power they pretend to have from God and his Vice-gerent at *Rome*" (Machiavelli, *Works*, sig. ***2r–v). For similar anticlericalism, see Harrington, *The Art of Lawgiving*: "Rome, which hath brought ignorance to be the mother of devotion, and indeed interest to be the father of religion" (Pocock, *Harrington*, p. 679).

249. In "Nicholas Machiavel's Letter to Zanobius Buondelmontius in Vindication of Himself and His Writings," Neville makes Machiavelli accuse "the blind devotion and ignorance of the *Goths, Vandals, Huns,* &c." for allowing the imposture of the clergy to take root and flourish (Machiavelli, *Works*, sig. ***2v).

250. After splitting from the Church of Rome in the 1530s, the Church of England sought to follow a via media between, on the one hand, the doctrines and

English Gentleman. You will know more of my *Church*,[251] when I have told you what I find the word *Church* to signifie in *Scripture*, which is to me the only rule of *Faith, Worship*, and *Manners*;[252] neither do I seek these additional helps, of *Fathers, Councels*, or *Ecclesiastical* history, much less *Tradition:* for since it is said in the word of God it self, *That Antichrist did begin to work even in those days*;[253] I can easily believe that he had brought his Work to some perfection, before the word *Church* was by him applied to the *Clergy:* I shall therefore tell you what I conceive that *Church, Clergy*, and *Ordination*, signified in the *Apostolical* times. I find then the word *Church* in the New Testament taken but in two sences; the first, for the *Universal Invisible Church*, called sometimes of the *First-born*; that is, the whole number of the true Followers of Christ in the World, whereever resident, or into what part soever dispersed. The other

---

traditions of Roman Catholicism (which denied the possibility of salvation to those outside the church, and which revered the traditions of the Church Fathers and the various general councils as contributing to the truth of Christian teach- , ing), and on the other, the principle of *sola scriptura* characteristic of more extreme Protestantism, which located Christian authority in the words of the Bible alone, and which therefore tended to devalue the writings of the Church Fathers as merely human commentaries prone to error. Accordingly, Articles 19, 20, and 21 carefully set out the Church of England's position concerning the authority of a church and of general councils, and acknowledged their liability to error. Such a via media was naturally unstable, and in the eyes of many contemporaries the Restoration Church of England was moving closer to Roman Catholicism, par-ticularly in its cultivation of patristic learning, thus reviving unwelcome memories of the Laudian church in the 1630s. See John Spurr, *The Restoration Church of England 1646–1689* (New Haven, CT: Yale University Press, 1991), and Jean-Louis Quantin, *The Church of England and Christian Antiquity: The Construction of a Confessional Identity in the 17th Century* (Oxford: Oxford University Press, 2009).

251. A suave correction of the Noble Venetian's assumption that the English Gentleman subscribes without reservation to the doctrines of the Church of England.

252. Neville makes plain his attachment to the principle of *sola scriptura* and also to its possible corollary, the rejection of sacerdotal authority.

253. A paraphrase of two passages from 1 John: "As ye have heard that antichrist shall come, even now are there many antichrists; whereby we know that it is the last time" (2:18), and "This is that spirit of antichrist, whereof ye have heard that it should come; and even now is it in the world" (4:3).

signification of *Church* is an *Assembly*,[254] which though it be sometimes used to express any *Meetings* (even unlawful & tumultuous ones) as well in Scripture as prophane Authors; yet it is more frequently understood, for a gathering together to the Duties of *Prayer, Preaching*, and *Breaking of Bread*; and the whole Number so Congregated is, both in the Acts of the Apostles, and in their holy Epistles, called the *Church*;[255] nor is there the least colour for appropriating that word to the *Pastors* and *Deacons*,

254. Harrington too had paid close attention to the original meaning of Εκκλησια as a congregation of the people in his *The Prerogative of Popular Government* (Pocock, *Harrington*, p. 515). Originally a point of Commonwealthman semantics, it would in a decade or so become a favorite of the freethinkers. In his *Discourse of Free-thinking* (1713), Anthony Collins would seize on the variable translations of Εκκλησια as an example of priestly cunning in manufacturing a spurious Biblical foundation for sacerdotal authority: "In the old Protestant Bible, printed in King Edward the VI's days, and in the beginning of Queen Elizabeth's Reign in the Year 1562. the word Εκκλησια was translated every where *Congregation*, and not *Church*; whereby great offence was given to the Papists: But the Reverend Translators of the present *Common Bible* have in some places render'd it *Assembly*, and in others *Church*, with design to have us believe that the word *Church* signifies the *Priest*. For wherever the word Εκκλησια manifestly signifies the *People*, as it does in *Acts* 19.32. there they render it *Assembly*: whereas had they said, *The Church* (instead of *Assembly*) *was confus'd, and the more part knew not wherefore they were come together*; the signification of the word *Church* would not have admitted of any doubt about its meaning. And wherever the meaning of the word Εκκλησια is not so clear from the Context as it is in the foregoing Passage of the *Acts*, there they translate it *Church*. . . . Whereas was the word in the Original translated universally alike, either every where *Church*, or every where *Assembly*, there could be no dispute who are meant by Εκκλησια; nor by consequence, to whom belong the great Privileges which are throughout the Scripture given to those who are signify'd by that word" (pp. 91–92). Cf. Matthew Tindal, *The Rights of the Christian Church Asserted* (1706), pp. lxxxv–lxxxvii. Swift would mock this free-thinking scruple when he compressed, traduced, and ventriloquised Collins's argument: "What should I mention the pious Cheats of the Priests, who in the *New Testament* translate the Word *Ecclesia* sometimes the *Church*, and sometimes the *Congregation*" (Swift, *Prose Writings*, vol. 4, p. 37; cf. vol. 2, p. 87, for his chiding of Tindal).

255. See Acts 2:47, 5:11, 8:1, 11:26, 14:23 and 27, 15:3 and 22, 18:22; Romans 16:5; 1 Corinthians 4:17, 14:4–5 and 23, 16:19; Ephesians 1:22, 3:10, 5:24, 25, 27, 29, and 32; Philippians 3:6, 4:15; Colossians 1:18 and 24, 4:15; 1 Timothy 5:16; Philemon 2; 1 Peter 5:13; 3 John 6 and 9.

who since the Corruptions of *Christian Religion* are called *Clergy*;[256] which word in the Old Testament is used, sometimes for *Gods whole People*, and sometimes for the *Tribe of Levi*, out of which the Priests were chosen: for the word signifies a *Lot*; so that *Tribe* is called *Gods Lot*, because they had no share alotted them when the Land was divided, but were to live upon *Tythe*, and serve in the functions of their *Religion*, and be *Singers*, *Porters*, *Butchers*, *Bakers*, and *Cooks*, for the Sacrifices, *&c.* So that this *Tribe* was stiled *Clergy* but figuratively, and the Allegory passed into the New Testament, where the Saints are sometimes called *Clergy*,

256. In *A Short Historical Essay, Touching General Councils, Creeds, and Impositions in Matters of Religion* (1676), Andrew Marvell had recently associated the adoption by the Christian priesthood of the term "clergy" with the corruption of Christianity introduced during the Council of Nicaea and its debates concerning the doctrine of the Trinity: "This Council [i.e., the Council of Nicaea] denounces every invention [not] of its own; (far from the Apostolic modesty, and the stile of the Holy Spirit) under no less then an Anathema. Such was their arrogating to their inferior degrees the style of *Clergy*, till custome hath so much prevailed, that we are at a loss how to speak properly either of the name or nature of their function. Whereas the *Clergy*, in the true and Apostolic sense, were only those whom they superciliously always called the *Laity*: The word *Clerus* being never but once used in the New Testament, and in that signification, and in a very unlucky place too, Peter 1.5.3 where he admonishes the Priesthood, *that they should not Lord it or domineer over*, the Christian People, *Clerum Domini* or *the Lord's Inheritance*" (Marvell, *Prose Works*, vol. 2, pp. 148–49). In "Nicholas Machiavel's Letter to Zanobius Buondelmontius in Vindication of Himself and His Writings," Neville makes Machiavelli speak in very similar terms: "I shall say but one word of their calling and original, and then leave this subject. The word *Clergy* is a term, wholly unknown to the Scriptures, otherwise than in this sence; a peculiar People or Gods lot, used often for the whole Jewish Nation, who are likewise called a Kingdom of Priests in some places. In the New Testament the word *Cleros* is taken for the true Believers, who are also called the Elect, and often the Church, which is the Assembly of the Faithful met together, as is easily seen by reading the beginning of most of St. *Paul's* Epistles, where writing to the Church, or Churches, he usually explains himself, *To all the Saints in Christ*; sometimes, *To all who have obtained like faith with us*; sometimes, *To all who in all places call upon the Name of the Lord Jesus*, &c. by which it appears, that neither the word Church nor Clergy was in those days ever appropriated to the Pastors or Elders of the flock; but did signifie indifferently all the people assembled together; which is likewise the literal construction of the word *Ecclesia*, which is an assembly or meeting; in these Congregations or Churches was performed their Ordination, which properly signifies no more than a decree of such Assembly; but is particularly used for an Election of any into the Ministry" (Machiavelli, *Works*, sig. ***2v).

but never the *Pastors* or *Deacons*, who were far from pretending in those days to come in the place of the *Aaronical Priesthood*.[257] The word *Ordination* in Scripture signifies lifting up of hands, and is used, first, for the giving a *Suffrage*, which in all popular Assemblies was done by stretching out the hand (as it is in the Common-Hall of *London*).[258] In the next place it is applied to the Order or Decree made by the *Suffrage* so given, which was then (and is yet too in all Modern Languages) called an *Ordinance*, and the *Suffrage* it self *Ordination*; which word proves that the first *Christian Churches* were *Democratical*; that is, That the whole *Congregation* had the *Choice* in this, as well as the *Soveraign Authority* in all *Excommunications*, and all other matters whatsoever that could occur; for in all *Aristocratical Commonwealths* the word for choice, is *Keirothesia*,[259] or *Imposition of hands*, (for so the Election of all Magistrates and Officers was made) and not *Keirotoniae*.[260] These *Pastors* and other *Officers* did not

257. In the course of his anticlerical analysis of the political history of the tribes of Israel in *Oceana*, Harrington had also drawn attention to the fact that the Levites had been excluded from the distribution of lands by lot: "The people by their first division, which was genealogical, were contained under their ten tribes, houses or families, whereof the firstborn in each was prince of his tribe and had the leading of it (Numbers, 1); the tribe of Levi only, being set apart to serve at the altar, had no other prince but the high priest. In their second division they were divided locally by their agrarian (Joshua, c. 13 to c. 42), or the distribution of the lands of Canaan unto them by lot, the tithe of remaining unto Levi: whence according unto their local division, the tribes are reckoned but twelve" (Pocock, *Harrington*, pp. 174–75); "The tribes thus planted, or to have been planted, were twelve. The thirteenth, or that of Levi, came in like manner unto the lot, for their forty-eight cities with their suburbs, and received them accordingly; as the lot came forth for the families of the Kohathites, and the rest. These Israel gave unto the Levites out of their inheritance; that is, these were such as the twelve tribes, before division, set apart for the Levites, with the tithes and the offerings, which, though this tribe had no other lands, made their portion by far the best" (*The Art of Lawgiving*, in Pocock, *Harrington*, p. 633).

258. I.e., a general meeting of the Corporation of the City of London at the Guildhall, assembled for the purpose of choosing the next Lord Mayor.

259. I.e., χειροθεσια, or the laying on of hands.

260. I.e., χειροτονια, or the show of hands. This distinction between the laying on and the showing of hands in the early church had been of interest to Hobbes in chapter 42 of *Leviathan*, because the fact that the officers of the early Christian church had been elected by a show of hands (χειροτονια) rather than by the laying on of hands (χειροθεσια) supported his argument that the clergy could legitimately

pretend to be by virtue of such *Choice* of a peculiar profession different from other Men, (as their *Followers* have done since *Antichrists* Reign) but were onely called and appointed (by the *Congregations* approval of their gifts or parts) to instruct or feed the Flock, visit the sick, and perform all other *Offices* of a *true Minister* (that is, Servant) of the *Gospel:* at other times they followed the business of their own *Trades* and *Professions*; and the *Christians* in those times (which none will deny to have been the *purest* of the *Church*)[261] did never dream that a true *Pastor* ought

claim no share of civil authority: "Now it is well enough known, that in all those Cities, the manner of choosing Magistrates, and Officers, was by plurality of suffrages; and (because the ordinary way of distinguishing the Affirmative Votes from the Negatives, was by Holding up of Hands) to ordain an Officer in any of the Cities, was no more but to bring the people together, to elect them by plurality of Votes, whether it were by plurality of elevated hands, or by plurality of voices, or plurality of balls, or beans, or small stones, of which every man cast in one, into a vessell marked for the Affirmative, or Negative; for divers Cities had divers customes in that point" (Hobbes, *Leviathan*, p. 366; cf. Pocock, *Harrington*, p. 81). In *A Short Historical Essay, Touching General Councils, Creeds, and Impositions in Matters of Religion* (1676), Marvell had paused in mock wonderment over the supposed distinctions of the Christian priesthood in relation to χειροθεσια and χειροτονια: "If they [i.e., the priesthood] were so peculiar from others, did the Imposition of the Bishops hands, or the lifting up of the hands of the Laity conferr more to that distinction?" (Marvell, *Prose Works*, vol. 2, p. 149). In *Oceana* and *Pian Piano*, Harrington had followed Hobbes in depicting theocratic Israel as a democratic, or chirotonised, state (Pocock, *Harrington*, pp. 262, 384–85, and—for a fulsome acknowledgment of the debt to Hobbes—423). It was an issue over which Harrington would later clash in detail with Henry Hammond and Lazarus Seaman in book 2 of *The Prerogative of Popular Government* (Pocock, *Harrington*, esp. pp. 516–63). Neville would put similar notions into the mouth of Machiavelli in the spurious "Nicholas Machiavel's Letter to Zanobius Buondelmontius in Vindication of Himself and His Writing" included in the 1675 edition of his works: "Whoever reads attentively the Historical part of the *Old Testament*, shall find that God himself never made by one Government for men, that this Government was a *Common-wealth* (wherein the *Sanhadrim* or *Senate*, and the Congregation or *popular Assembly* had their share) and that he manifested his high displeasure when the rebellious people would turn it into a *Monarchy*" (Machiavelli, *Works*, sig. **2v; cf. on the subject of χειροθεσια and χειροτονια, sig. ***3r).

261. Study of the institutions of the early Christian church had been undertaken by pious clergymen such as William Cave in order to identify the features of "true Christian piety and simplicity," which, if they were to be found anywhere, were surely present "*when* (as *S. Hierom* notes) *the blood of Christ was yet warm in*

to pretend to any *Succession*, to qualifie him for the *Ministry* of the word; or that the *Idle* and *Ridiculous Ceremonies* used in your *Church* (and still continued in that which you are pleased to call mine) were any way essential or conducing to Capacitate a person to be a true *Preacher* or *Dispencer* of the *Christian Faith*. And I cannot sufficiently admire why our *Clergy*, who very justly refuse to believe the *Miracle* which is pretended to be wrought in *Transubstantiation*,[262] because they see both the *Wafer* and

---

the breasts of Christians, and the faith and spirit of Religion more brisk and vigorous" (William Cave, *Primitive Christianity* [1673], "The Preface to the Reader," sig. A8ᵛ; cf. Grey, *Debates*, vol. 7, p. 313, and the speech of Sir Thomas Clarges in the Commons, 21 May 1679). However, freethinkers were quick to discern the utility of primitive Christianity (originally a weapon in the arsenal of Protestantism, forged to be used against Roman Catholicism) as a lens which brought into sharp focus the causes and trajectory of religious corruption and hence was apt to be deployed against all religious establishments whatsoever: cf., e.g., Matthew Tindal, *An Essay concerning the Power of the Magistrate* (1697), pp. 70, 79, 80, and 118. Cf. also Machiavelli, *Discourses*, 1.12: "Nor can any thing portend the ruine of our Church with more certainty, than that those who are nearest the Church of *Rome*, (which is the head of our Religion) should have less Religion than other people: and he who should consider the present practice, with the Primitive foundation, would find that either utter destruction, or some great judgment was hanging over our heads" (Machiavelli, *Works*, p. 284). In the spurious "Nicholas Machiavel's Letter to Zanobius Buondelmontius in Vindication of Himself and His Writings," Neville fashioned Machiavelli in his own image, making him anticlerical but also a zealot for the "true Religion" that the Church of Rome has obscured and corrupted (Machiavelli, *Works*, sig. ***1r).

262. The Roman Catholic doctrine that during the Mass the wafer and wine are really transformed into the body and blood of Christ. Among freethinkers this doctrine was the most egregious example of a purely human corruption introduced into the church to promote and secure sacerdotal authority: "Nothing wou'd expose Priestcraft more, than an Historical account, how, and upon what Motives the Clergy vary'd in their Notions and Practices concerning the Lord's Supper: As first, how they made it a Mystery in the Heathenish sense of that word, and for Heathenish Reasons, that they might have the same Power, as the Priests of Idols, to exclude whom they were pleas'd to term Unworthy. Which Power, when they had by this means sufficiently settled, nothing less wou'd serve 'em, in order to magnify their Consecration, than that it produc'd the Real Presence of the Body and Blood of Christ . . . and made it a Real Sacrifice, and the Ministers Real Priests, and the Communion-Table an Altar; which placing in the East, they made profound Bows and Cringes towards it" (Matthew Tindal, *The Rights of the Christian Church Asserted* [1706], pp. 101–2). Cf. Hobbes, *Leviathan*, chapter 44: "Nor did the Church of Rome ever establish this Transubstantiation, till the time

the *Wine* to have the same *Substance*, and the same *Accidents*[263] (after the *Priest* has mumbled words over those *Elements*[264]) as they had before, and yet will believe that the same kind of *Spell* or *Charm* in *Ordination* can have the Efficacy to Metamorphose a poor *Lay-Ideot* into a *Heavenly Creature*; notwithstanding that we find in them the same *humane Nature*, and the same *Necessities* of it, to which they were subject before such *Transformation*; nay, the same *Debauch*,[265] *Profaneness, Ignorance,* and *Disability* to preach the *Gospel*.

Noble Venetian. Sir, this discourse is very new to me. I must confess I am much inclined to joyn with you in believing, that the power *Priests Exercise* over *Mankind*, with the *Jurisdiction* they pretend to over *Princes* and *States*, may be a usurpation; but that they should not have a *Divine Call* to serve at the *Altar*, or that any person can pretend to perform those *Sacred Functions* without being duly *Ordained*, seems very strange.

English Gentleman. I am not now to discourse of *Religion*; it is never very civil to do so in Conversation of persons of a different belief; neither can it be of any benefit towards a *Roman Catholick*, for if his Conscience should be never so cleerly convinc'd, he is not yet *Master* of his own *Faith*, having given it up to his *Church*, of whom he must ask *leave* to be a *Convert*, which he will be sure never to obtain; But if you have the Curiosity

---

of *Innocent* the third; which was not above 500. years agoe, when the Power of Popes was at the Highest, and the Darknesse of the time grown so great, as men discerned not the Bread that was given them to eat, especially when it was stamped with the figure of Christ upon the Crosse, as if they would have men beleeve it were Transubstantiated, not only into the Body of Christ, but also into the Wood of his Crosse, and that they did eat both together in the Sacrament" (p. 423).

263. A term originating in Aristotelian philosophy, where it refers to those properties or qualities not essential to a substance or object; things that do not constitute an essential component; attributes (*OED*, s.v. "accident," I1a).

264. I.e., the bread and wine used in the sacrament of the Eucharist (*OED*, s.v. "element," 3).

265. I.e., the practice of excessive indulgence in sensual pleasures, particularly those of eating and drinking (*OED*, s.v. "debauch," 1 and 2).

when you come amongst the learned in your own *Country* (for amongst our *Ordination-Mongers*, there is a great scarcity of *Letters* and other *good Parts*) you may please to take the *Bible*, which you acknowledg to be the *Word* of *God* as well as we, and intreat some of them to shew you any passage, the plain and genuine sense of which can any way evince this *Succession*, this *Ordination*, or this *Priesthood*, we are now speaking of; and when you have done, if you will let your own excellent *Reason* and *Discourse* judg, and not your *Priest*, (who is too much concerned in point of Interest) I make no doubt but you will be convinced that the pretence to the dispensing of *Divine things* by virtue of a *humane Constitution*, and so ridiculous a one too, as the *Ordination* practised by your *Bishops* and ours (who descend and succeed from one and the same *Mother*) is as little Justifiable by *Scripture* and *Reason*, and full as great a *Cheat* and *Usurpation*, as the Empire which the *Ecclesiasticks* pretend to over the *Consciences* and *persons* of men, and the Exemption from all *Secular power*.

Noble Venetian. Well, Sir, though neither my *Faith* nor my *Reason* can come up to what you hold, yet the Novelty and the grace of this *Argument* has delighted me extreamly: and if that be a Sin, as I fear it is, I must confess it to my *Priest*; but I ask your pardon first, for putting you upon this long Deviation.

English Gentleman. Well, this Digression is not without its use, for it will shorten our business (which is grown longer than I thought it would have been) for I shall mention the Clergy no more, but when-ever I speak of Peerage, pray take notice that I mean both Lords Spiritual and Temporal, since they stand both upon the same foot of Property. But if you please, I will fall immediately to discourse of the Government of *England*, and say no more of those of our Neighbours, than what will fall in by the way, or be hinted to me by your Demands; for the time runs away, and I know the *Doctor* must be at home by noon, where he gives daily charitable audience to an Infinity of poor people, who have need of his help, and who send or come for it, not having the confidence to send for him, since they have nothing to give him; though he be very liberal too of his Visits to such, where he has any knowledg of them: But I spare his Modesty,

which I see is concerned at the Just Testimony I bear to his Charity.[266]
The Soveraign Power of *England* then, is in King, Lords, and Commons.
The Parliaments, as they are now constituted, that is, the assigning a
choice to such a Number of Burroughs, as also the manner and form of
Elections and Returns, did come in, as I suppose, in the time of *Henry*
the third,[267] where now our Statute-Book begins; and I must confess, I
was inclined to believe, that before that time, our Yeomanry or commonalty had not formally assembled in Parliament, but been virtually included, and represented by the Peers, upon whom they depended: but
I am fully convinced, that it was otherwise, by the learned Discourses
lately publisht by Mr. *Petit* of the *Temple*, and Mr. *Attwood* of *grays-Inne*,
being Gentlemen whom I do mention *honoris causa*; and really they deserve to be honor'd, that they will spare some time from the Mechanical[268] part of their Callings (which is to assist Clients with Counsel, and
to plead their Causes, and which I acknowledg likewise to be honourable) to study the true Interest of their Country, and to show how ancient
the Rights of the People in *England* are, and that in a time when neither
Profit nor Countenance[269] can be hop'd for from so ingenious an under-

266. Wood records that Lower had a plentiful and lucrative practice, although
he does not mention his charitable works: "In 1666 he [i.e., Lower] followed
Dr. *Willis* to the great City, and setling at first in *Hatton Garden*, practised under
him and became Fellow of the said *Society*. Afterwards, growing famous, he removed to *Salisbury Court* near *Fleetstreet*, and thence to *Bowstreet*, and afterwards
to *Kingstreet* near *Covent Garden*; where being much resorted to for his succesful
practice, especially after the death of Dr. *Willis*, an. 1675, he was esteemed the
most noted Physitian in *Westminster* and *London*, and no mans name was more
cried up at Court than his, he being then also Fellow of the *Coll. of Physitians*"
(Anthony à Wood, *Athenae Oxonienses*, 2 vols. [1692], vol. 2, p. 652).

267. Henry III reigned from 1216 to 1272. For the significance of his reign in the
late seventeenth-century debate on the antiquity of the House of Commons, see
below, n. 270.

268. I.e., the practical and applied, as opposed to the theoretical, part of their
profession (*OED*, s.v. "mechanical," AI2). At this time the pejorative connotation
of the word was available but not inevitable. In 1790 Burke would stigmatize the
lawyers of the French National Assembly as being for the most part "the inferior,
unlearned, mechanical, merely instrumental members of the profession" (Burke,
Reflections, p. 196).

269. I.e., monetary gain or patronage (*OED*, s.v. "countenance," *n. 1*, 8a),
respectively.

taking.[270] But I beg pardon for the deviation. Of the three branches of Soveraign Power which Politicians mention, which are Enacting Laws, Levying of Taxes, and making War and Peace, the two first of them are indisputably in the Parliament; and when I say Parliament, I ever intend with the King. The last has been usually exercis'd by the Prince, if he can do it with his own Money: yet because even in that Case it may be ruinous to the Kingdom, by exposing it to an Invasion, many have affirmed that such a Power cannot be by the true and ancient free Government of *England*, supposed to be Intrusted in the hands of one man: And therefore we see in divers Kings Reigns, the Parliament has been Consulted, and their advice taken in those matters that have either concerned War or Leagues; And that if it has been omitted, Addresses have been made to the king by Parliaments, either to make war or peace, according to what they thought profitable to the publick.[271] So that I will not determine

270. William Petyt (1640/41–1707), lawyer and politician; an associate of Neville's. William Atwood (d. 1712), lawyer and politician. The question of the antiquity of Parliament was intensely topical during the Exclusion Crisis of 1681. Filmer's *Freeholder's Grand Inquest*, republished in 1680, had argued against the antiquity of the House of Commons, noting that the earliest extant writ to the house was dated 1265, during the reign of Henry III (Filmer, *Patriarcha*, pp. 76, 80, and 84, drawing on John Selden's *Priviledges of the Baronage of England* [1642]). In his reply, *The Antient Right of the Commons of England Asserted* (1680), William Petyt had assembled a range of medieval materials to present the image of an ancient, pre-Conquest parliament that had possessed and exercised (and whose successors therefore still possessed and might exercise) the right to alter the succession. In the cause of defending the antiquity and authority of parliament, Petyt had been joined by his friend and associate William Atwood, whose *Jani Anglorum Facies Nova* (1680) and *Jus Anglorum ab antiquo* (1681) had argued in a similar direction. For comment, see John Pocock, "The Varieties of Whiggism from Exclusion to Reform: A History of Ideology and Discourse," in *Virtue, Commerce, and History* (Cambridge: Cambridge University Press, 1985), pp. 218–23; Corinne Weston and Janelle Greenberg, *Subjects and Sovereigns: The Grand Controversy over Legal Sovereignty in Stuart England* (Cambridge: Cambridge University Press, 1981); and Corinne Weston, *English Constitutional Theory and the House of Lords, 1556–1832* (London: Routledge and Kegan Paul, 1965).

271. Neville is pushing against the limits of English constitutional practice in suggesting that Parliament had any say in these matters except indirectly through the voting or withholding of supply, although the point had been debated in Parliament in 1654 (Burton, *Diary*, vol. 1, pp. xliv–xlvi); and, famously, as early as 1621 James I would remove from the Journal of the House of Commons a statement of

whether that power which draws such consequences after it, be by the genuine sence of our Laws in the Prince or no; although I know of no Statute or written Record which makes it otherwise. That which is undoubtedly the Kings Right, or prerogative, is to Call and Dissolve Parliaments, to preside in them, to approve of all Acts made by them, and to put in Execution, as Supream or Soveraign Magistrate, in the Intervals of Parliaments, and during their Sitting, all Laws made by them, as also the Common Law; for which Cause he has the nomination of all Inferiour Officers and Ministers under him, excepting such as by Law or Charter are eligible otherwise; and the Power of the Sword, to force Obedience to the Judgements given both in Criminal and Civil Causes.

Doctor. Sir, You have made us a very absolute Prince; what have we left us? if the King have all this Power, what do our Liberties or Rights signifie whenever he pleases?

English Gentleman. This Objection, *Doctor*, makes good what I said before, that your skill did not terminate in the body natural, but extend to the Politick; for a more pertinent Interrogatory could never have been made by *Plato* or *Aristotle:* In answer to which, you may please to understand, That

---

the Commons' claimed right to debate matters of foreign policy. On 7 February 1673, Secretary Coventry had congratulated the Commons on their prudence in refusing "to meddle with advising war; it is the King's just prerogative" (Grey, *Debates*, vol. 2, p. 10; cf. pp. 58 and 65). Charles had strongly defended this element of his prerogative in his address to the Commons of 20 May 1678: "The right of making and managing War and Peace is in his Majesty; and if you think he will depart from any part of that right, you are mistaken. The reins of Government are in his hands" (Grey, *Debates*, vol. 5, p. 62). It was a point of principle that could be made to rebound upon the Court, however, as William Sacheverell had noticed during debates on the impeachment of Danby, one of the charges against whom was that he had encroached on the royal monopoly of these matters: "Great stress is laid upon the words 'assuming, encroaching, or usurping Regal authority.' I would know, whether treating Peace and War without the King's consent is Treason? For that making Peace and War is in the King, no man will deny" (Grey, *Debates*, vol. 6, pp. 376–77). As late as the early eighteenth century, during the crisis of the Kentish Petition, William III would vigorously resist the notion that Parliament had any standing in questions either of war and peace or of alliances with foreign powers.

when these Constitutions were first made, our Ancestors were a plain-hearted, well-meaning People, without Court-reserves or tricks, who having made choice of this sort of Government, and having Power enough in their hands to make it take place, did not foresee, or imagine, that any thoughts of Invading their Rights could enter into the Princes Head; nor do I read that it ever did, till the *Norman* Line came to Reign;[272] which coming

---

272. The nature of the Norman Conquest, and its implications for English law, politics, and monarchy, had been a perennial topic for common lawyers since the time of Coke. Common lawyers had tended to argue that, in legal terms, the Conquest had made no breach in the continuity of English legal history, since one of the first acts of William I had been to confirm and codify the laws of his Saxon predecessor, Edward the Confessor—an argument which relied on documents we know now to be inauthentic. See, e.g., Edward Cooke, *A Seasonable Treatise* (1689). If on the other hand William had really made a conquest, and in consequence had been king by *jus conquestus*, all his acts—including the confirmation of the Saxon laws he had found here—had been made out of the plenitude of his unfettered, absolute sovereignty, and the English monarchy to this day retained that absolutist character. This had been the view of Thomas Hobbes, and it had drawn down upon him the opprobrium of his old friend Edward Hyde (Hobbes, *Leviathan*, chapter 24, p. 172; G. A. J. Rogers, ed., *Leviathan: Contemporary Responses to the Political Theory of Thomas Hobbes* [Bristol: Thoemmes Press, 1995], pp. 245–50)—hence the desire of the common lawyers from Coke to Blackstone to present William not as a conqueror but rather as a claimant to the crown under ancient law who had vindicated his claim by trial of battle; see, e.g., Philip Hunton, *A Treatise of Monarchy* (1643), in Wootton, *Divine Right*, pp. 198–99). It is interesting that Royalist writers until late in the seventeenth century had also tended to downplay the significance of the Conquest, being uneasy with such appeals to the sword. They had preferred instead to rest their defenses of Stuart monarchy on the presence of the royal prerogative within the scope of the ancient constitution. However, at just the moment when Neville was composing and publishing *Plato Redivivus*, Robert Brady and Sir William Dugdale, writing in opposition to Neville's allies Petyt and Atwood, had represented William as in every respect a conqueror of the most high-handed kind, who had imported feudalism into England, thereby displacing the earlier Saxon tenures and creating a watershed in English legal history: "Though we have many *Laws* and *Customs* from the *Northern* People, and North parts of *Germany*, from whence both Saxons and Normans came: yet after the *Conquest*, the Bulk and Maine of our Laws were brought hither from *Normandy*, by the Conqueror. For from whence we received our Tenures, and the Manner of holding our Estates in every respect, from thence also we received the Customs incident to those *Estates*. And likewise the quality of them, being most of them *Feudal*, and enjoyed under several Military Conditions, and Services, and of necessary consequence from thence, we must receive the

in by Treaty, it was obvious there was no Conquest made upon any but *Harold*, in whose stead *William* the First came, and would claim no more after his Victory, than what *Harold* enjoy'd, excepting that he might confiscate (as he did) those great men who took part with the wrong Title, and *Frenchmen* were put into their Estates; which though it made in this Kingdom a mixture between *Normans* and *Saxons*, yet produced no Change or Innovation in the Government; the *Norman* Peers being as tenacious of their Liberties, and as active in the recovery of them to the full, as the *Saxon* Families were.[273] Soon after the death of *William*, and possibly in his time, there began some Invasions upon the Rights of the Kingdom, which begat Grievances, and afterwards Complaints and Discontents, which grew to that height, that the Peers were fain to use their Power, that is, Arm their Vassals to defend the Government; whilst the Princes of that Age, first King

---

Laws also by which these Tenures, and the Customs incident to them were regulated, and by which every mans right in such Estates was secur'd according to the nature of them. But from *Normandy* (and brought in by the *Conqueror*) we received most, if not all our ancient *Tenures*, and manner of holding and enjoying our *Lands* and *Estates*, as will appear by comparing our *Ancient Tenures* with theirs" (Brady, *A Full and Clear Answer* [1681], p. 31). In 1686 Nathaniel Johnston would go further, arguing in *The Excellency of Monarchical Government* that the Conqueror had been an absolute monarch, and that in consequence all post-Conquest English laws and liberties were the result of grants and concessions made by other absolute monarchs. It is against the first stirrings of this neo-Royalist interpretation of the Conquest that Neville was writing. He had sketched his own view of the Conquest in Parliament on 8 February 1659: "William the Conqueror came in with an intent to seize all the lands. He was only prevented by the privilege of the Church; that saved us. I mean the Church of Rome, not our Church, if we have any" (Burton, *Diary*, vol. 3, p. 133; cf. Sidney, *Court Maxims*, pp. 13–15).

273. Cf. Harrington's very similar observations about the government of the Normans (or "Neustrians" as he calls them) in *Oceana*: "But the Neustrians— while they were but foreign plants, having no security against the natives but in growing up by their prince's sides—were no sooner well rooted in their vast dominions than they came up according to the infallible consequences of the balance domestic and, contracting the national interest of the baronage, grew as fierce in the vindication of the ancient rights and liberties of the saem as if they had been always natives; whence, the kings being as obstinate on the one side for their absolute power as these on the other for their immunities, grew certain wars which took their denomination from the barons" (Pocock, *Harrington*, pp. 195–96). Petyt and Atwood had similarly argued that the Conquest had made no rupture in the continuity of English legal and political life.

John, and then *Henry* the Third,[274] got Force together. The Barons call'd in *Lewis* the Dauphin,[275] whilst the King would have given away the Kingdom to the *Sarazens*, as he did to the Pope,[276] and armed their own Creatures; so that a bloody War ensued, for almost forty years, off and on; as may be read in our History: The success was, that the Barons or Peers obtained in the close two Charters or Laws[277] for the ascertaining their Rights, by which

274. In 1215–16 there was a civil war between King John and his barons, of whom two-thirds would abandon their king at his death in October 1216. Between 1258 and 1262 a magnate government, headed by powerful barons such as Simon de Montfort, had ruled England and in effect deposed Henry III. Conflict between Henry and his barons had revived between 1264 and 1267.

275. In the summer of 1215 barons rebelling against King John had appealed to the French dauphin, Louis, for military assistance. An advance guard of French troops was in London before the end of the year, and further troops arrived in the spring of 1216, quickly taking control of most of the counties south of the Tees. See *Antimonarchical Authors*, p. 201.

276. "He [i.e., John] is also thought to have sought aid from *Mirammula* King of *Affrica*, whilst he was in his Troubles, promising him the Kingdom of *England*, if he Conquered, and to renounce his *Christian* Faith" (George Meriton, *Anglorum Gesta* [1675], pp. 160–61). In the heat of the Exclusion Crisis, John Somers was not above repeating this story in his *A Brief History of the Succession* (1681), even though he must have realized that it was not well founded (p. 5; see below, appendix F, p. 404). Robert Brady would shortly dismiss the tradition as nothing more than a monkish calumny (Brady, *A Complete History of England* [1685], pp. 488–89). However, it is a fact that on 15 May 1213, in a desperate attempt to shore up his political position, John had surrendered his kingdom to the papacy and had promised to pay an annual tribute of 1000 marks, thereby succeeding in converting Innocent III from an inveterate enemy into an important ally.

277. I.e., Magna Carta and the Carta de foresta. Since Coke, these charters had been prized by common lawyers as the foundations of English liberty (see the commentary on Magna Carta that begins the second part of the *Institutes*: Coke, *Selected Writings*, vol. 2, pp. 755–913). During the 1690s the Whig clergyman and agitator Samuel Johnson would study Magna Carta and publish his findings in *The Second Part of the Confutation of the Ballancing Letter* (1700), arguing that it predated the time of King John and was untainted by rebellion. However, technically Magna Carta and the Carte de foresta were not laws, because they were grants of the Crown rather than acts of Parliament (for an example of the popular Whiggish ignorance of the legal status of Magna Carta, see Henry Care, *English Liberties* [1680], p. 19, where he seems to think that Magna Carta is an act of Parliament). Robert Brady would shortly use this fact in an attempt to undermine the popular belief that Magna Carta could be used to curb the power of the Crown, arguing that the charter itself was an act of the Crown and so could not be used to

neither their Lives, Liberties, or Estates, could ever be in danger any more from any Arbitrary Power[278] in the Prince; and so the good Government of *England*, which was before this time like the Law of Nature, onely written in the hearts of Men, came to be exprest in Parchment, and remain a Record in Writing; though these Charters gave us no more than what was our own before.[279] After these Charters were made, there could not chuse but

restrict the power from which it had proceeded: *"All the* Liberties *and* Priviledges *the People can pretend to, were the* Grants *and* Concessions *of the* Kings *of this Nation, and were derived from the Crown"* (Brady, *A Complete History of England* [1685], "To the Reader," sig. A4ʳ). In *Politicaster* Harrington would present Magna Carta as the site of repeated struggles between Crown and people: "If in England there have ever been any such thing as a government of laws, was it not Magna Charta? Well, and have not our kings broken Magna Charta some thirty times? I beseech you, sir, did the law govern when the law was broken? Or was that a government of men? On the other side, hath not Magna Charta been as often repaired by the people? And the law being so restored, was it not a government of laws, and not of men?" (Pocock, *Harrington*, p. 715). It might occasionally be treated with irreverence: see Grey, *Debates*, vol. 9, p. 306. Mahlberg notes that the forest laws were of close and material interest to the Neville family (Gaby Mahlberg, "Historical and Political Contexts of *The Isle of Pines*," *Utopian Studies*, 17, no. 1 (2006), p. 118).

278. Although "arbitrary," when used to qualify "monarchy," might either casually or for polemical purposes be confused with "absolute" (e.g., by Philip Hunton in his *Treatise of Monarchy* [1643], chapter 2, section 1 [Wootton, *Divine Right*, p. 178]), in fact the two terms were distinguishable. "Absolute" power was unqualified but operated within the bounds of law. "Arbitrary" power was not confined by law, as Locke had pointed out in a work composed contemporaneously with *Plato Redivivus*: "Even *absolute Power*, where it is necessary, is *not Arbitrary* by being absolute, but is still limited by that reason, and confined to those ends, which required it in some Cases to be absolute" (Locke, *Two Treatises*, 2, §139, p. 361). This distinction would be repeated in the next century by Blackstone, and it became the hegemonic ideology of British monarchy in the long eighteenth century: "I shall not (I trust) be considered as an advocate for arbitrary power, when I lay it down as a principle, that in the exertion of lawful prerogative, the king is and ought to be absolute; that is, so far absolute, that there is no legal authority that can either delay or resist him" (Blackstone, *Commentaries*, vol. 1, p. 243). See also J. W. Daly, "The Idea of Absolute Monarchy in Seventeenth Century England," *Historical Journal*, 21 (1978), pp. 227–50.

279. Neville is arguing that Magna Carta was merely declaratory and therefore had not created the liberties it described and defended. In this he was following the common law tradition of interpretation of Magna Carta. Coke in the "Proeme" to the second part of the *Institutes* had maintained that the charter was "for the most part declaratory of the principall grounds of the fundamentall Laws of

happen some encroachment upon them: but so long as the Peers[280] kept their greatness, there was no breaches but what were immediately made up in Parliament; which when-ever they assembled, did in the first place confirm the Charters,[281] and made very often Interpretations upon them, for the benefit of the People; witness the Statute *de Tallagio non concedendo*,[282]

England, and for the residue it is additionall to supply some defects of the Common Law; and it was no new declaration" (Coke, *Selected Writings*, p. 748). Cf. Burke, *Reflections*, p. 182.

280. Neville's aristocratic conviction that it is the Lords rather than the Commons that are the surest defense of liberty in the English constitution is once more evident here.

281. Coke had also laid heavy emphasis on the repeated confirmations of Magna Carta by Parliament: "It [i.e., Magna Carta] hath so often been confirmed by the wise providence of so many Acts of Parliament. . . . It is provided by Act of Parliament, that if any judgement be given contrary to any of the points of the great Charter, or *Charta de Foresta*, by the Justices, or by any other of the Kings Ministers, &c. it shall be undone, and holden for nought" (Coke, *Selected Writings*, p. 751).

282. Literally, "that tax may not be granted"; i.e., 25 Edw. I, a statute confirming Magna Carta passed in 1297, thought to give Parliament the right to assent to taxes before they could be levied. This act had been frequently invoked earlier in the century by opponents of Charles I and had figured prominently in the preamble to the *Petition of Right* (1642). Cf. John Lilburne, *The Opressed Mans Opression Declared* (1647), p. 15; *The Peoples Prerogative and Priviledges* (1648), p. 1; and John Rushworth, *Historical Collections* (1659), p. 596. The preamble was a favorite text of William Prynne's: see *An Humble Remonstrance* (1641), p. 4; *The Fourth Part of the Soveraigne Power of Parliaments and Kingdomes* (1643), p. 14; *A Legall Vindication of the Liberties of England* (1649), p. 2; *Reasons Assigned* (1649), p. 2; *A Declaration and Protestation Against . . . Excise in General* (1654), p. 8; *A Seasonable, Historical, Legal Vindication* (1654), p. 39 [36]; *A New Discovery of Free-State Tyranny* (1655), p. 13; *A Summary Collection of the Principal Fundamental Rights, Liberties, Proprieties of All English Freemen* (1656), pp. 3, 11, and 40; *Demophilos* (1658), p. 3; and *A Legal Vindication of the Liberties of England* (1660), p. 3. Immediately before the publication of *Plato Redivivus*, this statute had been cited by Henry Care in *English Liberties* (1680), p. 112, and by James Tyrrell in *Patriarcha Non Monarcha* (1681), p. 155; it had also been referred to by Neville's allies William Petyt and William Atwood (see above, p. 157, n. 270): cf. *Miscellanea Parliamentaria* (1680), p. 126, and *Jani Anglorum Facies Nova* (1680), p. 192. It was also invoked in parliamentary debate (Grey, *Debates*, vol. 2, p. 404, and vol. 7, p. 99; Burton, *Diary*, vol. 3, p. 170). Royalist writers, however, would have none of it. In *The Freeholders Grand Inquest* (1679), Filmer had doubted the very existence of the statute (p. 43); cf. Brady, *Complete History of England* (1685), p. xxxix. Notwithstanding those attempted underminings, this statute would continue to be cited by Whig writers later in the

and many others. But to come nearer the giving the *Doctor* an answer, you may please to understand, that not long after the framing of these forementioned Charters, there did arise a Grievance not foreseen or provided for by them; and it was such an one that had beaten down the Government at once, if it had not been Redressed in an Orderly way. This was the Intermission of Parliaments, which could not be called but by the Prince; and he not doing of it, they ceast to be Assembled for some years: if this had not been speedily remedied, the Barons must have put on their Armour again; for who can Imagine that such brisk Assertors of their Rights could have acquiesced in an Omission that ruin'd the Foundation of the Government, which consisting of King, Lords, and Commons, and having at that time Marched near Five hundred years upon three Leggs, must then have gone on hopping upon one; which could it have gone forward (as was impossible whilest Property continued where it was) yet would have rid but a little way. Nor can it be wonder'd at, that our great Men made no provision against this Grievance in their Charters, because it was impossible for them to imagine that their Prince, who had so good a share in this Government, should go about to destroy it, and to take that burden upon himself, which by our Constitution was undeniably to be divided between him and his Subjects: And therefore divers of the great Men of those times [283] speaking

---

century: see Roger Coke, *A Detection of the Court and State of England* (1697), pp. 207, 228, and 268; and James Tyrrell, *Bibliotheca Politica* (1694), pp. 122 and 400. Burke would recall it as late as 1790 in *Reflections on the Revolution in France* (Burke, *Reflections*, p. 173). In the 1670s, MPs nevertheless felt that the exclusive right of the Commons to grant taxes raised on the people needed reinforcement, so for instance in October 1675 "A Bill to prevent the illegal Exaction of Money from the subject," intended to "prevent the levying of any Tax, Tillage, or Subsidy, but by Parliament" had been introduced (Grey, *Debates*, vol. 3, p. 320).

283. Historians since Stubbs have recognized that the reign of Edward I saw the regularizing and strengthening of Parliament, not least in the inclusion of representatives of the commons (Stubbs, *Constitutional History*, vol. 2, pp. 183–304). But although Edward I held frequent parliaments, no provision was made for yearly meetings (even the Bill of Rights of 1689 goes no further than to say that "Parliaments ought to be held frequently," and until as late as 1780 the campaigner and associate of Wilkes, John Sawbridge, made regular motions in the Commons demanding annual parliaments, motions which were always defeated). Neville may have in mind the "Confirmatio Cartarum" of 1297, which had been granted by Edward under pressure from his magnates.

with that excellent Prince King *Edward* the First about it, he, to take away from his People all fear and apprehension that he intended to change the Ancient Government, called speedily a Parliament,[284] and in it consented to a Declaration of the Kingdoms Right in that point; without the clearing of which, all our other Laws had been useless, and the Government it self too; of which the Parliament is (at the least) as Essential a part as the Prince; so that there passed a Law in that Parliament that one should be held every year, and oftner if need be;[285] which like another *Magna Charta*, was

284. This is possibly a reference to the Salisbury parliament of 1297, where Edward was compelled to grant the "Confirmatio" in a manner that recalled the coercion of John in 1215 (Stubbs, *Constitutional History*, vol. 2, p. 295).

285. Although Neville is here ostensibly talking about the later Middle Ages, his wording would have recalled to the first readers of *Plato Redivivus* a dispute in 1677 about the legality of prorogation: "The Parliament of *England* had been prorogued for about a year and some months, by two different prorogations. One of these was for more than a year. So upon that it was made a question, whether by that the Parliament was not dissolved. The argument for it was laid thus. By the ancient laws [4 Ed. III. c. 14 and 36 Ed. III. c. 10] a Parliament was to be held *once a year, and oftener if need be:* It was said, the words, *if need be*, in one act, which were not in another that enacted an annual Parliament without that addition, did not belong to the whole period, by which a session was only to be held once a year if it was needful; but belonged only to the word *oftener:* So that the law was positive for a Parliament once a year: And if so, then any act contrary to that law was an unlawful act: By consequence, it could have no operation: From whence it was inferred, that the prorogation which did run beyond a year, and by consequence made that the Parliament could not sit that year, was illegal; and that therefore the Parliament could not sit by virtue of such an illegal act. Lord *Shaftsbury* laid hold on this with great joy, and he thought to work his point by it. . . . All the rest of the party [i.e., the Country party] was against it. They said, it was a subtilty: And it was very dangerous to hand so much weight upon such weak grounds. The words, *if need be*, had been understood to belong to the whole act: And the long Parliament did not pretend to make annual Parliaments necessary, but insisted only on a triennial Parliament: If there had been need of a Parliament during that long prorogation, the King by proclamation might have dissolved it, and called a new one. All that knew the temper of the House of Commons were much troubled at this dispute, that was like to rise on such a point. It was very certain the majority of both Houses, who only could judge it, would be against it. And they thought such an attempt to force a dissolution, would make the Commons do every thing that the Court desired" (Burnet, *History*, vol. 1, p. 401; cf. Grey, *Debates*, vol. 4, pp. 55–62, 65, 166–73; vol. 10, pp. 369–70). The Triennial Act of 16 Car. I. had been repealed in 1664 and replaced by a simple Declaratory Act which obliged the King to meet with Parliament at least every three years but which provided no machinery

confirmed by a new Act made in the time of *Edward* the Third,[286] that glorious Prince: nor were there any Sycophants in those days, who durst pretend Loyalty by using Arguments to prove that it was against the Royal Prerogative, for the Parliament to entrench upon the Kings Right of calling and Dissolving of Parliaments;[287] as if there were a Prerogative in the Crown, to chuse whether ever a Parliament should assemble, or no; I would desire no more, if I were a Prince, to make me Grand Seignior.[288] Soon after this last Act, the King, by reason of his Wars with *France* and *Scotland*, and other great Affairs, was forced sometimes to end his Parliaments abruptly, and leave business undone, (and this not out of Court-tricks, which were

---

of compulsion (Kenyon, *Stuart Constitution*, p. 361). Neville's sentiments seem to have been closer to those of the more intrepid members of Parliament, such as Shaftesbury. Cf. Carey, *Considerations*, p. 11: "Our annual Parliaments are established to us by Common-Law, Statute Law, and the Reason even of the Government it self." Such claims appear, in strict point of law, to have been exaggerated; although cf. Burton, *Diary*, vol. 1, p. 403, and vol. 3, p. 75. "Constant successive parliaments" had been an object of radical army agitation in 1647 and 1648 (Pocock, *Harrington*, pp. 8–9). On 19 March 1659, Sir Arthur Haselrig had declared in Parliament that it "is a fundamental law that there shall be a Parliament at least every year. The Triennial Bill provides for a Parliament every year. You will laugh at me, but it did provide so, that if the king did not call Parliaments once a year, the people might once in three years, in spite of the King" (Burton, *Diary*, vol. 4, p. 197). On demands for yearly elections—a significantly different point—see below, p. 301 and n. 609. For Thomas Goddard's denial of the existence of these acts of Edward III, see Goddard, *Plato's Demon*, pp. 327–30.

286. 4 Ed. III. c. 14 and 36 Ed. III. c. 10. In the so-called "Good Parliament" of 1376, the Commons had petitioned for annual parliaments, and the Crown had replied that they were already provided for in law (Stubbs, *Constitutional History*, vol. 2, p. 433). The apparent legal provision did not engender the reality: "That the Kings of *England* have not duely nor constantly observed these *Statutes* ever since their making, doth not render them of less force; For the Kings Omissions to fulfil a Law, or his personal Offences, can never be drawn into question Judicially, because the King is not under any compulsion, nor accountable to any Court, and is so far, and in such respect *Solutus legibus*; But all Acts of the king contrary to law, are adjudged to be in deceit of the king, and the law voids and nullifies all such Acts" (Carey, *Considerations*, p. 5). These statutes had been remembered during the constitutional debates of the 1650s: see, e.g., Streater, *Glympse*, p. 3.

287. Another neuralgic point for the first readers of *Plato Redivivus*. In 1681 Charles II would dissolve the Oxford Parliament only one week (21–28 March) after it had assembled.

288. See above, p. 127, n. 211.

then unknown) which produced another Act not long after, by which it was provided, That no Parliament should be dismist, till all the Petitions were answered; That is, in the Language of those times, till all the Bills[289] (which were then styled Petitions) were finished.

Doctor. Pray, Sir, give me a little account of this last Act you speak of; for I have heard in Discourse from many Lawyers, that they believe there is no such.

English Gentleman. Truly, Sir, I shall confess to you, that I do not find this Law in any of our Printed Statute-Books; but that which first gave me the knowledg of it was, what was said about three years ago in the House of Commons, by a worthy and Learned Gentleman,[290] who undertook to produce the Record in the Reign of *Richard* the Second; and since I have questioned many Learned Counsellors about it, who tell me there is such a one; and one of them, who is counted a Prerogative-Lawyer,[291] said it was so, but that Act was made in Factious times. Besides, I think it will be granted, that for some time after, and particularly

289. That is to say, draft legislation awaiting approval before passing into statute law. This was a point disputed by at least one of Neville's first readers: cf. *Antidotum*, pp. 84–85.

290. In fact on 14 April 1675 (which may suggest that this portion of the text predates publication by two years, whereas other portions were clearly written much closer to publication): "This day ye Commons met & ordered 3 old dormant statutes (one of Rich. ye second, another of Henry ye 4th and ye 3^d of Edward ye third) to be laid upon ye table: ye first was never printed, ye second printed by halves and ye 3^d of no great concern, but ye other two are look'd upon as of great advantage to ye Commons, ye first especially, which says y^t all petitions of ye people shall be heard in ful Parlem^t before they be separated, wch they looke upon as a securitie ag^st desolution, from haveing order'd these to be layd before y^m; one Sir Nicholas Cary very abruptly sayd y^t since they had found out statutes of y^t nature it were good to consider who transgress'd most ag^st y^m, & from thence fell upon ye D. of Lawderdale" (*Bulstrode Papers*, pp. 284–85). The instigator of the debate, presumably Neville's "worthy and learned Gentleman," is not identified, although it was possibly Sir Nicholas Carey or Carew (1635–88) himself, whose *Some Considerations* on this point would be published the following year. Cf. Marvell, *Prose Works*, vol. 2, p. 306.

291. I.e., a lawyer retained on behalf of the royal prerogative (*OED*, s.v. "prerogative," C2).

in the Reigns of *Henry* the *4th, Henry* the *5th,* and *Henry* the *6th,* it was usual for a Proclamation to be made in *Westminster-Hall,* before the end of every Session, that all those that had any matter to present to the Parliament, should bring it in before such a day, for otherwise the Parliament at that day should determine. But if there were nothing at all of this, nor any Record extant concerning it; yet I must believe that it is so by the Fundamental Law of this Government,[292] which must be lame

292. Fundamental laws are those which underwrite a constitution or form of government and to which subsequent laws should conform; a synonymous term, in Leveller writings, was "law paramount" (Morton, *Freedom,* pp. 40–41; cf. John Lilburne, *Legall Fundamentall Liberties* [1649]). For scholarly commentary in an English context, see J. W. Gough, *Fundamental Law in English Constitutional History* (Oxford: Clarendon Press, 1955). The concept of fundamental law had been embraced by common lawyers such as Coke, who had insisted that Magna Carta was simply declaratory of "the fundamentall Laws of *England*" (Coke, *Selected Writings,* vol. 2, p. 748; cf. Brady, preface to *History,* sig. B1r and p. xliii for mocking commentaries on this). "Fundamental law" was however a protean concept which might be deployed with equal ease by either side or any faction in the growing rift between Crown and Parliament. Pym had accused Strafford of endeavouring by "his words, actions and counsels to subvert the fundamental law of England and Ireland"; on 3 January 1642, Charles would instruct the Lord Keeper to impeach Lord Kimbolton and the five members of the Commons on the grounds that "they had endeavoured to subvert the fundamental laws and government of the kingdom" (Kenyon, *Stuart Constitution,* pp. 213 and 241); and in 1653 John Lilburne would claim that the purpose of resisting the king had been the "restauration of the Fundamental Laws and Rights of the Nation" (Morton, *Freedom,* p. 334). The *Grand Remonstrance* of 1641 had deplored "a malignant and pernicious design of subverting the fundamental laws and principles of government, upon which the religion and justice of this kingdom are firmly established" and had accused the senior clergy of making "canons that contain in them many matters contrary to the King's prerogative, to the fundamental laws and statutes of the realm, to the right of Parliaments, to the property and liberty of the subject, and matters tending to sedition and of dangerous consequence, thereby establishing their own usurpations, justifying their altar-worship, and those other superstitious innovations which they formerly introduced without warrant of law." Harrington had included fundamental laws of the agrarian and the ballot in the constitution of *Oceana,* defining fundamental law as "such as state what it is that a man may call his own, that is to say property, and what the means be whereby a man may enjoy his own, that is to say protection; the first is also called dominion, and the second empire or sovereign power" (Pocock, *Harrington,* pp. 230–31; cf. pp. 333–34). The language of fundamental law had been invoked in Parliament during the 1650s: see, e.g., Burton, *Diary,* vol. 2, pp. 48 and 81. Burnet would recall how the idea of fundamental law had been reinvigorated during the Exclusion Crisis, i.e.,

and imperfect without it; for it is all one to have no Parliaments at all but when the Prince pleases, and to allow a power in him to dismiss them when he will, that is, when they refuse to do what he will; so that if there be no Statute, it is certainly because our wise Ancestors thought there needed none, but that by the very Essence and Constitution of the Government it is provided for: and this we may call (if you had rather have it so) the Common-Law, which is of as much value (if not more) than any Statute, and of which all our good Acts of Parliament and *Magna Charta* itself is but Declaratory;[293] so that your Objection is sufficiently answered in this, That though the King is intrusted with the formal part of summoning and pronouncing the Dissolution of Parliaments, which is done by his Writ, yet the Laws (which oblige him as well as us) have determin'd how and when he shall do it; which is enough to shew, that the Kings share in the Soveraignty, that is, in the Parliament, is cut out to him by

---

at the moment when *Plato Redivivus* was published: "All lawyers had great regard to fundamental laws. And it was a maxim among our lawyers, that even an Act of Parliament against *Magna Charta* was null of it self" (Burnet, *History*, vol. 1, p. 458; cf. Grey, *Debates*, vol. 8, pp. 60 and 240, and *Of the Fundamental Laws or Politick Constitution of This Kingdom*, in *State-Tracts*, vol. 2, pp. 22–26). And in 1689 the Convention Parliament would cite as one of its reasons for declaring the throne vacant that James II had "violated the fundamental Laws" (Grey, *Debates*, vol. 9, p. 25). Nevertheless, the concept was arguably incoherent and empty: "The fundamental law or constitution was an ancient law or constitution; the concept had been built up by the search for precedents coupled with the common-law habit of mind that made it fatally easy to presume that anything which was in the common law, and which it was desired to emphasize, was immemorial" (Pocock, *Ancient Constitution*, p. 49). Accordingly, the concept of fundamental law was one on which later royalist writers such as Robert Brady delighted to pour scorn: "For here never was Pact between King and People, nor Fundamental Terms of Government agreed between them; nor indeed ever was there, or is it possible for any such thing to be in any Nation of the World: Matter of Fact so long as we have any Memorials of it in these Kingdoms, shews the contrary" (Brady, preface to *History*, sig. B2r–v; cf. *Antimonarchical Authors*, sig. B2v). It is also a phrase which Hobbes takes pleasure in mocking: see *Behemoth* (1679), p. 67. Equally, however, the concept of fundamental law might be discounted by a thinker of a much more populist character, such as John Warr, who coolly remarked in 1649 that it was "no such idol as men make it" (Wootton, *Divine Right*, p. 153). For Thomas Goddard's mockery of this point, see Goddard, *Plato's Demon*, pp. 373–74.

293. Cf. above, p. 162, n. 279. Cf. also Coke, *Selected Writings*, vol. 2, p. 748, where the phrasing is very similar.

the Law, and not left at his disposal. Now I come to the Kings part in the Intervals of Parliament.

Noble Venetian. Sir, before you do so, pray tell us what other Prerogatives the King enjoys in the Government; for otherwise, I who am a *Venetian*, may be apt to think that our Doge, who is call'd our Prince, may have as much Power as yours.

English Gentleman. I am in a fine condition amongst you with my Politicks: the *Doctor* tells me I have made the King Absolute, and now you tell me I have made him a Doge of *Venice*; But when your Prince has Power to dispose of the Publick Revenue, to name all Officers Ecclesiastical and Civil that are of trust and profit in the Kingdom, and to dispose absolutely of the whole Militia by Sea and Land, then we will allow him to be like ours, who has all these Powers.

Doctor. Well, you puzzle me extreamly: for when you had asserted the King's Power to the heighth, in Calling and Dissolving Parliaments, you gave me such satisfaction, and shewed me wherein the Law had provided, that this vast Prerogative could not hurt the People, that I was fully satisfied, and had not a word to say; Now you come about again, and place in the Crown such a Power, which in my Judgment is inconsistent with our Liberty.

English Gentleman. Sir, I suppose you mean chiefly the Power of the Militia, which was, I must confess, doubtful, before a late Statute[294] declar'd

---

294. 13 Car. II, c. 6, "An Act declaring the sole right of the militia to be in the King" (1661) had stipulated that the "command and disposition of the militia and of all forces by sea and land . . . ever was the undoubted right of his Majesty and his royal predecessors, Kings and Queens of England, and that both or either of the Houses of Parliament cannot nor ought to pretend to the same, nor can nor lawfully may raise or levy any war" (Kenyon, *Stuart Constitution*, p. 374). Control of the militia had been a point of tension between Charles I and Parliament in the early 1640s, as Neville might remember (May, *History*, lib. 2, pp. 39–43 and 99–100). In *Eikonoklastes* (1649) Milton had viewed control

it to be in the King: For our Government hath made no other disposal of the Militia than what was natural, *viz.* That the Peers in their several Counties, or Jurisdictions, had the Power of calling together their Vassals, either armed for the Wars, or onely so as to cause the Law to be executed by serving Writs; and in case of resistance, giving possession: which Lords amongst their own Tenants did then perform the two several Offices of Lord-Lieutenant, and Sheriff;[295] which latter was but the Earls Deputy, as by his Title of *Vice-Comes* do's appear. But this latter being of daily necessity, and Justice it self, that is, the Lives, Liberties and Estates of all the People in that County depending upon it, when the greatness of the Peers decay'd (of which we shall have occasion to speak hereafter) the Electing of Sheriff was referred to the County-Court, where it continued till it was placed where it now is by a Statute. For the other part of the Militia, which is, the Arming the People for War, it was *de facto* exercised by Commission from the King, to a Lord-Lieutenant (as an image of the Natural Lord) and other Deputies; and it was tacitely consented to, though it were never setled by Statute (as I said before) till His Majesties happy Restauration. But to answer you, I shall say, That whatever Powers are in the Crown, whether by Statute or by old Prescription, they are, and must be understood to be intrusted in the Prince,

---

of the militia as the key to the nation's liberty: "As for sole power of the *Militia* . . . give him but that, and as good give him in a lump all our Laws and Liberties" (quoted in Skinner, *Liberty*, p. 73). Cf. *A Letter from a Person of Quality*, in *State-Tracts*, vol. 1, p. 41. Neville had spoken in Parliament on 24 February 1659 on the subject of the militia (Burton, *Diary*, vol. 3, p. 461). Others, however, drew a distinction in respect of political consequences between militias and standing armies, such as the author of *A Letter from a Parliament-Man to His Friend*: "The *Militia* must, and can never be otherwise than for *English Liberty*, because else it doth destroy it *self*; but a *standing Force* can be for nothing but *Prerogative*, by whom it hath its *idle Living* and *Subsistance*" (*State-Tracts*, vol. 1, p. 70).

295. Respectively, the representative of the Crown in a county (*OED*, s.v. "lord lieutenant," 1b); and the representative of the royal authority in a shire (*OED*, s.v. "sheriff," 1a). The sheriff was the magistrate who presided in the shire-moot and was responsible for the administration of the royal demesne and the execution of the law.

for the preservation of the Government, and for the safety and interest of the People;[296] and when either the Militia, which is given him for the execution and support of the Law, shall be imploy'd by him to subvert it

296. In "Nicholas Machiavel's Letter to Zanobius Buondelmontius in Vindication of Himself and His Writings," Neville placed very similar sentiments in the mouth of Machiavelli, who deplores those princes that "make Magistracy, which was intended for the benefit of mankind, prove a Plague and Destruction to it" and who argues that his writings have taught that "the interest of *Kings*, and of their people is the same" (Machiavelli, *Works*, sig. **2v). A number of Boccalini's advertisements enforce the same mild, benevolent, and Epicurean view of the end of government, for instance, XXXV: "This man presenting himself before *Apollo*, in the name of *Hannibal* the Carthaginian, gave him that Lyon, which his Majesty was very well pleased withal; who asked the African what Art he had used to tame so fierce, ravenous, jealous, and cruel a Beast? The *African* answered, By feeding him continually with his own hand. *Apollo* then turned towards the Princes, who, for the honour of that Audience, were there in great numbers, and said unto them; Learn, Lords, by the Miracle of this Lyon which you see is become so tame, that fair treatment doth domestichize even savage beasts; do you the like by your Subjects, and make them not come hardly by their food through your angersom Taxes upon things necessary for human life; for, by so doing, you shall not be beloved, served, and honoured by your own natural Subjects only, but even by the more Forraign and Barbarous Nations of the earth" (Boccalini, *Advertisements*, p. 41; cf. pp. 85, 145, 151, and 165). Burke would echo this concept of the purpose of government in 1790: "Kings, in one sense, are undoubtedly the servants of the people, because their power has no other rational end than that of the general advantage"; "If civil society be made for the advantage of man, all the advantages for which it is made become his right. It is an institution of beneficence; and law itself is only beneficence acting by a rule"; "Government is a contrivance of human wisdom to provide for human *wants*" (Burke, *Reflections*, pp. 179, 217, and 218). David Wootton has suggested that the emergence of this view in an English context occurred at the end of the seventeenth century, when "it was even proposed that rulers and constitutions should be assessed in terms of their ability to ensure prosperity rather than godliness" (Wootton, *Divine Right*, pp. 18–19); of course, even then such opinions were far from hegemonic. Note, however, that Charles I, in his *Answer to the Nineteen Propositions* (1642), had conceded that the "high and perpetual power" of the prince should be exercised for the good of the people; that Roger Williams, in *The Bloudy Tenent of Persecution* (1644), had said that "civil government is an ordinance of God, to conserve the civil peace of people so far as concerns their bodies and goods" (Wootton, *Divine Right*, pp. 172 and 243); and that John Streater in 1653 had postulated that "Government should or ought to be for the conservation of mankind" (Streater, *Glympse*, p. 2). In the *Court Maxims* of 1664–65, Sidney's spokesman in the dialogues, the Commonwealthsman Eunomius, tells his interlocutor Philalethes that "if you say monarchy is the best government because

(as in the case of Ship-Money[297] it was) or the Treasure shall be mis-apply'd, and made the Revenue of Courtiers and Sycophants (as in the time of *Edward* the Second)[298] or worthless or wicked People shall be put into the greatest places, as in the reign of *Richard* the Second;[299] In this case, though the Prince here cannot be questionable for it (as the Kings

---

greatest conquests have been made by monarchs, you must show that the people have been bettered by those conquests; else you only show monarchy is good for monarchs. That is nothing to our purpose. We seek not what is good for a *man* but for a *nation*" (Sidney, *Court Maxims*, p. 15). The objective of the common good was clearly a principle that could be grasped from very different directions and applied to quite contrasting ultimate ends. However, in the late 1670s it was feared that Charles II's ministers had acquired very different principles of government during their time of exile: "One maxim they brought over . . . was, 'Make the people poor, and you will make them obedient'" (Grey, *Debates*, vol. 7, p. 51; cf. p. 190). Sidney has Philalethes, the courtier in the dialogues of his *Court Maxims*, confess the same: "There is nothing we learned more perfectly when abroad than that the number, strength, and riches of the people of England must be abated, and nothing has been more industriously sought by us" (Sidney, *Court Maxims*, p. 72). Cf. Goddard, *Plato's Demon*, pp. 137–38; and below, p. 320.

297. An ancient tax levied in time of war on the ports and maritime towns, cities, and counties of England to provide ships for the king's service. It had been revived by Charles I (with an extended application to inland counties) in order to raise funds during the Personal Rule but was finally abolished by statute in 1640 (*OED*, s.v. "ship money"). Although it seems to have been efficiently collected, and thus productive, it was profoundly resented: see, e.g., article 20 of the *Grand Remonstrance* (1641), where it is complained that "a new unheard-of tax of ship-money was devised, and upon the same pretence, by both which there was charged upon the subject near £700,000 some years, and yet the merchants have been left so naked to the violence of the Turkish pirates, that many great ships of value and thousands of His Majesty's subjects have been taken by them, and do still remain in miserable slavery." Technically, however, ship money was not a tax but a service, or payment-in-lieu. Neville's insinuation, that the militia was misused by the Crown to coerce payment of ship money, has seemed groundless to modern historians: see, e.g., Sharpe, *Personal Rule*, pp. 583–95.

298. A reference to Edward II's bestowing of lucrative positions on his favorite, Piers Gaveston (d. 1312). Gaveston had been a particular target of the ordinances imposed on Edward by his magnates in 1311. Cf. Sidney, *Discourses*, p. 524. Edward II's criminal indulgence of his favorites had been recalled in Parliament during the debates surrounding the Popish Plot and Charles II's pardon of Danby; see Grey, *Debates*, vol. 7, p. 25.

299. A reference to Richard's employment of lowborn instruments such as Robert Tresilian (d. 1388) to enforce his high-handed policies over taxation.

were in *Sparta*, and your Doges I believe would be) yet it is a great violation of the trust reposed in him by the Government, and a making that
Power, which is given him by Law, unlawful in the Execution. And the
frequent examples of Justice inflicted in Parliament upon the King's
Ministers for abusing the Royal Power, shews plainly that such authority
is not left in his hands to use as he pleases.[300] Nay, there have befallen sad
troubles and dangers to some of these Princes themselves, who have
abused their Power to the prejudice of the Subjects; which although they
are no way justifiable, yet may serve for an Instruction to Princes, and an
example not to hearken to ruinous Councils: for men when they are enraged do not always consider Justice of Religion, passion being as natural
to man as reason and vertue,[301] which was the Opinion of divine *Machiavil*. To answer you then, I say, That though we do allow such Powers in
the King, yet since they are given him for edification and not destruction, and cannot be abused without great danger to his Ministers, and
even to himself; we may hope that they can never be abused but in a
broken Government: And if ours be so (as we shall see anon) the fault of
the ill execution of our Laws is not to be imputed either to the Prince or
his Ministers; excepting that the latter may be, as we said before, justly
punishable for not advising the Prince to consent to the mending the
frame; of which we shall talk more hereafter: but in the mean time I will

300. Neville here touches lightly on the English political doctrine that the king
can do no wrong. Sometimes shallowly misunderstood as implying that the king's
actions, no matter how criminal or offensive in themselves, are ipso facto right in
virtue of being performed by the king, in fact the doctrine is a restraint on royal
power, because it means that a servant of the Crown cannot plead a royal command as sufficient warrant for the commission of an illegal act (the principle is
correctly explained by the authors of *A Just and Modest Vindication of the Proceedings of the Two Last Parliaments of King Charles the Second*: see *State-Tracts*, vol. 1,
p. 165; for another example, see p. 188).

301. A reference not to any authentic Machiavellian text but rather to Neville's
spurious "Machiavellian" composition, "Nicholas Machiavel's Letter to Zanobius
Buondelmontius in Vindication of Himself and His Writings," where he makes
Machiavelli say in defense of mild and humane rule that "let the terrour and the
guilt be never so great, it is impossible that humane Nature which consists of passion as well as virtue can support with patience and submission the greatest cruelty
and injustice" (Machiavelli, *Works*, sig. **2v).

come to the Kings other Prerogatives, as having all Royal Mines, the being serv'd first before other Creditors where mony is due to him, and to have a speedier and easier way than his Subjects to recover his debts and his Rents, &c. But to say all in one word, when there arises any doubt whether any thing be the king's Prerogative or no, this is the way of deciding it, *viz.* To consider whether it be for the good and protection of the people that the King have such a Power; For the definition of Prerogative is a considerable part of the Common Law, by which Power is put into the Prince for the preservation of his People.[302] And if it be not for the good of his Subjects, it is not Prerogative, not Law, for our Prince has no Authority of his own, but what was first intrusted in him by the Government, of which he is Head; nor is it to be imagined that they would give him more Power than what was necessary to Govern them.[303] For example, the power of pardoning Criminals[304] condemned, is of such

302. See above, p. 172, n. 296.

303. Cf. the statement of general principle in the anonymous pamphlet on the illegality of extensive and repeated prorogation included in Grey's *Debates*: "It is a fundamental and unquestionable maxim in the law of *England*, that the Kings of *England* are so bound by all Statutes made for the public good, that every command, order, or direction of them, contrary to the substance, scope, or intent of any such Statute, is void and null in law" (Grey, *Debates*, vol. 4, pp. 55–62; quotation on p. 57).

304. In 1679 the scope, nature, and possible limitations of the King's prerogative to grant pardons had been extensively debated in Parliament *à propos* the impeachment of Danby. Burnet summarized the arguments deployed on either side: "Upon this a great debate was raised. Some questioned whether the King's pardon, especially when passed in bar to an impeachment, was good in law: This would encourage ill Ministers, who would be always sure of a pardon, and so would act more boldly, if they saw so easy a way to be secured against the danger of impeachments: The King's pardon did indeed secure one against all prosecution at his suit: But, as in the case of murder an appeal lay, from which the King's pardon did not cover his person, since the King could no more pardon the injuries done his people, than he could forgive the debts that were owing to them; so from a parity of reason it was inferred, that since the offenses of Ministers of State were injuries done the publick, the King's Pardon could not hinder a prosecution in Parliament, which seemed to be one of the chief securities, and most essential parts of our constitution. Yet on the other hand it was said, that the power of pardoning was a main article of the King's Prerogative: None had even yet been annulled: The law had made this one of the trusts of the Government, without any limitation upon it: All arguments against it might be good reasons for the limiting it for the future: But what was already past was good in law, and could not be broke thro" (Burnet,

use to the Lives and Estates of the People, that without it many would be exposed to die unjustly; As lately a poor Gentleman,[305] who by means of the Harangue of a Strepitous[306] Lawyer was found guilty of Murder, for a Man he never kil'd; or if he had, the fact had been but Man-slaughter; and he had been inevitably murdered himself, if his Majesty had not been graciously pleased to extend his Royal Mercy to him; As he did likewise vouchsafe to do to a Gentleman convicted for speaking words[307] he never utter'd; or if he had spoken them, they were but foolishly, not malitiously spoken. On the other side, if a Controversie should arise, as it did in the beginning of the last Parliament, between the House of Commons, and the Prerogative-Lawyers, about the choice of their Speaker,[308] these latter having interested his Majesty in the Contest, and made him,

---

History, vol. 1, p. 453). Parliament was concerned in the later 1670s about the frequency with which royal pardons were being granted, and for the seriousness of the offenses to which such pardons were being applied (see, e.g., Grey, *Debates*, vol. 4, p. 134). As Thomas Bennet (c. 1640–c. 1702) had observed in the House of Commons on 22 March 1679, "If Pardons go on at this rate that the King has told us, we are in a desperate condition" (Grey, *Debates*, vol. 7, p. 20). Edward Vaughan (c. 1635–84) concurred: "It is a great and glorious Prerogative in the King to pardon offences, &c. but at this rate of pardoning, you may have all persons break loose, and all honest men in prison" (ibid., p. 30). Cf. John Brydall, *A New-Years-Gift* (1682).

305. This person is unidentified. On 6 November 1689, Sir Edward Hussey had defended the royal pardon in Parliament in terms that parallel Neville's example: "What if a murder be committed, and a man wrongfully condemned, shall he be hanged for want of the King's Power to pardon?" (Grey, *Debates*, vol. 9, p. 397).

306. I.e., noisy (*OED*, s.v. "strepitous," citing this passage).

307. This is possibly a very topical reference to the trial and conviction of Viscount Stafford in 1680; see Burnet, *History*, vol. 1, pp. 488–94.

308. Neville refers to a trial of strength between the House of Commons and the Crown that had occurred in the spring of 1679: "*Seimour* [i.e., Sir Edward Seymour (1633–1708), fourth baronet] had in the last Session struck in with that heat against Popery, that he was become popular upon it. So he managed the matter in this new Parliament, that tho' the Court named *Meres* [i.e., Thomas Meres (1634–1715)] yet he was chosen Speaker. The nomination of the Speaker was understood to come from the King, tho' he was not named as recommending the person. Yet a Privy Counsellor named one: And it was understood to be done by order. And the person thus named was put in the chair, and was next day presented to the King, who approved the choice. When *Seimour* was next day presented as the Speaker, the King refused to confirm the election. He said, he had other occasions for him, which could not be dispensed with. Upon this, great heats arose, with a long and violent debate. It was said, the House had the choice of their Speaker in them, and

by consequence, disoblige, *in limine*,[309] a very Loyal, and a very Worthy Parliament; and for what? for a Question, which if you will decide it the right way, will be none: for setting aside the Presidents, and the History when the Crown first pretended to any share in the Choice of a Speaker, which Argument was very well handled by some of the Learned Patriots then, I would have leave to ask, what man can shew, and what reason can be alledged, why the protection and welfare of the People should require that a Prerogative should be in the Prince to chuse the Mouth of the House of Commons, when there is no particular person in his whole Dominion that would not think it against his interest, if the Government had given the King Power to nominate his Bayliff, his Attorney, or his Referree in any Arbitration? Certainly there can be no advantage either to the Soveraign or his Subjects, that the person whose Office it is to put their deliberations into fitting words, and express all their requests to his Majesty, should not be entirely in their own Election and appointment; which there is the more reason for too, because the Speakers for many years past have received Instructions from the Court,[310] and have broken

---

that their presenting the Speaker was only a solemn shewing him to the King, such as was the presenting the Lord Mayor and Sheriffs of *London* in the Exchequer; but that the King was bound to confirm their choice. The debate held a week, and created much anger. A temper was found at last. *Seimour's* election was let fall: But the point was settled, that the right of electing was in the House, and that the confirmation was a thing of course. So another was chosen Speaker" (Burnet, *History*, vol. 1, pp. 452–53). Cf. *Antidotum*, pp. 97–103, and Grey, *Debates*, vol. 7, pp. 1–3.

309. I.e., on the threshold, at the very outset (*OED*, s.v. "in," *prep.* 2, I11).

310. On 9 March 1659, Sir Arthur Haslerig had stated in Parliament that it had always been the practice and concern of the Commons to choose a Speaker "that was no way influenced by the Court" (Burton, *Diary*, vol. 4, p. 91). Nevertheless, monarchical interference in the choice of a Speaker was common (see, e.g., Grey, *Debates*, vol. 2, p. 37), and the office of Speaker had for a number of years been a site of tension between Crown and Parliament: see, e.g., the debate on the Speaker on 27 October 1673, in which MPs objected to Sir Edward Seymour's closeness to the Court and to his being a Privy Counsellor, as well as to his dissolute way of life (Grey, *Debates*, vol. 2, pp. 186–88); Henry Powle had said that he would "never think that Privilege of Parliament is not violated as long as a Privy Counsellor sits in the Chair" (ibid., p. 208). A salient recent instance of conflict had occurred in May 1677 when Charles responded to an address of the Commons for an alliance with the Dutch States General by requiring the House to adjourn until July (for Charles's ostensible and actual motivation, see Grey, *Debates*, vol. 5, p. 2, n. *). The Speaker, Sir Edward Seymour, had carried out the instruction in the face of pro-

the Priviledges of the House, by revealing their Debates, Adjourning them without a Vote, and committed many other Misdemeanours, by which they have begotten an ill understanding between the King and his House of Commons, to the infinite prejudice both of his Majesties Affairs, and his People. Since I have given this rule to Judge Prerogative by, I shall say no more of it; for as to what concerns the King's Office in the Intervals of Parliament, it is wholly Ministerial, and is barely to put in Execution the Common Law and the Statutes made by the Soveraign Power,[311] that is, by Himself and the Parliament, without varying one tittle, or suspending,[312] abrogating, or neglecting the Execution of any

---

test and had renewed the adjournment on three further occasions (July and December 1677, and January 1678) in response to further instructions from the king (see Grey, *Debates*, vol. 4, pp. 389–91). When the House eventually resumed on 28 January 1678, William Sacheverell had tried to press a charge against Seymour for his conduct (MPs had reminded themselves that Sir John Finch had been forcibly prevented from adjourning on the king's instructions in 1629: Grey, *Debates*, vol. 4, p. 390; vol. 5, p. 1 n. *; and vol. 5, pp. 5–17). Seymour had already made himself an object of suspicion to some MPs for his closeness to Danby and his willingness to manage the Court's business in the Commons, and on 9 February 1678 the Commons held a debate on whether or not the Speaker had the right to adjourn the Commons on receipt of an instruction from the king (Grey, *Debates*, vol. 5, pp. 122–44). For commentary, see Paul Seaward, "The Speaker in the Age of Party, 1672–1715," in *Parliamentary History*, vol. 29, no. 1 (2010), pp. 90–101, esp. pp. 95–97.

311. Cf. Carey, *Considerations*, p. 6: "These Statutes are in pursuance of the Common Law, and the king cannot dispence with the Common Law. . . . It is a general rule in law, That the king cannot dispence with any Statute made *pro bono publico*."

312. Prior to 1689 the royal prerogative included a suspending power, whereby the monarch could cause a law to be for a period no longer in force, or to be abrogated or temporarily inoperative (*OED*, s.v. "suspend," 2e). During the reign of Charles II this prerogative power had become deeply controversial: the Declaration of Indulgence of 1673 had attempted to circumvent the penal laws against religious dissidents, and the House of Commons had forced its withdrawal (see Grey, *Debates*, vol. 2, pp. 61–69). James II would attempt something similar in 1687, and again the courts would not uphold it. The Bill of Rights of 1689 would abolish the suspending power of the Crown, specifying that one of the abuses practiced by James II had been his "assuming and exercising a power of dispensing with and suspending of laws and the execution of laws without consent of Parliament" and that in consequence "the pretended power of dispensing with laws or the execution of laws by regal authority without consent of Parliament is illegal."

Act whatsoever; and to this he is Solemnly Sworn at his Coronation:[313]
And all his Power in this behalf is in him by Common Law, which is
Reason it self, written as well in the hearts of rational Men, as in the
Lawyers Books.

Noble Venetian. Sir, I have heard much talk of the Kings Negative Voice
in Parliaments, which in my Opinion is as much as a Power to frustrate,
when he pleases, all the endeavours and labours of his People, and to
prevent any good that might accrue to the Kingdom by having the right
to meet in Parliament: for certainly, if we in *Venice* had placed any such
Prerogative in our Duke, or in any of our Magistracies, we could not call
our selves a free People.

English Gentleman. Sir, I can answer you as I did before, that if our Kings
have such a Power, it ought to be used according to the true and genuine
intent of the Government, that is, for the Preservation and Interest of the
people, and not for the disappointing the Counsels of a Parliament,
towards reforming Grievances, and making provision for the future execution of the Lawes; and whenever it is applyed to frustrate those ends, it
is a violation of Right, and infringement of the King's Coronation-Oath;
in which there is this Clause, That he shall *Confirmare consuetudines,*
(which in the Latine of those times is *leges*) *quas vulgus elegerit.*[314] I know

313. The first question in the coronation oath taken by Charles II had required
him to swear that he would "grant and keep, and by your Oath confirm, to the
People of *England,* the Laws and Customs to them granted, by the Kings of
England, your lawful and Religious Predecessors."

314. The relevant section of the old coronation oath in its Latin form is as follows: "Concedis justas leges et consuetudines esse tenendas, et promittis per te eas
esse protegendas, et ad honorem Dei corroborandas, quas vulgus elegerit, secun-
dum vires tuas? *Respondebit.* Concedo et promitto." The grammatical crux re-
volves around whether the verb *elegerit* is in the future perfect or the simple future,
since both these tenses form the third person singular as *elegerit*; hence, the language of the Latin form of the coronation oath is ambiguous. Cf. Harrington, *The
Prerogative of Popular Government* (Pocock, *Harrington,* pp. 391–92; cf. *Valerius and
Publicola,* ibid., pp. 786–87). For hostile but learned commentary, see *Antidotum,*
pp. 111–16. The point had occurred in debates in Parliament in 1659 (Burton,
Diary, vol. 3, p. 319), and Neville himself had quoted the tag in the House of

some Criticks, who are rather Grammarians than Lawyers, have made a distinction between *elegerim* and *elegero*, and will have it, That the King Swears to such Laws as the people shall have chosen, and not to those they shall chuse. But in my Opinion, if that Clause had been intended onely to oblige the King to execute the Laws made already, it might have been better exprest by *servare*[315] *consuetudines*, than by *confirmare consuetudines*; besides that he is by another clause[316] in the same Oath sworn to execute all the Laws. But I shall leave this Controversie undecided; those who have a desire to see more of it, may look into those quarrelling Declarations, *pro* and *con*, about this matter, which preceded our unhappy Civil Wars.[317] This is certain, that there are not to be found any Statutes that have passed, without being presented to his Majesty, or to some commissioned by him; but whether such Addresses were intended for Respect and Honour to His Majesty, as the Speaker of the House of Commons and the Lord Mayor of *London* are brought to him, I leave to the Learned to Discourse; onely thus much we may affirm, That there never were yet any Parliamentary Requests, which did highly concern the Publick, presented to any King, and by him refused, but such denials did produce very dismal effects, as may be seen in our Histories ancient and late; it being certain, that both the Barons Wars, and our last dismal

---

Commons (ibid., p. 341). Milton had commented in 1651 on Charles I's attempts to evade the implications of that clause: "Leges, *quas vulgus*; id est, communitas, sive plebeius ordo *elegerit*. Hanc clausulam, *quas vulgus elegerit*, Carolus, antequam coronam acceperit, ex formula juramenti regii eradendum curavit" (*Angli Pro Popvlo Anglicano Defensio* [1650], p. 237).

315. *Confirmare* means "to confirm or strengthen," *servare* "to preserve or protect."

316. The fourth question to which Charles was asked to swear in the affirmative was "Sir, will you grant to hold and keep, the Laws and rightful Customs, which the Commonalty of this your Kingdom have? And will you defend and uphold them, to the Honour of God, so much as in you lieth?"

317. This grammatical detail of the coronation oath had been a matter of furious altercation between Royalists and Parliamentarians in 1642: cf. *A Remonstrance, or The Declaration of the Lords and Commons* (1642), p. 6; *His Majesties Answer to a Printed Book* (1642), p. 9; Dudley Diggs, *An Answer to a Printed Book* (1642), pp. 24–25; "J. M.," *A Reply to the Answer* (1642), pp. 13–14; and William Prynne, *The Aphorismes of the Kingdome* (1642), p. 1. Cf. Rushworth, *Collections*, part 3, vol. 1, pp. 593–94.

Combustions,[318] proceeded from no other cause than the denial of the Princes then reigning to consent to the desires of the States of the Kingdom: and such hath been the wisdom and goodness of our present gracious Prince, that in twenty years and somewhat more, for which time we have enjoy'd him since his happy Restauration, he hath not exercis'd his Negative Voice towards more than one publick Bill; and that too, was to have continued in force (if it had passed into an Act) but for six Weeks, being for raising the Militia for so long time; and as for the private Bills, which are matters of meer grace, it is unreasonable his Majesty should be refused that Right that every *Englishman* enjoys, which is not to be obliged to dispence his favours but where he pleases. But for this point of the Negative Vote, it is possible that when we come to Discourse of the Cure of our Political Distemper, some of you will propose the clearing and explanation of this matter, and of all others which may concern the King's Power and the Peoples Rights.

Noble Venetian. But pray, Sir, have not the House of Peers a Negative Voice in all Bills? how come they not to be obliged to use it for the Publick Good?

English Gentleman. So they are, no doubt, and the Commons too; but there is a vast difference between a deliberative Vote which the Peers have with their Negative, and that in the Crown to blast all without deliberating. The Peers are Co-ordinate with the Commons in presenting and hammering of Laws, and may send Bills down to them, as well as receive any from them, excepting in matters wherein the People are to be Taxed: and in this our Government imitates the best and most perfect Commonwealths that ever were; where the Senate assisted in the making of Laws, and by their wisdom and dexterity, polisht, fil'd, and made ready things for the more populous Assemblies; and sometimes by their gravity and moderation, reduced the People to a Calmer State, and by their authority and credit stem'd the Tide, and made the Waters quiet,

---

318. I.e., the Civil Wars of 1642–49. "Combustions" are, in this context, disorders or tumults (*OED*, s.v. "combustion," 5b).

giving the People time to come to themselves. And therefore if we had no such Peerage now upon the old Constitution, yet we should be necessitated to make an artificial Peerage or Senate in stead of it: which may assure our present Lords, that though their Dependences[319] and Power are gone, yet that we cannot be without them; and that they have no need to fear an annihilation by our Reformation, as they suffered in the late mad times.[320] But I shall speak a word of the peoples Rights, and then shew how this brave and excellent Government of *England* came to decay.

The People by the Fundamental Laws,[321] that is, by the Constitution of the Government of *England*, have entire freedome in their Lives, Properties, and their Persons; neither of which can in the least suffer, but according to the Laws already made, or to be made hereafter in Parliament, and duly publisht: and to prevent any oppression that might happen in the execution of these good Laws, which are our Birth-right, all Tryals must be by twelve Men of our equals, and of our Neighbourhood; These in all Civil Causes judge absolutely, and decide the matter of Fact, upon which the matter of Law depends; but if where matter of Law is in question, these twelve Men shall refuse to find a special Verdict at the direction of the Court, the Judge cannot Controul it, but their Verdict must be Recorded. But of these matters, as also of Demurrers, Writs of Errour, and Arrests of Judgment,[322] *&c.* I have discours'd to this Gentleman

319. I.e., bodies of dependants; a retinue (*OED*, s.v. "dependence," 4b).

320. On 6 February 1649 the House of Commons had resolved to abolish the House of Lords and passed the necessary statute in March of the same year.

321. See above, p. 168, n. 292.

322. A demurrer is a pleading which, admitting for the moment the facts as stated in the opponent's pleading, denies that the opponent is legally entitled to relief and thus stops the action until this point be determined by the court (*OED*, s.v. "demurrer," 1a). Demurrers were topical in that they had figured prominently in the proceedings against Danby in 1679 (see, e.g., Grey, *Debates*, vol. 7, pp. 173–82). A writ of error is brought to procure the reversal of a judgment on the ground of error. An arrest of judgment is a stay of proceedings, after a verdict for the plaintiff or the Crown, on the ground of manifest error therein (*OED*, s.v. "arrest," 6). One

(who is a Stranger) before now; neither do's the understanding of the Execution of our Municipal Laws[323] at all belong to this discourse: Onely it is to be noted, that these Juries, or twelve Men, in all Trials or Causes which are Criminal, have absolute Power, both as to matter of Law and Fact (except the Party by Demurrer confess the matter of Fact, and take it out of their hands.) And the first question the Officer asks the Fore-man, when they all come in to deliver their Verdict, is this, Is he Guilty in manner or form as he is Indicted, or not Guilty? which shews plainly, that they are to Examine and Judge, as well whether, and how far the Fact committed is Criminal, as whether the person charged hath committed that Fact. But though by the Corruption of these times (the infallible consequences of a broken frame of Government) this Office of the Juries and Right of *Englishmen* have been of late question'd, yet it hath been strongly and effectually vindicated by a learned Author of late,[324] to whom I refer you for more of this matter. I shall say no more of the Rights of the People, but this one thing, That neither the King, nor any by Authority from him, hath any the least Power or Jurisdiction over any *Englishman*, but what the Law gives them; and that although all Commissions and Writs go out in the King's name, yet his Majesty hath no right to Issue out any Writ (with advice of his Council, or otherwise)

---

of the first actions of the Parliament of 1653 had been to "prepare an Act for redress of delays and mischiefs, arising on writs of error, writs of false judgment, and arrests of judgment" (Burton, *Diary*, vol. 1, p. iii). Neville himself had been personally involved in both an arrest of judgment and the possibility of a writ of error (Burton, *Diary*, vol. 3, pp. 52–53). Writs of error had figured in debates in the Commons concerning how that house could be adjourned, to which debates Neville also refers (Grey, *Debates*, vol. 5, p. 123; cf. vol. 9, pp. 523–26, 532–35), and also in the arraignment of the Five Lords in 1679 (Grey, *Debates*, vol. 7, p. 121).

323. I.e., the internal laws of a state, as distinct from international law (*OED*, s.v., "municipal law," A1).

324. A reference to William Penn, who in *Truth Rescued from Imposture* (1670) had defended the role of the jury to judge both law and fact: "If then the Indictment comprehends both *Law* and *Fact,* and that the Jury is to give their Judgment in *Manner* and *Form,* and that *Manner* and *Form* takes in, and includes the whole *Law* and *Fact of the Indictment* (as they manifestly do) then, with great strength and clearness we may infer, *That the Iury is Iudge of Law and Fact*" (p. 32).

excepting what come out of his Courts; nor to alter any Clause in a Writ, or add any thing to it. And if any person shall be so wicked as to do any Injustice to the Life, Liberty, or Estate of any *Englishman*, by any private command of the Prince, the person agrieved, or his next of kin (if he be assassinated) shall have the same remedy against the Offender, as he ought to have had by the good Laws of this Land, if there had been no such Command given; which would be absolutely void and null, and understood not to proceed from that Royal and lawful Power which is vested in his Majesty for the Execution of Justice, and the protection of his People.[325]

Doctor. Now I see you have done with all the Government of *England*; pray before you proceed to the decay of it, let me ask you what you think of the Chancery,[326] whether you do not believe it a Solecism in the Politicks to have such a Court amongst a free People; what good will *Magna Charta*, the Petition of Right,[327] or St. *Edwards* Laws[328] do us to defend

325. An explanation of the principle that the king can do no wrong, which rightly understood is protective of liberty in its rejection of the possibility that the king may legitimately authorize or command an illegal act.

326. The court of the Lord Chancellor of England, until the Judicature Act of 1873 the highest court of law below the House of Lords. It formerly consisted of two distinct tribunals, one ordinary, being a court of common law, the other extraordinary, being a court of equity. To the former belonged the issuing of writs for a new parliament and of all original writs. The second proceeded upon rules of equity and conscience, moderating the rigor of the common law, and giving relief in cases where there was no remedy in the common-law courts (*OED*, s.v. "Chancery," 2a). The Doctor refers to the latter. Suits in Chancery had the reputation of being unusually expensive, prolonged, and vexatious; hence the English Gentleman's speculation that the Doctor "had a Suit in Chancery" (below, p. 185), which explains his strength of feeling against that court.

327. The Petition of Right had been ratified by Charles I on 7 June 1628, albeit reluctantly. In it Parliament had specified a number of liberties of the subject that the king was prohibited from infringing.

328. The apocryphal *leges Edwardi Confessoris*, written versions of which exist only in manuscripts much later than the reign of the Confessor. They are a body of good, benevolent legislation that common lawyers imputed to Edward the Confessor and that they maintained had been adopted in 1066 by William the Conqueror; cf. the preface to part 8 of Coke's *Reports* (Coke, *Selected Writings*, pp. 245–49) and Somers's *A Brief History of the Succession* (*State-Tracts*, vol. 1, p. 385).

our Property, if it must be entirely subjected to the arbitrary disposal of one man, whenever any impertinent or petulant person shall put in a Bill against you? How inconsistent is this Tribunal with all that hath been said in defence of our rights, or can be said? Suppose the Prince should in time come so little to respect his own honour and the Interest of his People, as to place a covetous or revengeful person in that great Judicatory, what remedy have we against the Corruption of Registers,[329] who make what Orders they please; Or against the whole Hierarchy of Knavish Clerks, whilst not only the punishing and reforming misdemeanours depend upon him, who may without controul be the most guilty himself, but that all the Laws of *England* stand there arraigned before him, and may be condemned when he pleases? Is there, or ever was there any such Tribunal in the World before, in any Countrey?

English Gentleman. *Doctor*, I find you have had a Suit in Chancery, but I do not intend to contradict or blame your Orthodox Zeal in this point: This Court is one of those Buildings that cannot be repaired, but must be demolished. I could inform you how excellently matters of Equity are Administred in other Countries; And this worthy Gentleman could tell you of the Venerable *Quaranzia's*[330] in his City, where the Law as well as the Fact, is at the Bar, and subject to the Judges, and yet no complaint made or grievance suffered: but this is not a place for it, this is but the superstructure; we must settle the foundation first; every thing else is as much out of Order as this. Trade is gone, Suits are endless, and nothing amongst us harmonious: but all will come right when our Government is

---

Until 1688 the English coronation oath included a promise to observe the laws of St. Edward. See Janelle Greenberg, *The Radical Face of the Ancient Constitution: St. Edward's "Laws" in Early Modern Political Thought* (Cambridge: Cambridge University Press, 2001).

329. I.e., the keepers of the register of the court.

330. More correctly, *Quarantia*. The "Council of Forty" was one of the highest constitutional bodies in the Venetian Republic. Its members nominated the Doge and served as the judiciary of the state. See Jean Gailhard, *The Present State of the Republick of Venice* (1669), pp. 96, 109, 120, and 122–23; Boccalini, *Advertisements*, pp. 78–79. Neville's fondness for Venetian institutions and vocabulary irritated his critics: see *Antimonarchical Authors*, pp. 237 and 241–42. Cf. Pocock, *Harrington*, p. 668.

mended, and never before, though our Judges were all Angels: this is the *primum quaerite*; when you have this, all other things shall be added unto you;[331] when that is done, neither the Chancery (which is grown up to this since our Ancestors time) nor the Spiritual Courts,[332] nor the Cheats in trade, nor any other abuses, no not the Gyant Popery it self, shall ever be able to stand before a Parliament, no more than one of us can live like a Salamander in the fire.[333]

Noble Venetian. Therefore, Sir, pray let us come now to the decay of your Government, that we may come the sooner to the happy restauration.

English Gentleman. This harmonious Government of *England* being founded as has been said upon Property, it was impossible it should be shaken, so long as Property remain'd where it was placed: for if, when the ancient Owners the *Britains* fled into the Mountains, and left their Lands to the Invaders[334] (who divided them, as is above related) they had made an *Agrarian* Law[335] to fix it; then our Government, and by consequence our Happiness had been for ought we know Immortal: for our Constitution, as it was really a mixture of the three, which are *Monarchy, Aristocracy,* and *Democracy* (as has been said) so the weight and predominancy remain'd in the *Optimacy,* who possessed nine parts in ten of the Lands; And the Prince but about a tenth part. In this I count all the Peoples share to the Peers, and therefore do not trouble my self to enquire what proportion was allotted to them, for that although they had an Heredi-

331. An allusion to a passage from the Sermon on the Mount (Matthew 6:33), which in the Vulgate reads, "Quaerite autem primum regnum et iustitiam eius et omnia haec adicientur vobis." In the Authorized Version the passage reads, "But seek ye first the kingdom of God, and his righteousness; and all these things shall be added unto you."

332. I.e., the ecclesiastical courts. Before the Court Probate Act of 1857, the English ecclesiastical courts had jurisdiction to grant or withhold probate over the personal estates of the deceased, and it is probably their exercise of this jurisdiction over private property that has provoked the Doctor's resentment against them.

333. The salamander was a mythical lizard supposed to be able to survive in fire.

334. I.e., the Saxons.

335. See above, p. 109, n. 157.

tary right in their Lands, yet it was so clog'd with Tenures and Services, that they depended, as to publick matters, wholly on their Lords, who by them could serve the king in his Wars; and in time of Peace, by leading the people to what they pleased: Could keep the Royal Power within its due bounds, and also hinder and prevent the people from Invading the Rights of the Crown; so that they were the Bulwarks of the Government; which in effect was much more an *Aristocracy*, than either a *Monarchy* or *Democracy*: and in all Governments, where Property is mixt, the Administration is so too: And that part which hath the greater share in the Lands, will have it too in the Jurisdiction: And so in Commonwealths, the Senate or the People have more or less Power, as they have more or fewer possessions; as was most visible in *Rome*, where in the beginning, the *Patricii* could hardly bring the People to any thing; but afterwards, when the *Asiatick* Conquests[336] had inricht the Nobility to that degree, that they were able to purchase a great part of the Lands in *Italy*, the People were all their Clients, and easily brought even to cut the throats of their Redeemers the *Gracchi*,[337] who had carried a Law for restoring them their Lands. But enough of this before. I will not trouble my self nor you, to search into the particular causes of this change, which has been made in the possessions here in *England*; but it is visible that the fortieth part of the Lands which were at the beginning in the hands of the Peers and Church, is not there now; besides that not only all Villanage[338] is long since abolished, but the other Tenures are so altered and qualified, that they signifie nothing towards making the Yeomanry depend upon the Lords. The consequence is, That the natural part of our Government, which is Power, is by means of Property in the hands of the People, whilest the artificial part, or the Parchment, in which the Form of Government is written, remains the same. Now Art is a very good servant

336. Between approximately 270 and 120 B.C., Rome had expanded beyond Italy and had made a number of conquests in the eastern Mediterranean which had brought immense booty into the city. The classic statement of the deleterious effect that oriental riches produced on Roman character and Roman institutions is given by Sallust, *Bellum Catilinae*, 10–13.

337. See above, p. 110, n. 159.

338. I.e., feudal bondage (*OED*, s.v. "villanage," 2).

and help to Nature,[339] but very weak and inconsiderable, when she opposes her, and fights with her: it would be a very *Impar congressus*,[340] between Parchment and Power: This alone is the cause of all the disorder
you heard of, and now see in *England*, and of which every man gives a
reason according to his own fancy, whilest few hit the right cause: some
impute all to the decay of Trade, others to the growth of Popery; which
are both great Calamities, but they are Effects, and not Causes; And if in
private Families there were the same causes, there would be the same effects. Suppose now you had five or six Thousand pounds a year, as it is
probable you have, and keep forty Servants, and at length, by your neglect, and the industry and thrift of your Domesticks, you sell one Thousand to your Steward, another to your Clerk of the Kitchen, another to
your Bayliff, till all were gone; can you believe that these Servants, when
they had so good Estates of their own, and you nothing left to give them,
would continue to live with you, and to do their service as before? It is
just so with a whole Kingdom. In our Ancestors times, most of the
Members of our House of Commons thought it an honour to retain to
some great Lord, and to wear his blew Coat:[341] And when they had made

339. This has a proverbial air but perhaps can be traced back to Aristotle's *Physics*: "ὅλως τε ἡ τέχνη τὰ μὲν ἐπιτελεῖ ἃ ἡ φύσις ἀδυνατεῖ ἀπεργάσασθαι, τὰ δὲ
μιμεῖται"; "Indeed, as a general proposition, the arts either, on the basis of Nature,
carry things further than Nature can, or they imitate Nature" (2.8, 199a15).

340. I.e., an uneven contest.

341. A blue coat was the livery of a servant or retainer to a lord (*OED*, s.v. "blue
coat"). Marvell had used similar language in his *Growth of Popery* of 1677 (Marvell, *Prose Works*, vol. 2, p. 304). On 8 February 1659, Neville had spoken in Parliament on the topic of the medieval dependence of the Commons on the Lords:
"The Commons, till Henry VII., never exercised a negative voice. All depended
on the Lords. In that time it would have been hard to have found in this house so
many gentlemen of estates. The gentry do not now depend upon the peerage. The
balance is in the gentry. They have all the lands. Now Lords, old or new, must be
supported by the people" (Burton, *Diary*, vol. 3, p. 133). He returned to the same
point on 5 March: "There were so many blue coats in our father's remembrance,
that sat in this House, as we could see no other colours there. Near twenty
Parliament-men would wait upon one Lord, to know how they should demean
themselves in the House of Commons" (Burton, *Diary*, vol. 4, pp. 24–25). A very
similar observation is made in *A Copy of a Letter* in respect of the distribution of
power in medieval parliaments: "Although the Commons were named, it will be
found (if we look into Records, that they had little share, except to help bear up

up their Lord's Train, and waited upon him from his own House to the Lords House, and made a Lane for him to enter, and departed to sit themselves in the Lower House of Parliament, as it was then (and very justly) called; can you think that any thing could pass in such a Parliament that was not ordered by the Lords? Besides, these Lords were the King's great Council in the Intervals of Parliaments, and were called to advise of Peace and War; and the latter was seldom made without the consent of the major part; if it were not, they would not send their Tenants, which was all the Militia of *England* (besides the King's tenth part). Can it be believed, that in those days the Commons should dislike any thing the Lords did in the Intervals, or that they would have disputed their Right to receive Appeals from Courts of Equity,[342] if they had

---

the Lords, whose Blew-coats they wore against the King) and it will likewise appear, that they were never discontented at their small proportion" (appendix A, below, p. 324).

342. Most immediately an allusion to the language of the message sent by the Commons to the Lords on 4 June 1675 relating to the detention of lawyers who had brought a suit in the Lords against a member of the House of Commons, Thomas Dalmahoy (d. 1682), in breach of privilege: "The Commons cannot find, by *Magna Charta*, or by any other law, or ancient custom of Parliament, that your Lordships have any Jurisdiction, in cases of Appeal from Courts of Equity" (Grey, *Debates*, vol. 3, p. 258; cf. vol. 3, p. 277, and vol. 4, p. 30: "First resolve to assert your right, 'That no Appeal can be brought to the Lords from any court of Equity.'" For an indignant response from the Lords, see Shaftesbury's speech on Sherley's case, 20 October 1675, reprinted in *State-Tracts*, vol. 1, p. 58); the Commons' point was that, by 4. Edw. III. c. 6, the Lords were restricted to passing judgment on only their own Peers. But the judicature of the House of Lords had been a frequent bone of contention with the House of Commons in the 1660s and 1670s, key cases being *Skinner v. East India Company* and *Sherley v. Fagg* (for Serjeant Maynard's lengthy and interesting opinion on Skinner's case, see Grey, *Debates*, vol. 1, pp. 445–62; cf. vol. 4, pp. 27–49). The memory of this case lingered in the Commons: see ibid., vol. 9, pp. 409–10. For Marvell's comments in *An Account of the Growth of Popery and Arbitrary Government* (1677) on this and other "Appeales from the Court of Chancery," see Marvell, *Prose Works*, vol. 2, pp. 286 and 289. In 1667 it had been urged in the Commons that "where the common law does remedy, people are not to run to the House of Lords; where ordinary remedies fail only" (Grey, *Debates*, vol. 1, p. 101). In 1675 the House of Commons had gone so far as to vote that *"whosoever shall Sollicite or prosecute any Appeal against any Commoner of England, from any Court of Equity before the House of Lords, shall be deemed and taken a betrayer of the Rights and Liberties of the Commons of England, and shall be proceeded against*

pretended to it in those days, or to mend Money-bills?[343] And what is the reason, but because the Lords themselves at that time represented all their Tenants (that is, all the People) in some sort? and although the House of Commons did Assemble to present their Grievances, yet all great Affairs of high Importance concerning the Government, was Transacted by the Lords; and the War which was made to preserve it,

---

accordingly" (Marvell, *Prose Works*, vol. 2, p. 289). Algernon Sidney caught the mood of worsening suspicion, writing on 12 May 1679, "The last week was spent for the most part in janglings between the two Houses, upon *points of Privilege* relating unto the Rights the Lords pretend unto in points of *Judicatories*; which the Lords Frecheville, Berckely [*sic*], Ferrers, Aylesbury, Northampton, and some other equal unto them in understanding, eloquence and reputation, do with the help of the Bishops very magnanimously defend" (Sydney, *Letters*, p. 62: cf. Grey, *Debates*, vol. 7, pp. 215–16 and 296). See Grey, *Debates*, vol. 7, p. 94, for another example of resentment in the Commons at the high-handedness of the Lords. When Charles II prorogued this Parliament, he gave as one of his reasons for so doing the "differences between the two Houses," which promised "very ill effects" (Grey, *Debates*, vol. 7, p. 345; for similar sentiments, see vol. 3, pp. 261 and 289).

343. These were bills put before Parliament to meet government monetary requirements by the imposition or regulation of taxation. The House of Commons was jealous of its monopoly over money bills, which it traced back to medieval statutes establishing that only Parliament could grant taxes, and which had been reaffirmed in the Petition of Right of 1628, preamble and sect. 10; see above, p. 163, n. 282. Lord Whitlock had stated in Parliament on 7 January 1657 that "it is against the Instrument of Government, and the fundamental laws, to lay any tax, but in Parliament, by free consent" (Burton, *Diary*, vol. 1, p. 318; cf. pp. 406–8). Most recently, the Commons and the Lords had clashed over the issue in 1670–71 and 1678. The 13 April 1671 Resolution of the Commons had stipulated that "in all Aids given to the King, by the Commons, the Rate or Tax ought not to be altered by the Lords." The Resolution had been provoked by amendments made in the Lords to the Foreign Commodities Bill. On 17 April the Lords had responded by claiming that their right to make such amendments "is a fundamental, inherent, and undoubted Right of the House of Peers, from which they cannot depart." Lord Lucas had complained in the House of Lords on 22 February 1671 (in a speech that was later burned by the hangman) that "either your Lordships can deny or moderate a Bill for Money coming from the Commons, or if you cannot, all your great Estates are wholly at their disposal, and your Lordships have nothing that you can properly call your own" (*State-Tracts*, vol. 1, p. 356). The altercation on this occasion came to nothing, the king proroguing Parliament on 22 April. However, the matter had flared up again in 1678 when the Lords had amended the date of disbandment in a bill raising taxation to pay off troops. The Commons had once again resisted this interference on a point of principle, the

was called the Barons Wars,[344] not the War of both Houses: for although in antienter times the word *Baron* were taken in a larger sense, and comprehended the *Francklins* or *Freemen*; yet who reads any History of that War,[345] shall not find that any mention is made of the concurrence of any assembly of such men, but that *Simon Monford* Earl of *Leicester*,[346] and others of the great ones, did by their Power and Interest manage that contest. Now if this Property, which is gone out of the Peerage into the Commons, had passed into the King's hands, as it did in *Egypt* in the time of *Joseph*,[347] as was before said, the Prince had had a very easie and peaceable reign over his own Vassals, and might either have refused, justly, to have Assembled the Parliament any more; or if he had pleased to do it, might have for ever managed it as he thought fit: But our Princes have wanted a *Joseph*, that is, a wise Councellor; and instead of saving their Revenue, which was very great, and their expences small, and buying in those Purchases which the vast expences and luxury of the Lords made ready for them, they have alienated their own Inheritance; so that now the Crown-Lands, that is, the publick Patrimony, is come to make up the interest of the Commons, whilest the King must have a precarious Revenue out of the Peoples Purses, and be beholding to the Parliament for his Bread in time of Peace; whereas the Kings their Predecessors never asked Aid of his Subjects, but in time of War and Invasion: and this alone (though there were no other decay in the Government) is

---

3 July 1678 Resolution stating, "All Aids and Supplies, and Aids to his Majesty in Parliament, are the sole Gift of the Commons: And all Bills for the Granting of any such Aids and Supplies ought to begin with the Commons: And that it is the undoubted and sole Right of the Commons, to direct, limit, and appoint, in such Bills, the Ends, Purposes, Considerations, Conditions, Limitations, and Qualifications of such Grants; which ought not to be changed, or altered by the House of Lords." I am grateful to Paul Seaward for guidance and information on these matters.

344. A civil war waged from 1264 to 1267 between Henry III and a group of barons led by Simon de Montfort, who had sought more power for the baronial council.

345. See Sir William Dugdale, *A Short View of the Late Troubles in England* (1681), which explores parallels between seventeenth- and thirteenth-century England.

346. Simon de Montfort (c. 1208–65), magnate and political reformer.

347. See above, p. 92 and n. 103.

enough to make the King depend upon his People; which is no very good condition for a Monarchy.

Noble Venetian. But how comes it to pass that other Neighbouring Countries are in so settled a State in respect of *England?* does their Property remain the same it was, or is it come into the hands of the Prince? You know you were pleased to admit, that we should ask you, *en passant,* something of other Countries.

English Gentleman. Sir, I thank you for it, and shall endeavour to satisfie you. I shall say nothing of the small Princes of *Germany,* who keep in a great measure their ancient bounds, both of Government and Property; and if their Princes now and then exceed their part, yet it is in time of Troubles and War, and things return into their right Chanel of Assembling the several States, which are yet in being every where: But *Germany* lying so exposed to the Invasion of the *Turks*[348] on the one side, and of the *French* on the other; and having ever had enough to do to defend their several Liberties against the encroachments of the House of *Austria*[349] (in which the Imperial dignity is become in some sort Hereditary) if there had been something of extraordinary power exercised of late

348. Westward encroachment by the Ottoman Empire was a contemporary reality for Neville. It had been repeatedly warned against by Rycaut in his *History of the Turkish Empire* and would be his chosen keynote for *The Present State of the Ottoman Empire*: "It hath been the happy fortune of the Turk to be accounted barbarous and ignorant; for upon this perswasion Christian Princes have laid themselves open and unguarded to their greatest danger; contending together for one Palm of land, whilst this puissant Enemy hath made himself master of whole Provinces, and largely shared in the rich and pleasant possessions of Europe" (Rycaut, *Present State*, sig. A2ᵛ). That encroachment had begun with the capture of Belgrade in 1521 and the sieges of Vienna in 1529 and 1532. Ottoman ascendancy in Hungary had been recognized by the Hapsburgs in 1547. In 1669 the Ottomans had taken control of Crete following the successful siege of Candia. A final, unsuccessful, Ottoman attempt on Vienna would be launched in 1683.

349. During the sixteenth century the Hapsburgs had repeatedly sought land to the northwest in what is now Austria, the Czech Republic, Slovakia, and southern Germany.

years, I can say *Inter arma silent leges:*[350] but besides their own particular States, they have the Diet of the Empire,[351] which never fails to mediate and compose things, if there be any great oppression used by Princes to their subjects, or from one Prince or State to another. I shall therefore confine my self to the three great Kingdoms, *France, Spain,* and *Poland*; for as to *Denmark* and *Sweden,* the first hath lately chang'd its Government,[352] and not only made the Monarchy Hereditary, which was before Elective, but has pull'd down the Nobility, and given their Power to the Prince; which how it will succeed, time will shew. *Sweden* remains in point of Constitution and Property exactly as it did anciently, and is a well-Governed Kingdom. The first of the other three is *France*, of which I have spoken before, and shall onely add, That though it be very true, that there is Property in *France*, and yet the Government is Despotical at this present, yet it is one of those violent States, which the *Grecians* called Tyrannies: For if a Lawfull Prince, that is, one who being so by Law, and sworn to rule according to it, breaks his Oaths and his Bonds, and reigns Arbitrarily, he becomes a Tyrant and an Usurper, as to so much as he assumes more than the Constitution hath given him; and such a Government, being as I said violent, and not natural, but contrary to the Interest of the people, first cannot be lasting, when the adventitious props which support it fail; and whilst it does endure, must be very uneasie both to

350. "The laws are silent in time of war." A slightly garbled version of a famous remark by Cicero in his defence of Milo: "Silent enim leges inter arma ne se expectari iubent"; "When arms speak the laws are silent; they bid none to await their word" (*Pro Milone*, 4; cf. Quintilian, *Institutio Oratoria*, 5.14.17). Cicero is discussing those circumstances in which homicide is not a crime. In support of his argument that sometimes homicide is justifiable, he appeals to the natural law of the right to self-defense. The maxim was frequently invoked in the course of political discussion: see Hobbes, *Philosophicall Rudiments* (1651), in Wootton, *Divine Right*, p. 459; and later Burke, *Reflections*, p. 180. Sir Henry Vane had used the phrase in Parliament on 16 March 1659 with Neville present (Burton, *Diary*, vol. 4, p. 153; cf. p. 305).

351. The Imperial Diet was the deliberative and legislative body of the Holy Roman Empire. From 1663 it had sat in permanent session at Regensburg. It would be dissolved by Napoleon in 1806.

352. The Danish coup d'état of 1660 that had installed an absolutist monarchy would shortly be described by the commonwealth Whig Robert Molesworth in his *An Account of Denmark* (1694).

Prince and People; the first being necessitated to use continual oppression, and the latter to suffer it.

Doctor. You are pleased to talk of the oppression of the People under the King of *France*, and for that reason, call it a violent Government, when, if I remember, you did once to day extol the Monarchy of the *Turks* for well-founded and natural; Are not the people in that Empire as much oppressed as in *France*?

English Gentleman. By no means; unless you will call it oppression for the grand Seignior to feed all his People out of the Product of his own Lands; and though they serve him for it, yet that does not alter the Case: for if you set poor men to work and pay them for it, are you a Tyrant, or rather, are not you a good Commonwealths-man,[353] by helping those to live, who have no other way of doing it but by their labour?[354] But the King of

353. In general terms, one devoted to the common good (*OED*, s.v. "commonwealthman," 1), but with, at this time, the additional connotation of an adherent of the Parliamentary cause in the Civil War, and possibly also an advocate of republican government (2). For commentary, see Caroline Robbins, *The Eighteenth-Century Commonwealthman* (Cambridge, Mass.: Harvard University Press, 1959).

354. Cf. Harrington, *Oceana:* "If one man be sole landlord of a territory, or overbalance the people, for example, three parts in four, he is grand signor, for so the Turk is called from his property; and his empire is absolute monarchy. . . . It being unlawful in Turkey that any should possess land but the grand signor, the balance is fixed by the law, and that empire firm" (Pocock, *Harrington*, pp. 163–64). The same point had been made in *The Armie's Dutie* (1659): "Some kingdomes we say have been founded upon the Monarchs immediate interest, or property in the lands, as many ancient *Eastern* Kings, and the *Turk*, with other *Eastern* Princes at this day, who are sole proprietors or Landlords of the whole Territories where they reign, and the people their tenants at will, or at best for life, upon conditions of service in war, proportionable to the value of their farms, whereby the *Turk* keeps an absolute power over his subject by their dependance upon his will for their bread, and with his own proper revenue is able also to maintain an army of strangers to strengthen the other tie, he hath upon his vassals, and upon this root of his property, (to the eye of humane reason) his power hath grown to that monstrous height" (*Armie's Dutie*, p. 19). The troubling excellence of the Ottoman government is a theme touched on occasionally in the booklist: cf. Boccalini, *Advertisements*, pp. 37–38, 81–84, 85, 194–95, 220–22, 232–33, 286. Pocock explains the grounds of Harrington's respectful attention to the institutions of the Ottoman

France knowing that his People have, and ought to have Property, and that he has no right to their Possessions, yet takes what he pleases from them, without their consent, and contrary to Law; So that when he sets them on work he pays them what he pleases, and that he levies out of their own Estates. I do not affirm that there is no Government in the World, but where Rule is founded in Property; but I say there is no natural fixed Government, but where it is so; and when it is otherwise, the People are perpetually complaining, and the King in perpetual anxiety, always in fear of his Subjects, and seeking new ways to secure himself; God having been so merciful to mankind, that he has made nothing safe for Princes, but what is Just and Honest.[355]

Noble Venetian. But you were saying just now, that this present Constitution in *France* will fall when the props fail; we in *Italy*, who live in perpetual fear of the greatness of that Kingdom, would be glad to hear something of the decaying of those props; What are they, I beseech you?

Empire: "Harrington . . . knew the *feudum* to have been formerly a precarious or non-hereditary *beneficium*. The Roman and Turkish monarchies, he says, were alike in resting upon a distribution of benefices for life to soldiers, reinforced by a body of palace troops—praetorians or janissaries—to protect and sometimes to dispose of the person of the ruler" (Pocock, *Harrington*, p. 48). In *Oceana*, Harrington had presented the Ottoman polity as both perfect in its kind, and yet, apparently in virtue of that very perfection, unstable: "But for a monarchy by arms, as that of the Turk (which of all models that ever were cometh up unto the perfection of the kind), it is not in the wit or power of man to cure it of this dangerous flaw, that the janissaries have frequent interest and perpetual power to raise sedition, and to tear the magistrates, even the prince himself, in pieces. Therefore the monarchy of Turkey is no perfect government" (Pocock, *Harrington*, p. 179; cf. pp. 189 and 432; cf. Harrington's similar later judgments on the Ottoman Empire— perfect in its inferior kind—in *The Prerogative of Popular Government*, ibid., pp. 400, 446–47, and 566: "It is certain the perfection of the Turkish policy lies in this, that it cometh nearest to that of hell"). For a similar view of the simultaneously perfect and defective title of the Ottoman sultan expressed in Parliament in 1654, see Burton, *Diary*, vol. 1, p. xxx.

355. Neville's language here recalls Cicero's famous and influential discussion of the expedient (*utile*) and the morally right (*honestum*) in book 3 of *De Officiis*; see especially 3.7.

English Gentleman. The first is the greatness of the present King, whose heroick Actions and Wisdom[356] has extinguished envy in all his Neighbour-Princes, and kindled fear, and brought him to be above all possibility of control at home; not only because his Subjects fear his Courage, but because they have his Virtue in admiration, and amidst all their miseries cannot chuse but have something of rejoycing, to see how high he hath mounted the Empire and Honour of their Nation. The next prop is the change of their ancient Constitution, in the time of *Charles* the Seventh, by Consent: for about that time the Country being so wasted by the Invasion and Excursions of the *English*, The States then assembled Petitioned the King that he would give them leave to go home, and dispose of Affairs himself, and Order the Government for the future as he thought fit. Upon this, his Successor *Lewis* the Eleventh, being a crafty Prince, took an occasion to call the States no more, but to supply them with an *Assemble des notables*, which were certain men of his own nomination, like *Barbones* Parliament[357] here, but that they were of better quality:[358] These in succeeding reigns (being the best men of the King-

356. After assuming full control of the government of France in 1661, Louis XIV had enjoyed great success in the Franco-Dutch War of 1672–78, extending the boundaries of France to include Franche-Comté and additional territory in the Spanish Netherlands. In 1681, the year of publication of the second edition of *Plato Redivivus*, Louis had further extended French territory when he annexed Strasbourg.

357. An entirely nominated parliament that came into existence on 4 July 1653 and was dissolved on 12 December of the same year. Its members had all been nominated by Oliver Cromwell and the army's Council of Officers. Its name derived from that of the nominee for London, Praise-God Barebone.

358. Charles VII (1403–61) ruled France from 1422 until his death, when he was succeeded by his son Louis XI. After his return to Paris in 1437, Charles gradually assumed power from the Estates General, including crucially the right to levy directly taxes that previously had been levied by them. As power ebbed from the Estates, they began to meet less frequently. By the end of his reign, Charles directly ruled most of the vast territories previously held by his vassals; only Burgundy, Flanders, and Brittany still enjoyed their former independence. This mutation in the French government had been previously remarked by Harrington in *The Prerogative of Popular Government* (1658): "The estates, be they one, or two, or three, are such (as was said), by virtue of the balance, upon which the government must naturally depend. Wherefor constitutively the government of France (and all other monarchies of like balance)

dom) grew Troublesome and Intractable;[359] so that for some years the
Edicts have been verified (that is in our Language) Bills have been passed
in the Grand Chamber of the Parliament at *Paris*, commonly called the
Chambre d'audience, who lately, and since the Imprisonment of President

---

was administered by an assembly of the three estates, and thus continued until,
that nation being vanquished by the English, Charles the Seventh was put to
such shifts as, for the recovery of himself in the greatest distress, he could
make; unto which recovery, while the estates could not be legally called, he,
happening to attain without them, so ordered his affairs that his successors, by
adding unto his inventions, came to rule without this assembly; a way not suiting with the nature of their balance, which therefore required some assistance
by force and other concurring policies of like nature, whereof the foreign guards
of that monarchy are one; the great baits alluring the nobility another; and the
emergent interest of the church a third" (Pocock, *Harrington*, pp. 439–40).
Neville may be confusing an event of the reign of Louis XI with the develop-
ments of the reign of his father. Charles VII told the Estates of Languedoc in
1442 that he "did not wish such assemblies to meet in future . . . because it is
only a cost and expense for the poor common people"; however, it was the only
Estates General of the reign of Louis XI, meeting at Tours in 1468, that begged
not to be summoned again on grounds of inconvenience and expense (P. S.
Lewis, *Later Medieval France: The Polity* [London: Macmillan, 1968], pp. 372
and 342). In 1676 these events had been recalled in Parliament by Henry Powle:
"A learned *French* Lawyer tells us, 'That the first grants of Aids in *France* were
only temporary Supplies, and were perpetuated for ever after; as in *Charles*
VII's and *Lewis* XI's time. *Charles* VII. prayed a law of the States to order him
to raise money but till their next meeting, and that neither unless there were
occasion; which the Parliament, by inadvertency, granted, and have never met
since" (Grey, *Debates*, vol. 4, pp. 229–30). They would again be recalled in 1689
by Sir Robert Cotton: "*Lewis* XI of *France* desired only liberty to raise Money
till the next Parliament did sit; and he never called a Parliament, and they have
raised Money without Parliaments ever since" (Grey, *Debates*, vol. 9, pp. 266–
67). There was a strong sixteenth-century English tradition that had viewed
the doings of Louis XI with suspicion. Sir Thomas Smith in 1565 had identified
the reign of Louis XI as the moment when the French government had been
perverted from a "lawfull and regulate raigne" to an "absolute and tyrannicall
power and government" (Smith, *Republica*, p. 54). In 1580 in the House of Commons Sir Humphrey Gilbert had cited Louis XI as an illustration of his fear
that, as crowns became more free, so populaces became more enslaved (T. E.
Hartley, ed., *Proceedings in the Parliaments of Elizabeth I*, 3 vols. [Leicester:
Leicester University Press, 1981–95], vol. 1, pp. 224–25).

359. Aristocratic incursions against the power of the French monarchy had cul-
minated in the Frondes of 1648–49 and 1650–53.

Brouselles[360] and others during this King's Minority,[361] have never refused or scrupled any Edicts whatsoever. Now whenever this great King dies, and the States of the Kingdom are restored, these two great props of Arbitrary Power are taken away. Besides these two, the Constitution of the Government of *France* it self, is somwhat better fitted than ours to permit extraordinary Power in the Prince, for the whole People there possessing Lands, are Gentlemen; that is, infinitely the greater part; which was the reason why in their Assembly of Estates, the Deputies of the Provinces (which we call here Knights of the Shire) were chosen by, and out of the Gentry, and sate with the Peers in the same Chamber, as representing the Gentry onely, called *petite noblesse*.[362] Whereas our Knights here (whatever their blood is) are chosen by Commoners, and are Commoners; our Laws and Government taking no notice of any Nobility but the persons of the Peers, whose Sons are likewise Commoners, even their eldest, whilst their Father lives: Now Gentry are ever more

360. Pierre Broussel (1576–1654), *conseiller* in the Parlement de Paris. Broussel had been arrested on 26 August 1648 for organizing parliamentary resistance to a royal edict proposing a new tax on the tenants of royal lands. After popular unrest in Paris he was freed two days later on 28 August. In 1649 he was made governor of the Bastille. In 1652 he was by royal command stripped of his positions and banished. Priolo gives a circumstantial, if rhetorically heightened, account of the events of 26–28 August 1648 in Paris (Priolo, *History of France*, pp. 92–107). He includes the following character sketches of Broussel: "One *Peter Broussel*, a Member of the Parliament of Paris, most single in his carriage, easie of access, a vertuous and most honest man; of no ill Principles, but easie to be led by the designing party. Therefore he seemed fit to be made the subject of the tinkling Cymbal to sound for the publick discontent" (p. 92); "*Broussel* came home the next morning with joyful acclamations, to see his rejoicing Children and dear Friends. From that day forward he lived as before, in a constant tenour of honest conversation, innocent in his carriage: that heat of popular affection being somewhat cold: one bounded within his rank. A person of no ill design, over-born by the stream of the Factious through the publick storm, to run upon Shelves and Sands: [To teach posterity how vain and failing a stay it is, to lean upon such Props as will always be condemned, and continued to the perpetual ruine of both high and low.]" (p. 107; the text in brackets is in Priolo's original Latin; the brackets indicate a parenthetic comment, or *obiter dictum*).

361. Louis XIV was deemed to have attained his majority on 7 September 1651, having ascended the throne in 1643 and been born in 1638. His personal reign, however, began only with the death of Cardinal Mazarin in March 1661.

362. I.e., the lesser nobility.

tractable by a Prince, than a wealthy and numerous Commonalty; out of which our Gentry (at least those we call so) are raised from time to time: For whenever either a Merchant, Lawyer, Tradesman, Grasier, Farmer, or any other, gets such an Estate, as that he or his Son can live upon his Lands, without exercising of any other Calling,[363] he becomes a Gentleman. I do not say, but that we have men very Nobly descended amongst these, but they have no preheminence, or distinction, by the Laws or Government. Besides this, the Gentry in *France* are very needy, and very numerous;[364] the reason of which is, That the Elder Brother, in most parts of that Kingdom, hath no more share in the division of the Paternal Estate, than the Cadets or Younger Brothers, excepting the Principal House, with the Orchards and Gardens about it, which they call *Vol de Chappon*, as who should say, As far as a Capon can fly at once. This House gives him the Title his Father had, who was called Seignior, or Baron, or Count of that place; which if he sells, he parts with his Baronship, and for ought I know becomes in time *roturier*,[365] or ignoble. This practice divides the Lands into so many small parcels, that the Possessors of them being Noble, and having little to maintain their Nobility, are fain to seek their Fortune, which they can find no where so well as at the Court, and so become the King's Servants and Souldiers, for they are generally Couragious, Bold, and of a good Meen.[366] None of these can

363. Neville is here using an economic definition of a gentleman, namely, one whose personal estate is sufficient that he need not engage in any trade or profession. Among the gentry such a position of economic independence was thought a necessary condition for the impartial exercise of political judgment. In the Putney Debates, Henry Ireton had in general spoken in defense of private property, and in particular he had resisted "the introducing of men into an equality of interest in this government who have no property in this kingdom, or who have no local permanent interest in it" (Wootton, *Divine Right*, p. 295; see also above, p. 89, n. 97).

364. Cf. Harrington, *The Art of Lawgiving*, on the pattern of land tenure in France as compared with that of England: "The true cause whence England hath been an overmatch in arms for France lay in the communication or distribution of property unto the lower sort" (Pocock, *Harrington*, p. 688).

365. I.e., a person of low social rank; a commoner; in prerevolutionary France, a member of a social class comprising all those not nobles or clergy, that is, the bourgeois and villeins collectively (*OED*, s.v. "roturier," A1).

366. I.e., mien; bearing or manner (*OED*, s.v. "mien").

ever advance themselves, but by their desert, which makes them hazard themselves very desperately, by which means great numbers of them are kill'd, and the rest come in time to be great Officers, and live splendidly upon the King's Purse, who is likewise very liberal to them, and according to their respective merits, gives them often, in the beginning of a Campagne, a considerable sum to furnish out their Equipage. These are a great Prop to the Regal Power, it being their Interest to support it, lest their gain should cease, and they be reduced to be poor *Provinciaux*, that is, Country-Gentlemen again: whereas, if they had such Estates as our Country-Gentry have, they would desire to be at home at their ease, whilest these (having ten times as much from the King as their own Estate can yield them, which supply must fail, if the King's Revenue were reduced) are perpetually engaged to make good all exorbitances.

Doctor. This is a kind of Governing by Property too, and it puts me in mind of a Gentleman of good Estate in our Country, who took a Tenants Son of his to be his Servant, whose Father not long after dying, left him a Living of about ten pound a year: the young Man's Friends came to him, and asked him why he would serve now he had an Estate of his own able to maintain him: his Answer was, That his own Lands would yield him but a third part of what his Service was worth to him in all; besides, that he lived a pleasant Life, wore good Clothes, kept good Company, and had the conversation of very pretty Maids that were his Fellow-servants, which made him very well digest the name of being a Servant.

English Gentleman. This is the very Case; but yet Service (in both these Cases) is no Inheritance; and when there comes a Peaceable King in *France*, who will let his Neighbours be quiet, or one that is covetous, these fine Gentlemen will lose their Employments, and their King this Prop; and the rather, because these Gentlemen do not depend (as was said before) in any kind upon the great Lords (whose standing Interest is at Court) and so cannot in a change, be by them carried over to advance the Court-designs against their own good and that of their Country. And thus much is sufficient to be said concerning *France*. As for *Spain*, I believe there is no Country (excepting *Sweden*) in Christendom, where the Property has remained so intirely the same it was at the beginning; and the reason is, the great and strict care that is taken to hinder the Lands from passing out of the old owners hands; for except it be by Marriages, no man can acquire another man's Estate, nor can any Grandee, or Titulado,[367] or any other Hidalgo[368] there, alienate or ingage his Paternal or Maternal Estate, otherwise than for his Life; nor can alter Tenures, or extinguish Services, or dismember Mannors: for to this the Princes consent must be had, which he never gives, till the matter be debated in the *Consejo de Camera*, which is no *Junta* or secret *Consejo de Guerras*,[369] but one wherein the great men of the Kingdom intervene, and wherein the great matters concerning the preservation of the Government are transacted, not relating to Foreign Provinces or Governments,

367. I.e., a man of title; hence, an aristocrat.

368. A member of the Spanish nobility. Cf. Colonel Matthews in Parliament, 4 February 1658: "The word 'gentleman' is a title of no small honour. In Spain, it is of high esteem, and a saying there is 'As good a gentleman as the king'" (Burton, *Diary*, vol. 2, p. 456).

369. Respectively, the council of the chamber and the council of war. Edward Grimeston described the functions of these councils as follows: "The Councell of warre. It prouides for Generals, Colonels, Captaines, the Generall of the gallies, and for whatsoeuer concernes the war, with the aduice of his Majestie, who is president of this Councell. They punish all commanders and officers at warre that doe not their duties. And in like maner they dispose of the companies of men at arms appointed for the gard of the kingdom, and they giue order for the artillerie, munition, and fortifications, or any thing that is necessary for the warre. The counsellors haue no wages. . . . The Councell which they call de Camera. It hath a President and three Counsellors, of the most ancient of the Councell Royall, which haue no wages. In this Councell they prouide superiour officers for the Realme, and they dispose of Bishopricks, Chanonries, and other Ecclesiastical liuings, the king hauing the nomination from the Pope of Rome" (Mayerne, *Spaine*, pp. 1338–39). In a Spanish or Italian context a junta is simply a deliberative or administrative council or committee, without any pejorative connotation (*OED*, s.v. "junta," 1). In England since the Civil War, however, it was associated pejoratively with a small group of nobles who controlled access to the monarch with a view to subverting the constitution, and was effectively synonymous with "cabal" (*OED*, s.v. "junto," 1a). In 1714 Swift would deplore the fact that "those who are paid to be Defenders of the Civil Power will stand ready for any Acts of Violence, that a Junta composed of the greatest Enemies to the Constitution shall think fit to enjoin them" (*Some Free Thoughts upon the Present State of Affairs*, in Swift, *Prose Writings*, vol. 8, p. 90).

but to the kingdom of *Castile* and *Leon*, of which I only speak now. It is true, there have been one or two exceptions against this severe Rule, since the great calamities of *Spain*,[370] and two great Lordships have been sold, the *Marquisate del Monastero*, to an *Assentista Genoese*, and another to *Sebastian Cortiza* a *Portuguese*, of the same Profession: but both these have bought the intire Lordships, without curtailing or altering the condition in which these two great Estates were before; and notwithstanding, this hath caused so much repining amongst the natural *Godos*[371] (as the *Castilians* call themselves still for glory) that I believe this will never be drawn into an Example hereafter. Now the Property remaining the same, the Government doth so too, and the King's Domestick Government, over his natural *Spaniards*, is very gentle, whatever it be in his Conquer'd Provinces; and the Kings there have very great advantages of keeping their great men (by whom they Govern) in good temper, by reason of the great Governments they have to bestow upon them, both in *Europe* and the *Indies*;[372] which changing every three years, go in an Age through all the Grandees, which are not very numerous. Besides, *Castile* having been in the time of King *Roderigo* over-run and Conquered by the *Moors*,[373] who Governed there Despotically, some hundreds of years, be-

370. In addition to the economic adversity which overtook Spain in the seventeenth century, Neville presumably also has in mind a series of political and military reverses, including the achievement of independence by Portugal in 1640, the loss of the Netherlands, and defeats at the hands of the French in the Thirty Years' War.

371. I.e., Goths, or Visigoths, who had conquered and ruled Spain in the fifth century A.D.

372. At this time the Spanish crown possessed enormous territories in both North and South America; in the early sixteenth century it had conquered both the Aztec and the Inca Empires. Since 1556 the Spanish crown had also held the states of the Holy Roman Empire in the Low Countries; this was a territory equivalent to most of modern-day Belgium and Luxembourg, as well as parts of northern France, the Netherlands, and western Germany. The Spanish crown would retain these territories until the Treaty of Utrecht of 1714.

373. The Moorish or Ummayad conquest of Hispania began in 711 when a Berber army under the caliph Al-Walid I defeated and killed Ruderic (Neville's Roderigo), the Visigothic king of Hispania, at the battle of Guadalete. The resulting Caliphate of Cordoba occupied most of the Iberian Peninsula in the tenth century and still held substantial territory until the fall of the Nasrid kingdom of

fore it could be recovered again by the old Inhabitants, who fled to the Mountains; When they were at length driven out, the Count of *Castile* found a Tax set upon all Commodities whatsoever, by the *Moors*, in their Reign, called *Alcaval*,[374] which was an easie matter to get continued (when their old Government was restored) by the *Cortes*, or States; and so

---

Granada in 1492 (the so-called reconquista). In his *Court Maxims* (composed 1664–65), Sidney had recalled this passage of Spanish history as an example of how tyranny undermines public virtue and weakens a state: "King Roderico of Spain turned a legal kingly government into absolute tyranny by bringing the people low. The virtue of his subjects was the first enemy he sought to destroy, which he effected by corrupting and effeminating the nobility; taking away by poison, sword, or false witnesses those that otherwise could not be secured; he disarmed the people, impoverished, weakened them; left off military discipline. The issue was, after a few years' tyranny he and his people were utterly unable to resist a common enemy and were easily defeated in the first encounter with the Moors" (Sidney, *Court Maxims*, p. 79).

374. "The *Alcauales*, thirdes and other rentes, which the king of *Spaine* hath in all the Prouinces, Townes, villages and Countries of al his kingdomes and Lord-shippes, as also what euery towne with their territorie; and precinctes doe seuer-ally pay, that you may the plainelier see and vnderstand, you must first learne what these rents of *Alcauales* are, and what they do signifie: namely of all goods, marchandises, houses, lands, and of all other thinges whatsoeuer they may be (none excepted) it is the custome in *Spaine*, to pay ye tenth pennie to the king: and that at euery time and as often as such goods, wares, houses lands or whatsoeuer els, are sold from one to another: & this tenth pennie is called *Alcaual*: likewise all handie crafts men, Mercers, Haberdashers, and other trades, that buy and sell in their said trades, as also Butchers, Fishmongers, Inkeepers, or any other trade, occupation, victualling, or hand worke whatsoeuer, must euery man pay a tenth pennie of all thinges whatsoeuer, they sell, and as oftentimes as they doe sell any thing, where vpon euerie Citie, towne &c. doth compounde and agree with the king for a yearely somme to be paide into his coffers, so that there are certain which do farme the same of the king, & pay it yearely accordingly, which summes are receyued cleerely into the kings coffers, all costes and charges deducted. To the same end there are in euery chiefe towne and prouince of the countrey, diuers receyuers appointed to take all accounts and summes of money in the kings be-halfe, that arise of the said *Alcaualaos*, and again to pay out of the same the *Iuros*, that is, such summes of money as the king by warrant appointeth to be paide vnto certaine persons, as also other assignations, appointed likewise to be paide, which paymentes the said receyuers doe set downe in account for their owne discharge, and thereof as also of their receipts, do make a yearely and general account into the kings Exchequer" (Jan Huygen von Linschoten, *Discours of Voyages into Ye East and West Indies* [1598], p. 452).

it has continued ever since, as the Excise has done here, which being imposed by them who drove and kept out the King, does now since his happy Restauration remain a Revenue of the Crown.[375] This *Alcaval*, or Excise, is a very great Revenue, and so prevented, for some time, the necessities of the Crown, and made the Prince have the less need of asking Relief of his People, (the ordinary cause of disgust,) so that the *Cortes*, or Assembly of the States, has had little to do of late, though they are duly

375. Excise, as a source of money that was collected automatically and did not depend upon a parliamentary grant, was clearly a particularly congenial stream of revenue for a monarch. Excise tended also to be unpopular because of its regressiveness, and so it figures often as a grievance in Leveller pamphlets (see, e.g., Morton, *Freedom*, pp. 52, 191, 232, 273). As Sir Arthur Haslerig had said in Parliament on 8 March 1659, the "King laboured to bring in excise, and it was distasted" (Burton, *Diary*, vol. 4, p. 79). In 1643 Parliament had raised money to meet the cost of waging war with Charles I by means of a tax on alcohol manufactured in England. This was carefully called an "impost" to avoid the connotations of arbitrary government and invasion of the property of the subject which had clung to the word "excise" since an attempt had been made to introduce one by Charles I in 1628 (Sharpe, *Personal Rule*, p. 123; cf. Sir Robert Cotton, *The Danger Wherein the Kingdome Now Standeth* [1628], pp. 9–10; *An Elegy upon the Most Incomparable K. Charles I* [1648], p. 11; John Pym, *The Declaration . . . against Thomas Earle of Strafford* [1641], p. 14). It was no accident that the "Grand Remonstrance" of 1641 had deplored, among other unwelcome innovations, the "unjust and pernicious attempt to extort great payments from the subject by way of excise." By February 1647 riots against the "impost" had become frequent and menacing, to the point where Parliament in the summer of 1653 had urgently considered "how the Excise may be brought in with the greatest ease to the people, and how the oppressions and burdens which have been in the managing of that business, may be redressed for the future" (Burton, *Diary*, vol. 1, p. v). Nevertheless, in March 1654 Cromwell would extend the "impost" to almost all saleable commodities. Despite its unpopularity it would remain the financial mainstay of government during the Interregnum (Kenyon, *Stuart Constitution*, p. 272; cf. the long and interesting debates on the principles and practice of the excise during the Parliament of 1657 in Burton, *Diary*, vol. 1, pp. 324–31 and 344–45). In *Oceana* Harrington acknowledges the excise to be "the best, the most fruitful and easy way of raising taxes," but the frugality of his republic allows the excise to be suspended (Pocock, *Harrington*, p. 352). In 1660 the Convention Parliament had abolished purveyance and feudal tenures in return for a grant in perpetuity to the Crown of a portion of the excise (12 Car. II, c. 24). Additionally in 1661 Charles—the first English monarch to be granted the excise—had been granted a further portion of it (the so-called "Additional Excise") for the period of his life. In 1685 these arrangements would be continued for the new king James II.

assembled every year, but seldom contradict what is desired by the Prince; for there are no greater Idolaters of their Monarch in the World than the *Castilians* are, nor who drink deeper of the Cup of Loyalty: so that in short, the Government in *Spain* is as ours was in Queen *Elizabeths* time, or in the first year after his now Majesties Return,[376] when the Parliament for a time Complimented the Prince, who had by that means both his own Power and the Peoples: which days I hope to see again, upon a better and more lasting Foundation. But before I leave *Spain*, I must say a word of the Kingdom of *Arragon*, which has not at all times had so quiet a state of their Monarchy as *Castile* hath enjoyed; for after many Combustions which happened there, concerning their *Fueros* and *Privilegios*,[377] which are their Fundamental Laws, the King one day coming to his Seat in Parliament, and making his demands, as was usual, they told him that they had a Request to make to him first; and he withdrawing thereupon, (for he had no right of sitting there to hear their Debates) they fell into discourse how to make their Government subsist against the encroachments of the Prince upon them, and went very high in their Debates, which could not chuse but come to the king's ear, who walked in a gallery in the same Palace to expect the issue; and being in great Passion, was seen to draw out his Dagger, very often, and thrust it again into the sheath; and heard to say, *Sangre ha de costar*;[378] which coming to the knowledg of the Estates, they left off the Debate, and sent some of their number to him, to know what blood it should cost, and whether he meant to murder any body. He drew out his Dagger again, and pointing it to his breast, he said, *Sangre de Reys*;[379] leaving them in

376. Burnet had been struck by the compliant mood of Parliament in the period immediately following the Restoration: "After the King came over, no person in the House of Commons had the courage to move the offering propositions for any limiting of prerogative, or the defining of any doubtful points. All was joy and rapture. If the King had applied himself to business, and had pursued those designs which he studied to retrieve all the rest of his reign, when it was too late, he had probably in those first transports carried every thing that he would have desired, either as to revenue or power" (Burnet, *History*, vol. 1, p. 159).

377. I.e., rights and privileges.

378. I.e., "blood has to cost."

379. I.e., "royal blood."

doubt, whether he meant that his Subjects would kill him, or that he would do it himself.[380] However, that Parliament ended very peaceably, and a famous settlement was there and then made, by which a great person was to be chosen every Parliament, who should be as it were an Umpire between the King and his people, for the execution of the Laws, and the preservation of their Government, their *Fueros* and *Privilegios*, which

---

380. In this short and unparalleled excursion on Spanish history, Neville seems to be following Edward Grimeston's continuation of Louis Turquet de Mayerne's *The Generall Historie of Spaine* (1612), where the story of Philip II's secretary of state Antonio Perez and an account of the origin of the office of *el Justicia d'Arragon* are found together on pp. 1257–66. This "Edward Grimeston" was perhaps the son of Edward Grimston (1507/8–1600), the Tudor soldier and administrator; his similarly named son is recorded as sergeant-at-arms to James I and Charles I. Neville's grandfather, Sir Henry Neville, had been a patient of Louis Turquet de Mayerne's physician son, the celebrated Sir Theodore de Mayerne (1573–1655) (on whom see Hugh Trevor-Roper, *Europe's Physician: The Various Life of Sir Theodore de Mayerne* [New Haven, Conn.: Yale University Press, 2006], especially pp. 8 and 189). There is also a tantalizing possibility that the arguments mounted by Neville *fils* in *Plato Redivivus* were influenced by those of Turquet's *De la Monarchie aristodémocratique* (1611). Neville seems to have taken a particular interest in England's relations with Spain, particularly relations of trade between the two countries: see, e.g., Neville's speech in Parliament on 17 February 1659 (Burton, *Diary*, vol. 3, p. 314). Grimeston's account of the origins of the office of *el Justicia d'Arragon* does not coincide at all points with that given by Neville in *Plato Redivivus*: "Since the generall losse of Spaine, which hapned vnder King *Roderigo*, by the meanes of Cont *Iulian*, for that he had defloured his daughter *Caba*. The Moores or Sarazins held Spaine long, without either King or Lord. In the end the realme of Arragon freed it selfe from the power of the Moores, and the Arragonois made themselues their owne Maisters and Lords, not acknowledging any particular Prince, and without any Soueraignty but their owne. So as beeing weary of their rest and liberty, they required (as the children of Israell did sometimes to *Samuel*) to haue a King, and therein they demanded the Popes aduice: who answered them as *Samuel* had done the Israelits. But seeing they desired to haue a King, he did wish them to prescribe him lawes and conditions, and ouer him a Soueraigne Iudge, with assistants, to bridle his ambition. The Arragonois gaue credit to this Councell, and before they would choose them a King, they erected the dignity and preheminence of *El Iusticia* of Arragon, which is a Soueraigne Iudge aboue the King, with seuenteene Assistants. And they made a law which was called the *Lawe of manifestation*, for the preseruation of the Vassals right, against the out-rages and oppressions of the mighty, be hee King, Prince, or other Iudge. Which law, with other Statutes and Ordonances, together with their Priuiledges, are to be seene Printed, vnder the Kings royall authority, and haue continued many hundred yeares, to the honor

are their Courts of Justice, and their Charters. This Officer was called, *El Justicia d'Arragon*,[381] and his duty was to call together the whole Power of the Kingdom, whenever any of the aforesaid Rights were by open force violated or invaded, and to admonish the King, whenever he heard of any clandestine Councils among them to that effect. It was likewise made Treason, for any person of what quality soever, to refuse to repair upon due summons to any place where this *Justicia* should erect his Standard,

---

and reputation of their Kings, and especially of Don *Ferdinand* of Arragon, sur-named the Catholicke, who would not giue eare (being come to the crown of Castile, by D. *Isabella* his wife) to the bad councell which the Spaniards gaue him, tending to the abolishing of the said priuiledges, saying: *So long as the two ballances of the King and realme, shall be in a iust Counterpese, the king and realme shall continue and flourish together, but if one of the Scales seeke to weigh downe the other, the one or the other will fall to ruine, or it may bee both together.* Moreouer the Arragonois made a law of vnion, consisting in two points worthy the knowledge, for the cleering of this present discourse. The one is, that whensoeuer the king shall breake their lawes, they may choose an other. For you must vnderstand that they do not sweare vnto their Kings, but conditionally in these termes. *Nes que valemos tanto come vos, 'y vos tanto come nos, oz hazemo nuestro Rey y Sennor contal, que nos gardeys nuestros fueros, y libertades, sy no, no.* And hee must humble himselfe vpon his knee, bare-headed, before the Soueraigne Iudge, which is *El Iusticia*, and sweare first, and then the Arragonois after him. The second point of this vnion is, that the Princes and Noblemen of the realme, may make leagues and confederations against their King in case of oppression, or of breach of their priuiledges. And vpon these con-ditions they did choose their first King, who was a Knight of Arragon, called *Garci Ximenes,* and after him three or foure: But this election continued not long: for the King D. *Pedro,* called with the Poignard, desiring to make the realme suc-cesiue and hereditarie, insisted in an assembly of the Estates, to disanull this law of election; the which in the end was granted, by the foure members of the realme, reseruing all their other rights and priuiledges but that: the which he did willingly accept, and after this Accord made (holding the Charter of this Election in his hand) he drew out his Poynard and cut it in peeces, saying these words. *Que tal suero y fuero dy poder eligir Rey los vassallos, sangre de Rey auia de costar,* and withall stab'd himselfe through the hand: from which time the King was called Don *Pe-dro* with the Poynard: as his effigie is to bee seene at this day, in the royall hall of the deputation in the towne of Saragoça, whereas all the Kings his successors are, vnto *Philip* the second last deceased" (Mayerne, *Spaine,* p. 1265).

381. Cf. Pocock, *Harrington,* p. 805; and for the late eighteenth-century afterlife of this Commonwealthman *topos,* see Burke, *Reflections,* p. 180. For Algernon Sid-ney's recognition of the salutariness and importance of this office, see Sidney, *Dis-courses,* p. 167. It also receives mention in John Somers's *A Brief History of the Succes-sion* (*State-Tracts,* vol. 1, pp. 397–98; see below, appendix F, p. 421).

or to withdraw himself without leave, much more to betray him, or to revolt from him: Besides, in this *Cortes*, or Parliament, the old Oath which at the first Foundation of their State was ordered to be taken by the King at his admittance, was again revived, and which is, in these words: *Nos que valemos tanto camo vos, y podemos mas, os eligimos nuestro Rey, conque nos guardeys nuestros Fueros y Privilegios; y si no, no.* That is, We who are as good as you, and more Powerful, do chuse you our King, upon condition that you preserve our Rights and Priviledges; and if not, not. Notwithstanding all this, *Philip* the Second, being both King of *Castile* and *Arragon*, picked a quarrel with the latter, by demanding his Secretary *Antonio Perez*, who fled from the King's displeasure thither, being his own Country; and they refusing to deliver him (it being expresly contrary to a Law of *Arragon*, that a Subject of that Kingdom should be against his will carried to be tryed elsewhere) the King took that occasion to Invade them with the Forces of his Kingdom of *Castile* (who had ever been Rivals and Enemies to the *Aragoneses*) and they to defend themselves under their *Justicia*, who did his part faithfully and couragiously; but the *Castilians* being old Soldiers, and those of *Arragon* but County-Troops,[382] the former prevailed, and so this Kingdom in getting that of *Castile* by a Marriage (but an Age before) lost its own Liberty and Government: for it is since made a Province, and Governed by a Vice-Roy from *Madrid*, although they keep up the formality of their *Cortes* still.[383]

---

382. I.e., militia, rather than professional soldiers.

383. Antonio Perez (1534–1611), Spanish statesman and secretary to Philip II of Spain. Perez had instigated the murder on 31 March 1578 of Juan de Escobedo, the secretary to Philip's half-brother Don John of Austria, whom Perez had planted in Don John's household as a spy but who had become loyal to his new master. Philip II having succumbed to remorse, Perez was thereafter the object of a series of legal proceedings and imprisonments before escaping from Spain to France on 23 November 1591. He spent the rest of his life in exile in England and France and had an unexpected impact on English literature, allegedly being the person upon whom Shakespeare based the ludicrous character of Don Armado in *Love's Labours Lost*. In England, too, Perez would make the acquaintance of Neville's grandfather, Sir Henry Neville (Blair Worden, "Classical Republicanism and the Puritan Revolution," in *History and Imagination: Essays in Honour of H. R. Trevor-Roper*, ed. Hugh Lloyd-Jones, Valerie Pearl, and Blair Worden [London: Duck-

Doctor. No man living that knew the hatred and hostility that ever was between the *English* and *Scots*, could have imagined in the years 1639, and 1640,[384] when our King was with great Armies of *English* upon the Frontiers of *Scotland*, ready to Invade that Kingdom, that this Nation would not have assisted to have brought them under; but it proved otherwise.

English Gentleman. It may be they feared, That when *Scotland* was reduced to slavery, and the Province pacified, and Forces kept up there, That such Forces and greater might have been imployed here, to reduce us into the same condition; an apprehension which at this time sticks with many of the common People, and helps to fill up the measure of our Fears and Distractions. But the visible reason why the *English* were not at that time very forward to oppress their Neighbours, was the consideration, That they were to be Invaded for refusing to receive from hence certain Innovations in matters of Religion,[385] and the worship of God,

---

worth, 1981], p. 189, n. 29). Philip II, meanwhile, exploited the situation to extirpate the remnants of Aragonese independence. Grimeston (Mayerne, *Spaine*, pp. 1257–65) relates the treatment of Perez at the hands of Philip II as an instance of princely ingratitude and duplicity, which naturally recommended the episode to Neville for inclusion in the covertly republican *Plato Redivivus*.

384. Neville refers to the First Bishops' War (1639) and the Second Bishops' War (1640), so called because the point of contention was whether or not Scotland should have an episcopal church governance (i.e., a church governed by bishops) or, as many Scots themselves desired, a presbyterian form of church government. Charles I had not sought supplies from Parliament to wage this war against his Scottish subjects, instead raising forces numbering some 20,000 men from his own resources. Whether because Charles feared he was outnumbered, or because (as the Doctor implies) his troops refused to fight in such a cause with even their inveterate enemies, the Scots, the campaign was a military fiasco for Charles. The Scots occupied much of northern England, and the humiliating Treaty of Ripon (October 1640) stipulated that they should be paid £850 per day until an English Parliament was summoned, which could vote supplies to pay off the Scottish forces. These reversals and embarrassments would shortly be dwelt upon (with outward indignation and covert satisfaction) by Whig detractors of Stuart kingship (e.g., Coke, *Detection*, pp. 381–86; Jones, *Tragical History*, pp. 329–30).

385. A reference to the religious reforms introduced by William Laud (1573–1645), archbishop of Canterbury, who moved the Church of England away from Calvinism in respect of its theology, toward greater ceremonialism in respect of its ritual, and toward a more authoritarian church government. The Grand

which had not long before been introduced here; and therefore the People of this Kingdom were unwilling to perpetuate a Mungrel Church here, by imposing it upon them. But I do exceedingly admire, when I read our History, to see how zealous and eager our Nobility and People here were anciently to assert the right of our Crown to the Kingdom of *France*; whereas it is visible, that if we had kept *France* (for we Conquered it intirely and fully) to this day, we must have run the fate of *Arragon*, and been in time ruined and opprest by our own Valour and good Fortune; a thing that was foreseen by the *Macedonians*, when their King *Alexander* had subdued all *Persia* and the *East*; who weighing how probable it was, that their Prince having the possession of such great and flourishing Kingdoms, should change his *Domicilium Imperii*, and inhabit in the Centre of his Dominions, and from thence Govern *Macedon*, by which means the *Grecians*, who by their Vertue and Valour had Conquered and subdued the *Barbarians*, should in time (even as an effect of their Victories) be opprest and tyrannized over by them: and this precautious foresight in the *Greeks* (as was fully believed in that Age) hastened the fatal Catastrophe of that great Prince.[386]

Doctor. Well, I hope this consideration will fore-arm our Parliaments, That they will not easily suffer their eyes to be dazled any more with the false glory of Conquering *France*.

Remonstrance of 1641 had called for Laud's imprisonment, and after the passage of a bill of attainder he was executed on 10 January 1645. Opponents of Stuart kingship were content to take their view of Laud's character, inclinations, and ambitions from Parliamentarian publications such as John Rushworth's *Historical Collections*, which describes Laud as follows: "Doctor *Laud*, was looked upon in those times as an *Arminian*, and a fierce opposer of *Puritans*; and while he lived in *Oxford*, suspected to incline to Popish Tenents" (Rushworth, *Collections*, pp. 61–62). Rushworth's *Collections* depicts Laud as one of the principal evil counsellors who had perverted the judgment of first the Duke of Buckingham (p. 444, quoting the text of the Grand Remonstrance) and later of the king himself (p. 649).

386. A reference to Calamus's illustration of the nature of government in Plutarch, *Alexander*, 65. Cf. also Arrian, *Anabasis*, 4.11 (Callisthenes's speech rebuking Alexander for his affectations of divinity and his self-orientalizing), 5.25–28 and 7.6.

Noble Venetian. You need no great cautions against Conquering *France* at this present, and I believe your Parliaments need as little admonition against giving of Money towards new Wars or Alliances, that fine wheedle[387] having lately lost them enough already; therefore, pray, let us suffer our Friend to go on.

English Gentleman. I have no more to say of Foreign Monarchies, but only to tell you, That *Poland* is both Governed and Possessed by some very great Persons or Potentates, called *Palatines,*[388] and under them by a very numerous Gentry; for the King is not onely Elective, but so limited, that he has little or no Power, but to Command their Armies in time of War; which makes them often chuse Foreigners of great Fame for Military Exploits: and as for the Commonalty or Country-men, they are absolutely Slaves or Villains. This Government is extreamly confused, by reason of the numerousness of the Gentry, who do not always meet by way of representation as in other Kingdoms, but sometimes for the choice of their King, and upon other great occasions, collectively, in the Field,

387. See above, p. 146, n. 247.

388. "Next to the Bishops sit the Palatines or Woiwodes, and Castellanes. The Palatines are Governors of Dutchies or Counties, Commanders of their Militia in the general Expeditions of the Kingdom, appoint Conventions of the Nobles within their own Palatinate, and preside in them, and in Courts of Judicature, and have the patronage of the *Jews,* who are very numerous in *Poland.* They are the first order of the secular Senators" (Moses Pitt, *The English Atlas* [Oxford, 1680], p. 9). On the elective nature of the Polish monarchy, Pitt says, "At first the Kings of *Poland* were successive, as appears from the testimony of all their Historians: and it was the custom that the reigning Prince appointed his successour. So *Lescus* the Third appointed *Popielus:* so also *Boleslaus* the Chast, did *Lescus* the Black. Nay oftentimes the Kings of *Poland* divided the Kingdom amongst their sons, which is not usual in elective governments. This is evident from the example of *Boleslaus Crivoustus;* and is further confirm'd, in the *Polonian* Histories, by the precedent of *Boleslaus* the Curld. But in the reign of *Sigismund Augustus,* a Law was made that no King of *Poland* should presume to nominate, or impose on the Kingdom a successor: which law was not only renew'd in the *interregnum* after his death, but several times afterwards: the custom of Elections having encroached upon the Scepter for some while before, for want of issue of the true *Polish* Royal Family" (p. 4). In 1679 Sir Leoline Jenkins had cited Poland in the Commons as an illustration of the inconveniences of elective monarchy (Grey, *Debates,* vol. 7, p. 419).

as the Tribes did at *Rome*; which would make things much more turbulent if all this body of Gentry did not wholly depend for their Estates upon the favour of the Palatines their Lords, which makes them much more tractable. I have done with our Neighbours beyond Sea, and should not without your command have made so long a digression in this place, which should indeed have been treated of before we come to speak of *England*, but that you were pleased to divert me from it before: However, being placed near the Portraicture of our own Country, it serves better (as *contraria juxta se posita*)[389] to illustrate it: but I will not make this Deviation longer, by Apologizing for it; and shall therefore desire you to take notice, That as in *England* by degrees Property came to shift from the few to the many, so the Government is grown heavier and more uneasie both to Prince and People, the complaints more in Parliament, the Laws more numerous, and much more tedious and prolix, to meet with the tricks and malice of men, which works in a loose Government; for there was no need to make Acts *verbose*, when the great Persons could presently force the Execution of them: for the Law of *Edward* the First, for frequent Parliaments, had no more words than *A Parliament shall be holden every year*, whereas our Act for a Triennial Parliament, in the time of King *Charles* the First, contained several sheets of paper, to provide against a failer[390] in the Execution of that Law; which if the Power had remained in the Lords, would have been needless: for some of them, in case of intermission of Assembling the Parliament, would have made their Complaint and Address to the King, and have immediately removed the obstruction, which in those days had been the natural and easie way: but now that many of the Lords (like the Bishops which the Popes make at *Rome, in partibus infidelium*)[391] are meerly grown Titular, and purchased for nothing but to get their Wives place, it cannot be wondred at if the King slight their Addresses, and the Court-Parasites deride their Honourable undertakings for the safety of their Country.

389. The full proverb is "Contraria juxta se posita magis elucescunt"; "Contraries when juxtaposed are very illuminating."
390. I.e., failure.
391. "In the lands of the unbelievers," an addition to the name of the see of a titular (i.e., nondiocesan) bishop in the Roman Catholic Church.

Now the Commons succeeding, as was said, in the Property of the Peers and Church (whose Lands five parts of six have been alienated, and mostly is come into the same hands with those of the King and Peers) have inherited likewise, according to the course of nature, their Power; But being kept from it by the established Government, which (not being changed by any lawfull Acts of State) remains still in being formally, whereas virtually it is abolished; so that for want of outward Orders and Provisions, the people are kept from the Exercise of that Power which is faln to them by the Law of Nature; and those who cannot by that Law pretend to the share they had, do yet enjoy it by vertue of that Right which is now ceased, as having been but the natural Effect of a Cause that is no longer in being: and you know *sublata causa, tollitur*.[392] I cannot say that the greater part of the people do know this their condition, but they find very plainly that they want something which they ought to have; and this makes them lay often the blame of their unsetledness upon wrong causes: but however, are altogether unquiet and restless in the Intervals of Parliament; and when the King pleases to assemble one, spend all their time in Complaints of the Inexecution of the Law, of the multiplication of an Infinity of Grievances, of Mis-spending the Publick Monies, of the danger our Religion is in by practices to undermine it and the State, by endeavours to bring in Arbitrary Power, and in questioning great Officers of State, as the Causers and Promoters of all these Abuses;[393] in so much, that every Parliament seems a perfect State of War, wherein the Commons are tugging and contending for their Right, very justly and very honourably, yet without coming to a Point: So that the Court sends them packing, and governs still worse and worse in the Vacancies, being necessitated thereunto by their despair of doing any good in Parliament; and therefore are forced to use horrid shifts to subsist without it, and to keep it off; without ever considering, that if these

392. A common law maxim, which in full reads, "Sublata causa, tollitur effectus"; "When the cause is removed, the effect is gone."

393. As a recent example of what Neville is describing, consider the speech of Colonel Birch at the beginning of the session of Parliament on 25 October 1679, which is a pure litany of grievances arising from previous Parliaments (Grey, *Debates*, vol. 7, p. 350).

Counsellers understood their Trade, they might bring the Prince and People to such an Agreement in Parliament, as might repair the broken and shipwrack'd Government of *England*; and in this secure the Peace, Quiet and Prosperity of the People, the Greatness and Happiness of the King, and be themselves not only out of present danger (which no other course can exempt them from) but be Renowned to all Posterity.

Noble Venetian. I beseech you, Sir, how comes it to pass, that neither the King, nor any of his Counsellors could ever come to find out the truth of what you discourse? for I am fully convinced it is as you say.

English Gentleman. I cannot resolve you that, but this is certain, they have never endeavoured a Cure, though possibly they might know the Disease, as fearing that though the Effects of a Remedy would be, as was said, very advantagious both to King and People, and to themselves; yet possibly, such a Reformation might not consist with the Merchandize they make of the Princes Favour, nor with such Bribes, Gratuities and Fees as they usually take for the dispatch of all Matters before them. And therefore our Counsellors have been so far from suggesting any such thing to their Master, that they have opposed and quashed all Attempts of that kind, as they did the worthy Proposals made by certain Members of that Parliament in the beginning of King *James*'s Reign, which is yet called the Undertaking Parliament.[394] These Gentlemen considering

394. Neville here recounts some of the secret history of the "Addled" or "Undertaking" Parliament, the second Parliament of the reign of James I, which sat between 5 April and 7 June 1614 and which passed no legislation (hence the name "Addled"). Given that Neville's grandfather had taken a leading role in these initiatives, this was presumably in part a matter of Neville family tradition. What Sir Henry Neville had suggested to James was a more modest version of the "Great Contract," which had been proposed by Salisbury to Parliament in February 1610 but which had stalled and not been passed before the dissolution in February 1611. Salisbury's idea had been that Parliament should grant the Crown an income of £200,000 per annum in perpetuity in exchange for the Crown's abandonment of its rights of wardship, marriage, and purveyance. Neville's plan was less ambitious: Parliament would vote more subsidies if the king would relax the administration of his rights as a landlord; to ensure this, he and a group of like-minded MPs would undertake (hence the name) to manage Par-

what we have been discoursing of, *viz.* That our old Government is at an end, had framed certain Heads, which, if they had been proposed by that Parliament to the King, and by him consented to, would, in their Opinion, have healed the Breach; and that if the King would perform his part, that House of Commons would undertake for the Obedience of the People. They did believe that if this should have been moved in Parliament before the King was acquainted with it, it would prove Abortive: and therefore sent three of their number to his Majesty; Sir *James a Croft*,[395] Grandfather or Father to the present Bishop of *Hereford*;[396]

---

liament in the king's interest. But the scheme had come to nothing and would leave a bitter taste in James's mouth. Rushworth records the king saying, in the speech which opened his third parliament on 30 January 1620, "If I may know my Errors, I will reform them. I was in my first Parliament a Novice; and in my last there was a kind of beasts called *Undertakers*, a dozen of whom undertook to govern the last Parliament, and they led me" (Rushworth, *Collections*, p. 23). Contemporary manuscript copies of Neville's memorandum are plentiful: PRO, SPD, 14/74, nos. 45 i and 46; BL Harleian MS 4289, fols. 231–33; BL Harleian MS 3787, fols. 185–86; BL Lansdowne MS 486, fols. 17–20; BL Cottonian MS Titus F IV, fols. 13–14. For an overview of this Parliament, see Thomas Moir, *The Addled Parliament of 1614* (Oxford: Clarendon Press, 1958); see also, focusing specifically on Neville's project, Clayton Roberts and Duncan Owen, "The Parliamentary Undertaking of 1614," *English Historical Review*, vol. 93 (1978), pp. 481–98. The episode of "undertaking" was recalled in the Parliament of 1659 by Sir Walter Earle in the presence of Neville, who rose to both defend and apologize for the actions of his grandfather: "I blush for that my grandfather was one of those. There were eighty of them; and it was to good purpose. They were men of the best estates. Sir John Widrington questioned them, but could fasten nothing on them, that they went to the Court" (Burton, *Diary*, vol. 4, pp. 346–47). Sir Henry Neville's willingness to manage the Commons on behalf of the king, notwithstanding the purity of his intentions, is at odds with the republican principles of his grandson.

395. A slip for Sir Herbert Croft (c. 1565–1629), the father of the bishop of Hereford and a member of the "Addled" Parliament of 1614.

396. Herbert Croft (d. 1691). His father was Sir Herbert Croft (c. 1565–1629), and his grandfather was Edward Croft (d. 1601). Originally a Roman Catholic, the Bishop of Hereford was the author of *The Naked Truth: or, the True State of the Primitive Church* (1675), an appeal for religious comprehension which provoked in its defense against Francis Turner's attack on it *Animadversions* (1676), Marvell's *Mr. Smirke. Or, the Divine in Mode* (1676). For commentary, see Marvell, *Prose Works*, vol. 2, pp. 3–22.

Thomas Harley,[397] who was Ancestor to the Honourable Family of that Name in *Herefordshire*; and Sir *Henry Nevill,*[398] who had been Ambassador from Queen *Elizabeth* to the *French* King. These were to open the matter at large to the King, and to procure his leave that it might be proposed in Parliament: which, after a very long Audience and Debate, that wise Prince consented to, with a promise of Secresie in the mean time, which they humbly begged of His Majesty. However, this took Vent,[399] and the Earl of *Northampton,*[400] of the House of *Howard*, who ruled the Rost in that time, having knowledg of it, engaged Sir *R. Weston*, afterwards Lord Treasurer and Earl of *Portland,*[401] to impeach these Un-

397. Possibly an error for Sir Robert Harley (1579–1656), an active politician at this time and the man who had consolidated the Harley family's political power base in Herefordshire. Harley had been involved in the negotiations with James over the Great Contract but had failed to find a seat in the 1614 Parliament.

398. Sir Henry Neville (1561/62–1615), Neville's grandfather; English ambassador to France 1599–1600.

399. I.e., "became generally known" (*OED*, s.v. "vent" *n. 2*, 2a).

400. Henry Howard (1540–1614), Earl of Northampton; courtier, administrator, and author. For a modern assessment of his career as a whole, see L. L. Peck, *Northampton: Patronage and Policy at the Court of James I* (London: Allen and Unwin, 1982); for his role in the "Addled" Parliament, see pp. 205–12.

401. Richard Weston (1577–1635), first Earl of Portland, later Chancellor of the Exchequer. The journal of the House of Commons contains the following entry for 14 May 1614, when the concern over "undertaking" had reached its crisis: "Sir Roger Owen maketh Report for the Undertaking. That they have done him no Harm: That they have yet done no Harm, but Good: Yet done Injury, though not Damage.—His Memory like a Pidgeon House: If One fly in another flieth out. Sir H. Croftes:—That divers taxed, as Stars of the last Parliament, now Jelly.—That hereby an implicit concluding, that there are still Undertakers. The Paper read. Sir H. Nevill avoweth the Paper: Giveth the Reason: That his Majesty, in July was two Year, at Windsor, where his Charge lieth, called him to him to know his Opinion in Parliament. The One not pertinent to this: The other, whether he might trust to the Love of his People, for Relief.—Shewed him the Reasons why divers dissuaded a Parliament.—That he answered, he trembled to think that any should thus breed a Dislike between his People and him. That he then answered his Majesty; and whilst fresh in Memory, set them down; which will justify them upon his Oath.—That he told him, that divers of those Gentlemen he then.—That he thought—That then no House. That most of these Things contained in the Memorials the last Parliament.—That he called, and commanded.—That he never undertook to include all in this Paper: That divers of them of little Value to the King; of much Value to the People. Mr. Crew:—That this Question first well moved, now well removed. That we have fished long, and catched nothing.—Moveth to leave this, and prepare ourselves for the Conference

dertakers in Parliament before they could move their matters; which he did the very same day, accompanying his Charge (which was endeavouring to alter the established Government of *England*) with so eloquent an Invective, that if one of them had not risen, and made the House acquainted with the whole Series of the Affair, they must have been in danger of being impeached by the Commons: but however it broke their designe, which was all that *Northampton* and *Weston* desired, and prevented Posterity from knowing any of the Particulars of this Reformation; for nothing being moved, nothing could remain upon the Journal.[402] So that you see our Predecessors were not ignorant altogether of our condition, though the Troubles which have befallen this poor Kingdom since, have made it much more apparent: for since the Determination of that Parliament, there has not been one called, either in that King's Reign, or his Son's, or since, that hath not been dissolved abruptly, whilst the main businesses, and those of most concern to the publick, were depending and undecided.[403] And although there hath happened in

---

with the Lords; and go on with Things for the Good of King and Commonwealth. Sir Rich. Weston:—Cum duo faciunt idem, non est idem.—That he cometh hither for none, but for publick Ends. That the Business may be severed from the Person of Sir H. Nevill.—Misliketh the Proceedings.—That a House of Parliament not to suffer their Counsels to be led by any private Man.—Moveth an Entry of a Precedent, that no Papers shall be spread of Parliament Matters" (*CJ*, vol. 1, p. 485). Note that Sir Henry Neville's first conversation with James I on the subject of the management of Parliament had occurred at Windsor in July 1612, long before the opening of the "Addled" Parliament. The account in *Plato Redivivus*, however, seems to imply that the overture was made to James after writs had been issued summoning the Parliament on 19 February 1614. There may of course have been more than one such conversation between the two men.

402. The House of Commons journals contain no details about the contents of the "undertaking" memorial drawn up by Sir Henry Neville, beyond the discussion of it given above.

403. The power of the Crown to suppress unpalatable legislation by the expedient of dissolving Parliament had been a point of friction since 1641, when Parliament had brought forward "a revolutionary bill prohibiting the adjournment, prorogation or dissolution of the present parliament without its own consent" (Kenyon, *Stuart Constitution*, p. 192). It would be a recurrent source of discontent after the Restoration: "For opponents of crown policy, the principal political issue after April 1681 was the indefinite suspension of parliaments. The obstruction of parliaments had been the major political issue throughout this crisis, as under Charles I" (Scott, *Commonwealth Principles*, p. 125; cf. p. 332). On 25 October 1675 Sir Thomas Meres had complained, "Five or

this Interim a bloody War,[404] which in the Close of it, changed the whole Order and Foundation of the Polity of *England*, and that it hath pleased God to restore it again by his Majesty's happy Return, so that the old

---

six times Bills have been cut to pieces by Prorogations. We are tired with hearing them read" (Grey, *Debates*, vol. 3, p. 346). The author of *A Letter from a Parliament-Man to His Friend* had set it down as a principle that "*Parliaments ought not to be Prorogued, Adjourned, or Dissolved, till all Petitions are heard, and the Aggrievances of the People redressed*" (*State-Tracts*, vol. 1, p. 71; cf. vol. 2, pp. 67–71). In 1677 Lord William Cavendish, later first Duke of Devonshire, had argued that sustained prorogation amounted to dissolution and a frustration of parliamentary government, laying on the table as he did so the relevant Act from the reign of Edward III. Sir Henry Capel echoed the sentiment on 19 December 1678: "These last four or five years, we have had nothing but Prorogations and Adjournments of the Parliament, without doing any thing to purpose" (Grey, *Debates*, vol. 6, p. 355). On 15 February 1679 Buckingham had made a celebrated speech in the House of Lords attacking the practice of repeated prorogation as a frustration of Parliament (reprinted in *State-Tracts*, vol. 1, pp. 237–40). On 20 March 1679 Sir Thomas Clarges would demand that a report of a committee of the House should be "entered upon our books, we then have a good title to it, which, by a Dissolution of the Parliament, we have not else" (Grey, *Debates*, vol. 7, p. 7). The address to the king requesting that Halifax be removed from his counsels specified among his misdemeanours the practice of "frequent Prorogations" and the dissolution of the last Parliament by which Roman Catholics had been "greatly encouraged to carry on their hellish and damnable Conspiracies against your Royal Person and Government" (Grey, *Debates*, vol. 8, p. 51). Similar points would be made in a text published in the same year as *Plato Redivivus*, *A Just and Modest Vindication of the Proceedings of the Two Last Parliaments* (1681), which placed its demands in an historical context: "The Wisdom of our Ancestors has provided, by divers Statutes, both for the holding Parliaments annually, and oftner if need be; and that they should not be Prorogued or Dissolved till all the Petitions and Bills before them were answered and redressed" (*State-Tracts*, vol. 1, p. 165; for other examples, see pp. 192 and 463; for comment, see Scott, *Commonwealth Principles*, pp. 337–38). The fear was that "Excesses and arbitrary Proceedings" might flourish and take root during "Recesses of Parliament" (Grey, *Debates*, vol. 8, p. 67). Such had been the implication of the subtitle of Marvell's *An Account of the Growth of Popery and Arbitrary Government in England* (1677): "More Particularly, from the Long *Prorogation* of *November*, 1675. Ending the 15*th.* of *February*, 1676, till the last Meeting of *Parliament*, the 16 of *July* 1677." Consequently, in the Convention Parliament of 1689 William Sacheverell would stipulate as one of the key elements in any settlement that "Parliaments be duly chosen, and not kicked out at pleasure; which never could have been done, without such an extravagant Revenue that they might never stand in need of Parliaments. Secure the Right of Elections, and the Legislative Power" (Grey, *Debates*, vol. 9, p. 33).

404. I.e., the English Civil Wars. On the scale of mortality in those wars, see Charles Carlton, *Going to the Wars: The Experience of the British Civil Wars, 1638–*

Government is alive again; yet it is very visible that its deadly Wound is not healed, but that we are to this day tugging with the same difficulties, managing the same Debates in Parliament, and giving the same disgusts to the Court, and hopes to the Country, which our Ancestors did before the Year 1640, whilst the King hath been forced to apply the same Remedy of Dissolution to his two first Parliaments,[405] that his Father used to his four first,[406] and King *James* to his three last,[407] contrary to his own visible Interest, and that of his people; and this for want of having Counsellors about him of Abilities and Integrity enough to discover to him the Disease of his Government, and the Remedy: which I hope, when we meet to Morrow Morning you will come prepared to enquire into; for the Doctor says, he will advise you to go take the Air this afternoon in your Coach.

Noble Venetian. I shall think it very long till the morning come: But before you go, pray give me leave to ask you something of your Civil War

---

1651 (London: Routledge, 1992); and Stephen Porter, *Destruction in the English Civil Wars* (Stroud: Sutton, 1997). Blair Worden has evoked the destructive scale of the conflict: "The whole community was sucked into the war. Informed speculation . . . has suggested that one in every four or five adult English males was enlisted into an army at some point between 1642 and 1646. Over the course of the wars in England, it is estimated, at least 150 towns suffered serious destruction of property; around 11,000 homes were burnt or demolished and 55,000 people made homeless; nearly four per cent of the population died in fighting or from war-related disease, a much higher figure that that in the First World War" (Blair Worden, *Roundhead Reputations: The English Civil Wars and the Passions of Posterity* [London: Allen Lane, 2001], p. 3).

405. I.e., the Convention Parliament (summoned 16 March 1660, dissolved 29 December 1660) and the Cavalier Parliament (summoned 18 February 1661, dissolved 24 January 1679).

406. Charles I's first Parliament (summoned 2 April 1625, dissolved 12 August 1625), his second Parliament (summoned 26 December 1625, dissolved 16 June 1626), his third Parliament (summoned 31 January 1628, dissolved by the king in person 10 March 1629), and his fourth Parliament, the "Short" Parliament (summoned 20 February 1640, dissolved 5 May 1640).

407. The "Undertaking" or "Addled" Parliament (summoned 19 February 1614, dissolved 7 June 1614), James I's third Parliament (summoned 13 November 1620, dissolved 8 February 1622), and his fourth Parliament (summoned 30 December 1623, dissolved 27 March 1625).

here; I do not mean the History of it (although the World abroad is very much in the dark as to all your Transactions of that time for want of a good one) but the grounds or pretences of it, and how you fell into a War against your King.

English Gentleman. As for our History, it will not be forgotten; one of those who was in Employment from the Year 40. to 60. hath written the History of those 20 Years, a Person of good Learning and Elocution; and though he be now dead, yet his Executors are very unwilling to publish it so soon, and to rub a Sore that is not yet healed.[408] But the Story is writ with great Truth and Impartiality, although the Author were engaged both in Councils and Arms for the Parliaments side. But for the rest of your Demand, you may please to understand, that our Parliament never did, as they pretended, make War against the King; for he by Law can do no Wrong, and therefore cannot be quarrelled with: The War they declared was undertaken to rescue the King's Person out of those Mens hands who led him from his Parliament, and made use of his Name to levy a War against them.

Noble Venetian. But does your Government permit, that in case of a disagreement between the King and his Parliament, either of them may raise Arms against the other?

English Gentleman. It is impossible that any Government can go further than to provide for its own Safety and Preservation whilst it is in being, and therefore it can never direct what shall be done when it self is at an end; there being this difference between our Bodies Natural and Politick, that the first can make a Testament to dispose of things after his death, but not the other.[409] This is certain, that where-ever any two Co-

408. Neville is presumably referring to the *Memorials* of Bulstroke Whitlocke, which would be published in 1682. I owe this identification to the kindness of Blair Worden.

409. The principle that Parliament cannot bind the hands of its successors is familiar to us today, but it went against the ancient constitutionalism which fueled much seventeenth-century resistance to Stuart kingship. For ancient constitutionalists the fundamental laws of the kingdom, such as Magna Carta, were, if not

ordinate Powers[410] do differ, and there be no Power on Earth to reconcile them otherwise, nor any Umpire, they will, *de facto*,[411] fall together by the Ears. What can be done in this Case *de jure*,[412] look into your own

---

technically binding, then certainly to be reverenced and wherever possible followed. In Neville's lifetime it is only in Leveller writings and at moments in the contributions of Colonel Rainsborough to the Putney Debates that something like an opinion to the contrary is to be found. For instance, *An Agreement of the People* (1647) states, "*No Act of Parliament is or can be unalterable, and so cannot be sufficient security to save you or us harmlesse, from what another Parliament may determine*" (Morton, *Freedom*, p. 144). In a letter to Madison of 6 September 1789 Jefferson would take a clear stand on this question, which he believed wrongly to be virgin intellectual territory: "The question Whether one generation of men has a right to bind another, seems never to have been started either on this [*the letter is written from Paris*] or our side of the water. Yet it is a question of such consequences as not only to merit decision, but place also, among the fundamental principles of every government. The course of reflection in which we are immersed here on the elementary principles of society has presented this question to my mind; and that no such obligation can be transmitted I think very capable of proof. I set out on this ground which I suppose to be self evident, '*that the earth belongs in usufruct to the living*'; that the dead have neither powers nor rights over it." In *Rights of Man* Paine would state the principle clearly, in contradiction to Burke's very different view of the relationship between generations: "There never did, there never will, and there never can exist a parliament, or any description of men, or any generation of men, in any country, possessed of the right or the power of binding and controlling posterity to the 'end of time,' or of commanding for ever how the world shall be governed, or who shall govern it; and therefore, all such clauses, acts or declarations, by which the makers of them attempt to do what they have neither the right nor the power to do, nor the power to execute, are in themselves null and void.—Every age and generation must be free to act for itself, in all cases, as the ages and generations which preceded it. The vanity and presumption of governing beyond the grave, is the most ridiculous and insolent of all tyrannies" (Paine, *Rights of Man*, pp. 63–64).

410. For a mid-seventeenth-century attempt to address this problem, see Philip Hunton, *A Treatise of Monarchy* (1643), chapter 7, "Where the legal power of final judging in these cases does reside, in case the three estates differ about the same," in Wootton, *Divine Right*, pp. 209–11. Cf. Goddard, *Plato's Demon*, p. 313; and *Antimonarchical Authors*, pp. 178–79. Pocock finds the problem of coordinate powers at the root of the constitutional perplexities of the 1640s: "Two lawful authorities were competing for his [the Christian subject's] allegiance, and neither could destroy the legitimacy of the other; to decide that one or the other was not lawful was, in a traditionalist society, almost certainly to conclude that it had never been, and so to destroy tradition" (Pocock, *Harrington*, p. 22).

411. I.e., as a matter of fact.

412. I.e., in point of right or justice.

Country-man *Machiavell*,[413] and into *Grotius*,[414] who in his Book *De jure Belli ac Pacis*, treated of such matters long before our Wars. As for the ancient Politicians, they must needs be silent in the Point, as having no mixt Governments amongst them; and as for me, I will not rest my self in so slippery a Place. There are great disputes about it in the Parliaments Declarations before the War, and something considerable in the King's Answers to them;[415] which I shall specifie immediately, when I have satisfied you how our War begun; which was in this manner. The Long Parliament[416] having procured from the King his Royal Assent for their Sitting till they were dissolved by Act, and having paid and sent out the Scottish Army, and disbanded our own, went on in their Debates for the settling and mending our Government: the King being displeased with

413. Possibly a reference to *Discourses*, 1.6, and to the opening of book 3 of the *History of Florence* (Machiavelli, *Works*, pp. 275–77 and 50).

414. Hugo de Groot, or Grotius (1583–1645), Dutch jurist. Neville is perhaps thinking of a section of book 1, chapter 4, para. 13, of *De Jure Belli ac Pacis* where Grotius is reviewing the legitimate grounds for waging war upon a monarch: "*Sixthly*, If a King should have but one Part of the sovereign Power, and the Senate or People the other, if such a King shall invade that Part which is not his own, he may justly be resisted, because he is not Sovereign in that Respect. Which I believe may take Place, though in the Division of the Sovereignty, the Power of making War fell to the King, for that is to be understood of a foreign War: Since whoever has a Share of the Sovereignty must have at the same Time a Right to defend it" (Grotius, *War and Peace*, p. 376). The principle *Par in parem non habet imperium* ("Equals have no power over one another") was well established in English law, reaching back to Bracton (see Sidney, *Court Maxims*, p. 201 and n. 429).

415. See the resolutions passed by Parliament on 20 May 1642, with the accompanying declarations and the answer of the king (Rushworth, *Collections*, part 3, vol. 1, pp. 575–99; Clarendon, *History*, vol. 2, pp. 77–80). Neville himself indicates on p. 224 below that these are the documents he has in mind. For the "something considerable" in the king's answer to Parliament on this point, see, e.g., "His Majesty hath often heard of the great Trust, that by God and Mans Law is committed to the King, for the Defence and Safety of His People; but as yet hath never understood what Trust or Power is committed to either, or both Houses of Parliament without the King, they being summoned to Council and Advise the King; *but by what Law or Authority they possess themselves of His Majesty's proper Right and Inheritance; He is confident that as they have not, so they cannot shew*" (Rushworth, *Collections*, part 3, vol. 1, p. 576).

416. So-called because it lasted nearly twenty years, being summoned in September 1640, assembling on 3 November, and being dissolved on 16 March 1660.

them for it, and with himself for putting it out of his Power to dissolve them, now the business which they pretended for their Perpetuation was quite finished, takes an unfortunate Resolution to accuse five principal Men of the Commons House, and one of the Peers,[417] of High-Treason: which he prosecuted in a new unheard-of way, by coming with armed Men into the Commons House of Parliament, to demand their Members; but nothing being done by reason of the absence of the five, and Tumults of discontented Citizens flocking to *White-Hall* and *Westminster*, the King took that occasion to absent himself from his Parliament. Which induced the Commons House to send Commissioners to *Hampton-Court* to attend his Majesty with *a Remonstrance of the State of the Kingdom*,[418] and an humble Request to return to his Parliament, for the Redressing those Grievances which were specified in that Remonstrance. But the King, otherwise Counselled, goes to *Windsor*, and thence Northwards, till he arrived at *York*; where he summons in the *Militia*, that is, the Trained-Bands[419] of the County; and besides, all the Gentry, of which there was a numerous Appearance. The King addressed himself to the latter with Complaints against a prevailing Party in Parliament, which intended to take the Crown from his Head; that he was come to them, his loving Subjects, for Protection; and, in short, desired them to assist him with Moneys to defend himself by Arms. Some of these Gentlemen petitioned His Majesty to return to his Parliament, the rest went about the Debate of the King's Demands; who, in the mean time, went to *Hull*, to secure the Magazine there, but was denied Entrance by a Gentleman[420] whom the House had sent down to prevent the seizing it;

417. On 3 January 1642 the lord keeper had been instructed to impeach Lord Kimbolton and five members of the House of Commons (John Pym, John Hampden, William Strode, Denzil Holles, and Sir Arthur Haslerigg) on grounds of high treason (Kenyon, *Stuart Constitution*, pp. 240–41).

418. I.e., the Grand Remonstrance, a compendium of parliamentary grievances presented to Charles at Hampton Court on 1 December 1641 but which had been in preparation since November 1640 (Kenyon, *Stuart Constitution*, p. 194).

419. I.e., trained companies of citizen soldiery.

420. Hull was a place of military significance because it contained a magazine of cannon, arms, and munitions: "This Town thus situated, was by the State Polititians deemed the fittest place in the Northern Parts, for the *Kingdoms Magazine* in

who was immediately declared a Traytor,[421] and the King fell to raising of Forces: which coming to the Knowledge of the House, they made this Vote, *That the King, seduced by Evil Counsel, intended to levy War against his Parliament and People, to destroy the Fundamental Laws and Liberties of* England, *and to introduce an Arbitrary Government,* &c. This was the first time they named the King, and the last: For in all their other Papers, and in their Declaration to Arm for their Defence (which did accompany this Vote) they name nothing but Malignant Counsellors. The Kings Answer[422] to these Votes and this Declaration, is that which I mentioned;

the Expedition against the *Scots.* There was therefore sent hither great store of Ammunition, and *Arms* for about thirty thousand Men both Horse and Foot, all which were in the managing of Captain Leg, and his Assigns, and for the future security thereof, as also of the Castle, Forts and Block-houses, here was planted by the Earl of *Strafford* a Garrison of 1000 Soldiers, under the Command of Sir *Thomas Glemham,* who continued here almost a year after the *pacification* betwixt his Majesty and the *Scots,* until they were dismissed and disbanded by the Parliament, and then Magazine, Castle, Block-houses, and other Forts were committed to the care of the Townsmen, whose care in Watching and Warding was answerable to their trust" (Rushworth, *Collections,* part 3, vol. 1, p. 564; cf. Clarendon, *History,* vol. 1, p. 555). On 5 March 1642 Parliament had put Hull under the command of Sir John Hotham (1589–1645), who in the 1630s had been active in presenting Yorkshire's grievances to the king. When Charles appeared before the gates of the city on 23 April 1642 he was denied admittance, Hotham declaring that "he durst not open the gates, being trusted by the Parliament." Clarendon's account of the episode is colorful and circumstantial (Clarendon, *History,* vol. 2, pp. 45–50). His character of Hotham is noteworthy: "Hotham was, by his nature and education, a rough and a rude man; of great covetousness, of great pride, and great ambition; without any bowels of good nature, or the least sense or touch of generosity; his parts were not quick and sharp, but composed, and judged well; he was a man of craft, and more like to deceive than to be cozened. . . . [He] lamented his own fate, that, being a man of very different principles from those who drove things to this extremity, and of entire affection and duty to the King, he should now be looked upon as the chief ground and cause of the civil war which was to ensue, by his not opening the ports when the King would have entered into the town" (Clarendon, *History,* vol. 2, pp. 261–63). Cf. *Antimonarchical Authors,* pp. 223 and 344–45.

421. Cf. Rushworth, *Collections,* part 3, vol. 1, p. 567.

422. Neville perhaps is thinking of the following passage: "We say, with a clear and upright Conscience to God Almighty, whosoever harbours the least thought in his Breast of ruining or violating the publick Liberty or Religion of this Kingdom, or the just Freedom and Priviledg of Parliament, let him be accursed; and he

wherein His Majesty denies any intention of invading the Government, with high Imprecations upon himself and Posterity if it were otherwise: and owns that they have Right to maintain their Laws and Government. This is to be seen in the Paper it self now extant; and this Gracious Prince never pretended (as some Divines have done for him) that his Power came from God,[423] and that his Subjects could not dispute it, nor

---

shall be no Counsellor of Ours that will not say *Amen*" (Rushworth, *Collections*, part 3, vol. 1, p. 589).

423. On the theory of *jure divino* monarchy, see J. N. Figgis, *The Divine Right of Kings*, second edition (Cambridge: Cambridge University Press, 1914), especially pp. 137–76. James I had asserted the divine origin of monarchical authority in *The Trew Law of Free Monarchies* (1598), and Charles's own adherents had claimed the benefits of that theory on his behalf (Figgis, *Divine Right of Kings*, pp. 141–45). Roger Maynwaring, in sermons preached before Charles in 1627 that had to be suppressed because their doctrine was so offensive to Parliament, was particularly outspoken, extolling, e.g., "that most *high*, *sacred*, and *transcendent Relation*, vvhich naturally growes betweene *The Lords Anointed*, and their loyall *Subiects:* to, and ouer whom, their lawfull *Soueraignes* are no lesse then *Fathers*, *Lords*, *Kings* and *Gods* on earth," and roundly asserting, "All *Powers* created are of God; *no power, vnlesse it be giuen from aboue:* And *all powers*, that are of this sort, *are ordained of God*. Among al the *powers* that be ordained of God, the *Regall* is most *high*, *strong* and *large*: *Kings* aboue all, inferiour to none, to no *man*, to no *multitudes* of men, to no *Angell*, to no *order* of *Angels*" (Roger Maynwaring, *Two Sermons* [1627], first sermon, pp. 3–4 and 8). In the next century, however, Hume would note that the Tories were more attached to divine right theory than their political forebears the Cavaliers had been: "When we compare the parties of Whig and Tory with those of Round-head and Cavalier, the most obvious difference, that appears between them, consists in the principles of *passive obedience*, and *indefeasible right*, which were but little heard of among the Cavaliers, but became the universal doctrine, and were esteemed the true characteristic of a Tory" ("Of the Parties of Great Britain," in Hume, *Essays*, p. 70). Around 1680 the issue had become freshly topical. On 25 March 1679 the Earl of Shaftesbury had risen in the Lords and spoken out passionately against the revival of doctrines of divine right monarchy, as he had four years previously on 20 October 1675: "If this Doctrine [*jure divino* monarchy] be true, our *Magna Charta* is of no use, our Laws are but Rules amongst our selves during the King's pleasure. Monarchy, if of Divine Right, cannot be bounded or limited by Humane Laws; nay, what's more, cannot bind it self, and all our Claims of Right by the Law, or Constitution of the Government, all the Jurisdiction and Privilege of this House, all the Rights and Privileges of the House of Commons, all the Properties and Liberties of the People, are to give way, not only to the Interest, but the Will and Pleasure of the Crown" (*State-Tracts*, vol. 1, pp. 60–61).

ought he to give any Account of his Actions (though he should enslave us all) to any but him. So that our War did not begin upon a point of Right, but upon a matter of Fact; for without going to Lawyers or Casuists to be resolved, those of the People who believed that the King did intend to destroy our Liberties, joyned with the Parliament; and those who were of opinion that the prevailing party in Parliament did intend to destroy the King or dethrone him, assisted vigorously His Majesty with their Lives and Fortunes. And the Question you were pleased to ask never came; for both parties pretended and believed they were in the right, and that they did fight for and defend the Government:[424] But I have wearied you out.

Noble Venetian. No sure, Sir, but I am infinitely obliged to you for the great care you have taken and still have used to instruct me, and beg the continuance of it for to morrow morning.

English Gentleman. I shall be sure to wait upon you at nine a Clock, but I shall beseech both of you to bethink your selves what to offer, for I shall come with a design to learn, not to teach: nor will I presume in such a matter to talk all, as you have made me do to day; for what I have yet to say in the point of Cure, is so little, that it will look like the Mouse to the Mountain[425] of this days discourse.

424. On the proximity of the political views of Parliamentarians and Royalists before the outbreak of hostilities, see Kenyon, *Stuart Constitution*, pp. 190–91.

425. An allusion to famous lines in Horace's *Ars Poetica* ridiculing bombastic poetry: "Quid dignum tanto feret his promissor hiatu? / parturient montes, nasce-tur ridiculus mus" ("What will this boaster produce in keeping with such pomp-ous language? / The mountains will labour, and give birth to a laughable mouse" (ll. 138–39). It was a tag retorted against Neville by Thomas Goddard (Goddard, *Plato's Demon*, p. 301) and was familiar enough sometimes to be quoted in Parlia-ment (e.g., Grey, *Debates*, vol. 3, p. 246). It was also common in polemical literature of the time, for instance being quoted by Marvell in *The Rehearsal Transpros'd. The Second Part* (1672) (Marvell, *Prose Works*, vol. 1, p. 223), and possibly alluded to in the same author's *A Short Historical Essay, Touching General Councils, Creed, and Impositions in Matters of Religion* (1676) (Marvell, *Prose Works*, vol. 2, p. 139 and n. 183).

Doctor. It is so in all Arts, the Corollary is short, and in ours[426] particularly. Those who write of the several Diseases incident to humane bodies, must make long Discourses of the Causes, Symptomes, Signs and Prognosticks[427] of such Distempers; but when they come to treat of the Cure, it is dispatched in a few *Recipes.*[428]

English Gentleman. Well, Sir, for this bout,[429] I humbly take my leave of you; nay, Sir, you are not in a condition to use ceremony.

Doctor. Sir, I forbid you this door; pray retire: to stand here, is worse than to be in the open air.

Noble Venetian. I obey you both.

Doctor. I shall wait on you in the Evening.

426. I.e., medicine.
427. I.e., symptoms which indicate the probable course and outcome of a disease (*OED*, s.v. "prognosticks").
428. I.e., formulas for the composition of medicines; prescriptions (*OED*, s.v. "recipe").
429. I.e., "for the time being" (*OED*, s.v. "bout," *n. 2,* 2b).

The Third Day.

Noble Venetian. Gentlemen, you are very welcome: what, you are come both together!

Doctor. I met this Gentleman at the door: But methinks we sit looking one upon another, as if all of us were afraid to speak.

English Gentleman. Do you think we have not reason, in such a subject as this is? how can any Man, without Hesitation, presume to be so confident as to deliver his private opinion in a point, upon which, for almost 200 year[430] (for so long our Government has been crazy) no Man has ventured; and when Parliaments have done any thing towards it, there have been Animosities and Breaches, and at length Civil Wars?

Noble Venetian. Our work to day is, to endeavour to shew how all these troubles may be prevented for the future, by taking away the Cause of them, which is the want of a good Government; and therefore it will not be so much presumption in you, as charity, to declare your self fully in this matter.

430. Cf. above, p. 74, n. 67.

English Gentleman. The Cure will follow naturally, if you are satisfied in the Disease, and in the Cause of the Disease: for if you agree that our Government is broken, and that it is broken because it was Founded upon Property, and that Foundation is now shaken; it will be obvious, that you must either bring Property back to your old Government, and give the King and Lords their Lands again, or else you must bring the Government to the Property as it now stands.

Doctor. I am very well satisfied in your Grounds; but because this Fundamental truth is little understood amongst our People, and that in all conversations men will be offering their opinions of what the Parliament ought to do at their Meeting, it will not be amiss to examine some of those Expedients they propose, and to see whether some or all of them may not be effectual towards the bringing us to some degree of settlement, rather than to venture upon so great a change and alteration as would be necessary to model our Government anew.

English Gentleman. Sir, I believe there can be no Expedients proposed in Parliament that will not take up as much time and trouble, find as much difficulty in passing with the King and Lords, and seem as great a change of Government, as the true remedy would appear, at least I speak as to what I have to propose; but however, I approve your Method, and if you will please to propose any of those things, I shall either willingly embrace them, or endeavour to shew reason why they will be of little fruit in the settling our State.

Doctor. I will reduce them to two Heads (besides the making good Laws for keeping out Arbitrary Power, which is always understood:) the hindering the growth of Popery,[431] and consequently the providing against a Popish Successor;[432] and then the declaring the Duke of *Monmouth's*

431. See above, p. 76, n. 74.
432. I.e., Charles II's brother, the Duke of York and future James II.

Right to the Crown,[433] after it hath been examined and agreed to in Parliament.

English Gentleman. As for the making new Laws, I hold it absolutely needless, those we have already against Arbitrary Power being abundantly sufficient, if they might be executed; but that being impossible (as I shall shew hereafter) till some change shall be made, I shall *postpone* this point: and for the first of your other two, I shall divide and separate the consideration of the growth of Popery from that of the Succession. I am sorry that in the prosecution of this Argument, I shall be forced to say something that may not be very pleasing to this worthy Gentleman, we being necessitated to discourse with prejudice of that Religion which he professes; but it shall be with as little ill breeding as I can, and altogether without passion or invectives.

Noble Venetian. It would be very hard for me to suspect any thing from you that should be disobliging; but pray, Sir, go on to your Political discourse, for I am not so ignorant my self, but to know that the conservation of the National Religion (be it what it will) is essential to the well ordering a State:[434] and though in our City the doctrinals[435] are very different from what are professed here, yet as to the Government of the

---

433. James Scott (1649–85), Duke of Monmouth and first Duke of Buccleuch; illegitimate son of the future Charles II and Lucy Walter. Although there are no good grounds for believing the rumors that Charles and Lucy Walter were in fact married and that Monmouth was therefore legitimate (see, e.g., Grey, *Debates*, vol. 7, p. 455 and n.), once the future James II had apostasized to Roman Catholicism there was an understandable desire among Protestant Englishmen to explore the possibility of Monmouth's becoming the heir apparent to the English throne. In 1679 Charles II had sworn that Monmouth was not legitimate: "The King made a solemn declaration in Council, and both signed it and took his oath on it, that he was never married, nor contracted to that Duke's mother; nor to any other woman, except to his present Queen" (Burnet, *History*, vol. 1, p. 452).

434. The Venetian, true to the Laodiceanism of his city, adopts the principle of "cuius regio, eius religio" that had shaped the Peace of Augsburg (1555).

435. I.e., points of religious doctrine (*OED*, s.v. "doctrinal," B2).

State, I believe you know that the Pope or his Priests have as little influence upon it, as your Clergy have here, or in any part of the World.[436]

English Gentleman. I avow it fully, Sir, and with the favour you give will proceed. It cannot be denied but that in former times Popery has been very innocent here to the Government, and that the Clergy and the Pope were so far from opposing our Liberties, that they both sided with the Barons to get a declaration of them by means of *Magna Charta:*[437] It is true also, that if we were all Papists, and that our State were the same, both as to Property and Empire, as it was 400 years ago, there would be but one inconvenience to have that Religion National again in *England*, which is, That the Clergy, *quatenus* such,[438] had and will have a share in the Soveraignty, and inferiour Courts in their own Power, called Ecclesiastical; this is, and ever will be a Solecism in Government, besides a manifest contradiction to the words of Christ our Saviour, who tells us, his Kingdom is not of this World:[439] and the truth is, if you look into the Scriptures, you will find, that the Apostles did not reckon that the Religion they planted should be National in any Country, and therefore have given no precepts to the Magistrate to meddle in matters of Faith and the Worship of God; but Preach'd, That Christians should yield them obedience in all lawfull things.[440] There are many passages in Holy Writ which plainly declare, that the true Believers and Saints should be but a

436. During the sixteenth and seventeenth centuries, relations between Venice and the Papacy had been strained on account of the apparent lack of zeal for religion in, and the political independence of, the Venetians. Paul V had imposed an interdict on Venice in 1606. The animosity between Venice and the Papacy is touched on in a number of books in the booklist: see Amelot de la Houssaie, *Venice*, pp. 73–74; Gailhard, *Italy*, p. 20; and, above all, Nani, *Affairs of Europe*, pp. 64, 319–20, 364–65, 385–86, 414, and 519.

437. The church, led by Stephen Langton (c. 1150–1228), archbishop of Canterbury, had been instrumental in forcing John to seal Magna Carta in 1215 and—not coincidentally—had also been a principal beneficiary of the provisions of the charter.

438. I.e., simply in virtue of their quality (as clergy) (*OED*, s.v. "quatenus").

439. See John 8:23 and 18:36.

440. See Romans 13:1–7, which echoes the teaching of Matthew 22:21 and Mark 12:17.

handful,[441] and such as God had separated, and as it were taken out of the World; which would not have been said by them, if they had believed that whole Nations and People should have been true Followers of Christ, and of his Flock: for certainly none of them are to be damn'd, and yet Christ himself tells us, that few are saved, and bids us strive to get in at the strait gate;[442] and therefore I conceive it not to be imaginable, that either Christ or his Apostles did ever account that the true Religion should be planted in the World by the framing of Laws, Catechisms, or Creeds, by the Soveraign Powers and Magistrates, whether you call them Spiritual or Temporal, but that it should have a Progress suitable to its beginning: for it is visible that it had its Original from the Power and Spirit of God, and came in against the stream, not onely without a *Numa Pompilius*,[443] or a *Mahomet*,[444] to plant and establish it by humane Constitutions and Authority, but had all the Laws of the World to oppose it, and all the bloudy Tyrants of that age to persecute it, and to inflict exquisite torments on the Professors of it.[445] In *Nero's* time (which was very early) the Christians were offered a Temple in *Rome*,[446] and in what other

441. E.g., Matthew 20:16 and 22:14.

442. Luke 13:23–24.

443. In legendary Roman history, this was the successor to Romulus as king of Rome, during whose long and peaceful reign the Romans believed that many of their religious institutions (festivals, sacrifices, rites, the *pontifices*, and the Vestal Virgins) had been founded.

444. See above, p. 88, n. 95. On the utility of Mahomet as a stalking horse for the anticlerical writers and thinkers of Neville's generation, see Champion, *Priestcraft*.

445. A reference to the persecutions of the Christians by the Roman emperors. This had begun under Nero, when the Christians were accused of having set fire to Rome, and it continued under Domitian. But the persecutions were sporadic until the general persecution under Diocletian, which began in A.D. 303 and continued until A.D. 311, with Galerius's publication of an edict of toleration.

446. Possibly a reference to Nero's permission to St. Paul to pursue his ministry in Rome without hindrance (Eusebius, *Ecclesiastical History*, 2.22). Andrew Marvell had recently touched upon Nero's initial indulgence of the Christians in his *A Short Historical Essay, Touching General Councils, Creeds, and Impositions in Matters of Religion* (1676) (Marvell, *Prose Works*, vol. 2, p. 121; cf. Acts 28:16–31). For modern scholarly commentary on Nero's treatment of the Christians, see Paul Keresztes, "The Imperial Roman Government and the Christian Church. I. From Nero to the Severi," in *Aufstieg und Niedergang der römischen Welt*, part 2, vol. 23, no. 1

Cities they pleased, to be built to Jesus Christ, and that the *Romans* should receive him into the number of their gods; but our Religion being then in its purity, this was unanimously refused, for that such a God must have no Companions, nor needed no Temples, but must be Worshipped in Spirit and Truth. The Successors to these good Christians were not so scrupulous; for within some Ages after, the Priests to get Riches and Power, and the Emperors to get and keep the Empire (for by this time the Christians were grown numerous and powerful) combined together to spoil our Holy Religion, to make it fit for the Government of this World, & to introduce into it all the Ceremonious follies and Superstitions of the Heathen; and which is worse, the Power of Priests, both over the Persons and Consciences of Men.[447] I shall say no more of this, but refer you to innumerable Authors who have treated of this Subject, particularly to a *French* Minister, who hath written a Book, Entituled, *La Religion Catholique Apostolique Romaine instituee par Nume Pompile*;[448] and to the incomparable *Machiavel* in his *Posthume* Letter,[449] Printed

---

(Berlin: Walter de Gruyter, 1979), pp. 248ff.; and Keresztes, "Nero, the Christians, and the Jews in Tacitus and Clement of Rome," *Latomus*, 43, no. 2 (1984), pp. 404–13.

447. The corruption of primitive, pure Christianity into priestcraft was a favorite topic of anticlerical writers: see Champion, *Priestcraft*, chapter 5, "Prisca Theologia," pp. 133–69. It might also, however, be cited as an ideal by pious clergymen advocating a comprehension, such as Herbert Croft in *The Naked Truth* (1675): see above, p. 215, n. 396.

448. Untraced.

449. This spurious letter, dated long after Machiavelli's death, was printed in the edition of Machiavelli's *Works* with which Neville was associated. In this letter—which Neville himself may have composed in a spirit of playful imposture—Machiavelli is made vehemently to deplore the corruption of Christianity at the hands of the Roman clergy: "I do not deny but that I have very frequently in my Writings, laid the blame upon the *Church of* Rome, not only for all the misgovernment of *Christendom*; but even for the depravation and almost total destruction of Christian Religion it self in this Province. . . . The *Bishops* of *Rome*, by their insatiable ambition and avarice, have designedly, as much as in them lyes, frustrated the merciful purpose he had, in the happy restauration he intended the world by his Son, and in the renewing and reforming of humane Nature, and have wholly defaced and spoil'd Christian Religion, and made it a worldly and a Heathenish thing; and altogether uncapable, as it is practised amongst them, either of directing the ways of its Professors to virtue and good life, or of saving their Souls

lately in our Language, with the Translation of his Works. But I have
made a long digression; and to come back again, shall onely desire you to
take notice, when I say that anciently Popery was no inconvenience in
this Kingdom, I mean onely Politically, as the Government then stood,
and do not speak at all of the prejudice which mens Souls did and will
ever receive from the Belief of those impious Tenents,[450] and the want of
having the True Gospel of Jesus Christ preached unto them, but living in
perpetual Superstition and Idolatry: The consideration of these Matters
is not so proper to my present purpose, being to Discourse onely of Government. Notwithstanding therefore, as I said before, that Popery might
have suited well enough with our old Constitution, yet as to the present
Estate, which inclines to Popularity, it would be wholly as inconsistent
with it, and with the Power of the Keys,[451] and the Empire of Priests

---

hereafter. . . . The Faith and Religion Preach'd by Christ, and setled afterwards
by his Apostles, and cultivated by their sacred Epistles, is so different a thing from
the Christianity that is now profess'd and taught at *Rome*, that we should be
convinc'd, that if those Holy men should be sent by God again into the world,
they would take more pains to confute this *Gallimaufry*, than ever they did to
Preach down the tradition of the *Pharisees*, or the Fables and Idolatry of the *Gen-
tiles*, and would in probability suffer a new Martyrdom in that City under the
Vicar of Christ, for the same Doctrine which once animated the Heathen Tyrants
against them. Nay, we have something more to say against these Sacrilegious pretenders to Gods power; for whereas all other false worships have been set up by
some politick Legislators, for the support and preservation of Government, this
false, this spurious Religion brought in upon the ruines of Christianity by the
Popes, hath deformed the face of Government in *Europe*, destroying all the good
principles, and morality left us by the Heathen themselves, and introduced instead
thereof, sordid, cowardly, and impolitick notions, whereby they have subjected
mankind, and even great *Princes* and *States*, to their own *Empire*, and never suffered any Orders or Maxims to take place where they have power, that might
make a Nation wise, honest, great or wealthy. . . . I could infinitely wish, now Letters begin to revive again, that some Learned Pen would employ it self, and that
some person vers'd in the Chronology of the Church (as they call it) would deduce
out of the Ecclesiastical Writers, the time and manner how these abuses crept in,
and by what arts and Steps this *Babel* that reaches at heaven, was built by these
Sons of the Earth" (Machiavelli, *Works*, sig. ***ʳ).

450. I.e., opinions or dogmas; a variant form common in the seventeenth
century of the now more familiar word "tenets" (*OED*, s.v. "tenet," *n.*).

451. The papal insignia contains two crossed keys—one gold, one silver—
bound by a red cord. These represent the keys to the kingdom of heaven entrusted

(especially where there is a Forreign Jurisdiction in the case) as with the Tyranny and Arbitrary Power of any Prince in the World. I will add thus much in Confirmation of the *Doctor's* Assertion, That we ought to prevent the Growth of Popery, since it is now grown a Dangerous Faction here against the State.

Noble Venetian. How can that be, I beseech you, Sir?

English Gentleman. Sir, I will make you Judg of it your self; I will say nothing of those foolish Writings that have been put forth by *Mariana*,[452] *Emanuel Sa*,[453] and some others, about the lawfulness of destroying Princes and States in case of Heresie, because I know all the conscientious and honest Papists (of which I know there are great numbers in the World) do not only not hold, but even abhor such cursed Tenents; and do believe, that when the Pope, by Excommunication hath cut off any Prince from the communion of the Church, can go no further, nor ought to pretend a Power to deprive him of his Crown, or absolve his Subjects from their Oaths and Obedience: But I shall confine my self to the present condition of our Papists here. You know how dangerous it is for any Kingdom or State to have a considerable, wealthy, flourishing party amongst them, whose interest it is to destroy the Polity and Government of the Country where they live; and therefore if our Papists prove this Party, you will not wonder why this People are so eager to depress them. This is our Case: for in the beginning of Queen *Elizabeths* reign,[454] there

---

to the disciple Peter by Christ: "Thou art Peter, and upon this rock I will build my church; and the gates of hell shall not prevail against it. And I will give unto thee the keys of the kingdom of heaven: and whatsoever thou shalt bind on earth shall be bound in heaven: and whatsoever thou shalt loose on earth shall be loosed in heaven" (Matthew 16:18–19). St. Peter was the first bishop of Rome, from whom the popes derived their authority.

452. Juan de Mariana (1536–1624), Spanish Jesuit theologian whose writings taught the legitimacy of the assassination of tyrants (in which category were included princes adhering to religions other than Roman Catholicism). See especially *De rege et regis institutione* (Toledo, 1598).

453. Manuel de Sá (1530?–96), Portuguese Jesuit theologian.

454. The "alteration of Religion" to which Neville refers is the religious settlement achieved by Elizabeth's first Parliament in 1559. England's religion reverted

was an alteration of Religion in our Country, which did sufficiently enrage the Holy Father at *Rome*, to see that this good Cow would be Milked no longer. He declares her an Heretick and a Bastard,[455] (his Sanctity not having declared null that incestuous Marriage[456] which her Father had contracted before with his Brothers Wife, and which that King had dissolved to Marry her Mother) and afterwards Excommunicated our Queen, depriving her, as much as in him lay, of the Kingdom; some of the Zealots of that Party[457] (having a greater terrour for those Thunder-bolts

---

to Protestantism from the Roman Catholicism introduced by Mary I; the Act of Uniformity adopted the second Edwardian prayer book of 1552, in a slightly amended form. The convocation of 1563 approved the Thirty-Nine Articles of Religion, in which these changes were crystallized. There may, however, be a broader point behind Neville's recollection of these events. Nostalgia for the reign of Elizabeth I had, from the very early years of the reign of James I, been a lightly camouflaged way of expressing discontent with Stuart monarchy; see Anne Barton, "Harking Back to Elizabeth: Jonson and Caroline Nostalgia," chapter 14 of her *Ben Jonson: Dramatist* (Cambridge: Cambridge University Press, 1984), pp. 300–320.

455. *Regnans in Excelsis*, a papal bull issued on 25 February 1570 by Pope Pius V, declared Elizabeth to be a heretic ("haereticam, et haeriticorum fautricem") and a pretender to the throne of England ("pretensa Angliae regina"). It did not refer to her as a bastard, however, although that slur might be inferred from the allegation that she was a pretender. The prompt rejoinder was "An Act against the bringing in and putting in execution of bulls and other instruments from the see of Rome" (13 Eliz. I, c. 2), which made it high treason to obey the pope's instructions. *Regnans in excelsis* was renewed in 1588 by Pope Sixtus V. Elizabeth's bastardy was recalled in the Commons during a debate on Exclusion by Daniel Finch on 2 November 1680—thus very close in time to the publication of the first edition of *Plato Redivivus* (Grey, *Debates*, vol. 7, p. 411).

456. Henry VIII first married Katherine of Aragon, the widow of his elder brother Arthur, on 11 June 1509 (they had been betrothed since 25 June 1503). Notwithstanding the degree of proximity between Henry and Katherine, the union was declared legitimate on the grounds that the marriage between Arthur and Katherine was deemed not to have been consummated. On 23 May 1533 Cranmer pronounced the marriage between Henry and Katherine to be null, Henry having married Anne Boleyn, the mother of Elizabeth I, in January of the same year. On 17 May 1536 Cranmer declared Henry's marriage with Anne Boleyn to be null on the grounds of her adultery, and she was beheaded on 19 May.

457. In the early and mid-1580s there was much alarm about Catholic-inspired plots to assassinate Elizabeth, such as the Throckmorton plot of 1583 and the Babington plot of 1586.

than I believe many have now) began to Conspire against her; and Plots grew at length so frequent, and so dangerous, that it was necessary (as the Parliaments then thought) to secure the Queen, by making severe Laws[458] against a People, who did not believe themselves her Majesties Subjects; but on the contrary, many of them thought themselves in Conscience obliged to oppose and destroy her: and although that Excommunication, as also the pretended doubtfulness of the Title, both died with that renowned Queen, yet a new desperate Conspiracy[459] against the King her Successor and the whole Parliament ensuing, not long after her decease, those rigorous Laws have been so far from being repealed, that very many more, and far severer,[460] have been since made, and are yet in

458. The parliament of 1581 had prepared draconian anti-Catholic legislation of which the avowed purpose was "to retain the Queen's Majesty's subjects in their due obedience" (23 Eliz. I, c. 1). Heavy fines were imposed on those who celebrated and participated in the mass. (As originally drafted, the bill proposed that these offenses should be felonies, and so punishable by death; Elizabeth herself is thought to have been responsible for the reduction of the penalty to mere fines.) Recusancy (i.e., nonattendance at church) was punished with fines of up to £20 per month. Conversion to Roman Catholicism, if undertaken with a view to withdrawing allegiance, was treason. This was followed in 1593 by "An Act against popish recusants" (35 Eliz. I, c. 2). Roman Catholics had been barred from public office, the universities, and the professions.

459. I.e., the Gunpowder Plot of 1605, which had been provoked by the resolute enforcement of the penal laws against Roman Catholics following the discovery in 1603 of two Catholic plots, the "Bye Treason" and the "Main Treason."

460. Tudor anti-Catholic legislation was renewed and reinforced early in the reign of James I. In 1604 "An Act for the due execution of the Statutes against Jesuits, Seminary Priests, Recusants, etc." (1 & 2 Jac. I, c. 4) required that all existing anti-Catholic legislation be "put in due and exact execution." It was followed in 1606 by "An Act for the better discovering and repressing of Popish Recusants" (3 & 4 Jac. I, c. 4), which imposed a new oath of allegiance on Roman Catholics (this remained in force until 1688), and provided that, in lieu of the statutory fine of £20 per month, the government at its own discretion might "take, seize, and enjoy all the goods, and two parts as well of all the lands . . . of such offender . . . , leaving the third part only of the same . . . to and for the maintenance and relief of the same offender, his wife, children, and family." This was accompanied by "An Act to prevent and avoid dangers which may grow by Popish Recusants" (3 & 4 Jac. I, c. 5). Cf. "The Oaths Act" of 1610 (7 & 8 Jac. I, c. 6). The Long Parliament was ferocious toward Roman Catholics, the "Ordinance for sequestering notorious delinquents' estates" of 27 March 1643 allowing the estates of Royalist Catholics to be seized in their entirety. Those who had remained neutral lost two-thirds of

force. Now these Laws make so great a distinction between Protestants and Papists, that whereas the former are by our Government and Laws, the freest People in the World, the latter are little better than slaves, are confined to such a distance from their Houses, are not to come near the Court, which being kept in the Capital City, mostly deprives them from attending their necessary occasions; they are to pay two third parts of their Estates annually to the King,[461] their Priests are to suffer as Traitors, and they as Felons for harbouring them; in fine, one of us, if he do not break the Municipal Laws for the good Government of the Country, need not fear the King's Power, whereas their being what they are, is a breach of the Law, and does put them into the Princes hands to ruine them when he pleases; nay, he is bound by Oath to do it,[462] and when he does it not, is complained against by his People, and Parliaments take it amiss.[463] Now judge you, Sir, whether it is not the interest of these People

---

their estates and were subjected to double taxation. The lucrativeness of such measures meant that, as Waller said wittily in the Commons, "Popery was the King's meadow. We must not plough it up, but we may cut the grass from time to time" (Grey, *Debates*, vol. 7, p. 76). After the Restoration, Parliament was eager to pass further anti-Catholic legislation, notwithstanding (or perhaps because of) the king's expression of his indebtedness to Roman Catholics during his exile. The Test Acts of 1673 (25 Car. II, c. 2) and 1678 (30 Car. II, st. 2, c. 1) (sometimes referred to as the "Act disabling Papists") confirmed the exclusion of Roman Catholics from public life. Notwithstanding this impressive volume of legislation, however, at the very moment *Plato Redivivus* was published the sentiment in Parliament was that it had all been unavailing. Sir Henry Capel told the Commons on 26 October 1680, "I have sat here many years, and I find that every Session of Parliament we are still troubled with Popery. In the descent of four kings, still the parliaments have been troubled with Popery; laws have been made against it, and all fail" (Grey, *Debates*, vol. 7, p. 360). See Raymond D. Tumbleson, *Catholicism in the English Protestant Imagination: Nationalism, Religion, and Literature 1600–1745* (Cambridge: Cambridge University Press, 1998).

461. As provided for by "An Act for the better discovering and repressing of Popish Recusants" (3 & 4 Jac. I, c. 4) and confirmed by the "Ordinance for sequestering notorious delinquents' estates" of 27 March 1643 (see previous note).

462. In his coronation oath, Charles II had sworn to uphold "the true Profession of the Gospel established in this Kingdom," but the oath did not oblige him explicitly to persecute Roman Catholics.

463. "James I and Charles I both found it impossible to prosecute a successful foreign policy in a Europe still dominated by Catholic powers while they were persecuting their own Catholic subjects. The resultant slackening in persecution

to desire and endeavour a change, whilest they remain under these discouragements, and whether they are not like to joyn with the Prince
(whose connivance at the inexecution of those Laws is the onely means
and hope of their preservation) whenever he shall undertake any thing
for the increase of his own Power, and the depressing his Parliaments.

Noble Venetian. What you say is very undeniable, but then the Remedy is
very easie and obvious, as well as very just and honourable, which is the
taking away those cruel Laws, and if that were done they would be one
People with you, and would have no necessity, and by consequence no
desire to engreaten[464] the King against the Interest and Liberty of their
own Country.

English Gentleman. You speak very well, and one of the Reasons amongst
many which I have, to desire a composure of all our troubles by a setled
Government, is, that I may see these People (who are very considerable,
most of them, for Estates, Birth and Breeding)[465] live quietly under our

---

was always regarded with uneasiness by Parliament, and especially after the outbreak of the Thirty Years War. The Commons addressed a sharp memorial to
James I on the subject in 1621, but his son was no better, finding it difficult to evade
the provisions of his marriage treaty with Henrietta Maria. The plausible assertion that he and Buckingham were 'soft' towards Roman Catholicism did Charles
I lasting harm, and in the 1630's his attempt to enforce the recusancy laws again,
largely for financial motives, was offset by his wife's aggressive Catholicism, his
many contacts with leading Roman ecclesiastics, and the large number of conver-
sions which occurred at Whitehall. This was the raw material out of which the
parliamentary leaders fashioned the myth of a great Popish conspiracy" (Kenyon,
Stuart Constitution, p. 449).

464. I.e., aggrandize, increase in power (*OED*, s.v. "engreaten," citing this
passage).

465. "A sizeable minority of Catholics obstinately survived; their numbers have
been estimated at 27,000, and these are merely the recusants convict, and heads of
households into the bargain. A large allowance must be made for wives and dependants, and an even larger allowance for the 'church Papists,' those conformist
Catholics regarded with equal hostility by the English authorities and the Roman
Church. Moreover, a disproportionate number of these surviving recusants were
nobility and gentry, a fact of which Parliament showed itself aware in 1606 when it
authorised the government to refuse the recusancy fines, even if preferred, and
proceed against the estates of wealthy Catholics" (Kenyon, *Stuart Constitution*,

good Laws, and increase our Trade and Wealth with their expences here at home; whereas now the severity of our Laws against them, makes them spend their Revenues abroad, and inrich other Nations with the Stock of *England*; but as long as the State here is so unsetled as it is, our Parliaments will never consent to countenance a Party, who by the least Favour and Indulgence may make themselves able to bring in their own Religion to be National, and so ruine our Polity and Liberties.

Noble Venetian. I wonder why you should think that possible?

English Gentleman. First, Sir, for the Reason we First gave, which is the craziness of our Polity, there being nothing more certain, than that both in the Natural and also the Politick Body any sinister[466] accident that intervenes, during a very Diseased habit, may bring a dangerous altera-tion to the Patient. An Insurrection in a decayed Government, a thing otherwise very inconsiderable, has proved very fatal, as I knew a slight flesh-wound bring a lusty Man to his Grave in our Wars, for that he be-ing extreamly infected with the *French* Disease,[467] could never procure the Orifice to close; so although the designs both at home and abroad, for altering our Religion, would be very little formidable to a well-founded Government, yet in such an one as we have now, it will require all our care to obviate such Machinations. Another Reason is the little Zeal that is left amongst the ordinary Protestants, which Zeal uses to be a great Instrument of preserving the Religion establish'd, as it did here in Queen *Elizabeths* time; I will add the little Credit the Church of *England* hath amongst the People, most men being almost as angry with that Popery which is left amongst us[468] (in Surplices, Copes, Altars, Cring-ings, Bishops, Ecclesiastical Courts, and the whole Hierarchy, besides an

---

p. 448). The reference is to "An Act for the better discovering and repressing of Popish Recusants" (3 & 4 Jac. I, c. 4).

466. I.e., unlucky (*OED*, s.v. "sinister," 7).

467. I.e., syphilis.

468. I.e., the vestiges of Roman Catholicism that had been preserved in the Church of England. It was a habitual complaint of Puritans that the Church of England had been only imperfectly reformed.

Infinite number of Useless, Idle, Superstitious Ceremonies, and the Ignorance and Vitiousness of the Clergy in general) as they are with those *Dogma's* that are abolished; So that there is no hopes that Popery can be kept out, but by a company of poor People called Fanaticks,[469] who are driven into Corners as the First Christians were; and who only in truth Conserve the Purity of Christian Religion, as it was planted by Christ and his Apostles, and is contained in Scripture. And this makes almost all sober men believe, that the National Clergy, besides all other good qualities have this too, that they cannot hope to make their Hierarchy subsist long against the Scriptures, the hatred of mankind, and the Interest of this People, but by Introducing the *Roman* Religion, and getting a Foreign Head and Supporter, which shall from time to time brave and hector the King and Parliament in their favour and behalf, which yet would be of little advantage to them, if we had as firm and wise a Government as you have at *Venice*. Another Reason, and the greatest, why the *Romish* Religion ought to be very warily provided against at this time, is, That the Lawful and Undoubted Heir[470] to the Crown, if his Majesty should die without Legitimate Issue, is more than suspected to Imbrace that Faith; which (if it should please God to call the King, before there be any Remedy applied to our Distracted State) would give a great opportunity (by the Power he would have in Intervals of Parliament) either to Introduce immediately that profession, with the help of our Clergy, and other *English* and Foreign Aids, or else to make so fair a way for it, that a little time would perfect the work; and this is the more formidable, for that he is held to be a very Zealous and Bigotted *Romanist*; and therefore may be supposed to act any thing to that end, although it should manifestly appear to be contrary to his own Interest and Quiet; so apt are those who give up their Faith and the Conduct of their Lives to Priests (who to get to themselves Empire, promise them the highest Seats in Heaven; if they will sacrifice their Lives, Fortunes, and Hopes, for the

469. I.e., nonconformists and dissenters.

470. Charles II's brother, the Duke of York and future James II, who had converted to Roman Catholicism in 1672. However, his conversion was not official until 1676, when it was recognized by the pope. Neville's "more than suspected" looks like litotes.

Exaltation of their Holy Mother, and preventing the Damnation of an innumerable company of Souls which are not yet born) to be led away with such Erroneous and wild Fancies. Whereas *Philip* the Second of *Spain*,[471] the House of *Guise*[472] in *France*, and other great Statesmen, have always made their own greatness their first Aim, and used their Zeal as an Instrument of that; And instead of being cozen'd by Priests, have cheated them, and made them endeavour to Preach them up to the Empire of the World. So I have done with the Growth of Popery, and must conclude, that if that should be stopt in such manner, that there could not be one Papist left in *England*, and yet our Polity left in the same disorder that now afflicts it, we should not be one Scruple the better for it, nor the more at quiet; the Growth and Danger of Popery not being the Cause of our present Distemper, but the Effect of it: But as a good and setled Government would not be at all the nearer for the destruction of Popery, so Popery and all the Dangers and Inconveniences of it would not only be further off, but would wholly vanish at the sight of such a Reformation. And so we begin at the wrong end, when we begin with Religion before we heal our Breaches. I will borrow one Similitude more, with our Doctor's favour, from his Profession. I knew once a man given over by the Physitians, of an incurable *Cachexia*,[473] which they said proceeded from the ill Quality of the whole Mass of Blood, from great Adustion,[474] and from an ill habit of the whole Body. The Patient had very often painful Fits of the Chollick, which they said proceeded from the sharpness of the humour which caused the Disease; and, amongst the

---

471. Philip II (1527–98), king of Spain. Neville's view of Philip II may have been darkened as a result of the acquaintance of his grandfather with Antonio Perez (see above, p. 206, n. 380, and p. 208, n. 383). Certainly once in exile Perez was an enthusiastic denigrator of his former master: see Gregorio Marañón, *Antonio Pérez: El hombre, el drama, la época*, 2 vols. (Madrid: Espasa Calpe, 1951).

472. A prominent ultra-Catholic French noble family, allies of Philip II of Spain, and founders and leaders of the Catholic League. The senior line of the family, the Dukes of Guise, would shortly become extinct in 1688.

473. I.e., a depraved condition of the body in which nutrition is defective (*OED*, s.v. "cachexia").

474. I.e., a term of art drawn from humoral medicine, denoting a condition in which the humors of the body are adust, that is, scorched or parched (*OED*, s.v. "adustion").

rest, had one Fit which tormented him to that degree, that it was not expected he could out-live it; yet the Doctors delivered him from it in a small time: Notwithstanding, soon after the man died of his first Distemper. Whereas if their Art had arrived to have cured that (which was the Cause of the other) the Chollick had vanished of it self, and the Patient recovered. I need make no Application, nor shall need to say much of the Succession of the Crown (which is my next Province) but this I have said already, That it is needless to make any Provision against a Popish Successor if you rectifie your Government; and if you do not, all the Care and Circumspection you can use in that Particular, will be useless and of none effect, and will but at last (if it do not go off easily, and the next Heir succeed peaceably, as is most likely, especially if the King live till the People's Zeal and Mettle is over)[475] end probably in a Civil War about Title; and then the Person deprived may come in with his Sword in his Hand, and bring in upon the Point of it both the Popish Religion, and Arbitrary Power: Which, though I believe he will not be able to maintain long (for the Reasons before alledged,) yet that may make this Generation miserable and unhappy. It will certainly be agreed by all lovers of their Country, that Popery must be kept from returning, and being National in this Kingdom, as well for what concerns the Honour and Service of God, as the Welfare and Liberty of the People; and I conceive there are two ways by which the Parliament may endeavour to secure us against that danger; the first by ordering such a change in the Administration of our Government, that whoever is Prince, can never violate the Laws, and then we may be very safe against Popery; our present Laws being effectual enough to keep it out, and no new ones being like to be made in Parliament that may introduce it; and this remedy will be at the same time advantagious to us against the Tyranny and Incroachments of a Protestant Successor, so that we may call it an infallible Remedy both against Popery and Arbitrary power. The second way is by making a Law to disable any Papist by name or otherwise, from Inherit-

475. This indeed happened in 1685, when Sir John Reresby recorded that James II acceded to the throne "with all imaginable Tokens of Peace and Joy; not only in *York* itself, but afterwards throughout the whole County, and, indeed, the whole Kingdom" (*The Memoirs of the Honorable Sir John Reresby, Baronet* [1734], p. 108).

ing the Crown;[476] and this is certainly fallible, that is, may possibly not take place (as I shall shew immediately;) and besides, it is not improbable that an Heir to this Kingdom in future times, may dissemble his Religion, till he be seated in the Throne; or possibly be perverted to the Roman Faith after he is possest of it, when it may be too late to limit his Prerogative in Parliament; and to oppose him without that, will I fear, be Judged Treason.

Doctor. But Sir, would you have the Parliament do nothing, as things stand, to provide (at least, as much as in them lies) that whoever succeeds be a good Protestant?

English Gentleman. Yes, I think it best in the first place to offer to his Majesty the true Remedy; & if they find him averse to that, then to pursue the other which concerns the Succession, because the People (who are their Principals, and give them their Power)[477] do expect something

476. This would be done in the Bill of Rights, or (to give it its true title) "An Act Declaring the Rights and Liberties of the Subject and Settling the Succession of the Crown" (1689), which would provide that "whereas it hath been found by experience that it is inconsistent with the safety and welfare of this Protestant kingdom to be governed by a popish prince, or by any king or queen marrying a papist, the said Lords Spiritual and Temporal and Commons do further pray that it may be enacted, that all and every person and persons that is, are or shall be reconciled to or shall hold communion with the see or Church of Rome, or shall profess the popish religion, or shall marry a papist, shall be excluded and be for ever incapable to inherit, possess or enjoy the crown and government of this realm and Ireland and the dominions thereunto belonging or any part of the same, or to have, use or exercise any regal power, authority or jurisdiction within the same."

477. An explosive parenthesis, because of the challenge it poses to the traditional location of sovereignty in the king in Parliament. Filmer, in the opening paragraphs of *Patriarcha*, had identified the belief in popular sovereignty as what he intended to refute (Filmer, *Patriarcha*, pp. 2–3; cf. his contention in the preface to *Observations upon Aristotle's Politiques* [1652] that there "never was any such thing as an independent multitude who first had a natural right to a community" [Wootton, *Divine Right*, p. 110]). Nevertheless, the doctrine of constituent power residing in the people had flourished at midcentury and had in particular been explored during the Interregnum by the Levellers (Neville's phrasing here recalls that of Overton): "Wee are your Principalls, and you our Agents; it is a Truth which you cannot but acknowledge" (Overton, *A Remonstrance of Many Thousand Citizens* [1646], p. 3; cf. Lorenzo Sabbadini, "Popular Sovereignty and Representation in the English Civil War," in *Popular Sovereignty in Historical Perspective* [Cambridge: Cambridge University Press, 2017], pp. 164–86). See also William Walwyn, *Englands Lamentable Slaverie* (1645): "A Parliamentary

extraordinary from them at this time; and the most of them believe this
last the only present means to save them from Popery, which they judge

---

authority is a power intrusted by the people (that chose them) for their good safetie
and freedome; and therefore a Parliament cannot justlie do anything to make the
people lesse safe or lesse free then they found them" (p. 3; cf. Wootton, *Divine Right*,
pp. 51–52). And see Roger Williams, *The Bloudy Tenent of Persecution* (1644): "The
sovereign, original and foundation of civil power lies in the people" (Wootton, *Divine Right*, p. 243). It was a doctrine closely associated with regicide. On 4 January 1649, shortly before the execution of Charles I, Parliament had asserted that "the
people are, under God, the original of all just power" (quoted in Scott, *Commonwealth Principles*, p. 252). In the Putney Debates, Wildman had said plainly that "all
government is in the free consent of the people" (Wootton, *Divine Right*, p. 299), and
in 1653 John Streater would insist that "power is essentially in the people" (Streater,
Glympse, p. 2; cf. Burton, *Diary*, vol. 1, p. xxix). On 11 February 1659, writing to
George Downing, Andrew Marvell would allege that this was also Neville's creed:
"Their [i.e., Neville and his allies in the resistance to Richard Cromwell being recognized as Protector] Doctrine hath moved most upon their Maxime that all pow'r is in
the people" (Marvell, *Poems and Letters*, vol. 2, p. 294). But in Carolean England, the
doctrine of popular sovereignty remained unsurprisingly deeply heterodox to those
associated with the Court. As Sir Leoline Jenkins had said in the Commons on 11
November 1680, "I have always taken it, that the Government had it's original, not
from the People, but from God" (Grey, *Debates*, vol. 7, p. 447). In July 1683 the first of
the "damnable doctrines" that would be condemned by the University of Oxford was
the proposition that "All civil authority is derived originally from the people" (Kenyon, *Stuart Constitution*, pp. 471–74; Wootton, *Divine Right*, p. 121). The contrary
position was also vigorously held, for instance by the author of *The Character of a Popish Successour*, who argued that monarchy could arise in only two ways: either by conquest, or "By the Choice of the People, who frequently in the beginning of the World,
out of the natural desire of Safety, for the securing peaceful Community and Conversation, chose a single Person to be their head, as a proper Supreme Moderator in all
Differences that might arise to disquiet that Community. Thus were Kings made for
the People, and not the People for the King" (*State-Tracts*, vol. 1, p. 162). In *The Art of
Lawgiving*, Harrington's subtle position had been that popular sovereignty was a
necessary, fundamental, and yet also extraconstitutional element in a well-ordered
commonwealth: "An assembly of the people sovereign! Nay, and an assembly of the
people consisting in the major vote of the lower sort! Why sure, it must be a dull, an
unskilful thing. But so is the touchstone in a goldsmith's shop a dull thing, and altogether unskilled in the trade; yet without this would even the master be deceived"
(Pocock, *Harrington*, p. 676). On the deep historical roots and early modern flourishing of the doctrine of popular sovereignty, see most recently Daniel Lee, *Popular
Sovereignty in Early Modern Constitutional Thought* (Oxford: Oxford University Press,
2016), especially chapter 9; and for a survey by many hands of the concept over the
longue durée from antiquity to the present, see Richard Bourke and Quentin Skinner,
eds., *Popular Sovereignty in Historical Perspective* (Cambridge: Cambridge University
Press, 2017).

(and very justly) will bring in with it a change of Government. But then, I suppose, they may be encouraged to propose in the first place the true Cure; not only because that is infallible, as has been proved, but likewise because His Majesty in probability will sooner consent to any reasonable Demand towards the Reforming of the Government, and to the securing us that way, than to concur to the depriving his onely Brother of the Crown.[478] And possibly this latter (as I said before) may be the only way the Parliament can hope will prove effectual: For if you please to look but an Age back into our Story, you will find that *Henry* the Eighth did procure an Act of Parliament,[479] which gave him power to dispose of the Crown by his last Will and Testament; and that he did accordingly make his said Will, and by it devise the Succession to his Son *Edward* the Sixth, in the first place, and to the Heirs of his Body; and for want of such, to his Daughter *Mary*, and to the Heirs of her Body; and for want of which Heirs, to his Daughter *Elizabeth*, our once Soveraign of Immortal and Blessed Memory, and the Heirs of her Body; and for want of all such Issue, to the right Heirs of his Younger Sister, who was, before he made this Will, married to *Charles Brandon* Duke of *Suffolk*, and had Issue by him. By this Testament he disinherited his elder Sister, who

478. This had been demonstrated in 1679: "The main point in debate [in Parliament in 1679] was, what security the King should offer to quiet the fears of the Nation upon the account of the Duke's [i.e., the Duke of York's] succession. The Earl of *Shaftesbury* proposed the excluding him simply, and making the succession to go on, as if he was dead, as the only mean that was easy and safe both for the Crown and the people: This was nothing but the disinheriting the next heir, which certainly the King and Parliament might do, as well as any private man might disinherit his next heir, if he had a mind to it. The King would not consent to this. He had faithfully promised the Duke, that he never would. And he thought, if Acts of Exclusion were once begun, it would not be easy to stop them; but that upon any discontent at the next heir, they would be set on: religion was now the pretence: But other pretences would be found out, when there was need of them: This insensibly would change the nature of the *English* Monarchy: So that from being hereditary it would become elective" (Burnet, *History*, vol. 1, p. 455).

479. The so-called third Succession Act of 1544 (35 Henry VIII, c. 1). This act confirmed the king's right to bestow the crown by will but also expressed a desire for a more public definition of the succession. The will made by Henry in December 1546 bequeathed the crown in the manner described by the English Gentleman.

was married in *Scotland*; and by that means did, as much as in him lay, exclude His Majesty (who now, by God's Mercy, Reigns over us) as also his Father and Grandfather. And to make the Case stronger, there passed an Act long after,[480] in the Reign of Queen *Elizabeth*, That it should be Treason during that Queen's Life, and a Premunire[481] afterwards, to assert that the Imperial Crown of *England* could not be disposed of by Act of Parliament: yet after the Decease of that Queen, there was no considerable Opposition made to the peaceable Reception and Recognition of King *James* of happy Memory. And those who did make a little stir about the other Title, as the Lord *Cobham*,[482] Sir *Walter Rawleigh*,[483] and a few others, were apprehended & condemn'd according to Law. And, notwithstanding that, since, in the Reign of K. *Charles* the First, there was a bloody Civil War, in which Men's Minds were exasperated at a high rate; yet in all the Course of it, the Original Want of Title was never objected against His late Majesty. I do not urge this to aver that the Parliament, with the King's Consent, cannot do lawfully this, or any other great

480. "An Act whereby certain offences be made treasons" (13 Eliz. I, c. 1), clause IV of which states, "And be it further enacted, that if any person shall in any wise hold and affirm or maintain that the common laws of this realm not altered by Parliament ought not to direct the right of the crown of England, or that our said sovereign lady Elizabeth the Queen's Majesty that now is, with and by the authority of the Parliament of England, is not able to make laws and statutes of sufficient force and validity to limit and bind the crown of this realm and the descent, limitation, inheritance and government thereof . . . every such person . . . shall be judged a high traitor."

481. I.e., a writ charging a sheriff to summon a person accused of asserting or maintaining papal jurisdiction in England (originally, one accused of prosecuting abroad a suit cognizable by English law), so denying the ecclesiastical supremacy of the monarch (*OED*, s.v. "premunire," 1).

482. Henry Brooke (1564–1619), eleventh Baron Cobham. Shortly after the accession of James I in 1603, Cobham was drawn into a conspiracy, the "Bye and Main Plots" (see above, p. 238, n. 459), in which Sir Walter Ralegh was also deemed to be involved, which aimed at the overthrow and assassination of James I and his replacement by Arabella Stuart. Cobham was tried in November 1603 and found guilty, but he escaped the scaffold. Imprisoned in the Tower for many years, he died in penury.

483. Sir Walter Ralegh (1554–1618), courtier, author, and adventurer. Implicated in the "Bye and Main Plots" of 1603 (see above), he was imprisoned in the Tower from 1603 to 1616.

Matter; which would be an incurring the Penalty of that Law, and a Solecism in the Politicks: But to shew, that when the Passions of men are
quieted, and the Reasons other than they were, it happens oftentimes
that those Acts which concern the Succession fall to the Ground of
themselves, and that even without the Sword, which in this Case was
never adoperated.[484] And that therefore this Remedy in our Case may be
likely never to take place, if it please God the King live till this Nation be
under other kind of Circumstances.

Doctor. Sir, you say very well: but it seems to me, that the last Parliament[485] was in some kind of Fault, if this be true that you say; for I remember that my Lord Chancellor did once, during their Sitting, in His
Majesty's Name offer them to secure their Religion and Liberties any
way they could advise of, so they would let alone meddling with the Succession, and invited them to make any Proposals they thought necessary
to that end.

English Gentleman. Hinc illae lachrimae.[486] If this had been all, we might
have been happy at this time; but this Gracious Offer was *In limine,*[487]
accompanied with such Conditions that made the Parliament conjecture
that it was only to perplex and divide them;[488] and did look upon it as an
Invention of some new *Romanza*[489] Counsellors (and those too, possibly,
influenced by the *French*) to make them embrace the Shaddow for the
Substance, and satisfying themselves with this Appearance, to do their
ordinary Work of giving Money, and be gone, and leave the Business of
the Kingdom as they found it. For it was proposed, that whatsoever

484. I.e., brought into operation; employed or used (*OED*, s.v. "adoperate").
485. On 30 April 1679 the Lord Chancellor had invited the House of Commons
to formulate any measure to "secure Religion and Liberty against a Popish Successor, without defeating the Right of Succession itself," assuring them that Charles
would "most readily consent to it" (Grey, *Debates*, vol. 7, p. 159).
486. "Hence those tears" (Terence, *Andria*, l.126; cf. Horace, *Epistles*, I, 19, l.41).
487. See above, p. 177, n. 309.
488. A fair summary of the ensuing discussions: see Grey, *Debates*, vol. 7,
pp. 159–64.
489. I.e., a fanciful invention (*OED*, s.v. "romanza," 1).

Security we were to receive, should be both Conditional and Reversionable: That is, First, We should not be put into Possession of this new Charter (be it what it will) till after the death of His Majesty who now is; whereas such a Provision is desirable, and indeed necessary for us for this only reason, that when that unfortunate hour comes, we might not be, in that Confusion, unprovided of a Calm, Setled and Orderly, as well as a Legal Way to keep out Popery. Whereas otherwise, if we be to take Possession in that Minute, it must either miscarry, or be gotten by a War, if it be true that Possession be Nine Points of the Law in other Cases, it is in this the whole Ten: and I should be very unwilling, in such a Distraction, to have no Sanctuary to fly to, but a piece of Parchment kept in the Pells;[490] and to have this too, as well as other Advantages, in the Power and Possession of him in whose prejudice it was made: this had been almost as good an Expedient to keep out Popery, as the Bill which was thrown out that Parliament; which provided, that in the Reign of a King that should be a Papist, the Bishops should chuse one another upon Vacancies.[491]

490. I.e., the office of the Exchequer in which official documents were kept (*OED*, s.v. "pell").

491. Although concerns about the likely ecclesiastical policy of any future Catholic king had been raised as early as 1677 (see a long speech by Marvell touching on this in Grey, *Debates*, vol. 4, pp. 321–25), this is most immediately a very topical reference to the Bill for Securing the Protestant Religion, first read in the House of Lords on 29 November 1680, as an alternative to the Exclusion Bill, which the Lords had thrown out on 15 November. (An earlier bill, with a similar title and making similar provisions, had died in committee in 1677; see Marvell, *Prose Works*, vol. 2, pp. 313–23). On 30 April 1679 Charles had indicated his willingness to countenance such a measure: "In reference to the Church, his Majesty is content, that care be taken, that all Ecclesiastical Benefices and Promotions in the gift of the Crown may be conferred in such a manner, that we may be sure the Incumbents shall be always of the most pious and learned Protestants, and that no Popish Successor, while he continues so, may have any power to controul such Presentments" (Grey, *Debates*, vol. 7, p. 158). The bill set out a series of limitations on the power of any future Catholic monarch, which included (quoting from the report on the heads of the bill on 17 November in the Lords Journal, which echoes the language of the speech from the throne) "that all Ecclesiastical and Spiritual Benefices and Promotions, in the Gift of the Crown, may be conferred in such a Manner, that the incumbent shall always be of the most pious and learned Protestants; and that *James* Duke of *Yorke*, nor any Popish Successor, while he continues

Those Counsellors who put my Lord Chancellor upon this Proposal, were either very slender Politicians themselves, or else thought the Parliament so. If *Magna Charta* and *The Petition of Right* [492] had not been to take place till after the Decease of those Princes who confirmed them, neither had the Barons shed their Blood to so good purpose, nor the Members of the Parliament in *Tertio Caroli*, [493] deserved so Glorious an Imprisonment after it was ended. The other Condition in this renowned Proposal is, That all Provision and Security which is given us to preserve our Religion, shall cease immediately, whenever the Prince shall take a certain Oath to be penned for that purpose; and I leave it to all thinking men to determine what that will avail us, when we shall have a King of that Profession over us, who shall not have so much Zeal for his Religion, as he who is now the next successor hath; but shall possibly prefer

---

so, may have any Power to control such Presentments, nor to dispose of any the Premises belonging to, or in the Gift of, the Crown." My thanks to Paul Seaward for the foregoing information. Note the words of Hampden in the House of Commons on 11 May 1679: "For us to go about to tie a Popish Successor with Laws for preservation of the Protestant Religion, is binding *Sampson* with withes; he will break them when he is awake" (Grey, *Debates*, vol. 7, p. 243; William Sacheverell had also voiced skepticism in language close to that used by Neville: see ibid., pp. 159–61). Milton's *Samson Agonistes* had been published in 1671.

492. A Parliamentary petition to the Crown of 1628 that specified a number of liberties of the subject (e.g., freedom from non-Parliamentary taxation, billeting of soldiers, imprisonment without cause, imposition of martial law) that the Crown is prohibited from infringing.

493. I.e., 1628. That Parliament had been dissolved on 10 March 1629 in the midst of resentment over Charles's levying of Tunnage and Poundage, which he had been collecting without grant since his accession in 1625. On 2 March, in tumultuous scenes, the House of Commons had voted in support of a declaration deploring Charles's innovations in religion and his continued levying of Tunnage and Poundage. Charles dissolved the Parliament by proclamation and had nine of the ringleaders (Denzil Holles, Sir Miles Hobert, Sir John Eliot, Sir Peter Hayman, John Selden, William Coriton, Walter Long, William Stroud, and Benjamin Valentine) arrested. One of them, Sir John Eliot, would die in the Tower three years later. On 5 March 1659 Neville remarked in the House of Commons that Charles I "would have been glad to have had tonnage and poundage for ever," because it would have made his power immoveable: "If the King had stood in no need of money from the people, we had had no Parliaments. The great Turk had been among us" (Burton, *Diary*, vol. 4, p. 25).

his Ambition, and his desire to get out of Wardship, before the Scruples of his Confessor; and yet may afterwards, by getting Absolution for, and Dispensation from such Oaths and Compliance, employ the Power he gets himself, and the Security he deprives us of, to introduce violently what Worship and Faith he pleases. This Gracious Offer had the fatality to disgust one of the best Parliaments that ever Sate,[494] and the most Loyal; so that laying it aside, they fell upon the Succession, the only thing they had then left, and were soon after Dissolved, leaving the Kingdom in a more distracted Condition than they found it; and this can no way be composed, but by mending the Polity, so that whoever is King cannot (be he never so inclined to it) introduce Popery, or destroy whatever Religion shall be established: as you see in the Example of the Dutchy of *Hanover*, whose Prince some fourteen Years since, was perverted to the *Roman* Church, went to *Rome* to abjure Heresie (as they call the truth) return'd home, where he lived and Governed as he did before, without the least Animosity of his Subjects for his Change, or any endeavour of his to Introduce any in his Government or People, and dying this last Spring, left the Peaceable and undisturbed Rule of his Subjects to the next Successor, his Brother the Bishop of *Osnaburg*, who is a Protestant, and this because the Polity of that Dukedom has been conserved entire for many years, and is upon a right Basis:[495] and if our Case were so, we should not

494. Presumably the first Exclusion Parliament, summoned 6 March 1679 and dissolved 12 July 1679. To hold that Parliament in high esteem might be a sign of Exclusionist sympathies: cf. *A Word without Doors concerning the Bill for Succession*, in *State-Tracts*, vol. 2, p. 76.

495. More accurately, the Duchy of Brunswick-Lüneberg, which in 1696 would become the Electorate of Hanover. The apostate duke was Johann Friedrich (1625–79), who had converted to Roman Catholicism in 1651; Neville's "some fourteen Years since" is therefore either a mistake, or an indication that this part of the dialogue was composed in the mid-1660s. Cf. Edmund Everard, *Discourses on the Present State of the Protestant Princes of Europe* (1679), pp. 27–28; Bethel Slingsby, *The Interest of Princes and States* (1680), p. 155. Sir Leoline Jenkins, arguing against Exclusion, would mention this notable apostasy in Parliament on 7 January 1681 (Grey, *Debates*, vol. 8, p. 277). The "Bishop of *Osnaburg*" was Ernest Augustus (1629–98), Prince-Bishop of Osnabrück and, from 1679, Duke of Brunswick-Lüneberg; since 1658 he had also been married to Sophia, the daughter of Elizabeth of Bohemia and

onely be out of danger to have our Religion altered (as I said before) whoever is King, but should in other things be in a happy and flourishing
condition. But I have made a long and tedious digression to answer your
demands: Now 'tis time you assist me to find the Natural Cure of all our
Mischiefs.

---

thus a granddaughter of James I. The Act of Settlement of 1701 would associate the
English throne with the ruling dynasty in Hanover, in order to safeguard the Protestant character of the Church of England. But at the time of the Exclusion Crisis,
to glance at the recent history of the duchy of Hanover might bear a very particular
implication. Writing in 1683, Thomas Long underlined what he took to be Neville's
anti-Exclusionist point in referring to the apostate Duke of Hanover: "But as you
suppose the *Popish Successour may* be; so I suppose he *may not* be a Persecutor. And
for the proof of this, I appeal to your Friend *Plato Redivivus,* who in *p.* 207. gives
an instance in the Prince of *Hanover,* who was perverted to the *Roman* Church,
went to *Rome* to abjure *Heresie;* and returning home, lived and governed as he did
before, without the least animosity of his Subjects for his *change,* or any endeavour
to introduce any to his *Government* or *People;* and dying the last Spring, left the
peaceable and undisturbed Rule of his Subjects to the next Successour his Brother
the Bishop of *Osnaburg,* who is a Protestant" (*A Vindication of the Primitive Christians in Point of Obedience to Their Prince* [1683], p. 36). Edward Pelling, in a sermon
of 1685, would make the same point in virtually the same words: "It hath been
generally believed, that a Prince, who is in the communion of *another* Church,
must needs endeavour the alteration of the *Establisht* Religion, if it be different
from his own. Men are ready to think it must *necessarily* be thus, and that it cannot
possibly be *otherwise.* But this is a very great *mistake:* and to prove that it is so, I
appeal to a most memorable story, that I perceive is not taken notice of, and yet the
truth of it is acknowledg'd by one, that is well known to be of *Republican* Principles, and that a while ago wrote a very Seditious Book, to *Subvert* our *Monarchy,*
and to reduce our Government to the *Venetian* form; I mean, the Author of *Plato
Redivivus.* That very man tells us *(pag.* 207) that a few years since, a Duke of *Hanover* was reconciled to the *Roman* Church, and even went to *Rome* to abjure the
Protestant Religion. Yet upon his return home, he lived and govern'd as he did
before, without the least animosity of his *Subjects* for the change he had made, and
without any endeavour of his to introduce any change in his *Government* or *People,*
but reigned peaceably fourteen years, and then dying left the Establisht Government and Religion entire to his Brother, the Bishop of *Osnaburg,* who was a Protestant. Here now is plain *experience* and matter of *Fact,* which shews that 'tis very
possible for a Prince to Reign very quietly and peaceably over a Church, that is of
a different Faith in some things from his own" (*A Sermon Preached at Westminster-
Abbey* [1685], pp. 27–28).

Doctor. Stay, Sir, I confess my self to be wonderfully Edified with your discourse hitherto, but you have said nothing yet of the Duke of *Monmouth.*

English Gentleman. I do not think you desire it, though you were pleased to mention such a thing, for I suppose you cannot think it possible, that this Parliament (which is now speedily to meet by his Majesties Gracious Proclamation) can ever suffer such a thing to be so much as Debated amongst them.

Doctor. Sir, you have no reason to take that for granted, when you see what Books are Printed, what great and Honourable Persons frequent him in private, and countenance him in publick; what shoals of the middle sort of people have in his Progress this Summer met him before he came into any great Town, and what Acclamations and Bon-fires have been made in places where he lodged.[496]

496. Monmouth had returned to England from campaigning in Flanders in August 1678, having been appointed Captain-General in April, and was already being discussed in some quarters as a possible Protestant successor. In November of that year bonfires had been lit in London in celebration of remarks by Charles II that were taken to indicate his wish to make Monmouth his heir. Successful military campaigns in Scotland in 1679 served only to increase Monmouth's stature among the people, and in September to defuse the situation Charles exiled him temporarily to Utrecht. But it was only in the early months of 1680 that Monmouth seems to have begun actively to promote himself as a candidate for the throne, making tours into Essex in February and into the west country during the summer, while also attending public dinners in London with leading Whigs. During his tour of the west, Monmouth had been "caressed with the joyful Welcomes and Acclamations of the people, who came from all parts, 20 miles about, filling and lining the Hedges with Men, Women and Children, some going before, some following after for some miles in the High ways, all the way, and incessantly with hearty and great shouts crying, God bless our King *Charles,* and God bless the Protestant Duke. Some Towns and Parishes expressed also their Country-respects in strewing their streets and ways thorough which he passed, with herbs and flowers, as was seen at *Ilchester,* and *Pithyton,* &c. In some places where no other better present could be expected or made, the honest kind Goodwomen with rustick sincerity presented to him bottles of Wine, which he courteously accepted and tasted. Some of these good Dames could not restrain their joys,

English Gentleman. These things, I must confess, shew how great a Distemper the People are in, and the great reason we have to pray God of his Mercy to put an end to it by a happy Agreement in Parliament. But certainly this proceeds only from the hatred they have to the next Successour and his Religion, and from the compassion they have to the Duke of *Monmouth* (who as they suppose, hath suffered banishment and disfavour at Court, at his Instance)[497] and not from any hopes of expectations that the Parliament will countenance any pretence that can be made in his behalf to the Succession.

Doctor. It may be when we have discoursed of it, I shall be of your mind, (as indeed I am enclined already). But yet nothing in War is more dangerous than to contemn an Enemy; so in this Argumentation that we use to secure our Liberties, we must leave nothing unanswered that may stand in the way of that, especially the Duke of *Monmouth*'s Claim, which is pretended to confirm and fortifie them, for (say some

---

but in their homely phrase call'd out to him thus, *Master, we are glad to see you, and you are welcome into our Country.* And then some caught hold of his Feet, some took him by the Hand, some by the Coat, but all cried, Welcome, welcome, no *Popery*, no *Popery*, &c. When he drew near to Esq *Speaks* by 10 miles, he was met by 2000 persons on Horse back, who were so increast before they arrived at Mr. *Speaks*, that some conjectured they were in number near 20000, others said, they were many more" (*A True Narrative of the Duke of Monmouth's Late Journey* [1680], p. 2). Works supportive of the Duke of Monmouth published in 1680 alone include: Anonymous, *The Interest of the Three Kingdoms*; Anonymous, *The Protestants Joy*; Anonymous, *The Disloyal Forty and Forty One and the Loyal Eighty*; Henry Care, *The History of the Damnable Popish Plot*; Henry Clark, *His Grace the Duke of Monmouth Honoured in His Progress in the West of England*; and "Eye-Witness," *A True Narrative of the Duke of Monmouth's Late Journey.* Support for Monmouth was extensive and highly placed. On 10 January 1681 the House of Commons had requested the king to restore Monmouth to his offices and commands, from which they asserted he had been removed by the influence of the Duke of York (Grey, *Debates*, vol. 8, p. 290).

497. Monmouth and the Duke of York had fallen out in 1678 when York had insisted that Monmouth be described as Charles's "natural son" in his commission as Captain-General. Monmouth, increasingly the focus of Protestant agitation, had been ordered into exile in Utrecht in September 1679, returning without permission two months later.

Men) if you set him up, he will presently pass all Bills that shall concern the Safety and Interest of the People; And so we shall be at rest for ever.

English Gentleman. Well, I see I must be more tedious than I intended; First then, the reasoning of these men you speak of, does in my apprehension, suppose a thing I cannot mention without horrour, which is, That this Person should be admitted immediately to the Possession of the Crown to do all these fine Matters; for otherwise, if he must stay till the Death of our Soveraign who now Reigns (which I hope and pray will be many years) possibly these delicate Bills may never pass, nor he find hereafter the People in so good a humour to admit him to the Reversion, which if it could be obtain'd (as I think it impossible Politically) yet the Possession must be kept by a standing Army,[498] and the next Successour cannot have a better Game to play, nor a better Adversary to deal with, than one who leaps in over the Heads of almost all the Protestant Princes Families abroad, besides some Papists who are greater; and when we have been harrassed with Wars, and the miseries that accompany it some few

---

498. A standing army—that is to say, a permanent, professional military force—had been an object of suspicion and resentment in England for most of the seventeenth century as an instrument whereby the prince might impose his will upon the people. We first encounter the English phrase "standing army" in 1603, when Richard Knolles used it to refer to the domestic policy of Tamerlane: "He kept alwaies a standing armie of fortie thousand horse, and threescore thousand foot readie at all assaies" (Knolles, *Turkes*, p. 235: cf. Schwoerer, *Armies*, p. 2). For the next forty years or so the *OED* lists no more than a handful of further occurrences of the phrase, until we reach the outbreak of hostilities between Charles I and Parliament in 1642, when unsurprisingly it became much more common. However, although a fondness for a standing army is swiftly included in the list of despotic inclinations characteristic of the Stuarts, Cromwell too had seen its attractions. Clause XXVII of the Instrument of Government of 1653 had been particularly alarming: "The Instrument had . . . provided for a 'constant yearly Revenue' for the maintenance of '10,000 Horse and Dragoons, and 20,000 Foot, in England Scotland, and Ireland, for the Defence and Security thereof, and also for a convenient number of Ships for guarding the Seas.' . . . For Cromwell's critics these soldiers resembled the hired 'Janizaries' of the 'grand Senieur,' who aided in the enslavement of the people" (Mahlberg, p. 143; cf. Kenyon, *Stuart Constitution*, pp. 342–48). The Bill of Rights of 1689 would make it illegal for the king to maintain a standing army in England without permission of Parliament.

years, you shall have all these fine People, who now run after him, very weary of their new Prince: I would not say any thing to disparage a Person so highly born, and of so early merit; but this I may say, That if a Lawful Title should be set on foot in his favour, and a thousand *Dutch* Hosts, and such like, should swear a Marriage,[499] yet no sober Man, that is not blinded with prejudice, will believe, That our King (whom none can deny to have an excellent understanding) would ever Marry a Woman so much his Inferiour as this great Persons Mother was; and this at a time when his Affairs were very low,[500] and he had no visible or rational hopes to be restored to the Possession of his Kingdoms but by an assistance which might have been afforded him by means of some great Foreign Alliance. Well, but to leave all this, do these Men pretend that the Duke of *Monmouth* shall be declared Successour to the Crown in Parliament, with the King's Concurence or without it; if without it, you must make a War for it, and I am sure that no Cause can be stated upon such a point, that will not make the Assertors and Undertakers of it be condemned by all the Politicians and Moralists of the World, and by the Casuists of all Religions, and so by consequence, it is like to be a very unsuccessful War. If you would have this declar'd with the King's Consent, either you suppose the Royal assent to be given, when the King has his liberty either to grant it, or not grant it, to Dissolve the Parliament, or not Dissolve it, without ruine or prejudice to his Affairs: If in the first Case, it is plain he will not grant it, because he cannot do it without confessing his Marriage to that Duke's Mother, which he hath already declared against in a very solemn manner, and caused it to be Registred in Chancery;[501] and which not only no good Subject can chuse but believe, but which cannot be doubted by any rational person; for it would be a very unnatural, and indeed a thing unheard of, that a Father who had a Son in Lawful Matrimony, and who was grown to perfection, and had signalized himself in the Wars,[502] and who was ever intirely beloved by

---

499. See above, p. 231, n. 433.

500. That is, during the period of his exile on the continent.

501. See above, p. 184, n. 326.

502. Monmouth had been present at the Battle of Solebay in 1665, and in July 1673 he had acquitted himself with credit at the siege of Maastricht,

him,[503] should disinherit him by so solemn an asseveration (which must be a false one too) to cause his Brother to succeed in his room. And whereas it is pretended by some, that His Majesties danger from his Brothers Counsels and Designs may draw from him something of this; beside that they do not much Complement the King in this, it is clear, his Brother is not so Popular, but that he may secure him when he pleases, without hazard, if there were any ground for such an apprehension. But we must in the next place suppose that the King's Affairs were in such a posture, that he could deny the Parliament nothing without very great mischief, and inconvenience to himself and the Kingdom; then I say, I doubt not, but the Wisdom of the Parliament will find out divers Demands and Requests to make to His Majesty of greater benefit, and more necessary for the good of his People than this would be; which draws after it not only a present unsetledness, but the probable hazard of Misery and Devastation for many years to come, as has been proved. So that as on the one side the Parliament could not make a more unjustifiable War than upon this Account, so they could not be Dissolved upon any occasion wherein the People would not shew less discontent and resentment, and for which the Courtiers would not hope to have a better pretext to strive in the next Choice to make their Arts and endeavours more successful in the Election of Members more suitable to their Designs for the continuance of this present mis-government; For if this Parliament do mis-spend the Peoples Mettle, which is now up, in driving that Nail which cannot go,[504] they must look to have it cool, and so the Ship of this Commonwealth, which if they please may be now in a fair way of Entering into a Safe Harbour, will be driven to Sea again in a Storm, and must hope for, and expect another favourable Wind to save them; and God knows when that may come.

---

where he was in command of the British auxiliaries sent by Charles II to assist Louis XIV.

503. An allusion perhaps to the style in which Charles II referred to Monmouth in official documents after 1673: "our dearest and most entirely beloved son."

504. I.e., pursuing the project of securing the succession for the Duke of Monmouth.

Doctor. But Sir, there are others, who not minding whether the *Parliament* will consider the Duke of *Monmouths* concern, so far as to debate it, do yet pretend, that there is great reason to keep up the peoples affections to him; and possibly to foment the opinion they have of his *Title* to the *Crown*, to the end, that if the *King* should die *re infectà*,[505] that is, before such time as the Government is redrest, or the Duke of *York* disabled by Law to Succeed, the people might have an Head, under whose Command and Conduct they might stand upon their Guard, till they had some way secured their *Government* and *Religion*.

English Gentleman. What you have started is not a thing that can safely be discoursed of, nor is it much material to our design, which is intended to speculate upon our Government, and to shew how it is decayed: I have industriously avoided the argument of *Rebellion*, as I find it coucht in modern Polititians, because most Princes hold, that all Civil Wars in mixt Monarchies must be so, and a Polititian, as well as an Oratour, ought to be *Vir bonus*,[506] so ought to discourse nothing, how rational soever, in these points under a peaceable *Monarchy*, which gives him protection,[507] but what he

---

505. I.e., with the matter unfinished or imperfect (*OED*, s.v. "re infectà").

506. I.e., a good man.

507. Here Neville inserts an explosive political doctrine in an apparently casual parenthesis. The doctrine that obedience is predicated on protection (*protectio trahit subjectionem*) was, according to Hobbes, the central doctrine of his *Leviathan*: "Thus I have brought to an end my Discourse of Civill and Ecclesiasticall Government, occasioned by the disorders of the present time, without partiality, without application, and without other designe, than to set before mens eyes the mutuall Relation between Protection and Obedience; of which the condition of Humane Nature, and the Laws Divine, (both Naturall and Positive) require an inviolable observation" (Hobbes, *Leviathan*, p. 491: cf. pp. 484–85 and 153 ["the end of Obedience is Protection"]). Similar statements can be found in Hobbes's earlier writings: see *De Cive*, 6.3 and 14.12, and *Elements of Law*, 2.1.5. They were echoed in the writings of contemporaries such as Algernon Sidney, Anthony Ascham, and Marchamont Nedham (Sidney, *Court Maxims*, p. 160; Pocock, *Harrington*, pp. 33–34) and might at this time be heard in the House of Commons: "I will not say of what divine right Government is, but I will say, that obligation to obey the Government is as long as it can give me security to protect me, and I ought to defend that Government and Governors" (Sir Henry Capel, 11 May 1679, in Grey,

would speak of his *Prince* if all his *Councel* were present. I will tell you only, that these Authors hold, that nothing can be alledged to excuse the taking Arms by any *people* in opposition to their *Prince* from being *Crimen Lesae Majestatis*,[508] but a claim to a lawful Jurisdiction, or Co-ordination in the Government, by which they may judg of, and defend their own Rights, and so pretend to fight for, and defend the Government; for though all do acknowledg, that *Populi salus*[509] is, and ought to be the most Supreme, or

---

Debates, vol. 7, p. 252; cf. Grey, *Debates*, vol. 8, p. 166, where the principle of "protectio trahit subjectionem" is traced back to "Calvin's Case" in Coke's seventh *Report*; cf. ibid., p. 273). Such a pragmatic grounding of the duty of obedience on the provision of protection, with its ostensible unconcern about abstract questions of right, is in general characteristic of the "de factoist" political theory engendered in England during the mid-seventeenth century by the Civil Wars. For classic accounts of this theory, see the articles reprinted in Quentin Skinner, *Visions of Politics*, 3 vols. (Cambridge: Cambridge University Press, 2002), vol. 3, pp. 238–307. One of the reasons the Commons gave for declaring the throne vacant in 1689 was that "there is no person on the Throne, from whom the subject can have regal protection, therefore they owe no Allegiance to any" (Grey, *Debates*, vol. 9, p. 50).

508. Literally, "the offense of harming majesty"; hence, treason.

509. An abbreviation of "Salus populi suprema lex": "The safety of the people is the supreme law." See, e.g., Cicero, *De Legibus*, 3.3.8. For a conspicuous earlier seventeenth-century invocation of the principle, see Sir Francis Bacon, "Of Judicature": "*Judges* ought above all to remember the Conclusion of the *Roman Twelve Tables*; *Salus Populi Suprema Lex*; And to know, that Lawes, except they been in Order to that End, are but Things Captious, and Oracles not well Inspired" (Bacon, *Essayes*, p. 169). The implications of the saying had been explored from diverse perspectives at midcentury. Henry Parker had invoked the principle in his *Observations* of 1642 (p. 3). John Warr in 1649 had asserted that the "end of just laws is the safety and freedom of a people" (Wootton, *Divine Right*, p. 152; cf. p. 47). It was, however, an extremely common political maxim, often quoted in Parliament during the 1650s and after the Restoration (e.g., Burton, *Diary*, vol. 1, pp. 234, 240–41, 261, 281; vol. 3, pp. 108, 569; vol. 4, pp. 47, 94; Grey, *Debates*, vol. 1, p. 113; vol. 6, p. 329; vol. 9, pp. 98 and 101; cf. Sidney, *Court Maxims*, p. 126, and *State-Tracts*, vol. 2, pp. 23 and 24). Confining ourselves to merely the few years preceding publication of *Plato Redivivus* and to printed quotations, see, e.g., Robert Sanderson, *Nine Cases of Conscience* (1678), p. 169; Charles Blount, *An Appeal from the Country to the City* (1679), t.p.; William Denton, *The Ungrateful Behaviour of the Papists* (1679), p. 123; Sir Robert Filmer, *The Free-Holders Grand Inquest* (1679), p. 281; Thomas Hobbes, *Behemoth* (1679), p. 67; Sir Roger L'Estrange, *The Case Put, Concerning the Succession* (1679), p. 16; Bethel Slingsby, *The Interest of Princes and States* (1680), p. 262; Buckingham, *An Essay upon Satyr* (1680), p. 49; Robert Constable, *God and the King* (1680), p. 31; Thomas

Soveraign Law in the world; yet if we should make private persons, how numerous soever, judg of *Populi salus*, we should have all the Risings and Rebellions that should ever be made, justified by that title, as happened in *France*, when *La Guerre du bien publique*[510] took that name, which was raised by the insatiable ambition of a few Noble men, and by correspondency and confederacy with *Charles*, Son of the Duke of *Burgundy*,[511] and other enemies to that Crown.

Doctor. But would you have our people do nothing then, if the King should be Assassinated, or die of a natural death?

English Gentleman. You ask me a very fine question, *Doctor*: If I say, *I would have the people stir* in that case, then the King, and his Laws take hold of me; and if I should answer, *that I would have them be quiet*, the people would tear me in pieces for a *Jesuit*, or at least, believe that I had no sense of the Religion, Laws, and Liberty of my Countrey. *De facto*,[512] I do suppose, that if the people do continue long in this heat which now possesseth them, and remain in such a passion at the time of the Kings death without setling matters, they may probably fall into tumults and Civil War, which makes it infinitely to be desired, and prayed for by all good *English* men, that during the quiet and peace we injoy, by the blessing of his Majesties life and happy Reign, we might likewise be so wise and fortunate, as to provide for the safety and prosperity of the next generation.

Doctor. But if you would not have the people in such a case, take the Duke of *Monmouth* for their Head, what would you have them do?

Hobbes, *The Last Sayings* (1680), p. 1; John Humfrey, *A Peaceful Resolution of Conscience* (1680), p. 102; Sir John Monson, *A Discourse concerning Supreme Power* (1680), p. 141; and Thomas Otway, *The Poet's Complaint of His Muse* (1680), p. 16.

510. "The War of the Public Weal" (1465–67 and 1472), the name given to the conflicts between Charles the Bold and other allies of the Duchy of Burgundy on the one hand, and the French crown on the other. Cf. Commines, *Memoirs*.

511. Charles the Bold (1433–77), Duke of Burgundy from 1467 until his death.

512. I.e., as a matter of fact.

English Gentleman. Doctor, you ask me very fine questions; do not you know that *Machivel,* the best and most honest of all the modern *Polititians,* has suffered sufficiently by means of *Priests,* and other ignorant persons, who do not understand his Writings, and therefore impute to him the teaching Subjects how they should Rebel and conspire against their Princes, which if he were in any kind guilty of, he would deserve all the reproaches that have been cast upon him, and ten times more;[513] and so should I, if I ventured to obey you in this. I am very confident, that if any man should come to you, to implore your skill in helping him to a drug that might quickly, and with the least fear of being suspected, dispatch an enemy of his, or some other, by whose death he was to be a gainer; or some young Lass that had gotten a Surruptitious great Belly, should come to you to teach her how to destroy the fruit;[514] I say, in this case you would scarce have had patience to hear these persons out; much less would you have been so wicked to have in the least assisted them in their designs, no more than *Solon,*[515] *Lycurgus,*[516] *Periander,*[517] or any other of the *Sages* could have been brought to have given their advice to any persons who should have begged it, to enable them to ruine and undermine the government of their own Commonwealths.

Doctor. Sir, this Reprehension would be very justly given me, if I had intended by this question to induce you to counsel me, or any other how to rebel; my meaning was to desire you (who have heretofore been very fortunate in prophesying concerning the events of our changes here) to ex-

513. The spurious "Nicholas Machiavel's Letter to Zanobius Buondelmontius in Vindication of Himself and His Writings," included in the translation of Machiavelli's *Works* with which Neville was associated and very possibly composed by Neville himself, rebuts three influential misreadings of the Florentine's works: (1) that Machiavelli encourages the people to cast off monarchy; (2) that he vilifies the Roman Catholic Church; and (3) that he instructs and encourages princes to oppress their subjects (Machiavelli, *Works,* sigs. **ʳ–***4ʳ).

514. I.e., procure an abortion.

515. See above, p. 104, n. 137.

516. See above, p. 82, n. 84.

517. Ruler of Corinth, c. 625–c. 585 B.C., who, although stern, was reputed to be just and was included among the Seven Sages of Greece.

ercise your faculty a little at this time, and tell us, what is like to be the end of these distractions we are under, in case we shall not be so happy as to put a period to them by mending our Government, and securing our Religion and Liberty in a regular way.

English Gentleman. Doctor, I will keep the reputation of Prophecy, which I have gained with you, and not hazard it with any new predictions, for fear they should miscarry; yet I care not, if I gratifie your curiosity a little in the point, about which you first began to Interrogate me, by presaging to you, that in case we should have troubles, and combustions here, after his Majesties decease (which God avert) we must expect a very unsuccessful end of them, if we should be so rash and unadvised, as to make the great Person we have been lately speaking of, our head; and that nothing can be more dangerous and pernitious to us than such a choice. I have not in this discourse the least intention to except against, much less to disparage the personal worth of the Duke of *Monmouth*, which the world knows to be very great, but do believe that he hath Courage and Conduct proportionable to any imployment that can be conferred upon him, whether it be to manage Arms, or Counsels; but my opinion is, that no person in his circumstance can be a proper head in this case; for the people having been already put on upon his scent of the *title* to the *Crown*, will be very hardly called off, and so will force the wiser men, who may design better things, to consent that he be Proclaimed *King* immediately, except there be some other head, who by his Power, Wisdom, and Authority, may restrain the forwardness of the multitude, and obviate the acts of some men, whose interest and hopes may prompt them to foment the humours of the people. Now the consequences of hurrying a man to the Throne so tumultuously, without the least deliberation, are very dismal; and do not only not cure the politick distempers of our Countrey, which we have talked so much of, but do infinitely augment it, and add to the desease our State labours under already (which is a Consumption) a very violent Feaver too; I mean War at home, and from abroad, which must necessarily follow in a few years: nor is it possible to go back, when once we have made that step; for our *new King* will call a *Parliament*, which being *summoned* by his *will*, neither will nor can question his Title or Government, otherwise than by making Addresses, and by presenting Bills to him, as they do to his now Majesty.

Noble Venetian. It seems to me, that there needs nothing more than that; for if he consent to all Laws as shall be presented to him, you may reform your Government sufficiently, or else it is your own fault.

English Gentleman. We have shewed already, and shall do more hereafter, that no Laws can be executed till our government be mended; and if you mean we should make such as should mend that (besides that it would be a better method to capitulate[518] that, before you make choice of your *Prince*, as wise people have done in all ages, and the *Cardinals* do at *Rome* in the *Conclave* before they choose their *Pope*) I say besides this, it is not to be taken for granted that any Bills that tend to make considerable alterations in the administration, (and such we have need of, as you will see anon) would either in that case be offered or consented to; both *Prince* and *People* being so ready to cry out upon *Forty-one*,[519] and to be frighted with the name of a *Common-wealth*, even now when we think *Popery* is at

518. I.e., insist upon, stipulate (*OED*, s.v. "capitulate," 1).
519. I.e., recalling the Civil Wars, and drawing a comparison between that crisis of state and the Exclusion Crisis. For contemporary examples, see, e.g., William Mercer, *The Moderate Cavalier* (1675), p. 4; Marchamont Nedham, *A Pacquet of Advices* (1676), p. 30; John Nalson, *The Countermine* (1677), p. 71; Andrew Marvell, *An Account of the Growth of Popery and Arbitrary Government* (1677), in Marvell, *Works*, vol. 2, pp. 279 and 287; Anonymous, *A Letter to a Friend* (1679), p. 9; Anonymous, *The Protestants Congratulation to the City* (1679), p. 1; Sir Roger L'Estrange, *The Free-Born Subject* (1679), pp. 18–19, and *The Parallel* (1679), p. 11; Anonymous, *The Disloyal Forty and Forty-One and the Loyal Eighty* (1680); Anonymous, *A New Medley* (1680), p. 1; Anonymous, *A Relation of Two Free Conferences* (1680), pp. 4 ("the whole Band of Pensioners in the House of Commons were perpetually crying out, *Forty* and *Forty One*") and 10 ("how much the *E.* of *D.* thought himself concerned to cry out of the return of Forty One"); Anonymous, *A Wiltshire Ballad* (1680), p. 1; J. Dean, *The Badger in the Fox-Trap* (1680), pp. 3 and 7; David Fitzgerald, *A Narrative of the Irish Popish Plot* (1680), p. 8; "J. D.," *A Word without Doors concerning the Bill for Succession* (1680), p. 9; Richard Onslow, *A Sober Discourse of the Honest Cavalier* (1680), p. 16; Thomas Otway, *The Poet's Complaint of His Muse* (1680), p. 15; Samuel Palmer, *The Plotters Doom* (1680), p. 19 ("theirs that cry out on *Forty one*"); Nahum Tate, *The Loyal General* (1680), p. 6 (prologue, written by Dryden).

the door; which some people then will think farther off, and so not care to make so great alterations to keep it out; besides the great Men and favourites of the new *Prince* will think it hard that their King should be so bounded and limited both in power and Revenue, that he shall have no means to exercise his liberality towards them, and so may use their interest and eloquence in both Houses to dissuade them from pressing so hard upon a Prince who is a true zealous Protestant, and has alwaies headed that party and who is justly admired, if not adored by the people; and considering too that all the power they leave him, will serve but to enable him to defend us the better from Popery and Arbitrary power; for which latter Monarchy was first Instituted. Thus we may exercise during a *Parliament* or two, love-tricks between the Prince and his people, and imitate the hony-moon that continued for about two years after his Majesties Restauration till the ill management of affairs and the new grievances that shall arise (which will be sure never to fail till our true cure be effected, notwithstanding the care of the new King and his Councellors) shall awaken the discontents of the people, and then they will curse the time in which they made this election of a Prince, and the great men for not hindring them. Then men will be reckoning up the discontents of the Peers, sometime after they had made a rash choice of *H.* the 7th in the field, (who had then no title)[520] when they saw how he made use of

520. In *The Art of Lawgiving* Harrington had noted that Henry VII had been "conscious of infirmity in his title" and had in consequence embarked on that policy of diminishing the power of the peers which had in the end broken the old English constitution by gradually and progressively separating the exercise of political power from the ownership of land (Pocock, *Harrington*, pp. 606–7). More generally, Bacon's *Historie of the Raigne of King Henry the Seventh*, first published in 1622, had been republished in 1676, and this may have served to refresh interest in his reign. Bacon had also commented on the complexities and deficiencies of Henry's title: "The King immediately after the Victory . . . was himselfe with generall applause, and great Cries of Ioy, in a kind of *Militar Election* or *Recognition*, saluted King. . . . But King Henry in the very entrance of his Reigne, and the instant of time, when the Kingdome was cast into his Armes, met with a Point of great difficultie, and knotty to solue, able to trouble and confound the wisest King in the newnesse of his Estate; and so much the more, because it could not endure a *Deliberation*, but must be at once deliberated and determined. There were fallen to his lot, and concurrent in his Person, three severall *Titles* to the Imperiall Crowne. The first, the Title of the Lady *Elizabeth*, with whom, by precedent Pact

the power they gave him to lessen their greatness, and to fortifie himself upon their ruins;[521] when it comes to this, and that the Governing party

with the Partie that brought him in, he was to marry. The second, the ancient and long-disputed Title (both by *Plea*, and *Armes*) of the House of *Lancaster*, to which he was Inheritour in his owne Person. The third, the Title of the *Sword* or *Conquest*, for that he came in by victorie of Battaile, and that the King in possession was slaine in the Field. . . . But the King, out of the greatnesse of his own minde, presently cast the Die, and the inconueniences appearing vnto him on all parts; and knowing there could not be any *Interreigne* or suspension of Title; and preferring his affection to his own Line and Bloud, and liking that Title best which made him independent; and being in his Nature and constitution of minde not very apprehensiue or forecasting of future Euents a-farre off, but an Intertainer of Fortune by the Day; resolued to rest vpon the title of *Lancaster* as the *Maine*, and to vse the other two, that of *Marriage* and that of *Battaile*, but as *Supporters*, the one to appease secret Discontents, and the other to beate downe open murmur and dispute: not forgetting that the same Title of *Lancaster* had formerly maintained a possession of three Discents in the Crowne, and might have proved a *Perpetuitie*, had it not ended in the weakenesse and inabilitie of the last Prince. Whereupon the King presently that very day, being the two and twentieth of August, assumed the Stile of King in his owne name, without mention of the Lady Elizabeth at all, or any relation thereunto. In which course hee euer after persisted, which did spin him a threed of many seditions and troubles" (Bacon, *Henry VII*, pp. 1–6). In the context of Exclusion, however, the reign of Henry VII was charged with additional implications. In the first place, Englishmen had recently been reminded that the Stuart title to the throne of England derived much of its strength from Henry VII: "CHARLES I. King of Great *Britain*, *France* and *Ireland*, was the Son of *James* VI. King of *Scots*, and *Anne* his Wife a Daughter of *Denmark*. By His Father descended to him all the Rights (together with their blood) of all our Ancient both *Saxon* and *Norman* Kings to this Empire. For the Lady *Margaret*, Sister and sole Heir of *Edgar Atheling* the last surviving Prince of the *English Saxons*, being married to *Malcolme Conmor* King of *Scots*, conveyed to his Line the *Saxon*, and *Margaret* Daughter of *Henry* VII. married to *James* IV. did bring the *Norman* Titles and Blood" (Richard Perrinchief, *The Royal Martyr* [1676], p. 1; cf. John Price, *The Mystery and Method of His Majesty's Happy Restauration Laid Open to Publick View* [1680], p. 9). Secondly, the complexities of Henry's title could be manipulated into support for the Duke of York and resistance to exclusion: see, e.g., "W. B.," *The White Rose, or, A Word for the House of York, Vindicating the Right of Succession* (1680), p. 8. Harrington had referred frequently both to Bacon's *Essayes* and to his *Historie of the Raigne of King Henry the Seventh* (Pocock, *Harrington*, pp. 45, 157–58, and 197). The thinness of Henry VII's title had been repeatedly recalled in the House of Commons in the context of Exclusion and very close to the date of publication of the first edition of *Plato Redivivus* (see Grey, *Debates*, vol. 7, pp. 142, 252, and 457–59). Cf. Somers, *A Brief History of the Succession*, in *State-Tracts*, vol. 1, p. 390; and also below, appendix F, pp. 411–12.

521. Bacon characterizes Henry's firm policy toward the English aristocracy as follows: "*Hee kept a strait hand on his* Nobilitie, *and chose rather to aduance* Clergie-

comes to be but a little faction, the people (who never know the true cause of their distemper) will be looking out abroad who has the Lawful title (if the next Heir be not in the mean time with an Army of *English* and *Strangers* in the field here, as is most likely) and look upon the *Prince of Orange*,[522] or the next of kin, as their future Saviour (in case the *Duke*

men *and* Lawyers, *which were more* Obsequious *to him, but had less* Interest *in the* People; *which made for his* Absoluteness, *but not for his* Safetie. *In so much as (I am perswaded) it was one of the* Causes *of his troublesome* Raigne; *for that his* Nobles, *though they were* Loyall *and* Obedient, *yet did not* Co-operate *with him, but let euery man goe his own Way. Hee was not afraid of an* Able Man, *as* Lewis *the Eleuenth was. But contrariwise, hee was serued by the* Ablest Men *that were to bee found; without which his Affairs could not haue prospered as they did*" (Bacon, *Henry VII*, pp. 241–42). In *The Art of Lawgiving* (1659) Harrington had explained the subtle process whereby Henry had made his nobles dwindle into courtiers in order to further his own security (Pocock, *Harrington*, pp. 606–7), but he had a low opinion of the quality of Bacon's analysis of this reign (Pocock, *Harrington*, p. 659). The author of *A Copy of a Letter* makes a very similar point about the critical importance of the reign of Henry VII in the history of English government: "When *Henry the Seventh* had established himself King, and saw plainlie that he did owe his ac-cessed [*sic*] to the Crown, more to the favour of those Lords who assisted him, then either to his own *Sword* or *Title*, he began to consider in how ticklish a pos-ture he stood, whilst it was in the power of any small number of Lords to set up, or pull down a Soveraign at their will, and upon this contemplation he made it his whole aim and work to lessent and debase the nobilitie, that he might have the less to apprehend in his new-gotten royaltie, by which he laid the foundation of *destroying his Posterity, not considering at all that the Lords could not be diminished, but by advancing and inriching the Commons*, whose desire of power must neces-sarilie increase accordinglie, which if they could not obtain, it was then obvious that they must strike not at this or that Prince, but at the verie *Root of Monarchy it self*, as being a thing uselesse whollie to them, and indeed inconsistent with their Government and interest" (pp. 8–9; see appendix A, below, p. 324). Sidney's fourth court maxim was that "Monarchy is not secure unless the nobility be sup-pressed, effeminated, and corrupted" (Sidney, *Court Maxims*, pp. 66–70). In *A Letter from a Person of Quality*, the inverted reciprocal relation between the power of the aristocracy and the prevalence of despotism was stated as a political law of nature: "For the Power of *Peerage* and a *standing-Army*, are like two Buckets, the proportion that one goes down, the other exactly goes up; and I refer you to the consideration of all the Histories of ours, or any of our Neighbour Northern Monarchies, whether standing Forces, Military, and Arbitrary Government came not plainly in by the same steps, that the Nobility were lessened" (*State-Tracts*, vol. 1, p. 55).

522. William of Orange (1650–1702), the future William III, who was close to the English throne in two respects: he was himself the grandson of Charles I via his mother Mary, the Princess Royal; and his wife Mary, whom he had married in

be dead in the mean time, and so the cause of all their distrust taken away) thus most men, not only discontented persons, but the people in general, lookt upon his Majesty that now is, as their future deliverer during our late distractions, when his condition was so weak that he had scarce wherewithall to subsist, and his enemies powerful at home and victorious abroad, which will not be I fear, our case. I Prophesy then (because you will have me use this word) that if Nobles or people make any such unfortunate choice as this during the distractions we may be in upon his Majesties death, we shall not only miss our cure, or have it deferred till another Government make it; but remain in the confusion we now suffer under; and besides, that shall be sure to feel, first or last, the calamity of a Civil and Foreign War, and in the mean time to be in perpetual fear of it, and suffer all the burden and charge which is necessary to provide for it, besides all the other ill consequences of a standing Army.[523] To conclude, I assure you in the Faith of a Christian, that I have made this discourse solely and singly out of zeal and affection to the Interest of my Countrey, and not at all with the least intention to favour or promote the Cause or Interest of the D. of *York*, or to disparage the Duke of *Monmouth*, from whom I never received the least unkindness, nor ever had the honour to be in his Company; and to whom I shall ever pay respect suitable to his high Birth and Merit.

Noble Venetian. Well, Sir, your Reasoning in this point has extreamly satisfied me; and the Doctor, I suppose, was so before, as he averred; therefore pray let us go on where we left.

1677, was the elder daughter of James II. "The people" did indeed look to William as their "future Saviour" in 1688. We have no direct knowledge of Neville's opinion of the settlement of 1689, but his friend and associate John Wildman, who had come over with William of Orange, would argue trenchantly at the Convention Parliament on 7 February 1689 for the crown to be given jointly to the Prince and Princess of Orange as King and Queen of England (Grey, *Debates*, vol. 9, p. 70).

523. See above, p. 170, n. 294.

English Gentleman. I cannot take so much upon me as to be Dictator in the Method of our Cure, since either of you is a thousand times better qualified for such an Office, and therefore shall henceforth desire to be an Auditor.

Doctor. Pray, Sir, let us not spend time in Compliments, but be pleased to proceed in this business, and we doubt not but as you have hitherto wonderfully delighted us, so you will gratifie us in concluding it.

English Gentleman. I see I must obey you, but pray help me, and tell me in the first place, whether you do not both believe, that as the *causa causarum*[524] of all our Distractions is (as has been proved) the breach of our Government; so that the immediate Causes are two: First, The great distrust on both sides between the King and his People and Parliament; the first fearing that his Power will be so lessened by degrees, that at length it will not be able to keep the Crown upon his head: And the latter seeing all things in disorder, and that the Laws are not executed (which is the second of the two Causes) fear the King intends to change the Government, and be Arbitrary.

Noble Venetian. I am a Stranger, but (though I never reflected so much upon the Original Cause, as I have done since I heard you discourse of it) yet I ever thought that those two were the Causes of the Unquietness of this Kingdom: I mean the Jealousie between the King and his People, and the Inexecution of the great Laws of Calling Parliaments Annually, and letting them sit to dispatch their Affairs: I understand this in the time of His Majesties Grand-Father, and Father,[525] more than in His own Reign.

English Gentleman. Then whoever can absolutely lay these two Causes asleep for ever, will arrive to a perfect Cure; which I conceive no way of doing, but that the King have a great deal more Power or a great deal

524. "The cause of causes," i.e., the root cause.
525. I.e., James I and Charles I.

less: And you know that what goes out of the King must go into the People, and so *vice versa:* Insomuch that the People must have a great deal more Power, or a great deal less: Now it is no question, but either of these two, would rather increase their Power than diminish it; so that if this cannot be made up by the Wisdom of this Age, we may see in the next, that both the King will endeavour to be altogether without a Parliament, and the Parliament to be without a King.

Doctor. I begin to smell, that you would be nibbling at the pretence which some had[526] before his Majesties Restauration, of a Commonwealth or *Democracy.*

English Gentleman. No, I abhor the thoughts of wishing, much less endeavouring any such thing, during these Circumstances we are now in; That is, under Oaths of Obedience to a Lawful King. And truly if any

---

526. "Democracy" possessed a number of discrete and separable aspects: government directly by the people; government by the elected representatives of the people; the exclusion of a monarch and sometimes also aristocrats from government; and frequent election on a wide suffrage. John Streater had defined it in 1659 as follows: "*Democracy* is a Government, where the Governours are Elected by the People out of themselves; sometimes called Free-State, or Popular State, or Common-wealth: This kind of Government by the People, is the most Natural, and best sort of all Governments; they Elect their Magistrates, which are to continue in poweer but one year, or less; they Trust not their Arms in the hands of one Person, but are managed by a Councel: This is the best sort of Government, because that the persons do not continue long in Trust: the which is the onely means to keep them from Corruption or Oppression" (*The Government of Monarchie, Aristocracie, Oligarchie, and Democracie Described* [1659], sig. A2v). In an English context, the late 1640s had "sharply increased the element of democratic activism in English political thinking" (Pocock, *Harrington*, p. 25). Leveller manifestos, such as *An Agreement of the Free People of England* (1649), had demanded universal adult male suffrage, excluding only servants, those in receipt of alms, and those who had engaged on the side of the king in the Civil Wars (Morton, *Freedom*, p. 268). Harrington had denied that a pure democracy could exist: "Though for discourse sake politicians speak of pure aristocracy and pure democracy, there is no such thing as either in nature, art or example" (Pocock, *Harrington*, p. 611). As Daniel Lee has recently reminded us, although democracy seems to be cognate with popular sovereignty, in fact the two things are perfectly separable, particularly at this time (Lee, *Popular Sovereignty*, pp. 319–20).

Themistocles should make to me such a Proposal, I should give the same Judgment concerning it, that *Aristides* [527] did in such a Case. The Story is short; After the War between the *Greeks* and the *Persians* was ended, and *Xerxes* driven out of *Greece*, [528] the whole Fleet of the *Grecian* Confederates (except that of *Athens* which was gone home) lay in a great Arsenal (such as were then in use) upon the Coast of *Attica*; during their abode there, *Themistocles* harrangues one day the People of *Athens* (as was then the Custome) and tells them, that he had a design in his head, which would be of Infinite profit and advantage to the Commonwealth; But that it could not be executed without the Order and Authority of them, and that it did likewise require secresie; and if it were declared there in the Market place, where Strangers as well as Citizens might be present, it could not be concealed, and therefore proposed it to their consideration what should be done in it: it was at length concluded that *Themistocles* should propose it to *Aristides*, and if he did next morning acquaint the People that he gave his approbation to it, it should be proceeded in: *Themistocles* informs him that the whole Fleet of their Confederates in the War against the *Medes* [529] had betaken themselves to the great Arsenal

527. For Themistocles, see above, p. 128, n. 213. Aristides (530–468 B.C.), ancient Athenian statesman and general, known as "the Just." For the source of the anecdote, see Plutarch, "Aristides," XXII. Cf. Machiavelli, *Discourses*, 1.59: "*Themistocles* in an Oration to the *Athenians*, told them, That he had something to advise that would be infinitely to their advantage, but durst not communicate it in publick, because to publish it, would hinder the Execution; whereupon the people deputed *Aristides* to receive it; and act in it afterwards as he should think convenient. *Themistocles* acquainted him, That the whole *Grecian* Fleet (though under their passport and parole) were in a place where they might be all taken or destroyed, which would make the *Athenians* absolute Masters in those Seas; and *Aristides* reported to the people, That the Council of *Themistocles* was profitable, but would be a great dishonor to their State; upon which it was unanimously rejected" (Machiavelli, *Works*, pp. 329–30). Thomas Goddard interprets this detail of *Plato Redivivus* as Neville hinting at the desirability of violent revolution (Goddard, *Plato's Demon*, p. 305).

528. Xerxes I, or "the Great" (519–465 B.C.), king of Persia. In 480 B.C. Xerxes invaded the Greek mainland and occupied Athens after defeating the Spartans at Thermopylae. After losing the battle of Salamis, Xerxes retreated to Persia but left behind an occupying force that was defeated in 479 B.C. at the Battle of Plataea.

529. An ancient Iranian people, powerful in the Near East until conquered by Cyrus the Great in 549 B.C. Thereafter they were assimilated into the Persian Empire. Herodotus reports that there was a Median contingent in Xerxes's army (7.62).

upon their Coast, where they might be easily fired, and then the *Athenians* would remain absolute Masters of the Sea, and so give Law to all *Greece*; when *Aristides* came the next day to deliver his Judgment to the People, he told them that the business proposed by *Themistocles*, was indeed very advantageous, and profitable to the *Athenians*; But withal, the most Wicked and Villanous Attempt that ever was undertaken; upon which it was wholly laid aside. And the same Judgment do I give, *Doctor*, of your *Democracy* at this time. But to return to the place where I was, I do believe that this difference may easily be terminated very fairly, and that our House need not be pulled down, and a new one built; but may be very easily repair'd, so that it may last many hundred years.

Noble Venetian. I begin to perceive that you aim at this, That the King must give the People more Power, as *Henry* the Third,[530] and King *John*[531] did, or the Parliament must give the King more, as you said they did in *France* in the time of *Lewis* the Eleventh;[532] or else that it will come in time to a War again.

English Gentleman. You may please to know, that in all times hitherto, the Parliament never demanded any thing of the King, wherein the Interest and Government of the Kingdom was concerned (excepting Acts of Pardon) but they founded their demands upon their Right, not only because it might seem unreasonable for them to be earnest with him to give them that which was his own, but also because they cannot chuse but know, that all Powers which are Fundamentally and Lawfully in the Crown, were placed there upon the first Institution of our Government,

---

530. Henry III (1207–72), king of England, whose reign was marked by tension between the Crown and the magnates, led by Simon de Montfort (c. 1208–65), who demanded administrative reforms (the so-called "Oxford Provisions" of 1258) including more regular parliamentary government. De Montfort defeated Henry at the battle of Lewes (1264) and held him prisoner for a year before himself falling at the battle of Evesham (1265) to Henry's son, the future Edward I.

531. See above, p. 161, n. 277.

532. See above, p. 196, n. 358.

to capacitate the Prince to Govern and Protect his People:[533] So that for the Parliament to seek to take from him such Authority, were to be *felo de se*,[534] as we call a self-Homicide; but as in some Distempers of the Body the Head suffers as well as the Inferiour parts, so that it is not possible for it, to order, direct and provide for the whole Body as its Office requires, since the Wisdom and Power which is placed there, is given by God to that end; In which Case, though the Distemper of the Body may begin from the Disease of some other part, or from the mass of Blood or putrefaction of other Humours; yet since that noble part is so affected by it, that Reason and Discourse fails, therefore to restore this again, Remedies must be apply'd to, and possibly Humours or Vapours drawn from the Head it self, that so it may be able to Govern and Reign over the Body as it did before, or else the whole Man, like a Slave, must be ruled and guided *ab extrinseco*,[535] that is by some Keeper: So it is now with us, in our Politick Disease, where granting (if you please) that the Distemper does not proceed from the Head, but the Corruption of other parts, yet in the Cure, Applications must be made to the Head as well as to the Members, if we mean poor *England* shall recover its former perfect health; and therefore it will be found, perhaps, Essential to our being, to ask something (in the condition we now are) to which the King as yet may have a Right; and which except he please to part with, the *Phenomena* of Government cannot be salved:[536] That is, our Laws cannot be executed; nor *Magna Charta* it self made practicable; and so both Prince and People, that is, the Polity of *England*, must die of this Disease, or by this *Delirium* must be Governed, *ab extrinseco*, and fall to the Lot of some Foreign Power.

533. See above, p. 259, n. 507, on the correlation between legitimacy and the provision of protection.

534. I.e., an act of suicide.

535. I.e., from outside.

536. A translation of the Byzantine Greek σῴζειν τὰ φαινόμενα (e.g., in Proclus *Hypotyposis astronomicarum positionum* 5.10): to reconcile the observed or admitted facts with a theory or doctrine with which they appear to disagree (*OED*, s.v. "phenomenon," citing this passage).

Noble Venetian. But, Sir, since the business is come to this *Dilemma*, why may not the King ask more Power of the Parliament, as well as they of him?

English Gentleman. No question but our present Councellours and Courtiers would be nibbling at that bait again, if they had another Parliament that would take Pensions for their Votes;[537] But in one that is come fresh from the People,[538] and understand their Sense and Grievances very well, I hardly believe they will attempt it; for both Council[539] and Parliament must needs know by this time-a-day, that the Cause of all our Distractions coming (as has been said an hundred times) from the King's having a greater Power already than the condition of Property at this present can admit, without Confusion and Disorder; It is not like to mend Matters for them to give him more, except they will deliver up to him at the same instant their Possessions, and Right to their Lands, and become Naturally and Politically his Slaves.

Noble Venetian. Since there must be a voluntary parting with Power, I fear your Cure will prove long and ineffectual, and we Reconcilers shall, I fear, prove like our devout *Cappuchin*[540] at *Venice*; this poor Mans name was *Fra. Barnardino da Udine*, and was esteemed a very holy Man, as well as an excellent Preacher, insomuch that he was appointed to Preach the *Lent* Sermons in one of our principal Churches, which he performed at the beginning with so much Eloquence, and Applause, that the Church was daily crouded three hours before the Sermon was to begin; the esteem and veneration this poor Fryar was in, elevated his Spirit a little too high to be contained within the bounds of reason; but before his *Delirium* was perceived, he told his Auditory one day, that the true Devotion of that People, and the care they had to come to hear his word Preached, had been so acceptable to God and to the Virgine, that they had vouchsafed to Inspire him with the knowledg of an Expedient, which he did

---

537. On the "Pensioner Parliament" of 1661–79, see above, p. 73, n. 64.

538. The current Parliament had been summoned on 17 October 1679 and would be dissolved on 18 January 1681.

539. I.e., the Privy Council.

540. I.e., a friar of the Order of St. Francis (*OED*, s.v. "Capuchin").

not doubt, but would make Men happy & just even in this Life, & that the Flesh should no longer lust against the Spirit; but that he would not acquaint them with it at that present, because something was to be done on their parts to make them capable of this great Blessing, which was to pray zealously for a happy Success upon his Endeavours, and to Fast, and to visit the Churches to that end; therefore he desired them to come the *Wednesday* following to be made acquainted with this blessed Expedient. You may Imagine how desirous our People were, to hear something more of this Fifth-Monarchy;[541] I will shorten my Story, and tell you nothing of what crouding there was all night, and what quarrelling for places in the Church; nor with what difficulty the *Saffi*,[542] who were sent by the Magistrate to keep the Peace, and to make way for the Preacher to get into the Pulpit, did both; But up he got, and after a long preamble of desiring more Prayers, and Addressing himself to our Senate to Mediate with the Pope, that a week might be set apart for a Jubilee[543] and Fasting three days all over the Christian World, to storm Heaven with Masses, Prayers, Fasting and Almes to prosper his Designs; he began to open the Matter, That the Cause of all the Wickedness and Sin, and by Consequence of all the Miseries and Affliction which is in the World, arising from the enmity which is between God and the Devil, by which means God was often cross'd in his Intentions of good to Mankind here, and hereafter, the Devil by his temptations making us uncapable of the Mercy

541. Generally, the last of the five great empires referred to in the prophecy of Daniel (Daniel 2:44), in the seventeenth century identified with the millennial reign of Christ predicted in the Apocalypse. More specifically, in the context of recent English history, it refers to a member of one of the sects which had flourished during the Interregnum who believed that the Second Coming of Christ was immediately at hand and that it was the duty of Christians to be prepared to assist in establishing his reign by force, in the meantime repudiating all allegiance to any other government. Cf. Burton, *Diary*, vol. 2, pp. 369 and 390.

542. I.e., bailiffs (*OED*, s.v. "saffo").

543. Originally, a year instituted by Boniface VIII in 1300 as a period of remission from the penal consequences of sin, during which plenary indulgence might be obtained by a pilgrimage to Rome, the visiting of certain churches there, the giving of alms, fasting for three days, and the performance of other pious works; hence, more generally, a period of indulgence and remission of sins (*OED*, s.v. "jubilee," 2).

and Favour of our Creator; therefore he had a Design (with the helps before mentioned) to mediate with Almighty God, That he would pardon the Devil, and receive him into his Favour again after so long a time of Banishment and Imprisonment; and not to take all his power from him, but to leave him so much as might do good to Man, and not hurt; which he doubted not but he would imploy that way, after such reconciliation was made, which his Faith would not let him question. You may judge what the numerous Auditory thought of this; I can only tell you, that he had a different sort of Company at his return, from what he had when he came, for the Men left him to the Boys, who with great Hoops instead of Acclamations, brought him to the *Gondola*,[544] which conveyed him to the *Redentor*,[545] where he lodged; And I never had the curiosity to enquire what became of him after.[546]

Doctor. I thank you heartily for this Intermess;[547] I see you have learnt something in *England*: for, I assure you, we have been these twenty Years turning this, and all serious Discourses into Ridicule; but yet your Similitude is very pat; for in every Parliament that has been in *England* these sixty Years, we have had notable Contests between the Seed of the Serpent, and the Seed of the Woman.[548]

---

544. A skiff employed on the Venetian canals.

545. The Chiesa del Santissimo Redentore, commonly known as Il Redentore; a Palladian church in Venice.

546. The source of the anecdote is untraced. Udine is a city in northeastern Italy close to Venice: see Gailhard, *Italy*, p. 31. Robbins speculates that the Noble Venetian is alluding to "Friar Bernardino Occhino (1487–1564), a well-known preacher and critic of social vices of Venetians, and later a reformer who migrated to Geneva and then Moravia" (Robbins, *Republican Tracts*, p. 176, n. 1). Occhino's *A Dialogue of Polygamy* had been translated into English and published in 1657, and there had been several English translations of his sermons and his antipapal writings published in the sixteenth century.

547. I.e., something served between the courses of a banquet (*OED*, s.v. "intermess").

548. An allusion to the curse placed by God upon the serpent: "I will put enmity between thee and the woman, and between thy seed and her seed; it shall bruise thy head, and thou shalt bruise his heel" (Genesis 3:15).

English Gentleman. Well Sir, we have had a *Michael* here in our Age, who has driven out *Lucifer,*[549] and restored the true Deity to his Power: but where Omnipotency is wanting (which differs the Frier's Case and mine) the Devil of Civil War and Confusion may get up again, if he be not laid by prudence and Vertue, and better Conjurers than any we have yet at Court.

Noble Venetian. Well Gentlemen, I hope you have pardoned me for my Farce. But, to be a little more serious, pray tell me how you will induce the King to give up so much of his Right as may serve your turn? Would you have the Parliament make War with him again?

English Gentleman. There cannot, nor ought to be, any Change, but by his Majesty's free Consent; for besides, that a War is to be abhorred by all Men that love their Country, any Contest of that kind in this case (*viz.* to take away the least part of the Kings Right) could be justified by no man living. I say, besides that, a Civil War has miscarried in our days, which was founded (at least pretendedly) upon Defence of the People's own Rights: In which, although they had as clear a Victory in the end, as ever any Contest upon Earth had, yet could they never reap the least advantage in the World by it: but went from one Tyranny to another, from *Barebones* Parliament,[550] to *Cromwell's* Reign;[551] from that, to a Committee of Safety;[552] leaving those Grave Men, who managed Affairs

549. An obscure comment, perhaps deliberately so, but it may be an extravagantly panegyrical reference to Charles II himself. Milton's *Paradise Lost* had been published in 1667.

550. See above, p. 196, n. 357.

551. Oliver Cromwell ruled England as Lord Protector from 1653 to 1658. Neville was a strong critic of the Cromwellian regime, as is clear from writings such as *A Copy of a Letter from an Officer in the Army* (1656) and *Shufling, Cutting, and Dealing* (1659); and see immediately below, pp. 282–83. Such undisguised disaffection had led to Neville's being banished from London by Cromwell in 1654.

552. The Committee of Safety was a Parliamentary body set up initially in 1642 to pursue the war against Charles I and which remained in being until 1644. It was succeeded in 1647 by a new committee established by the Presbyterians to safeguard London from the New Model Army. Finally, in 1659 there were two Committees of Safety (sometimes also referred to as Councils of State). The first was established in May to replace Richard Cromwell's Council of State. It was suc-

at the beginning, amazed to see new Men, and new Principles Governing *England*. And this induced them to Co-operate to bring things back
just where they were before the War. Therefore this Remedy will be
either none, or worse than the Disease: It not being now as it was in the
Barons time, when the Lord who led out his Men, could bring them back
again when he pleased, and Rule them in the mean time, being his Vassals. But now there is no Man of so much Credit, but that one who be-
haves himself bravely in the War, shall out-vye him; and, possibly, be
able to do what he pleases with the Army and the Government: And in
this corrupt Age, it is ten to one, he will rather do Hurt than Good with
the Power he acquires. But because you ask me how we would perswade
the King to this? I answer, by the Parliament's humbly Remonstrating to
His Majesty, that it is his own Interest, Preservation, Quiet and true
Greatness, to put an end to the Distractions of his Subjects, and that it
cannot be done any other way, and to desire him to enter into debate with
some Men Authorized by them, to see if there can be any other means
than what they shall offer to compose things; if they find there may, then
to embrace it, otherwise to insist upon their own Proposals: and if in the
end they cannot obtain those Requests, which they think the only essential means to preserve their Country, then to beg their Dismission, that
they may not stay, and be partakers in the Ruin of it. Now, my Reasons
why the King will please to grant this, after the thorough discussing of it,
are two. First, Because all great Princes have ever made up Matters with
their Subjects upon such Contests, without coming to Extremities. The
two greatest, and most Valiant of our Princes, were *Edward* the First,[553]
and his Grandchild *Edward* the Third:[554] these had very great Demands
made them by Parliaments, and granted them all; as you may see upon

---

ceeded by the Committee of Safety established in October 1659 by the leaders of
the New Model Army, and it is to this final committee that Neville refers. Neville
was himself a member of both the committees of 1659.

553. Edward I (1239–1307), king of England.
554. Edward III (1312–77), king of England.

the Statute-Book. *Edward* the Second,[555] and *Richard* the Second,[556] on the contrary, refused all things till they were brought to Extremity. There is a Memorable Example in the Greek Story of *Theopompus* King of *Sparta*; whose Subjects finding the Government in disorder for want of some Persons that might be a Check upon the great Power of the King, proposed to him the Creation of the *Ephores*[557] (Officers who made that City so great and Famous afterwards). The King finding by their Reasons (which were unanswerable, as I think ours now are), that the whole Government of *Sparta* was near its Ruin, without such a Cure; and considering that he had more to lose in that Disorder than others, freely granted their desires; for which being derided by his Wife, who asked him what a kind of Monarchy he would leave to his Son? answered, a very good one, because it will be a very lasting one.[558] Which brings on my Second Reason, for which I believe the King will grant these things; because he cannot any way mend himself, nor his Condition, if he do not.

555. Edward II (1284–1327), king of England.

556. Richard II (1367–1400), king of England.

557. I.e., a body of five Spartan magistrates empowered to exert control over the kings.

558. Theopompus was a Europontid king of Sparta in the late eighth or early seventh century B.C. For the anecdote and its political significance, see Aristotle, *Politics*, 5.9: "It is clear that monarchies, speaking generally, are preserved in safety as a result of the opposite causes to those by which they are destroyed. But taking the different sorts of monarchy separately—royalties are preserved by bringing them into a more moderate form; for the fewer powers the kings have, the longer time the office in its entirety must last, for they themselves become less despotic and more equal to their subjects in temper, and their subjects envy them less. For this was the cause of the long persistence of the Molossian royalty, and that of Sparta has continued because the office was from the beginning divided into two halves, and because it was again limited in various ways by Theopompus, in particular by his instituting the office of the ephors to keep a check upon it; for by taking away some of the kings' power he increased the permanence of the royal office, so that in a manner he did not make it less but greater. This indeed as the story goes is what he said in reply to his wife, when she asked if he felt no shame in bequeathing the royal power to his sons smaller than he had inherited it from his father: 'Indeed I do not,' he is said to have answered, 'for I hand it on more lasting.'" Cf. Valerius Maximus, 4.1 ext. 8, and Plutarch, *Lycurgus*, 7. The anecdote was also recalled by Sidney in his *Court Maxims* (Sidney, *Court Maxims*, pp. 79–80).

Noble Venetian. You have very fully convinced me of two things: First, That we have no reason to expect or believe that the Parliament will ever increase the Kings Power: And then, that the King cannot by any way found himself a New, and more absolute Monarchy, except he can alter the Condition of Property, which I think we may take for granted to be impossible. But yet, I know not why we may not suppose that (although he cannot establish to all Posterity such an Empire) he may, notwithstanding, change the Government at the present; and calling Parliaments no more, administer it by force, as it is done in *France*, for some good time.

English Gentleman. In *France* it has been a long Work; and although that Tyranny was begun, as has been said, by Petition from the States themselves, not to be assembled any more;[559] yet the Kings since, in time of great Distraction, have thought fit to convocate them again; as they did in the Civil Wars thrice: Once at *Orleans*, and twice at *Blois*.[560] I would not repeat what I have so tediously discoursed of concerning *France* already, but only to intreat you to remember that our Nation has no such poor and numerous Gentry, which draw better Revenues from the King's Purse, than they can from their own Estates; all our country people consisting of Rich Nobility and Gentry, of Wealthy Yeomen, and of Poor Younger Brothers who have little or nothing, and can never raise their Companies, if they should get Commissions, without their Elder Brothers Assistance amongst his Tenants, or else with the free consent and desire of the People, which, in this case, would hardly be afforded them. But we will suppose there be idle People enough to make an Army, and that the King has Money enough to Arm and Raise them: And I will grant too, to avoid tediousness (although I do not think it possible) that the people will at the first, for fear, receive them into their Houses, and Quarter them against Law;[561] nay, pay the Money which shall be by

559. See above, p. 196 and n. 358.

560. The French States General had convened at Orléans in 1560 and at Blois in 1576 and 1589.

561. A recurrent source of grievance in the years leading up to Civil Wars. The Petition of Right (1628) had deplored how "of late great companies of soldiers and mariners have been dispersed into divers counties of the realm, and the inhabit-

illegal Edicts, imposed upon the Subjects to pay them;[562] Yet is it possible an Army can continue any time to enslave their own Country? Can they resist the Prayers, or the Curses of their Fathers, Brothers, Wives, Mothers, Sisters, and of all Persons wherever they frequent? Upon this Account all the *Greek* Tyrants were of very short Continuance; who being in chief Magistracy and Credit in their Commonwealths, by means

---

ants against their wills have been compelled to receive them into their houses, and there to suffer them to sojourn against the laws and customs of this realm, and to the great grievance and vexation of the people"; cf. Grey, *Debates*, vol. 7, p. 70; cf. also vol. 2, p. 221. The Grand Remonstrance (1641) had complained of "the charging of the kingdom with billeted soldiers in all parts of it, and the concomitant design of German horse, that the land might either submit with fear or be enforced with rigour to such arbitrary contributions as should be required of them." The burden of quartering had become freshly topical in 1679 and 1680: "These *Fears* [of invasion] obliged us to maintain a considerable *Force* at *Land* and *Sea*, which, lying *idle*, corrupted, as *standing-Water* in a *Pool*, and every moment threaten'd fresh *Combustions*, as they were blown up this way or that way by their new *Masters;* but at the best (like our old *Lord-Danes*) they were most insupportably burthensome and odious to the *Country*, by their Quartering; and to keep them as much in *action* as possibly we could, we were fain either to be perpetually amusing them with pretended Discoveries of some *new-feigned Plot* or other, or else to engage them in *Forreign Wars*" (Anonymous, *The Interest of the Three Kingdoms* [1680], pp. 10–11; cf. the remarks by Sir Henry Capel in the Commons in Grey, *Debates*, vol. 7, pp. 64–65). William of Orange would be so aware of this resentment that in his *Declaration* of 1688 he would underline that the troops he brought with him would be kept "under all the Strictnes of Martiall Discipline: and [we shall] take a speciall Care, that the People of the Countries thro which wee much march, shall not suffer by their means."

562. A reference either to forced loans, which had notoriously been used by Charles I, or non-Parliamentary taxation. Again, Neville touches on one of the most sensitive neuralgic points in earlier seventeenth-century English experience. The Petition of Right (1628) had requested that "no man hereafter be compelled to make or yield any gift, loan, benevolence, tax, or such like charge, without common consent by act of parliament; and that none be called to make answer, or take such oath, or to give attendance, or be confined, or otherwise molested or disquieted concerning the same or for refusal thereof." The Grand Remonstrance (1641) had inveighed against "the exacting of the like proportion of five subsidies, after the Parliament dissolved, by commission of loan, and divers gentlemen and others imprisoned for not yielding to pay that loan, whereby many of them contracted such sicknesses as cost them their lives," "great sums of money required and raised by privy seals," and "an unjust and pernicious attempt to extort great payments from the subject by way of excise, and a commission issued under the seal to that purpose."

of Soldiers and *Satellites*, usurped the Soveraignty. But did ever any of them, excepting *Dionysius*, leave it to his Son? Who was driven out within less than a year after his Fathers death.[563] Many Armies of the Natives have destroyed Tyrannies: So the *Decemvirate*[564] was ruined at *Rome*, the *Tarquins*[565] expelled before that: Our own Country has been a Stage, even in our time, where this Tragedy has been sufficiently acted; for the Army, after the War was done, fearing the Monarchy should be restored again, held Councils, got Agitators; and though there were often very severe Executions upon the Ring-leaders, did at length, by their perseverance, necessitate their Officers to joyn with them (having many good Headpieces of the Party to advise them); and so broke all Treaties.[566] And the Parliament too, adhering to a small Party of them who consented to lay aside Kingly Government, and afterwards drove them away too, fearing they would continue to Govern in Oligarchy.[567] I am far from approving this way they used, in which they broke all Laws, Divine and Humane, Political and Moral: But I urge it only to shew how easily an Army of Natives is to be deluded with the Name of Liberty, and brought to pull down any thing which their Ring-leaders tell them tends to enslaving their Country. 'Tis true, this Army was afterwards cheated by their General;[568] who without their Knowledge, much less Consent, one Morning, suddenly made himself Tyrant of his Country. It is as true, that their Reputation (not their Arms) supported him in that State for some time; but it is certain that they did very often, and to the last, refuse

563. Dionysius I and II were successive tyrants of the Sicilian city of Syracuse; the father ruled from 405 to 367 B.C., and his son succeeded him until he was expelled by Dion in 357 B.C.

564. A reference to the so-called second Decemvirate, one of several ten-man commissions established during the Roman Republic. The second Decemvirate foundered on the tyrannical behavior of one of its members, Appius Claudius Crassus in 452 B.C.; see Livy, 3.33.

565. The Roman royal dynasty, expelled in 510 B.C. by the patricians led by Lucius Junius Brutus.

566. For Neville's role in this recent crisis of state, see Mahlberg, pp. 47–48.

567. A reference to the forcible dissolution of the Rump Parliament on 19 April 1653 by Oliver Cromwell, supported by forty musketeers who entered the chamber with lighted matches.

568. I.e., Oliver Cromwell.

to be instrumental to levy Moneys, though for their own pay: and so he, against his Will, was fain to call from time to time Parliamentary Conventions.[569] And it is most certain that he did, in the Sickness of which he died, often complain that his Army would not go a step farther with him: and, *de facto*, some Months after his death, they did dethrone his Son,[570] and restore the Remainder of the old Parliament,[571] upon promise made to them in secret (by the Demogogues of that Assembly) that a Commonwealth should be speedily framed and setled.

Noble Venetian. Sir, I am satisfied that an Army raised here on a sudden, and which never saw an Enemy, could not be brought to act such high things for the Ruin of their own Government; nor possibly, would be any way able to resist the Fury and Insurrection of the people. But what say you of a Forreign Army, raised by your King abroad, and brought over, whose Officers and Soldiers shall have no Acquaintance or Relations amongst the people here?

English Gentleman. All Forces of that kind must be either Auxiliaries or Mercenaries: Auxiliaries are such as are sent by some Neighbour Prince or State, with their own Colours, and paid by themselves: though possibly, the Prince who demands them may furnish the Money. These usually return home again, when the occasion, for which they were demanded, is over: But whether they do or not, if they be not mixed and over-ballanced with Forces which depend upon the Prince who calls them, but that the whole Weight and power lies in them, they will certainly, first or last, seize that Country for their own Soveraign. And as for Mercenaries, they must be raised ('tis true) with the Money of the Prince who needs them, but by the Authority and Credit of some Great

569. During the Protectorate (1653–58), parliaments were summoned and dissolved as follows: (1) Barebones Parliament (June 1653–12 December 1653); (2) the Second Protectorate Parliament (10 July 1656–4 February 1658).

570. Richard Cromwell was appointed Lord Protector on the death of his father on 3 September 1658 and was ejected by the army on 25 May 1659.

571. I.e., the Rump Parliament, the purged remnant of the Long Parliament which had been forcibly dissolved by Cromwell in 1653.

Persons who are to Lead and Command them: And these, in all Occasions, have made their own Commander Prince; as *F. Sforza* at *Milan* drove out by this trick the *Visconti*,[572] ancient Dukes of that State; and the *Mamalukes* in *Egypt* made themselves a Military Commonwealth.[573]

572. In 1448 Francesco Sforza made himself Duke of Milan, ejecting his former employers, the Visconti. Cf. Machiavelli, *The Prince*, chapter 12: "Upon the death of Duke *Philip*, the *Milanesi* entertained *Francesco Sforza* against the *Venetians*, and *Francesco*, having worsted the Enemy at *Caravaggio*, joyned himself with him, with design to have mastered his Masters" (Machiavelli, *Works*, p. 215).

573. The mamalukes were members of the régime established and maintained by emancipated white military slaves that ruled Egypt as a sultanate from 1250 until 1517, continuing as a ruling military caste of Egypt as a pashalik under Ottoman sovereignty until 1812, and of Syria from 1260 to 1516 (*OED*, s.v. "Mameluke," *n.*); "a light-horseman (in the Syrian and Arabian tongues) the Mamalukes were an order of valiant horse-men in the last Empire of Egypt" (Thomas Blount, *Glossographia* [1661]). The mamalukes were renowned as an example of the conversion of military prowess into political ascendancy: "It is woonderfull to tell vnto what a strength and glorie this order of the Mamalukes was in short time grown, by the care of the Aegyptian kings: By them they mannaged their greatest affaires, especially in time of wars; and by their valour, not onely defended their countrey, but gained many a faire victorie against their enemies, as they did now against the French. But as too much power in such mens hands, seldome or neuer wanteth danger, so fell it out now betwixt the late Sultan *Melech-sala*, and those masterfull Mamaluke slaues: who proud of their preferment, and forgetfull of their dutie, and seeing the greatest strength of the kingdome in their hands, traiterously slew *Melech-sala* their chiefe founder, setting vp in his place (as aforesaid) one *Turquiminus*, a base slaue, one of their owne order and seruile vocation, but indeed otherwise a man of a great spirit and valour" (Knolles, *Turkes*, p. 107; cf. Sidney, *Discourses*, pp. 155 and 197). Like the janissaries, the mamalukes were occasionally invoked pejoratively in the context of the English Civil War: "The Eleven Impeached Members, before mentioned, who had superseded themselves, and were newly re-admitted, (the Army not being able to produce their Charge, upon pretence of more weighty affairs) now altogether withdrew, and had Passes, (though some staid in *London*) some for beyond Sea, and other for their homes; in the way whither, one of them (Mr. *Nichols*) was seized on, and basely abused by *Cromwel:* another, Sir *Philip Stapleton*, one who had done them very good service, passed over to *Calice*, where falling sick, as suspected, of the Plague, he was turned out of the Town, and perished in the way near to *Graveling*; whose end was inhumanely commented on by our *Mamaluke* like Saints, who inscribed it to the Divine Vengeance" (James Heath, *A Chronicle of the Late Intestine War* [1676], p. 142). James Harrington had spoken of the mamalukes in very similar terms in *Oceana*: "The Mamelukes (which, till any man show me to contrary, I shall presume to have been a commonwealth consisting of an army, whereof the common soldier was the people, the commission-officer the senate, and the general the prince)" (Pocock, *Harrington*, p. 168).

So that the way of an Army here would either be no Remedy at all, or one very much worse than the Disease to the Prince himself.

Noble Venetian. Well Sir, I begin to be of Opinion, that any thing the King can grant the Parliament (especially such a Parliament as this is, which consists of Men of very great Estates, and so can have no interest to desire Troubles) will not be so inconvenient to him, as to endeavour to break the Government by force. But why may he not, for this time, by soothing them, and offering them great Alliances abroad for the Interest of *England*, and ballancing Matters in *Europe* more eaven than they have been; and, in fine, by offering them a War with the *French*, to which Nation they have so great a hatred; lay them asleep, and get good store of Money, and stave off this severe Cure you speak of, at least, for some time longer?

English Gentleman. There has been something of this done too lately; and there is a Gentleman lies in the Tower,[574] who is to answer for it. But you may please to understand, that there is scarce any amongst the middle sort of People, much less within the Walls of the House of Commons, who do not perfectly know, that we can have no Alliance with any Nation in the

---

574. A reference to the current disgrace of Thomas Osborne (1632–1712), Lord Danby, Marquess of Carmarthen, and later Duke of Leeds; a prominent but mistrusted statesman under Charles II and William III. Danby had been Lord Treasurer from 1673 to 1679. In the mid-1670s he had worked hard to create a Court party in Parliament by the use of pensions (see above, p. 73, n. 64). He was also thought to have raised supply from Parliament, ostensibly for a war against France, which was then applied to remedy the general weakness of the Crown's finances. In December 1678 Danby was impeached, the charges specifying that he had "encroached to himself regal power" through his conduct of foreign affairs, that he had endeavored to introduce arbitrary power by raising an army on pretense of a war, and that he was "popishly affected" and had concealed the Popish Plot. He was imprisoned in the Tower in April 1679, where he would remain until 1684. The publication of *Plato Redivivus* in 1681 had coincided with a lively pamphlet war over Danby's case. His own vindication, *An Impartial State of the Case of the Earl of Danby* (1679) had been answered by Sir Robert Howard's hostile *An Examination of the Impartial Case* (1679). Danby had replied in *The Answer of the Earl of Danby to a Late Pamphlet* (1680), which had provoked a further riposte from Howard and yet a further reply from Danby, *The Earl of Danby's Answer to Sr Robert Howard's Book* (1680).

World that will signifie any thing to them, or to our selves, till our Government be redressed and new modelled. And therefore, though there were an Army Landed in this Island, yet that we must begin there, before we are fit to repulse them, or defend our selves. And the fear and sense of this People universally is, that if we should have any War, either for our own Concerns, or for those of our Allies, whilst Matters remain as they do at home, it would certainly come to this pass, that either being beaten, we should subject this Kingdom to an Invasion, at a time when we are in a very ill condition to repell it; or else, if we were Victorious, that our Courtiers and Counsellors *in flagrante*[575] (or as the *French* cry, *d'emblée*[576]), would employ that Mettle and good Fortune to try some such Conclusions at home as we have been discoursing of. And therefore, if any War should be undertaken without Parliament, you should see the People rejoyce as much at any disaster our Forces should receive, as they did when the *Scots* seized the four Northern Counties in 1639.[577] Or before that, when we were beaten at the Isle of *Rhee*,[578] or when we had any Loss in the last War with *Holland*.[579] And this

575. I.e., ardently.

576. I.e., at once, or straightaway.

577. Following the English failure in the first Bishops' War in 1639, in August of the following year the Scots Covenanter army invaded and occupied the counties of Northumberland and Durham. The humiliating Treaty of Ripon (October 1640) recognized the Scottish occupation of this English territory.

578. An English military debacle of 1627. In an attempt to destabilize Richelieu, the chief minister of Louis XIII, Charles I's favorite, George Villiers, Duke of Buckingham, planned a combined forces operation to relieve the Huguenots besieged in La Rochelle. Arriving off the southeastern tip of the island of Ré on 12 July 1627, the English troops were successfully landed, and invested the citadel of St. Martin into which the French defenders had withdrawn. By the end of September the garrison was close to capitulation. However, Richelieu, who had taken personal charge of the French forces on the nearby mainland, dispatched a convoy of small ships that slipped through the English blockading fleet and brought supplies to the starving garrison. There was no prospect now of a swift victory, and Buckingham gave the order for withdrawal, in the course of which the English suffered heavy casualties; cf. May, *History*, lib. 1, p. 9. Late seventeenth-century Whig historians regarded this fiasco with fierce indignation as an illustration of the fecklessness of the Stuarts: see, e.g., Jones, *Theatre of Wars*, pp. 82–89, and Ludlow, *Memoirs*, vol. 1, pp. 3–5.

579. I.e., the Third Dutch War (1672–74), in which the Royal Navy suffered a series of demoralizing defeats at the hands of the Dutch admirals De Ruyter and

Joy is not so unnatural as it may seem to those who do not consider the Cause of it; which is the breach of our old Government, and the necessity our Governors are under to make some new experiments: And the fear we are in, that any Prosperity may make them able to try them, either with Effect, or at least with Impunity. Which Consideration made a Court-Droll say lately to His Majesty, (who seemed to wonder why his subjects hated the *French* so much); Sir, it is because you love them, and espouse their Interest: And if you would discover this Truth clearly, you may please to make War with the King of *France*; and then you shall see, that this People will not only love them, take their parts, and wish them Success; but will exceedingly rejoyce when they are Victorious in sinking your Ships, or defeating your Forces.[580] And this is sufficient to answer your Proposal for Alliances abroad, and for a War with *France*. Besides this (to wind all up in a Word) it is not to be imagined, that so good and wise a Prince as we have at this time should ever be induced (when he comes to understand perfectly his own Condition) to let his own Interest (granting his Power to be so, which is very false) contest with the Safety and Preservation of his People, for which only it was given him; or that he will be any way tenacious of such Prerogatives, as now, by a natural Revolution of Political Circumstances, are so far from continuing useful to his Governing the People, that they are the only *Remora*[581] and Obstacle of all Government, Settlement and Order. For His Majesty must needs know, that all Forms of regulating Mankind under Laws were ordained by God and Man, for the Happiness and Security of the Governed,[582] and not for the Interest and Greatness of those who rule;

Tromp: the Battle of Solebay (1672), the First and Second Battles of the Schooneveld (1673), and the Battle of the Texel (1673).

580. Unidentified.

581. I.e., an obstacle or impediment (*OED*, s.v. "remora," 2).

582. That the purpose of government is to secure the well-being of the people in this world rather than the next is a principle that had often been invoked in the earlier part of the seventeenth century, for instance by Philip Hunton in his *A Treatise of Monarchy* (1643): "God's ordinance is not only power, but power for such ends, scil. the good of the people" (Wootton, *Divine Right*, p. 207). Cf. Anonymous, *England's Miserie and Remedie* (1645): "The one is but the servant of the other (the House of Commons, I mean, of the people), elected by them to provide

unless where there is *Melior Natura*[583] in the Case. So God Governs Man for his own Glory only, and Men Reign over Beasts for their own Use and Service; and where an Absolute Prince rules over his own Servants whom he feeds and pays (as we have said), or the Master of a great and numerous Family Governs his Houshold; they are both bound by the Law of God and Nature, and by their own Interest, to do them Justice, and not *Insaevire*[584] or Tyranize over them, more than the necessity of preserving their Empire and Authority requires.

Doctor. But Sir, considering the difficulty which will be found in the King, and possibly in the Parliament too, to come up to so great an alteration at the first, and the danger that may happen by our remaining long in this unsetled Condition, which does hourly expose us to innumerable hazards, both at home, and from abroad; why may we not begin, and lay the Foundation now, by removing all His Majesty's present Council by Parliament; which is no new thing, but hath been often practised in many Kings Reigns?

English Gentleman. First, the Council, that is, the Privy Council which you mean, is no part of our Government,[585] as we may have occasion to

---

for their welfare and freedoms against all in-bred tyranny or foreign invasion" (Wootton, *Divine Right*, p. 277). Cf. also the Leveller Petition of 1647: "The end of all Government is the safetie and freedome of the governed" (Morton, *Freedom*, p. 91). According to Burnet, it was the essential political principle of those who advocated Exclusion: "Government was appointed for those that were to be governed, and not for the sake of Governors themselves: Therefore all things relating to it were to be measured by the publick interest, and the safety of the people" (Burnet, *History*, vol. 1, p. 457). Accordingly, it had been appealed to by John Locke in his *Second Treatise*, para. 163, composed during the Exclusion crisis although first published later: "For the End of Government being the good of the Community." The principle survived into the following century, Bolingbroke in his *Idea of a Patriot King* maintaining that "the good of the people is the ultimate and true end of government." For further discussion of this fundamentally Epicurean understanding of the purpose of government, see above, p. 172, n. 296.

583. I.e., better nature, or natural superiority.

584. I.e., literally, to fall into a passion.

585. Neville will of course shortly recommend the creation of a complex suite of councils to guide the monarch in the exercise of his prerogative. His objection to

shew hereafter; nor is the King obliged by any Fundamental Law, or by any Act of Parliament to hearken to their Advice, or so much as to ask it; and if you should make one on purpose, besides that it would not be so effectual as what we may propose, it would be full as hard to go down either with King or Parliament. But besides all this, you would see some of these Counsellours so nominated by Parliament, perhaps prove honest, and then they would be forced to withdraw as some lately did,[586]

---

the Privy Council is that it was selected by the monarch and thus tended to come between the king and Parliament. A recognition of the need for the king to be guided by a council was not by any means confined to republicans, as Clarendon's explanation of its utility makes clear: "The truth is, the sinking and near desperate condition of monarchy in this kingdom can never be buoyed up but by a prudent and steady Council attending upon the virtue and vivacity of the king; nor be preserved and improved when it is up but by cherishing and preserving the wisdom, integrity, dignity, and reputation of that Council: the lustre whereof always reflects upon the king himself, who is not thought a great monarch when he follows the reins of his own reason and appetite, but when, for the informing his reason and guiding his actions, he uses the service, industry, and faculties of the wisest men. And though it hath been, and will be, always necessary to admit to those Councils some men of great power who will not take the pains to have great parts, yet the number of the whole should not be too great, and the capacities and qualities of the most [should be] fit for business; that is, either for judgment and despatch, or for one of them at least; and integrity above all" (Clarendon, *History*, lib. 3, §53; vol. 1, p. 261). Cf. *Antidotum*, pp. 217–27. The matter was topical when *Plato Redivivus* was first published. On 21 April 1679 Charles had informed Parliament that "he had this day established a new Privy Council, the number of which should never exceed thirty: That he had made choice of such persons as were worthy, and able to advise, and was resolved, in all his weighty and important affairs, next to the advice of his Great Council in Parliament . . . to be advised by this Privy Council" (Grey, *Debates*, vol. 7, p. 129). See immediately below, n. 586. Cf. Waller's comments in the House of Commons on 23 November 1692: "'Cabinet-Council' is not a word to be found in our Law-books. We knew it not before; we took it for a nick-name. Nothing can fall out more unhappily than to have a distinction made of the 'Cabinet' and 'Privy-Council'" (Grey, *Debates*, vol. 10, p. 276).

586. A reference to a recent administrative experiment. After the fall of Danby in 1679 (see above, p. 145, n. 245) "Charles tried to overcome his difficulties by a reconstruction of the ministry which was also intended, perhaps not seriously, to inaugurate a new constitutional system. It was undertaken partly or mainly on the advice of Sir William Temple, and he was probably the inventor of its curiously doctrinaire constitutional arrangement. The privy council had grown too large. It was dismissed and a new council set up, which was to have some thirty members arranged in categories. Half were to be ministers and half without office. There

because they found, I suppose, that till the Administration be alter'd, it is impossible that their Councils can be imbraced, or any thing be acted by them which may tend to the good of their Country; those who have not so great a sence of Honour and Integrity, will be presently corrupted by their own Interest, whilst the Prince is left in possession of all those baits and means to answer such Mens expectations: It being most certain, that if you have a musty Vessel, and by consequence dislike the Beer which comes out of it, and draw it out, causing the Barrel to be immediately fill'd with good and sound Liquor, it is certain by experience, that both your new Drink, and all that ever you shall put into the Cask, till it be taken in pieces, and the Pipes shaved, and new model'd, will be full as musty, and unsavoury as the first which you found fault with.

Noble Venetian. Now, Sir, I think we are at an end of our Questions, and I for my part am convinced, that as the King cannot better himself any way by falling out with his people at this time, so that his goodness and wisdom is such, that he will rather chuse to imitate the most glorious and generous of his predecessors, as *Edward* the First, and *Edward* the Third,

---

were to be two ecclesiastics, two dukes, two earls, and so on. This body, the king announced, was to transact all business, and there was in future to be no hole-and-corner cabinet. On its political side this was an attempt to combine both parties in the king's service: Shaftesbury was made president of the council. But no constitutional conjuring trick could alter the disposition of forces and reconcile their conflicts. The new council soon proved in its turn too large, and the main business was settled in private meetings of ministers which resembled cabinets though they were not so called. The king, instead of accepting the advice of the majority of the council, preferred that of the ministers who were on the side of the prerogative, such as Sunderland and Laurence Hyde, later earl of Rochester, and first lord of the treasury. He did not win over the opposition leaders, and the resistance of parliament went angrily on. . . . Charles therefore gave up the new scheme of government" (Sir George Clark, *The Later Stuarts 1660–1714*, second edition [Oxford: Clarendon Press, 1955], pp. 97–98; see also Macaulay, "Sir William Temple," in his *Critical and Historical Essays* [London: Longmans, 1877], pp. 442–54, and E. R. Turner, "The Privy Council of 1679," *English Historical Review*, 30 (1915), pp. 251–70). For a contemporary response, see Sydney, *Letters*, pp. 31–35. As Ralph Montagu (1638–1709) had said disparagingly in the House of Commons, this new council "is to put new wine into old bottles, and new cloth to piece up an old garment" (Grey, *Debates*, vol. 7, p. 189).

than those who were of less worth, and more unfortunate, as *Edward* the Second, and *Richard* the Second. And therefore we are now ready to hear what you would think fit to ask of so excellent a Prince.

English Gentleman. I never undertook to be so Presumptuous; there is a Parliament to sit speedily,[587] and certainly they are the fittest every way to search into such matters; and to anticipate their wisdom would be unreasonable, and might give them just offence. But because all this tittle tattle may not go for nothing, I shall presume to give you my thoughts, how the Cure must be wrought, without descending to particulars. The Cause Immediate (as we have said) of our Disease, is the inexecution of our Laws; and it is most true, that when that is alter'd for the better, and that all our Laws are duly executed, we are in health; for as we can never have the entire benefit of them, till our Government is upon a right Basis; so whenever we enjoy this happiness, to have the full benefit of those Constitutions, which were made by our Ancestors for our safe and orderly living, our Government is upon a right Basis; therefore we must enquire into the Cause why our Laws are not executed, & when you have found and taken away that Cause, all is well. The Cause can be no other than this, That the King is told, and does believe, that most of these great Charters or Rights of the people, of which we now chiefly treat, are against his Majesties Interest, though this be very false (as has been said) yet we will not dispute it at this time, but take it for granted, so that the King having the Supreme execution of the Laws in his hand, cannot be reasonably supposed to be willing to execute them whenever he can chuse whether he will do it or no; it being natural for every man not to do any thing against his own Interest when he can help it; now when you have thought well what it should be that gives the King a Liberty to chuse whether any part of the Law shall be currant or no, you will find that it is the great Power the King enjoys in the Government; when the Parliament hath discovered this, they will no doubt demand of his Majesty an abate-

587. After the dissolution on 12 July 1679, Parliament would next assemble on 21 March 1681.

ment of his Royal Prerogative [588] in those matters only which concern our enjoyment of our All, that is our Lives, Liberties and Estates, and leave his Royal Power entire and untoucht in all the other branches of it; when this is done, we shall be as if some great Heroe had performed the adventure of dissolving the Inchantment we have been under so many years. And all our Statutes from the highest to the lowest, from *Magna Charta* to that for burying in Woollen, [589] will be current, and we shall neither fear the bringing in Popery, nor Arbitrary Power in the Intervals of Parliament, neither will there be any Dissentions in them; all Causes of Factions between the Country and Court-party [590] being entirely abolisht; so that the People shall have no reason to distrust their Prince, nor he them.

588. I.e., the special right or privilege exercised by a monarch over all other persons (*OED*, s.v. "prerogative," 2a). In England the royal prerogative included the right of sending and receiving ambassadors, making treaties, making war and concluding peace, conferring honors, nominating to bishoprics, choosing ministers of state, summoning Parliament, refusing assent to a bill, and pardoning those under legal sentence; with many other political, ecclesiastical, and judicial privileges. The origin, scope, and exercise of the prerogative created a point of friction between the Crown and Parliament in the later seventeenth century; see above, p. 175, n. 304. The defenders of Stuart monarchy tended to think of the royal prerogative as above or outside the law; others, such as Andrew Marvell in *An Account of the Growth of Popery and Arbitrary Government* (1677), insisted that the king's "very Prerogative is no more then what the Law has determined" (Marvell, *Prose Works*, vol. 2, p. 225)—in other words, that the prerogative was subsequent, not antecedent, to law. For Neville's summary of those elements in the prerogative that were in his opinion burdensome or a drag upon efficient and just administration, see below, pp. 293–96. With *Plato Redivivus* Neville was hoping to strike during a crisis in Stuart monarchy and at a moment when Charles himself seemed to realize that he could not simply invoke his prerogative and needed to gather around himself a broader political coalition, as Algernon Sidney had noted as recently as 1679: "The *King* certainly inclines not to be so stiff as formerly in advancing only those that exalt *Prerogative*" (Sydney, *Letters*, p. 24).

589. The Burying in Woollen Acts (18 & 19 Cha. II c. 4, 30 Cha. II c. 3, and 32 Cha. II c. 1) required the dead to be buried in English woollen shrouds to the exclusion of foreign textiles. The last of these acts had been passed in 1680, so here Neville is once again very topical. Waller had wittily objected to the bill introduced in 1678, observing, "Our Saviour was buried in Linnen. 'Tis a thing against the Customs of Nations, and I am against it" (Grey, *Debates*, vol. 5, p. 155).

590. In "Of the Parties of Great Britain," Hume would define these two groupings as the fundamental parties of principle in English politics: "Were the British government proposed as a subject of speculation, one would immediately perceive

Doctor. You make us a fine Golden Age; but after all this, will you not be pleased to shew us a small prospect of this *Canaan*,[591] or Country of rest; will you not vouchsafe to particularize a little what Powers there are in the King, which you would have discontinued? would you have such Prerogatives abolished, or placed elsewhere?

English Gentleman. There can be no Government if they be abolished. But I will not be like a Man who refuses to sing amongst his Friends at their entreaty, because he has an ill Voice; I will rather suffer my self to be laught at by you in delivering my small Judgment in this Matter, but still with this protestation, that I do believe that an Infinity of Men better qualifi'd than my self for such sublime Matters, and much more the House of Commons, who represent the Wisdom as well as the Power of this Kingdom, may find out a far better way, than my poor parts and Capacity can suggest. The powers then which now being in the Crown do hinder the execution of our Laws, and prevent by consequence our happiness and settlement, are four; The absolute power of making War and peace, Treaties and Alliances with all Nations in the World, by which means, by Ignorant Councellours, or Wicked Ministers, many of our former Kings have made Confederations and Wars, very contrary,

---

in it a source of division and party, which it would be almost impossible for it, under any administration, to avoid. The just balance between the republican and monarchical part of our constitution is really, in itself, so extremely delicate and uncertain, that, when joined to men's passions and prejudices, it is impossible but different opinions must arise concerning it, even among persons of the best understanding. Those of mild tempers, who love peace and order, and detest sedition and civil wars, will always entertain more favourable sentiments of monarchy, than men of bold and generous spirits, who are passionate lovers of liberty, and think no evil comparable to subjection and slavery. And though all reasonable men agree in general to preserve our mixed government; yet, when they come to particulars, some will incline to trust greater powers to the crown, to bestow on it more influence, and to guard against its encroachments with less caution, than others who are terrified at the most distant approaches of tyranny and despotic power. Thus are there parties of Principle involved in the very nature of our constitution, which may properly enough be denominated those of Court and Country" (Hume, *Essays*, pp. 64–65).

591. The promised land of the Israelites; hence, by extension, any ideal or sought-after place or situation.

and destructive to the Interest of *England*, and by the unfortunate management of them, have often put the Kingdom in great hazard of Invasion: Besides that, as long as there is a distinction made between the
Court-party and that of the Country, there will ever be a Jealousie in the
people, that those wicked Councellours (who may think they can be safe
no other way) will make Alliances with powerful Princes, in which there
may be a secret Article [592] by which those Princes shall stipulate to assist
them with Forces upon a short warning to curb the Parliament, and possibly to change the Government. And this apprehension in the People
will be the less unreasonable, because *Oliver Cromwel* (the great Pattern
of some of our Courtiers) is notoriously known to have Inserted an Article in his Treaty with Cardinal *Mazzarin*, during this King of *France*'s
Minority, That he should be assisted with ten thousand Men from *France*
upon occasion to preserve and defend him in his Usurped Government,
against His Majesty that now is, or the People of *England*, or in fine, his
own Army, whose revolt he often feared.[593] The Second great Prerogative

592. By the Secret Treaty of Dover (1 June 1670) between England and France it
had been agreed (1) that Charles would convert to Roman Catholicism; (2) that
England would support a French invasion of the Dutch Republic with sixty war-
ships and 4,000 troops; (3) that Louis would pay Charles a yearly pension of
£230,000; and (4) that 6,000 French troops would be sent to England in the event
of any rebellion against Charles.

593. On the dates of the minority of Louis XIV, see above, p. 198, n. 361.
Cromwell negotiated two treaties with Cardinal Mazarin, one signed on 24 October 1655 and the other on 13/23 March 1657 (the Treaty of Paris). Cromwell had been
concerned that the French would support domestic attempts to unseat him, and on
10 April 1655 Mazarin wrote to Bordeaux, the French ambassador in England, asking him to assure Cromwell that "we are not to be persuaded to be interested in all
those attempts, which are made to weaken his authority. . . . We would never hearken here, directly or indirectly, to any propositions of commotions in England" (*A
Collection of the State Papers of John Thurloe*, 7 vols [1742], vol. 3, p. 327). It was the
second of these treaties that contained secret articles providing for mutual military
aid, although worded in less inflammatory language than Neville suggests. Cf. *Antidotum*, p. 185, and *Antimonarchical Authors*, p. 225. For censure of Cromwell's policy toward France, broadly contemporary with *Plato Redivivus*, see Slingsby Bethel,
The World's Mistake in Oliver Cromwell (1668), reprinted in *State-Tracts*, vol. 1,
pp. 366–74, relevant passages on pp. 370–71. For modern scholarly commentary on
the question of Interregnum diplomacy, see David L. Smith, "Diplomacy and the
Religious Question: Mazarin, Cromwell, and the Treaties of 1655 and 1657," *E-rea*,

the King enjoys, is the sole Disposal and Ordering of the Militia[594] by Sea and Land, Raising Forces, Garisoning and Fortifying places, Setting out Ships of War, so far as he can do all this without putting Taxations upon the People; and this not only in the Intervals of Parliament, but even during their Session; so that they cannot raise the Train-bands[595] of the Country or City to Guard themselves, or secure the Peace of the Kingdom. The third point is, That it is in His Majesties Power to Nominate and Appoint as he pleases, and for what time he thinks fit, all the Officers of the Kingdom that are of Trust or profit, both Civil, Military, and Ecclesiastical, (as they will be called) except where there is *Jus Patronatus*;[596] These two last Powers may furnish a Prince who will hearken to ill designing Councellours, with the means either of Invading the Government by Force, or by his Judges and other Creatures undermining it by Fraud; Especially by enjoying the Fourth Advantage, which is the Laying out and Imploying, as he pleases, all the Publick Revenues of the Crown or Kingdom, and that without having any regard (except he thinks fit) to the necessity of the Navy, or any other thing that concerns the Safety of the Publick. So that all these Four great Powers, as things now stand, may be adoperated[597] at

---

II, no. 2 (2014); François Saulnier, *La diplomatie française et la République d'Angleterre, 1649–1658*, diss., Université de Paris IV Sorbonne, 1999; and Steven Pincus, *Protestantism and Patriotism: Ideologies and the Making of English Foreign Policy, 1650–1668* (Cambridge: Cambridge University Press, 1996).

594. The preamble to the Militia Act of 1661 (13 Car. II c. 6) begins, "Forasmuch as within all his Majesty's realms and dominions the sole supreme government, command and disposition of the militia and of all forces by sea and land and of all forts and places of strength is and by the laws of England ever was the undoubted right of his Majesty and his royal predecessors, Kings and Queens of England, and that both or either of the Houses of Parliament cannot nor ought to pretend to the same, nor can nor lawfully may raise or levy any war, offensive or defensive, against his Majesty, his heirs or lawful successors, and yet the contrary thereof hath of late years been practised, almost to the ruin and destruction of this kingdom, and during the late usurped governments many evil and rebellious principles have been distilled into the minds of the people of this kingdom, which unless prevented may break forth, to the disturbance of the peace and quiet thereof" (Kenyon, *Stuart Constitution*, p. 374).

595. See above, p. 223, n. 419.

596. In ecclesiastical law, the right possessed by a private person of presenting a clerk to a benefice.

597. See above, p. 249, n. 484.

any time, as well to destroy and ruine the good Order and Government of the State, as to preserve and support it, as they ought to do.

Noble Venetian. But if you divest the King of these Powers, will you have the Parliament sit always to Govern these Matters?

English Gentleman. Sir, I would not divest the King of them, much less would I have the Parliament assume them, or perpetuate their Sitting: They are a Body more fitted to make Laws, and punish the Breakers of them, than to execute them. I would have them therefore petition His Majesty by way of Bill, that he will please to exercise these four great *Magnalia*[598] of Government, with the Consent of four several Councils to be appointed for that end, and not otherwise; that is, with the Consent of the Major part of them, if any of them dissent. In all which Councils His Majesty, or who he pleases to appoint, shall preside; the Councils to be named in Parliament; first all the number, and every Year afterwards a third part: So each Year a third part shall go out,[599] and a Recruit of an equal number come in: And in three Years they shall be all new, and no Person to come into that Council, or any other of the four, till he have kept out of any of them full three Years, being as long as he was in. And this I learnt from your *Quarantia's*[600] at *Venice:* and the Use is excellent; for being in such a Circulation, and sure to have their intervals of Power, they will neither grow so insolent as to brave their King, nor will the Prince have any occasion to corrupt them, although he had the means to do it, which in this new Model he cannot have. These Men in their several Councils should have no other instructions, but to dispose of all

598. I.e., great or wonderful things (*OED*, s.v. "magnalia"); in 1680 already on the verge of becoming obsolete; occasionally used in Parliament in the mid-seventeenth century (e.g., Burton, *Diary*, vol. 4, p. 143).

599. An introduction into English politics of the Venetian principle of the rota, which had made so strong an impression on both James Harrington and Neville himself. See, in particular, Harrington's *The Manner and Use of the Ballot* (Pocock, *Harrington*, pp. 361–67). It was perhaps elements such as this in *Plato Redivivus* that led some of Neville's first readers to the conclusion that he proposed to cast the English constitution into a Venetian form: see, e.g., Edward Pelling, *A Sermon Preached at Westminster-Abbey* (1685), pp. 27–28.

600. See above, p. 185, n. 330.

things, and act in their several Charges, for the Interest and Glory of *England*; and shall be Answerable to Parliament, from time to time, for any malicious or advised Misdemeanor: only that Council which manages the Publick Revenue, shall (besides a very copious and Honourable Revenue which shall be left to His Majesty's disposal for his own Entertainment, as belongs to the Splendor and Majesty of the Government) have Instructions to serve His Majesty (if he pleases to command them, and not otherwise) in the regulating and ordering his Oeconomy and Houshold; and if they shall see it necessary, for extraordinary Occasions of treating Foreign Princes and Ambassadors, or Presenting them, and the like Ostentation of Greatness; to consent with His Majesty moderately to charge the Revenue to that end. I verily believe that this Expedient is much more effectual than either the *Justitia* of *Aragon*[601] was, or the *Ephores* of *Sparta*:[602] Who being to check the King almost in every thing, without having any share in his Councils, or understanding them, could not chuse but make a sullen posture of Affairs; whereas these both seem, and really are the King's Ministers, only obliged by Parliament to act faithfully and honestly; to which, even without that, all other Councellors are bound by Oath. As for the other Council, now called the Privy Council, the King may still please to continue to nominate them at his pleasure, so they act nothing in any of the Matters properly within the Jurisdiction of these four Councils, but meddle with the Affairs of Merchants, Plantations, Charters, and other Matters, to which the Regal Power extendeth. And provided that His Majesty call none of the Persons employed in these other four Councils during their being so, nor that this Council do any way intermeddle with any Affairs, Criminal or Civil, which are to be decided by Law, and do belong to the Jurisdictions of other Courts or Magistrates, they being no established Judicatory, or Congregation, which either our Government or Laws do take notice of (as was said before) but Persons congregated by the King, as his Friends and faithful Subjects, to give him their Opinion in the Execution of his Regal Office. As for Example, the King does exercise, at this time, a Negative Voice as to Bills presented to him by the Parliament, which he

601. See above, p. 207, n. 381.
602. See above, p. 279, n. 557.

claims by Right; no Man ever said that the Privy Council had a Negative Voice; yet former Kings did not only ask their Advice as to the passing or not passing of such Bills, but often decided the Matter by their Votes; which, although it be a high Presumption in them, when they venture to give him Council contrary to what is given him by his greatest Council, yet never any of them have been questioned for it; being looked upon as private Men, who speak according to the best of their Cunning, and such as have no publick Capacity at all. But if this be not so, and that this Council have some Foundation in Law, and some publick Capacity, I wish in this new Settlement it may be made otherwise, and that His Majesty please to take their Counsel in private; but summon no Persons to appear before them; much less give them Authority to send for in Custody, or Imprison any Subject, which may as well be done by the Judges and Magistrates; who, if Secrecy be required, may as well be Sworn to Secrecy as these Gentlemen; and I believe can keep Counsel as well, and give it too.

Noble Venetian. But would you have none to manage State-Affairs, none Imprisoned for secret Conspiracies, and kept till they can be fully discovered? you have made an Act here lately about Imprisonments, that every Person shall have his *Habeas Corpus*,[603] I think you call it: so that no Man, for what occasion soever, can lie in Prison above a Night, but the Cause must be revealed, though there be great cause for the concealing it.

---

603. The act of 1641 abolishing the Star Chamber (16 Car. I, c. 10) had established that any man imprisoned by order of the king or the council was entitled to a writ of habeas corpus from King's Bench or Common Pleas, and that in response the jailer must certify the cause of imprisonment. But the scope of this act did not cover the increasingly common case of imprisonment on the orders of a secretary of state; nor did it cover imprisonment in the Channel Islands (see, e.g., Burton, *Diary*, vol. 3, p. 46, and vol. 4, pp. 159 and 162, in respect of the imprisonment of Overton in Jersey; cf. Grey, *Debates*, vol. 1, p. 237, and vol. 2, p. 349). In the 1670s various attempts were made to remedy these defects, but they were lost either in the Lords or by the prorogation of Parliament. Finally in 1679 the "Habeas Corpus Amendment Act" (31 Car. II, c. 2) was passed, which strengthened the existing legislation by specifying the procedure for the issuing of the writ, setting a time limit for the hearing, and forbidding the transportation of prisoners overseas. See G. Davies and E. L. Klotz, "The Habeas Corpus Act of 1679 in the House of Lords," *Huntington Library Quarterly*, 3, no. 4 (1940), pp. 469–70.

English Gentleman. This Act you mention, and a great many more[604] which we have to the same purpose, that is, against Illegal Imprisonments, shews that for a long time the Power over Men's Persons has been exercised (under His Majesty) by such as were very likely, rather to employ it ill than well; (that is) would rather Imprison ten Men for Honourable Actions; such as standing for the People's Rights in Parliament, refusing to pay Illegal Taxes, and the like; than one for projecting and inventing Illegal Monopolies, or any other kind of oppressing the People. This made first *Magna Charta*, then the *Petition of Right*,[605] and divers other Acts besides this last, take that Power quite away, and make the Law and the Judges the only Disposers of the Liberties of our Persons. And it may be, when the Parliament shall see the Fruit of this Alteration we are now discoursing of, and that State-Affairs are in better hands, they may think fit to provide that a Return, or Warrant of Imprisonment from one of these Four Councils (which I suppose will have a Power of Commitment given them, as to Persons appearing Delinquents before them) wherein it shall be expressed, That if the Publick is like to suffer or be defrauded, if the Matter be immediately divulged; I say in this Case, the Parliament may please to make it Lawful for the Judge to delay the Bailing of him for some small time, because it is not to be judged, that these Councellours so chosen, and so instructed, and to continue so small a time, will use this Power ill; especially being accountable for any abusing of it to the next Parliament. And I suppose the Parliament, amongst other Provisions in this behalf, will require that there shall be a Register kept of all the Votes of these several Councils, with the names as well of those who consented, as of such who dissented: And as to the former part of your Question, whether I would have none to manage State Affairs; I think there are very few State Affairs that do not concern either Peace and War, and Treaties abroad, the management of the Arms, Militia, and *posse Comitatus*[606] at home; the management of all the Publick Moneys, and the Election of all Officers whatsoever; the other parts, of State Affairs, which are Making and Repealing of Laws, punishing

604. See above, p. 298, n. 603.
605. See above, p. 184, n. 327.
606. See above, p. 93, n. 106.

high Crimes against the State, with Levying and Proportioning all manner of Impositions upon the People, this is reserved to the Parliament it self; and the Execution of all Laws to the Judges, and Magistrates; And I can think of no other Affairs of State than these.

Doctor. Do you intend that the Council for chusing Officers shall Elect them of the King's Houshold, that is, his Menial Servants?

English Gentleman. No, that were unreasonable, except any of them have any Jurisdiction in the Kingdom, or any place or preheminence in Parliament annexed to such Office; but in these things which concern the powers and Jurisdictions of these several Councils (wherein, *la guardia della liberta*, as *Machiavil* calls it,[607] is now to be placed) I shall not presume to say any thing, but assure your self, if ever it come to that, it will be very well digested in Parliament, they being very good at contriving such Matters, and making them practicable, as well as at performing all other Matters that concern the Interest and greatness of the Kingdom.

Doctor. I have thought that the *Ephores* of *Sparta* were an admirable Magistracy, not only for the Interest of the People, but likewise for the preservation of the authority of the Kings, and of their lives too; for *Plutarch* observes that the Cities of *Mesene* and *Argos* had the same Government with *Lacedemon*, and yet for want of erecting such an Authority as was in the *Ephores*, they were not only perpetually in broils amongst themselves, and for that reason ever beaten by their Enemies, whereas the *Spartans* were always victorious, but even their Kings were the most miserable of Men, being often call'd in question Judicially, and so lost their Lives, and many of them murdered by Insurrections of the People: And at last in both these Cities, the Kings were driven out, their Families extirpated, the Territory new divided, and the Government turn'd into a *Democracy*.[608] And I ever

607. Machiavelli had praised the tribunes as the "guardia della libertà romana" in *Discourses*, lib. 1, cap. 4 (Machiavelli, *Works*, p. 273: "They were constituted as Guardians and Conservators of the Roman liberty").

608. "τῷ γὰρ ὄντι τὸ ἄγαν ἀποβαλοῦσα μετὰ τοῦ φθόνου διέφυγε τὸν κίνδυνον, ὥστε μὴ παθεῖν ἃ Μεσσήνιοι καὶ Ἀργεῖοι τοὺς παρ' αὐτοῖς βασιλεῖς ἔδρασαν,

thought that this expedient you propose (for I have heard you discourse of it often before now) would prove a more safe, and a more noble reformation than the Institution of the *Ephores* was, and that a Prince who is a lover of his Country, who is Gracious, Wise and Just, (such a one as it has pleased God to send us at this time) shall be ten times more absolute when this Regulation is made, than ever he was or could be before; and that whatsoever he proposes in any of these Councils will be received as a Law, nay, as an Oracle: And on the other side, ill and weak Princes shall have no possibility of corrupting Men, or doing either themselves or their People any kind of harm or mischief: But have you done now?

English Gentleman. No, Sir, when this Provision is made for the Execution of the Laws, (which I think very effectual, not to say Infallible) although it is not to be doubted, but that there will be from time to time many excellent Laws Enacted; yet two I would have passed immediately, the one concerning the whole Regulation of the Elections to Parliament, which we need very much, and no doubt but it will be well done; that part of it which is necessary to go hand in hand with our Settlement, and which indeed must be part of it, is, that a Parliament be Elected every year[609] at a certain day, and that without any Writ or Summons, the People Meeting of course at the time appointed in the usual place (as

---

μηδὲν ἐνδοῦναι μηδὲ χαλάσαι τῆς ἐξουσίας ἐπὶ τὸ δημοτικὸν ἐθελήσαντας": "And in fact, by renouncing excessive claims and freeing itself from jealous hatred, royalty at Sparta escaped its perils, so that the Spartan kings did not experience the fate which the Messenians and Argives inflicted upon their kings, who were unwilling to yield at all or remit their power in favour of the people" (Plutarch, *Lycurgus*, 7).

609. On the various laws governing the frequency of parliaments, and the means available to monarchs to avoid holding parliaments, see above, p. 165, n. 285. Calls for yearly elections to Parliament had figured in Leveller manifestos, such as *An Agreement of the Free People of England* (1649), clause 8: "And for the preservation of the supreme Authority (in all times) entirely in the hands of such persons only as shal be chosen thereunto—we agree and declare: That the next & al future Representatives, shall continue in full power for the space of one whole year: and that the people shall of course, chuse a Parliament once every year" (Morton, *Freedom*, p. 270; cf. pp. 40 and 190). *An Agreement of the People* (1647), clause 3, had called for biennial elections (Morton, *Freedom*, p. 140).

they do in Parishes at the Church-House[610] to chuse Officers) and that the Sheriffs be there ready to preside and to certifie the Election. And that the Parliament so Chosen shall Meet at the time appointed, and Sit and Adjourn as their business is more or less urgent: But still setting yet a time for their coming together again; but if there shall be a necessity (by reason of Invasion or some other Cause) for their Assembling sooner, then the King to Call the Councellors of these Four Councels all together, and with the consent of the major part of them, intimate their Meeting sooner; but when the day comes for the Annual Meeting of Another Parliament, they must be understood to be Dissolved in Law, without any other Ceremony, and the new one to take their place.

Doctor. I would have this considered too, and provided for, That no Election should be made of any person who had not the majority of the Electors present to Vote for him; so the Writ orders it, and so Reason dictates; for else, how can he be said to represent the County, if not a fifth part have consented to his choice, as happens sometimes, and may do oftener? for where seven or eight stand for one vacant place, as I have know in our last Long Parliament, where the Votes being set in Columns, he who has had most Votes, has not exceeded four hundred of above two thousand who were present.

Noble Venetian. This is a strange way; I thought you had put every Man by himself, as we do in our Government, and as I understood they do in the House of Commons, when there is any nomination, and then, if he has not the major part, he is rejected.

English Gentleman. This is very Material, and indeed Essential; but I make no doubt, but if this Project should come in play in Parliament, this and all other particulars (which would be both needless and tedious to discourse of here) will be well and effectually provided for. The next Act I

---

610. I.e., a house owned by a church; a building next to a church in which social events, meetings, and other events connected with the church are held; a church hall. Also: a house provided by the church for a member of the clergy; a parochial house (*OED*, s.v. "church house").

would have passed, should be concerning the House of Peers, that as I take it for granted, that there will be a Clause in the Bill concerning Elections, that no new Boroughs shall be enabled to send Members to Parliament, except they shall be capacitated thereunto by an Act; so it being of the same necessity as to the Liberty of Parliament, that the Peers (who do and must enjoy both a Negative and Deliberative Voice in all Parliamentary Transactions, except what concern Levying of Money Originally) be exempted from depending absolutely upon the Prince, and that therefore it be declared by Act, for the future, that no Peer shall be made but by Act of Parliament, and then that it be Hereditary in his Male Line.[611]

Noble Venetian. I am not yet fully satisfied how you can order your Matters concerning this House of Peers, nor do I see how the Contests between the House of Commons and them, can be so laid asleep but that they will arise again: Besides the House of Commons must necessarily be extreamly concerned to find the House of Peers, which consists of private persons, though very great and honourable ones, in an Instant dash all that they have been so long hammering for the good of all the People of

---

611. Neville's desire to remove the Crown's power to create peers and thereby to influence the decisions of the House of Lords looks forward to those moments in the early eighteenth century when mass creations of peers were used as an instrument of the Crown; for instance, the creation of twelve new peers by Queen Anne in December 1711 to secure a majority for the Court party. Against the background of such mass creations, in 1719 the Stanhope-Sunderland ministry would introduce a Peerage Bill that had three objectives: (1) to protect the ministry from impeachment should the then–Prince of Wales succeed to the throne; (2) to settle the unsatisfactory Scottish representation in the Lords; and (3) to maintain the existing peerage's social position, by limiting creations. The bill laid down that the king could create only six more peerages, then further peers only on the extinction of titles. The sixteen Scottish elected peers were to be replaced by twenty-five hereditary ones. The bill easily passed the Lords but was defeated in the Commons. On Neville's general strategy of preserving externalities but reforming underlying principles, see Machiavelli, *Discourses*, 1.25: "He who desires to set up a new form of Government in a Common-wealth, that shall be lasting, and acceptable to the people, is with great caution to preserve at least some shadow and resemblance of the old, That the people may (if possible) be insensible of the innovation; for the generality of Mankind do not penetrate so far into things, but that outward appearance, is as acceptable to them as verity it self" (Machiavelli, *Works*, p. 296).

England whom they represent; were it not better now, you are upon so great alterations, to make an Annual Elective Senate, or at least one wherein the Members should be but for Life, and not Hereditary.

English Gentleman. By no means, Sir, the less change the better, and in this Case the Metaphysical Maxime is more true than in any, *viz. Entia non sunt multiplicanda sine necessitate*;[612] for great alterations fright Men, and puzzle them, and there is no need of it at all in this Case. I have told you before, that there is a necessity of a Senate, and how short this Government would be without it, and how confused in the mean time; the *Roman* Senate was Hereditary amongst the *Patricii*, except the Censor left any of them out of the Roll during his Magistracy, for some very great and scandalous offence;[613] and in that case too there was an Appeal to the People, as in all other Causes, witness the Case of *Lucius Quintius* and many others. To shew that there can be no need of such a change here as you speak of, you may please to consider, that all differences between the several parts of any Government, come upon the account of Interest; now when this Settlement is made, the House of Peers, and the House of Commons, can have no Interest to dissent; For as to all things of private Interest, that is, the Rights of Peers, both during the sitting of Parliaments, and in the Intervals, is left to their own House to judge of, as it is to the House of Commons to judge of their own Priviledges; And as for the contest of the Peers Jurisdiction as to Appeals from Courts of Equity; Besides that I would have that setled in the Act which should pass concerning the Lords House; I believe it will never happen more, when the Government is upon a right Foundation; it having been hitherto fomented by two different Parties, the Court-party sometimes blowing up that difference to break the Session, lest some good Bills for the People should pass, or that the King by rejecting them, might discontent his People; to avoid which *Dilemma*, there needed no more, but to procure some person to prosecute his Appeal be-

---

612. "Entities should not be multiplied unnecessarily," a statement of the scientific preference for simplicity usually referred to as Occam's razor, although anticipations of it can be found in philosophical writing before William of Occam (c. 1287–1347).

613. See Plutarch, "Marcus Cato," 17.

fore the Lords; some honest Patriots afterwards possibly might use the same policy which they learnt from the Courtiers, to quash some Bill very destructive, in which they were out-voted in the Commons House; otherwise it is so far from the Interest of the Commons to hinder Appeals from Courts of Equity, that there is none amongst them, but know we are almost destroyed for want of it: And when they have considered well, and that some such Reformation as this shall take place; they will find that it can never be placed in a more honourable and unbyas'd Judicatory than this; And I could wish that even in the Intermission of Parliamentary Sessions, the whole Peerage of *England*, as many of them as can conveniently be in Town, may sit in their Judicial Capacities, and hear Appeals in Equity, as well as Judge upon Writs of Errour.[614] Now as to your other Objection (which is indeed of great weight) that the House of Commons must needs take it ill, that the Lords should frustrate their endeavours for the Peoples good by their Negative; If you consider one thing, the force of this Objection will vanish; which is, That when this new Constitution shall be admitted, the Lords cannot have any Interest or temptation to differ with the Commons, in any thing wherein the Publick good is concerned, but are obliged by all the ties in the World, to run the same course and fortune with the Commons, their Interest being exactly the same; so that if there be any dissenting upon Bills between the two Houses, when each of them shall think their own Expedient conduces most to the advantage of the Publick; this difference will ever be decided by right reason at Conferences;[615] And the Lords may as well convince the Commons, as be convinced by them; and these contests are and ever will be of admirable use and benefit to the Commonwealth;[616] the reason why it is otherwise now, and that the House of Peers is made use of to hinder many Bills from

614. See above, p. 182, n. 322.

615. I.e., joint sessions of the Commons and Lords.

616. A translation into an English setting of the Machiavellian principle that dissension in a state can be a source of strength: "Those who object against the tumults betwixt the Nobles and the People [of Rome], do in my opinion condemn those very things which were the first occasion of its freedom, regarding the noise and clamours which do usually follow such commotions, more than the good effects they do commonly produce, not considering that in all Common-wealths there are two opposite humours, one of the People, the other of the Nobless; and

passing, that are supposed to be for the ease of the People, is, that the great Counsellors and Officers which sit in that House, do suggest (whether true or false) that it is against his Majesties Will and Interest that such an Act should pass, whereupon it has found Obstruction; but hereafter if our expedient take place it cannot be so, first, because our King himself cannot have any designs going (as was proved before) which shall make it his advantage to hinder any good intended his people, whose prosperity then will be his own. And then because in a short time, the Peers being made by Act of Parliament, will consist of the best Men of *England* both for Parts and Estates, and those who are already made, if any of them have small Estates, the King if he had the Interest, would not have the means to corrupt them, the Publick Moneys, and the great Offices being to be dispensed in another manner than formerly; so their Lordships will have no Motive in the World to steer their Votes and Councils, but their own Honour and Conscience, and the preservation and prosperity of their Country. So that it would be both needless and unjust to pretend any change of this kind. Besides, this alteration in the administration of our Government being proposed to be done by the unanimous consent of King, Lords, and Commons, and not otherwise, it would be very preposterous to believe, that the Peers would depose themselves of their Hereditary Rights, and betake themselves to the hopes of being Elected; it is true, they have lost the Power they had over the Commons, but that has not been taken from them by any Law, no more than it was given them by any; but is fallen by the course of Nature, as has been shewn at large; But though they cannot lead the Commons by their Tenures, as formerly, yet there is no reason or colour that they should lose their Co-ordination,[617] which I am sure they have by Law, and by the Fundamental Constitution of the Government; and which is so far from being prejudicial to a lasting Settlement (as was said) that it infinitely contributes to it, and prevents the Confusion which would destroy it. If I should have proposed any thing in this Discourse which should

---

that all the Laws which are made in favour of liberty, proceed from the differences betwixt them" (Machiavelli, *Discourses*, 1.4, in Machiavelli, *Works*, p. 273).

617. I.e., the condition of being placed in an equivalent order or rank (*OED*, s.v. "co-ordination," 2).

have Intrenched upon the King's Hereditary Right, or that should have
hindred the Majesty and Greatness of these Kingdoms from being represented by his Royal Person, I should have made your Story of the *Capu-
chine* Fryar[618] very Applicable to me.

Noble Venetian. I see you have not forgiven me that Novel[619] yet; but pray
give me leave to ask you one Question: Why do you make the Election of
Great Officers, to be by a small secret Council, that had been more
proper for a Numerous Assembly; as it is in most Commonwealths?

English Gentleman. It is so in Democracies, and was so in *Sparta,*[620] and
is done by your Great Council in *Venice;*[621] but we are not making such a
kind of Government, but rectifying an ancient Monarchy, and giving the
Prince some help in the Administration of that great Branch of his Re-
gality; besides, it is sufficient, that our Parliament chuses these Councils,
(that is always understood the Lords and Commons, with the Kings
Consent) besides, it is possible, that if such a Regulation as this come in
Debate amongst them, the Parliament will reserve to it self the Approbation of the Great Officers, as Chancellor, Judges, General Officers of an
Army, and the like; and that such shall not have a settlement in those
Charges, till they are accordingly allowed of; but may in the mean time
exercise them. As to particulars, I shall always refer you to what the Par-
liament will judge fit to Order in the Case; but if you have any thing to
Object, or to shew in general, that some such Regulation as this cannot

618. See above, pp. 274–76.

619. I.e., a fable (*OED*, s.v. "novel," 4a).

620. A reference to the Spartan senate, or Council of Elders; Plutarch, *Lycur-gus*, 5–6.

621. "The *Grand Council* is a General Assembly of the *Nobles*, which meets on *Sundays* and *Holydays* for the Election of *Magistrates*" (Amelot de la Houssaie, *Venice*, p. 7; cf. Gailhard, *Italy*, p. 122). Amelot de la Houssaie also drew a compari-son with Sparta in respect of the Venetian Grand Council: "So that the rights of Majesty being equally divided betwixt the *Grand Council*, which consists of all the *Nobles*, and the Senat, which is a select party; the *Republick* of *Venice* may be said to be almost an *Aristo-Democracy*, like that in *Sparta* after the institution of the *Ephori*" (*Venice*, p. 16).

be effectual towards the putting our Distracted Country into better Order; I shall think my self oblig'd to Answer you, if you can have Patience to hear me, and are not weary already; as you may very well be.

Noble Venetian. I shall certainly never be weary of such Discourse; however I shall give you no further trouble in this matter; for I am very fully satisfied, that such Reformation, if it could be compassed, would not only Unite all Parties, but make you very Flourishing at home, and very Great abroad: but have you any hopes that such a thing will ever come into Debate? what do the Parliament-men say to it?

English Gentleman. I never had any Discourse to this purpose, either with any Lord, or Member of the Commons house, otherwise than as possibly some of these Notions might fall in at Ordinary Conversation: For I do not intend to Intrench upon the Office of God, to teach our Senatours Wisdom. I have known some men so full of their own Notions, that they went up and down sputtering them in every Mans Face they met; some went to Great Men during our late troubles; nay, to the King himself, to offer their Expedients from Revelation.[622] Two Men I was acquainted with, of which one had an Invention to reconcile differences in Religion; the other had a project for a Bank of Lands to lye as a Security for summs of Money lent;[623] both these were Persons of Great Parts and Fancy; but yet so troublesome at all Times, and in all Companies, that I have often been forced to repeat an Excellent Proverb of your Country:[624] God deliver me from a man that has but one business; and I assure you there is no Mans Reputation that I

---

622. Apparently a mocking reference to the political schemes of religious radicals, such as the Ranters, of which the language often recalls that of the book of Revelation. See, e.g., Joseph Salmon, *A Rout, a Rout* (1649), in *A Collection of Ranter Writings from the Seventeenth Century,* ed. Nigel Smith (London: Junction Books, 1983), p. 193.

623. Robbins speculates that Neville may here be referring to Nicholas Philpot, whose proposal for a land registry, *Reasons and Proposals,* had been published in 1671, and to the anonymous author ("a Gent of the Middle Temple") of the more recent *The Grounds of Unity in Religion* (1679).

624. Perhaps "Dio mi guardi da chi studia un libro solo," or "Fear the man of one book."

envy less, than I do that of such Persons; and therefore you may please to believe that I have not imitated them in scattering these Notions, nor can I Prophesie whether any such Apprehensions as these will ever come into the Heads of those men who are our true Physitians. But yet to answer your Question, and give you my Conjecture; I believe that we are not Ripe yet for any great Reform; not only because we are a very Debauch'd People; I do not only mean that we are given to Whoring, Drinking, Gaming and Idleness; but chiefly that we have a Politique Debauch, which is a neglect of all things that concern the publick welfare, and a setting up our own private Interest against it; I say, this is not all, for then the Polity of no Country could be Redrest: For every Commonwealth that is out of order, has ever all these Debauches we speak of, as Consequences of their loose State. But there are two other Considerations which induce me to fear that our Cure is not yet near. The first is, because most of the Wise and Grave Men of this Kingdom are very silent, and will not open their Budget[625] upon any terms: and although they dislike the present Condition we are in as much as any Men, and see the Precipice it leads us to, yet will never open their Mouths to prescribe a Cure; but being asked what they would advise, give a shrug like your Countrymen. There was a very considerable Gentle-man[626] as most in *England*, both for Birth, Parts, and Estate, who being a Member of the Parliament that was called, 1640.[627] continued all the War with them; and by his Wisdom and Eloquence (which were both very great) promoted very much their Affairs. When the Factions began be-tween the Presbyters and Independents, he joyned Cordially with the lat-ter, so far as to give his Affirmative to the Vote of No Addresses;[628] that is,

625. I.e., speak their mind candidly (*OED*, s.v. "budget," 1c).

626. William Pierrepont (1607–78), presbyterian and moderate Parliamentarian statesman; member of the 1642 Committee of Safety (see above, p. 277, n. 552); younger son of Robert Pierrepont (1584–1643), first earl of Kingston-upon-Hull.

627. I.e., the Long Parliament.

628. On 17 January 1648, on learning that Charles I was entering into an engagement with the Scots, the Long Parliament broke off negotiations with the king. Four resolutions were passed: "1. That the Lords and Commons do declare that they will make no further addresses or applications to the King. 2. That no application or addresses be made to the King by any person whatso-ever, without the leave of both Houses. 3. That the person or persons that shall

to an Order made in the House of Commons, to send no more Messages to the King, nor to receive any from him. Afterwards, when an Assault was made upon the House by the Army, and divers of the Members taken violently away, and Secluded;[629] he disliking it (though he were none of them) voluntarily absented himself, and continued retired; being exceedingly averse to a Democratical Government, which was then declared for, till *Cromwell*'s Usurpation; and being infinitely courted by him, absolutely refused to accept of any Employment under him, or to give him the least Counsel. When *Cromwell* was dead, and a Parliament called[630] by his Son, or rather by the Army, the chief Officers of which did, from the beginning, whisper into the Ears of the Leading Members, that if they could make an honest Government, they should be stood by (as the Word then was) by the Army. This Gentleman, at that time, neither would be Elected into that Parliament, nor give the least Advice to any other Person that was; but kept himself still upon the Reserve. Insomuch that it was generally believed, that although he had ever been opposite to the late King's coming to the Government again, though upon Propositions; yet he might hanker after the Restoration of His Majesty that now is. But that Apprehension appeared groundless when it came to the pinch: for being consulted as an Oracle by the then General *Monk*,[631] whether he should restore the Monarchy again or no, would make no Answer, nor give him the least Advice; and, *de facto*, hath ever since kept himself from Publick Business; although, upon the Banishment of my Lord of *Clarendon*,[632] he was visited by one of

---

make breach of this order shall incur the penalties of high treason. 4. That the two Houses declare they will receive no more any message from the King; and do enjoin that no person whatsoever do presume to receive or bring any message from the King to both or either of the Houses of Parliament, or to any other person."

629. A reference to the purging of the Long Parliament ("Pride's Purge") on 7 December 1648, when the army arrested forty-one members of Parliament.

630. The so-called Third Protectorate Parliament, summoned on 9 December 1658 and dissolved on 22 April.

631. George Monck or Monk (1608–70), Parliamentarian army and naval officer, later first Duke of Albemarle; broker and architect of the restoration of Charles II in 1660.

632. Edward Hyde (1609–74), Royalist statesman and historian of the Civil Wars; later first Earl of Clarendon. In the aftermath of a series of disasters and the unsuccessful conclusion of the Second Dutch War (1664–67), Clarendon was sac-

the Greatest Persons in *England*,[633] and one in as much Esteem with His Majesty as any whatsoever, and desired to accept of some great Employment near the King; which he absolutely refusing, the same Person, not a Stranger to him, but well known by him, begged of him to give his Advice how His Majesty (who desired nothing more than to unite all his People together, and repair the Breaches which the Civil War had caused, now my Lord *Clarendon* was gone, who by his Counsels kept those Wounds open) might perform that Honourable and Gracious Work: but still this Gentleman made his Excuses. And, in short, neither then, nor at any time before or after (excepting when he sate in the Long Parliament of the Year 40.) neither during the distracted Times, nor since His Majesty's Return, when they seemed more reposed, would ever be brought, either by any private intimate Friend, or by any Person in Publick Employment, to give the least Judgment of our Affairs, or the least Counsel to mend them, though he was not shye of declaring his dislike of Matters as they went. And yet this Gentleman was not only by repute, and esteem a wise Man, but was really so, as it appeared by his management of business, and drawing Declarations, when he was contented to act; as also by his exceeding prudent managing of his own Fortune, which was very great, and his honourable Living and providing for his Family; his Daughters[634] having been all Marryed to the best Men in *England*; and his Eldest Son[635] to the most accomplisht Lady in the World. I dare assure you, there are above an hundred such Men in *England*, though not altogether of that eminency.

Noble Venetian. Methinks these persons are altogether as bad an extreme as the loquacious men you spoke of before. I remember when I went to

---

rificed to appease public discontent. He was dismissed on 10 October 1667 and impeached on charges including high treason on 11 November. On 30 November he went into exile in France, where he died on 9 December 1674.

633. Unidentified.

634. The marriages contracted by Pierrepont's three daughters were Frances (1629/30–95) to Henry Cavendish (1630–91), second Duke of Newcastle in 1653; Grace (d. 1702) to Gilbert Holles (1633–89), third Earl of Clare in 1655; and Gertrude (1640/41–1727) to George Savile (1633–95), first Marquess of Halifax in 1672.

635. Pierrepont's eldest son, Robert Pierrepont, married Elizabeth, née Evelyn (d. 1692). Their son, Evelyn (1667–1726), was the first Duke of Kingston upon Hull, and the father of Lady Mary Wortley Montagu.

School, our Master, amongst other Common-places in the commenda-
tion of silence, would tell us of a Latine saying,[636] That a Fool whilst he
held his peace did not differ from a Wise man; but truly I think we may
as truly say, That a wise man whilst he is silent does not differ from a
Fool; for how great soever his Wisdom is, it can neither get him credit,
nor otherwise advantage himself, his Friend, nor his Country. But let me
not divert you from your other point.

English Gentleman. The next Reason I have to make me fear that such an
Expedient as we have been talking of, will not be proposed suddenly, is the
great distrust the Parliament has of men, which will make most Members
shy of venturing at such matters, which being very new, at the first motion
are not perfectly understood, at least to such as have not been versed in Authors who have written of the Politicks;[637] and therefore the Mover may be
suspected of having been set on by the Court-party to puzzle them, and so
to divert, by offering new Expedients, some smart mettlesome Debates they
may be upon concerning the Succession to the Crown, or other high
matters: For it is the nature of all Popular Counsels (even the wisest that
ever were, witness the people of *Rome* and *Athens*, which *Machiavil* so much
extols)[638] in turbulent times, to like discourses that heighten their passions,
and blow up their Indignation, better than them that endeavour to rectifie
their Judgments, and tend to provide for their safety. And the truth is, our
Parliament is very much to be excused, or rather justified in this distrust
they have of persons, since there hath been of late so many and so successful
attempts used by the late great Ministers, to debauch the most eminent
Members of the Commons-House, by Pensions and Offices;[639] and therefore it would wonderfully conduce to the good of the Common-wealth, and
to the composing our disordered State, if there were men of so high and

636. In fact, a Biblical saying: "Even a fool, when he holdeth his peace, is
counted wise" (Proverbs 17:28).
637. A comment which hints at the purpose of the initial booklist (see above,
pp. 51–53).
638. See *Discourses*, 1.4 (for Rome) and 1.58 (for Athens) (Machiavelli, *Works*,
pp. 273 and 328).
639. A reference to the "Pensioner Parliament" of 1661–79; see above, p. 73,
n. 64.

unquestionable a Reputation, that they were above all suspicion and distrust, and so might venture upon bold, that is (in this case) moderate Counsels, for the saving of their Country. Such men there were in the Parliament of 1640. at least twenty or thirty, who having stood their ground in seven Parliaments before, which in the two last Kings Reigns had been dissolved abruptly and in wrath, and having resisted the fear of Imprisonment and great Fines for their love to *England*, as well, as the temptation of Money and Offices to betray it, both inferred by the wicked Councellours of that Age,[640] tending both to the ruine of our just Rights, and the detriment of their Masters Affairs;[641] I say, having constantly, and with great magnanimity and honour made proof of their Integrity, they had acquired so great a Reputation, that not only the Parliament, but even almost the whole People stuck to them, and were swayed by them in Actions of a much higher Nature than any are now discoursed of, without fear of being deserted, or as we say, left in the lurch, as the people of *France* often are by their Grandees, when they raise little Civil Wars to get great Places, which as soon as they are offered, they lay down Arms, and leave their Followers to be hang'd;[642] but although these two reasons of the silence of some wise men, and the want of reputation in others, does give us but a sad prospect of our Land of Promise,[643] yet we have one Consideration, which does incourage us to hope better things ere long. And that is the Infallible Certainty that we cannot long Continue as we are, and that we can never Meliorate,[644] but by some such Principles, as we have been here all this while discoursing of, and that without such helps and succours as may be drawn from thence, we must go from one distraction to another, till we come into a Civil War, and in the close of it be certainly a prey to the King of *France*, who (on which side it matters not) will be a Gamester, and sweep Stakes[645] at last; the

640. Principally Thomas Wentworth (1593–1641), first Earl of Strafford, and William Laud (1573–1645), archbishop of Canterbury; see above, p. 168, n. 292, and p. 209, n. 385.

641. Robbins finds this claim "substantially accurate" (Robbins, *Republican Tracts*, p. 199, n. 2). She refers the reader to Mary F. Keeler, *The Long Parliament* (Philadelphia: American Philosophical Society, 1954), p. 16, n. 76.

642. As Neville has pointed out already; see above, p. 200.

643. I.e., Canaan; see above, p. 293, n. 591. See Deuteronomy 27:3.

644. I.e., improve or progress.

645. I.e., win everything.

World not being now equally ballanced between two Princes alike powerful, as it was during our last Civil War;[646] and if as well this danger, as the only means to prevent it, be understood in time, (as no doubt it will) we shall be the happiest and the greatest Nation in the World in a little time; and in the mean time, enjoy the best and most just easie Government of any People upon Earth. If you ask me whether I could have offer'd any thing that I thought better than this, I will answer you as *Solon* did a Philosopher, who askt him whether he could not have made a better Government for *Athens?* Yes, but that his was the best, that the People would or could receive.[647] And now I believe you will bear me witness, that I have not treated you as a Wise man would have done in silence; but it is time to put an end to this tittle-tattle which has nauseated you for three days together.

Noble Venetian. I hope you think better of our Judgments than so; but I believe you may very well be weary.

Doctor. I am sure the Parish Priests are often thanked for their pains, when they have neither taken half so much as you have, nor profited their Auditory the hundredth part so much.

English Gentleman. The answer to Thank you for your pains, is always, Thank you, Sir, for your patience; and so I do very humbly both of you.

Noble Venetian. Pray, Sir, when do you leave the Town?

English Gentleman. Not till you leave the Kingdom. I intend to see you, if please God, aboard the Yacht[648] at *Gravesend.*

Noble Venetian. I should be ashamed to put you to that trouble.

---

646. I.e., Louis XIV of France and Philip IV of Spain.

647. See above, p. 104, n. 137. For the anecdote, see Plutarch, "Solon," 15: "ὅθεν ὕστερον ἐρωτηθεὶς εἰ τοὺς ἀρίστους Ἀθηναίοις νόμους ἔγραψεν, Ὧν ἄν,' ἔφη, 'προσεδέξαντο τοὺς ἀρίστους'"; "Therefore when he was afterwards asked if he had enacted the best laws for the Athenians, he replied, 'The best they would receive.'"

648. At this time a light, fast sailing boat reserved for official government business (cf. Grey, *Debates*, vol. 7, pp. 432–33). An entry in Evelyn's diary for 1 Octo-

English Gentleman. I should be much more troubled if I should not do it; in the mean time I take my leave of you for this time, and hope to wait on you again to morrow. What, *Doctor,* you stay to Consult about the Convalescence? Adieu to you both.

Doctor. Farewell, Sir.

Nullum numen abest si sit prudentia.[649]

FINIS.

---

ber 1661 suggests the relative novelty of this kind of craft: "I sailed this morning with his *Majestie* on one of his Yaachts (or Pleasure boates) Vessells newly known amongst us, til the *Dutch* E. India Comp. presented that curious piece to the King, & very excellent sailing Vessels" (Evelyn, *Diary,* vol. 3, p. 296).

649. If we act wisely, then God will not be wanting to us. The maxim appears to be an adaptation of the final lines of Juvenal's tenth satire: "Nullum numen habes, si sit prudentia: nos te, / nos facimus, Fortuna, deam caeloque locamus"; "O Fortune, you would have no divine power if we had prudence. It is we who make you a goddess and place you in heaven" (Juvenal, 10.365–66). However, in Neville's time it was widely received as a variant reading of those lines: see John Speed, *The History of Great Britaine* (1611), p. 728; Robert Dallington, *Aphorismes Ciuill and Militarie* (1613), p. 185; Thomas Jackson, *A Treatise of the Divine Essence and Attributes* (1629), p. 259; *Analecta poetica Graeca* (1643), p. 18; Sir Richard Baker, *A Chronicle of the Kings of England* (1643), "The Raigne of Queen Elizabeth," p. 5; John Wall, *Ramus Olivae* (1653), p. 45; Barten Holyday, *Motives to a Good Life* (1657), p. 160; Archibald Campbell, *Instructions to a Son* (1661), p. 97; Henry More, *Divine Dialogues* (1668), p. 170; Thomas Allestree, *A Funeral Handkerchief* (1671), p. 160; John Langston, *Lusus Poeticus Latino-Anglicanus* (1675), p. 66. The reading "abest" for the now-preferred "habes" occurs in at least two Juvenalian manuscripts: codex Parisiensis 7900[A] and codex Vrbinus 661, Vaticanus. The maxim was a popular choice of epigraph, having also served as the concluding epigraph of the anonymous Royalist and anti-Machiavellian tract *Aurora* (1648), p. 20; and as the initial epigraph of the 1670 Edinburgh printing of Bacon's *Union of the Two Kingdoms of Scotland and England,* of Martin Blochwich's *Anatomia Sambuci* (1677), and (in a modified form) of the anti-Exclusionist tract *A Letter on the Subject of the Succession* (1679). Most significantly, perhaps, this Juvenalian tag had been quoted by Neville's friend Harrington in the "Epistle Dedicatory" to *The Prerogative of Popular Government* (1657) (Pocock, *Harrington,* p. 390), and by Andrew Marvell in *The Rehearsal Transpros'd* (1672) (Marvell, *Prose Works,* vol. 1, p. 101). It had also been quoted in the House of Commons by John Sadler on 19 March 1659 in Neville's presence (Burton, *Diary,* vol. 4, p. 200).

Appendix A

A Copy of a Letter from an Officer of the Army in Ireland, to his Highness the Lord Protector, concerning his changing of the Government.

My Lord,

I do not at all doubt but that your Highness will wonder to receive a letter, and of this length, from so mean a person; but when you shall be pleased to weigh that, no man who is not too mean to be calumniated, can be too inconsiderable to defend himself; I make no question but you will think this boldness a necessitie, and so pardon it: It is now neer five years since I left *England* in your Companie, and under your Command, ever since which time I have constantlie resided with my charge here, one bare moneth excepted, for which space I had leave to dispatch some affairs in *England*. Now for that my Superiours here do refuse at present to give me permission to wait upon your Highness in person, as also that I have small hopes otherwise, that your many weightie imployments can ever admit me to be heard by you at large, I have presumed to write these few lines, beseeching you to beleeve the contents of them, as proceeding from an unfaigned heart, and to take a measure of me and my principles from hence, and not from such Clandestine reports as may possibly be Instill'd into your Eares, by those that are my Enemies, and will be yours,

Transcribed from the first edition, printed in 1656. For discussion of Neville's possible involvement in the authorship of this pamphlet, see the Introduction (above, pp. xx–xxi).

when they shall have prevailed with you, *to disgrace those that have bin old servants to the cause of libertie, and to your person,* and to put your selfe wholly at their mercy and discretion, whose deep policy hath made them desert their country for this last five years, dureing which time they have been little lesse then Martyrs to *Charles Steward,* and his interest: My Lord, I cannot answer to these objections against me, for which I am traduced to your Highness, because I yet never heard them in particular, nor is there any charge against me that yet I can learn news of, only a rumor speaks me disaffected to your present power, and so not fit to be trusted any longer, to give answer to this, it would be necessary to understand *the drift of this government we are now under* which I protest I cannot, I mean, whether we are in the way to a glorious *Commonwealth for which we have ingaged,* & to which the great power which you are Possessed of, may make us much neerer, if you please, or upon a transition, thinking *the case of our liberty desperate,* from a free state, to a lasting *setled Monarchy,* when it shall appear to be the latter, I shall not at all conceale my disaffection, nor desire to retaine my imployment, that may give me a relation to that *government,* to expose which my life hath been so often hazarded, and my hand and my heart to so many *solemn declarations against it,* which together with mine own light and reason, would haunt and persecute mee, like so many revenging furies, if I should dare to harbour *an apostate thought of being* instrumentall to revert, *as if it was nothing in the eyes of God and Good men, to imbrew two Nations in blood, to execute a great Prince, to destroy so many considerable persons and families, who now all beg their bread in forrain Lands, and to take the food out of the mouthes of the poore, and their beds from under them for taxes and impositions, and all this to the intent to support that liberty which nature hath bestowed upon mankind,* and then to make no more use of the most miraculous mercies of God, and the precious blood and tears of so many worthy and religious Patriarks, then to make them instrumentall to pull down a *Legall Monarchy,* for being somwhat too tenatious of certaine power prejudiciall to common freedom, and at the same time to set up, and introduce *without form of law,* justice, or consent (no not of the armie it selfe as is suggested) an arbitrary boundlesse power solely subservant to the exorbitant wil and unsupportable ambition of one single person, and that for ever, who is to have thirty thousand men, who are not to bee disbanded, nor the money for their entertainment laid or altered by *Parliament,* these are to be his *Janizaries,* and their work to inslave the people in these nations, to the lusts of their grand *Senior.* For if hee have any forraine emergencies hee may raise more: what hardhearted men were those in *Parliament,* who thought the *Earle* of Stratford worthy of death, for telling *the late King,* he had an Army in Ireland, which hee might imploy to reduce his subjects here to their obedience, and how severe were these grave and learned lawyers, who judged that speech treason, even at the *Common Law,* and now thinke it none for themselves, to act in seats of Judicatory, execute laws, and hang men, and yet have no power to authorize them therein, but what is derived from such another trick, as that *Earle* would have then plaid; to be short, if I should examine that paper called the *Government,* I should hardly find a line *in it, which is not* destructive *to our cause and liberty,* soe that it appears plainly to be a Monarchy bottomed in the sword, or to come neerer the right name, a Common-Wealth established in a Lord Protector, and thirty Thousand men, *these considerations my Lord, do prevaile with me, to believe that your Highness do not intend to continue this form of government upon us, but have assumed the power for a time, that you may be able to accomplish the worke of Libertie amongst us,* which the Parliment consisting of divers Persons, of several and different capacities, was not able to establish, and this seems more probable to me, not onely from your *owne Oaths, protestations, and excellent principles against Monarchy,* but even from the consideration of the ticklish and slipperie Posture in which al Monarchies do stand, who have no foundation of their right and Government, but an armed force; how often have the Pretorian bands, the Turkish & Rushian Armies proved more fatal and tyrannical to their own princes, then to their poor oppressed vassalls, and it seemes to be agreeing both to divine justice, and humane reason, that an armed multitude, which by the perswasions *of one man, hath broken all the bonds of Law and conscience, to serve his interest, and inslave their country; should when the tide of their fancy or passion turnes, thinke themselves as well absolv'd and disingaged from all reverence and obedience to their owne Captaine.*

Since I have said thus much it will be needless to speake more in praise of a free state, for that the best and most limited *Monarchies* are but perpetuall contests between the interest of Mankind, and that of one person, each striving industriously which shall ruine and undermine the other, & in that Government flattery and unworthy insinuations are turned up Trump, without which noe man can win in such a game, which gives a plaine reason why the most vertuous Princes, as *Marcus Aurelius, Antonius Pius,* and others, could never make their people so; the interest of their Government being wholly contrary thereunto; for if the principle of vertue and justice should be sowne, and come up, they would have that growth and increase, which would in short time overtop the interest of one person, & so destroy the state; as hath been seen by the experience of those Governments which have erected themselves out of the ruine of Monarchy, where the Prince hath been so unadvised, to suffer his people to attaine to riches, and so get good education, for that the great concernment, *or reason of state in Kings and Tyrants, is to keep mankind poore and ignorant,* which the Greeks and Romans understood well, when they stiled those nations who lived under the command of one man, *Barbarians,* just point blank contrary to this, are the principles and maximes of a *Commonwealth,* which is the nursery of vertue, valor, and industrie, where no Court whispers, no pimping projecting, or such arts, can bring advantage to those who practise them, but onelie a publike spirit exprest in just and honorable actions, must advance and prefer persons to the highest offices and imployments, this laies a foundation for the constant succession of generous and worthie Patriots, this makes a people rich and free, happie at home, and formidable abroad, and historie, which is the best reason in this point, will plainlie shew, that the worst and meanest of commonwealths, have been more rich, powerful and populous, then the same Countrie could ever be under a Prince; I take the most factious and corrupt estate in storie; to have been that of *Florence,* yet did that Common-wealth for many years together give Law to *Italy,* and when they had war with part of their own Territories, as *Pisa,* and its Countrie, did for manie yeares maintain *sixty thousand men,* whereas the same Dominions now under a Duke, with the addition of the state of *Sienna,* is not able to raise or maintaine *twelve thousand* men; for when the present Prince was necessitated in the yeare one thousand six hundred and fourtie three, to make an inconsiderable war against the Pope in companie of *Parma, Modena,* and the *Venetian,* and that for but one summer, he was reduced to such extremitie, that he hath been forc'd to sell his Gallies, and whollie to neglect the Sea, and yet those people that are left in his Dominion, are much more opprest by impositions, then in the daies of libertie; I will not speak of *England,* because it was never yet a Commonwealth, though it hath past a civill war, and all other sufferings which belongs to a Change, yet this must and will be said, that all those actions of Honour, which our *Kings* for six hundred years have performed, did not bring more renowne; nor so much advantage to these Nations, as the atchievements of the same People when they had no *Prince,* and but the Name only *of a free state*; and if for our sins it be decreed that we shal never be so; I dare almost prophecy that the actions of succeeding *Monarchyes* wil not outdo, nor perhaps not Equall these, and then Posterity will have leave to thinke, that all the wisedome, valor, and activity of these Nations was not residing in one single person; but I have dwelt too long upon this, and shall onlie *conclude, that if all Kingdomes be neer their period and ruine, when the subjects under them grow rich, wise, and capable of understanding their own good, and contrariwise, that Common-wealths do not decay, but when their people in general grow poore; and ignorant, and the riches of the Nation comes to be ingrossed by a few,* who by that meanes can buy voices to get into command, and then bribe souldiers to uphold them in their ambitious designes, to inslave their Countrie, the povertie and abjectness of the people, making them fit for the impression; then it must necessarilie follow, that those in whose hand and power it is to settle and establish what form of Government they please, ought to improve that power for erecting a *Free State,* or a *Commonwealth;* this is the case of your Highnesse, who besides your oaths and trust, have this obligation more, that you know, and are perswaded in your conscience, that this is a more excellent form then Monarchie, as you have thousand of times exprest your self, and particularlie in that Declaration which you composed here, and published when you entered the Province of *Munster,* 1649. in which you have most excellent and unanswerable Reasons for a Popular Government, which shall make mee say no more of this businesse; but come to bring it to our present condition, because it is Alledged (and indeed to that we owe this Change, which hath brought upon us so much distraction & unsettlement, that we were not capable being a free state, And so that you by necessitie have been forc'd upon these Courses, to prevent confusion) I am not ignorant, that nothing is more commonly said and believed amongst the Vulgar, then this Error, and it is besides industriously fomented by some subtil grandees, who knows their great Riches, titles, knavish cunnings, and such useless Qualities, will not prefer them to that dignitie and Eminencie in such a Government, as they hope to injoy under a Prince, whom they can sooth and flatter, I must confesse, to look upon the present humor of the People, as they are divided into factions, & animated against the Parliaments managing affairs, a rational man might believe, that as their passions do hinder them from seeing the advantage of a Comonwealth, so they would likewise hinder them from Obeying it; but those who shall consider on the one hand their punctuall Obedience, not only to all laws, but even to these ordinances, which are now called so, and that undoubtedly against their Judgement, as well as their affections; and on the other side their genuine inclinations, and before this warr, when they were free from factions, and in *Puris naturalibus,* to freedom, which was plainely seene by their joyning unanimously with the House of Commons, in their contest against their *King:* I say whosoever shall observe that, must needs say, that a small force joyned with Good Principle, and honest Governors, will soon reduce them to their naturall disposition and temper againe, *If thirty thousand men can support this Government, then ten thousand might maintaine Freedome,* which would quickly come to subject by it self without any force at al; which al states do, that are Established upon a right Basis, viz *upon the natural temper and humor which the posture and condition of the people puts them into, if they be poore and low, Monarchy may serve their turn, if rich, they wold look to have share, Rule & magistracy themselves:* whosoever then wold, found a Government which he intends not, shal subject by force (for if he do it, matters not what he makes it) might above all things, observe these accidences, which ruind the precedeing state, for every form of Government which crumbles and fals to ruine, by the weakness of its owne pillars, must have a new fabrick, or mend the old, one just in the place, first breake, if it be capable of it, and whosoever shall looke backe into the turnes and revolutions of state; will find, that all changes in Government have been mending of old frames, or making of new ones, & as Legislators or Senats, have gone to the root of nature in this, have not palliated or patched up the cure, so Nations have been happie or unhappie, free or slaves, governed by force continually, or by consent, and states durable, or short lived, is true, that our unhappiness is that great alterations seldom come without intestine wars, it being hard (especially in populous and flourishing Cities), to bring the multitude to give so great a power to one man as is necessary to redress a disordered State, and for that men are generally short sighted, and cannot foresee great inconveniences till they are too late to remedy, but by force, this makes the cure oftentimes miscarry, as in the case of the *Gracchi* at *Rome,* and of *Agis* and *Cleomenes* at *Sparta,* in both which examples, there was an endeavour to reduce those two excellent States, to their first principles, but it was too late attempted, when the corruption was growne to too great a height, which if they had found, and would have been contented to erect a new form more suitable to the inequalitie of mens estates at that time, they might possiblie have succeeded, if not to have introduced so good and excellent a model as they fell from, yet one able to have prevented the ruine and slaverie which soon after befell both these people; not to make the business longer, I will instance in the example of our own Nation, the first historie of which, (it is not esteemed fabulous) is that we were invaded and *conquered by* William *the* Norman, *who either ruled by his own will, or made the Law rule, which he gave at his own pleasure;* his French Lords left posteritie behind them, who in process of time grew so rich and powerful, that they did not think it fit to be governed by the discretion of one man, but believed, they might deserve and share in rules themselves, for there is nothing more fundamental by nature, then that those who possess a land will desire, and by all means attempt to govern it, which is the true reason of what was alledged before, viz. *That it is against the interest of a Monarchy, to let his subjects grow rich;* from this contest of the Lords, with succeeding Kings, began the *Barons Wars,* and in the close of them our Government, by *Kings, Lords,* and *Commons,* wherein, although the Commons were named, it will be found (if we look into Records, that they had little share, except to help bear up the Lords, whose Blew-coats they wore against the King) and it will likewise appear, that they were never discontented at their small proportion, and the reason is the same with the former, viz. that either they possessed no lands at all, or else they held them as servants to their loving Lords and Clergie, so that this State was founded with great wisdome, upon the verie condition of the People, which had it continued the same it then was, could never have been shaken, but by a forraign war; but all great bodies are well politique as natural, receive great alteration and corruption, and though in good mixtures they commonlie tend to decay and ruine, yet where the Crasis is bad, there may be accedents which may incline to amend it, and that without the knowledg of the parties, who are the subject matter of the change, and as Wine changes it self by working, so many times the natural humor of a Nation tends from the corruption of a *Monarchy, to the erecting of a Popular State,* though whilst they are in motion, they may not possiblie understand whether their own impulse doth incline and lead them, this will prove to be the case of *England;* for when *Henry the Seventh* had established himself King, and saw plainlie that he did owe his accession to the Crown, more to the favour of those Lords who assisted him, then either to his own *Sword* or *Title,* he began to consider in how ticklish a posture he stood, whilst it was in the power of any small number of Lords to set up, or pull down a Soveraign at their will, and upon this contemplation he made it his whole aim and work to lessen and debase the nobilitie, that he might have the less to apprehend in his new-gotten royaltie, by which he laid the foundation of *destroying his Posterity, not considering at all that the Lords could not be diminished, but by advancing and inriching the Commons,* whose desire of power must necessarilie increase accordinglie, which if they could obtain, it was then obvious that they must strike not at this or that Prince, but at the verie *Root of Monarchy it self,* as being a thing uselesse whollie to them, and indeed inconsistent with their Government and interest: *Henry the Eight* continued in

the same policie, and amongst many other accidents of increasing the
power of the Common-wealth, to the setling the *Militia* in Deputie
Lievtenant, it happened in his daies that religious houses being taken
away, most of the Lands and Mannours belonging to them, some for
moneys, others for Donations, fell into the hands of the *Commons;* this
was the first time they began to bear up with the Lords, who since have
been abased and impoverished by manie accidents, as by finding a means
to cut off Intailes, whereby it came to be in the power of those who were
in present possession, to sell their posteritie and revenues, and so to ruine
the Lords who succeeded them, (which estates too) being most what
spent in Court vices and luxurie, lost the interest of the Peers in their
Countries, and made them contemptible to the whole Nation, and slaves
to the Citizens, who by their prodigalities grew into great wealth, and
possest their lands; about this time trade beyond Sea increased, and
abuses in the Law growing up, made that a wealthie profession, so that
incensiblie foundations of great families amongst the Commons were
laid, whilst the Lords grew dailie to decay, and that which brought them
to nothing at last, was doubtless the Scotch race of Kings, who whether
by design, or for want of prudence, is not known, made so many worthless persons Peers here, as well Scotch as English, and those too for the
most part so inconsiderable in point of estate, *that the people did univer-*
sally detest the Government, as we may observe by the constant unquietness of their Representors in Parliament, there scarce having been one in
the two last Kings raigns, which were not dissolved abruptlie by them, so
little complying were they to his Government: Now though I am no
waies ignorant that the dissentions which happened between those Kings
and their Parliaments, had verie good ground on the peoples side, as the
taking away grievances, and the like, yet the natural cause (and which
was a long time collecting) *was the height of the Commons, and the mean-*
ness of the Lords, and the King, who had by this time sold and given away
all his revenues; and this too will appear to have been the original of
these civil wars, for although the last action, which drove us into it, will
ever be acknowledged to have been the *Kings misgovernment,* yet as we
are apt to say in Malignant fevers, that the last excesse we made drove us

into it, though the bodie had been gathering that pestilential Mass many years before; so in this case the essentiall and natural cause of this State disease, was much longer in collecting, *then the Ship-money, or the Loan;* and this is clear, for that the people did support much more then those from their Prince and Landlords too, whilst they were poor, and never did stomack to be governed, even arbitrarilie, by those upon whom they were necessarilie to depend in point of estate and subsistance, it being then, *my Lord,* so clear and evident, *That the riches of the people in general, is the natural cause of destruction to all Regal States:* I desire to bring this to our present discourse, and will beg leave to ask your Highness leave, whether the Commonaltie of *England* be grown poorer then they were when this was began, or rather, whether they are not become so much more *rich,* as the *Lands* and *Mannours* of *King, Bishops, Dean* and *Chapters,* and of all the great *Delinquent Lords,* together with *Free-farm Rents,* could make them; if this be granted, it must be then concluded, that we are farther off from a capacitie of being governed by *Monarchy* again, then when we first began this quarrell; so that you see that it is so far from being true, that the Nation of *England* is not fit at all to be a Commonwealth, *that indeed it is wholly impossible to make it any other, without an excessive force and violence;* so that my Lord, if your Highness shall yet resolve to detain from us our liberties, with which you were intrusted, you will not onlie offend against your owne Oaths and Principles, against common right and justice, but even against God and nature too, for that it will be impossible for you *to mend this frame where it first brake,* except *you can take from the people their estates, and confer them upon old or new Lords,* which will be hardlie safe for you to attempt, it hath been my unhappiness to make this discourse somewhat too long for a letter, but I have been forc'd to rove too far into the nature of Government in generall, before I could shew the principles of a *Free-State,* and how neer we are to it, if you please, so neer, that the Cavaliers themselves in their hatred to the Parliament, and now to your self, do fully manifest, that they abhor all Superiours, and are impatient to be governed by others; and this verie humor in them, is a secret impulse towards a *Commonwealth,* which although they do not now understand to be so, yet they would soon do it, if they had what they immediatelie desire, for I am fullie perswaded, if their Darling *Charles Stewart* could be brought in by them, and all his opposers whollie rooted out, he would not be able without a standing Armie to maintain the old Government, even amongst his own partie, so much is the case altered now, and so strong and natural the motives which draw towards *Liberty*. I must confess these speculations were no part of the cause which induced me first to take up armes first for the *Parliament*, but did come into my thoughts since by discourse, what I did originallie look at, was the justness and honestie of the cause, the excellencie of libertie, the glorie of advancing and promoting the interest of mankind, the making my Nation more wise, valiant, happie, and honest then before, as well as more free, *which I cannot yet dispair of whilst I see you alive*, whose noble and unwearied endeavours to that end, can never be forgotten, when the *King*, the *Scots*, and half the *Parliament* combin'd against us, you could not be daunted, when your own Grandees would have perswaded you out of those *principles*, you would not be circumvented, but did often say, that towards the attaining of a just and upright Government, *an ounce of honesty and resolution, was worth a pound of sneaking policie:* Oh let not those men who have suffered for your enemies get that upon you, by soothing your ambition, which they could never doe by opposing *your reason*, let not those instruments, who have deserted the cause of libertie, be now made use of to destroy it, and by advising you to purge the Armie, make those *Janizaries*, whose glorie it was once, they would not acknowledg themselves to be *Mercenaries*, put not your self upon the discretion of those whose love is not to you, but to *Monarchy*, and when they shall have made you a while the instrument of their ambition and avarice, will in the least adversitie look back to the old line again, which they scarce ever yet *offended*, and when that shall be understood by *Charles Stewart* and his Hectors, and that there shall be nothing standing in their way hither, but *your life, the antient asserters of libertie being laid by with shame*, and those who were once outed for opposing it, stept into their places, in how hazardous and desperate a condition is that life of yours like to be, which hath been hitherto so precious to all the honest partie in these Nations; Consider therefore that those

Grandees are like fire and water, good servants, but verie dangerous masters, *let them do your drudgery*, but let them not steer your counsels, *trust this Nation with their freedome, posterity with your fame, and God for a reward;* we know we cannot be free without your help, till we have undergone a thousand confusions in the way, our factions will not suffer us to agree in any thing, *except you lead us* into that frame which will fit us, and to make which, you may find persons enough to assist you, if you please to seek them; and who knows but that the wise providence of God, seeing the failings of the *Parliament* hath permitted you to assume this great power, to that end, do not offend that God whom you have so often *called to witness of the integrity of your heart;* Consider, that if you will not build us up that fabrique of a *Free State*, you must be the first to lose your own libertie; do but weigh the feares and the uncertainties you will be in, whilst you live, and the almost inevitable necessitie that *your posterity* must be destroyed when you are gone, as well as ours, or let this prevaile with you, at least to make us a Commonwealth, *because you can make us nothing else;* if you believe your selfe not safe without this power, pray consider how many plots and designs there were against you when you were our General, and how many nights sleep you brake then in examinations, nay remember, if during the Triall of the late King, you did not walk the streets often with one servant, or without one, whereas now, new Troops and Regiments must be raised, and the old recruited, and all thought too little to preserve you, and yet the lives of all the honest Patriots in *England* were then wrapt up in yours, as much as now, and their interest more; but if yet after all this, that detestable poyson of ambition, and desire of domination, have taken so far possession of you, that no Antidote can expell it, and that nothing will satisfie you, but to destroy that libertie which you were appointed Guardian to; and to outdoe him whom you have pull'd downe and executed: I must professe to all the world, that though I shall ever acknowledge *that I owe much of my being setled in the principles of freedome, which I now adhere to, to your former excellent discourses, and most excellent actions;* yet that I cannot finde any thing in my conscience that will perswade me to change vvith you, but shall vvash my hands from the guilt and infamie of your vvaies, and vvithall lay dovvn my commands, and all other relations to your Government, that so I may deliver you from the apprehensions, vvhich I believe you are in, that you cannot finde a specious pretence to discharge me from my imployments, though the series of your former behaviour in that kind tovvards your friends, makes me believe you vvill be soon provided of a cause to lay me by, for you have hitherto (as I may so say) rid so fast, that you have seemed to be mounted rather upon Posthorses, then those vvhich vvere your ovvn, leaving them still at their stages end, and taking fresh ones; one vvhile none but *Barkley Legg* and *Ashburnham* must serve your turne, and the King must either be brought in, or it must be thought so, soon after, vvhen his head comes to be cut off, the Levellers must be cajol'd, when that is well over, the Presbyterian must be Courted till the war of *Scotland* be ended, and their nest fired; next to this an expedient in Religion must be thought upon, and a Committee for Propagation appointed, into which, as into the Ark, all kind of creatures must enter, soone after this Blackfriers men must be incouraged to cry this downe, and the Parliament too, for going on too fast with it, and for not reforming the Laws, till at length they being preach'd ripe for destruction, the members of Parliament must be removed, and such honest godlie persons chosen to succeed them, as may make the people forget Monarchie; but these are presentlie cashiered too, for endeavouring to perform what they were called for, as if they had been summoned onlie to beat a Commonwealth out of the Pit, and serve for a foil for the new Monarchie; next, because we have no more varieties of fashions or instruments, we must revert to our Monarchical Grandees againe, these are now the onlie wise men, for having distrusted you, and foreseen all this, the only firme States men, for sticking to their principles, these must now be called the honest partie, whilst those who were so the last year are stiled factious fellowes, and to make this relish the better, there must be sought out instruments of an inferiour capacitie to the Grandees, who never had any other principles then fear and avarice, and who never disdained to be flatterers in any age, I mean Divines and Lawyers, whom the late fright they were in for Tythes and Reformation, hath made them now more supple then formerlie; the first of these must now preach up tyrannie, as much as ever they have done libertie, they who once said the people, or the Saints, were the Lords Annointed, must now recant that Doctrine, and say its the Lords Protector, and must even prostitute the *Jus Divinum* of their Ordination it self, to an Ordinance of your Highness, and for the latter, they must make that just and honorable in you, which they thought Treason in the Earle of *Stafford;* those who condemned Ship-money, must cry up the monethlie Taxes in their Circuits and charges, and such who scrupled Councel-Table Orders formerlie, must now sweare to, and judg by such Laws, as you can make a dozen in an hour, without the trouble of twice reading or ingrossing, nay, the same persons must be a High Court, and hang men for striving to oppose Monarchie to day, who yesterday did the same to them who would have brought it in: *But my Lord, we will have patience to expect the end, it will be that which must give the denomination to all this, which if it terminate in libertie, will be esteemed prudent policy, if in the contrary, it will have another name;* but least your Highness should think, that either my selfe, or any honest man here, do place our hopes of a good issue to this business in the next Parliament, as you call it, I will presume to disabuse you in that particular, and give you that which I conceive to be the judgement of the world concerning it, as well as mine: First, then my Lord, it is understood to be a creature of your will and power, the definition of the places, the qualification of the persons, the summons, and all other incidents belonging unto it, deriving themselves wholly from you, and your assumed office, so that if there be a flaw in the justice of legalitie, of that which is the foundation, what can be hoped for in the superstructure? it might be objected in the next place, the people having alreadie chosen a Parliament, which have not received any formal, (or as it was once called) legal determination, could not be in a capacitie to chuse another, because this would seem to grant, that any prevailing violence might, even in that sense of Law, dissolve a Parliament; but I leave this as that which comes too neer Treason; another thing which renders the whole scrupellous is, that your Highness should think the people fit to have a share in Government, and give Laws, and yet should make your selfe so far Paramount to them at the same time, as to confine them by the Instrument and Indentures, what power they shall delegate to their Trustees, if the original of all just power be in the people, as we have beene taught by the Parliament, how comes there to be a Jurisdiction superiour to theirs, which must command them what to do with that power, and what instructions to give those who represent them? but if that Doctrine be not true, what need they be disturbed in their harvest work, to chuse and send needless Cyphers up to *London?* and why cannot you rather, either as you do now, make Lawes still with the consent of the major part of seven men, or without it, or else take the paines, as you did latelie, to name the persons, to be summoned your self, this had savoured of much more ingenuitie, and would have made us hope this deplorable estate we are now in, had been to last no longer then till you, with the advice of wise and honest Patriots, had been able to frame a moddle of present freedome for us, whereas things standing thus, there are sad apprehensions, that the countenance of a Parliament, and not their counsel, is sought for, and that specious pretence to deceive the vulgar are more aimed at and desired, then either the present good of the Nation, or any designe of settlement for the future, and reallie what advantage could have been expected from the last Parliament, if the King, which called it, had incombred it with an Indenture, that they should have power onelie to have secur'd his ends, but not to alter the Government, though he had taken them man by man, and murthered them, and doubtless this must be a president for all Kings and other usurped Powers, which shall succeed in *England,* to put all their Commands, Lusts and Projects into writing, and deliver them for a lesson to the people at their choice, till they have made their Indentures as long as *Drury House* Conveyance, till such time as the people of those Nations, like the Natives under the *Spaniard* in the *Indies,* shall be capable of no other office or imployment, but to summon and bring in their fellows to the mines, and make them slaves; one advantage more towards tyrannie in this businesse is, that those blocks laid in the way, will discourage many wise and honest Patriots, from suffering themselves being elected, and so the credit and reputation of this new *Junto,* will be as small as its Authoritie, onelie this will render them somewhat more fit to serve the end for which they are appointed, *viz.* either to confirm this power as it is, or settle the old Royaltie in your line, or else perhaps finde out some mungrell expedient, by which they will seem to retrench some part of this arbitrary Soveraignty, and by that means, as much as in them lies, authenticate the rest; but the truth is, they do perform all that by summoning in; and not only so, but make all these poor blind people who elect them, to submit themselves to a voluntary slavery, by owning an authority destructive to their freedom, *for either those they send, must not attempt to do them any service, or if they do, be perfidious and break their trust,* since the only call they can pretend to, is the peoples choice, and even by them they are confused by an instruction to approve this Government, *and so undoe all that hath been building up towards our Libertie for these fourteen years:* Next my Lord, because it is Commonly reported here that your Highness intends to resign your power, entirely and absolutely into the hands of those men when they are met, I will crave leave to say a word to that, to the end, you may perceive that there are some honest people even *in Ireland* who are undeceived in that point. First then they Conceive you may, as well and justly Resign it to your Council, they being equally your Creatures, and then they observe the falacie of Leaving those men free, whom you have Caused to be bound ere they came there, and with such Chaines as you your selfe cannot loosen, no more then a Foraigne *Prince* can Give an *Embassador* sent from hence Authority to Negotiate beyond his *Commission,* and those bonds which you have Laid upon them are concerning the very Essence of our Liberty, *viz. the Government by one Person, which you were once so fully perswaded of* that you said in your Declaration here, that you did believe that *God* was entering into a contest with *Kings* and *Priests,* and would very suddenly open the eies of the *Nations,* so that within few years, there should not be either left in the whole *world.* Cease then, my *Lord,* to *Flatter* your selfe any longer with an Opinion that the well affected people of any of these Nations will think any better of *your Monarchy* then they now doe, when you shall seemingly have Laid it down to those men who have no power for any thing, but to restore it to you; and who are besides a product of your own will. A Civill Army Raised by your selfe to handle the Estates of your people, as the other perhaps doe their persons when they are purged and fitted to the principles of *A Turkish Empire,* and possibly you had this, this thought when you made this Modle, that because it was probable (and it fell out since) that the *Most wise and honest part of the Gentlemen of England would not suffer themselves to be perswaded to come into your Council,* nor own your Government, therefore you would make the people of that Nation your Lictors, who should send you *four hundred men bound hand and foot* to perform your commands, and who should have power to tax, poll, and oppresse them, but not the least shadow of any to relieve them: And here I cannot chose but touch at one thing often alledged; and it is, that if you do rightly and duly administer justice, the Nation will be happy that you tooke this power, for it matters not who Governs so they Govern well, for my part I wholly dissent from, and detest this opinion, and do conceive it to have been invented first by some Lawyer or other flatterer, meerly to satiate their present Apostacy, for if it will be granted that there is in the most pure and incorrupt part of mankind, a natural instinct or inclination to Liberty in Government (which is for ought I know) the only thing that distinguishes them from beasts for that the creature hath no Reason, or no Religion, cannot infallibly be said by us as it can, that they never attempt to rule themselves by Lawes but suffer a Monarchy over them, to be either in the strongest of themselves, or in us, without ever attempting to assert their freedom) then it will likewise be confest that it is a vile and an unnatural Passion in us which makes us prefer a state, much more a little quiet or ease, before that liberty which is so essential to us, and for this I have the example of all those excellent Persons and Nations whom their own hazards and adventures in this behalf have styled so in the universal esteem of all mankind; indeed if the contrary to this were true, it would follow as Mr. *Goodwin* holds, that any Person who believeth in his conscience that he could govern better then others do, might, nay is bound to use all means to attain to power, and acquire the Government, the consequence of which will be that if any man will call his Ambition Conscience, no known Laws, no Constitution of Estate, no Common Right, *in fine* nothing divine or humane ought to stand in this way. I dare go yet farther and affirm that nothing can be more pernitious to these Nations at this present, then for you to govern well, for it would Palliate the assumed Power, and so hide it from the just indignation of this age, and prove like the guilding of poysonous pills, or Painting of Sepulchers, and be a bribing us out of our Rights and Liberties with a seeming justice, nothing but this can Lull asleep so many Patriots, who have been often awakened with Drums and Trumpets, to adventure their lives against a Tyrant; neither indeed could any other thing then the just and happy Reign of *Augustus Caesar*, have given the last defeat to the Roman liberty, or made way for those Monsters who succeeded. You see then my Lord what a businesse you have undertaken, when you have made it the interest of honest men to wish that you may commit all Excesses, and use more violence, break more Laws and ties, in carrying on this arbitrary Soveraignty then you have done in the assuming of it. My Lord, I beseech your Highnesse to pardon the length of this Letter, which could not well have been made shorter, for that the intention thereof is to evince, first, that to continue this present government upon us or any thing like it, would be most injurious in you, not onely because it is most contrary to your own trust and Oathes but even against common right and justice, and in the next place that there is no necessity of a new erected Royalty, the nature and Condition of those Nations being so proportionable to a Commonwealth that we are no way fit to receive any other form, but by an outward force and violence, besides that we have spent our blood and fortunes for it, and in the last place to shew that we are not easily deluded into a belief, that either the next assembly or any expediencies that arise from thence have any right or likelihood to mend our conditions; I shall next give your Highnesse a short account of my self, and then humbly take my leave. I took up Armes with the first in the quarrel of the Parliament, not as a mercinary, as not having before my eyes the temptation of my Masters pay or the spoile of their enemies, but purely and solely out of a conscientious desire to free my Nation from slavery and oppression, and having confirmed my judgement in this, I did examine my zeal and resolution, and believed it had enough of both to hazard my self, for such a cause; in which expectation I thank the Lord, I have not yet found my self deceived; How I have behaved my self since I came under your command, it would seem vanity for me to relate, if my former and present usage did not make it necessary for me to say that for my Justification, which I should never have said for boasting; this excuse makes me bold to lay before you some of my services, as wel as my personal discouragements: your Highness may please to Remember, (here some particulars are left out which would detect the person who wrote the letter) notwithstanding all which I am yet satisfied to go on with my imployment here, and to be faithful in it, as being for the advancement of the Common Cause and against the Common Enemy, and yet if I were assured that you did intend to perpetuate upon us this slavery (after you had disolved the Parliament, for an imputation of endeavoring to perpetuate themselves) I should have many scruples against serving you in *Scotland,* whither we are very lyable to be transported; for what Reason is there that we should not give them leaves to be Governed by their Native King, and whom they had received by their Parliament? and at the same time seeke to impose upon them by force another Prince of our Nation, whom we had chosen for them, or rather had chosen himself, what can you think my Lord the just God, who hath been used to deside upon appeales would do in this quarrel, if they should have recourse to him with faith and prayer? Alas my Lord you do not consider how much these thoughts do weaken the hands and hearts of those poor righteous and precious souls, who are yet left in the Army and who poure forth their tears and prayers daily before the Lord on your behalf, that you may find mercy in this day of your temptation, that so they may not be traduced to have slain so many men as Bravoes to your designes, and that you would make use of the Great power you are now possest of to settle and transmit to succeeding ages a state of Lasting freedome which a small trouble and force would accomplish, whereas this Government must be eternally supported by violence, no unnaturall things being permanent without it, or if this cannot be, their prayers and desires are that you would summon a free unlimitted Parliament (consisting of such that have not forfeited their liberties) not bound or fettered by Indentures, and devesting your selfe of all power and Command, you would leave the whole sway & Government to them, and swear the Army to obey them, by this means the Nation would either enjoy their liberty, or have the choice & imposition of their own yoak; nor is there any Reason except you will do one of these, upon which you can excuse the dismission of the Parliament, for that it was within their power and design to make Indentures in the behalf of Liberty, which would have had an unquestionable Authority as well as a more Noble end, then those you have compelled for the Contrary; If you shall wholly refuse all things of this kinde, and obstinately resolve to goe forward in your way you now take, you will want the hands, hearts and prayers of all Gods people in these Nations; and though the principles of some of them may not give leave as private men to make you any further opposition, yet they will wash their own hands, and deliver their own Souls, and beseech the just God of Heaven and earth, who hath appeared so visibly and Miraculously for this Cause of freedom, and whom no hypocrosie can deceive, no false Oathes, nor teares prevaile upon to judge between you and these poor oppressed and deluded people, but if yet you shall Answer their hungry expectations of Liberty; you will give Glory to God, increase to his Church, flock and Religion, which hath been grievously dishonoured by those actions, Immortall fame to your self, safty to your Posterity, happiness to mankinde, and will have the lives of many thousands intirely at your service and Command, and amongst the rest that of

Waterford this
24 Iune 1654.

> *Your most humble and most*
> *faithful Servant*
> R. G.

POSTSCRIPT

Reader, that this letter should not be exposed to publique view so long after the date thereof, I hope will not possess thee with any prejudice against it the honesty and reason of the tract and faithfulnesse of the Author to that good old principle of common justice, equity and liberty, secured in the most noble form of government, viz. The peoples representative may commend it to thee, indeed that hath been the Axletree of the cause which God so signally blessed us in, and since it was broken (although upon pretence of going faster on in the obtaining of our liberties) hath blasted us, wherein that saying is verified Melius in via claudicare quam extra viam currere. *It was the design of the old, so it is of the new Court, to estrange the people from, and work them out of love with Parliaments, many honest well meaning men being too much led away with that mistake. The Author mentioneth his fear of the last Representative not of their judgement in, & affection to the publique cause of liberty, but by reason of that restriction in the indenture framed to serve the intrest of the present Pro-tector. But indeed the Gentlemen deserve an honourable esteem from all En-glish men, who though they could not do the good desired by us, and doubtlesse intended by them, yet would not do us the evil (which a powerful party en-deavoured to court and threaten them unto) in perpetuating by any act of theirs our vassalage to the present Grandees, or revoke those acts which maketh it treason for any single person to assume the supream Magistracy. I shall only adde this as the earnest desire of myself and of many who are friends to the good old cause, that the Lord would be pleased to guide us in the attayning of a free Representative, which may assert our liberties, and secure them to posterity, which will be a glorious answer to the faith, prayer, expence of blood and trea-sure, both of the godly and likewise of the rest of the freeborn people of England who have been faithful to the common cause of justice and liberty.*

FINIS.

Appendix B

Neville's Major Speeches in Parliament, 1659

1. 2 February 1659

Mr. Neville. I am glad that what you did yesterday passed with so much unanimity. I would have something go, hand in hand with it, for the liberties of the people. The two great flaws in the Government, one in the sovereign power, and another in the executive power, were the negative voice and the militia.

The King would not concur, which produced war; and it was determined on the people's side. I would have nothing of aspersion. It is in good hands now; so that the propositions sent to the King, in all things, will not agree. As to the propositions of the militia, about putting it in Sheriffs and Deputy-Lieutenants, I would have a Committee of able persons appointed to prepare a law, that your negative voice may not be many, without doors, and the militia be entrusted in safe hands, that it may not be oppressive. I shall not bring in an Act, but offer my thoughts.

(Vol. 3, p. 34)

2. 3 February 1659

Mr. Neville. You have been often told you sit here on the Petition and Advice. I hope you sit here by the people's choice. I would not have that urged here, *sit liber judex*. You are judges of the law.

All texts taken from *The Diary of Thomas Burton*, ed. John Towill Rutt, 4 vols. (London: Henry Colbourn, 1828).

The oath of allegiance was done by as free consent as ever; yet it was resolved in the Long Parliament to dispense with it in some cases. Oaths are of a subtle nature. Not but that any man may safely take this oath; for they are not part of the legislature till they sit here, and it does not bind us not to alter the legislature. We are free to debate any part of it.

(Vol. 3, pp. 72–73)

3. 8 February 1659

Mr. Neville. I wish the questions were regularly before you, that we might speak to them. There are three questions before you.

1. To lay the recognition aside.
2. To commit it, which is proper and regular.
3. To declare a previous vote.

I wish a Bill had been brought in.

It has been said that the Chief Magistrate is King, and that his office is hereditary. If nothing has been done to take away those powers, then Charles Stewart has undoubted right.

I am for a single person, a senate, and a popular assembly; but not in that juggling way. King, Lords, and Commons I cannot like. This man is, at least, actually, if not legally, settled the Chief Magistrate.

As to the objection of fears, never was greater quiet and peace for three months, than when the last Government was in debate, and why should it not be so now.

Since the dissolving the old Government, we have had many alterations without success, which hath happened because every Government hath had some flaw in it which hath not yet been seen.

It was not the civil war that altered our Government, but tendencies to the alteration of Government that caused the civil war. It is in your power, as the sovereign power of the nation. *Imperium fundatur in dominatione*, that is an infallible maxim. The people are not like a young heir that hath squeezed wax, by which being once bound, it is too late after for him to repent. If one have power to do any thing, he may and will do it.

William the Conqueror came in with an intent to seize all the lands. He was only prevented by the privilege of the Church; that saved us. I mean the Church of Rome, not our Church, if we have any.

The Barons got a great share, and having a considerable part of the land, and no part in the Government, they began to stir and ruffle with the King; and in fine got authority, and gave laws both to King and Commons, until King Henry VII.'s time. He designed to weaken the hands of the nobility and their power. But Henry VIII. did more by dissolving many of the abbeys, and distributing their lands among the Commons.

The Commons, till Henry VII., never exercised a negative voice. All depended on the Lords. In that time it would have been hard to have found in this house so many gentlemen of estates. The gentry do not now depend upon the peerage. The balance is in the gentry. They have all the lands. Now Lords, old or new, must be supported by the people. There is the same reason why the Lords should not have a negative voice, as that the King should not have a negative; to keep up a sovereignty against nature. The people of England will not suffer a negative voice to be in those who have not a natural power over them. And for the Militia, that power which was to be employed for the preserving of laws, that was employed against them. No power will acquiesce in the taking away their own power. When we are naturally free, why should we make ourselves slaves artificially?

Let us not return to the Government of the Long Parliament. It was an oligarchy, detested by all men that love a Commonwealth: so that whosoever lays that upon us, it was not the Government contended for. We that are for a Commonwealth, are for a single person, senate, and popular assembly; I mean not King, Lords, and Commons. I hope that will never be admitted here. I shall speak to it afterwards.

The Petition and Advice settled power in a prince to have kingly authority over a people. Never think that settling such powers as are not consistent with a free people, can do your business. There will be hauling and pulling, and irregular proceedings: witness many late exorbitances in the Government, of which I will not say you ought to call them to a severe account that have been instrumental; but this I will say, that either you ought to call them to account, or to mend the constitution, so as there may be no danger for the future. It will be in vain to recognize any body, till you have provided for the liberty of the people.

I shall move that this Bill be laid aside, and to declare the Protector to be Chief Magistrate. He is the fittest person of any man in England. I would have him so; but leave it not to Westminster-hall to interpret what is meant by the Chief Magistrate. I could wish he were a magistrate, as supreme as the nation will bear at this day; but I know not what misrepresentations may be made of it.

Your David, that had shed a great deal of blood, was as safe as any man, while you were settling the Government. There is not danger of this pious person. I would have you declare this man to be Chief Magistrate, under such rules and limitations as you shall agree upon. And let this be debated in a Grand Committee.

(Vol. 3, pp. 132–35)

4. 11 FEBRUARY 1659

Mr. Neville. The word magistrate signifies to execute. I first moved you for the additional words. I affirm it, this is the same quarrel that was in 1640. Inevitably a civil war must follow. If you give up the liberties of the people, you lay the foundation for it. Chief Magistracy continued three hundred years because the barons' interest supported it; but the Petition of Right not three months, because the King had not interest to support it. I would have a Committee to pen the question against tomorrow.

(Vol. 3, p. 229)

5. 17 FEBRUARY 1659

Mr. Neville. I think the last proposition, whether you will have another House, not material now; but when the whole Petition and Advice comes in debate, another House perhaps may then be thought convenient; but it is not necessary you should take the old way into consideration. You may have another House, and not a negative voice. You are not going to build upon the old constitution. The Other House may be such a House as is only preparatory to this, as, among popular assemblies in other commonwealths, there was an assembly to propound laws, and another to enact them, and a single person to put all in execution. Commonwealth was a good title, but grubbed up by the title of Chief Magistrate.

The negative voice will not at all touch the Other House. It is presumed we are going to something else, though what are men? Therefore it is not fit to debate whether it shall be in the power of any person or persons to strangle the debates and pains of this House.

(Vol. 3, pp. 320–21)

6. 18 FEBRUARY 1659

Mr. Neville. It is all one. You will either have the Lords' House, or none. If you will have none, then you can have no negative. If you have one, how can that, the House of Lords, be a boundary to the kingly power? You have no such House of Peers now, which hath an interest answerable to be able to do it. Here will be a negative upon you, and the Chief Magistrate shall have the power of that. There is no intent to cheat. Whenever a House of Peers comes to be debated, it will not be found that a House of Peers shall be of that use now as formerly. We are upon alterations, and no thought now is to be taken of what was done by John of Gaunt, and such fellows. The Lords much outweighed before, and now the Commons and the people outweigh; and your King, not long since, before the Parliament, did oversway. So you build upon an ill foundation if you aim at the old way. You cannot build up that which God and nature have destroyed. We are upon an equal balance, which puts out Turkish government and peerage. Laws are made to preserve things that are, not things that are destroyed. You are invested with all legal power. If you will say, all power is in the sword, that is one thing; if in the people, that is another. But it is in the people, in you, in consent. You have laid a good foundation, a single person. It now concerns you to build upon that, and to bound him, that he may lay claim to no more power than now you give him. You are in a good way. Go on.

(Vol. 3, pp. 330–31)

7. 21 FEBRUARY 1659

Mr. Neville. The account is very satisfactory and accurate. Here hath been something offered of interest of state, of trade, and of religion.

For this last it is certain, that the Protestant cause or the Protestant religion are different things. When a war is begun upon account that the Protestant religion is in persecution, as in France and Spain formerly, there is a great concernment, and it ought to move us before all things else. There is no such war now, as I take it.

But I call that a Protestant interest or cause, when several particulars agree and league together for maintaining their respective dominions.

As to this quarrel, I can see nothing of religion or Protestant religion. There are Calvinists and Lutherans on both sides. Brandenburgh, Holland, Denmark, are all Protestants; and as good, if not better than the Swede; and therefore I cannot see how the Protestant religion is particularly concerned in this.

England, indeed, cannot subsist without trade, and interests of state may, peradventure, far engage us. I know not how it comes, unless it is because of your interest against Spain, that the Emperor is in alliance with Spain. It is told you, the interest of the Baltic Sea is material to your trade. Therefore, our question will be: -

How far forth our engaging now, by intermeddling with the business of the Sound, can advance our interest, either for the strength or for the trade of this nation? And it seems to me to be for our service to preserve it in Denmark's hands, where it hath been this long time; your friend's, whose right it is, and where it was and will be well enough, if we please ourselves. The King of Denmark hath but the door into the Sound. But what if we should help to put it into the hands of Sweden, that hath both the door and the house too? Consider whether thus to trust them be for your service.

Your recommending it, may include peace or war; to decree which is our work. The management, indeed, may be elsewhere, but we must well consider the inconveniences we may be engaged in, if we undertake a war, and therefore you must resolve what you mean to do by setting forth our ships. It is one thing to maintain a fleet at home, another thing to maintain a war abroad. Contending for that trade, we are like two rivals, that go a wooing to one woman.

It grieves my heart to think what hath been the event of the breaking of the peace with Spain. We had a war with Holland. I am ashamed to say upon what terms the peace was made.

I cannot give a rational account of it, unless it were to establish the Government over us, which was set after on foot, so that England was conquered, instead of conquering Holland. For if the Hollander had come into conditions with us, as was fairly offered, that Government would never have expected any place in this nation: but the abrupt war with Spain, and the dishonourable peace with the Dutch, gave opportunity to what after followed. I am afraid, if you engage now against Holland, they will be too hard for you. We are exhausted for money. It is not for a *hierarchy* to maintain that war.

If we put the Sound into the Swede's hand, we must, for ever after, trade but at his courtesy; for he will have not only all the dominion of the Sound, but all the Baltic in his own hands, and the territories adjoining to it in his power. Thus Sweden is able to maintain that trade himself. I know not that it is fit to trust Sweden with it. Why may we not assist Denmark?

I suppose the danger from the Emperor is not considerable. He is not like to sit down by the Sound. His dominions lie far off. He hath enough to do to defend himself against the Turk; and though he hath sent forces into Flanders, yet I presume you may have terms of security, at least of neutrality from him.

Besides all this, I apprehend it will be no easy matter to get monies to carry on this war. I would have it our first business, that by peace we may remain umpire, rather than engage upon such a hard service in a war. Therefore, I shall move for a further day to be appointed, that gentlemen may consider of this; that we bethink ourselves what to offer in this business; unless you think fit, now, to send ambassadors for a mediation.

(Vol. 3, pp. 387–92)

8. 24 FEBRUARY 1659

Mr. Neville. I doubt this will lead into a long debate. The militia hath been in several hands according as the balance of government hath varied. It has sometimes been asserted to be in the King, sometimes in the Lords, sometimes in the Commons.

By the Petition and Advice the militia is entrusted in the Parliament, sitting the Parliament. I suppose you will consider where it is now. It is no where in the world by any law, for the Petition and Advice is out of doors.

I doubt the business of the Sound will hardly keep cold corked up, till you have considered these things, and settled the debate concerning the militia. I would have you, then, quite put this off at present.

Let it pass now and declare your sense, whether you think it fit to engage in this war, whether this fleet shall go into the Baltic sea, or whether they shall have your instructions along with them what to do.

(Vol. 3, p. 461)

9. 1 March 1659

Mr. Neville. You are not now about transacting with the other House; and therefore to move that we shall transact with them begs the question. You are upon a single vote, in order to preparing a Bill.

I hear it not yet answered that the Petition and Advice being personally addressed to his late Highness is personal; therefore the Protector that now is, is not obliged, nor indeed empowered to call another House; so that by what is offered, you will swallow the Petition and Advice at once.

That question of transacting with them, was the debate of many days, last Parliament, and that lies unresolved yet, and it might have been better insisted upon, then.

Your proper question, and I pray hold us to it, is whether the House you intend shall be the other House mentioned in the Petition and Advice.

(Vol. 3, p. 564)

10. 5 March 1659

Mr. Neville. All the motions are irregular. I am for another House, but not for this, nor that, but another. I am, in truth, against both these Houses.

I think you are going to vote that which cannot be, though you should vote. There were two ends of the other House.

1. For a balance, and that is impossible now to be. No power in England can be a balance. There can be no support, no subsistence

for it, but by force. That which made them a balance before, was their great power and interest in the nation. Then every lord of the manor was called. They represented their tenants. Thus the whole nation was truly represented by the Lords, and no need of a House of Commons.

The Commons will be apt to say, shall we have a vote stand between us and home? The people will never return to them without force, or be subject long. We have known when the Lords refused to consent to a Bill, the Commons sent up a messenger to know the face of that Lord that refused it. Another time, this House sent them word, by Sir John Evelyn, that if they would not pass an ordinance, they would pass it without them. This will not be endured by the people, to have a sort of privileged persons to obstruct the passing their laws.

The Commons at present are much more considerable than at that time, and the Lords much less. Therefore, as to the balance of power, it will come to nothing. Heretofore the Lords' House paid this. There were so many blue coats in our father's remembrance, that sat in this House, as we could see no other colours there. Near twenty Parliament-men would wait upon one Lord, to know how they should demean themselves in the House of Commons. The Lords paid the Commons then, and we must now pay the Lords.

The King would have been glad to have had tonnage and poundage for ever. We are now having an excise for ever. If this be at any time thought grievous, you can never lessen the charge nor grievance of the nation. You give them salaries to be your balance. For these persons, they depend upon the single person, and they are paid by the public revenue as well as the single person, so as you will have two negatives upon you, both in pay by that revenue, when you think to diminish it. If the King had stood in no need of money from the people, we had had no Parliaments. The great Turk had been amongst us.

The second use of another House is to bar the sudden and precipitate passing of laws, for that, indeed, I would have the other House, either to consider of laws before or after they are considered by you; but I would have them chosen either by the people or by you, so that they might rise or fall with you.

I shall move you, that you will not transact with those persons. There is much more to be said for the old peerage being neuters. They have no dependency. They are but as rich commoners now. They are no more. Let us have them rather than the other; as much more fit and indifferent.

(Vol. 4, pp. 23–25)

II. 18 MARCH 1659

Mr. Neville. I intended not to have troubled you in this debate.

The manner of this Union has been fully related to you. I was at the drawing of that declaration. The Union of that nation was then calculated for a Commonwealth, and not for a Monarchy. England was then, by the blessing of God, governed by its own representatives.

I conceive you are not bound by that Union, and you, first, ought to consider what constitution you will be at. You invited them to the same constitution with yourselves, and they received it.

As to the point of right. If they had right, and if writs had not been sent, they might have demanded it at your doors. Yet, if Edinburgh had come and demanded that right, you would not have granted it.

It is agreed, on all hands, that the Chief Magistrate cannot send writs to choose knights. Writs he may send to boroughs, but must first grant a patent to make them boroughs.

As to prudence. It is dangerous, at this time of day, to endow the Chief Magistrate with such a power to issue out writs to what place he pleases, to send whom they please, when you know not how you will bound him and limit him.

It cannot be prejudicial to that nation not to send members. It is much charge to them. They have a law which cannot be applicable to our laws. They must not have Englishmen imposed upon them by letters to enslave them and us too. None can be chosen there but of their own sheriffdom. It is absolutely to enslave and reduce them to a province. You are not ripe at this time to admit them; and though I differ from that gentleman in the means, I shall agree with him in the end, that the question be, whether, as things now stand, they have a legal right to sit here?

(Vol. 4, p. 188)

12. 1 APRIL 1659

Mr. Neville. I am so far from blaming the gentleman that brought in this Bill, that I would have brought it in, myself. I believe there are some defects in the levy, that unless you do something in this, they cannot act so cheerfully, that act in it.

The ends of Parliament have ever since King James's time been untimely ends. The people were wise, and would not serve those ends that they were called together for.

Our new monarchy had the same influence on Parliament. The Instrument of Government had made good humane provision for the maintenance of thirty thousand men, with whose pay you could not meddle. It was not thought so good to be on a military account, but upon a legal, which you know has its flaw.

If there had not been a necessity for calling you, you had not been here. You are here to serve turns, to strengthen the government, and to pay two millions of money.

You have a single person in a possessory right, put in by the Council; that call themselves a council, I know not by what law. You have made several votes. I hope, if ever the Bill comes on again, we shall speak to that point of the single person. Consider your own constitution before you settle your revenue. This is *hysteron proteron.* It may be, you will think fit to retrench the Chief Magistrate's charge, that he may not go out with his chariots and horses, the powers of the heathen.

I would have no excise levied after this Parliament, unless confirmed by the Parliament.

(Vol. 4, pp. 322–23)

Appendix C

The Armies Dutie (1659)

To the Reader.

Reader, Whoever thou art, 'tis fit thou should know that the following Letters were sent to the Lord *Fleetwood,* and read by him before the calling of the late Parliament, but were not intended to be published, because those that wrote them, hoped that this advice would have been followed, and they so much wished the Lord *Fleetvvoods* Honor, that they desired the good he should do might appear to be from the impulse of his own mind, but now finding that our Country hath languished so many months since, and seeing the distraction and confusion, that his neglect hath now brought upon us, and finding the general Counsel of Officers, to have expressed their sense of our dangers and impending ruine; and to have interposed in the dissolving the Parliament: when they found by experience, that a settlement would not be made by them, we thought fit to make these Letters publick, hoping that it may in some measure quicken up the Lord *Fleetvvood* himself, upon a second reading of them, and also those Officers that are now concerned by the utmost perill of their lives, to procure a settlement of that common freedome, which hath cost so much bloud and treasure, we have only to request your reading these Letters, with respect to the season wherein they were written, and without

Transcribed from the first edition, printed in 1659. For discussion of Neville's possible involvement in the authorship of this pamphlet, see the Introduction (above, pp. xiv and xix).

prejudice upon your minds, and the Lord: Cause you to understand and do the things that belong to our Countreys Peace and Welfare.

H. M. H. N. I. L.
I. W. I. I. S. M.

My Lord,
You have long been the object of many good mens pity and prayers, who have judged in charity that the temptations of your late Fathers Court have been too mighty for you. But now you are become the object of their prayers and great expectations; hitherto they thought you unable to prevent the wickednesse and apostacy which you have often seemed to mourn for in secret. But now the chief military power derived from any lawfull authority being fallen upon you, and all such Officers and Souldiers in the Army as have any sense of justice and honesty in their use of arms, being ready to be commanded by you, and to rejoyce in their return to their first principles. They believe that God hath made your way plain before you to vindicate the profession of Religion from the black reproaches that rest upon it, to restore the peoples liberties, the Armies honour, and price of their bloud. And therefore they hope and pray that the Lord may say effectually to you upon this opportunity: *Be thou strong and of a good courage in this my work, and I will be with thee.* But if you should now sit still, they think as *Mordecai* said to *Esther that deliverance and enlargement shall arise to the people from another; but you and your fathers house shall be destroyed.* Now my Lord, do not imagine us either vain Enthusiasts or busie bodies that thus mind you, what is expected from you. We are such as engaged with you in the war against the late King, and do believe that you and we must render an account to the dreadfull God of the justice and sincerity of our intentions therein, and our souls are deeply afflicted to behold our righteous ends perverted, the bloud of our friends shed in the quarrell, trampled upon, the binding power of trusts, promises, and oaths, slighted, and the same (if not worse) principles of Arbitrary power, Tyranny, and oppression exercised, asserted, and maintained, against which we have so earnestly contended with a prodigall expence of our bloud and estates; and our hearts are wounded to hear our old cause now made a mock and by-word by our enemies, and to see such a

black brand of infamy set upon all the Parliaments adherents, as if they
had been all the vilest hypocrites, who made pretences of Religion, and
faithfulnesse to their Countries Laws and Liberties, to be only a cloak
for the blackest wickednesse, as if none of them had ever intended any
more, then by force and fraud to fat up themselves upon the bloud and
ruines of other families. But your Lordship knows, that the Kings invasion of our properties and liberties, by taxes, illegall imprisonments, and
opposition of the Parliament in their supreme trust of ordering the Militia for the peoples safety, did necessitate us to defend it by arms, as our
native right, that the trust of the peoples safety and welfare, their
strength, and purses, was only in the hands of their successive Parliaments, and that they ought to be governed only by the Laws: And their
consciences, persons, or estates, to be at no mans will or mercy; And
doubtlesse the defence of these Liberties is essentially necessary to the
well being of any Nation, and to the being of publick morall righteousness
amongst men. And your Lordship knows that all the successes and victories have been owned, as from the wonderfull appearance of God for
his people in this honest cause, and that you caused the exercise of the
chief Magistracie in *England* by a single person to be abolish'd, because
it was dangerous to this righteous cause, as well as uselesse and burdensome. Now my Lord, let us appeal to your conscience whether we ought
not to expect those things we do, we are unwilling lest it should wound
too deep to make a comparison between the principles of Tyrannie and
oppression that were attempted to be practised by the late King, and were
declared by you to be begotten by the blasphemous arrogance of Tyrants
upon their servile parasites, and those that have been practised & avowed
since God gave us victorie in the defence of our Liberties (and though we
confesse the greatest number of honest men have hitherto least smarted
under them, yet they will infallibly have the greatest weight of them
upon their backs hereafter, should those principles get root amongst us,
they being the only likely men to destroy them, and however, injustice
against Enemie ought to be abhorred by righteous Men.) But let us tell
your Lordship that it is the secret sigh of every honest heart: Oh that
God would now take away the reproach from this People, and their eyes
are much upon you in it, and shoud you slight our eyes and expectations

in this case, assuredlie the blood of our friends shed in the Cause, will crie aloud for vengeance against you.

We have better thoughts of your Lordship, then that you should seek to shelter your self in your omission of so great a Dutie, or in your proceeding in the evils begun under those vain subterfuges which have been used of late: Oh be not deceived with pretences of Providences of God, leading you from your old Cause into things not to be justified by the morall Lawes. The holie God directs his People only into the paths of Righteousnesse, that is such Actions as agree with his Lawes, 1, *Iohn* 3. 7, 8, 10. *He that doth not Righteousness is not of God,* His Providences and his Lawes alwaies speak the same things, neither let any man deceive you with pretence of necessitie that constrains you to desert your old Principles for the People of Gods sake and to advance Christs Kingdome; For 'tis not possible there should be necessitie to transgresse a Divine naturall Law that is Eternall, there may be cases of extream inevitable necessitie, that may disoblige a man from some Divine positive Lawes, because a Superior that is a Divine, naturall Law may oblige him in that case; Therefore in everie case of highest necessities, the immutable Lawes of Nature ought to be Guides and Commanders of what is to be done: And if your Lordship can make your Actions or Omissions consist with those, neither God nor his People will blame you. And in so doing onelie, you can advance Christs Kingdome: For then is he exalted when supream Reverence, and absolute subjection is given to his Fathers Lawes in the deniall of our selves in all Countermands and Temptations, and when the sword of the Spirit is used to increase the number of such Subjects: For this Scepter, Throne and Wars are of and in Righteousness.

Therefore, we beseech your Lordship without hesitation or delay, pursue the exaltation of Christ and his Kingdom, in following in simplicity and integrity of heart after those righteous ends you proposed and declared in the late warre, and unto which you have obliged your self by all the sacred Bonds of humane societie: be not affrighted with some Parasites, bugbears of Confusion, if you shake the *Diana,* by which they hope to subsist, fear not assistance from every honest heart in *England,* and though some pretenders to honesty, may out of cowardise, or ambition, or covetousness, cry, ther's a Beare and a Lion in the way, yet even they shall run after you when they see you forward in your way; And to avoid delayes, let us beseech your Lordship first to examine your conscience presently what you can answer to the blood of any poor Saint shed, that cries in your ears to settle that Libertie and Justice in his Countrie for which he shed his blood under your command.

Secondly, what you can answer to the blood of Thousands of the enemies, which are esteemed by God as murdered by you if the Iustifick cause of the war be not effectually prosecuted. Will not their blood crie to God, and say, Lord, this *Fleetwood* killed us upon pretence that we should have destroied the Liberties of the People of God, in imposing Arbitrarie power upon them, which we did ignorantlie? And he hath done the same thing, and made or suffered more heavie Yokes to be imposed; Pray remember it, The Scripture saith, *Thinkest thou O Man, that judgest another, and doest the same things thy selfe, that thou shalt escape the iudgement of God*, Rev. 1. 3, 4.

Thirdly, We beseech you to examine what Cause you now maintain with constant expence of blood, and the Peoples Estates, and how you can give an account to God for it. Remember what are the causes for which God alloweth mens blood to be shed without blood-guiltinesse in him that causeth it; and trie whether that be one, to make a Nation greater slaves to *Iohn* a *Styles* and his Confederates, then they would have been to *Iohn* a *Nokes*. But we praie your Lordship if it be possible that anie pretence can be found for it, state a justifick Cause of your present posture of Arms, that thousands of tender consciences may be satisfied how to pray for you in any of your present designes, if God should not honour you in the work which they now expect from You.

Now My Lord, if we would plead with you by worldly Arguments or motives, that concern your self, it were easie to evince, that safetie, honour, and greatness to your self, and familie, can be certainlie compassed by no other means, then by returning to the Principles from whence you are fallen, your daily terrors that now attend you and your Counsells, would soon vanish, you might have above threescore thousand men of honest principles that would take themselves concern'd to be in armes at an houres warning to assist you, and this without second charge, and an armie of praiers 2. times as great, indeed who would or could hurt you, if you were a naked sincere follower of that which is good. We appeal to your conscience, whether you do not believ that your late Father was more safe with a Foot-boy onelie following him in the streets when he was believed to intend that good that your Lordship may if you please effect, then he was afterwards (when he was believed to intend his own ambition) invironed with Guards, and enclosed with locks, and bolts without number; Indeed the onelie meanes of safetie for such as will exercise great power over a people to the subjection of their liberties, is a mercenarie Armie. And if that consists of some of the same people, their interest will change as often as they get estates that are of more value then their pay, and then they will be readie to conspire with any of the people to provide libertie and securitie of their estate for their children, and then the power of the Tirants shake, And of how manie slaughters of the Kings of Israell do we read by their own service; & if mercenarie strangers be intended to be Guards for Rulers in England, our Ancestors taught us the way, when they were not so well instructed in their libertie to ridd our selves of them in a night, But if your own person could be secure for a while; what will be the portion of your familie, if their persons and estates be left to the mercie of him that gets uppermost, And if you expect greatnesse or honor, consider whose names are delivered to us from former ages with reverence, and esteem, and who have been most admired, honored, and obeyed, by their countrey and people: Can a *Dionysius* compare, command or fain with a *Tymoleon;* was ever great *Cyrus* or *Alexander* obeyed like the poor young Fisher-boy *Massinello* in *Naples,* whil'st the people imagin'd he sought a settlement of their libertie? But we suppose the sense and remembrance of your dutie to God and his people, should be of greater weight in your Lordships heart then all the conceits of the earth, & therefore we also forbear to mind you of the improbabilitie of setling this Nation according to the rules of pollicie, upon anie other basis then their libertie; the lands & interests of this Nation being so dispersed & with so much equalitie, that whosoever shall attempt to invade our liberties will not find an interest able to overballance the peoples interest, and therefore cannot long maintain a Dominion over them; But we forbear to mention this Capital politick consideration to your Lordship at present, onlie let us beg your serious consideration how much the honor of the profession of the Gospel is concerned in what we move your Lordship to, & expect from you; And that you would say to your self, is it not better that I & mine perish, then that a publick scandal be brought upon Gospel profession by my injustice & treacherie to my Countrie under a shew of holiness; & if we shall observe by your Lordships actions from henceforth that there are some apearances, that God hath begun to imprint upon your heart the sense of your publick dutie, and that he will put that honor & greatness upon you to be the restorer of his peoples liberties in this Nation, we shall then think our selves obliged to write again to your Lordship or wait upon you to strengthen your hands; In the interim, we shall praie without ceasing, that wisdom, courage and strength may be given you from the Father of all mercies, and that out of his fulness you may be in all things prepared for the accomplishing his own work of righteousness; And if in judgement to this Nation your heart should be hardned by these poor lines, your Lordship will be left more inexcusable, and however some satisfaction in the discharge of your duties will arise to the Consciences of

> My Lord, Your Lordships
> Most affectionate humble servants
> So far as you follow Christ—

My Lord,
We presumed lately to mind your Lordship of your present oportunity, and most important duty, and our souls wish that the secrets of your thoughts upon it were revealed, that our hearts and prayers might be towards you, and for you accordingly we must tell your Lordship that you have since wounded the hearts of many precious Saints, by conducting your Armie officers, in an action of such gross hypocrisie, and palpable flattery, as that addresse you made to your new Protector, we have reason to believe that it had been impossible for your Lordship to have said privately to an honest man without blushing, what you have said there to the world under your hand, and if your Lordship will remember (with God in your eye) what is said of your father, and your brother in it, and of an unknown connexion between his person and your cause, which also you cannot now, and as now (state to your own conscience as just,) we are

confident your heart will smite you, and if your own heart condemn you, God is greater then your heart, and must much more condemn you. Truly my Lord, we were much startled in our hopes from you, and praiers for you, (and we hear the same of others) when we saw that addresse, yet our remembrance of your secret expressions even with tears, of your sense of the Armies backslidings, and your earnest intreaties of us to pray for you, together with the great respect we have, for your Lordship hath inclined us strongly to the best thoughts of you, sometimes saying one to another, surely he had not read our letter before his Addresse, yet we have been so stumbled, that we had troubled your Lordship no farther in this kind, if God had not so placed the interest of his cause and people upon our spirits, that we are restlesse within our selves, untill we have said so much, as may be either effectuall upon your heart, or at least discharge our consciences, and leave you inexcusable. If therefore the Lord hath made us his remembrancers to you, and revived his fear in your heart, whilest you considered what we sent you, we have reason to conclude that you are come to these resolves in your owne breast, viz. 1. That the peoples arms of this nation have been committed to your charge in your severall capacities, as a steward of that high trust for them, to imploy them for their benefit, in preserving their rights and freedome, and that you must give an account to the eternall God of that stewardship.

2. That you are under all possible sacred and indispensable obligations to be faithfull in your trust.

3. That the cause for which you were trusted was to defend and maintain the peoples right to make laws for themselves, and thereby provide for their own welfare and safety, by such persons as they should chuse, and that without the negative controule of the King, and also to defend the freedome of their consciences, persons, and estates, in being over the only government of their own laws, without subjection to the will or mercie of any man.

And we suppose you may also conclude that you have now power and oportunitie cast upon you to secure this libertie unto Gods people, according to humane prudence beyond the reach of wicked men, and that if you should hide your talent of power, in the napkins of fear, cowardise, ambition, or self-interest, you will be condemned from the mouth of your own conscience, for an unprofitable and unfaithfull servant.

Now if God hath enabled your Lordship thus to consider, with a pure understanding, and with integritie of heart thus to resolve, we know you are continually saying within your self, men and brethren what shall I doe, to shew my faithfulnesse to the cause of God, and the people, and to vindicate my possession from scandall; and in hopes that God hath thus disposed your heart, we shall endeavour to inquire into your particular dutie.

And in our search we may assert this generall maxime, as an infallible pillar to guide you in your present dutie to your generation, *viz.* that the peoples liberties cannot be lastingly secured to them by any other means, then an institution of sense, wise order or method, wherein the people may make and execute their own laws, and use their own arms and strength, for the common good of the whole societie. This may direct all your Lordships thoughts and debates, about a settlement, and keep in your eie perpetually the white mark wherein all your designes and contrivances of publick concernment, ought to centre; this may prepare you, to passe a quick sentence upon all the ambitious proposals of your Court-parasites, this may cut off all those Court debates, about impowering a Prince, to check and controul the people by his negative, in their making their laws. It ought to be no question, whither the people should make their own laws, God himself having resolved it, the very point being the single point whereupon you joyned Battell at first with the King, you defending that the Parliaments Ordinance for the *Militia,* was a Law without the Kings consent, and he denying it to be of any force, and affirming those Traitors, that obeied that, and not his *Commissions of Array* (this by the Kings Confession was the first quarrel) this libertie then being their bloud, cannot be taken from them, but by the highest robberie and contempt of Obligations to God and Man. Therefore your Lordships dutie is no more then to contrive the best, most prudent form, and order, wherein the people may injoy their own, with the least hazard of being preyed upon by Tirants, or being disquieted by their own ignorant disorders and confusions: Your dutie to the people, is like to that of a Guardian to an Heir, Not to give them an Estate, but to set down rules, how it shall be ordered for them, and they put in quiet Possession of it, to their most advantage and securitie, and this dutie is the more incumbant upon you, because you have broken, and trampled to pieces, beyond repair all those old Christian forms, wherein they formerly injoyed their liberties, though with continuall Disputes, and subject to daily injuries and oppressions.

Now before we propose to your Lordship any Form or Order to be settled, it is fit that we discover to you the Errours and inconsistencies, of your present practices, and appearing design, both in themselves, and in relation to the peoples liberties.

First, it's a grand errour in the foundation, if you imagine it possible to secure libertie or justice to the people, onelie by advancing good men to power over them, and trusting to the grace in their hearts, to rule in righteousnesse, good men upon the single account of mortalitie, can be no lasting bottom, whereupon to settle liberty and justice. It's beyond the wisdome of man, to contrive an infallible provision, in the present age that the ruling power in the succeeding age, shall fall onelie into good mens hands, but what age ever produced men of such enlightned pure minds? that of themselves could discern right at all times, without the least cloud of their private interest upon their understandings, and also pursue such dictates of their minds, without interruptions by corrupt affections; we mention this, not as if our Souls did not wish, that all powers were vested in the best of men, but because we know that every man is vanitie, and a Lie; and yet we believe, it is often whispered in your eares, by some weak well meaning men, that honest mens liberty would then be secure, and they satisfied, if they could see good men put into power, saying we should then need no lawes, for they would be a law to themselves, having Gods law in their hearts, but those that thus by consequence beg advancement, know not what they ask, scarce intending to be the peoples lords and to rule them as their slaves, which is necessarily employed in the arbitrarie power they ask; neither do they apprehend, what horrid impietie it is, for any man in England now to erect, and exercise an arbitrarie power, they see not the blasphemous arrogancy of such as rule without lawes, being indeed, an attempt to erect their throne, in it's kind, higher then Almightie Gods, who rules and judges onelie according to his lawes, without which there is neither justice, nor injustice in things humane, or divine, therefore the peoples security of libertie, and justice, must be founded upon excellent lawes, or constitutions, for the continued order, from generation to generation, wherein the people shall chuse their own lawes and magistrates, and if good men in power, will in simplicitie and integritie joyn heads, hearts, and hands to establish such an order, or forme of Government, they will be worthilie esteemed the founders, though not the foundation of our Liberties.

Secondlie, 'tis a grosse mistake, to think that the securing the peoples Liberties, and the creating of a Soveraign Prince over them, (under whatsoever title) can consist together, we mean such a Prince or Potentate, the tenure of whose power, shall not be upon the people, and who shall not be subject, and accomptable to the Lawes of this Commonwealth, doubtlesse the people may not be free, where there shall be a chief Magistrate, whose deserved real honour and greatnesse, may justly make him disdain to look down upon the Throne of the greatest Monarch, yet if he shares in the Soveraigntie, he subverts Libertie and the foundation of his own glorie: the very essence or formall reason of a Nations freedom, consists in the peoples making their own Lawes and Magistrates, and therefore it is a contradiction to say, we are free under a Prince controling our Lawes in their Creation, or Execution, and imposing his Officers upon us at his will and the consequence of that practice, even in our late Kings, hath caused all our present bloudie ruines, his Officers being naturally inclined, and resolved to serve their Creator, to the subversion of our Lawes and Liberties; besides, if a Prince be invested with the least Punctilio of the Soveraigntie, it is exceeding vain to imagine, that he should not naturally aspire to the top of it: every thing having an innate desire of its owne perfection, and there being no other visible meanes to preserve from the peoples reach, that part which hee hath, but the destruction of their Libertie, you may as well suppose, fire not to ascend, as such a Prince not to be wishing and aspiring to be an absolute Lord, if he had neither ambition, nor pride in himself, nor in his appendixes, his Court Parasites, yet the unavoydable reciprocall fear, in the people, and such a Prince, least each should dispoil the other of his share of Soveraigntie, will compell the Prince to provide for his own securitie, and do your

Lordship think he will believe himself safe, untill he hath set himself above the peoples reach, and brought them to depend upon his will? It may be he that you would create Prince with a small share of Soveraignty, would at first thinke his power great, yet in continuance he would esteem it smal, men naturally reaching beyond what they have attained; Liberty therefore and Principalitie, are incompatible, and can never last together: It seems strange to a People, that they should be free, and yet serve, and be imposed upon it's strange to a Prince, that he should be chief Lord and not command; The meane of Libertie, is the Mother of Murder, and Tyrannie; any Freedome from Princes Commands being intollerable to them, they by Violence take it away, or attempt it, and that forceth a Violent brutish Tyrany, instead of Government, We need not look farre for an instance of this, the bloud and sufferings of our Ancestours, and our own Age, witnesse it, hath not our Princes and Ancestours been alwayes strugling for four hundred yeares, and thousands perished in it, that are known, besides the ruine of many Worthies which no History durst mention, unlesse with Infamie, to please the Tyrants, And your Lordship hath seen, with what an Earth-quake, Libertie subverted Principalitie, when it found Opportunitie. Therefore, if you wish us, and our Posterities no greater good then onely Quiet, it behooveth you to make us wholly Free, or wholly Slaves.

Thirdly, It is no small fayler of foresight, that you may imagine it feasible in this Nation, at this time, to establish a Principalitie, or Monarchie, of any probable continuance, unlesse you can destroy all present Reall Properties and vest all, or most of the Lands of *ENGLAND,* in your Monarch. Every Princes Power of Command must arise either from a voluntarie Submission, and willingnesse of a People to serve him, as their Lord, or from a Violent Compulsion, of them to be subject to Him, and both those are founded upon an inequalitie, between him and them, either reall or apparent. A Peoples willingnesse to serve a Prince (if any such be) ariseth from their apprehension of some great inequality and disproportion between him and them, either in vertue, interest, or power. The two first are proper to a Prince in his native countrey, or one that hath dominion over only a sovereign Prince, who may be thought powerfull to one people, the last may be proper to protect a people, and that may be chosen as the least of some impudent mischiefs; but if any people ever were, or shall be voluntarily subject to a Prince, upon their high opinion of his unequall transcendent vertue, that related only to his person, and never was or can be a solid foundation for an hereditary Monarchy, but an unequall interest in the lands, may be, and is the common cause, either of a voluntary or constrained subjection: no man serves for nought, 'tis the need that people have of the Lords interest, that procures him servants, and enables him to compell subjection: so *Joseph* that new moulded the *Egyptian* Monarchy, devised a way for the King to get all the possessions into his hands, that so the people might serve *Pharaoh*, which was a necessary consequence. 'Tis evident that the relation of masters and servants would soon be banished the world, if all mens interests, vertues, and strength were equall, and much sooner would the names of princes and subjects be for ever razed out of memory; surely then (my Lord) 'tis beyond dispute that if you intend to settle a Monarchy over us, it must be by violence, for it cannot enter into your heart, to imagine, that you shall find a man, whose glorious vertues shall be as a Sun amongst the stars compared with all the vertues in this nation, and those also to be surely intailed upon his heirs, neither can your Lordship pretend, to find any family, whose interest in the lands is now so unequall, to the bulk of the people, that the nation should be induced by their interest to serve them.

Now that a compulsive subjection to a Monarchy, must be the product of an unequall power, is as good as written with a Sunbeam, he that forceth must be stronger then he that is forced, and 'tis as evident, that such a power is the only naturall fruit of an unequall interest in the lands, upon which the beast of force must graze, that bears the Monarch power to force a nation, cannot be inherent in a single person, and multitudes of hands, neither can nor will serve him to subject a nation, unless they be hired, (Christ himself says no man goes to warfare at his own charge) and nothing can afford the constant growing hire of the Princes own, but his interest in the lands, and if he put the hirelings to rob and pilfer for their own hire, upon the fruits of the lands, which the people esteem their own, (that is by taxes) the basis and root of the power, by which the forces live, hath not an appearance to be in the Monarch, nor do his forces seem to have a necessary dependance upon him, but may as well rob for themselves, and at best, they must remain a fluctuating body without root, the Monarch not being able to plant them upon his lands with conditions of service; and therefore they will be esteemed of the land owners, only as the common thieves, whose hands are against every man, and ought to have every mans hand against them, and the robbery being in such a case, to be renewed continually upon the land-owners, and the wound alwaies smarting, 'tis of more constant danger, to subvert the Monarch, then it were for him to cut the throats of ten thousand land-owners at once, and possesse the lands, to plant his forces upon, as their standing-quarters upon their masters own lands, either for their lives, or during his pleasure. Surely (my Lord) it's not to be denied, that a Monarch in his domestick dominions, hath no greater rooted continuing power over a nation, then he hath an interest in the lands, surmounting in value, the interest of the whole people, as that interest grows, by murders, oppression, and the other common artifices of Princes, (unlesse the wrath of God interposeth) so doth his power root, and flourish, all other seeming power of a Monarch, hangs as the ignorant use to say, by Geometry, and is without bottome; 'tis a tree whose root is dead, and may be kept up a little while by dead props that decays with it. 'Tis like an armies foraging into an enemies countrey, and plundering, not being able to gain the possession of a town, castle, or house there, as a root of power over it. Indeed, no form of domestick government can be establisht to be of duration, in a nation, chiefly living upon their lands, if property in the land do not accompany the Empire, that is, if that order which governs (be it one man, or the few, or the people) do not possesse a greater share of the land of that countrey, then the rest of the people that are governed; and therefore where the Administration is most popular; servants, and all such as have no estates are reckoned to have no share, or voices in the government. And we conceive, that the founders of governments, have either framed their models, according to the ballance of property, which they found amongst the people, or else have divided the property, and reduced it to their form. And your Lordship may remember when God himself formed the people of Israel, by *Moses* hand, into a free Commonwealth, there was not only a suitable division of the lands at the first, but a perpetuall law of Jubilee, to prevent alienation of lands, and the growth of any to such unequall interest, as his power might be dangerous to the government, and when that people rejected Gods form of their Common wealth for a Monarch, he foretold them, 1 *Sam.* 8. 11. 17. that the first work of their King would be to alter the modell of property in the lands, settled by God and take away the best of their fields, vineyards, and olive-yards, and give them to his servants, for strengthening himself, and so they should become his servants. And if we should not trouble your Lordship too much, we would shew from History, that all the lasting Monarchies that ever were in the world, have been built upon this foundation, of possessing the greatest interest in their countreys lands, either immediately, or by their Peers and their powers, being the naturall result of that, they have had their births, decays, and deaths together. Some kingdomes we say have been founded upon the Monarchs immediate interest, or property in the lands, as many ancient *Eastern* Kings, and the *Turk,* with other *Eastern* Princes at this day, who are sole proprietors or Landlords of the whole Territories where they reign, and the people their tenants at will, or at best for life, upon conditions of service in war, proportionable to the value of their farms, whereby the *Turk* keeps an absolute power over his subject by their dependance upon his will for their bread, and with his own proper revenue is able also to maintain an army of strangers to strengthen the other tie, he hath upon his vassalls, and upon this root of his property, (to the eye of humane reason) his power has grown to that monstrous height. Others kingdomes have been built upon the property in the lands, which the Monarchs, Peers, have had joyntly with and under him: so were these *Western* dominions after their conquest by the *Northern* people, who divided a land, when conquered, into so many parcels, as they had great Officers, leaving the choice of the best and largest share to their Prince or leader, he becoming their King, and the chief Officers, holding their large shares on him by some small acknowledgements, became his Dukes, Counts, and Earls; and the common souldiers (who came indeed to seek a countrey to inhabit) holding together with the poor natives some small parcels of land under those great men upon such conditions as made them wholly dependant upon their Landlords, and thus these Dukes and Earls paying homage and fealty and small acknowledgements to the Prince, became princes in their own divisions, and thus the interest of the King and his Peers overweighed the properties of all other the Inhabitants, whereupon the power of our ancient Monarchy was founded, and the Kings chief Officers were the tenants and vassalls of his Peers, to whom he sent upon occasion of trouble forreign or domestick to leavy arms, who gathered their vassalls together, and either assisted the King, or fought against him as they liked the quarrell, their souldiers never daring to dispute their Lords commands knowing no immediate Lord but them.

Thus was the Kings power lesse or greater, as he agreed with his Peers they having been able (as your Lord ship knows) to make and unmake Kings of *England* as they pleased, and if their propertie in the lands had so remained, nothing could have shaken the Monarchs power, if he had kept an union with them, but the inferiour people grew by degrees to better their tenures, and to make some of their estates hereditary upon easie fines at every change, as our coppy-holders of inheritance and some to have their estates their own free hold, and in fine they came to abolish in *England* the tenures of vassailage & villainage, which is yet in practice amongst our neigh-bour nations, (whose Monarchies stand by so much the stronger) and the people having got a better interest in the lands, soon obtained some share in the government they were then thought fit to be summoned to the national meetings then called Gamont, since a Parliament, to consider what way to supply their King with money, which was to come only from their purses and properties (the nobles then (as now in *France*) paying no Tax or Tollage) and the sense they had of their own properties in the lands made them soon after challenge it as their right, that their King could take no tax, toll, or tollage, unlesse they were pleased to give it him in their Parliaments, and then the peoples yoakes, growing more easy, their wealth increased, and lands being commonly suffered to be alienated, the multitude became the purchasers, and some bought off their services that still remained due to their Lords, and others bought their Lords lands, who proved prodigalls, and as occasion was offered, the Churches lands, and this together with some Kings endeavours to abate the power of their Peers in their Countreys, reduced the English Peerage to an empty name, the greatest quantity of the lands, and with those, the power being fallen into the Commons hands, before the Warr, who being then sensible, they neither depended upon the King nor his Peers for their Bread, conceived themselves obliged to serve none but God, and therefore ought not to be commanded, or to have lawes imposed upon them by the King or his Peers, judging it the right of a people, whose property rendred them free, and independent to chuse their own lawes and Magistrates, being intended onely for the preservation of their own properties and liberties; and thus did our House of Commons gradually grow to that power which in latter time proved formidable to the Kings, there wanting nothing to the destruction of the Throne, whose pillars were broken, but an occasion for the people to feel the power they had, & this was the naturall cause of our late Kings projecting to have brought *German* Horse, or an *Irish* Army into England, a mercenary Army being the last refuge of a Monarch, devested of his Nobility, (though that also will prove but a violent dead prop, and soon rotten, unlesse he can suddainly reassume a greater property, & give them root by an interest in the lands upon conditions of serving him). And this was the cause of the Kings raising his Guard at *York,* and leaving the VVarre; being the last means to support his power; therefore we may say, that the dying pangs of a Monarchial power in England, caused our VVarrs, as his violent stranglings for life, much rather, then that the VVarre caused the destruction of Monarchiall power; the Parliaments Army did indeed prevent a possibility of the resurrection of that power, by a forcible changing the property in the lands, and so reviving a new Monarchy; but the old was dead by a kind of natural desolution before the Parlament voted it uselesse, burdensome, and dangerous; for surely 'tis neither of the three, where, and so long as it's single property in the lands, or in union with his Nobility, makes the people live upon him and them, though 'tis most certainly all the three, where it must be fed upon the peoples properties; like the Snake in the Rustick's house, till it be able to oppresse them.

My Lord, wee hope it will be clear to your Lordship, that England is now become an unnatural soyl for a Monarch. The Governor of the World by various providences hath so divided the land amongst the bulk of the people, that they can live of themselves without serving, and it is preposterous to impose a Monarch upon us, as to make a law, that the weaker shall alwaies binde the stronger; we believe it no less impossible to establish a lasting Monarch in England without alteration of the interest, the multitude hath in the lands, and naturall power, then it were to settle a firm lasting free State, or Commonwealth in the Turkish Territories, suffering the *Ottoman* Family to remain the sole Landlord of the Territories, as now he is; and we suppose, that obvious objection, that England hath been a Monarchy for many hundred years, is clearly answered, from what we have said, if you will take us as conquered, as much by your Army, as by the *Normans,* and think to settle a Monarchy like theirs, in a new line; you see the Materialls, for your building and theirs, are of a different form, and can never make a like building; England then yielded earth to the Conqueror, by vast Earldomes, and Baronies, for the plantation of his new Potentates, and a few confiscations or forfeitures made his own and his creatures interest in the lands to exceed all the rest; besides, the temper of the people, to whom any property in the land was left, was much different from that you now finde, they being then bred to learn, and know no better; now being bred in some liberty, and the continuall claim of the whole. Neither can your Lordship with reason hope to prop up a new Monarchy, by an Army of Natives, to be paid by Taxes, if you consider how soon their Estates of inheritance and naturall love to posterity, with their independency upon the Monarch, a disgust of the universall Odium, they must live under by extorting Taxes, will make them espouse the nationall interest as their own, as did the forreign plants of the *Normans,* when rooted in lands of inheritance, so that no sort of Armes, to be maintained by a meer Tax, can long support a Monarch, because the very Tax, if nothing else, create's and maintain's him Enemies that have roots in his dominions, when his friends have none: we could now shew your Lordship invincible difficulties (as our Case is) to found a Monarchy though you should confiscate to your selves most of the peoples ends, to make your land property over weigh al the rest but we believe the confiscation of a people, that have never fought against you, but whose armes you have borne, to be an act so unnaturall and so full of blacknesse and horrour, that it can never be admitted room in your thoughts, and therefore we shall say nothing of it.

Fourthly, but my Lord there is a fourth mistake that deserves the first place in the file of Errors, that is, to conceive it possible to settle your Brother *Richard* and his heirs as our Prince, to share in the Sovereign power, if the wounds of Monarchiall power in England, were not mortall, doubtlesse his art and experience renders not him to be a Surgeon fit for the cure; it was poverty and famine that shot his deadly arrow into the heart of our Monarchy, and no plaister can heal it, but Mammon to make it self new friends, and do your Lordship judge his estate and property sufficient to make him friends enough to compell this Nation to subjection? what can a prudent man fancy as a foundation of his Empire? wherein is the equality between him and the people, even in your opinion, or the dictates of the present Armies conscience? it was said in the last Parlament frequently, that he was a stranger to the people of God, unknown to the Army, having never actually drawn sword, and one that was never observed to have had any affection for the Parlaments Cause; if your Lordship please to consider it, you will finde such disadvantages attends your Brother, in his aspiring to the Throne, as would render his settlement very doubtfull, if the basis for Monarchy stood firm in England; We pray your Lordship think of the primary of his Education, the tenderness of his years, the meanenesse of his natural Authority, the slenderness of his reputation as soldier, or Counseller, and above all, the hatred and contempt the people hath conceived him; either of which, is sufficient to ruine a settled Prince; and adde unto these, the claime and pretence he sets up, by pretending to be our Prince, for *Charles Stewart* against himselfe: (whose interest and friends forreign and domestique may at the least be put in the ballance with your Brothers) which gives life to a growing root of a civill Warr; and adde farther, your rendring all knowing conscientious men desperate of their liberty bought with their bloud, & then remember the feeble interest and repute of his Lords, who in stead of supporting his Throne, as their predecessours did their Princes have need to be supported by it. And once more adde, that his onely hope and refuge being an army for Gods assistance in such designes, ought not to be expected) that those are natives, not his servants, nor obliged to any dependance upon him, who must against their trust and oaths, fight against their own countrey, and their own interest, (which is to transmit

to posterity their estates in security and freedome) and that all their pay
must be extorted from the people (wherein their relations are concerned)
by taxes and collages, and that your Brother must have the greatest share
of them to subsist upon in his pomp, and that many of those think their
own merit and value equall to your Brothers, and may not be full proof
against ambition, and that they will not discern what aid he contributes
to the paying of the taxes, whereof he spends so much; nor what need
have they of him. Then your Lordship will passe a deliberate resolve,
whether it be probable to settle your Brother as your Monarch, especially
if your Lordship remember with what difficulty fear and danger your
father was supported for three or foure years only under most of the contrary advantages, and above all his pretence to army and people (believed
by many) that he abhorred the thoughts of the reviving the old Monarchy, and intended to procure a settlement of true liberty.

Now my Lord, when we think upon these things, and the work you
are called to, 'tis evident to us that God hath hedged up all the by-waies
from your duty with thorns, or rather seas and mountains of difficulties,
and made the path of righteousnesse plain and easy. 'Tis your duty to
restore the people to their liberty, and lay solid foundations of common
right and justice amongst them, and in the natural course and order of
things, it appears almost impossible to make them slaves. Oh then give
glory to God, vindicate the profession of religion, and make your own
name as sweet odours to all generations in doing your duty, as a freewill-
offering, chearfully and speedily, least your own necessities, and the
peoples confusions should extort it from you. Your only businesse then
my Lord is to settle the order for the continuall successive assemblies of
the people, to make their own laws and Magistrates, all present forms
being broken by you, and an absolute necessity upon you, to appoint what
shall be next, though you would return back to that imperfect form of
Parliaments that's now become unsuitable for us as a free people. For it is
essentially necessary to the securitie of freedome, that the same assem-
blie should never have the debating and finally resolving power in them,
least it suddenly degenerates into an Oligarchie or Tyrannie of some few,
that assembly being in such a case able to perpetuate themselves. Of this
the providence of God hath given as an experiment in the long Parlia-

ment, who exercising both the debating and determining power, were strongly tempted to have made themselves perpetually legislators, and what else they please, and to have governed according to their private interests, which if it had taken effect, would have as much destroyed the common interest and common right, vertue and liberty, as the same power exercised by a single person, who doth also naturally make his whole government, centre in his particular interest. Therefore the order that hath alwaies been in effect amongst free people, (although with some variation of names and circumstances) hath been this: They have ranked themselves into three orders, the people, the Senate, and the Magistrate, whereby they have made themselves partakers of all the benefit of the naturall Democracy, Aristocracy, and Monarchy; that is, they have had the good effects of all the excellent endowments for rule and order, which God hath dispensed to any of their people, and by the wise distribution of the power amongst them, with controuls to every of their corrupt affections, unto which they were prone, they have prevented the mischiefs apt to ensue, when the governing power happened to be placed solely in any of the three. By the people is to be understood, (in large populous places where the body of the people is too large to meet) the popular assembly chosen by the body of the people of interests and estates, who have right of suffrage amongst us. This Counsell or Assembly ought to be numerous, as one thousand or more, and their function ought to be, to give their affirmative or negative to all laws, matters of peace, warre, and leveys of money, and that without debate, or arguing, which would bring in confusion in so great an assembly. Therefore the matters ought always to be proposed by the Senate, a convenient time before, that the popular assembly may be fully advised of them, before their meeting, and then they are to be summoned to meet, by one of their own choice for that purpose: and therefore they ought to reside near the chief Citie, for the time of their power, which may be for two or three years, one third going out of Office every year the Assembly being filled by a new choice, and this is called the Power of the Common wealth; The Senate is the wisedom and Authoritie of the Common-wealth, which is a select Company, not very numerous, chosen by the whole People at the same time and in the same manner with the popular Councell, and to continue for the same space, with the same changes and recruits: The Office of this Councell, is to manage affairs of Peace and Warrs, when the people hath Decreed it, and to prepare all Lawes and Decrees, ready for their Sufferage, to command the Forces by Sea and Land, according to such Lawes and Orders as shall be either Fundamental to the Government, (for there ought to be an Instrument of Government) or made from time to time by the Senate, and the people. So that the Senate is to debate and propose, and the people to Decree and resolve all Lawes going in the name of both of these Deputies, both Senate and People ought to have moderate Sallaries allowed them, to prevent corruption, and in some recompence for the neglect of their private affairs, those of the popular Assembly may have fourty shillings *per* week, & those of the Senate may have five hundred pound *per annum*, their pains, care, and expence, being to be probably much greater, regard being also had to their qualitie, now if it should not be provided in the foundation, that the Popular Assembly should not assume the debate, it would come to an Anarchie; but *Athens*, which perished by that means: and if the Senate should take upon them the result, it would soon be an Oligarchy, (or Tyranny of a few) For they might with a Vote perpetuate themselves, and govern the Nation according to their private interest; but both Counsels can never agree to perpetuate themselves, for the popular Assemblies Office, being not of profit, but burden, and being capable when out of that Office, to be chosen into the Senate, which is of more profit and authoritie, it would be against their interest, which is the most certain Bond upon Mankind) to perpetuate themselves, and the yearly change of a third in each Councels, bringing the whole number by Successive Changes, so suddenly into their private Capacities, to enjoy the Good, or suffer the harmes of what is done by the Councell, in an equalitie with the whole people, it is of naturall impulse, that the whole Government, should be onely according to the publicke reason and interest, and cannot be imagined to deviate from the proper ends of Government, neither can any Brazen-wall, be so firm and lasting, against the private Interest and Pretence of *Charles Stuart*, as the moulding the people into these Orders, there being no danger, that the Senate and people should agree to de-throne themselves, to be yoaked by a Monarch: And we may safely say, that no people formed into

these Orders, if their number held any neer proportion to lie under Monarchie, were ever yet subdued by a Monarch, from the beginning of the
World, untill this Day, unlesse they were first broken in pieces by themselves, through some inequalitie in the Constitution of their Orders, but
mightie Monarchs have been often led Captives by such people.

The third Order, is the Magistracy, wherein some are Chiefe, some
subordinate, some Senatorian, some Popular, and are chosen accordingly,
being all changeable, at certain times, and wholly subject to the Lawes
and Order of the Common-wealth. And the Office of these, is to execute
impartially all the Lawes made as is before expressed. It is possible it may
consist with the Common Interest, to have one chiefe Magistrate, in
whom the Title & Honour of the Common-wealth, may reside in publicke Solemnities and addresses; So that no publick Action bee left to his
discretion, We shall not mention the Excellent Order of Armes, that is
the Consequence of Casting a People into this Forme, whereby they subsist, and become invincible by their own Armies, not by Mercinaries. We
onely mention the first Forme, wherein the Foundation of Libertie to a
people ought to be laid, that is by Establishing the Popular Assembly, the
Senate, and the Magistracy; these are Essentiall unto true Libertie, the
Superstructures have differed amongst severall free People, according to
divers accidents, We shall not presume so well of our selves as to offer
any Direction to your Lordship in them: but if God shall prepare your
heart for such a Worke of Righteousness and Honour, we shall readily
throw in our Mite of Advice to your Treasury.

My Lord, We have now not onely Cleared it to be your Lordships
Duetie, to make us free, but shewed wherein the Foundation of our Libertie must be laid, and the ground is digged to your hand, the Lands
being so distributed, that no one Man, or small number of Men can overpower the whole People, by their possessions. If we thought it needfull to
quicken your Affections to your Duetie, we could tell you from Reason and
Experience how strangely such a settlement of Libertie would transforme
the manners of the people; Luxurie would Change into Temperance,
Haughtinesse and Envie into Meeknesse, and mutuall Love and Emulation of Goodnesse, servilitie and basenesse of minde, into Noblenesse and
Generositie. Who would not follow Vertue for the Love? When neither

alliance, flattery or any Vice, could make great, but a Generall Sentence from Popular Assemblies of Worth and Goodnesse, we might tell you it would wash foule Garments from the staines of bloud, and the Armies honour from the black reproach that now covers it, and above all the profession of religion from scandall and infamy; this would shew that you had nobler ends then yet the world believes to be in Christians: If ambition pricks in your breast, for your self or your brother; in thus doing you may set him upon a Throne more noble, lofty, and commanding, then ever the *Stuarts* possessed or designed. His free conjunction with your Lordship in this work may give him merit of greatnesse in the souls of those that now disdain him, you may make your swords shine with a radiant glory beyond those of *Alexander* and *Caesar*, whose honour was only the same with that of the Plague and Pestilence to destroy mankind, yours may restore liberty to England, and propagate it to mankind. And what should hinder your Lordship, surely you can fear no resistance in giving the people their right, when you feared none in many destructive attempts to their right & freedomes, besides you have an Army whose interests, consciences, ingagements, yea their very passions and affections lead them this way, and in doing this you may extinguish all fears, and secure against all plots, and make all knowing men your voluntary vas-salls in thankfulnesse for their liberty. But if your private interest should blind your Lordships eies, and lead you out of the paths of mercie, righ-teousnesse and peace, to hew out a bloudy way to empire against the naturall course of things, We believe it will not be long before oppression and confusion, the consequences of such violent actings wil extort that from you, which with little more trouble then to moddle the elections for a Parliament (as they ought) you might give us above to your eternal hon-our. So wishing the God of mercy and peace to direct you, we remain

My Lord,
Your affectionate servants in Christ.

FINIS.

Appendix D

The Humble Petition (1659)

To the
Supream Authority,
THE
Parliament *of the* Commonwealth
of England.
The Humble Petition of divers
well-affected Persons.

SHEWETH,

That your Petitioners have for many years observed the breathings and longings of this Nation after Rest and Settlement, and that upon mistaken grounds they have been ready even to sacrifice and yield up part of their own undoubted right, to follow after an appearance of it.

And your Petitioners do daily see the bad effects of long continued distractions, in the ruines and decayes of Trade Forraign and Domestique; And in the advantages that are taken to make Confederacies to involve the Nation in Blood and Confusion, under pretence of procuring a Settlement.

Transcribed from the first edition, printed in 1659. For discussion of Neville's possible involvement in the authorship of this pamphlet, see the Introduction (above, p. xv).

That it hath been the practice of all Nations upon the subversion of any form of Government, to provide immediately a new constitution, suitable to their condition; with certain successions and descents, that so both their Law-givers and Magistrates, might use their several Trusts, according to the established constitution; and the Peoples mindes be setled secure, and free from attempts of introducing several forms of Governments, according to the variety of their fancies, or corrupt interests.

That God hath preserved this Nation wonderfully without example many years, since the dissolution of the old form of Government, by King, Lords, and Commons, there having been no fundamental Constitutions of any kind duly setled, nor any certain succession provided for the Legislative power; but even at this instant, if by any sudden sickness, design or force, any considerable numbers of your persons should be rendered incapable of meeting in Parliament, The Commonwealth were without form of successive Legislature or Magistracy, and left to the mercy of the strongest faction. Yet we have reason to remember in these years of unsettlement, the expressible sufferings of this Nation, in their strength, wealth, honour, liberty, and all things conducing to their well-being; And we have like reason now, sadly to apprehend the unpending ruine; And we cannot discern a possibility of your Honours unanimous, and expeditious proceedings towards our Countries preservation, and relief from its heavy pressures, whilest your mindes are not setled in any known Constitution of Government or fundamental Orders: according to which, all Lawes should be made; but diverse or contrary interests may be prosecuted upon different apprehensions of the Justice and Prudence of different forms of Government, though all with good intentions.

Your Petitioners therefore conceiving no remedy so effectual against the present dangers, as the settlement of the peoples mindes, and putting them into actual security of their properties and liberties, by a due establishment of the Constitution under which they may evidently apprehend their certain enjoyment of them; and thereupon, a return of their Trade and free Commerce, without those continual feares, that maketh such frequent stops in Trade, to the ruine of thousands.

And your Petitioners also observing, that the Interest of the late Kings Sonne, is cryed up, and promoted daily, upon pretence, that there will be nothing but confusion and Tyranny, until he come to govern; and that such as de-

clare for a Commonwealth, are for Annarchy and confusion, and can never agree amongst themselves, what they would have.

Upon serious thoughts of the premises, your Petitioners do presume with all humility, and submission to your Wisdom to offer to your Honours, their Principalls and Proposalls concerning the Government of this Nation: Whereupon, they humbly conceive, a just and prudent Government ought to be established, viz.

I.

That the Constitution of the Civil Government of *England* by King, Lords, and Commons, being dissolved, whatever new Constitution or Government can be made or settled according to any Rule of righteousness, It can be no other then a wise Order or Method, into which the free Peoples Deputies shall be formed for the making of their Lawes; and taking Care for their Common safety and welfare in the execution of them: For, the exercise of all just authority over a free People, ought (under God) to arise from their own Consent.

II.

That the Government of a free People ought to be so settled, that the Governours and Governed may have the same Interest in preserving the Government, and each others Proprieties and Liberties respectively; That being the onely sure foundation of a Commonwealth's Unity, Peace, Strength, and Prosperity.

III.

That there cannot be an Union of the Interests of a whole Nation in the Government, where those who shall sometimes Govern, be not also sometimes in the Condition of the Governed; otherwise the Governours will not be in a capacity to feel the weight of the Government, nor the Governed to enjoy the advantages of it: And then it will be the interest of the *Major* part to destroy the Government; as much as it will be the interest of the *Minor* part to preserve it.

IV.

That there is no security that the Supream Authority shall not fall into factions, and be led by their private Interest to keep themselves alwayes in power, and direct the Government to their private advantages; If that Supream Authority be setled in any Single Assembly whatsoever, That shall have the entire power of Propounding, Debating, and resolving Laws.

V.

That the Soveraign Authority in every Government of what kind soever, ought to be certain in its perpetual Successions, Revolutions or Descents: and without possibility (by the Judgement of humane prudence) of a death or failer of its being, because the whole forme of the Government is dissolved, if that should happen, and the people in the utmost imminent danger of an absolute Tyranny, or a War amongst themselves; or Rapine and confusion. And therefore where the Government is Popular, the Assemblies in whom reside the Supream Authority, ought never to die or dissolve: though the persons be annually Changing: neither ought they to trust the Soveraign care of the strength and safety of the people out of their own hands, by allowing a Vacation to themselves, lest those that should be trusted be in love with such Great Authority, and aspire to be their Masters, or else fear an Account, and seek the dissolution of the Common-wealth to avoyd it.

VI.

That it ought to be declared as a Fundamental Order in the Constitution of this Common-wealth, that the Parliament being the Supream Legislative Power, is intended only for the exercise of all those Acts of Authority that are proper and peculiar unto the Legislative Power; and to provide for a Magistracy, unto whom should appertain the whole Executive Power of the Lawes: and no Case either Civil or Criminal to be Judged in Parliament, saving that the last Appeals in all Cases, where Appeals shall be thought fit to be admitted, be only unto the Popular Assembly;

and also that unto them be referred the Judgement of all Magistrates in Cases of Male Administrations in their Offices.

And in prosecution of these Principles,

Your Petitioners Humbly propose for the
Settlement of this Commonwealth,
that it be Ordained,

1. *That the Parliament or the Supreme Authority of* England, *be chosen by the free People, to represent them with as much equality as may be.*

2. *That a Parliament of* England *shall consist of two Assemblies, the lesser of about three hundred, in whom shall reside the entire power of consulting, debating, and propounding Lawes: the other, to consist of a farre greater number, in whom shall rest the sole power of resolving all Lawes so propounded.*

3. *That the free People of* England, *in their respective divisions at certain dayes and places appointed, shall for ever annually choose one third part to each Assembly, to enter into their Authority, at certain dayes appointed: the same dayes, the Authority of a third of each of the said Assemblies to cease, onely in the laying the first Foundation in this* Commonwealths *Constitution: the whole number of both the Assemblies to be chosen by the People respectively, (viz.) One third of each Assembly to be chosen for one year, One third for two years, and one third for three years.*

4. *That such as shall be chosen, having served their appointed time in either of the said Assemblies of Parliament shall not be capeable to serve in the same assembly during some convenient intervall or vacation.*

5. *That the Legislative power doe wholy refer the execution of the Laws unto the Magistracy, according to the sixth principle herein mentioned.*

6. *That in respect to Religion and Christian liberty, It be ordained that the Christian Religion by the appointment of all succeeding Parliaments, be taught, and promulgated to the Nation, and publique Preachers thereof maintained; and that all that shall professe the said Religion, though of different perswasions in parts of the Doctrine, or Discipline thereof, be equally protected in the peaceable profession, & publique exercise of the same; and be equally capeable of all elections, Magistracies, preferments in the commonwealth, according to the order of the same.* Provided alwaies, *that the publique exercise of no Religion contrary to Christianity be tollorated: nor the publique exercise*

of any Religion, though professedly Christian, grounded upon, or incorporated into the interest of any Forraign State or Prince.

These your Petitioners humbly conceive, to be the Essentials of the form of a free Commonwealth, which if they were made fit for practise by your Honers appointing the numbers, times, places, and all other necessary circumstances, and setled as the fundamental Orders of the Commonwealth, would naturally dispose those that should hereafter be chosen into the Parliaments, from the love of their own interest to seek the common good being obliged by the constitutions here humbly offered to partake with the whole body of the people, of the good or evil that shall happen to the Commonwealth, having no probable temptations or means left, to compass any private or factious ends in matters Religious or Civil, And your Petitioners cannot imagine a greater security for the cause and interest contended for with such effusion of blood, Then by disposing the free people into this kind of order, whereby the same cause would become their common interest. Yet if your Honours should think it necessary or convenient for securing the minds of such as are doubtful, and jealous, that the people may betray their own liberties; There may be inserted into the fundamental orders of the Commonwealth, these following Expedients, *Viz.*

I

That for securing the government of this Commonwealth, & of the Religious and Civil freedom of the good people thereof, it may be for ever esteemed & judged Treason against the Commonwealth, for any member of either Assembly of Parliament, or any other person whatsoever to move or propose in either of the said Assemblies, the restitution of Kingly Government, or the introduction of any single Person to be chief Magistrate of *England,* or the alteration of that part of the fundamental order herein contained that concerns the equal freedom and protection of Religious persons of different perswasions.

II

That about the number of twelve persons of the most undoubted fidelity and integrity, may be authorised and impowred for some certain number of yeers next ensuing to seize, apprehend, and in safe custody to detain any person or persons whatsoever till he or they be in due form of law, delivered as is hereafter specified; That shall move or propose in either of the said Assemblies of Parliament the restitution of Kingly Government, or the Introduction of any single person to be chief Magistrate of this Commonwealth, or the alteration of that part of the fundamental order herein contained, that concerns the equal freedom, and protection of Religious persons, of different perswasions. But for no other matter or cause whatsoever; And when it shall happen that any person or persons shall be arrested or seized for any of the causes aforesaid, in manner aforesaid; a Commission *of Oyer and Terminer* may issue forth in due form of Law, unto the said Twelve or any Six of them to proceed in due form of law, within one moneth after the apprehension of any such person or persons: to the arraignment and publique trial of every such person or persons, and upon the legal conviction of him or them by the testimony of two sufficient witnesses of any of the Treasons herein declared, to condemn to the pains of death; and to cause the same Judgment to be duly executed, and the keeper or keepers of the great seal of England that shall be for the time being may be authorised and required from time to time during the Term of yeers to issue out Commissions unto the said twelve or any six of them authorizing them to proceed as aforesaid.

And if your Honours shall further judge it convenient, the fundamental orders of the Government may be consented unto or subscribed, by the people themselves, if their express pact shall be esteemed any additional security; other Nations upon the like occasions of expulsion of their Kings, having taken the peoples oathes against their returning, And the same may be proclaimed as often as our Ancestors provided for the proclaiming of *Magna Charta* and any further security also added, if any can be found amongst men, that hath a foundation in justice.

Now your Petitioners having with humble submission to your grave wisdomes, thus declared their apprehensions of the present condition of this distracted Nation, and the only effectual means under God to prevent the impending mischiefs; They do most humbly pray,

That such speedy Considerations may be had of the premises as the Condition of this Nation requires, and that such a method may be setled for the debating, and consulting about the Government, that your wise Results may be seasonable for the healing all the breaches of the Commonwealth and establishing sure foundations of Freedom, Justice, Peace, and Unity.

And your Petitioners shall always pray, &c.

Wednesday, July the 6.
1659.

The house being informed that divers Gentlemen were at the door with a Petition, they were called in, and one of the Petitioners in the Behalf of himself and the rest said, we humbly present you a petition, to which we might have had many thousand hands, but the matter rather deserves your serious consideration then any publique attestation, and therefore we do humbly present it to this honourable House: which after the petitioners were withdrawn was read and was entituled, The humble Petition of divers well affected persons.

Resolved.

That the Petitioners have the thankes of the House.

The Petitioners were again called in and Mr. Speaker *gave them this answer.*

Gentlemen,

The House hath read over your Petition, and find it without any private end, and only for publique interest, And I am commanded to let you know that it lyeth much upon them to make such a settlement, as may be most for the good of posterity. And they are about that worke, and intend to goe forward with it with as much expedition as may be, And for your parts they have commanded me to give you thankes: and in their names I do give you the thanks of this House accordingly.

Tho. St. Nicholas *Clerke*
of the Parliament.

APPENDIX E

Manuscripts Relating to Sir Henry Neville

Neville's grandfather Sir Henry Neville (1561/62–1615) had served as Elizabeth I's ambassador to France and had been a prominent statesman in the early part of the reign of James I, coming close to being nominated as Secretary of State. His attempt in the so-called Undertaking Parliament of 1614 to manage the House of Commons on behalf of James I had come to nothing. However, the episode had been recalled in Parliament on 5 April 1659 by Sir Walter Earle, and Sir Henry's republican grandson had evidently felt some awkwardness about it (Burton, *Diary*, 3:346–47). In one sense, that embarrassment is understandable. The schemes of his grandfather were the reverse of Neville's own political projects, for while Sir Henry had offered to manage Parliament on behalf of the king, his grandson aspired to manage the king on behalf of Parliament. Nevertheless, Sir Henry's state projects, sketched in the following documents, may have influenced the design of the remedies for England's broken constitution that Neville advanced in *Plato Redivivus*.

An Advice Touching the Holding of a Parliament

There is a question grown and much debated amongst us, whether the King should relieve himself in his great want (whereof the world taketh knowledge both at home and abroad), by a Parliament, or by some projects and devices to raise money, which may be set on foot to that purpose. For my part, I will not examine what these projects may be, although by experience of such as have been put in use since the dissolution of the last Parliament, I am induced to believe that either they will fail or fall short in the practice, howsoever they may appear likely in the theory; or that they will prove like some medicines, which do rather take away sense of pain for the present than cure the grief for which they were applied. But admit there may be other ways devised to relieve the King, yet am I clearly of opinion that there is none so fit, so honourable, and so necessary as by a Parliament. My reason is this; I consider on what terms the King and the last Parliament parted at the dissolution, full of distaste and acrimony on His Majesty's part, and not without some discontentment on theirs, I consider also that from the Parliament, the apprehensions that are taken there are spread and dispersed over the whole realm. And further that the knowledge of these misunderstandings between His Majesty and the Parliament is not confined within this kingdom only but is flown abroad into all foreign parts that have any commerce or dealing with us. Now what disadvantage this opinion may breed us, and what hopes it is like to raise both in our enemies abroad and our discontented persons at home may easily be gathered. For, as there is nothing that more upholds the reputation of any Prince than the opinion of his strength at home, which consisted principally in the love and concord between him and his people from whence there followeth naturally a sequence of all other duties on their part to make him strong and able to help and hurt his neighbours; so there is nothing that emboldeneth more an enemy, either open or secret, to attempt the disturbance of the peace of any State than the imagination that the Prince and people stand not in

State Papers, Domestic, lxxiv. 44; reprinted from Samuel Rawson Gardiner, *History of England from the Accession of James I. to the Disgrace of Chief-justice Coke: 1602–1616*, 2:389–94 (London: Hurst & Blackett, 1863).

kind and loving terms. And to this purpose I remember a story of Antigonus, one of the immediate and mightiest successors of Alexander, who, being solemnly set in great state to give audience to some other prince's ambassador; as he was in that solemnity, his son Demetrius came in from hunting, and being arrayed in his hunting attire, with his darts in his hand, presented himself so unto his father, and after a salutation given according to the manner of that people, sat down by him. The audience being ended, and the ambassadors retiring themselves, Antigonus called them again, and willed them to report one thing more to their masters, namely, in what fashion they had seen his son and him converse together, intending that it would be taken for a great argument of his strength and a great assurance of his safety that his son and he lived in that confidence and concord. If this were true in that case between the father and the son, how much more is it verified between the Prince and the people? And hereupon I conclude that the world being possessed with a conceit that the last Parliament ended with some sourness and distaste on the King's part, and not with the best satisfaction on theirs, there is nothing more necessary for the King's Majesty, either in regard of honour or safety, than to deface that opinion, and to make it apparent to the world that as he was received into the kingdom at his first entry, with the greatest demonstrations of the love and joy of his people that ever Prince was, so he is still rooted and established in their hearts; and that whatsoever cloud or mist might seem to have darkened or overshadowed the kind respects between them at that time, it was no other but that which happeneth often by some distemper, between a tender father and dutiful children which quickly vanish when the distemper of either side is removed.

For the effecting of this I can think of no other way but by another Parliament, for there this error grew, and there and no where else it must be repaired. The harsh conclusion of the former Parliament bred that ill-conceit, and the sweet close of another must beget a better. And by this means two notable effects will be wrought together if matters be well handled; the removing of that erroneous and dangerous conceit of a misunderstanding between the King and his people, and the relieving of the King's present necessities in a sure speedy and plentiful manner; whereas that other cause of projects may happily prove slow and fail in the most, and in very few succeed according to the first design. And for rectifying the misconceit between the King and his people there is no hope at all that way. It is rather to be feared it will do hurt, and rather aggravate than cure that malady if there be not great judgment used in the choice of the projects, and much dexterity in the managing of them. Against this opinion there are two objections. The one that the Parliament may still continue adverse and unwilling to relieve the King at all, and so no hope of making up the breach, the other that as long as it is conceived the King cannot help himself without them, they will play upon the advantage of his necessities and extort some unreasonable demands from him before they yield to do anything for him. Both these objections are grounded upon the same false foundation, namely, that whatsoever the last Parliament did in that kind, they did it out of evil affection, which I do know, and do confidently avow to be otherwise, and have before in speech delivered the true reasons of that averseness, as one that lived and conversed inwardly with the chief of them, that were noted to be most backward and know their inwardest thoughts on that business. So I dare undertake for the most of them that the King's Majesty proceeding in a gracious course toward his people, shall find those gentlemen exceeding willing to do him service, and to give him such contentment, as may sweeten all the former distastes, and leave both His Majesty and the world fully satisfied of their good intentions, and of the general affection of his subjects. It is true (as I lately delivered unto His Majesty), that some things will be desired and expected of him by way of grace, which may both give some contentment to them that shall pay what is given, and justify the care and honest regard of them that shall give it. And, without this, I dare promise nothing; for it is most certain that, as in private families and all other societies, where the straitest bonds of nature or election do concur to unite affections, there is almost a continual necessity of mutual offices of kindness to nourish and maintain that love, so in kingdoms, besides that great bond of protection and allegiance between the sovereign and the subject, there is a like necessary use of the frequent interchange of mutual effects of grace and love to cherish and foster that tender affection that daily is to be renewed between them. But what be the things that will be demanded or expected by the Parliament on behalf of the people will be hard for any one man to set down. Yet what I have collected out of the desires of sundry of the principal and most understanding gentlemen that were of the last Parliament, and are like to be of this, I will be bold to deliver in a memorial hereunto adjoined, whereby it shall appear that they aim not at anything unjust or unreasonable, or that may derogate from His Majesty in point of sovereignty further than His Majesty hath already been pleased to offer in writing to the last Parliament (which no doubt will be maintained) nor in point of profit to any matter of certain and considerable value, but only at such things as being now of small moment and loss to His Majesty to depart with, because they have been sifted and ransacked to the bottom, may yet be valued to the subjects, both in opinion and truth, at a high rate, because they shall thereby enjoy a great repose and security from vexation which any of them may otherwise be subject unto.

These things being taken into His Majesty's consideration, and receiving His gracious approbation as matter not unfit to be yielded of grace unto his subjects, the next points to be thought of are the time of holding the Parliament, the things preceding to be done by way of preparation, and the manner of proceeding with the House of Commons when the Parliament is assembled. For the first I see no cause why it should be deferred longer than Michaelmas, for after the session there must be a time proportionable for the Commissioners to sit, and for the money to be levied and brought into the Exchequer, which the sooner it is done, the sooner will the King be eased of his debts for which he payeth interest, and the sooner will his reputation be recovered and settled, which is the thing that most deserves to be respected. If the Parliament begin at Michaelmas, the Term may be adjourned to Hollantide; or if not, yet till that time there is little business done, so as the lawyers may well attend the Parliament, whose absence will otherwise breed delay. And I do not see but in a month or five weeks this point of supplying the King and of his retribution will be easily determined if it be proposed betimes and followed close afterwards. For the second, which concerns matter of preparation, these be the things that I would humbly offer to His Majesty's gracious consideration, to forbear to use any speech that may irritate, and to seem rather confident than diffident of their affections, casting the fault of any former error upon evil offices done on both sides, and want of true understanding rather than want of good affection. To speak graciously and benignly to the people that shall flock to see His Majesty this progress. And especially to take notice of the principal gentlemen, and let them kiss his hand, and do them some other grace. To give order to the Archbishop to prohibit all books and invective sermons against the Parliament, so as notice may be taken of His Majesty's commandment before the meeting. To peruse the grievances exhibited the last Parliament, and if His Majesty would please to be gracious in any of them, to do it of himself before he be pressed. For a small thing in that manner will give more contentment than much more obtained with importunity. And especially to call to mind if His Majesty promised anything to the last Parliament which is not yet performed; for upon the performance of that men will be like to ground their trust and hopes in those things which shall be offered now. For the last point concerning the manner of proceeding, I wish that His Majesty will be pleased to make his propositions by himself or by his ministers and servants that are of their own body, and not by mediation of the Lords. For the Commons will be rather willing to make oblation of their affections themselves unto His Majesty than that any others should do it, and intercept both the merit and thanks from them. I wish also that the King should forbear to nominate any particular men to be sent unto him from the Commons to treat upon any point or occasion, but after His Majesty hath declared his own desires and made likewise known his gracious inclination to gratify his subjects with any favours and graces that with reason and moderation they can desire for them, His Majesty may be pleased to require the House to nominate a competent number of thirty or forty or fewer which may repair unto him with their demands, and be authorized both to ask and answer such questions as the debate about them shall beget without concluding or binding the House in any point, but only to clear things and report all back to the House. This course, I conceive, will much expedite the business, avoid jealousies, and give good satisfaction to the most, when they shall see that the King shall understand their desire immediately from themselves without any interposition, or danger of misinterpretation, and that upon any point of doubt they shall be admitted to clear their own intentions and not to be subject to the construction of other. Matters being thus prepared beforehand, and thus managed at the time, and His Majesty being pleased to be gracious to his people in the points proposed or any other of the like nature which may be thought of by the House, when they meet (for beforehand no man can precisely say these things will be demanded and no other) I have no doubt, but am very confident, that His Majesty shall receive as much contentment of this next Parliament as he received distaste of the former, and that all things will end in that sweet accord that will be both honourable and comfortable for His Majesty and happy for the whole realm. And when His Majesty hath made use of his people's affection to put him out of want, any fit projects that shall be offered may be the boldlier entertained to fill his coffers. For whatsoever shall be done in that kind will be the less subject to offence when there is a perfect renewing of affections gone before; whereas otherwise whiles dislikes continue *seu benè, seu malè facta premunt.*

In this advice it may evidently appear that I have proceeded with more zeal to His Majesty than caution or wariness for myself; for I am not ignorant what a hazard I run if things should fall out contrary to my expectation. But love and faith cast no perils. And I hold it a matter of that consequence both to King and people to have these misunderstandings cleared as well in truth as in opinion, that I would think my life of little value in respect of it, and had rather hazard anything that may befall me than leave such an office unattempted. Wherein if I fail, howsoever my discretion may be censured, yet I am sure the honest purpose and sincerity of my heart cannot be reproved.

A Collection of Sum Graces

[231v] A collection of sum graces, wch ye King may perfourm to ye subiect, wth out preiudice to his honor & proffitt: wch was dispersed abrode before ye beginning of ye Parlament the 5. of Aprill. 1614. These have been by severall persons desired to be obtained of his Ma.^{ty} for ye good of his people.

1. A law to be made for ye declaration of all treasons.
   Heerby it is meant not to alter ye law, or to make any thing not to be treason, y^t now is: but only to declare what is treason, y^t every man may know it, avoyd it, & not fall uppon a hidden rock before he be aware. And y^t it may not be in ye power of a iudge, (by inference, or superinduced interpretation,) to ruine a man & his posterity.

2. That it may be lawfull for ye subiects to pleade not guilty to any inform/a/tion of intrusion pro/ex/hibited by ye Kings atturney; & in ye mean time, till ye matter be tryed, keepe ye possession.
   This can no ways prejudice ye Kings iust tytle, for if he fall right must take place for all his pleadings, & for ye possession chiefly it rellieveth ye subiects in sutes commenced against them in ye Kings name, uppon a surmyse: when it standeth wth great iustice to help them untill ye surmyse be prooved.

3. That no man be forced to answear, or traverse any office, or inquisition found for ye King, out of any court, untill there were notice first given to ye parties, whom it concerneth, & who are to receaue prejudice by it.
   [232r] The meaning of this is to preuent ye secret fynding of offices, wthout calling them to it, whom it doth concern, wherby many men ar infinitly vexed & trubbled, who if they had been called at ye first, would have shewed sufficient matter for their discharge. And can no way preiudice ye King, but only serveth to free ye subiect from infinit vexation.

4. That ye Kings grants, & his progenitors be construed as common persons grants: & y^t all ye Kings, & his progenitors pattents of laws & leases not allreddy overthrown by iudgment, may be confirmed.

British Library, Harleian MSS 4289, fol. 231–33.
Convention of transcription: // enclose material inserted above the line.

This is a matter of great grace, yet agreeing wth ye rules of generall equity; & not likely to preiudice his Ma.^ty muche in proffitt; becaws all pattents haue been allreddy so narrowly sifted, y^t whosoeuer hath not been impeached, may be well presumed to be wth out defect.

5. That no fees henceforth be payd in ye Exchecker by sheriffs, escheators, or collectors of subsidies, tenths, fifteens, & aydes, uppon their accounts: & y^t a time may be limited to all officers respectively to whom it may appertayn to receaue their accounts after they be tendered, & to giue them a discharge, uppon a paine; seeing these men take payns in ye Kings seruice wth out any reward.

This concerneth his Ma.^ty nothing, but only restraineth ye unmeasurable couetousnes of ye Exchecker men, who exact uppon ye accountants beyond all reason, under cullor of expedition, & suche other deuises.

6. That no man be forced to pleade any alienation in ye Exchecker, for wch he hath taken any pardon, or lycense under ye great seale: but ye clarks of ye court to take notice of y^t lycense or pardon (beeing of record) at their perill,: or at ye least, uppon ye sight of ye lycense or pardon to forbear to trubble him, who seweth them out.

This likewise concerneth ye King nothing at all, but only ye officers of ye Exchecker, or their clarks, who for their pryuat gayn inforce men to pleade y^t, wch was of record before: by wch ye King hath no proffitt.

7. That a liberall pardon may be granted by his Ma.^ty wherin these points following may be included, besyds those contained in ye last pardon; viz. All detts arysing before y^e ~~dea~~ death of Queen Elsabeth, except suche as ar stalled by a yearly payment.

This is much in shew, & euery man will be glad to be secured: yet is nothing to ye King to grant, becaws ye detts of ye crown before y^t time, haue been so narrowly sifted, as ther is small ~~pro~~ probability, y^t there remaineth any thing unlevied.

8. All alienations uppon state of inheritance, or estates for life, before ye last of March anno 9.° of ye Kings Ma.^ty

Ther is no great dowt, but ye alienations made before, & not compounded for, haue been by this time discovered, or if any thing have escaped, it is so little, as is not considerable. And besyds, this [232v] is a thing was allways used to be pardoned untill ye 13.th of Queen Elizabeth, when my Lord of Lester had a purpose to farm ye fynes for alienations at a rent.

9. All concealed wards, whose ancestors dyed before ye last of March anno i.^{mo} of ye Kings Ma.^{ty} & no office found.

It may well be presumed y^t ye diligence of feodaries, & escheators, & ye greedines of suche, as gape after suche sutes, haue left nothing unsifted, & undiscouered of y^t kynd: & therfore it will be a matter of small loss to ye King to grant, & may secure ye subiect from vexation y^t we know by common experience, they suffer under y^t pretense.

io All fynes, & amercements in any of ye Kings courts of iustice, imposed before ye last of 7.^{br} anno 9.º of ye King, & not yet leuied.

These proffits ar ~~not~~ granted away for ye most part, & ye grantees do not use to be slack in ye leuying of them: therfore it may well pass in ye rank of ye former.

ii. All trespasses concerning vert, & venison, in forrests, parks, & chases.

If it be examined what proffit ye King hath made of ye justice seales, wch haue been houlden since his raigne: I think ther will ~~be~~ no suche benefitt appear, y^t ye King should be discurraged from granting this grace to his people in this point, wch I confess I haue inserted ye rather, becaws ye former do all concern landed men of sum wealth, & this may happily breed a peace, & contentment to ye poorer sort, wch must not be altogether neglected.

These points I haue collected from ye desires of seuerall men, sum gentlemen, sum lawyers, who, if they haue miscarried my iudgment in any point out of ye cumpass of my profession, I hope I shall be pardoned: but for tryall of it, I humbly desire his Ma.^{ty} will be pleased to call his lerned councell vppon a suddayn, & examin them what loss, or dammage certayn, or what prejudice they conceaue it will be to his Ma.^{ty} to depart wth these things & of what valew they do esteem them. For surely we ayme not to take from his Ma.^{ty} any more of valew, but only sum small things, wch may be abundantly recompensed in ye guift he may expect from his people: & if it fall out otherwise in ye particulars, we ar mistaken in them. Besyds these, ther were 8. other points offered to ye Lords (as I remember) in ye Kings name, & deliuered in wryting, after ye treaty of contract was ~~brok~~ broken: viz.

1. That 60. years possession should be sufficient against yᵉ King.
2. That no lease of yᵉ Kings land should be auoided for non payment of rent at a iust day,: but yᵉ penalty for default, to be dubble yᵉ rent.
3. Respitt of homage to be clean taken aw‸/a/ay.
4. No asserts, or drownd lands to be called into question.
5. No impositions vppon commodities exported, or imported, from henceforth to be [233r] raised, without consent of Parlament.
6. No statute to be repealed, concerning yᵉ altering of yᵉ Laws of Wales.
7. Obsolete, & vnproffitable laws to be repealed.
8. Forfeytures vppon penall laws to be turned into sum other kynde of correction.

Thes‸/e/ I meddle not wᵗʰ, becaws they were publikely offered, & many coppies dispersed of them: & therfore I shall need to giue no reason for them: becaws they were [*illeg.*] free offers on his Ma.ᵗʸ part, out of his abundant grace, wherof ther is no reason to be giuen, but his abundant goodnes.

[John Somers], A Brief History of
the Succession (1681)

A Brief
HISTORY
OF THE
SUCCESSION,
Collected out of the RECORDS, and the most
Authentick HISTORIANS.

Written for the Satisfaction of the EARL of *H.*

Men generally, at present, busy themselves in discoursing about the Succession, and therefore cannot but be pleased to have a short History of it
set before them: For by seeing how the Crown has descended, and in
what manner,[1] and upon what grounds the natural Course of the Descent hath been changed, they will be enabled to judge what has been the
Opinion of all Ages, in this so controverted a Point, and thereby may
safely direct their Own.

Nothing certain has come down to us of the Nature of the Government of this Island before the *Romans* came hither; only this we learn
from *Caesar,* and *Strabo,* and *Tacitus,* That the *Britans* were subject to

---

Transcribed from the first edition, printed in 1681.

1. *Caes.* de Bell. Gall. lib. 5. *Tacitus* in vitae *Jul.* Agricolae *Strab.* lib. 4.

many Princes and States, not confederate, nor consulting in common, but always suspecting, and frequently warring with one another.

During the *Heptarchy,* whilst every Kingdom was govern'd by different Laws, we cannot think they agreed in one Rule of Succession: But, if that does not, I am sure, the reading the many Changes and Confusions of those Times must convince any man, that their Rule was uncertain, or else that they had no Rule at all.

Those seven Kingdoms were at last united under *Egbert:* But yet our Historians who lived nearest those Times, exprest themselves so odly in this Matter, and do so constantly mention the Election of almost every King before they tell us of his Coronation, that some learned men have doubted, whether before the Conquest the Government of this Island was ever grown up into a settled Hereditary Monarchy. Surely if it were so, yet all must agree, that[2] then the Succession was not guided by the same Rules, as some men believe or pretend it ought now to be. *Egbert* himself, the first *English* Monarch, came to the Crown, not by Succession but Election, being no way related to *Brissicu,* the last of the *West-Saxon* Kings; and when he died, he gave the Kingdoms of *Kent* and *Essex* to his second Son.[3] *Ethelwolf* divided the whole Island between his two Sons *Ethelbald* and *Ethelbert.*[4] *Athelstan* (though a Bastard) succeeded his Father, and was preferred to his ligitimate Brothers.[5] *Edred,* the younger Brother of King *Edmond,* was advanced to the Throne, though the deceased Prince had two Sons, *Edwin* and *Edgar,* who did both of them reign afterward successively. *Edgar* left a Son at his Death; but yet there hapned a mighty Contest about his Successor,[6] some of the great men contending for the Election of *Egelred* his Brother. But at last the Interest of *Edward* the Son prevail'd, and he was in a full Assembly elected, consecrated, and anointed King. That which *Ailredus,* Abbot of *Rievallis,* in

2. Pol. *Virg.* Hist. Angl. l. 4. in fine. *Will. Malmes.* l. 1. c. 2. fol. 16. l. 2. c. 1. fol. 36.
3. *Hen. Hunt.* l. 5 fol. 348. *Will. Malmes.* lib. 2. c. 3. f. 41.]
4. *Will. Malmes.* l. 2. c. 6. f. 48.
5. *Will. Malmes.* l. 2. c. 6. f. 55. *Rog. Hoved.* par. 1. f. 423. *Hen. Hunt.* l. 5. f. 355.
6. *De Rege Eligendo magna inter Regni Primores oborta est dissentio* Simeon Dunelm. *an. 975. f. 160 Edwardum* Elegerunt Electum consecraverunt, & in Regem unxerunt *Sim.* Dunelm ubi supra.

his Life of *Edward* the Confessor, gives an account of, seems very remarkable to our purpose. King *Ethelred*[7] (who was no tame and easie
Prince) desirous to establish his Successor in his Life-time,[8] summon'd a
great Council expresly for that purpose, and proposes the thing to them.
The Council were divided, some of them appearing for *Edmond* his eldest Son, and some for *Alfred* his second Son by Queen *Emma*. But at
last, upon some superstitious Fancy, they agreed to pass by both of them,
and elected the Infant that was in the Queens Womb. To which Election
the King gave his[9] Royal Assent, and the whole Assembly swore Fealty
to the Child whilst yet unborn. Undoubtedly this Story makes it plain,
that it was not enough at that time to entitle one to the Crown, that he
was the Kings Eldest Son, for then *Ethelred* would never have suffer'd a
Debate about the Election of a Successor, nor summon'd a Parliament
expresly for that purpose, which you see he thought necessary to be done.
And notwithstanding all his care it seems upon the Death of *Ethelred*,
Canutus had so great an Interest, that by an unanimous consent in a full[10]
Counsel he was elected King, and all the Issue of the last Prince rejected.
'Tis true, the *Londoners* stood firm to *Edmond* Ironside, (the approbation
of that renowned City had then no little Influence on the Succession)
and there were divers Battels fought between them; but at last they came
to an Agreement, and *Edmond* dying, the *Dane* ruled the whole Island
peaceably whilst he lived.

Immediately upon the Death of *Canutus*, there was assembled at *Oxford*[11] a great Council to determine who ought to succeed; where notwithstanding all the Interest which *Godwin* Earl of *Kent*, and the *West
Saxon* great men, could make on the behalf of *Hardiknute*, the legitimate

7. Gloriosus Rex *Ethelridus Ailred* Rievalis fo. *372.*
8. Fit magnus coram Rege Episcoporum Conventus *Reival.* ubi supra.
9. Praebet Electioni Rex consensum *Ailr.* Ab. *Reival.* ubi supra.
10. Episcopi Abbates Duces Quique nobiliores *Angliae* in unum congregati pari
consensu Canutum in Dominium & Regem Eligere omnem progeniem Regis
Ethelredi repudiantes *Sim. Dunelm an. 1016.* f. *173. Brompt f. 903. Rog. Hovedon 1
par. f. 434.*
11. Placitum magnum de Regni Successione apud *Oxonium* factum est *Brompt.
932.* Canuto mortuo facta est apud *Oxonium* magna alteratio de Regni Successione
Hen. Knyht. de event *Angl. Hen. Hunt l. 6. f. 364.*

Son of the dead King, they were over-voted, and *Harald Harefoot* (his Bastard, begotten on *Ailena* or *Elgiva*) was elected. *Harald* dy'd in the 5th. year of his Reign, and[12] then the People were content to accept of *Hardiknute* for their King, and to that end sent for him out of *Flanders;* but he dying Issueless, it was ordained in a[13] General Council, that never any *Dane* should for the future be admitted to Reign in *England.* After which they proceeded to elect *Alfred,* the Son of *Ethelred,* and he being murder'd by the Treachery of Earl *Godwin,* they chose his Brother *Edward,* commonly called *Edward the Confessor.* Nor were these Elections of theirs made with any respect to nearness of Bloud, more than those whereof we have heard before; for *Edmond Ironside,* their Elder Brother, had a Son then alive,[14] whose Name was *Edward,* and who was Father to *Edgar Atheling,* living also at the same time. And though this *Edward* had an undoubted Title to the Crown, if proximity of Blood could have given it, yet the *Confessor* was so far from suspecting any danger from such a Title, as that he invited his Nephew into *England,* and welcom'd him when he came with the greatest expressions of Joy, and entertain'd him with the greatest Confidence. Nor had the People any regard to this Royal Bloud upon the Death of the *Confessor,* but elected *Harald,* the Son of Earl *Godwin,* who had no pretence of Kindred to the *Saxon* Line.

These few, among many other Instances which may be given, will shew plainly enough, how men entituled themselves to the Crown in those days, and that then it was no strange thing to hear of a Parliaments medling with the Succession. Therefore I suppose the men who seem astonished at the boldness of a Parliament, in presuming to speak of it at this time, will say, that they ought not to be troubled with Presidents before the *Norman* Conquest; and that though the *Saxons* might be guilty of preferring a brave and deserving *Bastard,* before a *cruel* or a *silly legitimate* Prince, and of many other Irregularities, yet no such things are to be found in our Histories since the time of *William* the first, whose Reign is the great *Epoche,* from

12. *Post mortem* Heraldi Hardeknute *Electus Rex,* Hen. Hunt l. 6. f. 365.

13. Omnes *Anglorum* magnates ad invicem tractantes de communi Concilio & Juramento statuerunt, quod nunquam temporibus futuris aliquis Dacus super eos in Angliâ regnaret. *Brompt. 934.*

14. Brompt. 945.

whence we do compute our Kings. Let us therefore go on more particularly to observe what has been done since that time, and we shall see whether they who wonder so much, have any reason to do so.

William the *Conquerour* was himself illegitimate, and yet succeeded his Father in the Dutchy of *Normandy,* and therefore had no reason to set any great value upon that sort of Title, which is derived from a Right of Bloud. And it seems he did not much regard it; for passing by *Robert* his eldest, he gave the Crown[15] by his last Will, to *William Rufus* his younger Son, disposing only with regard to his own Inclinations, the Crown which himself had gain'd.

But his Son was too wise to rely upon this Disposition as a sufficient Title, and therefore had recourse to a more sure one:[16] For calling together the Nobles and wise Men of the Kingdom, he acquainted them in a full Council, with his Fathers Will, and desired their Consent to it; who after a long Consultation, did at last unanimously agree to make him their King, and thereupon he was Crown'd by *Langfranck,* Archbishop of *Canterbury.* I cannot but observe one thing farther, that though some men make use of the absolute Victory which the *Conquerour* had made, and affirm, that thereby the *English* were wholly broken, and all the old Laws and Customs of the Realm were destroy'd, yet it is plain that at this time the *English* Interest was so great, that it kept the Crown upon *William Rufus*'s Head, in spight of all that the *Normans* could do in behalf of *Robert,* though they universally joyn'd with him.[17] For the King calling together the *English,* and opening to them the Treason of the *Normans,* and[18] promising them a compleat Restitution of their ancient Laws, they stood firm to him, and soon put an end to all the Attempts of his Brother, and his *Norman* Accomplices.

15. A patre ultima valetudine decumbente in Successorem adoptatus. Guil. Malmsb. *lib. 4. fol. 120.* Sim. Dunel. *anno 1087. fol. 213.* Brompt. *f. 980.*

16. Convocatis terrae magnatibus. *Brompt. 983.* Optimates frequentes ad *Westmonasterium* in Concilium convenere, ubi loci post longam Consultationem *Guilielmum Rufum* Regem fecere. *Mat. Paris,* Flores hist. fol. *231.* Volentibus omnium Provinciarum animis in Regem acceptus. *Mat. Paris* in vit *Gull 2.* fol. *14.* anno *1088.*

17. Rex fecit convocare Anglos. *Sim. Dunelm* an. *1088.* fol. *214.*

18. Angli cum fideliter juvabant, *&c. Sim. Dun.* ubi supra.

Upon the Death of *William Rufus, Robert* had a fair pretence to renew his Claim to the Crown,[19] but that Prince had discover'd too much of the *Cruelty of his Disposition, of his aversion to the* English *Nation, and of his proneness to Revenge;* so that by the full Consent and Counsel of the whole Body of the Realm, assembled at *Winchester,* he was finally rejected, and they did concur to elect the *Conqueror's* third Son *Henry* for their King, (as *Mar. Westminster* expresses it). Nor did they do this but upon Terms; for both the Clergy and Laity said, that if he would restore them their ancient Liberties, and confirm them by his Charter, and abrogate some severe Laws which his Father had made, *they would consent to make him King.* And this prudent and learned King was not ashamed or unwilling to own this Title; for he does at large recite it in his Charter whereby he confirms their Liberties,[20] *Sciatis me misericordia Dei, & communi consilio Baronum Regni Angliae, ejusdem Regni Regem Coronatum esse,* &c.

Henry the first you see had reason to believe and own the Power of the Kingdom, in setting the Crown upon what head they pleased, and therefore he desired to secure it that way to his Posterity. To that end, in the *13th.* year of his Reign,[21] he summon'd a Council, and procured all the great and powerful men of the Kingdom to swear that his Son *William* should succeed him: But afterwards this Son of his was unfortunately drown'd, and the King dy'd, leaving no other Issue but *Maud* his Daughter, who had been married to the Emperor, and afterward to *Geoffery Plantaginet,* Earl of *Anjou.* No dispute can be made, but that she had all the Right which proximity of Bloud could give; yet *Stephen,* Earl of *Boloign,* who was the Son of *Adela,* one of the *Conquerors* Daughters, and whose elder Brother *Theobald,* Earl of *Blois,* was then living, stept in before her, and by representing to them the Inconvenience of a Feminine

---

19. Hic *Robertus* semper contrarius & adeo innaturalis extiterat Baronibus Regni Angliae, quod plenario consensu & consilio totius Communitatis Regni, ipsum refutaverunt & pro Rege omnino recusaverunt, & *Henricum* fratrem in Regem erexerunt, *H. de Knyght. c. 8. 2374.* Post mortem *Willielmi Rufi* electus est *Henricus* frater ejus *M. Paris 55.* in vita *H. 1.* an. *1100.* & *62.* anno *1105, Mat. West, 235.* Apud *Winton.* in Regem electus est. *Brempt. 997.*

20. Rich. Hagulstad *310.* Brompt. *10.21.* Mat. Paris *240.*

21. Coacto Concilio fecit omnes Principes & Potentes Anglicani Regni adjurare terram & Regnum *Willielmo* filio suo, *&c. Gervas Cron. 1138.*

Government, and promising them to consent to such good and gentle Laws as they should devise, prevail'd[22] with the Estates of the Realm to elect him King. And in this Charter, which he made soon after, he owns this Title, beginning it thus, *Ego* Stephanus *Dei gratia, assensu Cleri & Populi in Regem Angliae electus,* &c. And the *Pope,* in his Charter of Confirmation, sent to him in the first year of his Reign, tells him, That he was *Communi voto & unanimi assensu tam Procerum quam etiam Populi in Regem electus.* And then he adds, That since so universal an Assent could not be directed but by the Divine Grace, he therefore allows his Title, and confirms him in the Kingdom.

'Tis true that afterwards *Mawd* the Empress, together with her Son *Henry,* having, after some years, gained many to their side, gave him great disturbance; till at last *Stephen* having lost his Eldest Son *Eustace* (in whom he placed his hopes[23] and used all means, whilst he liv'd, to have got him declared his Successor, but without Success) came to an Agreement with the Empress and her Son, and[24] the Parliament, (who alone could give a Sanction to such Agreement,) was assembled at *Winchester* to confirm it; and then *Stephen* publickly Adopts *Henry* for his Son, and with their full consent declares him his Heir; and with the same consent *Henry* gives *Stephen* the name of Father, and agrees that he should continue to be King, during his Life, and they all Swore, That if *Henry* surviv'd, he should without opposition obtain the Crown, and

22. A primoribus Regni cum favore Cleri & populi Electus est à *Wil. Cant.* Archiepiscopo in Regem Consecratur. *R. Hagulstad, an. 1156. f. 312.* Consentientibus in ejus promotionem *Willielmo Cantuariensis* Archiepiscopo & Clericorum & Laicorum universitate apud *London, Jo. Hagulstad 250.* Predictus *Stephanus* à cunctis in Regem Electus, *Gervas Chron. f. 340.* Congregatis *Londiniis* terrae magnatibus, *Mat. Paris 74.*

23. Hen. Hunt. l. 8. f. 395. R. Hag. de gestii. Steph. 314.

24. Facto *Wintoniae* conventu publica, Rex *Stephanus* ipsum Ducem cunctis videntibus adoptavit in Filium, utque, interposito omnium Juramento, concessit & confirmarit ei totius *Angliae* principatum, Dux autem suscepit eum in locum genitoris, contendens ei omnibus diebus vitae suae nomen & rem Regii culminis obtinere, *Gervas. f. 1375.* In conventu Episcoporum & aliorum de Regno optum *Mat. Westm. f. 246.* an. *1153.* & *282.* an. *1154.* Consenserunt in hoc omnes principes Regni *Jo. Hagulstad f. 282. Mat. pacis 86. Hen. Hunt. l. 8. f. 398. Jo. Hagalstad 282. an. 1154.*

Stephen by his Charter, which is set down at large in *Brompton* publishes this Agreement, *Brompt.* 1037.

In all this Transaction certainly there was no consideration had of any other Right, but that which universal consent conferred; For if *Stephen's Heir* had any pretence, he had a Son then living, whose Name was *William*, and who by the same Agreement was to have all the Possessions which his Father enjoyed before he was made King. If the *Heir* of *Henry* the first had any Title, that was vested in *Mawd* the Empress, who was then also living; so that neither of the parties had any other colour of Right to the Crown, than what the consent of the People gave them.

According to this Parliamentary Agreement and Limitation, *Stephen* enjoy'd the Crown peaceably during his Life, and after his Death *Henry* the *Second* came to it as peaceably; but he remembred by what Title, and therefore was desirous to secure it to his Son in the same manner, that he took a very dangerous and unusual way to do it.[25] For Summoning a Parliament to meet at *London*, he procures his Son *Henry* to be declared King together with himself, by their consent, and thereupon he was Crowned by the Archbishop of *York*, and Fealty Sworn to him by all. This was the occasion of Civil Wars between them, for the Father meant hereby only to have secured the Succession to him, and the Son was impatient of having only the bare Title of a King, all along pretending to an Equal Authority, as doth sufficiently appear by what he writes to the Prior and Convent of *Canterbury*, where he takes notice, That his Father did attempt some Invasions upon them, which he ought not to have done without his assent.[26] *Qui, ratione Regiae unctionis, Regnum, & totius Regni curam suscepiemus,* and therefore he appeal'd to the Pope in that behalf. Nay, the Father himself paid that Respect to his Sons Dignity, That when he at last subdued him and his Rebellious Brothers,[27] he would not suffer him to do him Hommage with his other Sons, (though he offered it.) But *Henry* the Son dying in the Life of his Father, *Richard*

25. Convenerunt interim die statuto ex mandato Regis *Londoniam* totius *Angliae* Episcopi Abbates Comites Barones vicecomites prepositi Aldermanis cum fidejussoribus, *Gervas H 2. f 1412.*

26. Gervas H. 2. f 1425.

27. Brompt. f. 1100.

was then his Eldest Son surviving, and consequently had all the Right which a next Heir could claim. But the wise and wary King had not confidence enough to rely upon this (now so much talk'd of) sacred Right; but though he had already suffered so much from disobedient Sons, was glad to get the Succession confirmed to him in his Life-time. And, the Truth is, there was reason enough that he should do so; for he had all his Children by *Eleanor* the Daughter of *William* Duke of *Guyen*,[28] who was before the Wife of *Lewis* the *7th* King of *France,* who was still living, and she onely Divorced *causa Adulterii,* which being not a Divorce *à vinculo Matrimonii,* she could not, either by the Canon-Law universally received, or the Laws of *England,* lawfully Marry with any other Husband.

After his Father's Death, *Richard* came to *London,* to which place all the Clergy and Laity were summoned; and[29] after he had been solemnly and duely Elected by the whole Clergy and Laity, (they are the very words of the Historian) and taken the usual Oaths, he was Crowned. And when he undertook the holy War, he[30] declared *Arthur* Son of his next Brother *Geoffery* the Duke of *Britain,* the next Heir to the Crown.

Richard dying without Issue, this *Arthur* ought to have succeeded, and his Sister *Elianor* also had a Title before her Uncle: But *John* the younger Brother, without regarding this divine Right of his Nephew, applies himself to the People for a more sure, though but a humane Title,[31] who being summon'd together, elected him King. And[32] *Hubert* the then Archbishop of *Canterbury,* did at his Coronation, preach a Doctrine, which would have sounded very strangely to the Convocation in 1640. *(viz.)* No one could make any title to the Crown, *nisi ab universitate Regni unanimiter Electus.* And that he who was most worthy ought to be preferred. But (as he goes on) if any one of the Race of the deceased

---

28. M. Paris 84.

29. Post tam cleri quam populi solemnem & debitam Electionem *R. de daeto f 647. R. H. par. 2. f. 6. 56.*

30. Flo. Hist. An. 1190.

31. Praelatorum Comitum & aliorum Nobilium multitudo infinita, *Brompt. 1281.*

32. *Mat. Paris, 197. An. 1199.* Si aliquis ex stirpe Regis Defuncti aliis praepolliret pronius & promptius in electionem ejus esse consentiendum.

King, was more deserving than others, as *John* the Brother of the deceased King was, the People ought more readily to elect him, than a Stranger to the Royal Bloud. This was all the Title King *John* pretended, and this was then sufficient to put by his Nephew. And in his[33] Charters, he does more than once own, that he owed his Crown to the election and favour of his Subjects.

But when King *John* gave over to dissemble his Nature, and went about to change his Religion[34] (for he made offers of that sort to the King of *Morocco*) when he discovered himself not to be that worthy man which the People supposed him to have been; they remembred whence he derived his Title, and proceeded, upon the same reason that they had chosen him, to make a new Election,[35] chusing *Lewis* Son of *Philip* King of *France,* who was next Heir to the Crown in the right of *Blanch* his Wife, Neece to King *John,* and Daughter to his Sister *Elianor,* both the Children of *Geoffery* Duke of *Britain,* being dead before that time.

When King *Philip* heard of their choice, he consented to send his Son, being the rather induced thereto by this reason,[36] That *John*'s Bloud being corrupted by an Attainder of Treason in the Life-time of his Brother *Richard,* he was uncapable of taking the Crown by Descent, and unworthy to take it any other way.

Lewis coming to *London,* was there Elected and Constituted King, swearing to preserve the Peoples Laws, and they swearing Allegiance to him: But he soon forgot his Coronation-Oath, and attempted several ways to introduce an Arbitrary Government, before he was well Established in his Throne, which the *English* as soon resented: And King *John* happening to die very opportunely, The *Earl-Marshal,* calling together the Great men of the Kingdom, and placing *Henry* the third, then an

33. Charta Moderationis feodi Magni sigilli, *an. 1 Jo.* ex vet. Reg. in Archivis Arch. *Cant. he says he came to the Crown,* Jure Hereditario & mediante tam Cleri quam Populi unanimi Consensu & Favore.

34. Necnon & Legem Christianum, Quam, vanam censuit relinquens, Legi *Mahometis* fideliter adhaereret, *Mat. Par. 243.*

35. Mat. Par. 279. Flo. Hist. an. 1216.

36. Volens fratrem suum Regem *Ricardum* à Regno *Angliae* injuste privare & inde de proditione accusatus & coram eo convictus, Damnatus fuit per judicium in Curia ipsius Regis, *Mat. Westm. 275. Mat. Par. 281.*

Infant, in the midst of them, perswaded them to make him King, who was altogether innocent of his Fathers faults:[37] The Earl of *Gloucester* said this was contrary to their Oath to *Lewis:* To which the Marshal replied, that *Lewis* by breaking his Oath had absolved them from theirs; and that he despised the *English* to set up the *French;* and that he would be the destruction of the Realm. With whose Reasons the whole Assembly being convinced, cried out unanimously, *Fiat Rex;* and accordingly they Crown'd King *Henry* the third, and soon after compelled *Lewis* to renounce all pretences to the Crown.

Henry the Third dying,[38] after a long and troublesome Reign, his Son *Edward* the First, a Prince of great hopes, and whose Life answered the highest expectations, succeeded; but whether he was the eldest Son of his Father, remains a doubt in History. The House of *Lancaster,* who derived themselves from his Brother *Edmond,* pretending always that *Edmond* was the Elder, and *Edward* the Younger Brother, and that *Edmond* was put by the Crown, by *common Consent,* for his Deformity.

After the Death of *Edward* the First,[39] his Son *Edward* the Second succeeded, but he degenerating from so great a Father, the People grew weary of his Irregular and Arbitrary Government. And a Parliament being by him summoned at *Westminster,*[40] as all our Writers say, or as *Polydor Virgil* words it, *Principes Convocato Concilio pervenerunt* Londini (which I observe, only that we may know what *Polydor* means, when he makes use of the expression of *Principes in Concilio Congregati;*) They presently entred into a consideration of the miserable state of the Nation;[41] and a Paper being publickly read, containing many Instances of the King's Misgovernment, all which he had confessed, they concluded he was unworthy to Reign any longer, and that he ought to be deposed; and sent to him to let him know their Resolution, and to require him to renounce his Crown and Royal Dignity, otherwise they would proceed as

37. Mat. West. 275. Hen. de Knyght f. 2426 *c.* 15. *l.* 2.
38. Hen. de Knight *f.* 2472. *c.* 16. *l.* 2.
39. Tho. Walsingh. in Vit. Ed. 2. f. 126.
40. Pol. Virg. l. 18. f. 352.
41. Froissart 1. vol c. 14. Fructus Temporum. Part 7. f. 107. Hen. de Knight l. 3. c. 15. f. 2549.

they thought good. And they appointed Commissioners to go to him in their Names: The *Bishop* of *Ely* for the *Bishops;* The *Earl* of *Warren* for the *Earls;* Sir *Henry Piercy* for the *Barons;* and Sir *William Frussel* for the *Commons,* to resign their Homage up to him: which *Frussel* pronounced in all their Names, and formally deprived him of all Royal Power; the form of which is particularly set down by *Knighton.* The King read this sad Sentence with extraordinary grief, and many complaints of those evil Counsellors who had seduced him; but in the midst of his Sorrow[42] he gave them thanks that they Elected his Son to reign after him. Thus was that glorious Prince *Edward* the Third elected King in his Fathers Lifetime, *Et huic Electioni universus populus consensit. Walter* Arch-Bishop of *Canterbury,* who preached the Coronation-Sermon, took this for his Text; *Vox Populi vox Dei.* By this we may see that all his Predecessors were not of Archbishop *Lawd's* minde, but thought there was a Divine Right somewhere else than where he placed it. Upon the death of *Edward the black Prince,* there was some Dispute whether *John of Gaunt,* the eldest surviving Son of *Edward* the Third, should Succeed *Jure propinquitatis,* or *Richard* the Son of the *Black Prince;* whereupon *Edward* the Third procured the Parliament to confirm the Succession to *Richard* the *Second.* And afterwards, when *Edward* the *Third* dyed,[43] *Polidorus Virgil* says,[44] *Principes Regni habito Concilio apud* Westm. (you know what *Polidor* means by *principes) Richardum, Edwardi principis Filium, Regem dicunt, by their* common Suffrages.[45]

In the 21 year of *Richard's* Reign, a Parliament being assembled at *Westminster,* they drew up, by their common Consent, a Form whereby he did resign the Crown, and the name and power of King, discharging all his Subjects from all Oaths which they had taken of Allegiance to him, confessing himself thereby insufficient for the Government; and swearing never to make any pretences to the same for the future. All which he Pronounced and Subscribed, wishing, (if it were in his power,)

42. Quod Filium suum *Edwardum* post se Regnaturum Eligissent, *Knyght 2550.*
43. Pol. Virg. 20. f. 295; Juri Hereditario ac etiam voto communi singulorum, *H. Knyght l. 5. f. 2630.*
44. Rot. Parl. 1 *H.* 4.
45. Pol. Virg. l. 5.

to have *Henry* Duke of *Lancaster* for his Successour; but since it was not, he desired the Commissioners to signifie his Desires to the States of the Realm. The next day all the States of the Realm accepted his Resignation, and when that was done, they proceeded to read publickly his Coronation-Oath, and all the Breaches of it, that so it might appear how justly he had deserved to be deposed. All which are contained in Thirty three Articles, entred at large in the Rolls of Parliament, (and well deserve to be read) whereupon the States adjudged that he shall be Depos'd, and appoint Commissioners *ad Deponendum eundem* Richardum *Regem ab omne Dignitate, Majestate & honore Regiis, vice nomine & authoritate omnium statuum praedictorum, prout in Consimilibus casibus de antiqua consuetudine dicti Regni fuit observatum:* which the Bishop of St. *Asaph* did, in full Parliament, in their names, and by their directions. The same Commissioners were also to resign up to him their Homage and Fealty, and intimate the Sentence of Deposition; which they did accordingly, by the Mouth of Sir *William Thirning,* whose words are at large entred upon Record. Then did the Parliament proceed to choose *Henry* the Fourth King; And upon this Title onely did he rely, though he mentioned some other trifling ones, as that he challenged it, being then void, by Force, as Descended to him from King *Henry* the Third.

But this could give him no Title, for 'tis plain that whilst any of the Issue of *Lionel* Duke of *Clarence*, the Third Son of *Henry* the Third, were in being, no right of Blood could Descend to him, who derived his Pedigree onely from *John* of *Gaunt*, who was but his Fourth Son. And he plainly shewed what a good Opinion he had of a Parliamentary Title to the Crown, when in the *7th* year of his Reign,[46] he procured an Act of Parliament to pass, whereby the Inheritance of the Crown and Realms of *England* and *France* were setled upon himself for Life, and the Remainder entail'd upon his four Sons by name, and the Issue of their Bodies begotten. He was contented that it should be limited no farther, but that after failure of his own Issue, it should go according to the general direction of the Law. And he made a Charter soon after, whereby he setled

46. 7 H. 4. cap. 2.

the Crown pursuant to this Act of Parliament:[47] *Post ipsum successive hae-redibus suis de ipsius Corpore legitime procreandis;* which Charter was again confirm'd in Parliament, the 22 *December,* 8 *H.* 4. and the Original Charter is still to be seen in the *Cotton* Library.

Immediately upon the Death of *Henry* the Fourth, a Parliament met at *Westminster,* and there, according to the custom of the Realm, it was debated who should be King: But all Men had entertained so good thoughts of Prince *Henry,* that without staying till the whole Assembly had declared him King, divers of them began to swear Allegiance to him. A thing strange, and without President, as only occasioned by the extraordinary Opinion which was generally conceived of him before.

And the certain Title vested in him by an Act of Parliament.

Princeps Henricus, *facto Patris sui funere, Concilium Principum apud* Westmonasterium *Convocandum Curat, in quo de 8 Rege Creando, more Majorum, agitabatur. Continuò aliquot Principe ultro in ejus Verba jurare coeperunt, quod Benevolentiae Officium Nulli, priusquam Rex re-nunciatus esset, praestitum constat. Adeo* Henricus *ab ineunto aetate spem omnibus optimae Indolis fecit,* Pol. Virg. l. 22. Hist. Angl. in Vit. H. 5.

Henry the Fifth dying, and leaving but one Son, who was an Infant of Eight Months old, *Titus Livius* says there was some doubt whether he should be accepted as King;[48] but as soon as his Fathers Funerals were Solemnized, the Estates of the Realm of *England,* Assembling and Consulting together, they declared *Henry* the Sixth to be their Sovereign.

In the Thirty fifth year of *Henry* the Sixth, a new Limitation of the Crown was made by Parliament, for though the King had a Son then living, yet it was Enacted,[49] That during his own Life onely, *Henry* the Sixth should hold and enjoy the Crown, and that during his Life, *Richard* Duke of *York* should be reputed and stil'd Heir Apparent to the Crown, and that it should be Treason to compass his Death;[50] and after the Death, Resignation, *&c.* of *Henry,* the Crown was limited in Re-

47. Bucks Hist. R. 3. l. 2. f. 50.
48. Titus Liv. Ms. in Bibl. Bod. Cott. Record. f. 666.
49. Hubington's Hist. E. 4. f. 10.
50. Cott. Rec. 670. Fructus Temp. part 7. f. 162.

mainder to *Richard* and his Heirs, with a Proviso, that if *Henry,* or any in his behalf, should endeavour to disanul or frustrate this Act, that then *Richard* should have the present possession of the Crown. And by force of this Act of Parliament, the same Duke of *York,* taking advantage of *Henry's* Violation of it, did lay claim to,[51] and attempt the recovery of the Kingdom, as also did his Son *Edward* after him with better success; and *Edward* did openly insist upon this Title in the Speech which he made at his Coronation.

It was also Declared by *Edward's* first Parliament, in the first year of his Reign, that *Henry* the Sixth having broken the aforesaid Concord in many particulars, the Crown was duely devolved to *Edward* the Fourth by vertue thereof.

Afterwards *Edward* the Fourth being driven out of the Kingdom, in the Tenth year of his Reign, the Parliament did again entail the Crown on *Henry* the Sixth, and the Heirs Male of his Body, with the Remainder to *George* Duke of *Clarence,* Brother to *Edward* the Fourth, who was thereby also declared Heir to *Richard* Duke of *York.*

'Tis worthy observation, that both the Families of *York* and *Lancaster* claimed a Title by Act of Parliament; and as long as that Title continued, the Issue of *Henry* the Fourth had never any Disturbance from the Pretences of the House of *York,* who had undoubtedly the Right of Blood on their side:[52] But as soon as *Richard* Duke of *York* had a Title vested in him, by the Statute made in the Thirty ninth year of *Henry* the Sixth, then he thought it was worth contending for; nor did he and his Son desist till they had driven out *Henry* the Sixth.

Edward the Fourth did recover the Kingdom again as suddenly as he lost it, and prevail'd with his Parliament to repeal that Law which was made during his Expulsion, and so left the Crown to that young unfortunate Prince *Edward* the Fifth, who held it not long enough to have it put on him with the usual Solemnity; for though he was Proclaimed, he was never Crowned King: For his Uncle *Richard* Duke of *Gloucester* having secured him and his Brother in the *Tower,* did cunningly insinuate

51. Hubingt. *E.* 4. f. 73.
52. *Buck's* Hist. *Rich.* 3. lib. 1. fol. 20.

the Bastardy of his Nephew, and that *Edward* the Fourth had another Wife living at the time of his Marriage to their Mother, and also at the time of their Birth.

The Report found Credit universally, in so much that the Duke of *Buckingham* coming to him at *Baynards*-Castle, with most of the great Lords and wise men of the Kingdom, and the Mayor and Aldermen of *London*, the Duke did in their Names acquaint him, that they had unanimously thought fit to elect him King, as being Heir to the Royal Blood of *Richard* Duke of *York*, upon whom the Crown was entail'd by the High Authority of Parliament.

'Tis very remarkable, that in the midst of their highest Flatteries and Courtship to him, they tell him only of this great and sure Title by Act of Parliament; although if he had been indeed (what was pretended) the Heir of the House of *York*, his Right by Descent from *Edward* the Third was unquestionable.

Richard (after some feigned Excuses) did at last accept of their Offer and Election; and the Parliament being soon after Assembled,[53] they presented a Bill to this effect: *Please it your Grace to understand the Consideration, Election and Petition under-written, of the Lords Spiritual and Temporal, and of the Commons*, &c. And thereby they Declare the Children of *Edward* the Fourth illegitimate,[54] and that his Brother *George* Duke of *Clarence* was attainted of High-Treason by Parliament, in the 17th year of *Edward* the Fourth's Reign, *by reason whereof all the Issue of the said* George *were and are disabled and barr'd of all Right and Claim, that in any case they might have or challenge by Inheritance to the Crown and Dignity Royal of this Realm, by the ancient Laws and Customs of the same.* After which, considering that none of the uncorrupted lineal Blood of *Richard* Duke of *York* could be found but in his Person, (say they) We have chosen and do choose you our King and Sovereign Lord. Then the Bill proceeds, in reciting that all the Learned in the Laws do approve his Title, and declaring him King as well by Right of Consanguinity and Inheritance, as by lawful Election, and entails the Crown on him and the Heirs

53. *Cott.* Rec. fol. 709.
54. *Bucks Rich.* 3. lib. 1. fol. 22.

of his Body, and declares his Son Heir Apparent. To which the King gave his Royal Assent in these words: *Et idem Dominus Rex, de Assensu dictorum trium Statuum Regni, & Authoritate praedicta, omnia & singula praemissa, in Billa praedicta contenta concedit, & ea pro vero & indubio pronunciat, decernit, & declarat.*

But the barbarous Murder of his Nephews did soon beget such an universal Detestation of *Richard* in the minds of the People, that they resolved he should no longer Reign over them; and so, taking hold of a Pretence which *Henry* Duke of *Richmond* set up, they joyn'd with him against *Richard.* Though *Henry*'s Title was indeed no more than a meer Pretence; for not only the Right of the *House* of *York,* (as far as Blood could give Right) was before that of the House of *Lancaster,* but also he had no manner of Interest in that Title which the *Lancastrian Line* had, since his Claim was under a Bastard, begotten in Adultery; and besides, his Mother, *Margaret* Countess of *Richmond,* as Heir to whom he pretended he claim'd, was then living. Therefore *Comines,* the most judicious Writer of that Age, and who knew well what was the sence of *Europe* concerning his Title, says plainly, (though he wrote in the time of *Henry* the Seventh) *Qu'il n'avoit Croix, ne Pile, ne nul Droit, (comme Jeo Croy) a la Couronne d'Angleterre.*

Nevertheless, *Henry* having slain *Richard* in *Bosworth*-field, the Crown was there put on his Head by the Lord *Stanley,* with the general Acclamation of the People. But he was wise enough to think his Title to it was not very good, till it was made so by an Act of Parliament, and therefore in the first year of his Reign he procured one to pass in these words:

For the Wealth,[55] *Prosperity, and Surety of this Realm of* England, *and for avoiding of all Ambiguities and Questions,* (The wisest of our Princes you see had no little Opinion of the Authority of a Parliament in this point,) *Be it Ordained,* &c. *That the Inheritance of the Crown of the Realms of* England *and* France, *with all the Preheminences and Dignities Royal to the same appertaining, and the Ligeances to the King belonging, beyond the Seas,* &c. *shall be, rest, remain and abide in the most Royal Person of our Sovereign Lord* Henry *the Seventh, and in the Heirs*

55. *Bucks Rich.* 3. lib. 5. fol. 145.

of his Body lawfully coming perpetually, with the Grace of God, and so to endure, and no other.

Thus did the wisest of our Kings establish himself,[56] and the best of our Historians mentions it as one of the greatest Instances of his Wisdom, That he did not press to have this as a Declaration or Recognition of Ancient Right, but onely as an Establishment of the possession which he then had; nor to have the Remainder limited to any person after the determination of his Estate, but was content with the Settlement upon himself, and the Issue of his own Body, leaving it to the Law, to decide what was to follow upon the failure of such Heirs.

Nor can any thing be more clear, than that *Henry* the *Seventh* depended entirely on this Parliamentary Title, without extending any pretences of his, or his Wives, (who was Heir of the House of *York*,) beyond this Establishment, in as much as the Oaths of Allegiance and other publick Tests and Securities, which were required at that time of the Subjects, were not in general Terms, to the King, his Heirs, and Successors, but only to the King,[57] and the Heirs Male of his Body lawfully begotten. An Instance of this, (without going any further) may be seen amongst the Records Printed at the end of the late History of the Reformation, where Cardinal *Adrian*, when he was promoted by *Henry* the Seventh to the Bishoprick of *Bath* and *Wells*, renounces all Clauses in the Popes Bulls, which may be prejudicial *Domini meo supremo, & Haeredibus suis corpore suo legitime procreatis*, Angliae *Regibus*; and he does afterwards swear Allegiance to him in the very same Words, without taking any notice of Remoter Heirs.

Henry the *Eighth*, the Heir to this Entail, Succeeded his Father; and though he attempted as much for Arbitrary Power, and used Parliaments with as little respect as any of his Predecessors; Yet even he never doubted of their Power in settling the Succession, but valued it much, and resorted to it frequently.

56. Lord *Bacon H.* 7. f. 11, 12.
57. *Burnet*'s. Hist. of the Reformation, Collect. ad lib. 2. fol. 3, 4.

In the *25th* year of his Reign an Act passed,[58] wherein the Parliament say, they were *bounden to provide for the perfect surety of the Succession;* (they did not certainly reckon themselves bound to do a thing that was not in their Power.) And then they take notice of the great Mischiefs and Effusions of Bloud which had happened by reason of the doubtfulness of the true Title; and *for the avoiding of all future Questions,* do Enact, *That the Imperial Crown of this Realm shall be to King* Henry *8th, and the Heirs of his Body Lawfully begotten on Queen* Anne, *and the Heirs of the Bodies of such several Sons respectively, according to the course of Inheritance; and for default of such Issue, then to the Sons of his Body in like manner; and upon failure of such Issue then to the Lady* Elizabeth, *and after her to any other Issue, in Tail, and then the Remainder is limited to the right Heirs of* Henry the *8th.* By the same Statute every Subject at his full Age is oblig'd to take an Oath to defend the Contents of it, and the refusal is made Misprision of Treason. And the next *Parliament,*[59] which was held in the year following, does particularly Enact an Oath for that purpose.

Some few years after these Acts were Repealed,[60] and the *Parliament Entailed* the *Crown* upon the King, and the Heirs of his Body by *Queen Jane;* And Power is given the King for want of Issue of his Body to dispose of the Succession by his Letters Patents, or his last Will.

It is also made Treason, if any Usurp upon those to whom it is so appointed. Here the *Parliament* do not only use their power of changing the Succession, but they *Delegate it to another.*

And in the *thirty fifth* Year of this King's Reign,[61] the *Parliament* by another Act take notice of the great and high Trust which the Subjects had in him, in putting into his hands wholly the Order and Declaration of the Succession; Yet the King being then ready to go into *France,* they do Enact, that after his Death, and the Death of *Prince Edward,* without Issue, the Crown should be to the *Lady Mary,* and the *Heirs* of her Body; but both subject to such Conditions as the King should limit by his Letters

58. St. 25 *H.* 8. cap. 22.
59. 26 *H.* 8. c. 2.
60. 28 *H.* 8. *Rast.* Crown 4.
61. 35 *H.* 3. cap. 1.

Patents, or by his last Will, sign'd with his Hand: And if the *Lady Mary* performed not those Conditions, that then the Crown should go to the *Lady* Elizabeth, *as if the Lady* Mary *had been dead without Issue;* and if the Lady *Elizabeth* neglected to perform such Conditions, then it should go to such other Person as the King should appoint, in the same manner as before, as if the Lady *Elizabeth* had *been dead without Issue.* And Authority is given to him, by his Letters Patents, or his last Will, signed with his own Hand, to appoint the Crown to remain to such Person or Persons, and for such Estate, and under such Conditions as he should please.

An Oath also for observing this Statute is appointed, and it is made *Treason* to refuse it, or to disturb or interrupt any Person to whom it is limited by this Act, or should be by the King, pursuant to the Power given him thereby.

This is abundantly sufficient to prove, That it was *the universal Opinion of that Age, That the Succession was wholly under the Controul of Parliament,* who not only limited it as they pleased themselves, but *subjected it to Conditions,* and *to the Appointments of others.* But the thing was in its own Nature so evident, that they who had the greatest Reason, and were most concern'd to do it, did never presume to question the Power of a Parliament in this Point.

Lethington,[62] *Secretary* of *Scotland,* in a Letter of his, written to Sir *William Cecill,* then *Secretary* of State here, wherein he argues in behalf of the Title of his *Mistriss,* Mary Queen *of* Scots, to succeed Queen *Elizabeth,* against a pretended Disposition made by the last Will of *Henry* the Eighth, to his *Neece,* the Lady *Frances,* Daughter to the *French Queen,* if his own Issue fail'd, says of these Statutes that gave the King Power to dispose of the Crown, That they were against Equity to disinherit a Race of Forreign Princes, and that they were made in an abrupt Time, (as he terms it;) but yet he confesses, that since the thing was done, it was now valid and unavoidable, unless some Circumstances did annihilate the Limitation and Disposition made by King *Henry*'s Will.

And so he proceeds to prove that the power which was given to the King by these Statutes, was not pursued, (which it ought to have been

62. *Burn.* Hist Reform. Collect. 268.

most strictly, and in a precise Form,) for that the King never signed the Will, but that his name, set to it, was forged: Nay, I will venture to say that in all the Books which were written to support the Claim of the *Scottish Queen* against *King Henries* Will, (though the whole power and wealth of the *Guises* were employed to set every wit at work on that Design) there was never any stress laid upon it,[63] or so much as a pretence that these Acts of Parliament were void or ineffectual in themselves. In that Discourse which was published by *Philips,* and composed by Sir *Anthony Brown* one of the Justices of the Common Pleas, who was (in judge *Dodderidges* opinion) a person of an incomparable sharpness of Wit, There was all the help that learning either in Divinity, Civil or Common Laws could give; yet there the Authority of the Parliament in the case, and the validity of these Statutes is all along admitted. Indeed they endeavour to put some other construction upon the Statutes, but their great Argument is, That King *Henry,* as King, had no power to dispose of the Crown, and therefore these Laws only gave him an Authority, and made him only as it were a Commissioner, and therefore, as all other Authorities, (especially being in Derogation of the course of the Common Line,) was to be strictly followed. They allow that he had sufficient power to Devise, and that he might Honourably have used that Power; but that he ever did exercise that Authority, is the thing denyed. But it is time for us to go on.

Edward the Sixth succeeded his Father, and took upon him a power, which surely no King ever had, to dispose of his Crown by the Will. But that disposition serving to no other purpose but to the Ruine of the *Lady Jane Gray,* His *Sister Queen Mary* first, and after *Queen Elizabeth* enjoy'd the Crown according to the Limitation of the Statute 35 *H.* 8. *c.* 1. and that one of them had no other Title, must be agreed by all: For Queen *Catherine* was alive at the time when *Elizabeth* was born: so that if the first Marriage was unlawful, Queen *Mary,* and if the second was unlawful, Queen *Elizabeth* must necessarily have been Illegitimate.

---

63. Treatise of the Title of Queen *Mary* to the Succession, *pag.* 38, 39. *&c. lib.* 2. *Dodd.* Engl. Lawyer. *pag.* 8.

I cannot but observe one passage to our present purpose, which I meet with in the time of Queen *Mary*. Sir *Edward Montague* first Lord Chief Justice of the Common Pleas,[64] and afterwards of the Kings Bench (one who had the reputation of the ablest and wisest Lawyer of his Age,) being accused to have drawn the Will of *Edward* the Sixth, whereby that Queen was to have been disinherited, and being in great danger upon that account; drew up a State of his own case, and therein sets forth that the great reason which prevailed with him to obey the King in that particular, and upon which he did still rely for his indemnity, was, that if Queen *Mary* came to the Crown,[65] she took it by force of the Act of Parliament which did limit it to her in Remainder, so that she came in as a purchaser and not in privity of estate to her Brother, and consequently could not punish Treasons or offences committed in his time.

I must needs also observe, that in the Articles made upon the Marriage of Q. *Mary* with *Ph.* of *Spain*, which were confirmed by Act of Parliament,[66] the several Crowns and Territories of *Philip* are distributed part to *Charles* the Infant of *Spain*, part to the *Issue* of the intended Marriage. Whereby it does appear not only what opinion all *Europe* had of the power of an English Parliament, but also that by the consent of the Estates of other Realms, Crowns might be limited and disposed out of the ordinary course of Descent.

In the *first* year of Queen *Elizabeth*, The Parliament recognize her Title to the Crown,[67] with express Relation to the *Statute* 35 *H.* 8. which invests it in her and the heirs of her Body, and do enact that the Limitation made by that Statute shall stand and remain as Law for ever, and all Sentences,[68] Judgements and Decrees to the contrary are declared to be void, and appointed to be cancell'd. And the several offences which are made Treason by another Statute in the same year, are all restrain'd to the Queen and the Heirs of her Body only. The Parliament intending to

64. *Mores* Reports 827. & 828.
65. *Fullers* Church-History *lib.* 8. *fol.* 5.
66. *1* Mar. Parl. *2.* cap. *2.*
67. 1 *Eliz. c.* 3.
68. 1 *Eliz. c.* 5.

extend that new security no further than her Estate in the Crown (which she took by that Parliamentary limitation) did extend.

In her *Thirteenth* year it was Enacted,[69] That if any person claim Title to the Crown for himself or any other, during her Life, or shall not upon Demand acknowledge her Right, *He shall be disabled during his Life to have the Crown in Succession, as if he were naturally Dead.* And to affirm Right of Succession in such claimer or usurper, (after Proclamation made of such claim or usurpation,) is made Treason. Nor does the Statute stop there, but makes it Treason, during the life of the Queen, and forfeiture of all Goods and Chattels after her decease, to affirm that the Queen, with and by the Authority of Parliament, is not able to make Laws and Statutes of sufficient force and validity to limit and bind the Crown of this Realm, and the Descent, Limitation, Inheritance and Government thereof, or that this or any other Statute made by Parliament, with the Queens assent, is not or ought not to be for ever of sufficient force to bind and Govern all persons, their Rights and Titles that may claim any *Interest* or *Possibility* in *or to the Crown in Possession, Remainder, Inheritance, Succession or otherwise.* It were well if some rash men, who presume in their discourses to restrain the power of the Parliament, (that is, the King, Lords and Commons,) in the great business of the Succession, would be so wise as to remember this Act, (which is still in force) and the penalty to which they subject themselves by such sawcy Talk. That incomparable States-man the Lord *Burleigh* had another kind of opinion of the Security which an Act of Parliament could give his Royal Mistress,[70] by making the Scottish Queen *(the Popish Successor of that time)* unable and unworthy of the Succession; as appears in a Letter which he wrote about this time to Sir *Francis Walsingham,* then Ambassadour in *France.*

In the *Twenty Seventh* year of Queen *Elizabeth,*[71] it was enacted that if any Invasion was made, or Rebellion or other thing tending to the hurt of Her person by or for, or with the privity of any one who should or might pretend Title to the Crown, and the same should be adjudged in

69. 13 *Eliz. c.* 1. *Rast.* Treason. 27.
70. Compleat Ambassad. *fol.* 219.
71. 27 *Eliz. cap.* 1.

such manner as that Law appoints, then every person against whom such Judgment should be given, should be *excluded and disabled for ever to have or claim the Crown;* And that the Subjects of this Realm lawfully might by all forcible and possible means, pursue all such offenders: And their Issues assenting or privy thereto, are in like manner disabled and to be pursued. And this Act was made in pursuance of an Association enter'd into by the People in the vacancy of Parliament out of their great zeal for the preservation of the life of that excellent Princess.

By vertue of his Statute *Mary* Queen of *Scotland* was afterwards executed,[72] as appears by the Commission for her Tryal.

King *James* her Son who was a wiser Prince, and not wholly *govern'd by Priests as his Mother was,* though he had the same pretences that she had, yet never disputed his Right, or set on foot any Title during the life of the ever Renowned Queen; *though she would never suffer him to be declared her successor.* He was too wise to incur the like disability as his Mother had done, and *to contest a Title Establisht by Parliament.*

After Queen *Elizabeths* Death, The Act of Recognition made upon King *James* his coming to the Crown, doth particularly insist upon that Title, which was raised by Act of Parliament to *Henry* the *Seventh,* and the Heirs of his body, and that immediately upon the *Queens* decease the Crown descended and came to King *James;* so that you see the Title of Queen *Elizabeth* is again acknowledged by Parliament; And the entail made by the Statute of 35 *H.* 8. being spent upon her death without Issue, King *James* comes in as next Heir to the old entail made the *first* year of *Henry* the Seventh.

Thus have I set down before you the whole course of the English Succession as plainly, as truly, and as briefly as is possible. I shall leave every man to make his own observations on this Historical Deduction: But this one observation I believe all men must make from it, That it hath been the constant opinion of all ages that the Parliament of *England* had an unquestionable power to Limit, Restrain and Qualify the Succession as they pleased, and that in all Ages they have put their power in prac-

---

72. *Strangways* Hist. of *Mary* Queen of *Scotland, fol.* 179.

tice; and that the Historian had reason for saying that seldom or never the third Heir in a right Descent enjoy'd the Crown of *England*.[73]

It were as easie to shew that in all other Kingdoms the next of Blood hath been frequently excluded from the Succession, but the History of our own Countrey is our business; yet I cannot forbear reciting the *Speech* which *Ambassadors* sent from the States of *France,* made to *Charles* of *Lorrain,* when they had solemnly rejected him (though he was Brother to *Louys d' Outremes* and next Heir to the Crown) and had elected *Hugh Capet* for their King. They told him that every one knew that the Succession of the Crown of *France* belonged to him, and not *Hugh Capet*.[74] But yet (say they) the very same Laws which give you this Right of Succession, do judge you also unworthy of the same; for that you have not hitherto endeavoured to frame your manners according to the Prescript of those Laws, nor according to the usages and customs of your Countrey, but rather have ally'd your self with the *German* Nation our old Enemies, and have loved their vile and base manners. Wherefore seeing you have forsaken the ancient virtue and sweetness of your Countrey, we have also forsaken and abandon'd *you;* and have chosen *Hugh Capet* for our King, and put you back, and this without any scruple of Conscience at all, esteeming it better and more just to live under him, enjoying our Ancient Laws, Customs, Priviledges and Liberties, than under you the Heir by Blood in oppression, strange Customs and Cruelty. For as those who are to make a Voyage at Sea do not much consider whether the Pilot be owner of the Ship, but whether he be skilful and wary; so our care is to have a Prince to Govern us gently and happily, (which is the end for which Princes were appointed) and for these ends we judge this man fitter to be our King.

Certainly it were a most dangerous thing to have an opinion prevail, that the King in concurrence with his Parliament should not have power to change the direct order of Succession, though the preservation both of him and his people did depend upon it. For it does directly tend to Anarchy, and makes the Government to want power to defend it self, by

73. Daniel, fol. *5.* in vita H. *1.*
74. Gerr. du Hail. lib. *6.* an. *988.*

making such Alterations as the variety of Accidents in several ages may make absolutely necessary. There must be a supreme uncontroulable power lodged somewhere. And the men who talk at this rate, can hardly find where it is lodged in *England,* if not in the King, Lords and Commons in Parliament.

But when a man begins to ask a Reason of this Doctrine of theirs, that proximity of Blood does give a Title unchangeable by any Humane Laws; The teachers of it differ exceedingly; some of them tell us of a Divine Patriarchal Right, which Kings as Natural Fathers of their People have derived down to them from *Adam.* And this Notion though it be no older than the present Age, has been very frequent in mens Mouths and Books, and has much pleased of late (as new things use to do). But they consider not that if this be true, there never can be but one Rightful Monarch in the Universe, That is He only who is the direct and Lineal Heir of *Adam* then living. And thus these great Patrons of Absolute Power, instead of supporting, do shake the Thrones of all the Princes in the world, since none of them at this day can make out any such Title.

There are others who being desirous to bestow upon the Crown a Complement of the like nature, which they were at the same time obtaining from it, have declared in general, That Monarchy is of Divine Right, That Princes succeed by the Laws of God, That their Title is not subject to any earthly cognizance, nor owing to any consent of the People. But the consequences of this opinion are not once consider'd by these men, that thereby the property of all Subjects, and the Laws of all Countreys, are destroy'd together. For no Humane Laws or Contracts can bind or restrain a Power divinely Instituted.[75] (Or if you like it better in the words of a great Cardinal) A Jurisdiction which is of Divine Right, is not alterable by the will or power of man.

Besides all communities which live under another Form of Government, must be guilty of violating this Divine Institution. And perhaps there are few others besides the Great *Turks* Dominions, which are govern'd as they ought to be.

---

75. Card. Pullav. Hist. conc. Trid. l. *18.* cap. *15.*

In what a damnable condition are the *Venetians* and the *Netherlands,* who admit no Monarch at all? *Poland* and the *Empire,* who Elect their Princes, and will not hear talk of this Divine Right of Succession?

Aragon, where they do not only elect their King, but tell him plainly at his Coronation, that they will Depose him if he observes not the conditions which they require from him, and have a setled Officer call'd *El' Justitia* for that purpose? Nay, even *France* it self, which 'tis notoriously known, does exclude Women from this Divine Right?

That Government is of Nature, and derived from God, is manifest. Nothing is more natural in Man than the Desire of Society, and without Government Society would be intolerable. But can it be proved from hence that the Government cannot be moulded into several Forms agreeable to the Interest and Dispositions of several Nations, and may not be varied from time to time as occasion requires, by the mutual consent of the Governours, and of those who are Governed?

And after all pretences of this kind, let any place of Scripture be produced wherein God obliges a people to this or that Form, till they have first obliged themselves to it by some Act of their own?

I do agree that if God by any extraordinary Revelation has ordain'd any sort of Government, or by any immediate Denomination has conferr'd a Kingdom on any Family, and has directed in what order the Crown shall discend, that all men are bound to submit to it and acquiesce in the Divine Will, as soon as it is clearly and evidently made out to them, but they must not be angry if men expect such an Evidence.

There is a third sort of men, who tell us this Realm being entirely subdued by the Conquerour, and by him left to descend to his Heirs, none of these Heirs who derive a Title under him, can deprive those who are to succeed of any Right which they ought to have, but must leave the Crown as free to them as they themselves received it from their Ancestors.

I will not here insist upon the danger that any Prince runs into who founds his Title in force, because it will be hard to prove that such a one does not leave as good a Title open for every man who can make himself strong enough. Nor need I trouble my self to shew, that all Conquest does not put the Conquerour into an Absolute Right. Though it be most evident in the case of *William* the *First,* who did by his Sword prosecute a claim of another nature, and meant only to acquire that Right, and after conquest rested in it. He pretended to the Crown as the Gift of King *Edward,* and to vindicate that Title he enter'd with Arms. And though his Relation to the Crown was more remote than that of *Edgar Atheling,* (then a child) yet his Title was better than *Harolds* the present Usurper, who could pretend no kindred at all, and who had himself Sworn to support the Grant to *William.* Nor did he claim a Power by conquest, (though the name of Conquerour was given him by after times, says *Daniel*) but submitted to the orders of the Kingdom, desirous rather to have his Testamentary Title, than his Sword to make good his succession. But I will admit that he made an absolute conquest, and then these men will grant that he might himself dispose of this conquer'd Kingdom. Therefore if he did not leave it to descend in such a manner as they would have it go, nor did institute any such sort of Succession, surely this Argument of theirs will fall to the ground. Now 'tis plain that he never design'd that the Crown should descend, but gave it to his second Son, and thereby gave an early example *of excluding and pretermitting the unworthy.*

Lastly, Others object that the Fundamental Laws of the Land against which no Act of Parliament can be of force, have so establisht the Succession that the course of it cannot be alter'd. This is surely a new discovery unknown to our Fore-fathers, as the foregoing History does abundantly prove. But let these objectors be asked by what Authority these imaginary Laws were made? For if an Authority equal to that which made them be still in being, That Authority may certainly repeal them when ever it pleases to exert it self. If the King alone made them, no doubt but that he may change them too. If they will say they were made by the diffusive body of the people, they run before they are aware into the guilt of worshipping that Idol The Multitude, and make a great step towards placing the foundation of the Government upon contract and consent. But then let them produce those Laws or some Authentick memorial of them, before it be exacted from us to believe there were ever any such.

Yes, they will say, there is such an ancient Law acknowledged by all the Judges, and known to every man, that the Descent of the Crown purges all Defects whatsoever. This Maxim as it is usually repeated is in these words, and this might be admitted, and yet could not be pertinently apply'd to a case where the Descent it self is prevented by a Law. But I will not take advantage of their words, but will consider the Objection, as it stands in that Book where the first mention of it was made,[76] and that is in the *Year Book* of *Henry* the *Seventh,* it being said there by the Judges, That the King was a person Able and Discharged of any Attainder *eo facto,* that he took upon him the Government, and to be King.

First, This was not only an extra-judical opinion, but was not pertinent to the Question referr'd to their consideration, Whether those who were chosen into the House of Commons, and were at that time attainted of Treason might sit in Parliament, till their Attainders were Reversed; and they all agree that their Attainders should first be annulled. But then they proceed to say that there was no necessity that the Kings Attainder should be Reversed, for that he might enable himself, and needed not any Act of Reversal. But surely they said very wisely in what they said, for he who had won a Crown in the field, had gone a great way towards enabling himself to wear it. Most sure it is that if an Act of Reversal were necessary before he could sit, that then it was impossible he ever should sit there, because no such Act could be made without the Royal Assent. *Henry* the *Seventh* was then King *de facto,* and in possession of the Throne, and it was somewhat of the latest to consider whether he was qualified or not. Certainly it had been strange self-denyal in the Judges, and a neglect of themselves, (which is not usual with them) to have alledged an Incurable Disability in the King, from whom they had their Patents and Authority.

In the next place let us consider what precedent the Judges cite to justifie this opinion of theirs, and how apposite it is. *Henry* the *Sixth* being driven out of the Kingdom by *Edward* the *Fourth,* The Conquerour call'd a Parliament, and got an Act to pass, whereby *Henry* was disabled

---

76. *1* H. 7. f. 4. b. Que le Roy fuist person able & discharge d'auscun attainder eo facto qu' il prist sur lui le Reign & estre Roy.

to hold the Crown. About ten years after, *Henry* regains the Kingdom, and upon this re-accession to the Crown (as 'tis usually call'd) This Act is never repeal'd. But does not every Child see the Reasons of it? For if *Henry* was Lawful King, (and before he was not to doubt that) The Act it self was void in as much as it wanted the Royal Assent. So that for him to have procured an Act of Repeal had been to affirm a Title to the Crown in *Edward*. But without doubt this opinion of the Judges as it is apply'd by the Objectors, was new and unheard of before. We see the *King* of *France* was otherwise informed by the learned men in the time of King *John*, for they thought his Blood corrupted,[77] and him uncapable of taking the Crown by Descent, because he was Attainted of Treason, which prevailed with that King to send over his Son *Lewis*, to put in his claim in right of his wife, who was the next Heir. It also ought to be observed that the true Reason why the generality of the Nation did so long approve the Title of the House of *Lancaster*, was because all the Princes of the House of *York* were Attainted of Treason, and their Blood corrupted. But as soon as ever this corruption was purged, and *Richard Duke* of *York* was declared Heir Apparent by Parliament, the people soon forsook the *Lancastrians*, and set the *House* of *York* in the Throne.

Nay, the very learned men of the same Age with these Judges, thought quite otherwise, as will appear beyond contradiction in this famous case which follows. *Richard* the *Third* had two Elder Brothers, *Edward* and *George* Duke of *Clarence*. *Richard* designing to secure the Crown to himself, had procured the Children of *Edward* to be declared Illegitimate, yet still the Duke of *Clarence* had Issue living which might pretend. But observe what the Parliament say (as to this) in the first year of *Richard* the *Third*:[78] "That in the seventeenth year of *Edward* the *Fourth*, *George* Duke of *Clarence* was Attainted of Treason, by reason whereof all the Issue of the said *George* was, and is Disabled and Barred of all Right and Claim, that in any case he or his Issue might have or challenge by Inheritance to the Crown and Dignity Royal of these Realms. After that we consider that you be the undoubted Heir, *&c.*" And so they proceed af-

---

77. Mat. Westm. *275.* v. supra.
78. V. Sup. & Cott. Rec. *709.*

firming that all Learned men in the Laws do approve his Title. You see within less than three years before this opinion of the Judges, The whole Parliament do not only give their opinion, but assure you that all Learned men of that time held clearly that an Attainder did hinder the descent of the Crown, and incapacitate the person to take it. Nay, what goes yet further in this matter, *Richard* himself, though he was as jealous to secure his Title as ever Tyrant was, and had as good advice to discern the most distant danger: though he was always restless in endeavouring to get the *Earl* of *Richmond* into his Hands, who was a very remote pretender, and only descended from a Bastard of the House of *Lancaster,* yet he fear'd nothing on this side. He knew how he had wrong'd the Children of his Brother *Edward,* and could not be at ease till he had sent them out of the World, but he let the Children of his Brother *Clarence* live, without apprehending any danger from them because their blood was corrupted, and all possibility of Descent taken from them by the Attainder of their Father. It was this only preserved them alive, and not any remorse of Conscience or any niceness in sending another Nephew out of the World after those whom he had dispatcht before. This notable case attended with these circumstances, will convince every man either that the Judges intended no such thing by their opinion as some men fancy, or else at least that extra-judicial opinions were then as Apocryphal as they have been since.

Consider Lastly, the unreasonableness of this Doctrine which tends directly to subvert Government, and to put the life of the King Regnant into the hands of his Successor. The next Heir may commit Rapes and Murders and Treasons, Burn Cities or Betray Fleets, may conspire against the life of his Prince, and yet after all, if by *Flight* or *Force* he can save himself, till some of his accomplices can get the King dispatcht, in spight of all Laws and Justice he must come to the Crown, and be Innocent.

But when I reflect what sort of men I am arguing with, and how willingly they use to submit to Authority, I think I shall convince them best by citing the opinions of two great men, the one a Cardinal, the other a Lord Chancellour, both of them Martyrs for the Papal Supremacy, I mean *Fisher* and Sir *Thomas Moor.* And if their Judgments approve the power of Parliaments in the business of the Succession, it cannot but weigh very much on such occasions as this. 'Tis well known how resolution even to death they refused the Oath of Succession which the Parliament had framed,[79] because therein the Kings Supremacy was avow'd, and therefore they cannot be suspected to dissemble, when at the very same time they declared, that if that of Supremacy was left out, they would willingly Swear an Oath to maintain the Succession of the Crown to the Issue of the Kings present Marriage, as it was then establisht by Parliament, and gave this reason for it, that this was in the power of a Parliament to determine; but not who was supreme head of the Church. Sir *Thomas Moor* went further, and own'd a very strange opinion of their power in this point. But he says expresly at the same time, that the Parliament had unquestionable Authority in the ordering of the Succession, and that the people were bound to obey them therein.

After the Testimonies of these two great Papists, it will be little to add the Testimony of a Protestant. But yet I will mention what Sir *Walter Rawleigh* (who was no inconsiderable man, though a Protestant) says in his Incomparable Preface to the History of the World: Without doubt (says he) Humane Reason would have judged no otherwise but that *Henry* the *Fourth* had rendred the Succession as unquestionable by the Act of Parliament which he had procured to entail it on his Issues, as by his own Act he had left his enemies powerless.

But sinking men catch hold of every thing, and when they cannot object to the validity, they will tell us, That such an Act of Parliament to disinherit the next Heir is unjust and without a sufficient ground.

I will not at present enter into the dispute how far the difference of Religion, which will also necessarily draw on a change in the Government, does justifie men in seeking to present the two dearest things on earth in an orderly and lawful way. I will not (though I safely might) challenge these men to tell me, where ever any settled Nation which had Laws of their own, and were not under the immediate force of a Conquerour, did ever admit of a King of another Religion than their own. I will not insist on it that the Crown is not a Bare Inheritance, but an In-

79. Burn. Hist. Ref. lib. *2.* fol. *156.*

heritance accompanying an Office of Trust, and that if a mans defects render him uncapable of the Trust, he has also forfeited the Inheritance. I need not say how far a Nation is to be excused for executing Justice summarily, and without the tedious formalities of Law, when the necessity of things requires haste, and the party flies from Justice, and his confederates are numerous and daring, and the Princes life in danger.

But this I will say, that if the Parliament have power in this thing, which I need not prove, by shewing that the ordinary course of Law allows Heirs to be disinherited of Fines and Recoveries, and that the Parliament in all ages has frequently done it by making Acts to alter the strongest Settlements, where Equity has Dictated it, though the Heirs were never in any wise criminal. There according to Sir *Thomas Moors* opinion the people are bound in conscience to obey their Laws, and must not pretend to enquire whether they were made upon just grounds. For by the same Reason they may pretend that all other Laws were made without just cause, and refuse obedience to any of them. And surely those that should do so, would be an Excellent *Loyal Party*. God defend this Nation from such Loyalty, as opposes it self to the King and the Laws, and God defend the King from the pretended Duty and Submission of those men, who whilst they talk of his power so much Renounce it openly, and oppose what would be the greatest security of his person, and in effect set up his Successor above him, even in his life time.

FINIS.

Appendix G

Thomas Hollis's Life of Henry Neville

SOME ACCOVNT OF H. NEVILLE

Henry Neville, second son of Sir Henry Neville, of Billingbeare in Berks, knight, was educated at Oxford.

In the beginning of the civil war, he travelled into Italy and other countries, whereby he advanced himself much as to the knowledge of modern languages and men; and returning in 1645 or thereabout, became Recruiter in the Long Parliament for Abingdon in Berkshire, at which time he was very intimate with Harry Marten, Thomas Chaloner, Thomas Scot, James Harrington, and other zealous Commonwealths men.

In Nov. 1651, he was elected one of the Council of State, being then a favorite of Oliver; but when he saw that Person gaped after the government by a single Person, he left him, was out of his favor, and acted little during his government.

In 1658 he was elected burgess for Reading, to serve in Richard's Parlament, and / when that Person was deposed and the Long Parlament shortly after restored, he was again elected one of the Council of State.

— He was a great Rota-man, was one of the chief persons of James Harrington's club of commonwealths men, to instil their principles into others, he being esteemed to be a man of good parts, and a well-bred gentleman. At the appearance of "The Commonwealth of Oceana,"

Transcribed from the presentation copy of Hollis's edition of *Plato Redivivus* (1763) in the British Library, shelf mark C.108.bb.4, pp. 1–8. [/ = page break.]

which for the practicableness, equality, and compleatness of it, is the most perfect form of such a government that ever was delineated by any antient or modern pen, it was greedily bought up, and coming into the hands of Thomas Hobbes of Malmesbury, he would often say, that Harry Neville had a finger in that pye, and those that knew them both were of the same opinion. By that book, and both their smart discourses and inculcations daily in Coffee houses, they obtained many proselytes. In 1659, in the beginning of Michaelmas term, they had every night a meeting at the then Turk's head, in New Palace Yard, Westminster, called / Miles's Coffee house, to which place their Disciples and Virtuosi would commonly repair; and their discourses about government and ordering of a Commonwealth, were the most ingenious and smart that ever were heard, the arguments in the Parlament House being but flat to those. They had a balloting box, and balloted how things should be carried by way of Tentamens, which not being used or known in England before, on that account, the room every evening was very full. Beside the author and Harry Neville, who were the prime men of this Club, were Cyriac Skinner, a merchant's Son of London, an ingenious Young Gentleman, a scholar to John Milton, which Skinner sometimes held the Chair, Major John Wildman, Charles Wolseley of Staffordshire, Roger Coke, William Poultney, afterward a knight, who sometimes held the Chair, John Hoskyns, John Aubrey, Maximilian Pettie of Tetsworth in Oxfordshire, a very able man in these matters and who had more than once turned the Council board / of O. Cromwell, Michael Mallet, Philip Carteret of the Isle of Guernsey, Francis Cradock, a merchant, Henry Ford, Major Venner, Thomas Marriett of Warwickshire, Henry Croone, Physician, Edward Bagshaw of Christ Church and Robert Wood of Lincoln College, Oxford, James Arderne, then or soon after a Divine, with many others; beside auditors and antagonists of note. Dr. William Pettie was a Rota-man. The Doctrine was very taking, and the more, as there was no probability of the king's return. The greatest of the Parlament men hated this design of rotation and balloting, as being against their power. Eight or ten were for it, of which number Harry Neville was one, who proposed it to the House, and made it out to the Members thereof, that except they embraced that way of Government they would be ruined. The Model of it was, that the third part of the Senate or House should rote out by ballot every year, so that every third year the Senate would be wholly altered. No magis- / trate was to continue above three Years, and all to be chosen by ballot, than which nothing could be invented more fair and impartial, as was then thought, though opposed by many for several reasons. This Club of Commonwealths men lasted till about feb. 21, 1659; at which time the secluded Members being restored by Monke, all their models vanished.

At the Restoration, he absconded; but being seized, was, among others, imprisoned, though soon after set at Liberty.

He published,

The Parlament of Ladies: Or divers remarkable Passages of Ladies in Spring Garden, in Parlament assembled. Printed 1647, in two sheets in quarto. Soon after was published, "The Ladies, a second time assembled in Parlament. A continuation of the Parlament of Ladies," etc. Printed 1647, in two sheets in quarto, written, as was thought, by the same hand.

Shuffling, cutting, and dealing, in a Game at Piquet, being acted from the year 1653 to 1658, by Oliver, Protector, / and others. etc. Printed 1659, in one sheet, in quarto.

The Isle of Pines: Or a late discovery of a fourth Island near Terra australis incognita. By Hen. Cornelius Van Sloetten. etc. Printed, London, 1668, in four sheets and a half in quarto. This, when first published, was looked upon as a meer piece of Drollery.

Plato Redivivus: Or a Dialogue concerning Government, wherein, by Observations drawn from other Kingdoms and States, both ancient and modern, an endeavour is used to discover the present politic distemper of our own; with the Causes and Remedies. Printed, London, 1681, in small octavo. This Book, which was first published in the month of october 1680, against the resitting of Parlament, was very much bought up by the members thereof and admired. It came out soon after, in the same year 1681, "with additions."—Plato Redivivus and the Oceana are both founded on one and the same political maxim, that of Empire's always following the Ballance of Property. / But there is this considerable difference in those works, viz. that the Oceana is only an imaginary scheme for a Commonwealth; whereas Plato Redivivus contains in it, the method of rendering a Monarchy, and particularly the monarchy of Great Britan, both happy at home and powerful abroad: the means for which are proposed distinctly and fully in the concluding Dialogue of that work. The Characters of the Persons engaged in those Dialogues are real. The Stranger, was a Nobleman of Venice, who had gone through several offices in that State; the English Gentleman is Harry Neville himself; and the Physician his great friend the celebrated Doctor Lower.

He likewise translated Machiavell's works, which were printed at London, in English, 1674 and 1680, in folio; wrote the preface to them; and first published and translated a Letter of Machiavell's, the much aspersed Nicolo Machiavelli, to Zanobio Buondelmonti, in vindication of himself and of his writings, brought by him from Italy, in 1645, on his return from his Travels. /

He hath also written divers copies of verses, which are printed in several books; and was esteemed a good Poet: but as for that Pamphlet called his "Poetic Offering," to which came out "The answer of Edward Colman's Ghost," printed, in one sheet, in folio, at London, in december, 1678, it is not his, but fathered on him.

This accomplished, faithful, magnanimous Englishman, Henry Neville, died sept. 20, 1694, and was buried at Warfield, in Berkshire. Reader, shouldst thou pass that way, strew Oak Leaves on his Tomb!

Appendix H

Corrections to Copy-Texts

page.line	error	correct reading
The Isle of Pines		
5.8	surreptiously	surreptitiously
5.10	accasion	occasion
6.8	couse	course
8.4	Wat Eylant is dit? [in blackletter]	"Wat Eylant is dit?"
8.16	in whole World	in the whole World
8.20	we eat	we ate
9.2	adorned vvith	adorned with
9.22	fll	fell
12.9	come there,	come there)
13.13	Waters,	Waters),
13.18	drowed)	drowned)
13.20	Tinder-hox	Tinder-box
13.22	dry, with	dry. With
13.28	Fowls.	Fowls).
14.14	Centry) we	Centry). We
15.13	finde us out:	finde us out).
15.15	towards the Sea)	towards the Sea,
15.20	equl distance	equal distance

page.line	error	correct reading
16.26	accompanined	accompanied
17.22	failng	failing
18.8	np	up
19.7	Chrilden	Children
20.11	from me	from me)
20.17	vvith	with
20.19	Ater	After
20.25	apointed	appointed
21.18	according	(according
22.11	podueeth	produceth
23.25	as before,	as before.
23.27	Brideappeared	Bride appeared
27.21	*GEOGE*	*GEORGE*
28.5	Countrey; which	Countrey. Which
28.6	*England.* Yet	*England,* yet
29.20	themselvesa	themselves
29.20	lltogether	all together
29.24	too	two
30.3	nakednss	nakedness
31.11	strenthening	strengthening
31.14	vvere forced	were forced
31.15	vve vvere	we were
31.16	vvhich	which
31.16	vve had	we had
31.16	here vve	here we
31.18	vve came	we came
32.1	Tovvn	Town
32.3	vve unladed	we unladed
32.3	vvhich caused	which caused
32.4	vvhich space	which space

page.line	error	correct reading
32.5	vvent abroad	went abroad
32.5	vvhich I	which I
32.7	vvhom thy	whom they
32.8	vvhom they	whom they
33.14	wa^n	way
34.9	to to	to
34.15	vere	very
35.6	us!	us,
35.7	safele	safely
37.13	acconnt	account

Plato Redivivus

page.line	error	correct reading
47.20	*lived. And*	*lived, and*
51.10	*dj*	*di*
60.3	mav	may
65.7	we speakall	one speak all
65.13	History of Christ:	History of Christ.
67.15	any think	any thing
68.2	aswell	as well
69.2	too early	~.
73.3	*Buisie*	*Busie*
76.3	Oxon	Oxen
80.17	so;	so,
88.14	Mocarchies,	Monarchies,
95.6	Philosopher	Philosophers
95.12	*Antonius*	*Antoninus*
97.14	keek	keep
98.2	*Iessu*	*Iussu*
100.13	Government)	Government).
100.13	we pitcht	We pitcht

page.line	error	correct reading
101.5	aud generally	and generally
102.18	Centleman;	Gentleman;
103.8	*Demacracies*	*Democracies*
105.18	Renowed	Renowned
105.20	doth	both
105.27	*Roman's*	*Romans'*
105.29	*Roman's*	*Romans*
106.10	oposition	opposition
106.14	ought	aught
107.8	run	ran
108.18	assoon	as soon
109.11	*Comtia,*	*Comitia,*
110.14	endeavour	endeavoured
113.1	infalliably	infallibly
113.8	you Assertion,	your Assertion,
114.1	*Decem-viri*	*Decemviri*
114.2	are first	at first
115.12	notwithstaning	notwithstanding
116.4	*Romulu*s	*Romulus*
116.5	Infalliable	Infallible
116.12	accquainting	acquainting
117.8	Represention	Representation
118.10	go one	go on
124.2	paricularly,	particularly,
126.6	comited	committed
130.2	Mercinary	Mercenary
133.6	Crmmonwealths,	Commonwealths,
137.1	Statsemen	Statesmen
137.8	ought	aught
148.4	aditional	additional

page.line	error	correct reading
151.5	*London.)*	*London).*
154.7	*Profanness*	*Profaneness*
167.3	aswered	answered
174.20	them ending	the mending
182.12	nether of	neither of
185.5	to come so little	come so little to
185.21	for, it	for it,
189.9	tenth part.)	tenth part).
193.3	great oppresson	great oppression
196.2	heriock	heroick
198.8	Asembly	Assembly
202.4	*Assent ista*	*Assentista*
205.18	Debates, whch	Debates, which
207.1	called.	~,
208.5	*nos*	*vos*
209.3	1640.	~,
222.8	manner:	manner.
231.17	assential	essential
233.16	Professors of it,	~.
234.16	*and* to the	and to the
242.13	and Paliament	and Parliament
249.16	*ille*	*illae*
249.20	*Romanza,* (Counsellors and	*Romanza* Counsellors (and
252.6	disguist	disgust
255.11	already)	~.
257.19	unsuccesful	unsuccessful
258.16	unjustfiable	unjustifiable
261.14	Riligion,	Religion,
263.2	destractions	distractions

page.line	error	correct reading
263.10	unsuccesful	unsuccessful
265.14	grevances	grievances
265.21	who (had	(who had
272.9	belive	believe
273.25	Foregin	Foreign
274.16	ineffectul,	ineffectual,
274.21	begining	beginning
275.12	keep the Paece,	keep the Peace,
275.13	preamable	preamble
276.8	thoughr	thought
282.21	It as true,	It is as true,
286.10	*in fragrante*	*in flagrante*
286.10	*d'emble*	*d'emblée*
290.6	ectpectations:	expectations:
300.11	*laberta,*	*liberta,*
300.11	persume	presume
302.4	Adjuorn	Adjourn
302.9	day day comes	day comes
311.25	hefore.	before.
313.6	wrath, aud	wrath, and

Appendix I

Textual Collation of the First and Second Editions of *Plato Redivivus*

page.line	*second edition reading] first edition reading*
39.15	The Second Edition, with Additions.] *om.*
39.17	and Sold by *R. Dew*, 1681.] in the Year M DC LXXXI.
41.7	*to the end]* ~,
41.11	*scurrulous]* Scurrulous
43.9	*Modesty:]* ~;
45.1	*was written:]* ~:
47.8	*Judgement]* Judgment
47.21	*lived, and]* lived. And
51–53	*om.*
55.2	*Commonwealth]* Common-Wealth
56.5	*in his Countrey.]* in his Country.
57.4	*two Moneths,]* two Months,
57.11	*abroad:]* ~:
57.13	*human]* humane
57.14	*Latine]* Latin
59.15	Countrey] Country
60.10	injoys] enjoys
60.22	Countryman] Country-man
60.22	here:] ~:

page.line	second edition reading] first edition reading
60.23	whilst] whilest
60.23	this vent] his vent
61.4	Modesty:] ~:
61.11	purpose] purpofe
62.3	reprehension] Reprehension
62.4	mav] may
63.14	Civility;] ~:
63.16	whilst] whilest
64.3	*Greeks*] *Geeeks*
64.4	Craziness] craziness
64.8	publique] publick
65.7	one speakall] one speak all
65.8	familiar] familliar
65.13	Christ:] ~.
66.17	troublesom] troublesome
67.1	scarce understand:] ~;
67.15	any think] any thing
67.16	my self] myself
69.2	too early] ~.
70.2	speak it:] ~:
70.9	skillful] skillfull
71.11	whole world] whole World
71.25	Mony] Money
73.1	*Evil Counsellors*] Evil Counsellors
73.2	*Pensioner-Parliament*] Pensioner-Parliament
73.2	*Thorowpac'd Judges*] Thorow-pac'd Judges
73.2	*Flattering Divines*] Flattering Divines
73.3	*Buisie* and *Designing Papists*] Busie and Designing Papists
73.3	*French Counsels*] *French* Counsels

page.line	second edition reading] first edition reading
73.4	*Causes* of our *Misfortunes*] Causes of our Misfortunes
73.4	*Effects*] Effects
74.1	*Primary Cause*] Primary Cause
74.1	*the Breach and Ruin of our Government*] the Breach and Ruin of our Government
74.4	*Political* Life] Political Life
74.5	*Courtiers*] Courtiers
74.8	with *Parliaments*] with Parliaments
74.8	*House of Commons*] House of Commons
74.10	*Adjourning*] Adjourning
74.10	*Proroguing*] Proroguing
74.10	*Dissolving*] Dissolving
75.1	the *Law*)] the Law)
75.1	our *late King*,] our late King,
75.2	*Majesties* that *now is*] Majesties that now is
75.2	our *Counsellors*] our Counsellors
75.3	the *Foundation*,] the Foundation,
75.3	the *Politicks*)] the Politicks)
75.4	to the *King*] to the King
75.4	call a *Parliament*,] call a Parliament,
75.6	piecing] pieceing
75.9	whilst it is Curable] whilest it is Curable
75.11	the *Counsellors*] the Counsellors
75.11	skilful Physicians] skillful Physicians
75.15	the *Ministers of State*] the Ministers of State
75.18	setting themselves] setting things
76.1	*Prince* nor *People*] Prince nor People
76.3	Oxon] Oxen
76.4	ill usage] ill Usage
76.5	unserviceable:] ~:

page.line	second edition reading] first edition reading
76.5	weathring out] weathering out
76.6	body of Man] Body of Man
76.8	in the humors] in the humours
76.9	the life] the Life
76.11	skillful Physician:] ~:
76.14	Commonwealth] Common-Wealth
76.19	*the growth of Popery*] the growth of Popery
77.9	living can:] ~;
78.2	no argument] no Argument
78.4	whilst all the rest] whilest all the rest
80.13	any Countrey,] any Country,
80.17	so;] ~,
81.5	Methinks, Sir,] Methings, Sir,
81.9	*Plutarch* tell] *Plutarch* tells
81.19	man-kind] Man kind
82.14	Meditation] Mediation
82.14	vertuous] Vertuous
83.2	Preservation] preservation
83.3	greatness] Greatness
83.3	Govern:] ~:
84.3	abovesaid] above-said
84.10	best Forms] best forms
84.11	Government:] ~:
85.6	*Seth*:] *Sethe*:
85.14	first-born,] first born,
85.16	*Commonwealth.*] *Common-Wealth.*
86.15	their Commonwealth] their Common wealth
87.12	Countrey] Country
88.13	Shadow] Shaddow
88.14	Mocarchies,] Monarchies,

page.line	second edition reading] first edition reading
89.2	*Property.*] ~:
89.4	undeniable] undenyable
90.2	*France?*] ~?
90.13	possessions] Possessions
91.3	Monarchy:] ~:
92.20	*Joseph's*] ~'s
94.16	ever read;] ~:
95.6	Philosopher said] Philosophers said
95.10	Commonwealth] Common-wealth
95.12	*Antonius:*] *Antoninus:*
96.15	Commonwealth] Common-wealth
96.17	Government:] ~:
96.18	ancient *Optimacies,*] ancient*Optimacies,*
97.13	the People;] the people;
97.14	keek] keep
98.2	*Iessu*] *Iussu*
98.9	Commonwealth] Common-wealth
99.10	little Rocks,] littleRocks,
100.1	way of law,] way of Law,
100.5	daily,] dayly,
100.7	*Sarazens*] *Saracens*
101.3	for ever,] ~;
101.4	the People,] the people,
101.5	aud generally] and generally
101.9	Under this] Uunder this
101.14	envy,] Envy,
102.1	of it:] ~;
102.3	leave the People] leave the people
102.4	keep them] keepthem
102.10	own People] own people,

page.line	*second edition reading] first edition reading*
102.18	Centleman;] Gentleman;
103.1	observation;] Observation;
103.2	Heroes] ~,
103.8	*Demacracies] Democracies*
104.3	*Athenians,]* ~
105.11	went to the] went to visit the
105.18	Renowed] Renowned
105.20	doth] both
105.21	the greatest,] the Greatest,
105.27	*Romans'] Roman's*
105.29	*Romans* having] *Roman's* having
105.29	omitted] ommitted
106.10	oposition,] opposition,
106.14	aught] ought
107.3	Warlike:] ~:
107.6	fear'd] feared
107.8	ran] run
107.8	*Hannibal;] Hanibal;*
107.12	Judgement] Judgment
107.18	before the land army of *Darius*] his Land Army
108.2	gain'd] gained
108.6	Citizens;] ~?
108.10	imagined] immagined
108.11	but that the] but the
108.18	as soon] assoon
109.11	*Comitia,] Comtia,*
110.5	Armed,] ~
110.14	late;] ~:
111.1	persons,] ~
111.2	intermission] Intermission

page.line	*second edition reading] first edition reading*
111.4	inriched] inrich'd
111.9	the Common] theCommon
111.11	Dependents] Dependants
111.14	joyne] joyn
111.15	Countrey,] Country,
111.15	redeemers,] Redeemers,
111.18	endeavour] endeavoured
112.8	*Peloponnesian] Peloponesian*
112.11	*Spartans:*] ~:
113.1	infalliably] infallibly
113.1	corrupted,] Corrupted,
113.2	corruption] Corruption
113.6	*Aristocracy*] ~,
113.8	you Assertion,] your Assertion,
113.11	lawes] Laws
113.11	state,] State,
113.12	Lawes] Laws
113.18	Example,] example,
113.24	violence,] Violence,
114.1	*Decem-viri] Decemviri*
114.2	are first] at first
114.5	not so:] not so;
114.10	Lawes,] Laws,
114.13	Proposing Lawes] Proposing Laws
115.3	*ripigliar] rupigliar*
115.6	originally] Originally
115.7	afterwards)] ~,)
115.12	notwithstaning] notwithstanding
115.16	well-regulated] well regulated
115.21	shal pass] shall pass

page.line	second edition reading] first edition reading
115.22	Policies.] Policy.
116.2	interrupt] Interrupt
116.4	*Romulus*] *Romulus*
116.5	Infalliable] Infallible
116.12	accquainting] acquainting
116.14	termed] tearmed
117.4	continued still] ~,
117.4	severall] several
117.5	popular] Popular
117.7	a Senate,] ~
117.8	a body.] a Body.
117.12	*Populi,*] *populi,*
119.1	instituted,] Instituted,
120.13	two kinds,] two kindes,
121.5	severall] several
121.9	*Aristocraticall,*] *Aristocratical,*
122.2	state of War,] State of War,
122.21	*Urnuscaperie*] *Urnscaperie*
123.1	something to him,] ~
123.6	oddly] odly
123.7	Meridian,] ~
123.14	wealth,] Wealth,
123.15	knowledge] Knowledge
123.18	powerfull] powerful
123.21	whilst] whilest
123.22	go one] go on
123.24	Ballat] Ballot
123.24	chiefe] chief
123.24	excellency:] ~;
124.1	read many] had many

page.line	second edition reading] first edition reading
124.2	paricularly,] particularly
124.3	know more] know most
124.8	Counsels] Councils
125.2	are contented] were contented
125.4	handfull;] handful;
125.5	who govern] who Govern
125.12	Common People] common People
126.4	revengeful] revengful
126.13	Traffick,] Traffique,
126.13	employing] Imploying
126.13	the Money] their Money
126.15	employ] Imploy
126.21	Possessor] possessor
126.21	wish that] wish more that
126.21	Countrey,] Country,
126.25	so merry,] merry,
127.9	But the Monarchy] but the Monarchy
127.10	somthing] something
128.9	and to private] and private
129.3	*Greece*;] ~,
129.3	possibly take] possibly bring
129.9	Knights-Fees,] Knights Fees,
129.12	whilst] whilest
130.2	Mercenary] Mercinary
132.1	as well] aswell
132.7	of their] off their
132.12	Employment] Imployment
133.2	Emperours:] ~;
133.3	Italy?] ~?
133.6	Crmmonwealths,] Commonwealths,

page.line	*second edition reading] first edition reading*
133.15	bloody wars] Bloody Wars
135.4	people,] People,
135.23	in general.] in General.
136.12	preserve] reserve
136.12	plenty,] ~
136.13	prosperity,] ~
136.14	and Statsemen] and Statesmen,
137.4	Discourse:] ~;
137.8	aught] ought
139.3	improve:] Improve:
139.9	half:] ~;
139.11	concerned:] ~:
139.16	Improved] Improv'd
140.3	limited] limitted
140.11	Latin Church,] LatineChurch,
141.1	ourselves] our selves
141.9	setled,] settled,
141.22	*Allodiali.*] *Allodiati.*
142.1	Land.] Lands.
142.9	Fealty:] ~:
142.11	Offices] ~;
142.14	Servants] servants
143.5	as I suppose] and suppose
143.8	setled,] ~
144.5	besides,] ~
144.6	Institution,] ~
144.10	given,] ~
144.16	onely,] only,
144.17	Towns,] ~
144.19	others,] ~

page.line	*second edition reading] first edition reading*
144.22	Clergy;] ~,
144.25	any:] ~,
145.1	at the first:] ~;
145.2	Solecism] Solecisme
145.3	intervened] intervene
145.7	Lay-Ideots,] Lay Ideots,
145.8	Spiritual.] ~:
145.11	truely] truly
146.5	*that they . . . the next*] Roman font
146.18	notorious] ~,
146.19	*Princes,*] Princes,
146.19	*other great Men*] other great Men
146.22	*that if . . . great possessions*] Roman font
146.24	*to . . . them nothing*] Roman font
147.5	*Monastery,*] Monastery,
147.5	*Abbey,*] Abbey,
147.5	*Religious House*] Religious House
147.9–155.20	Sir, you maintain . . . long Deviation.] *om.*
155.23	when-ever] when ever
155.26	discourse] Discourse
155.28	Demands;] ~,
155.32	give him;] ~,
155.33	knowledg] knowledge
156.6	third,] Third,
156.9	but I am] But I am
156.11	*grays-Inne,*] Grays-Inn,
156.12	*causa;*] ~,
156.13	honor'd] honour'd
156.15	acknowledg] acknowledge
157.4	in the Parliament;] ~,

page.line	second edition reading] first edition reading
157.5	King.] ~;
157.6	Money:] ~,
157.12	to the king] to the King
157.13	war or peace,] War or Peace,
158.4	prerogative,] Prerogative,
158.9	Officers] ~,
158.11	Judgements] Judgments
158.12	Prince;] ~,
158.12	left us?] ~,
158.13	Power,] Power?
158.18	*Plato*] ~,
158.18	*Aristotle:*] ~:
160.2	would claim] could claim
160.5	Estates;] ~,
162.3	onely written] only written
162.5	our own before.] ~:
163.1	upon them:] ~;
163.5	the People;] ~,
164.1	many others.] ~:
164.2	forementioned] forementiond
164.7	some years:] ~;
164.13	upon one;] ~,
164.14	little way.] ~:
165.4	of which,] ~
166.3	to prove] ~,
166.8	with *France*] ~,
167.10	knowledg] knowledge
167.12	Second;] ~,
167.14	Prerogative-Lawyer,] Prerogative Lawyer,
168.1	4*th*,] ~.

page.line	second edition reading] first edition reading
168.1	*5th,*] ~.
168.1	*6th,*] 6th,
169.7	than any] then any
169.9	aswered] answered
170.11	Civil] ~,
170.11	Kingdom,] Kingdome,
170.14	puzzle] puzle
170.14	extreamly:] ~;
170.17	could not] couldnot
171.4	or onely] or only
171.5	possession:] ~:
171.7	Lord-Lieutenant,] Lord Lieutenant,
171.8	Earls] Earles
171.13	Statute. For] Statute; for
171.15	Lord-Lieutenant] Lord Lieutenant
171.16	Deputies;] ~,
171.18	Restauration.] ~;
171.18	But to answer] but to answer
173.4	reign] reigne
173.4	Second;] ~.
174.6	he pleases.] ~;
174.10	Councils:] ~;
174.12	*Machiavil.*] ~:
174.20	may be,] ~
174.20	said before,] ~
174.21	them ending] the mending
174.22	frame;] ~,
175.2	mony] Money
175.3	way than] way then
175.5	kings's] King's

page.line	second edition reading] first edition reading
175.6	of the people] of the People
175.13	Govern them.] ~;
175.14	power] Power
176.3	Lawyer] ~,
176.4	kil'd;] ~,
176.10	Commons,] ~
176.11	Prerogative-Lawyers,] Prerogative Lawyers,
177.10	interest,] ~?a
177.10	if] If
177.12	Arbitration?] arbitration,
177.12	Certainly] certainly
177.15	appointment;] ~,
178.6	Kings] King's
179.8	accrue] acrue
179.9	Parliament:] ~;
179.12	can answer] could answerss
179.14	Preservation] preservation
179.15	people,] People,
179.15	Counsels] Councils
179.17	Lawes;] Laws;
179.18	Coronation-Oath;] Coronation Oath;
180.4	intended onely] intended only
180.8–9	besides . . . all the Laws] *om.*
180.9	But I shall] but I shall
180.16	onely thus] only thus
180.18	presented to any King,] presented to his Majesty,
181.2	Kingdom:] ~;
181.8	for the private] for private
181.23	to them,] ~
181.27	wisdom] ~,

page.line	*second edition reading] first edition reading*
181.27	fil'd] filed
181.28	ready] ~,
181.29	Calmer] calmer
182.3	Peerage or] Peerage, or
182.6	annihilation] Annihilation
182.7	peoples Rights,] Peoples Rights,
182.12	nether of] neither of
182.14	publisht:] ~,
182.20	Controul] Controll
182.22	Arrests] Arrest
182.22	&c.] &c.
183.2	Onely it is] Only it is
183.8	which shews] Which shews
183.10	committed] commited
184.1	Courts;] ~,
184.6	Land,] ~;
184.7	given;] ~,
184.7	understood] ~,
184.11	*England*;] ~,
184.13	Solecism] Solecisme
185.1	Property,] ~;
185.3	you?] ~:
185.3	How] how
185.6	revengeful] revengful
185.7	Registers,] ~;
185.8	please;] ~:
185.9	Clerks] Clearks
185.10	controul] control
185.12	pleases?] ~.
185.13	Countrey?] Country?

page.line	second edition reading] first edition reading
185.17	demolished.] demollished;
185.21	suffered:] ~;
185.21	for, it] for it,
185.22	superstructure;] ~,
185.23	as this.] ~;
185.23	Suits] Suites
185.24	harmonious:] ~,
186.1	Angels:] ~;
186.12	placed:] ~;
186.14	they had] They had
186.16	Happiness] ~,
186.16	Immortal:] ~;
187.3	Wars;] ~,
187.3	leading the people] leading the People
187.5	prevent the people] prevent the People
187.6	Crown;] ~,
187.6	Government;] ~,
187.7	*Monarchy*] ~,
187.8	and in all] And in all
187.12	possessions;] Possessions;
187.18	Lands. But] Lands, but
187.20	but it is] But it is
187.22	besides] ~,
187.23	abolished,] abollished,
187.24	Yeomanry] Yeomandry
188.2	with her:] ~;
188.3	cause:] ~;
188.6	Popery;] ~,
188.12	Clerk] Cleark
188.12	Kitchen,] Kitchin,

page.line	second edition reading] first edition reading
188.13	gone;] ~,
188.16	times,] time,
188.17	Commons] ~,
189.7	and War;] ~,
189.9	part.) Can] part;) can
190.1	those days] ~,
190.1	Money-bills?] ~.
190.3	sort?] ~;
190.3	and although] although
191.1	for although . . . manage that contest.] *om.*
191.13	that is,] ~
191.13	Councellor;] Counsellor,
191.17	Crown-Lands,] Crown Lands,
191.21	and this] And this
192.1	his People;] ~,
192.4	settled] setled
192.6	ask you,] ~
192.14	*Turks*] *Turk*
193.1	*leges:*] ~,
193.2	mediate and compose] Mediate and Compose
193.3	great oppresson] great oppression
193.4	subjects,] Subjects,
193.9	succeed,] ~
193.10	well-Governed] well Governed
193.12	onely] only
193.15	Tyrannies:] Tyrannies.
193.15	that is,] ~
193.16	Bonds,] Bounds,
193.20	the people,] the People,
193.21	endure,] ~

page.line	*second edition reading] first edition reading*
194.5	extol] extoll
194.6	well-founded] well founded
194.9	grand] Grand
194.10	Case:] ~,
196.2	heriock] heroick
196.3	Neighbour-Princes,] Neighbour Princes,
196.5	Virtue] Vertue
196.9	Seventh,] seventh
196.9	Consent:] ~,
196.10	*English,*] ~;
196.13	fit.] ~:
198.2	whenever] when-ever
198.5	somwhat] somewhat
198.7	part;] ~,
198.8	Asembly] Assembly
198.11	onely,] only,
199.3	whenever] when-ever
199.4	other, gets] other get
199.7	distinction,] ~
199.11	Cadets] ~,
200.5	often,] ~
200.6	Campagne,] ~
200.6	Equipage.] ~:
200.9	Country-Gentlemen] Country Gentlemen
200.9	again:] ~;
200.10	Country-Gentry] Country Gentry
200.31	Court-designs] Court designs
200.31	Country.] ~;
200.32	And thus] and thus
201.5	ingage] engage

page.line	*second edition reading] first edition reading*
201.5	Paternal] ~,
201.6	Life;] ~,
201.7	Mannors:] ~,
201.12	Provinces] ~,
202.1	*Castile*] ~,
202.1	now.] ~:
202.4	*Assent ista*] *Assentista*
202.5	*Cortiza*] ~,
202.5	Profession:] ~,
202.10	hereafter.] ~:
202.14	great men] great Men
202.16	*Indies*;] ~,
202.19	numerous.] ~:
203.4	*Alcaval*,] *Alcavat*,
203.5	States;] ~,
204.3	*Alcaval*,] *Alcavat*,
204.6	People,] ~
205.5	Parliament] ~,
205.6	time] ~,
205.7	Peoples:] ~,
205.7	again,] ~
205.9	times had so] times so
205.14	they told] They told
205.14	first;] ~,
205.15	(for] for
205.16	Debates)] Debates,
205.16	discourse] ~,
205.18	Debates, whch] Debates, which
205.18	king's] King's
205.19	gallery] Gallery

page.line	second edition reading] first edition reading
205.20	Passion,] passion
205.20	Dagger,] ~
205.21	sheath;] ~,
205.24	body.] ~;
205.24	He drew] he drew
205.25	his breast,] his own breast,
205.25	*Reys*;] ~,
206.2	himself.] ~;
206.2	However,] however,
206.5	his people,] his People,
206.5	the Laws,] their Laws,
206.6	preservation] Preservation
207.1	called. *El*] called, *El*
207.3	whenever] when-ever
207.4	whenever] when-ever
208.1	betray him,] ~
208.4	which is,] ~
208.5	words:] ~,
208.6	*Fueros*] *fueros*
208.6	*Privilegios*;] ~,
208.8	Priviledges;] ~,
208.13	Subject] Snbject
208.15	*Castile*] ~,
208.19	County-Troops,] County Troops,
208.21	Government:] ~;
208.21	Vice-Roy] Vice Roy
209.3	1640,] ~.
209.8	imployed] employed
210.1	here;] ~,
210.3	upon them.] ~:

page.line	second edition reading] first edition reading
210.5	right] Right
210.12	inhabit] inhabite
210.13	Centre] Center
210.16	them:] ~,
211.9	onely] only
211.11	War;] ~,
212.1	*Rome*;] ~,
212.9	it:] ~;
212.18	words than] words then
212.20	paper,] Paper,
212.29	Court-Parasites] Court Parasites
213.5	Government,] ~
213.5	which (not] (which not
213.8	people are] People are
213.9	Nature;] ~,
213.12	being:] ~,
213.12	*causa*,] ~
213.13	the people] the People
213.17	Parliament;] ~:
213.20	Monies,] Moneys,
213.20	practices] practises
213.25	Point:] ~:
214.1	Counsellers] Counsellors
214.2	Parliament,] part,
214.4	Greatness and] Greatness &
214.7	beseech you,] ~
214.10	certain,] ~
214.13	advantagious] advantageous
214.20	Reign,] ~;
215.9	*Hereford*;] ~;

page.line	*second edition reading] first edition reading*
216.1	*Thomas Harley,*] one *Harlow* a Knight, whose Christian Name I remember not,
216.9	knowledg] knowledge
217.1	matters;] Matters,
217.2	day,] ~;
217.7	designe,] design,
217.14	abruptly,] ~;
217.15	publick,] Publick
218.3	his Majesty's] His Majesty's
218.3	Return, so] Return. So
219.5	1640,] ~.
219.6	Parliaments,] ~
219.8	people;] People;
219.10	which I hope,] which, I hope,
219.12	afternoon] Afternoon
219.13	morning come:] Morning come:
220.3	grounds] Grounds
220.3	pretences] Pretences
220.20	other?] ~.
220.22	being,] Being,
220.24	end;] ~,
220.24	Politick,] ~;
220.26	his death,] its death,
221.3	Case] ~,
221.3	*de jure,*] ~?
221.3	look] Look
222.1	Book] ~,
222.5	Place.] place.
222.8	manner:] manner.
223.2	the business] their business

page.line	*second edition reading] first edition reading*
223.4	High-Treason:] High Treason:
223.5	unheard-of] unheard of
223.11	*Hampton-Court*] *Hampton Court*
223.11	*a Remonstrance of the State of the Kingdom*,] a Remonstrance of the State of the Kingdom,
223.15	*York*;] ~:
223.16	Trained-Bands] Trained Bands
224.8	Kings Answer] King's Answer
226.3	Fact;] ~,
226.4	People who] People, who
226.5	Parliament;] ~,
226.8	never came;] ~,
226.15	wait] waite
226.17	teach:] ~,
226.18	to day;] ~,
227.4	Distempers;] ~,
227.8	retire:] ~,
226.8	here,] ~
229.1	welcome:] ~;
229.1	what,] ~
229.2	together!] ~.
229.3	door:] ~:
229.5	reason,] ~
229.6	is?] ~?
229.9	ventured;] ventered;
230.2	Disease:] ~,
230.4	shaken;] ~,
230.4	it will be] It will be
230.8	Grounds;] ~,
230.10	men will] Men will

page.line	second edition reading] first edition reading
230.25	understood:)] ~)
230.25	hindering] hindring
231.7	point:] ~,
231.7	two,] ~
231.7	divide] ~,
231.12	professes;] ~,
231.16	self,] ~
231.17	assential] essential
231.18	State:] ~,
231.18	doctrinals] Doctrinals
232.4	proceed.] ~:
232.7	declaration] Declaration
232.13	this is,] ~
232.13	Solecism] Solecisme
232.15	World:] ~;
232.16	that the Apostles] That the Apostles
232.18	matters] Matters
232.20	lawfull] lawful
232.20	things.] ~:
232.21	a handful,] an handful,
233.2	World;] ~,
233.4	Flock:] ~,
233.11	beginning:] ~,
233.12	not onely] not only
233.13	*Mahomet,*] *Pythagoras*
233.15	bloudy] bloody
233.16	Professors of it,] Professors of it.
234.5	Truth.] ~,
234.5	The Successors] the Successors
234.6	scrupulous;] ~,

page.line	second edition reading] first edition reading
234.6	Priests] ~,
234.11	Heathen;] ~,
234.15	*Pompile*;] ~,
234.16	*and* to] and to
235.1	Works.] ~:
235.2	digression;] ~,
235.2	shall onely] shall only
235.4	mean onely] mean only
235.6	receive] recive
235.9	onely of] only of
236.9	*Emanuel*] *Emmanuel*
236.10	States] ~,
236.12	Tenents;] ~,
236.13	Excommunication] ~,
236.14	communion] Communion
236.20	live;] ~,
236.21	them. This] them; this
236.22	Case:] ~,
237.3	longer.] ~,
237.4	Marriage] ~,
238.1	her:] ~;
238.7	died] dyed
238.9	Successor] ~,
238.10	rigorous] vigorous
239.6	occasions;] ~,
239.10	what they are,] ~
239.14	judge] judg
240.1	change,] ~
240.3	onely means] only means
240.4	whenever] when-ever

page.line	second edition reading] first edition reading
240.6	but then] but when
240.13	setled] settled
240.15	Estates,] ~
241.2	at home;] ~,
241.4	unsetled] unsettled
241.9	First gave,] first gave,
241.10	certain,] ~
241.15	flesh-wound] flesh wound
241.16	Disease,] ~
241.18	well-founded] well founded
241.20	Reason] ~,
241.22	establish'd,] established,
241.24	most men] most Men
241.26	Bishops,] ~
242.3	abolished;] ~:
242.4	company] Company
242.5	First Christians] first Christians
242.8	sober men] sober Men
242.10	mankind,] Mankind,
242.11	*Roman* Religion,] ~;
242.13	King and Paliament] King and Parliament
242.16	time, is,] ~;
242.22	profession,] Profession,
242.27	Quiet;] ~,
243.24	humour] Humour
244.10	useless] ~,
244.14	Title;] ~:
244.19–245.6	It will certainly . . . Judged Treason.] *om.*
245.10	it best] it is their duty,
245.10	his Majesty] His Majesty

page.line	*second edition reading] first edition reading*
245.11	&] and
247.4	probability] ~,
247.6	concur] concurr
247.6	onely] only
247.11	Testament;] ~:
247.12	Will,] ~;
248.1	married in] married into
248.7	yet] Yet
248.11	apprehended &] apprehended and
248.11	condemn'd] condemned
248.12	K.] King
249.1	Matter;] ~:
249.1	Solecism] Sollecism
249.2	shew,] ~
249.3	oftentimes] often times
249.13	meddling] medling
249.16	ille] illae
249.20	*Romanza*, (Counsellors and] *Roman* Counsellors (and
250.1	receive,] ~
250.5	hour] Hour
250.11	piece] peice
251.9	whenever] when-ever
251.10	thinking men] thinking Men
251.13	next successor] next Successor
252.5	fatality] fatallity
252.6	disguist] disgust
252.10	Polity, so] Polity. So
252.13	*Hanover*,] *Hanouer*,
252.13	whose Prince] ~,
252.18	Successor,] Successour,

page.line	second edition reading] first edition reading
253.1	onely] only
253.3	condition. But] condition; but
255.1	These things,] ~
255.11	already).] already)
256.10	years)] years
257.2	Prince:] ~;
257.3	born,] ~
257.6	prejudice,] ~
257.11	means of] *om.*
257.14	Concurence] Concurrence
257.19	unsuccesful] unsuccessful
257.20	Royal assent] Royal Assent
257.21	not grant it,] ~;
257.22	Affairs:] ~:
257.30	intirely] entirely
258.15	So that as] So that
258.16	unjustfiable] unjustifiable
258.19	pretext] ~,
258.20	endeavours] Endeavours
258.21	this present] their present
259.1–268.21	But Sir, there are . . . Birth and Merit.] *om.*
268.23	before,] ~
268.23	averred;] ~,
269.23	Affairs:] ~,
270.4	increase] encrease
270.9	his Majesties] His Majesties
270.9	Restauration,] ~
271.11	secresie;] ~,
271.14	in it:] ~,
272.5	advantageous,] advantagious,

page.line	*second edition reading] first edition reading*
272.9	belive] believe
272.24	Government,] ~;
273.8	putrefaction] putrifaction
273.18	perfect health;] ~,
273.19	being,] Being,
273.23	*England*,] ~
273.25	Foregin] Foreign
274.2	of the Parliament,] ~
274.3	Councellors] Counsellors
274.7	attempt it;] ~,
274.16	ineffectul,] ineffectual,
274.28	knowledg] knowledge
275.6	that end;] ~,
275.12	Paece,] Peace,
275.13	preamable] preamble
275.18	That the Cause] that the Cause
276.1	Creator;] ~,
276.4	Imprisonment;] ~,
276.15	*England*:] ~:
276.16	Discourses] ~,
277.4	prudence] Prudence
277.11	his Majesty's] His Majesty's
278.4	Disease:] ~:
278.17	things;] ~:
278.21	partakers] Partakers
278.24	Contests,] Contest,
279.3	a Memorable] Memorable
279.7	so great] so Great
279.7	afterwards).] afterwards.)
279.8	are),] are,)

page.line	*second edition reading] first edition reading*
280.9	In *France*] in *France*
280.11	been said,] heen said,
280.11	States] State
280.13	thoughr] thought
280.20	Younger Brothers] ~,
280.20	nothing,] ~.
280.23	the people] the People
281.1	illegal] Illegal
281.1	possible an] possible An
281.4	frequent?] ~.
282.2	Son?] Family?
282.2–282.3	Who was . . . death.] *om.*
282.11	Headpieces] Head-pieces
282.11	them);] them;)
282.14	in Oligarchy.] in an Oligarchy.
282.21	It as true,] It is as true,
283.1	pay:] Pay:
283.4	with him:] ~:
283.7	Demagogues] Demagogue
283.12	people.] People.
283.15	people here?] People here.
283.18	themselves:] ~;
283.23	power] Power
284.3	State;] ~,
285.5	interest] Interest
285.12	Money,] Mony,
286.7	this pass,] ~;
286.10	(or] or
286.10	*d'emble*),] *d'emble*,
286.15	Or before] or before

page.line	*second edition reading] first edition reading*
287.3	experiments:] Experiments:
287.7	much);] much;)
288.6	*Insaevire]* *Insaenire*
290.3	Country;] ~,
290.6	ectpectations:] expectations:
290.15	his people] his People
290.17	predecessors,] Predecessors,
291.2	hear] ~,
291.4	Presumptuous;] presumptuous;
291.19	told,] ~
291.20	the people,] the People,
291.23	Supreme] Supream
292.3	of it;] ~,
292.7	Woollen,] ~
293.1	Age;] ~,
293.1	all this,] ~
293.3	particularize] particularise
293.4	discontinued?] ~:
293.10	protestation,] Protestation,
293.13	poor parts] poor Parts
293.14	powers] Power
293.17	peace,] Peace,
293.18	Councellours,] Counsellours,
294.2	of them,] ~
294.4	Court-party] Court Party
294.4	the people,] the People,
294.5	Councellours] Counsellours
294.6	powerful] Powerful
294.7	Article] ~,
295.2	Garisoning] Garrisoning

page.line	*second edition reading] first edition reading*
295.5	Session;] ~,
295.6	Guard] guard
295.9	profit,] Profit,
295.11	Councellours,] Counsellours,
296.2	support it,] ~
296.20	intervals] Intervals
296.24	instructions,] Instructions,
297.18	Councellors] Counsellors
298.5	Council contrary] Counsel contrary
298.16	State-Affairs,] State Affairs,
299.3	Persons] Purses
299.7	the like;] ~,
299.13	State-Affairs] State Affairs
299.19	Lawful] ~,
299.21	Councellours] Counsellours
299.29	War,] ~
299.31	parts,] ~
300.11	persume] presume
300.26–27	the Territory new divided,] *om.*
301.6	before;] ~,
301.8	Oracle:] ~:
301.17	Settlement,] Setlement,
302.4	and Adjuorn] and Adjourn
302.4	still setting] still Adjourn, setting
302.6	sooner,] ~;
302.7	Councellors] Counsellors
302.7	Councels] Counsels
302.9	day day comes] day comes
302.16	sometimes] some times
302.16	oftener?] ~,

page.line	*second edition reading] first edition reading*
302.21	way;] ~,
303.4	by an Act;] ~,
303.7	concern] concerns
303.10	and then] & then
303.12	Contests] Contest
303.13	asleep] ~,
304.5	*viz.*] ~,
304.12	that case] that Case
304.13	*Quintius*] *Quintus*
304.16	Government,] ~
304.16	Interest;] ~,
304.18	that is, the] that is the
304.22	Appeals from] Appeal from
304.26	Court-party] Court Party
305.15	If you] But if you
305.26	Commonwealth;] ~,
306.2	Counsellors] Counsellours
306.4	if our expedient take place] *om.*
306.7	his people,] his People,
306.13	formerly;] ~,
306.17	administration] Administration
307.8	Commonwealths?] Common-Wealths?
307.15	Consent)] Consent;)
308.9	Parliament-men] Parliament men
308.11	Commons house,] Commons-house,
309.2	imitated] immitated
309.7	Whoring,] Whoreing,
309.9	welfare,] wellfare,
309.11	Commonwealth] Common-Wealth
309.19	Countrymen.] Country-men.

page.line	second edition reading] first edition reading
309.24	Independents,] Independants,
311.9	Excuses.] ~:
311.21–22	and his Eldest . . . World.] *om.*
311.22	I dare] and I dare
311.24	extreme] extream
311.25	hefore.] before.
312.1	Common-places] Common places
312.14	Court-party] Court Party
312.18	people] People
312.19	passions,] Passions,
312.23	persons,] Persons,
313.5	Parliaments before,] Parliaments, before
313.6	wrath, aud] wrath, and
313.7	Fines] ~,
313.7	as well,] ~
313.8	Councellours] Counsellours
313.14	Nature] nature
313.15	people] People
313.18	although] altho
313.26	*France,* who] ~,
314.11	silence;] ~,
314.12	tittle-tattle] tittle tattle
314.21	Kingdom.] ~,
315.6	*prudentia.*] ~

INDEX

Abraham (biblical), 85
Achaean League, 121*n*194
Act for a Triennial Parliament (1641),
165*n*285, 212
Act of Settlement (1701), 145*n*245,
253*n*495
Act of Uniformity (1558), 237*n*454
Adam (biblical), 85
Adams, John, 137*n*232
Addled Parliament (1614), 214*n*394,
217*n*401, 219*n*407
adjournment of Parliament, 74*n*69
Aetolian League, 121*n*194
Agis IV (king of Sparta), 112, 112*n*162,
112*n*165
Aglionby, William, 91*n*100, 122*n*196;
*The Present State of the United
Provinces*, 121*n*192
agrarian laws, 108, 109*n*157, 111, 186
*An Agreement of the Free People of
England* (1649), 270*n*526, 301*n*609
Alamanni, Niccolò, xxxi
alcohol, 28*n*101, 204*n*375
Alexander the Great, 121*n*193, 210
Algiers, 34*n*127
alliances: of France, 139*n*236; of
Greece, 112*n*163; of Ottoman

Empire, 139*n*236; Parliament and,
158*n*271, 211, 285–87; royal prerogative and, 293–94
Al-Walid I, 202*n*373
anarchy, 114, 115
Ancus Marcius, 117*n*180
Anne (queen), 303*n*611
anticlericalism, 146*n*246, 147*n*248,
151*n*257, 233*n*444, 234*n*447
Antipater, 121*n*193
Antoninus Pius, 95, 95*n*115
Appius Claudius Crassus, 282*n*564
Aquinas, Thomas, 63*n*48
Aragon, Kingdom of, 205–8,
210, 297
arbitrary power, 71, 77*n*74, 92, 162*n*278,
198, 213, 230–31, 244, 265
architecture metaphor for
government, 46
architraves, 46, 46*n*13
Aristides, 271–72, 271*n*527
aristocracy, 91–92, 96–97, 101, 103, 113,
125, 186–87
Aristotle, 63*n*48, 79, 79*n*77, 81*n*82, 92,
95*n*110, 113*n*166, 158; *Metaphysics*,
40*n*2; *Physics*, 188*n*339; *Politics*,
279*n*558

473

The Armie's Dutie (anonymous), xiv–xv, xix, 91n100, 92n103, 103n132, 143n242, 194n354, 351–74
arrests of judgment, 182, 182n322
Artaxerxes I, 128n213
Asclepius, 59, 59n34
Assyrians, 127
Athens, 104–5, 107, 112n163, 114–15, 114n168, 115n175, 271–72, 314
Attila the Hun, 78n76, 99n125
Atwood, William, 156, 159n272, 160n273, 163n282; *Jani Anglorum Facies Nova,* 157n270; *Jus Anglorum ab antiquo,* 157n270
Aubrey, John, 43n8
Augsburg, Peace of (1555), 231n434
Augustus (emperor), 131n219, 133, 133n224, 134n225
Augustus, Ernest, 252n495
Aulus Gellius, xix
Austria, 192, 192n349
Aztec Empire, 202n372

Babington Plot (1586), 237n457
Bacon, Francis, 266n521; *Historie of the Raigne of King Henry the Seventh,* 265n520; *Union of the Two Kingdoms of Scotland and England,* 315n649
bailiffs, 275
balloting, 123–24, 124n202, 296n599
Barcelona, Treaty of (1493), 115n175
Barebone, Praise-God, 196n357
Barebones Parliament (1653), 196, 196n357, 277, 283n569
Barnardino da Udine, 274
Baxter, Richard, 30n107
Baynes, Captain, xii, 93n105
Belisarius, 140n238
Bembo, Giovanni, 55n23
Bennet, Thomas, 176n304
Bentivoglio, Cardinal Giulio, x; *Della guerra di Fiandra,* 122n196
Bias of Priene, 64n49
biblical references. *See* scriptural references

Bill of Rights (1689), 178n312, 245n476, 256n498
Birch, John, 64n48, 213n393
bishops, 145n245
Blochwich, Martin: *Anatomia Sambuci,* 315n649
blue coats, 188n341
Boccalini, Trajano, 55n23, 172n296
Bodin, Jean, 87n94; *Six livres de la république,* 95n110
Boleyn, Anne, 237n456
Bolingbroke, Henry St. John, Viscount, 288n582
Boniface VIII (pope), 275n543
Book of Sports (1618), 24n89
Boyle, Robert, 48n20, 72n62
Braddon, Laurence, 73n65
Brady, Robert, 143n242, 144n243, 159n272, 161n276, 161n277, 169n292
Brand, Thomas, 56n26
Brandon, Charles, Duke of Suffolk, 247
Brasile (mythical island), 4, 4n11
Brennus, 107n146
Brooke, Henry. See Cobham, Baron
Broussel, Pierre, 198, 198n360
Browne, William, 18n66
Buckingham, George Villiers, Duke of, xviii, 218n403, 286n578
Bulteel, John, xviin23
Burgundy, Duchy of, 261n510
Burke, Edmund, 73n65, 78n75, 156n268, 172n296, 221n409; *Second Letter on a Regicide Peace,* 44n9
Burnet, Gilbert, xxvii–xxviii, 42n4, 72n63, 175n304, 205n376, 288n582
Burton, Thomas, xii
Burying in Woollen Acts (1680), 292n589
Bye and Main Plots (1603), 238n459, 248nn482–83
Byzantine Empire, 100n127

Cain (biblical), 85
Calcutta, India, 31n114
Caliphate of Cordoba, 202n373

Callias, 47, 47n19
Calvin, Jean, 140, 140n239
Calvinism, 209n385
Canary Islands, 6nn18–19, 27n97
Capel, Henry, 77n74, 218n403, 239n460, 281n561
Cape Verde islands, 6, 6nn20–21
Capponi, Ferrante, 56n26
Care, Henry, 161n277, 255n496; *English Liberties*, 163n282
Carew, Thomas: "A Pastorall Dialogue," 18n66
Carey, Daniel, xxiin35
Cary, Nicholas, 167n290
Castile, 202–3, 205, 207–8
Catholicism. *See* Roman Catholicism
Catholic League, 243n472
Cavalier Parliament (1661–79), 76n74, 219n405
Cave, William, 152n261
Cavendish, Henry, 311n634
Cavendish, William, 218n403
Cebes, 47, 47n19
Chaloner, Thomas, x, 56n26
Chancery Court, 184n326, 185
Charles I: *Answer to the Nineteen Propositions*, 172n296; *Book of Sports* issued by, 24n89; coronation oath of, 180n314; divine right and, 225n423; excise and, 204n375; execution of, 246n477; First Bishops' War (1639) and, 209n384; forced loans and, 281n562; foreign policy of, 239n463; Grand Remonstrance (1641) and, 173n297, 204n375, 209n385, 223, 223n418, 281nn561–62; militia and, 170n294, 256n498; Parliament and, 219n406, 277n552; Petition of Right and, 184n327; in *Plato Redivivus*, 75n70, 212, 248; Scots and, 309n628; taxation by, 163n282, 173n297
Charles II: coronation oath of, 179nn313–14, 239n462; Danby and, 173n298, 285n574; "debonair" used to describe, 9n30; ecclesiastical power

and, 250n491; English Civil Wars and, x–xii, 71n60, 218n404, 219–26, 264n519; *The Isle of Pines* and, xxv; James II as potential successor to, 72n61; Monmouth and, 231n433, 254n496, 258n503; on Ottomans, 127n211; Parliament and, 73n64, 74n69, 166n287, 190n342; in *Plato Redivivus*, xxx; Privy Council and, 288–89, 289nn585–86; Restoration of, 71n59; royal prerogative and, 178n312; Treaty of Dover (1670) and, 73n66, 294n592
Charles V (Spain), 115n175
Charles VII (France), 196, 196n358
Charles the Bold, 261, 261nn510–11
Chiesa del Santissimo Redentore (Venice church), 276, 276n545
Christianity: anticlericalism and, 146n246, 147n248, 151n257, 233n444, 234n447; in *Plato Redivivus*, 144–56
Churchill, John, xvi
Churchill, Winston, xvi, 89n98
Church of England, 24n89, 147n250, 209n385, 241, 241n468, 253n495
Cicero, 79, 79n77, 193n350, 195n355
civic humanism, 83n84, 91n100
Clarendon, Earl of, 289n585, 310–11, 310n632
Clarges, Thomas, 153n261, 218n403
Clark, Henry, 255n496
Clement VII (Italy), 115n175
Cleobulus of Rhodes, 64n49
Cleomenes III (king of Sparta), 112, 112n162, 112n165
Cobham, Henry Brooke, Baron, 248, 248n482
coffeehouses, 61, 61n43
Coke, Roger, 162n279, 163n281, 168n292, 260n507
Collinges, John, 30n107
Collins, Anthony: *A Discourse of Free-thinking*, 149n254
colonialism, xxiv, 25n93
commerce, absence of, 24n90

Committee of Safety (Parliament), 277–78, 277*n*552

common good, 173*n*296, 194*n*353

"Confirmatio Cartarum" (1297), 164*n*283, 165*n*284

constituent power doctrine, 245*n*477

Contarini, Domenico, 48*n*20, 56*n*24, 124*n*203

Convention Parliament (1660), 204*n*375, 219*n*405, 268*n*522

Convention Parliament (1689), 169*n*292, 218*n*403

Cooke, Edward, 159*n*272

A Copy of a Letter from an Officer of the Army in Ireland, to His Highness the Lord Protector, Concerning His Changing of the Government (1656), xxi, xxii*n*31, 90*n*99, 188*n*341, 267*n*521, 277*n*551, 317–38

Corinthian architecture, 46*n*13

Coriton, William, 251*n*493

coronation oath, 179*nn*313–14, 185*n*328, 239*n*462

Cortiza, Sebastian, 202

Cosimo III (Grand Duke of Tuscany), xvi, xvi–xvii

Cotton, Robert, 127*n*211, 197*n*358

Council of Nicaea, 150*n*256

council of the chamber, 201*n*369

council of war, 201*n*369

Court Probate Act (1857), 186*n*332

Courts of Equity, 189–90, 305

Covent Garden, London, 3*n*7, 61*n*43

Cranmer, Thomas, 237*n*456

Craterus, 121*n*193

credible, definitions of, 3*n*6

Crino, Anna Maria, xvi*n*17, 77*n*74

Croft, Edward, 215*n*396

Croft, Herbert (father), 215, 215*nn*395–96

Croft, Herbert (son, Bishop of Hereford): *The Naked Truth: or, the True State of the Primitive Church,* 215*n*396, 234*n*447

Cromwell, Oliver: Barebones Parliament and, 196, 196*n*357, 277, 283*n*569; death of, 111*n*159; dissolution of Parliament by, xiv, 310; foreign policy of, 294; Neville banished from London by, 277*n*551; Parliament and, xii–xiv, 282*n*567, 283*n*569; standing army and, 256*n*498; taxation and, 204*n*375; treaties with France, 294*n*593

Cromwell, Richard, xi, 277*n*552, 283*n*570

Cujas, Jacques, 142*n*242

Cyrus the Great, 103, 103*n*134, 271*n*529

Dalmahoy, Thomas, 189*n*342

Dampier, William, 6*n*17

Danby, Thomas Osborne, Earl of, xvii, 145*n*245, 158*n*271, 173*n*298, 175*n*304, 178*n*310, 182*n*322, 285*n*574, 289*n*586

David (biblical), 132

Decemvirate (Roman Republic), 114, 282, 282*n*564

decemviri (ten-man commissions), 114*n*170

Defoe, Daniel, 7*n*23; *Jure Divino,* 94*n*108; *Robinson Crusoe,* 25*n*93

democracy, 46, 91–92, 97–98, 104–5, 113–15, 115*n*174, 125, 186–87, 270, 270*n*526, 300

demurrers, 182, 182*n*322

Denmark, 193, 266*n*520

De Ruyter, Admiral, 286*n*579

Diocletian, 233*n*445

Dionysius I, 282, 282*n*563

Dionysius II, 282*n*563

divine right of kings, 86, 86*n*91, 225*n*423

doctors, trope of patients killed by, 33*n*123

Domitian (emperor), 111*n*161, 233*n*445

Don John of Austria, 208*n*383

Doric architecture, 46*n*13

Dover, Treaty of (1670), 73*n*66, 294*n*592

Dryden, John, 11*n*39

Dugdale, William, 159*n*272

Duport, James, 106*n*144

Dutch East India Company, 11*n*39

Earle, Walter, 215*n*394
East India Company, 7*n*23
ecclesiastical courts, 186, 186*n*332, 241,
    250*n*491, 295
Edward I, 164*n*283, 165, 165*n*284, 212,
    272*n*530, 278, 278*n*553, 290
Edward II, 173, 173*n*298, 279, 279*n*555, 291
Edward III, 65*n*51, 166, 218*n*403, 278,
    278*n*554, 290
Edward VI, 247
Edward the Confessor, 159*n*272, 184–85,
    184*n*328
Egypt: Ottoman Empire and, 138*n*235;
    in *Plato Redivivus*, 92–93, 128,
    137–38, 191; political history in,
    284*n*573
elections, 123–24, 123*n*202, 296*n*599,
    301–2, 306–7
Eliot, John, 251*n*493
Elizabeth I, 2*n*3, 19*n*74, 216, 236–38,
    236*n*454, 237*nn*455–57, 238*n*458,
    247, 248
Elizabeth of Bohemia, 252*n*495
England's Miserie and Remedie (1645),
    287*n*582
English Civil Wars, x–xii, 71*n*60,
    218*n*404, 219–26, 264*n*519
Escobedo, Juan de, 208*n*383
Etruscans, 108*n*153
Eucharist, 153*n*262, 154*n*264
Euripides, 106*n*144
Evelyn, John, 9*n*30, 125*n*205, 314*n*648
excise, 204, 204*n*375. *See also* taxation
Exclusion Bill Parliament (1679),
    74*n*69, 76*n*74, 252*n*494
Exclusion Crisis, xxvii, xxix, xl, 40*n*1,
    41*n*4, 168*n*292. *See also* James II

Ferdinand (Spain), 207*n*380
Ferdinand II (Grand Duke of
    Tuscany), xvi, 56*n*26
feudalism, 129*n*216, 141–42, 142*n*242
Filmer, Robert, 87*n*94, 109*n*156,
    163*n*282; *Freeholder's Grand Inquest*,
    157*n*270; *Observations upon Aristotle's*

Politiques, 117*n*178; *Patriarcha*, 84*n*87,
    245*n*477
Finch, Daniel, 237*n*455
Finch, John, 178*n*310
firearms, 25*n*93
First Bishops' War (1639), 209*n*384,
    286*n*577
flattery, 60*n*38, 61*n*39
fleshly, definitions of, 18*n*68
Fletcher, Andrew, 129*n*216
Florence, Italy, 114–15, 114*n*172
forced loans, 281*n*562
Foscarini, Sebastiano, 48*n*20, 56*n*24
Fox, Stephen, 73*n*64
France: alliances of, 139*n*236; Assembly
    of Estates, 198; Cromwell and,
    294*n*593; Franco-Dutch War
    (1672–78), 123*n*201, 196*n*356; in *Plato
    Redivivus*, 88–90, 123, 139–40, 143,
    144, 166, 192, 193, 194–200, 210–11,
    243, 272, 287; political structures in,
    196*n*358, 198*n*360; property in, 195,
    199–200, 280; Secret Treaty of Dover
    (1670), 294*n*592; Thirty Years' War
    and, 202*n*370; Treaty of Paris and,
    294, 294*n*593. *See also specific kings*
Francis I (France), 139*n*236
Franco-Dutch War (1672–78), 123*n*201,
    196*n*356
fundamental laws, 168–69, 168*n*292, 182

Gaius Licinius Calvus Stolo, 106*n*142,
    109*n*157
Gaius Marius, 107*n*145
Gaius Sempronius Gracchus, 109*n*157,
    110, 110*n*159, 111, 187
Galerius, 233*n*445
Gardiner, Samuel, 30*n*107
Gascoigne, Bernard, xv–xvi
Gaveston, Piers, 173*n*298
Genghis Khan, 88, 88*n*96
Germany: in *Plato Redivivus*, 67, 120,
    121, 192; political structures in,
    120*n*190; Roman Republic and,
    140*n*237

Giannotti, Donato, 124*n*203
Gibbon, Edward, 89*n*98, 134*n*224
Gilbert, Humphrey, 197*n*358
Giustinian, Ascanio, II, 56*n*24
Glemham, Thomas, 224*n*420
Goddard, Thomas, 226*n*425, 271*n*527
Godwin, Francis: *The Man in the Moone*, 2*n*1
Golden Age, 10*n*33, 16*n*59, 24*n*90, 25*n*94, 26*nn*95–96. *See also* utopian themes
Goths, 99, 99*n*125, 101, 106, 119*n*187, 124*n*203, 129, 140, 140*n*237, 140*n*238, 142, 143, 145*n*244, 202*n*371
Grand Remonstrance (1641), 173*n*297, 204*n*375, 209*n*385, 223, 223*n*418, 281*nn*561–62
Greece (ancient): alliances of, 112*n*163; architecture of, 46*n*13; Athens vs. Sparta in, 112*n*163, 112*n*165; in *Plato Redivivus*, 64, 92, 101, 113–14, 129, 271
Greenblatt, Stephen, 25*n*93
Grey, Anchitell, xxvii
Grimeston, Edward, 201*n*369, 206*n*380, 209*n*383
Grimston, Edward, 206*n*380
Grotius, Hugo de: *De jure Belli ac Pacis*, 222, 222*n*414
The Grounds of Unity in Religion (anonymous), 308*n*623
Guasconi, Bernardo, 56*n*26
Guise family, 243, 243*n*472
Gunpowder Plot (1605), 238*n*459

habeas corpus, 298–99, 298*n*603
Habeas Corpus Amendment Act (1679), 298*n*603
Habeas Corpus Parliament, xl, 41*n*4
Hall, Thomas, 30*n*107
Hamden, John, x, 56*n*26
Hammond, Henry, 152*n*260
Hampden, John, 223*n*417
Hampden, Richard, 77*n*74
Hannibal, 107
Hanover, Duchy of, 252, 252*n*495

Hapsburgs, 192, 192*nn*348–49
Harley, Robert, 40*n*2, 216, 216*n*397
Harrington, James: on agrarian laws, 109*n*157; *Aphorisms Political*, 100*n*126, 118*n*185; *The Art of Lawgiving*, 92*n*103, 199*n*364, 246*n*477, 265*n*520, 267*n*521; *The Commonwealth of Oceana*, xi, xvi, xxi, 40*n*1, 43, 44*nn*9–10, 45*n*11, 48*n*21, 56*n*23, 80*n*79, 83*n*84, 86*n*93, 89*n*97, 90*n*99, 91*n*100, 94*n*108, 99*n*125, 109*n*156, 116*n*178, 119*nn*186–87, 121*n*192, 124*n*202, 142*n*241, 151*n*257, 168*n*292, 195*n*354, 204*n*375, 284*n*573; on democracy, 270*n*526; on excise, 204*n*375; on French political structures, 196*n*358; on fundamental law, 168*n*292; on Henry VII, 74*n*67; Heylyn and, 31*n*111; influence of, x–xi, xv, xxix, xxxiii–xxxiv, 43*n*9; on mamalukes, 284*n*573; *The Manner and Use of the Ballot*, 296*n*599; medicinal metaphor for politics used by, 63*n*48; on monarchy, 88*n*94; Neville's friendship with, 43*n*8, 56*n*26; on Ottoman Empire, 128*n*212, 195*n*354; *Politicaster*, 136*n*232, 162*n*277; on popular sovereignty doctrine, 246*n*477; *The Prerogative of Popular Government*, 86*nn*92–93, 91*n*100, 117*n*178, 120*n*190, 136*n*232, 149*n*254, 152*n*260, 195*n*354, 196*n*358, 315*n*649; on Roman Republic, 110*n*159; *Valerius and Publicola*, 118*n*185
Harvard College, vii
Harvey, William, 48*n*20
Haslerig, Arthur, xii, 166*n*285, 177*n*310, 204*n*375, 223*n*417
Hayman, Peter, 251*n*493
Henrietta Maria, 240*n*463
Henry III, 156, 156*n*267, 161, 161*n*274, 191*n*344, 272, 272*n*530
Henry IV, 168
Henry V, 168
Henry VI, 168

Henry VII, xxix, 74n67, 265n520, 266n521
Henry VIII, 237n456, 247
Heraclides, 93, 93n104
hereditary principle of succession, xxiv, xxvi, xxix
Hereford, Bishop of. *See* Croft, Herbert (son)
Herodotus, 271n529
Heylyn, Peter, xxvi, xxvin44, 31n111, 31n114, 32n120; *Cosmographie*, 127n208
Hippocrates, 57, 57n31, 76n73
Hobbes, Thomas, xi, xxxiii–xxxiv, 43n8, 80n79, 82n83, 83n85, 95n111, 136n232, 152n260, 159n272, 169n292; *Horae Subsecivae*, 134n224; *Leviathan*, 63n48, 95n110, 116n178, 151n260, 259n507
Hobert, Miles, 251n493
Holland: Franco-Dutch War (1672–78), 123n201, 196n356; in *Plato Redivivus*, 56, 67, 123; Third Dutch War (1672–74), 286, 286n579; Union of Utrecht (1579) and, 121n195
Holles, Denzil, 145n245, 223n417, 251n493
Holles, Gilbert, 311n634
Hollis, Brand, x
Hollis, Thomas, vii–viii, xviii, 61n43; "Life of Henry Neville," 429–32
Horace: *Ars Poetica*, 226n425
Hotham, John, 224n420
Hotman, François, 142n242
Houssaie, Amelot de la, 78n76, 117n179, 124n202, 307n621
Howard, Henry, 216, 216n400, 217
Howard, Robert, 285n574
Howard, Thomas, 125n205
Howell, James, 2n2
Huberinus, Caspar, xxiin33
Huguenots, 286n578
The Humble Petition (Neville), xv, 375–82
Hume, David, 43n9, 225n423; "Of the Parties of Great Britain," 292n590; "That Politics May Be Reduced to a Science," 137n232
Huns, 99, 99n125, 140n237

Hunton, Philip, 30n107, 159n272; *A Treatise of Monarchy*, 143n242, 221n410, 287n582
Hussey, Edward, 176n305
Hutchinson, John, xv
Hutchinson, Lucy, xv
Hyde, Edward, 159n272, 310n632
Hyde, Laurence, 290n586

Il Redentore (Venice church), 276, 276n545
Inca Empire, 202n372
incest, 19n71, 21
India, 31n111, 31n114
indulgences, 275n543
inheritance laws, 90n99, 186–87, 199, 200
Innocent III (pope), 161n276
Instrument of Government (1653), 256n498
Ionic architecture, 46n13
Ireton, Henry, 89n97, 199n363
Isaac (biblical), 85
Isla de Pinos (Cuba), 2n1
The Isle of Pines, 1–38; corrections to copy-text, 433–35; "The Isle of Pines, Discovered," 5–36; notes on texts, xxxix–xl; overview, xxii–xxvi; "Post-Script," 37–38; publication of, xvi; "Two Letters Concerning the Island of Pines," 3–4
Israel (ancient), 86, 119n186, 151n257
Italy: Neville in, x, xv–xvii, xvin17, 56n26, 62n45; in *Plato Redivivus*, 62, 67, 81, 99, 101, 108, 111, 195. *See also specific cities*

Jacob (biblical), 85
James I: accession of, xxxii; anti-Catholic legislation under, 238n460; *Book of Sports* issued by, 24n89; divine right and, 225n423; foreign policy of, 239n463; Parliament and, 157n271, 214n394, 217n401, 219n407; *The Trew Law of Free Monarchies*, 64n48, 86n91, 95n110, 225n423

James II: accession to throne, 244n475, 247n478; Burnet on character of, 72n63; Exclusion Crisis and, xxvii, 42n4, 72n61, 169n292, 230n432; Lower's opposition to, 48n20; military career of, 72n62; Monmouth and, 255n497; Roman Catholicism and, 242n470; royal prerogative and, 178n312

Janissaries, 130n218, 132, 132n223, 137, 256n498

Jefferson, Thomas, 221n409

Jenkins, Leoline, 211n388, 246n477, 252n495

Jethro the Midianite, 116n178

Johann Friedrich (Hanover), 252n495

John (king), 161, 161n274, 165n284, 232n437, 272

Johnson, Samuel (1649–1703): *The Second Part of the Confutation of the Ballancing Letter*, 161n277

Johnson, Samuel (1709–1784), 61n40, 66n55

Johnston, Nathaniel: *The Excellency of Monarchical Government*, 160n272

Joseph (biblical), 92, 191

Judicature Act (1873), 184n326

Julius Caesar, 133n224

jure divino. *See* divine right of kings

Justinian (emperor), 140n238

Juvenal, 111n161, 315n649

Katherine of Aragon, 237n456

Keating, Geoffrey, 85n88

Keresztes, Paul, 233n446

Khambhat, India, 31n111

Khan, Abulghazi Bahadur, 85n88

Kimbolton, Lord, 168n292, 223n417

Knolles, Richard, 129n215, 256n498

The Ladies, a Second Time, Assembled in Parliament (Neville), xix

Langton, Stephen, 232n437

La Rochelle, France, 3nn8–9

Latin language, 61n40, 66, 66n55

Laud, William, 24n89, 31n111, 209n385, 313n640

Lawrence, Thomas, 61n40

Lee, Daniel, 270n526

A Letter from a Parliament Man to His Friend (anonymous), 218n403

A Letter from a Person of Quality (anonymous), 267n521

A Letter on the Subject of Succession (anonymous), 315n649

A Letter to His Highness from an Officer in Ireland (anonymous), xi, 44, 45n10, 317–38

Leveller Petition (1647), 288n582, 301n609

Levites, 150

Lewkenor, Lewes, 124n203

libertinism in *The Isle of Pines*, xx, xxiv

Lilburne, John, 168n292

Littleton, Adam, 30n107

Livy, 46

Locke, John, xxxiii–xxxiv, 80n80, 82nn82–83, 84n85, 127n211, 162n278, 288n582; *An Essay concerning Human Understanding*, 35n138

Lombards, 99, 99n125

Long, Thomas, 253n495

Long, Walter, 251n493

Long Parliament (1640–60), 222, 222n416, 238n460, 283n571, 302, 309n628, 310n629

Louis (Dauphin of France), 161, 161n275

Louis XI (France), 196, 196n358, 272

Louis XIII (France), 286n578

Louis XIV (France), xviii, 73n66, 89n98, 123n201, 196n356, 198n361, 294n592, 314n646

Louis XV (France), 89n98

Louis XVI (France), 89n98

Lower, Richard, xviii, 48n20, 57n30, 61nn42–43, 126n207, 156n266

Lucas, Lord, 190n343

Lucius Junius Brutus, 118n182, 282n565

Lycurgus, 82*n*84, 96–97, 103, 104*n*137, 111–12, 112*n*162, 112*n*165, 262
Lysander, 112, 112*n*164, 114*n*168

Macedonians, 210
Machiavelli, Niccolò: on ancient Greece, 112*n*165; *The Art of War,* 110*n*159, 131*n*219; Calvin and, 140*n*239; *Discourses,* 91*n*100, 95*n*114, 100*n*128, 101*n*129, 107*n*148, 108*n*151, 118*n*184, 120*n*190, 133*n*224; on dissension as source of strength, 305*n*616; on Florence, 106*n*143; *History of Florence,* 114*n*172, 140*n*237, 222*n*413; influence of, xvii, xxxii; medicinal metaphor for politics used by, 63*n*48; in *Plato Redivivus,* 75, 98, 107, 174, 222, 234, 300, 312; *The Prince,* 75*n*71, 98*n*123, 102*n*130, 120*n*190, 128*n*212, 133*n*224; on Roman Republic, 56*n*23, 83*n*84, 114*n*170; Starkey's translation, publication of, xvii, xxxi*n*50
Madagascar, 7, 7*nn*23–24
Magalotti, Lorenzo, 48*n*20
Magna Carta, 161*n*277, 162*n*279, 163*nn*281–82, 165–66, 168*n*292, 169, 184–85, 220*n*409, 232, 232*n*437, 251, 292, 299
Mahlberg, Gaby, 162*n*277
Mahomet, 88, 88*n*95, 233, 233*n*444
Maltzahn, Nicholas von, 76*n*74
mamalukes, 137, 284, 284*n*573
Mantua, 135*n*228
Marcus, Leah, 24*n*89
Marcus Aurelius Antoninus, 95–96, 95*n*113, 95*n*115, 140*n*237
Mariana, Juan de, 236*n*452
Marten, Henry, x, 56*n*26
Marvell, Andrew: *An Account of the Growth of Popery and Arbitrary Government,* 76*n*74, 188*n*341, 218*n*403, 292*n*588; "The Garden," 24*n*90; on James II, 72*n*62; *Mr. Smirke, or The Divine in Mode,*

42*n*4, 215*n*396; on Neville, xvi*n*19; on popular sovereignty doctrine, 246*n*477; *The Rehearsal Transpros'd; The Second Part,* xxi*n*31, xxvi, 42*n*5, 226*n*425; republicanism and, x, 56*n*26; on royal prerogative, 292*n*588; *A Short Historical Essay, Touching General Councils, Creeds, and Impositions in Matters of Religion,* 150*n*256, 152*n*260, 233*n*446; "Upon Appleton House," 18*n*66
Mary I, 237*n*454, 267–68*n*522
Matthews, Colonel, 201*n*368
maxims, 46*n*17
Mayerne, Theodore de, 206*n*380
Maynard, Serjeant, 189*n*342
Maynwaring, Roger, 225*n*423
Mazarin, Cardinal, 198*n*361, 294, 294*n*593
Medes, 104, 271, 271*n*529
medicinal metaphor for politics, 46, 63, 63*n*48, 78*n*75
medievalism, 65*n*51
Meres, Thomas, 176*n*308, 217*n*403
Michiel, Francesco, 56*n*24
Miles's Coffee House, 61*n*43
militia, 170–71, 170*n*294, 181, 189, 208*n*382, 223, 295
Militia Act (1661), 295*n*594
Milo, 193*n*350
Miltiades, 107*n*149
Milton, John, x, 56*n*26, 66*n*55, 180*n*314; *Eikonoklastes,* 170*n*294; *Paradise Lost,* 16*n*59, 18*n*66, 26*nn*95–96, 88*n*94, 277*n*549; *Samson Agonistes,* 251*n*491
Molesworth, Robert, 193*n*352
monarchy: arbitrary power and, 162*n*278; Aristotle on, 95*n*110; divine right of kings, 86, 86*n*91, 225*n*423; in Egypt, 93; in France, 142*n*242; as government form, 91–92, 91*n*100; Harrington on, 119*n*187; in Israel, 87*n*94; James I on, 95*n*110; mixed, 93, 186–87; Norman Conquest and, 159*n*272; in Ottoman Empire,

monarchy: (continued)
94n108, 127, 127n211, 130; peerage
and, 115n174, 119n187; in Persian
Empire, 127n210; in publisher note to
Plato Redivivus, 47; in Roman
Empire, 116, 117n180, 134n224;
Sidney on, 172n296. *See also specific
monarchs*
Monck, George, 310, 310n631
Mongol Empire, 88n96
Monmouth, James Scott, Duke of,
127n211, 230–31, 231n433, 254–57,
254n496, 255n497, 257n502, 258n503,
259, 263, 268
Montagu, Mary Wortley, 311n635
Montagu, Ralph, 290n286
Montfort, Simon de, 161n274, 191,
191n344, 191n346, 272n530
Moorish conquest of Spain, 202–3,
202n373
Morosini, Giovanni, 56n24
Moses (biblical), 85, 103, 116–17, 119
Moulin, Pierre de, 136n232
Mount Teide, 6n18
Moyle, Walter, 40n2
Muhammad. *See* Mahomet

Nani, Giovanni Battista, 55n23, 56n24,
69n57; *Affairs of Europe*, 126n206;
History of Europe, xxxi$n$50
necessity, 81n82
Nedham, Marchamont, 104n137,
259n507
Nepos, 112n164
Nero, 233, 233n446
Neville, Henry: chronology of life,
li–liii; Civil War and, x–xii; in
Covent Garden area, 3n7; in
Cromwell's Parliament, xii–xv;
family background and early life,
ix–x; final years, xviii–xix, 3n7;
literary career, xix–xxxiii; major
speeches in Parliament, 339–50;
opposition to Cromwell, x–xii;
political career, x–xv; return to
England, xvi–xviii; Stuart restora-
tion and, xv–xvi. *See also titles of
specific works*
Neville, Henry (grandfather): manu-
scripts relating to, 383–94; as patient
of Theodore de Mayerne, 206n380;
Perez and, 208n383; political career
of, ix, 214n394, 216, 216n398; in
Undertaking Parliament (1614),
214n394, 216n401
Neville, Richard, xvi, 56n26
Newes from the New Exchange (Neville),
xix, xx, 32n120
New Model Army, 277n552
Nicaea, Council of, 150n256
*Nicholas Machiavel's Letter to Zanobius
Buondelmontius in Vindication of
Himself and His Writings* (Neville),
146n248, 147n249, 150n256, 153n261,
172n296, 174n301, 234n449, 262n513
Nimrod (biblical), 87–88, 87n94
Noah (biblical), 85
Norman Conquest, 159–60, 159n272,
160n273
Numa Pompilius, 82n84, 117n180, 233

obedience to government, 215, 259n507
Occam, William of, 304n612
Occhino, Bernardino, 276n546
Octavian, 135n228
Octavius Musa, 135n228
oligarchy, 282
Osborne, Thomas. *See* Danby, Earl of
Ostrogoths, 140n238
Othman, 129n215
Ottoman Empire: alliances of, 139n236;
Egypt and, 138n235, 284n573;
expansion of, xxxiii$n$52, 192n348;
Harrington on, 194n354; influence
of, xxxii; Janissaries in, 130n218, 132,
132n223, 137, 256n498; monarchy in,
94n108, 127, 127n211, 130; in *Plato
Redivivus*, 192, 194; political history
of, 127–29, 128n212, 129n215, 129n217;
Rycaut on, xxxii–xxxiii, 132n223;
Venice and, 126n206
Ovid, xxii$n$33

Owen, Roger, 216n401
Oxford Parliament (1681), 166n287
Oxford Provisions (1258), 272n530
Oxford University, ix, 126, 246n477

Padua, Italy, 98, 125–26, 125n205
Paine, Thomas: *Rights of Man,*
  221n409
Palatines, 211–12
Papirius Praetextatus, xix
pardons: of Danby, 145n245, 173n298; in
  The Isle of Pines, 22; as royal prerogative, 145n245, 175–76, 175n304,
  292n588
Paris, Treaty of (1657), 294, 294n593
Parker, Henry, 260n509
The Parlament of VVomen (anonymous),
  xix–xx
Parliament: Addled Parliament (1614),
  214n394, 217n401, 219n407; alliances
  and, 158n271, 211, 285–87; antiquity
  of, 157n270; Barebones Parliament
  (1653), 196, 196n357, 277, 283n569;
  bishops in, 145n245; Cavalier
  Parliament (1661–79), 76n74,
  219n405; Charles I and, 251n493;
  during Civil War, 24n89; Committee of Safety, 277n552; Convention
  Parliament (1660), 204n375, 219n405,
  268n522; Convention Parliament
  (1689), 169n292, 218n403; dissolution
  of, 166n287, 274n538; Exclusion Bill
  Parliament (1679), 74n69, 76n74,
  252n494; fundamental laws and,
  168–69; Grand Remonstrance (1641)
  and, 173n297, 204n375, 209n385, 223,
  223n418, 281nn561–62; Habeas Corpus
  Parliament, xl, 41n4; laws governing
  frequency of, 212, 301n609; Long
  Parliament (1640–60), 222, 222n416,
  238n460, 283n571, 302, 309n628,
  310n629; Magna Carta and, 163n281;
  militia and, 170n294, 256n498;
  Oxford Parliament (1681), 166n287;
  Pensioner Parliament (1661–79), 73,
  73n64, 274n537, 312n639; prorogation

of, 74n69, 165n285, 175n303; royal
  prerogative and, 179, 291–92; Rump
  Parliament, xiv, 282n567, 283n571;
  Second Protectorate Parliament
  (1656–58), 283n569; Third Protector-
  ate Parliament (1658–59), 310n630;
  Undertaking Parliament (1614), 214,
  214n394, 216–17, 216n401, 219n407
The Parliament of Ladies (Neville),
  x–xi, xix, 32n120
parochialism, xxxii
patriarchalism, xxiv, xxvi, 84–85, 84n87
Paul (saint), 65, 233n446
Paul V (pope), 232n436
Pausanias (king of Sparta), 114n168
Peace of Augsburg (1555), 231n434
peerage, 89–90, 115n174, 142, 181–82,
  213. *See also* aristocracy
Pegu (Burma/Myanmar), 127, 127n208
Pelling, Edward, 253n495
Peloponnesian War, 112, 112n164,
  114n168, 115n175
Penn, William: *Truth Rescued from
  Imposture,* 183n324
Pensioner Parliament (1661–79), 73,
  73n64, 274n537, 312n639
Perez, Antonio, 206n380, 208, 208n383,
  243n471
Periander of Corinth, 64n49, 262,
  262n517
Persian Empire, 107n149, 127, 210,
  271n528
Peter (saint), 236n451
Petition of Right (1628), 184–85,
  184n327, 190n343, 251, 251n492,
  280n561, 281n562, 299
Petty, William: *An Essay concerning
  the Multiplication of Mankind,* 2n5
Petyt, William, 156, 157n270, 159n272,
  160n273, 163n282; *The Antient Right
  of the Commons of England Asserted,*
  157n270
Phaedo of Elis, 47, 47n19
Philip II (Spain), 206n380, 208,
  208n383, 243, 243nn471–72
Philip IV (Spain), 314n646

Philpot, Nicholas, 308*n*623
Pierrepont, Evelyn, 311*n*635
Pierrepont, Frances, 311*n*634
Pierrepont, Gertrude, 311*n*634
Pierrepont, Grace, 311*n*634
Pierrepont, Robert, 309*n*626, 311*n*635
Pierrepont, William, 309*n*626
pines, meanings of, 2*n*1
Pittacus of Mitylene, 64*n*49
Pius V (pope), 237*n*455
Plato, 63*n*48, 79, 79*n*77, 158; *Phaedo,*
    47*n*19; *The Republic,* 95*n*112
Platonic dialogue, 40*n*1
Plato Redivivus, 39–315; "The Argu-
    ment," 55–57; "The First Day,"
    59–68; "The Second Day," 69–228;
    "The Third Day," 229–315; book list
    for, 51–53; corrections to copy-text,
    435–38; disclaimer concerning
    authorship, 41, 41*n*3; notes on texts,
    xl; overview, xxvi–xxxiii; publication
    of, xviii, xxviii, 41*n*4; textual
    collation of first and second editions,
    439–70
Plutarch, 46, 46*n*12, 81, 104, 104*n*138,
    110*n*159, 112, 112*n*162, 112*n*164,
    210*n*386, 300
Pocock, John, 73*n*64, 194*n*354,
    221*n*410
Poland: in *Plato Redivivus,* 144, 193,
    211; political history in, 211*n*388
Polybius, 46, 46*n*12, 91*n*100
polygamy, xxiv, 276, 276*n*546
Poole, William, 2*n*1
Pope, Alexander: *The Rape of the Lock,*
    xi*n*4
Popery, 76–77, 76*n*74, 188, 230–32, 235,
    239*n*460, 242, 243, 250, 264–65
Popish Plot, xviii, xxvii, 173*n*298,
    285*n*574
popular sovereignty doctrine, 245*n*477,
    270*n*526
populism, 115*n*174
Portugal: independence of, 202*n*370;
    slave trade on Madagascar by, 7*n*23;
    trade in Southeast Asia, 11*n*39

Powle, Henry, 76*n*74, 177*n*310,
    197*n*358
Praetorians, 131, 131*n*219, 135
Prestor-John, 127, 127*n*209
Price, John, 30*n*107
Priolo, Benjamin, 77*n*75, 198*n*360
Privy Council, 274*n*539, 288–89,
    289*nn*585–86, 297
Procopius of Caesarea, 140, 140*n*238;
    Secret History, xxxi
promiscuous, definitions of, 8*n*26
property: economic independence and,
    199*n*363; in England, 212; forms of
    government and, 44*n*9, 92–93, 136;
    in France, 44*n*9, 195, 199–200, 280;
    inheritance laws and, 90*n*99, 186–87,
    199, 200; monarchy and, 280;
    political authority grounded in,
    89*n*97, 92–93, 136, 199*n*363; power
    founded in, 93*n*105; in Spain,
    200–201
prorogation of Parliament, 74*n*69,
    165*n*285, 175*n*303
proscription, 134, 134*n*226
Protestantism, 19*n*74, 148*n*250, 153*n*261,
    209*n*385, 237*n*454, 239
Prynne, William, 163*n*282
Putney Debates (1647), 89*n*97, 199*n*363,
    221*n*409, 246*n*477
Pym, John, 56*n*26, 168*n*292, 223*n*417

Quakers, 66*n*54
Quarantia (Council of Forty), 185,
    185*n*330, 296
quartering of troops, 281*n*561

race in *The Isle of Pines,* xxiv, 12,
    17–18
Rainsborough, Colonel, 221*n*409
Ralegh, Walter, 248, 248*nn*482–83
Ranters, 308*n*622
regicide, 246*n*477, 261
religion: anticlericalism and, 146*n*246,
    147*n*248, 151*n*257, 233*n*444, 234*n*447;
    Calvinism and, 209*n*385; in *Plato
    Redivivus,* 144–56; in Scotland,

209–10. *See also* Protestantism; Roman Catholicism

Reresby, John, 244*n*475

Reuben (biblical), 85

Richard II, 167, 173, 173*n*299, 279, 279*n*556, 291

Richelieu, 286*n*578

Ripon, Treaty of (1640), 209*n*384, 286*n*577

Robbins, Caroline, 41*n*4, 276*n*546, 308*n*623, 313*n*641

Roman Catholicism: anti-Catholic legislation and, 238*n*458, 238*n*460; anticlericalism and, 146*n*246, 147*n*248, 151*n*257, 233*n*444, 234*n*447; Church of England and, 147*n*250; in England, 237*n*454; Eucharist and, 153*n*262, 154*n*264; James II and, 231*n*433; Johann Friedrich and, 252; Marvell on, 76*n*74; in *Plato Redivivus*, 154–55; sacerdotal authority and, 148*n*252, 149*n*254, 153*n*262; transubstantiation and, 153*n*262. *See also* Exclusion Crisis; Popery

Roman Empire: Christian persecution in, 233–34, 233*n*445; civil war in, 134*n*225; Decemvirate in, 114, 282, 282*n*564; economic problems in, 110*n*159; expansion of, 187*n*336; Liberators' civil war (44–42 B.C.), 134*n*225; Perusine war (41–40 B.C.), 134*n*225; in *Plato Redivivus*, 93, 95–96, 106–8, 110, 133–34, 187; political structures in, 114*n*170; Sicilian revolt (44–36 B.C.), 134*n*225. *See also specific rulers*

Romulus, 81, 93, 103, 106, 116–18, 117*n*180, 233*n*442

Rota Club, xv, 2*n*5, 61*n*43

royal prerogative, 158–59, 166, 170, 174, 178*n*312, 291–95, 292*n*588

Rudbeck the Elder, Olaus: *Atlantica*, 85*n*88

Rump Parliament, xiv, 282*n*567, 283*n*571. *See also* English Civil Wars

Rushworth, John, 210*n*385, 215*n*394

Russell, William, xviii

Rycaut, Paul, 47*n*17, 88*n*94, 119*n*187, 126*n*206, 127*n*212, 129*n*217, 132*n*223, 138*n*235; *History of the Turkish Empire*, 192*n*348

Rye House Plot, xviii

Sá, Manuel de, 236, 236*n*453

sacerdotal authority, 148*n*252, 149*n*254, 153*n*262

Sacheverell, William, 158*n*271, 178*n*310, 218*n*403

Sadler, John, 315*n*649

St. John, Henry, Viscount Bolingbroke, 288*n*582

Salisbury, Lord, 214*n*394

Salway, Richard, xv

Samnites, 108*n*151

Samuel (biblical), 86

Sanderson, Robert, 136*n*232

sanhedrin, 119, 119*n*186

Savile, George, 311*n*634

Sawbridge, John, 164*n*283

Scot, Thomas, xii

Scotland: English wars with, 166, 209–10, 209*n*384, 224*n*420, 254*n*496, 286, 286*n*577; Long Parliament and, 222; in *Plato Redivivus*, 248; religion in, 209–10; Treaty of Ripon (1640) and, 209*n*384, 286*n*577

Scott, James. *See* Monmouth, James Scott, Duke of

SCRIPTURAL REFERENCES

Genesis 1:2, 10*n*36

Genesis 3:15, 276*n*548

Genesis 7:23, 20*n*77

Genesis 9:18–19, 85*n*88

Genesis 10:1–32, 85*n*88

Genesis 10:8–10, 87*n*94

Genesis 27:28, 20*n*78

Genesis 27:39, 20*n*78

Genesis 40:1, 92*n*102

Genesis 47:13–26, 92*n*103

Genesis 49:1–33, 85*n*89

Exodus 9:15, 20*n*77

Exodus 18:1–24, 116*n*176

SCRIPTURAL REFERENCES
(continued)
Exodus 18:17–24, 117n178
Exodus 19:16, 116n176
Exodus 20–22, 20:18, 22n83, 116n176
Leviticus, 17n63
Leviticus 18:9, 19n71
Numbers 1:1–3, 20n75
Numbers 26:55, 85n90
Numbers 33:54, 85n90
Numbers 34:13, 85n90
Deuteronomy 27:3, 313n643
Joshua 7:9, 20n77
Joshua 13:6, 85n90
1 Samuel 8:1–22, 86n92
1 Chronicles 27:1, 132n222
Psalms 109:15, 20n77
Psalms 133, 27n98
Proverbs 2:22, 20n77
Proverbs 17:28, 312n636
Proverbs 25:3, 57n32
Ecclesiastes 10:8, 29n107
Ecclesiastes 11:1, 10n36
Jeremiah 17:9, 57n32
Ezekiel 47:22, 85n90
Ezekiel 48:29, 85n90
Daniel 2:44, 275n541
Daniel 4:15, 20n78
Daniel 4:23, 20n78
Daniel 4:25, 20n78
Nahum 2:13, 20n77
Matthew 6:33, 186n331
Matthew 16:18–19, 236n451
Matthew 20:16, 233n441
Matthew 22:14, 233n441
Matthew 22:21, 232n440
Mark 12:17, 232n440
Luke 13:23–24, 233n441
John 8:23, 232n439
John 18:36, 232n439
Acts 2:47, 149n255
Acts 5:11, 149n255
Acts 8:1, 149n255
Acts 11:26, 149n255
Acts 14:23, 149n255
Acts 14:27, 149n255
Acts 15:3, 149n255
Acts 15:22, 149n255
Acts 18:22, 149n255
Acts 19:32, 149n254
Romans 13:1–7, 232n440
Romans 16:5, 149n255
1 Corinthians 4:17, 149n255
1 Corinthians 14:4–5, 149n255
1 Corinthians 14:23, 149n255
1 Corinthians 16:19, 149n255
Ephesians 1:22, 149n255
Ephesians 3:10, 149n255
Ephesians 5:24, 149n255
Ephesians 5:25, 149n255
Ephesians 5:27, 149n255
Ephesians 5:29, 149n255
Ephesians 5:32, 149n255
Philippians 3:6, 149n255
Philippians 4:15, 149n255
Colossians 1:18, 149n255
Colossians 1:24, 149n255
Colossians 4:15, 149n255
1 Timothy 5:16, 149n255
Philemon 2, 149n255
1 Peter 5:13, 149n255
1 John 2:18, 148n253
1 John 4:3, 148n253
3 John 6, 149n255
3 John 9, 149n255
Seaman, Lazarus, 152n260
seasonality, absence of, 16n59
Seaward, Paul, 251n491
Second Bishops' War (1640), 209n384
Second Dutch War (1664–67), 310n632
Second Protectorate Parliament
    (1656–58), 283n569
Second Punic War (218–202 B.C.), 107n147
Selden, John, 86n93, 251n493; *De
    Synedriis*, 116n178; *Priviledges of the
    Baronage of England*, 157n270; *Titles
    of Honour*, 143n242
Selim I, 137, 138n235
Seller, Abednego: *History of Passive
    Obedience since the Reformation*, 96n116

Sermon on the Mount, 186*n*331
Servius Tullius, 109*n*156, 117*n*180, 125*n*204
Settled Land Act (1882), 90*n*99
sexual ethics in *The Isle of Pines*, xxiv, xxv–xxvi, 16–17, 17*n*63, 19*n*71
Seymour, Edward, 176*n*308, 177*n*310
Sforza, Francesco, 284, 284*n*572
Shaftesbury, Earl of, 77*n*74, 115*n*174, 119*n*187, 225*n*423, 247*n*478, 290*n*586
sheriffs, 171, 171*n*295, 302
ship-money (tax), 173, 173*n*297
Shuffling, Cutting, and Dealing in a Game of Pickquet (Neville), xi, xx–xxi, xxii, 277*n*551
Sidney, Algernon: *Court Maxims*, 42*n*5, 111*n*161, 172*n*296, 267*n*521, 279*n*558; *Discourses concerning Government*, 42*n*5, 85*n*87, 207*n*381; execution of, 41*n*3; on forms of government, 91*n*100; on French monarchy, 89*n*98; on Heylyn, 31*n*111; on Lower, 48*n*20; on obedience to government, 259*n*507; on Parliament, 190*n*342; on population increases, 2*n*5; republicanism and, x, 56*n*26; on royal prerogative, 292*n*588; Rye House Plot and, xviii, 41*n*3; on Spanish history, 203*n*373
Simmias of Thebes, 47, 47*n*19
Sixtus V (pope), 237*n*455
slavery, 7*n*23, 12
Smith, Francis, 30*n*107
Smith, Thomas, 109*n*156, 197*n*358; *De Republica Anglorum*, 91*n*100
Socrates, 47, 47*n*19, 95*n*112
sola scriptura principle, 148*n*250, 148*n*252
Solon, 64*n*49, 82*n*84, 104–5, 104*n*137, 111, 262, 314
Somers, John, 161*n*276; *A Brief History of Succession*, 395–428
Spahis, 132, 132*n*220

Spain: Aztec Empire and, 202*n*372; Inca Empire and, 202*n*372; Moorish conquest of, 202*n*373; in *Plato Redivivus*, 143, 144, 193, 200–208, 243; political history in, 202*n*370, 206*n*380; property in, 200–201; taxation in, 203*n*374; Thirty Years' War and, 202*n*370; Visigoths conquering and ruling, 202*n*371. *See also specific kings*
Spartans, 93, 96–97, 103, 112, 112*n*163, 114*n*168, 174, 279, 279*n*558, 297, 300, 307
Spelman, Henry, 142*n*242, 144*n*243
Spencer, Charles. *See* Sunderland, Earl of
Sphinx, 70, 70*n*58
Stafford, Viscount, 176*n*307
standing army, 256*n*498
Star Chamber, 298*n*603
Starkey, John, xvii, xxxi*nn*49–50
Staverton, Elizabeth, ix
Stillingfleet, Edward, 145*n*245
Streater, John, 172*n*296, 246*n*477, 270*n*526
Strode, William, xi–xii, 223*n*417
Stroud, William, 251*n*493
Stuart, Arabella, 248*n*482
Stuart, Charles, xv–xvi
Succession Act (1544), 247*n*479
Suffolk, Charles Brandon, Duke of, 247
Suleiman (sultan), 139*n*236
Sulla, 135*n*226
Sunderland, Charles Spencer, Earl of, 290*n*586, 303*n*611
Sweden, 193
Swift, Jonathan, 40*n*2, 78*n*76, 93*n*107, 149*n*254, 201*n*369; *Argument against Abolishing Christianity*, 32*n*120
Swinnock, George, 30*n*107
Switzerland, 120–21, 120*n*191

Tacitus, 136*n*232
Tarquinius Priscus, 117*n*180
Tarquinius Superbus, 117*n*180, 118*n*182

taxation: Catholics subject to, 239n460;
under Charles I, 204n375, 281n562; in
Egypt, 139; Parliament and, 190n343;
Petition of Right and, 251n493, 299;
under Richard II, 173n299; royal
prerogative and, 163n282; ship-
money, 173, 173n297; in Spain, 203,
203n374; standing army maintenance
via, 139, 295
Temple, William, 289n586
Teneriffe, 6n18
Test Acts (1673), 239n460
Thales, 64n49
Thebes, 114
Themistocles, 128, 128n213, 271–72,
271n527
Theopompus, 279, 279n558
Theseus, 81, 81n81, 103, 104, 116
Third Dutch War (1672–74), 286,
286n579
Third Protectorate Parliament
(1658–59), 310n630
Thirty Years' War, 202n370, 240n463
Thomas Hollis Library, vii–viii
Throckmorton Plot (1583), 237n457
Thucydides, 46, 46n12, 97, 112n163,
128n213
Tiberius Sempronius Gracchus,
109n157, 110, 110n159, 111, 187
Timaeus, 47, 47n19
timariots, 129n217, 132
Titus Livius, 46n12
Toland, John, 40n1, 43n9, 44n10,
45n11
transubstantiation, 153–54, 153n262
trapan, definitions of, 42n5
Treaty of Barcelona (1493), 115n175
Treaty of Dover (1670), 73n66, 294n592
Treaty of Paris (1657), 294, 294n593
Treaty of Ripon (1640), 209n384,
286n577
Tresilian, Robert, 173n299
Triennial Act (1641), 165n285, 212
Tromp, Admiral, 287n579
Tropic of Capricorn, 7n23

Tullus Hostilius, 117n180
Turner, Francis: Animadversions,
215n396
Turquet de Mayerne, Louis: The
Generall Historie of Spaine, 206n380
Tyrrell, James: Patriarcha Non
Monarcha, 163n282

Ulphilas, 145n244
Undertaking Parliament (1614), 214,
214n394, 216–17, 216n401, 219n407
Union of Utrecht (1579), 121, 121n195
utopian themes, 10n33, 16n59, 18n66,
28n101

Valentine, Benjamin, 251n493
Vandals, 106, 119, 119n187, 124n203,
140n238
Vane, Henry, xii, 193n350
Vaughan, Edward, 77n74, 176n304
Venetian Republic: balloting in,
296n599; Grand Council in, 307,
307n621; Harrington on, 124n203;
Ottoman Empire and, 126n206;
Papacy and, 232n436; political
history of, 78n76, 99n125, 142n241;
Quarantia (Council of Forty), 185,
185n330, 296
Villiers, George. See Buckingham,
Duke of
Virgil, 135n228
Visigoths, 202n371

Waller (member of Parliament),
239n460, 289n585, 292n589
Walter, Lucy, 231n433
War of the Public Weal (1465–67 and
1472), 261n510
Warr, John, 260n509
Weaver, John, xii
Wentworth, Thomas, 313n640
Weston, Richard, 216, 216n401, 217
Whitlock, Lord, 190n343
Whitlocke, Bulstroke, 220n408
Widrington, John, 215n394

wife as "second self," 36, 36*n*139

Wildman, John, xvii–xviii, 246*n*477, 268*n*522

William I (William the Conqueror), 159*n*272, 160, 184*n*328

William III (William of Orange), 88*n*94, 96*n*116, 158*n*271, 267, 267*n*522, 281*n*561, 285*n*574

Williams, Roger: *The Bloudy Tenent of Persecution,* 172*n*296, 246*n*477

Willis, Thomas, 48*n*20, 57*n*30

Wiseman, Susan, xxiv*n*40

Wood, Anthony à, 3*n*7, 48*n*20, 156*n*266

Wootton, David, 172*n*296; *Divine Right,* 143*n*242

Worden, Blair, 56*n*26, 219*n*404, 220*n*408

Wordsworth, William: *The Prelude,* xi*n*4

writs of error, 182, 183*n*322, 305

Xenophon: *Hellenica,* 112*n*163

Xerxes I (Persia), 107, 107*n*149, 128, 128*n*213, 271, 271*n*528

This book is set in Adobe Caslon Pro, a modern adaptation by Carol Twombly of faces cut by William Caslon, London, in the 1730s. Caslon's types were based on seventeenth-century Dutch old-style designs and became very popular throughout Europe and the American colonies.

Printed on paper that is acid-free and meets the requirements of the American National Standard for Permanence of Paper for Printed Library Materials, Z39.48-1992. ∞

Book design by Louise OFarrell
Gainesville, Florida

Typography by Westchester Publishing Services
Danbury, Connecticut

Index by Indexing Partners, LLC
Rehoboth Beach, Delaware

Printed and bound by Sheridan Books, Inc.
Chelsea, Michigan